The Planning and
Design Approach

The Planning and Design Approach

GERALD NADLER

University of Wisconsin-Madison
and
The Planning, Design and Improvement Methods Group, Inc.

A WILEY-INTERSCIENCE PUBLICATION

JOHN WILEY & SONS

New York • Chichester • Brisbane • Toronto

Library of Congress Cataloging in Publication Data:

Nadler, Gerald.
    The planning and design approach.

    ''A Wiley-Interscience publication.''
    Includes bibliographical references and index.
    1. Planning.   2. System design.   I. Title.

HD30.28.N33   658.4'012   81-1448
ISBN 0-471-08102-7   AACR2

Printed in the United States of America

10 9 8 7 6 5 4 3 2 1

Preface

Doing planning and design (P&D) is what this book is about. The format is operational, so that a person or group can be more effective doing P&D for real projects. P&D is a process to create or restructure a situation-specific solution. The results may be a house, legislation, an information system, a corporate plan, an appropriate technology transfer, a regional housing plan, a product design, a course outline, a factory layout—almost anything.

Simply talking about change, the future, and emerging needs does not ensure results. Everyone can agree that change is constantly occurring, that today's choices create the future, and that we have many options in planning and designing for emerging needs. This is a necessary backdrop for P&D, but effective P&D involves far more.

The planning and design approach (PDA) translates ideas into action. It provides a theoretical framework and methodology for P&D. It significantly increases the probability that innovative and effective solutions for the right problem will be developed and implemented. It is a plausible way of arriving at a desired and continuously improving future that may not have otherwise been considered. It also increases the likelihood that P&D resources will be used effectively.

To achieve these ends, this book emphasizes the conceptual and operational aspects of P&D in the "real world." Unlike much P&D literature, it does not make a fetish of techniques and models, although they are noted briefly with references in Appendix A. In-stead, the book proceeds on the premise that the big idea and enduring direction of creating or restructuring situation-specific solutions that are implemented govern P&D. It also operates on the premise that we should listen to what P&D professionals say in surveys taken two or more years after graduation—80 to 85% of what they needed to learn was not included in their education.

Therefore, this book concentrates on those topics most books dismiss or fail to make operational: problem definition, creativity in real-world settings, implementation, solution specification, interpersonal relations, P&D roles, and organizational integration.

Oliver Wendell Holmes said in the early 1900s, and it's just as true today, "At this time we need education in the obvious more than investigation of the obscure." This book contains a great number of obvious ideas put in an operational format.

The specific operational methods of P&D outlined in PDA rest firmly on basic theories, research results, and concepts. They establish the P&D context and setting for the nature of reality (metaphysics). They set out methods of knowing and understanding what is happening during the P&D process (epistemology). They clarify what is meant by change and stability (dynamics). The framework is thus the result of intensive theoretical and empirical investigations into the characteristics of *effective* P&D.

Some of the basic premises of PDA differ from those of conventional P&D. These include:

1 Specific human and organization realities—attitudes, needs, and behaviors—are the starting point of an approach, rather than the tools and techniques of any one P&D profession.

2 Individuals and organizations are unique. In the real world, there are no identical entities, regardless of what "statistics" may proclaim. Therefore, the P&D approach adapts itself to the specific situation, and not the situation to the approach.

3 P&D is only one of many human purposeful activities and is carried out in the context of overall human needs, values, and objectives.

4 The P&D approach is descriptive and prescriptive within a theoretical framework based on some simple truths (axioms), supportable assertions (propositions), and empirical evidence about effective P&D (principles). This changes the interpretation of available research. For example, research shows that people fail to use solutions that are "not invented here." Conventional P&D interprets this to show that people resist changes. PDA interprets this as a human reality that requires continuing joint real-world and P&D interaction right from the start of a project.

5 The P&D approach operationalizes the "whats" and "whys" of P&D into specific, day-by-day, week-by-week methods of interrelating with the human and organizational "real worlds."

6 Such an operationalization includes the notions that in defining a problem situation the focus is on purposes (what is desired and needed) rather than on what is wrong; that preparation for solution implementation begins when the individual or organization perceives there is a problem, not after the solution has been proposed; implementation requires continuous interaction with the people in the client's world; and every solution should contain the seeds of its own change and improvement.

7 Any approach or set of factors used to describe P&D will be incomplete. P&D is a holistic and interdisciplinary endeavor greater than the sum of its parts. Thus, the approach includes methods enabling each person who uses it to continually change and improve it.

A timeline scenario is used to operationalize PDA. It integrates the factors now considered essential to effective P&D with the client's world over time. Many illustrations and case histories using P&D concepts in usual (factory, government agency, bank) and unusual (education, recipe development, health care delivery) situations ground the approach in reality. The emphasis, however, is on what the concepts make possible, not on exalting what has been done.

The total PDA approach engenders a mind-set that enables practitioners to take advantage of as well as cope with the demands of ever changing real-world conditions. It provides a methodology that combines the best of the visionary and pragmatic traditions in P&D. By stressing implementation it prevents P&D from entanglement in utopian designs, but by focusing on purposes it ensures that P&D is directed toward normative goals and values.

The individual components of PDA are not new. What is new is integrating them into a holistic timeline scenario. This permits teachers and practitioners to focus on what is important in effective P&D, and *how* to achieve it.

Practitioners, instructors, administrators, and researchers can use this book to improve professional practice, enlarge the P&D context for students, increase accountability for producing innovative and timely results, and identify research topics essential in determining good P&D practices. Students can be exposed to different sections of the book in different course configurations. Each P&D professional area will have to supplement the book with exercises, projects, principles of "good" solutions, and cases of its own. The cases in Appendix B illustrate a wide range of applications, but all possible P&D fields could not be included. Some of the ways I have used this book in teaching follow. In all cases, I supplemented the text with exercises, readings, and projects:

· Required course, "Theory of Design," for senior industrial engineers: Parts Two and Three with some cases in Appendix B.

· Elective course, "Sociotechnical Design Concepts," for social science and humanities seniors and graduate students: Parts One and Three, with many cases in Appendix B.

· Elective course, "Planning Large-Scale Complex Systems," for any graduate students (plus selected industrial engineering seniors): Chapters One, Nine, Ten, Thirteen, and Seventeen and Appendix A.

· Required industrial engineering master's seminar, "Systems Synthesis": Chapters Two, Three, Ten, and Seventeen.

The changing nature of even the P&D approach, let alone the solutions P&D efforts develop, is so much a part of this book (Chapter Seventeen is particularly germane) that I seriously considered asking the publishers to put "Trial Edition" or "Draft" on the cover. Then the next version would be Trial Edition 2 or Draft 2. Because *everything* in P&D is subject to change and improvement, I would especially welcome your comments and suggestions about any and all parts of the concepts and operational approach. All of us should partake in the excitement of keeping P&D approaches alive and well in each succeeding year.

GERALD NADLER

Madison, Wisconsin
April 1981

Acknowledgments

Where does one start?

With all humans past and present? Their drive to better conditions of life led to P&D.

With all the people (clients, colleagues all over the world, organizational officers, researchers, workers) who influenced me? So many pages would be filled that it is not practical. Just those listed in my previous books would require two or three pages.

With all my graduate and undergraduate students? They are so many in number that five or six pages would be needed. Their research, independent studies, projects, and classroom questions will instead receive my accolades.

With those directly involved in preparing *this* book? Even this could get a bit out of hand, but some who significantly shaped the presentation are William Bozeman, Willow Diller (especially), Dan Gat, David Hinds, David Ralston, Alan Scharf, James Thomson, Jr., and Wilbur Walkoe.

All are important. So, even though most of them are unnamed here, my thanks—my deepest gratitude—to all those groups of people mentioned above, and others too. And, for supplying throughout the birth of this book a high threshold of encouragement and support, unremitting appreciation goes to my wife, Elaine.

G. N.

Contents

The Planning and
Design Approach

Introductory Overview

Anyone who seeks to create or restructure and implement a system is doing planning and design (P&D). The person whose career centers on providing assistance to specific people and organizations wanting such creation or change is a P&D professional.

Planning and design are classified together here because their definitions overlap. The words are often used interchangeably as in "Planning a vacation," or "designing a health care delivery system." No purpose is served by saying that "planning" is open-ended while "design" is specific, or that the former has a longer time horizon, or that the latter is project- rather than program-oriented. Whether it be an architect's blueprint, a five-year land-use map, or a family's financial plan, solution specifications are detailed, resource allocations are proposed, innovation is encouraged, and purposes are defined—and this is planning and design.

Planning and design is a long-standing and proliferating human endeavor. Over 30 P&D professions exist. Most sectors of government have a planning agency, and business is not far behind. Every person does a significant amount of personal P&D: career planning, designing a house, planning children's education.

Generally any P&D activity has three basic objectives:

- To maximize the effectiveness of a recommended solution.
- To maximize the likelihood of its implementation.
- To maximize the effectiveness of resources used in the P&D effort.

Regrettably, these objectives are seldom realized. In current planning and design, between the idea and reality falls the shadow, to paraphrase the poet T. S. Eliot. The best-laid plans may fail, not in spite of planners but because of them. P&D is rife with perfectly right solutions for absolutely wrong problems, with grand designs that are never implemented, and programs too narrow in scope because their parameters cannot exceed those of the latest model or computer system.

This book is designed to increase significantly the probability of realizing the three objectives of P&D. It provides a rationale and methodology for a theory of planning and design, with prescriptions general enough for use by individuals, neighborhood activists, or multinational corporate strategists. Two ingredients separate the planning and design approach (PDA) presented in this book from other theories of planning and design. First, PDA has as its conceptual basis a timeline perspective, a purpose-oriented strategy, and a prescriptive systems outlook. P&D is perceived as a holistic process with five main factors: pursuing a strategy, specifying the solution framework, involving people, using knowledge and information, and arranging for continual change and improvement. Successful P&D involves the integrated performance along the timeline of these factors in a flexible and interactive way.

Second, PDA specifies methodologies and techniques for operationalizing its conceptual basis. PDA is not a vast array of "shoulds"; it spells out the "hows." A PDA scenario incorporates the following components:

- A strategy focusing on purposes to be achieved rather than upon details of existing problems.
- The development of a purpose hierarchy to enlarge the solution space and ensure that the right issues are addressed.
- Techniques to foster innovation and creativity throughout the process.
- The use of a solution matrix for plan preparation.
- Continual contact between the client's world and the P&D professionals.
- Involvement of all persons necessary to detail and implement a solution, including administrator, workers, experts and affected groups.
- Techniques to foster commitment throughout the process.
- An initial focus on those conditions that occur most frequently or are most important.
- Generation of many alternative solutions, and selection of one to serve as a long-term target that is ideal and feasible.
- Methods for encouraging multichanneled or pluralistic solutions to fit real-world diversities.
- Arranging for continual review and change.
- Limiting the amount of data collection to satisfy only the needs of the efforts.
- Limiting the use of models and analysis techniques to situations where they are necessary to achieve purposes.

Before expanding on PDA theory and practice let's ground it in the real world by observing the PDA scenario in actual settings. In the following case histories, PDA is used for business purposes, in an engineering design, and for a health care delivery system. Note that although the process remains the same it is easily adapted to the unique conditions of each situation.

SOME CASE HISTORIES

A.   Marking Room in a Department Store

Situation

A department store, employing 4000 persons, is a member of a nationwide association of stores that compare cost and productivity indices on a monthly

basis. The store's 70-person marking room had a cost index of 150% of the association average.

The vice-president of general operations wanted a 33% cost reduction in his marking room. He asked me to apply work measurement and scheduling, as he had just returned from a conference where these two techniques were reported to have lowered costs in another store's marking room. I suggested that immediately tying ourselves to these techniques might be limiting, so he agreed to use PDA.

First, a project team composed of the manager of materials handling, the supervisor of the marketing area, a key worker, and a P&D professional listed many possible purposes of the marking room system. The hierarchy they developed after trying out several other ones is shown in Figure 1-1. Criteria for selecting the specified level for PDA application were: time available for the project, management desires, control factors from other departments, potential savings, and resources available for the project. Measures of effectiveness for the selected level were cost savings, in-process time for merchandise, degree of inventory control, space needed, and flexibility.

As the project team considered both the selected purpose level and the larger levels in the hierarchy, many solution ideas were generated. Some would have eliminated the need for the selected purpose. One idea, for example, was to send the merchandise directly from the manufacturer to the consumer. Another was to put no prices on the merchandise and place it in appropriate bins and racks marked with the individual prices. A third idea would require that a price code be placed on the merchandise by the manufacturer.

A target system was then developed that incorporated part of the second idea. The target system called for the department store to preprint tags with a punched hole price code and other control information to attach to the merchandise. The tags also served a checking function. Items selling for less than 50 cents were not marked, but their containers were.

Then, alternative solutions were developed for handling the irregular occurrences, such as merchandise that did not arrive in cardboard cartons, or did not match exactly the purchase order. Then recommended system details were completed. These included obtaining estimates of the number of people and pieces of equipment needed to carry out the plan and the system's overall cost.

Continual review of the PDA efforts was provided by the team, two workshop groups, an outside consultant, and frequent meetings with top management. Many suggestions were made and incorporated, and some were tested to determine workability along with components of the basic proposal. Implementation

Adapted from "Increasing the Effectiveness of Productivity Services through a Systems Perspective," by Gerald Nadler, in *Proceedings, 1977 Congress of European Federation of Productivity Services*, Vienna, 22 April 1977.

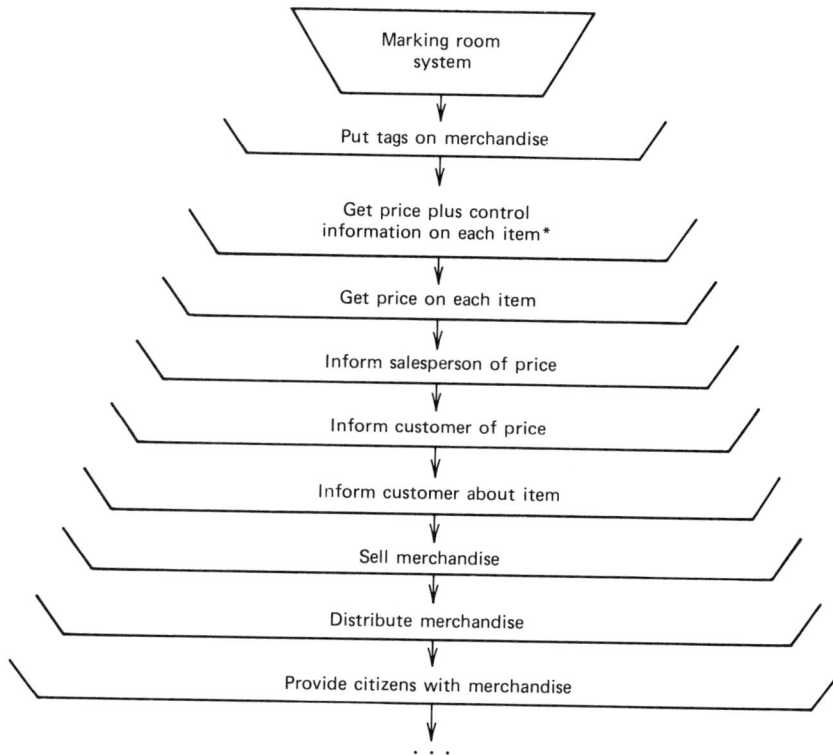

Figure 1-1 Purpose hierarchy for marking room system. Asterisk indicates selected level.

was completed after explanation and training sessions for several groups of people had been held, including detailed training for the marking room personnel.

Summary

The solution was multichanneled. The manager of materials handling said it would revolutionize the industry. Seventy percent of the total cost was saved. Over 25% of the original marking room space was saved. The time for processing merchandise from receipt until it is placed on the selling floor was reduced from 16 working hours to 4. Continuing administrative procedures for work measurement and scheduling procedures, originally requested by the vice president, were unnecessary.

The advantages of PDA in this situation are clear. By concentrating on the purposes in their marking room, rather than on applying techniques, a *direct* savings over twice that requested was achieved. Concentration on purposes and what "ought to be" rather than on measurements and data and/or how bad things were, provided a positive orientation for all the people in the marking room.

The approach enabled participants in the project to concentrate on the most frequently occurring and most important conditions first, and thus eliminated the confusion caused by trying to design for everything at once. It also allowed for the generation and consideration of a wide range of possible solutions. Further, PDA maximized the efficient use of planning resources. A relatively short period of time elapsed between the beginning of the project in late February and its installation in June. No one spent more than 35% of their working time on the project.

B. Fuel Reservoir Filler Cap

Situation

The United States Army Mobility Command (AMC) wanted a new fuel reservoir filler cap design for combat tank vehicles, which would cost less to produce than the cap currently in use. AMC sponsored a national design contest for engineering students, specifying the following performance characteristics: The cap must be free-breathing when the tank is on land (a valve must open when between 2 and 3 pounds per square inch of internal reservoir pressure is present), and it must be capable of sealing the filler neck of the reservoir to prevent leakage when the tank enters a body of water.

Working alone and using PDA, University of Wisconsin-Madison student Ferrill Stillson first listed

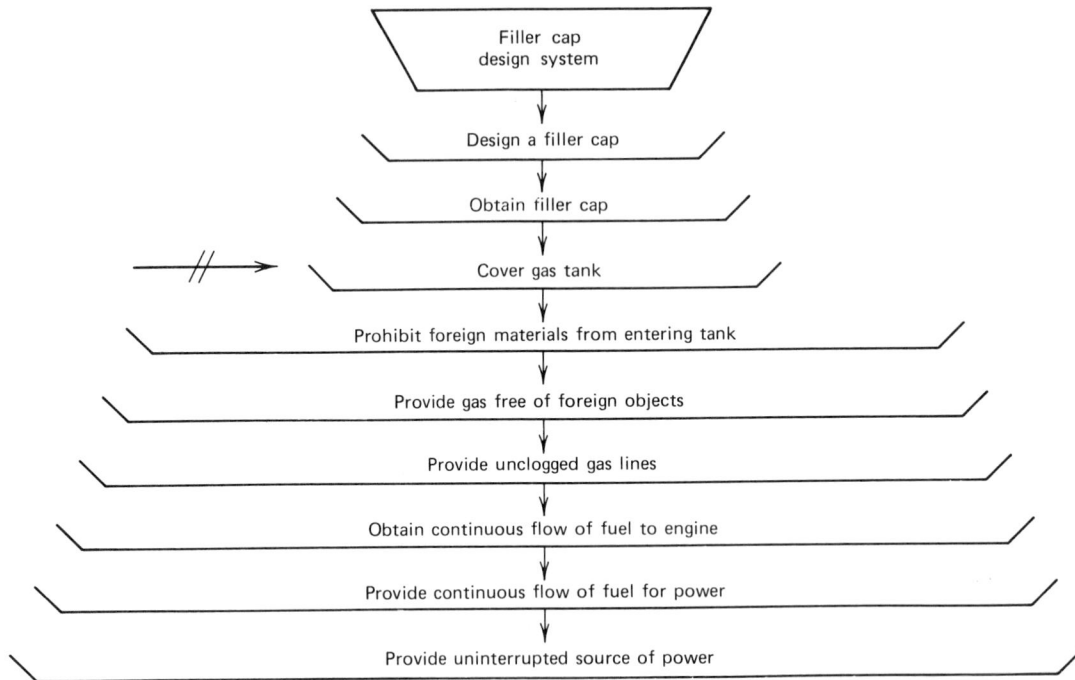

Figure 1-2 Function hierarchy for fuel tank filler cap. This is the hierarchy the student actually prepared. It contains statements the guides provided in Chapter Twelve would label as ineffective. However, the *concept* it portrays is the purpose of the illustration.

all the possible purposes the filler cap might have to fulfill, and from this list constructed a hierarchy of purposes (see Figure 1-2). Purpose number 3, "cover gas tank," was selected as the level at which he would focus his design efforts, but only after he determined that the contest did not enable him to argue for a bigger function level to provide greater potential savings.

Next, he used several creativity techniques to generate ideas for ideal solutions to the problem. Twelve major ideas resulted, including minor modifications of the current cap design, a new cap based on a snorkel tube, designing a different fuel storage system based on collapsible plastic containers, and seeking another source of power, such as a solar cell or small nuclear reactor for the tank. By focusing on the purpose rather than on the parts and materials of the existing filler cap design, Ferrill found he could identify many new and innovative ways to solve the problem, ways that went far beyond the original design. They were organized into two lists, one of "utopian" ideas and another of feasible ones. Details for each of the feasible ideas were investigated, and flawed and difficult-to-implement ideas were eliminated.

From the two major alternatives that remained (a snorkel tube, with a ping-pong-type ball to close the air vent when submerged, and a solution employing two separate caps, one for venting and the other sealing), the snorkel tube idea was selected, even though it was estimated to cost one-third more than the two-cap solution. The latter method required the caps to be changed by the vehicle operator as the situation required, a procedure far too error-prone.

Stillson refined the snorkel cap idea. After successive improvements a design with a ball in a small chamber, an internal air chamber, and a protective cover plate was produced.

When the design was completed the student developed the system necessary to produce the selected design. Costs were carefully estimated for each step in production to complete the recommendation to be submitted to contest officials.

This design won first prize in the U.S. Army Mobility Command national contest. Entries were submitted by 47 universities. Each of the entries from other universities was selected from 20 or 25 separate designs submitted by students to an instructor. As far as can be determined all other entries used conventional design methods.

Summary

Using PDA gave the student in this case several advantages he would not have had if he had followed a conventional approach: (1) the use of the purpose

Ferrill S. Stillson, 1969, industrial engineering student, University of Wisconsin-Madison.

hierarchy enabled him to free himself from past problem limitations and seek solutions that were unrelated to the old design but would still successfully accomplish the purpose; (2) the approach provided an effective, easy-to-learn framework for designing without a great deal of outside assistance; (3) it enabled him quickly and effectively to generate, organize, and evaluate a large number of alternatives; (4) by keeping the designer focused on seeking best possible or most ideal solutions rather than on collecting and analyzing data about the problem, the approach led to a superior recommendation; and (5) it maximized utilization of the limited design resources.

C. A System of Patient Care Based on Patient Needs

Situation

When the hospital administrators in the 33-member Hospital Council of the Greater Milwaukee Area decided to do something about the nurse shortage, members of the Milwaukee League for Nursing asked to work with the administrators. The result was a joint committee of six members. The committee concluded that the probability was high that the nurse shortage resulted as much from poor utilization as from an actual shortage. They agreed that no real benefits had been obtained from existing nurse utilization studies.

The committee enlarged its membership, including representatives from varied nursing educational programs, the state board of nursing, and the area hospital planning council. Also included were a physician, a consumer, additional administrators, and a hospital public relations director. The administrator of St. Mary's Hospital, Milwaukee, Wisconsin, offered the facilities of that hospital for a demonstration unit. Funding was provided by the Wisconsin Regional Medical Program, Inc., (WRMP) as of September 1969.

In the process of preparing a purpose hierarchy (Figure 1-3) the committee changed the focus of the project from level 2, how nurses are utilized, to levels 8 and 9, systems for care of patients. It was agreed that if effective systems to serve patient needs are implemented, nurses will be utilized correctly.

The new focus necessitated identifying what was meant by the expression "patient needs." Twenty-one needs in physical, sociopsychological, and environmental categories were identified. This led to a revi-

This case history is based on the following: J. M. Kraegel, V. Schmidt, R. K. Shukla, and C. E. Goldsmith, "A System of Patient Care Based on Patient Needs," *Nursing Outlook*, Vol. 20, No. 4, April 1972, pp. 247–264; E. P. Lewis, Editorial, *Nursing Outlook*, same issue; J. M. Kraegel et al., *Patient Care Systems*, Philadelphia: Lippincott, 1974.

sion of the project's selected purpose, which became "to observe, interpret and regulate patient's physical and sociopsychological function to meet his needs."

The needs for which patient care systems would be designed were: sleep and rest, food and fluids, plan of care, communication, verbal observation, vital signs, sociopsychology, physical hygiene, elimination, materials supply, infection control, patient orientation, patient education, medication, and discharge.

Each system was specified in terms of the inputs, outputs, procedures, equipment, environment, and workers required to meet the specific purpose for which it was being designed. A list of measures of effectiveness was developed for each system, with the identified needs playing an important role. For example, the need for privacy was a prime criterion in the elimination system, safety in the medication system, and security in the sleep and rest system.

As the component parts were integrated into the final patient care system the committee was surprised by what emerged. They had started without any preconceived ideas, the system's functions and procedures developing from the PDA process. They ended up, for instance, without a nurses station, because it never became evident throughout the entire design process that such an area could contribute toward meeting patient needs. Instead, the patient's plan of care, and doctor's notes, are always kept near each patient. Small work groups, each one responsible for a limited number of patients, were set up to provide each person with in-depth knowledge of a small number of patients. Standard supplies are kept in each patient room in a dual-access supply cabinet with a sealed-off disposal bin. A medication profile of the patient is on the inside of the supply cabinet door. A timer for the next medication causes a light to go on outside the room door as a reminder. Many other such features indicated that an innovative yet usable system had been designed.

The new solution was tested in a 39-bed unit. Evaluation of its performance showed that the same number of nurses could care for 48% more patients than in the previous system. This percentage is far higher than any previously achieved in efforts to "improve nurse utilization." In addition, the nurses expressed greater satisfaction with their work. Although the physicians initially balked at the time they would have to spend with each patient and at the change in their "routine," the essential elements of the system were incorporated in a new 500-bed hospital the board had built. Designing the project to achieve the purpose of caring for patients gave the committee an important insight as to the proper focus of nursing education and hospital design.

1. To obtain information about the way
hospital nurses spend their working hours

2. To determine how nurses are utilized in hospitals

3. To establish the characteristics
and magnitude of the hospital nursing shortage

4. To identify the critical nurse
characteristics and skills needed in hospitals

5. To define the needed nurse roles in a hospital

6. To relate nursing roles to hospital patient needs

7. To establish a pattern of
providing needed nurse roles in a hospital

8. To establish a system of providing
needed nursing care to hospital patients

9. To develop a system of providing nursing
services that meet the needs of hospital patients

10. To develop a system of providing services in hospital patient care units

11. To have available the services that meet the needs of hospital patients

12. To give patients hospital care

13. To give patients pre—, in—, and post —hospital care

14. To give patients continuing health care services

15. To give patients health care services

16. To produce socioeconomically well patients

17. To provide health care to citizens

18. To have a healthy population

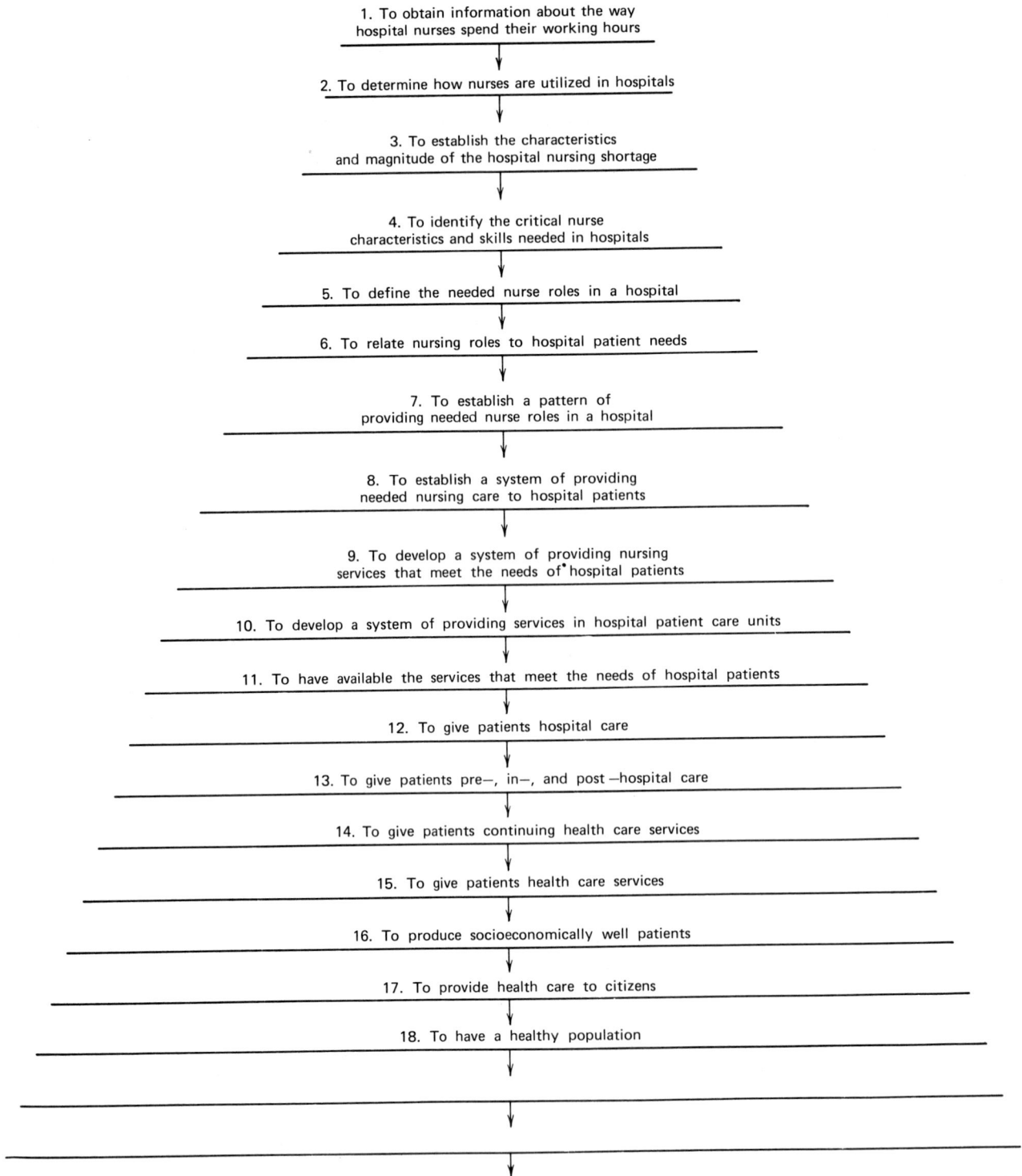

Figure 1-3   A simplified version of the function/purpose expansion for the nurse utilization project.

Summary

Using PDA resulted in important benefits. The purpose hierarchy insured that the committee sought a solution for the right problem, which as it turned out was not a shortage in the number of nurses. The target system improved nurse utilization when other methods failed, giving the hospital a unique solution suited to its needs.

THE TIMELINE SCENARIO COMMON TO ALL P&D

The PDA process illustrated in these cases is a flexible flow of holistic and multidimensional behavior that moves from a perceived problem to an implemented solution containing the seeds of its own change and improvement. Although it isn't possible to model the PDA reality in its totality, it is the identification and operationalization of five factors along a timeline that distinguishes PDA from most P&D theories. Their focus does not generally go beyond the strategy process. Seldom is a rationale provided that incorporates purposes, joint interaction with the client's world, and arranging for continuing change and improvement.

In addition, PDA sets the process in the context of time. Time is the only basis for a comprehensive theory of P&D. In the absence of crystal balls the business of planning for the future is risky at best. Time is irreversible, it cannot be capsulized in static snapshots for the convenience of P&D professionals, and the various factors in the process do not remain the same or change equally while the P&D professional works on one and then another snapshot. As a result, recommendations developed at one point in time may, before the proverbial ink is dry, be obsolete, because new data emerges, new technologies are developed, or the client's perception of the problem is no longer that of the P&D professional.

Conventional P&D compounds this dilemma. Generally, the "experts" collect large amounts of data and withdraw to their offices to "plan." Contact with the client occurs on a disjointed occasional basis. Seldom are the people in the client's world incorporated into the process. Defensiveness and skepticism result. Meanwhile the data collection effort changes the P&D experts' perception of the problem. Their solutions reflect these new perceptions. At the same time the client's world changes; perceptions, priorities and understanding of the problem alter. The scope and context of the project may differ dramatically from its initial conception.

Consequently, when the P&D experts make their recommendations the client rejects them. The premises underlying how each views the proposals are simply too divergent. The solution finally adopted, if any, is far too often a compromise neither party particularly likes. Lack of creativity, unachieved purposes, unmet objectives and failure to implement frequently characterize the results.

The PDA avoids this deadlock by integrating the changing realities of the client's world with the P&D process. The two worlds are kept in frequent contact, and techniques to build consensus and commitment to change are employed at each step. Successful implementation requires modifying the behavior and perceptions of the real-world people throughout the entire (PDA) process.

PDA accomplishes this by employing a timeline as the basis of its theory and methodology. The timeline scenario (Figure 1-4) does justice both to the complexity of P&D and to the problem of time. It provides a picture of the interaction of the five factors with each other and the client's world, day by day from the beginning of a project.

Although other factors may be identified in the future, research and empirical evidence about what successful P&D professionals do suggest that these five are currently sufficient. Most P&D theories at best merely offer exhortations advising professionals to think in holistic terms and to get people involved. PDA translates these and other concerns into operational parts of a timeline.

At first glance the timeline scenario looks complex and confusing. Do not be alarmed! The following chapters explain what the timeline is and how to use it. The timeline is a picture of PDA. This book is a journey through the territory of "good" planning and design. The timeline is the map of that journey. For now, it is enough to describe the five factors in the timeline running parallel to the "real world" of the client.

A note of caution: the structure of the timeline may suggest that PDA is a rigid step-by-step approach. It is not. Every P&D situation is unique, and its own specific PDA scenario will reflect that uniqueness. Terms may differ, for example, objectives may be called goals, or project teams may be called task forces. Strategy steps do not always proceed directly from numbers 1 to 19. Steps may occur out of sequence and be redone as the situation demands. What is important is the spirit of the timeline scenario, its pattern of reasoning, and its emphasis on holistic P&D.

Pursuing an Effective P&D Strategy

The PDA strategy is divided into five phases:

1 Develop a hierarchy of purpose statements from

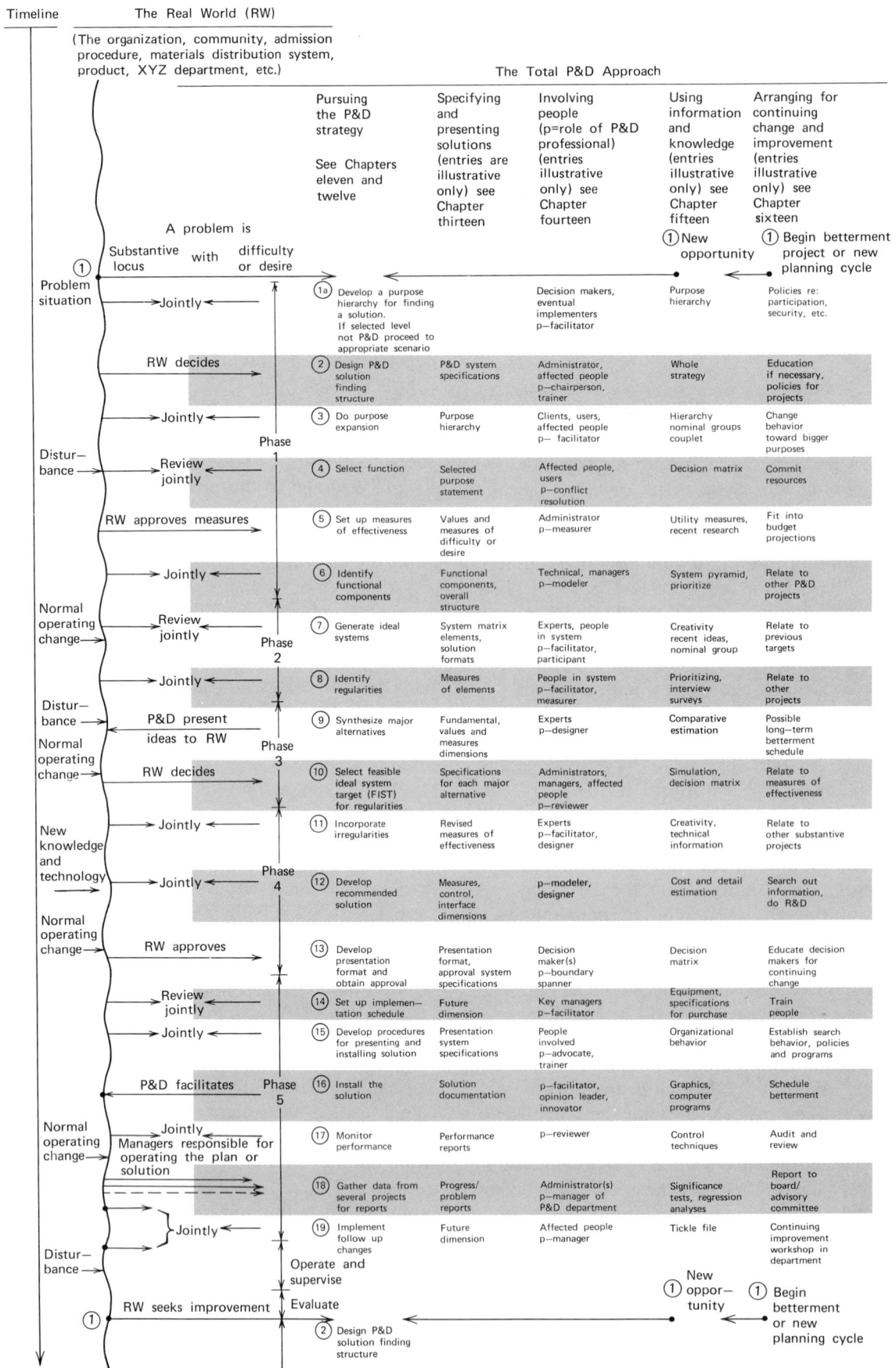

Figure 1-4 showing the planning and design scenario. Timeline (left), The Real World (RW), and The Total P&D Approach.

The Real World (RW)
(The organization, community, admission procedure, materials distribution system, product, XYZ department, etc.)

The Total P&D Approach

Step	Pursuing the P&D strategy (See Chapters eleven and twelve)	Specifying and presenting solutions (entries are illustrative only) see Chapter thirteen	Involving people (p=role of P&D professional) (entries illustrative only) see Chapter fourteen	Using information and knowledge (entries illustrative only) see Chapter fifteen	Arranging for continuing change and improvement (entries illustrative only) see Chapter sixteen
				(1) New opportunity	(1) Begin betterment project or new planning cycle
1a	Develop a purpose hierarchy for finding a solution. If selected level not P&D proceed to appropriate scenario		Decision makers, eventual implementers p-facilitator	Purpose hierarchy	Policies re: participation, security, etc.
2	Design P&D solution finding structure	P&D system specifications	Administrator, affected people p-chairperson, trainer	Whole strategy	Education if necessary, policies for projects
3	Do purpose expansion	Purpose hierarchy	Clients, users, affected people p-facilitator	Hierarchy nominal groups couplet	Change behavior toward bigger purposes
4	Select function	Selected purpose statement	Affected people, users p-conflict resolution	Decision matrix	Commit resources
5	Set up measures of effectiveness	Values and measures of difficulty or desire	Administrator p-measurer	Utility measures, recent research	Fit into budget projections
6	Identify functional components	Functional components, overall structure	Technical, managers p-modeler	System pyramid, prioritize	Relate to other P&D projects
7	Generate ideal systems	System matrix elements, solution formats	Experts, people in system p-facilitator, participant	Creativity recent ideas, nominal group	Relate to previous targets
8	Identify regularities	Measures of elements	People in system p-facilitator, measurer	Prioritizing, interview surveys	Relate to other projects
9	Synthesize major alternatives	Fundamental, values and measures dimensions	Experts p-designer	Comparative estimation	Possible long-term betterment schedule
10	Select feasible ideal system target (FIST) for regularities	Specifications for each major alternative	Administrators, managers, affected people p-reviewer	Simulation, decision matrix	Relate to measures of effectiveness
11	Incorporate irregularities	Revised measures of effectiveness	Experts p-facilitator, designer	Creativity, technical information	Relate to other substantive projects
12	Develop recommended solution	Measures, control, interface dimensions	p-modeler, designer	Cost and detail estimation	Search out information, do R&D
13	Develop presentation format and obtain approval	Presentation format, approval system specifications	Decision maker(s) p-boundary spanner	Decision matrix	Educate decision makers for continuing change
14	Set up implementation schedule	Future dimension	Key managers p-facilitator	Equipment, specifications for purchase	Train people
15	Develop procedures for presenting and installing solution	Presentation system specifications	People involved p-advocate, trainer	Organizational behavior	Establish search behavior, policies and programs
16	Install the solution	Solution documentation	p-facilitator, opinion leader, innovator	Graphics, computer programs	Schedule betterment
17	Monitor performance	Performance reports	p-reviewer	Control techniques	Audit and review
18	Gather data from several projects for reports	Progress/problem reports	Administrator(s) p-manager of P&D department	Significance tests, regression analyses	Report to board/advisory committee
19	Implement follow up changes	Future dimension	Affected people p-manager	Tickle file	Continuing improvement workshop in department
	Operate and supervise / Evaluate			(1) New opportunity	(1) Begin betterment or new planning cycle
2	Design P&D solution finding structure				

Timeline (left column): Problem situation; Disturbance; Normal operating change; Disturbance; Normal operating change; New knowledge and technology; Normal operating change; Normal operating change; Disturbance.

Real World (RW) actions: A problem is Substantive locus with difficulty or desire (1); Jointly; RW decides; Jointly; Review jointly; RW approves measures; Jointly; Review jointly; Jointly; P&D present ideas to RW; RW decides; Jointly; Jointly; RW approves; Review jointly; Jointly; P&D facilitates; Jointly — Managers responsible for operating the plan or solution; Jointly; RW seeks improvement.

Phases: Phase 1; Phase 2; Phase 3; Phase 4; Phase 5.

Figure 1-4 The planning and design scenario.

8

small to large, wherein each larger one describes the purpose of its predecessor(s). From this hierarchy, select the purpose a solution should achieve. Identify measures of effectiveness that indicate successful achievement of the selected purpose. More than one hierarchy and selected level may be involved.

2   Generate solution ideas that achieve both the selected and bigger purposes.

3   Group and shape ideas into major alternatives from which the most feasible ideal solution, the target solution, is selected. This solution considers only factors occurring with the greatest frequency, or having the greatest importance, otherwise known as regularity conditions.

4   Detail the recommended solution incorporating all necessary irregularities and exceptions, staying as close as possible to the target solution.

5   Install the solution, letting purposes and the target solution guide detailed installation. Create and maintain an environment conducive to continuing change and improvement.

By focusing on purposes, Phase 1 immediately pushes a P&D team into exploring alternative reasons for the effort. Constructing a purpose hierarchy expands the mental space in which solutions can be found by indicating the larger purposes the project can seek to accomplish. Pursuing these at the beginning is essential because there is no way of knowing whether a ''breakthrough'' solution can be attained. The process provides far greater certainty that a purpose which needs to be achieved will be selected than do conventional strategies. It ensures that the project will avoid focusing on the wrong problem and will have a worthwhile payoff. You will recall that in the three case histories it was the redefinition of stated purposes in a purpose hierarchy that led to effective innovative solutions.

Phase 2 focuses individual and group creativity on generating ''ideal'' solutions for the selected purposes within the context of the hierarchy. Many creativity techniques, such as morphological arrays, analogies, stimulator lists, and free association, are used to remove conceptual blocks and widen the choice of alternatives.

Phase 3 shapes the ideas into possible major alternatives. In this phase PDA encourages playing the ''believing game.'' This means focusing on how to make ideal solutions work, rather than on the reasons they won't—''trying on'' ideas to see how they fit. Specifying how an idea can be made operational often raises questions that need to be answered by data collection, research, or modeling techniques. It is then possible to select a feasible ideal solution target for

regularity conditions. This serves as a guide for developing recommendations. The regularity concept fosters creativity by allowing people to focus initially on one set of conditions rather than the many usually present.

Phase 4 works in the necessary exceptions and irregularities while seeking to maintain the desired qualities of the target solution. As a result, PDA solutions will often be multichanneled and pluralistic, involving more than one set of steps and even outcomes. Why discard the excellent solution that copes with 95% of the conditions because another 5% cannot directly fit into it? In this phase the solution is detailed. As much of the target solution as possible is incorporated to maintain a high potential for achieving ''ideal'' results.

Phase 5 uses the purposes, purpose hierarchy, suggestions for ideal solutions, target, and regularities in making the many, often minor, decisions that are necessary to install a solution. The continual interchanges between the P&D world and other members of the client's world make installation a natural action, rather than a sudden change ''they'' (the P&D world) impose. Even if real-world factors make full installation of the recommended solution impossible at this point in time, it remains a guide for the future.

Specifying and Presenting the Solution

The PDA solution framework provides a systematic basis for prescriptive notation of design specifications and plan preparation. It assures that important considerations will not be overlooked, and that possible consequences can be assessed. The framework separates the solution into eight elements, each with six dimensions, forming a 48-cell matrix (Figure 1-5). Many detailing benefits arise with the matrix: Each element can itself be viewed as a 48-cell matrix, each cell can as well, and most dimensions (e.g., control system) can also be viewed as a matrix. Each of these can also be extended if needed.

As one illustration of the prescriptive nature of the solution framework, consider briefly the *sequence* element of the marking room case. (1) Fundamental: buyer orders merchandise, tags are preprinted on the basis of purchase order, tags are put with merchandise when it arrives, tags are attached and used to check quantity, merchandise is sent to floor. Other flows and unit operations are also specified for stocking tags, information flow, merchandise received in wooden crates, handling scrap cardboard, as soon. (2) Values: minimize number of different jobs, assure that only quality merchandise is sent to sales floor, minimize in-process time in the marking room, and so on. (3) Measures: cost of roller conveyors, schedule of working time for employees, times of arrival for ship-

Dimensions

Elements	Fundamental: Basic or Physical, Characteristics—What, How, Where, or Who	Values: Motivating Beliefs, Global Desires, Ethics, Moral Matters	Measures: Objectives (Criteria, Merit and Worth Factors), Goals (How Much, When, Rates, Performance Specifications)	Control: How to Evaluate and Modify Element or System as It Operates	Interface: Relation of All Dimensions to Other Systems or Elements	Future: Planned Changes and Research Needs for All Dimensions
Purpose: mission, aim, need, primary concern, focus						
Inputs: people, things, information to start the sequence						
Outputs: desired (achieves purpose) and undesired outcomes from sequence						
Sequence: steps for processing inputs, flow, layout, unit operations						
Environment: physical and attitudinal, organization, setting, etc.						
Human agents: skills, personnel, responsibilities, rewards						
Physical catalysts: equipment, facilities, etc.						
Information aids: books, instructions, etc.						

Figure 1-5 Solution framework (system matrix). *Agents*, *catalysts*, and *aids* help process inputs into outputs without becoming part of outputs.

ping manifests. (4) Controls: "exception supervisors" to review merchandise that differs from purchase order statements, verifier to maintain counts on tags used for quantity checking. (5) Interfaces: accounts payable requirements for certifying receipt, notifying selling department about coming shipment. (6) Future: new computer to be word processer as well as tag producer, autonomous work groups, flexi-time work scheduling, automatic signal to selling departments.

Involving People

The need to maintain continual contact between the P&D professionals' and clients' worlds requires effective involvement of the clients throughout the PDA process. A P&D professional will probably guide a project team and may also work with an advisory group and many others connected with the client's world. By functioning in a variety of roles, such as facilitator, catalyst, modeler, expert, or coordinator at appropriate points in the strategy, the P&D professional can encourage participation. Group and individual techniques, such as delphi, interactive computers, and nominal groups enable people to take part as equals. Participation with purposes and targets paves the way for acceptance and implementation of solutions.

Arriving at effective implemented solutions ultimately depends on people—their understanding and their willingness to take action. The typical outcomes of conventional P&D—blueprints, flow diagrams, and proposed legislation—are not the endgoals of PDA. They may be interesting snapshots of the future, but they are only models of solutions. Implemented solutions require translating models into action. Successful implementation requires the people in both the P&D and client worlds to jointly modify their perceptions and behavior. Continuous interaction over time significantly increases the probability that commitments necessary to implementation will be made.

Using Knowledge and Information

A tidal wave of data and analytical techniques threatens to engulf the P&D professions. Budget programming, systems analysis, demand models, and multiattribute utility assessments may be needed occasionally on a project, but they do not in themselves constitute P&D. Quantitative techniques never mirror even a fraction of the real world. Overemphasizing them leads to model building rather than finding and implementing solutions. PDA rejects none of these techniques, but insists on using them in appropriate contexts identified in the PDA process.

The PDA approach to data collection is similar. By focusing on what purposes ought to be achieved rather than on what activities exist, PDA minimizes the amount of information formally collected and the number of experts needed. Effective involvement of people provides far more pertinent information in its proper context than any technique, model, or databank could ever produce. For example, if you want information about the regularity conditions for the form in which merchandise comes into a marking room (cardboard boxes, wooden crates, etc.), you can conduct a week-long sampling study at great expense, or you can simply ask the merchandise handlers.

Arranging for Continuing Change and Improvement

Time tarnishes even the best solutions. The most successful implemented solution is incomplete if it doesn't incorporate the seeds of its own improvement. An implemented solution should be treated as "provisional." Why wait until serious difficulties arise and people are threatened before making improvements? PDA encourages change, taking risks and recognizing the need for continual P&D in all areas of an organization, not just selected projects. PDA encourages an atmosphere of change by suggesting cyclical (every year or so) P&D to update target solutions. Each organization ought to have its own unique arrangements for continuing change and improvement. Throughout a project, the important perspectives suggested by these arrangements need to be incorporated.

THE THEORETICAL RATIONALE FOR THE PDA

Several basic premises and principles form the basis of the PDA scenario. They comprise a PDA mind-set that improves the ability to use the approach. Because real projects require a unique set of scenario adaptations, a professional who understands the premises and principles will make more effective decisions along the way. The rest of this chapter provides a broad overview of the conceptual basis for PDA. Those wanting in-depth insight can refer directly to Chapters Two through Ten.

The rationale has four components. First is a set of axioms, which are the basis of PDA, followed by a set of propositions describing PDA. Third is a set of principles based on the propositions and timeline, useful both in setting up a P&D system and doing the actual work on a project. Finally, P&D is situated in the context of other human purposes. Isolating P&D from other human concerns undermines its effectiveness.

Axiom 1   A continuous (rather than discrete) timeline is the fundamental basis for understanding the past, present or future of any phenomenon.

Axiom 2   Humans perform purposeful activities that influence and are influenced by the time-variant objectives and goals they seek to attain.

Axiom 3   Everything is a system.

Axiom 4   Each system is part of at least one hierarchy of systems.

Corollary 4a. Each system is part of at least one larger system.

Corollary 4b. Each system is composed of smaller systems.

Corollary 4c. Each system exists parallel to other systems.

Axiom 5   Each system can at any point in time be identified in one of three conditions of existence—future, satisfactory, or unsatisfactory.

Corollary 5a. A system tends toward unsatisfactory existence.

Axiom 6   A word is only a representation of a reality, not the real thing.

Corollary 6a. Models are incomplete representations of real-life phenomena.

Corollary 6b. A solution on paper is not the desired change or implementation.

Axiom 7   No two situations or things are identical.

Corollary 7a. There is no such thing as certainty in the future.

Corollary 7b. A solution for a specific problem in one organization differs from the solution for a similar problem in another organization.

Corollary 7c. An analogy cannot prove that a premise should be accepted.

Axiom 8   A system processes inputs into outputs that achieve and satisfy a purpose or purposes through the use of human, physical, and information resources in a sociological and physical environment.

Corollary 8a. Each element can be specified or detailed in terms of dimensions, properties, or attributes.

Corollary 8b. Each element and dimension of a system is a system.

Corollary 8c. Each cell of a system matrix is a system.

Axioms

Axioms are the starting point of a structure of inference. They are truths that need not be necessarily proved, because people are willing to accept them on face value. The axioms are explained at length in Chapters Six through Nine; they are presented here to indicate the basis for the propositions and principles that follow (see Table 1-1).

P&D Propositions

Propositions describe the features of PDA helpful to practitioners in real-world efforts. Many of these will be familiar, as they form the background of the PDA scenario previously described. They are drawn from the axioms.

The propositions demonstrate that PDA is designed to cope with the uncertainties of the future, as the real-world timeline illustrates. They emphasize that planning is a human endeavor, and therefore cannot be removed from the context of human needs and perspectives. The propositions explain why a P&D approach must be oriented toward changing perceptions and behavior. They remind professionals that even the most technical P&D effort has social and political dimensions requiring client participation.

The propositions illustrate that the objectives of P&D itself are related to those of the larger organization, company or city of which it is a part. A P&D system, like any other, may not yet be in existence, may be satisfactory, or be in need of improvement. But whatever the state of the planning system, of utmost importance is that there be action along a timeline to insure implementation of its solutions. The solution framework presented previously is a particularly useful implementation tool. The PDA scenario, taken as a whole, both provides a protocol (a P&D system) for planning, and assures a higher probability of solution implementation.

Proposition 1   *P&D efforts take place along a timeline parallel with the real-world entity in which the problem or need emerges.*

Corollary Proposition 1a   *The real world entity changes along the timeline and is thus different at various points in time after the parallel P&D effort begins.*

Corollary Proposition 1b   *P&D must adapt to and provide opportunities for real world consideration of various process steps and appropriate interim and recommended solutions.*

Corollary Proposition 1c   *P&D includes the incorporation of proposed plans and designs into operating activities. Plans and designs, by themselves, are insufficient P&D outcomes.*

Corollary Proposition 1d   *Successful P&D develops supporting links with the real-world entity's valued elements of the past and present.*

Proposition 2   *P&D is a purposeful activity in which humans want to engage.*

Proposition 3   *P&D is a system.*

Proposition 4   *P&D is part of at least one hierarchy of purposes.*

Corollary Proposition 4a *P&D at any level is open to and a part of a larger system (division, organization, city, company, etc.).*

Corollary Proposition 4b *P&D is composed of smaller P&D levels.*

Corollary Proposition 4c *P&D parallels other organizational activities and purposes as well as other internal and external P&D.*

Proposition 5 *P&D as part of its larger system (e.g., in a company) at any point in time can be in one of three conditions of existence—future, satisfactory, or unsatisfactory.*

Corollary Proposition 5a *P&D tends toward unsatisfactory existence.*

Proposition 6 *A planned P&D effort is not the same as effective P&D.*

Proposition 7 *The structure of a P&D effort operating satisfactorily in one setting should not be transferred to another effort or organization.*

Proposition 8 *A P&D system processes inputs into outputs of implemented plans, designs, or solutions that achieve and satisfy a P&D purpose through the use of human, physical, and information resources in a social and physical environment.*

Corollary Proposition 8a *Each element and dimension of the P&D system can be treated as a system.*

Corollary Proposition 8b *Each cell of the P&D system matrix can be treated as a system.*

Corollary Proposition 8c *The elements and dimensions of a P&D system are interdependent.*

Proposition 9 *A purpose design strategy or path of reasoning along a timeline significantly increases the probability of maximizing the effectiveness of a recommended solution, the likelihood of its implementation, and the effectiveness of resources used in the P&D effort.*

Proposition 10 *A universally applicable, prescriptive system matrix is a cost-effective framework for specifying and presenting the needed conditions of a P&D solution.*

Proposition 11 *Involving people in the P&D system as inputs, outputs, part of the environment, actors in following the P&D strategy, information aids, and human agents can maximize the number and effectiveness of implemented solutions and the effectiveness of utilizing P&D resources.*

Proposition 12 *Knowledge, information, and models aggregate data which can be used cost-effectively in P&D if each aggregation includes statements about its relative inability to predict an occurrence or performance value of a future specific instance or case, emphasizes the importance of its integration with the other four P&D factors, and is presented with accuracy and precision values to reflect past and present conditions.*

Proposition 13 *An implemented P&D change can be considered complete only when the solution includes a closely interwoven set of future specifications, just as the people working where its changes occur should continually search for improvements in all current systems and for solutions to meet new needs.*

PDA Principles

The timeline scenario and the propositions result in a set of principles embodying the operational aspects of PDA. They are listed below. Following each principle are the relevant PDA factors, and the numbers of related axioms and their corresponding propositions.

1 Each organization and project is unique. Don't initiate P&D by trying to install a solution from somewhere else. (Strategy, Involving people, Search for change—1,7)

2 Think PURPOSE. Think purpose hierarchy. Continually ask "for what purpose/function," or "what is to be accomplished." (Strategy, Solution framework—4,6)

3 Aim toward what the solution would be if you could start fresh, rather than starting with what presently exists. (Strategy, Involving people—4,5,6,7)

4 Develop many alternatives (as ideal as possible) and keep them as options for as long as possible before selecting one. (Strategy, Involving people—2,5)

5 Develop a feasible ideal TARGET for regularities to serve as a guide for continual changes. (Strategy, Involving people, Search for change—5,6,7)

6 Don't worry about everything at once. Treat regularities before irregularities. Separate activities that have different purposes. (Strategy, Involving people, Using knowledge—1,4,7)

7 Treat each problem as a system, regardless of size, including the "problem" of setting up the solution-finding structure. (Solution framework, Using knowledge—3,4,5,8)

8 Gather information only when necessary to an-

swer a specific question. Avoid redundancy. (Involving people, Using knowledge—6)

9   Develop solutions that fit users. These are likely to be pluralistic and multichanneled while using appropriate (low, intermediate, high) technology. (Solution framework, Involving people, Using knowledge, Search for change—1)

10 Give people affected the continual OPPORTUNITY to be involved in P&D. (Involving people, Search for change—2)

11 Specify only the minimum number of critical details and controls. Give some flexibility to people operating the system. (Solution framework, Involving people, Using knowledge—2)

12 Set up a schedule for change and improvement when implementing a solution. (Search for change—5,8)

Extensive empirical evidence indicates the PDA is superior to conventional P&D. Case histories as well as controlled experiments demonstrate that development of purpose hierarchies produces high-quality results; that group process techniques are more effective than interactive discussions; and that solution implementation starts at the beginning, not the end, of a project.

Nature of Human Purposeful Activities and Problems

Humans consciously seek to better their condition. Consequently, every human faces problems, as does every human group. Defining the word *problem* provides a basis for understanding the relationship between problems and P&D. A problem is a substantive matter about which there is a human concern. The substantive matter of a problem is both the specific problem situation and the type of purposeful activity involved. The human concern is a function of basic social values and particular goals and objectives for the situation.

The specific settings of problems cannot be adequately addressed in any general theory, but an analysis of human purposeful activities is possible and useful. The following categorization of purposeful activities illustrates the range of activity types:

1   *Assure self-preservation and survival* of the species.
2   *Operate and supervise* an existing system.
3   Create or restructure a situation-specific solution (*planning and design*).
4   Search for generalizations and causes (*research*).

5   *Evaluate* performance of solutions or other purposeful activities.
6   Gain skills or acquire knowledge (*learn*).
7   Experience *leisure*.

Many secondary purposeful activities appear frequently within each one at many points.

Clearly, it is toward (3), the problems and questions associated with planning and design, that PDA is directed. Nevertheless it is important to situate PDA in the context of other human and societal purposes. Unfortunately, much conventional P&D is considered an end in itself, independent of other human concerns.

Establishing that humans are involved in different purposeful activities leads to the notion that each activity type requires a different solution-finding approach. The mind-set and methods for each will be essentially different. This has profound implications for P&D, whose methodology heretofore has resembled that of research or operating and supervising with their emphasis on reductionism and collecting data. The inappropriateness of such methodologies is underscored when one considers the radically different results sought by planners and researchers and consequently their different mind-sets. Without detailing the differences at length, it is enough to note that the P&D person attempts to change specific solutions and systems, while the researcher hopes to keep them in the same state for observation and generalization purposes. This is not to say that there will not be methodological overlaps. A timeline scenario, for example, could form the basis of a separate total approach to each purposeful activity. PDA forms such an approach to planning and design. But its directives are not written in stone; they continue to change and improve. PDA's benefits accrue from the significantly greater probability that the three basic objectives of P&D will be met.

WHAT'S NEXT

This chapter began with case histories and the PDA timeline and methods. It then presented the axioms, propositions, and principles that form the conceptual basis of the PDA scenario. Lastly, it touched on human purposeful activities, assumptions, and perceptions, that explain the setting from which the rest arose. The remainder of this book reverses the order of coverage. Part One concerns purposeful activities, assumptions, and perceptions, Part Two discusses axioms and propositions, and Part Three deals with the operational scenario and methods. Appendix A indexes techniques and models appropriate for P&D. Appendix B presents other case histories to complement those with which this chapter opened.

PART ONE

The Setting

Planning and design encompass a big world. But that world is only a part of a much larger one. It is possible to consider P&D by itself. However, successful implementation of effective solutions is far more likely to occur if the larger vista serves as a guide. Part One describes this larger vista and lays the groundwork for a total approach to P&D.

Chapter Two situates P&D in the context of six other human purposeful activities. It presents a two-part perspective on the nature of problems and classifies them in terms of the seven purposeful activities.

Chapter Three considers various problem-solving approaches. It synthesizes them into a holistic perspective which can currently be explained in terms of five factors integrated along a timeline. The five factors become the foundation for operationalizing approaches to meet the specific needs of each purposeful activity.

Chapter Four explores the characteristics of P&D as a purposeful activity. It focuses on the objectives common to over 30 P&D professions, and describes the problems that thwart their realization.

Chapter Five considers conventional P&D approaches and their failure to promote effective implemented solutions. It describes the basic human realities, behaviors, and perceptions that must be incorporated into a total approach to P&D if solutions are to be effective and implemented.

CHAPTER TWO

A Perspective
on Problems

All organisms face problems. Nonhuman organisms encounter a limited range of them, and their resolution is most often the result of genetic programming.

Humans, conversely, constantly confront a baffling array of problems or needs, from the simple to complex: What to eat? When to marry? Which career? When to sleep? In addition, humans form innumerable groups, each with its own particular problems. Their resolution is seldom programmed or simple, depending instead on human intelligence, attitude and knowledge base.

Nonetheless, philosophically speaking, there is no such thing as a problem. At least not in the same way that there are chairs, computers, or tornadoes. Some thing or situation becomes a problem or need only if humans identify it as one. Problems exist solely because of human purposes and aspirations.

This chapter establishes a framework for conceptualizing the word *problem*. This is essential for P&D. Planners and designers are above all problem solvers. Defining the problem is critical; it structures both the solution-finding approach and the solution.

"The primary task of the problem solver is the formulation of what the problem is rather than a determination of a decision. The resulting decision is implicit in the way the problem is formulated."[1]

PROBLEM—A DEFINITION

The dictionary defines a problem as a substantive matter about which there is concern. A substantive matter may be a question, situation, phenomenon, person or issue. A concern may be an uncertainty, obstacle, desire, difficulty, or doubt. Other formulations abound. Dewey calls a problem a "felt difficulty"; for Davis it is "a stimulus situation for which an organism doesn't have a ready response";[2] for deBono "a difference between what one has and what one wants."[3] Generic ideas include a gap, dissatisfaction, and obstacle. Whatever the formulation, a problem remains something that causes concern.

This formulation designates the "something," the substantive aspect, and "the concern," the values aspect. The substantive aspect includes both the type of problem and its specific locus. The locus is the "what, where, when, and who" unique to each problem situation. The values aspect encompasses the desires, aspirations and needs that have made the substantive aspect a matter of concern. For example, in the case history (Chapter One) concerning patient care, the substantive aspect was designing a health care delivery system for a specific hospital; the values aspect was providing good patient care and using nurses effectively. This formulation differs in some important respects from others suggested by P&D practitioners and scholars, both in specifying a values aspect and categorizing problems by activity type. Such a conceptualization, as will be demonstrated, is essential to effective P&D.

A careful investigation of each aspect follows. In the substantive aspect, a format is proposed that classifies problems in the context of human purposeful activities. This enables a person to identify the type of problem they have and the appropriate methodology for solving it. The values aspect explores the human motivations that make something a problem or need. Is such an investigation just another exercise in academic futility? Consider the positive benefits to actual problem solving:

- Defining the substantive aspect of a particular problem assures that an appropriate methodology will be used. For example, a particular situation may pose a planning and design problem. If it is approached as a research problem the end product is likely to be a series of "studies," not an operational solution. Strict attention to a problem type and locus significantly reduces the possibility of an error of the third kind: finding the "perfect" solution for the wrong problem.[4]
- A clear idea of a problem's locus centers the problem-solving effort on the specifics of each unique situation. Rather than a solution being transferred from another situation, say, an evaluation of a procedure, each solution is tailored to specific needs, values, and resources. The abysmal failure of attempts to transfer American agricultural solutions to Third World Countries underscores this point.
- Designating a problem's value aspects places problem solving squarely in the context of human aspirations and needs. This forestalls the unhappy tendency of P&D professionals, for example, to become specialists with a "limited sense of ethical responsibility,"[5] whereby it is assumed that problems will be defined simply to fit into available techniques; and that solutions will reflect normative concerns. Swift's modest proposal—eat children to end overpopulation and hunger—is clearly satire but it evokes the specter of valueless solutions.

The Substantive Aspect of a Problem

What is a problem? What kinds of problems are there? Formats and taxonomies abound. Because practitioners and scholars seek solutions they classify problems. Ironically, classification both leads to and reflects solution approaches. Taxonomies range from the minimal—since there is only one problem-solving approach (the research method) there is no need to clas-

sify problems—to the mind-boggling. *The Futurist*, the magazine of the World Future Society, identifies 2653 problems humanity faces, ranging from nuclear war to art forgery. The classifications thus include:

- *Classification by a Problem Typology* Business tends to classify problems in the categories of finance, personnel, marketing, manufacturing, administration, and product development. Historians usually categorize problems as ones of art, religion, economics, science, politics, or language. Problems can be arranged by interest groups or estates: political, professional, administrative, and scientific.[6] Often problems are classified by discipline: engineering, astrophysics, sociology, and so on.
- *Classification by Solution-finding Method* In these formats problems are subsumed under a single method, usually a variant of the research approach. Some illustrations include the Kepner-Tregoe Process,[7] Management by Objectives,[8] and the systems approach.[9]
- *Classification by Analytical Technique* This is a variant of classification by solution-finding method. It admits that not all problems can be solved by the same technique but that problems can be categorized according to the specific technique *assumed* to solve them, such as linear programming, cost-benefit analysis, statistical inferences, or work measurement.

These classifications have serious deficiencies. The result is often ineffective problem solving. First, few formats point to a specific problem-solving methodology. Those that do focus on a single "correct" approach. The existence of many "correct" approaches suggests that exclusive reliance on any one may be risky.

Second, formats based on analytical techniques lead to deterministic thinking and rigid definitions of problems. For instance, long lines at bus stops are subsumed under the rubric of a "queueing theory problem." The tendency is for the problem solver to reach for a technique rather than grapple with larger issues outside his specialty or too messy to quantify. The existence of analytic techniques may even create "made" problems, for example, attempts to define problems to fit the parameters of new computer systems. The possibility of working on the wrong problem increases dramatically.

Finally, classification by type tends to be based on physical or structural similarities rather than purposes or functions. Physical and structural categories engender little prescriptive understanding of what to do about the problem. Also, categories are based on existing problems, that is, they are constructed on hindsight. Hindsight is hardly the way, particularly for P&D, to determine the type or nature of new problems and solutions.

These deficiencies mandate a different perspective on problems. Such a perspective should meet the following criteria:

- Categories should minimally overlap but still encompass all the problems associated with all activities in which humans engage.
- While identifying problems, categories should focus on the purposes with which humans confront a situation rather than on the problems themselves. To do otherwise unnecessarily restricts the solution-finding space. Philosophers and psychologists have noted also that a focus on the problems indicates a society is ill and is "going downhill."[10]
- The categories should produce a prescriptive understanding of what to do about the problem, that is, suggest a methodology.
- Categories should enhance the probability of working on the right problem and developing creativity in solution finding.

The following classification organizes problems on the basis of purposeful activities, that is, on the repertoire of behavior we employ day in and day out in the process of living. This classification emerges from the imperatives of the preceding criteria.

Human Purposeful Activities

Purpose implies aim or intention. Activities are the behaviors associated with aim or intention. The following categories are the fundamental human purposeful activities:

1 Assure self-preservation and survival of the species: *self-preservation*.
2 Operate and supervise an existing solution or system: *operate and supervise*.
3 Create or restructure a situation-specific solution or system: *plan and design*.
4 Search for generalizations: *research*.
5 Evaluate performance of previous solutions or other purposeful activities: *evaluate*.
6 Gain skills or acquire knowledge about existing information and generalizations: *learn*.
7 Experience leisure: *leisure*.

These types are deliberately presented as a set of ideas rather than words. The words *design* and *evaluate*, for instance, have specific connotations in various professions, but shouldn't interfere with the reader's grasp of the behaviors they are meant to convey.

You should note immediately that, unlike other classifications by type, this one does not focus on an issue or object. For example, food as a problem could be associated with all seven. The types enable you to identify whether food in a specific situation poses a problem of self-preservation, operate and supervise, plan and design, learn, leisure, or research. For example, in relation to food, you may be planning a diet, operating and supervising one, or evaluating it.

The types are not mutually exclusive: each may be involved with, and depend on, the other. For example, successful planning and design frequently requires, at various points in a project, research, evaluation, learning, and operating and supervising.

Assure Self-Preservation and Survival of the Species

These are paramount purposes shared by humans and animals. Included are all life support systems: food, shelter, safety, and procreation. Studies with animals as well as humans suggest that love and self-esteem are necessary to survival.[11] Self-preservation may also depend on satisfaction of social and creative needs.

The scope and type of these activities vary with the dictates of history and environment. The civil rights movement and women's liberation can be considered in a very real sense to be self-preservation activities.

Operate and Supervise an Existing Solution or System: Operate and Supervise (O&S).

Human capabilities enable us to change our environment. These changes require operation and supervision to maintain their structure and function. To some extent everyone engages in O&S. A father and mother operate and supervise the system called a family, a student a study schedule, a mayor a city. The activities of O&S range from those of a janitor to a minister operating and supervising the religious system, to those of bureaucrats and business managers. O&S concerns systems and solutions that people participate in routinely, expecting fairly standardized results. A society without such systems would be in chaos.

Ironically, this purposeful activity poses a real threat to our society: the exponential growth of bureaucracy. People operating bureaucracies often fail to understand the purpose of the system. Consequently, the system may be operating beautifully and simultaneously be counterproductive to the original purposes for which it was established.

Create or Restructure a Situation-Specific Solution or System: Plan and Design

Human history is the story of innovative solutions: plows, Roman aqueducts, the Mona Lisa, the Constitution, computer systems. Throughout the ages, individuals have emerged with the gift of imagination. Planning and design activities result in custom-made solutions, policies, and designs that restructure existing systems or create new ones. As a purposeful activity, P&D is concerned with inventing the specifics of how a particular locus ought to be arranged. Good P&D develops those specifics to satisfy as much as possible the desires and values motivating the effort. P&D is concerned with imagining, designing, and implementing new and restructured systems and solutions, O&S with maintaining them. The latter stresses standardization and routine, the former flexibility and innovation. Imagination and foresight are P&D hallmarks. P&D provides informed recommendations about decisions affecting the future.

Search for Generalizations: Research

The desire for explanation is pervasive. We want to know "how the world is created, how it developed and brought forth humankind, and how one day it will end."[12] This boundless curiosity flowered into science and other bodies of systematic thought. Frequently the result of this activity is new knowledge in the form of laws and theories explaining the relationships among, and the characteristics of, phenomena and events.

Pure research develops generalizations for their own sake, applied research meets the needs of other purposeful activities. There is a certain tension between those who seek truth for itself and those who believe, like Francis Bacon, that "knowledge is not to be sought for the pleasure of the mind . . . but for the benefit and use of life."[13]

Developing generalizations is not the exclusive domain of philosophers, scientists, and the myriad number of professionals engaged in research. Even the homeowner testing the relationship of certain types of fertilizer to lawn health is doing research.

The reliability and utility of generalizations vary with the phenomena where connections are sought. The physical and natural sciences produce the most reliable (or noncontroversial) ones, religion the least. Obviously, the importance of generalizations is not solely a function of "objective predictability."

Evaluate Performance of Previous Solutions or Other Purposeful Activities: Evaluate

How well did a solution work? Did it achieve its purpose? These are questions posed in an evaluation. The aim of evaluation or auditing is to provide information about performance, assure accountability, and lead to improvement. It occurs at all levels, at the level of the individual class session or the entire course, of one individual patient or of total hospital care. Evaluation occurs in relationship to every other purposeful activity. A board of directors' evaluation of capital expenditure paybacks and assessment of compliance with employment regulations occur in the process of operating a particular system. Evaluation of a pilot project is frequently an integral feature of P&D.

Gain Skills or Acquire Knowledge: Learn

If everyone were forced to rediscover all knowledge and skills previously developed, civilization would be in sad shape. Learning is the purposeful activity by which knowledge and techniques are transmitted. Learning takes place in a variety of structured and unstructured situations. Its results vary from the development of analytic and predictive ability to the development of the capacity for synthesis, decision making, and insights. Successful accomplishment of other purposeful activities depends on people who know the appropriate generalizations and techniques.

Experience Leisure

Leisure provides relaxation or recreation. It represents demand-free time for self-determined activities and pleasures. Leisure ranges from doing absolutely nothing to highly structured endeavors often resembling "work." Many forms of leisure may actually be another purposeful activity. Painting, composing, and sculpting clearly involve planning and design. Leisure and the problems associated with it underscore the notion that problems are not merely the result of avoiding noxious stimuli, as is common to most psychological problem models, but are also a result of stimulus seeking.[14]

Secondary Purposeful Activities

The primary purposeful activities include a number of secondary ones. These secondary purposeful activities are not exclusive to any single primary activity but occur frequently in all. They include:

Make a decision.

Maintain a standard of achievement (control or micro-O&S).

Resolve a conflict (of opinion, personality, etc.).

Make a model of or abstract a phenomenon.

Develop creative ideas.

Establish priorities.

Practice and exercise.

Focus and motivate individual efforts.

The fundamental purposeful activity sets the context for the secondary ones. Make a decision about what—operate and supervise, or plan and design a solution? Resolve a conflict about what—evaluation or learning? Develop creative ideas about what? Model a situation for what purpose? Establish priorities for what reason? Practice a skill for what reason? The primary activities spell out the alternatives about which a decision is to be made, the characteristics of the phenomenon to be modeled, and the categories to be prioritized.

The Values Aspect of a Problem

Why does something become a problem? Why do humans seek to better the world and themselves? What does "better" mean anyway? Where do aspirations and ideals come from? Such questions are essentially unanswerable and far beyond the scope of this book. But even if we cannot know the causes of human motivations and values, we can assess, albeit incompletely and inaccurately, their expression. What follows is a clarification of the values, goals and objectives forming the "why" aspect of a problem. It should be noted that these values reflect a Western bias.

Contemporary theorists argue that values, ethics, and motivation stem from human instincts, wants, and desires for certainty and security. The nature of these "needs" has been explored by various authors. The needs hierarchy constructed by Abraham Maslow is one of the best known.[15] It delineates the multifaceted aspect of "needs," and acknowledges a wide variety of human behaviors. (It validates human needs often relegated by reductionists to the metaphysical garbage bin.) The hierarchy is (1) physiological existence, and (2) security needs, (3) social and affiliative needs, (4) esteem and reputation, (5) autonomy and independence, and (6) self-actualization. Two other needs were initially suggested but not rigidly included: (7) cognitive need to learn and understand, and (8) esthetic. As a person's needs are met at one level, they are likely to seek the next.

In discussing human motivations it is essential to define the word *better*. *Better* can have many meanings. It never reflects a single desire or need. For example, a better understanding (search for generalizations) of rain means concern for accuracy, precision, completeness, level of water supply, impacts and so forth. When the desire for "better" is directed towards some thing or situation, it can be expressed on three levels: as values, as objectives, and as goals. In the preceeding example, "better" embraces *the values* of "learning for its own sake" and the desire to apply knowledge about rain to meet human needs.

Values are also beliefs, desired end states, societal and individual aspirations and desiderata. For example, safety, convenient schedules, and passengers' comfort, are values in a city mass transit system. These values are then expressed in specific objectives and goals (measures). *Objectives* are the criteria for determining how well a particular value for a purposeful activity is achieved (accident rate, time between buses, rider complaints). *Goals* are the performance levels or amount of an objective to be attained within specified time and cost limits (reduce accident rate by two percentage points in one year, maintain current 10 minutes between buses, reduce complaints by 50% in six months).

The words *values, objectives,* and *goals* will be used with these meanings throughout this book. These words along with *purpose* and *function* are often used interchangeably in usual P&D literature. The meanings of *objective* and *goal* are often reversed. The reader should use whatever *word* best suits the circumstances but maintain the distinction of *meanings* noted here. In defining a problem, people need to assess the values, objectives, and goals of the particular purposeful activity in which they are engaged and those of the specific problem locus. After all, it is the desire for "better" as expressed in the values and measures of human purposeful activities that makes "a problem" of a particular phenomenon. An effective solution will reflect and deliver more of the values than were present at the recognition of the "problem." Objectives and goals operationalize values for a specific locus.

What are these values? The values of a society reflect those of the individuals and groups composing it, now and in the past. It is virtually impossible for people to agree on one formulation of them, but the high degree of similarity among various value systems is striking. Most reflect a "belief in the values of the past, acceptance of the worth of economic and technological growth, faith in reason and in the kind of scientific and scholarly knowledge that can come from reason alone, and belief in the intrinsic importance, the ineffaceable worth of life on this earth."[16] The desire for "better" is the basis for these values. What does "better" entail in this context? One component is the desire to achieve greater effectiveness. Ideas associated with greater effectiveness are listed in Table 2-1.

Greater effectiveness is largely concerned with harnessing limited natural and human resources to do more. Although this could be an end in itself, inquiry into its result or value reveals another component of "better."

The result of seeking greater effectiveness is attainment of a higher quality of life. The values associated with such attainment are concerned primarily with the physical goals of life. Overemphasizing them

Table 2-1   Ideas Involved in the Societal Value of
Achieving Greater Effectiveness

(a) *Greater productivity,* increase the results of utilizing
any resource such as person-hours, or getting the same
results with less cost or time

(b) *Increased efficiency,* a component of productivity;
minimize costs and waste of human, information,
physical, and environmental resources

(c) *Improved profits* or return on investment (or assets or
equity) for private sector organizations, or apparently
increased discretionary income for nonprofits (hospitals, museums)

(d) *Improved services* per dollar, or the same services for
fewer dollars

(e) *Improved quality* of products, services, R&D results
(utility, pleasantness of services, ease of effort, reduced
waiting time, pluralism of solutions, etc.), and increased
degree to which necessary purposes are achieved

(f) *Increased market share* or target population served

(g) *More built-in and continuing change* within any solution

(h) *Improved relationships* with various constituencies,
such as customers (clients), suppliers, community, and
labor representatives

(i) *Improved capacity to increase quantity of goods and
services,* including reindustrialization, retrofitting of old
facilities, and remanufacturing or recycling of artifacts
that are considered worn out

Table 2-2   Ideas Involved in the Societal Value
of Attaining a Higher Quality of Life

(a) *Peace* among nations, elimination of aggression, international and national order, minimization of conflicts
among groups

(b) *Standard of living,* including improved or optimum food
and clothing, attractive housing, vacations, health
status, recreation, number of work hours per week,
general pleasantness and sociability, diets, medicines
and vitamins, length of life, and labor-management relationships

(c) *Cost and level of health care delivery* in all situations
(accidents, diseases, prevention, etc.)

(d) *Transportation and mobility systems*

(e) *Security in retirement and in the face of misfortune,*
such as floods, tornadoes, hurricanes and sudden accidents

(f) *Enforcement of laws*

(g) *Defense of the country*

(h) *Full employment*

(i) *Physical ease in work,* including the household

(j) *Availability of leisure time and resources,* such as
community recreation facilities, swimming pools, art
museums, music, parks, and theaters

(k) *Good environment* concerning air and water pollution,
waste disposal and landfill sites, esthetically pleasing
highway surroundings

(l) *Concern for those less fortunate,* including neighbors
and developing countries

engenders a materialistic attitude, which may be detrimental to other values. Ideas associated with attaining a higher quality of life are listed in Table 2-2.

Again, a higher quality of life can be an end in itself. But doesn't it result in the enhancement of human
dignity? Ideas associated with enhancing human dignity are listed in Table 2-3.

What is the result of enhancing human dignity? Its
result is individual betterment. This value recognizes
that people are equal, have the capacity to grow and
choose a unique path in life. Protection of individual
rights and encouragement of individual development
are the cornerstones, for example, of American democracy. America's dynamism is due "to the social
mobility, the individual responsibility, the egalitarian
thrust of American life, and above all, to the determination to invest in human beings, especially through
the promotion of education."[17]

As with the other values, the desire for individual
betterment is an end in itself. But if we ask "what is its
result?" the answer seems to be: to enable societies
and individuals to achieve greater effectiveness. Dia-
gramatically the relationship of the four value conno-

tations of "better" can be expressed as shown in Figure 2-1.

Societal values can be represented as circular in
nature. Any one could be selected as a starting point.
But the continual search for a "better" condition in
the other three values leads back to the first. This cir-
cularity means that concentration on any one value
affects, intentionally or not, the entire set. All four are
critical, one alone is insufficient. Overemphasis on one
may be detrimental to the others. For example, in the
Industrial Revolution, emphasis on greater effectiveness resulted, temporarily, at least, in the diminishing
of human dignity. Many external factors—economic
conditions, social beliefs, technological breakthrough,
and so on—can create this imbalance.

This array of circular values can be portrayed with
time as a third dimension. Assuming an upward improvement scale produces the spiral effect shown
schematically in Figure 2-2. An historically accurate
spiral would show an uneveness of movement along
the spiral. Trade-offs and imbalances among values are
historical facts. The spiral suggests that both the

Table 2-3 Ideas Involved in the Societal Value of Enhancing Human Dignity

(a) Each human has inherently unique capacities and qualities that should be respected as long as the uniqueness of others is also untrammeled

(b) Each person has many rights and freedoms: vote, speech, assembly, and freedom of thought and beliefs (religion, politics)

(c) Additional private time permits the pursuit of the unique activities that provide recognition, art, self-respect, culture, pleasure, and identification of individual sources of inner well-being and guidance

(d) We place a high value on each human life

(e) Features recently attained attesting to societal concerns for human dignity:

Improved safety regulations

Greater individual justice

Work humanization, quality of working life efforts, and corporate democracy

Corporate bill of rights for workers (free expression, security, protection regarding malfeasance, speedy and public hearing, due process, etc.)

Engineering awareness of the technology-human dignity idea

Societal concern with the mentally ill, retarded and aged

Relocation and retraining by organizations of workers when technological changes reduce the need for them

Questioning by science and society of permissible limits to and proper conditions for experimentation with human beings and animals

Enhancement of individual privacy and freedom of information

Opportunities to learn for learning's sake alone or to satisfy curiosity

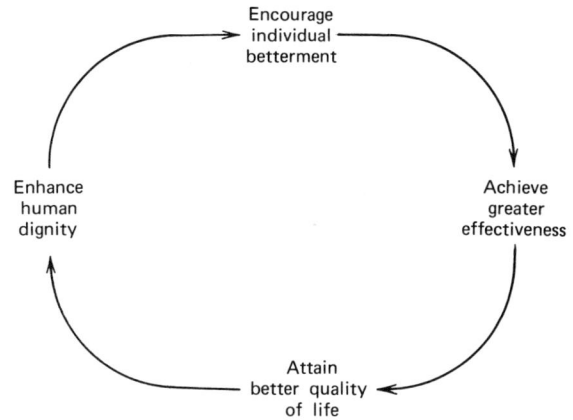

Figure 2-1 Relationship of four societal values.

definition and realization of values expand over time. The amounts of a single value, human longevity for instance, are greater now than 150 years ago. "Progress" for any society may in fact be defined as a relatively smooth upward movement along the spiral.

The values aspect includes the values, goals, and objectives unique to each purposeful activity and every problem locus. The problem solver must understand that those associated with the purposeful activity pursued and the specific problem situation differ from those of another situation. Clearly what is a value in one situation may be a goal or objective in another. Creating cultural opportunities, for example, may be the guiding value of a city repertory theater. But it is only one objective of a city council concerned with overall public health, safety, and welfare. And the

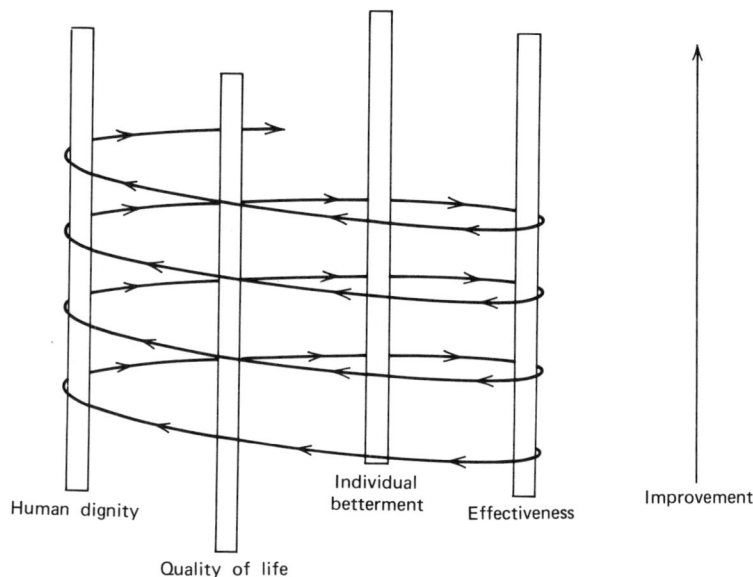

Figure 2-2 The spiral nature of societal values.

Table 2-4A   The Concept of Problem

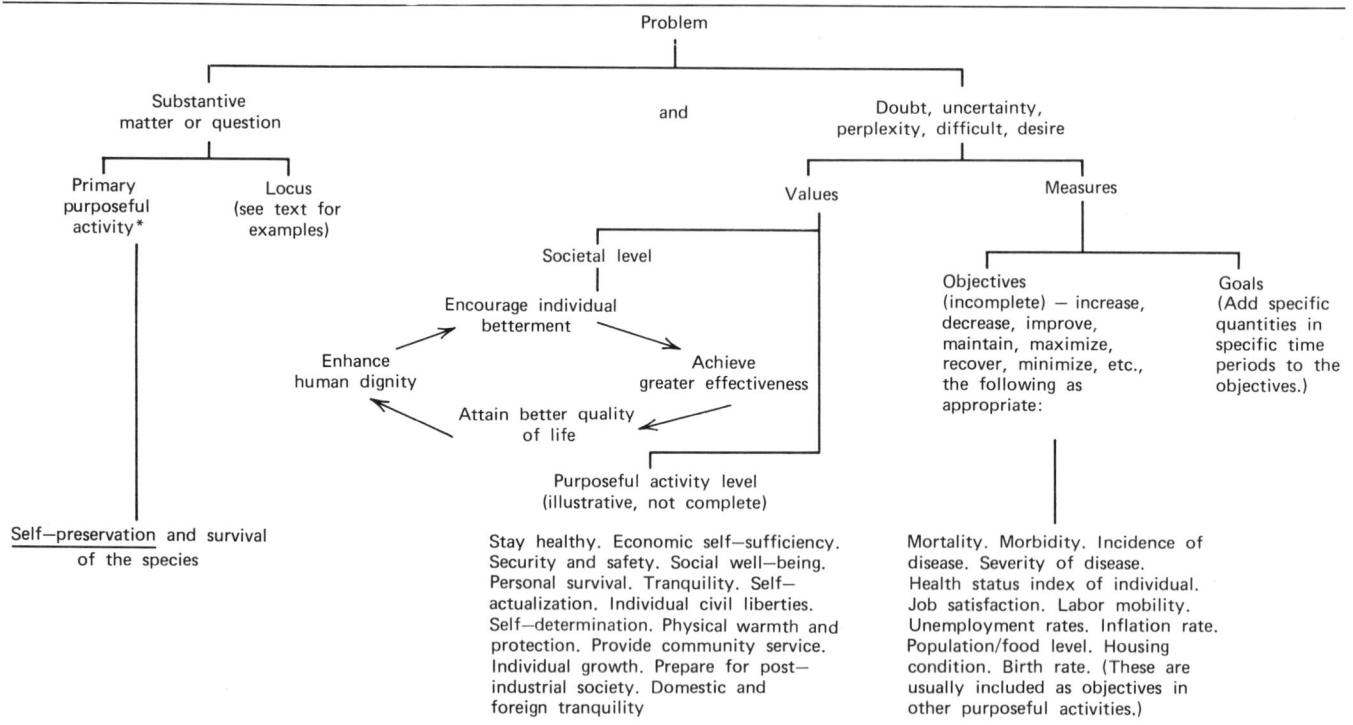

```
                                    Problem
            ┌──────────────────────────┼──────────────────────────┐
      Substantive                     and               Doubt, uncertainty,
   matter or question                                 perplexity, difficult, desire
     ┌──────┴──────┐                              ┌──────────┴──────────┐
  Primary        Locus                          Values               Measures
 purposeful   (see text for
  activity*    examples)
                                            Societal level      ┌───────────┴───────────┐
                                                 │          Objectives              Goals
                                        Encourage individual  (incomplete) — increase, (Add specific
                                            betterment        decrease, improve,     quantities in
                                     Enhance        Achieve   maintain, maximize,    specific time
                                  human dignity →  greater    recover, minimize, etc., periods to the
                                            ← effectiveness   the following as        objectives.)
                                    Attain better quality     appropriate:
                                         of life
  Self—preservation and survival    Purposeful activity level
          of the species            (illustrative, not complete)

                                    Stay healthy. Economic self—sufficiency.    Mortality. Morbidity. Incidence of
                                    Security and safety. Social well—being.     disease. Severity of disease.
                                    Personal survival. Tranquility. Self—       Health status index of individual.
                                    actualization. Individual civil liberties.  Job satisfaction. Labor mobility.
                                    Self—determination. Physical warmth and     Unemployment rates. Inflation rate.
                                    protection. Provide community service.      Population/food level. Housing
                                    Individual growth. Prepare for post—        condition. Birth rate. (These are
                                    industrial society. Domestic and            usually included as objectives in
                                    foreign tranquility                         other purposeful activities.)
```

* Several secondary purposeful activities may appear one or more times within a primary one: Make a decision; maintain a standard of achievement (control); resolve a conflict; develop creative ideas; establish priorities; observe, model, or abstract a phenomenon; practice or exercise; and focus and motivate individual efforts. None of these can be achieved without reference to a primary purposeful activity—make a decision about what, model a phenomenon when for what purposes, be creative about what, and so on. Chapter Three discusses the secondary purposeful activities and approaches to achieving them.

city's values are only objectives from the perspective of the four basic societal values! The dividing lines among values, objectives, and goals are fuzzy. Most of the fuzziness disappears when they are identified with reference to a specific purposeful activity or problem situation.

Recognition of the values aspect of a problem has important implications for planning and design.

1   Developing clearly stated values, objectives and goals in a specific situation clarifies decision making. Trade-offs can be shown and their impacts understood.

2   Understanding that the idea of values includes objectives and goals moves P&D from only vague "motherhood and apple pie" type statements toward specific criteria and measurable goals that seek to operationalize basic values.

3   Values clarification enables participants in a P&D effort to understand one another, reducing the disruptive potential of hidden agendas. It leads toward a collective sense of the purposes of a particular

P&D effort, significantly influencing both solution and implementation.

4   Acknowledgment of the values aspect precludes the "objective" stance of the P&D expert. It incorporates subjectivity and human concerns. It removes P&D efforts from the realm of narrow disciplines and techniques. It forces the solution measures to transcend the merely quantifiable and to incorporate critical subjective factors. (No one has or probably will set the worth of a human life. Amounts calculated from, say, the number of prisoners released in Cuba for an American "payment," are meaningless for all P&D purposes.) Because P&D solutions affect so many people as well as the environment it is crucial that solutions reflect larger social values.

SUMMARY

This chapter began with the assertion that there is no such thing as an "objective" problem. Instead, something or situation is perceived as a problem or need be-

Table 2-4B   The Concept of Problem

Primary Purposeful Activity*	Purposeful Activity Level (of Values)	Objectives
Operate and supervise a specific solution or system at its "good" design or desired specifications. (Illustrative problems: arrange a working capital loan for next quarter; determine whether vice-president for engineering should be replaced; revise organizational goals for the next three years.)	Ensure equity. Administer fairly. Maintain adaptability to environment. Reduce complexity and uncertainty. Ensure organizational integrity and stability. Improve quality of community relationships. Early warning about operational difficulties. Seek tranquility or nondestructive conflict. Resolve puzzles.	Number of factors for which operating system is not producing the norm. Profit. Cost per service. Cash flow. Discretionary income. Resource utilization. Morale. Quality of service or product. Operationality. Utility of administrators. Feasibility. Time to respond to current deviations. Customer and community attitudes about organization. Gross domestic product.
Create or restructure a situation-specific solution, system, or artificial (see Chapter Four). (Illustrative problems: develop a region-wide health delivery plan for next five years; design a house for client X; set up policies for allocating research funds.)	Innovate. Provide for individual and organizational growth and development. Achieve greater productivity and effectiveness. Increase ability to cope with complexity. Achieve humanitarian and social ideals. Enhance quality of working life. Build in recycling benefits to save materials and energy. Local participation. Maximize options open to future decision makers.	Cost of generating solution. Effectiveness of continuing change program. Elapsed time and person-hours to solution. Resource (materials, energy, manpower, financial, facilities) utilization. Consequence assessment. Number of people involved in finding the solution. Operationality and feasibility of solution. Return on investment. Attainability. Environmentally and socially sound.
Search for generalizations, theories, and laws about natural, social, and human-made phenomena (Illustrative problems: relate political trends to educational needs; identify factors causing airplane engine failure; establish a progress function base for types of equipment.)	Improve understanding. Increase amount of information and knowledge. Satisfy curiosity. Increase degree of relationship with natural environment. Explore depths of causal relationships. Establish state-of-the-art.	Ability to explain many observations. Potential utility to organization. Degree to which curiosity is satisfied. Number of papers produced. Breakthrough potential. Accuracy and precision. Prediction capability.
Gain skills or acquire knowledge about existing information and knowledge in a particular field or topic of study. (Illustrative problems: have board of directors' members gain insights into environmental implications of factories; orient new management trainees in organizational policies; become a computer programmer.)	Expand range of knowledge. Improve understanding. Encourage individual betterment and growth. Enhance intellectual enterprise. Practice solving puzzles.	Rate of learning. Standardized levels of basic skills. Interpretive capability of learner. Amount of dissemination of information.
Evaluate effectiveness of a previous solution or any specific purposeful activity. (Illustrative problems: determine effectiveness of the two-year-old exit interview program; assess the effectiveness of new regional sales offices; determine the accountability perspectives of professionals.)	Desire to assess whether program or solution performed as wanted. Curiosity about success in achieving another purposeful activity. Establish feedback about results.	Accountability measures. Acceptability measures. Modernity of facilities. Appropriateness and operationality measures. Affordability measures. Degree of innovation. Percentage of conformance of operation and performance with desired specifications.
Experience leisure and demand-free or unrestricted time for self-determined activities and pleasures while remaining respectful of the rights of others.	Be happy. Obtain enjoyment, at home and at work. Refresh and renew oneself.	Degree of pleasure, rest, or relaxation obtained (attitudinal as well). Amount of interest in activity. See objectives of other purposeful activities for those that may apply.

* Several secondary purposeful activities may appear one or more times within a primary one: Make a decision; maintain a standard of achievement (control); resolve a conflict; develop creative ideas; establish priorities; observe, model, or abstract a phenomenon; practice or exercise; and focus and motivate individual efforts. None of these can be achieved without reference to a primary purposeful activity—make a decision about what, model a phenomenon when for what purposes, be creative about what, and so on. Chapter Three discusses the secondary purposeful activities and approaches to achieving them.

cause of purposeful human activities, motivations, and aspirations. Because planning and design professionals seek to solve problems, the definition of what a "problem" is must become the basic starting point. A problem or need has a values aspect and a substantive one. The former includes the values, objectives, and goals implicit in human purposeful activities and those specific to a particular problem locus. The substantive aspect includes both the type of problem—operating and supervising, research, planning and design, learning, or evaluation—and the problem locus. (Self-preservation and leisure will be shown in Chapter Three to become one of the other five.) The locus is the specific what, when, who, and where of a particular situation.

Table 2-4, which illustrates this formulation of the concept of "problem," provides people with the opportunity to clarify what type of problem they confront, the specifics of the problem, and the values and measures associated both with the type of problem and the specific situation. It suggests to the problem solver an appropriate solution-finding approach (Chapter Three explores the methodologies associated with specific problem types) and is a critical beginning to ensuring that the "right problem" will be solved. The table begins with the two aspects of a problem. Under the substantive are listed the five purposeful activities. Other criteria for determining which purposeful activity is being pursued will be provided in Chapters Three, and Ten to Twelve. The locus column is empty, as it depends on the particular situation. The values aspect lists the values and objectives for each type of purposeful activity. The list is by necessity incomplete. Also, many values, self-actualization and comfort for instance, occur in relation to one or more purposeful activities. The goals column, like the locus, remains empty, as the specified amounts of an objective are unique to each situation.

CHAPTER THREE

Approaches to Problem Solving

The vital link between the perception of a problem and implemented change is the problem-solving approach. An approach is a mode of conduct directed in a given way toward a particular set of circumstances to attain desired results.[1]

An approach consists of principles of action and a methodology operationalizing them. Often, neither the principles nor the methodology are explicitly articulated. Even random or intuitive processes constitute a problem-solving approach.

The decision to do something about a problem automatically gives rise to the question of how this something is to be done. The key word is *how*—how to proceed, how to formulate a problem, how to seek and implement solutions. *How* means explicit and predictive methods, not simply a set of exhortations. It means providing, for example, specific techniques for transforming a problem as stated into a statement of the right problem, not merely proclaiming, "Be sure you formulate the problem correctly." *How* must address all aspects of an approach: determining the problem type and locus, the timing sequence for problem-solving activities, who should be involved, what group of techniques will be most effective, methods for ensuring continual solution change and improvement, and so on.

Everyone uses some kind of approach for problem solving. Ask any group of individuals how they would approach a particular problem and a variety of responses results. This was done several times as an experiment using the nurse utilization project described in Chapter One.[2] Eighteen responses were obtained in one trial; each was different. One respondent suggested, "Find out what hospitals in other cities are doing." A second said, "Determine the actual shortage amounts." Another suggested, "Find out the areas of potential cost savings." What is important to note here is that each of these approaches leads to different types of solutions and a search for different kinds of information. The first response might lead to a survey of other hospitals or hospital literature. A solution might then be "imported" from another hospital situation to this particular one. The third might involve budget and expenditure review sessions with management personnel, and an analysis of the areas in which other hospitals have cut costs. The solution might ask the board of trustees to arbitrarily cut department costs by a constant percentage.

Confronted by this array of approaches the crucial question becomes: which approach, if any, is most likely to assure the best results? How can we evaluate approaches? Five criteria immediately come to mind by virtue of their obviousness.

1   Is the approach fully descriptive and prescriptive, that is, does it describe a mode of action and operationalize it?

2   Is the approach adaptable enough to meet the multiple values and objectives of different human pur-

poseful activities and thus divergent problem situations?

3 Does the approach maximize the likelihood of arriving at beneficial change (even if this change is merely a reaffirmation of an existing solution)? The nature of this change is clearly a function of the purposeful activity pursued. The beneficial change sought by research, for example, might be improved accuracy and precision of a generalization; of planning and design, a food stamp delivery system that is less costly per unit output.

4 Does the approach maximize the likelihood of implemented change? Obviously an approach that arrives at solutions but can't assure implementation is futile.

5 Does the approach maximize the effectiveness of human and other resources? An approach that minimizes cost and time is superior to one that does not, if the results are equal.

In the remainder of this chapter we look at four types of problem-solving approaches:

The do-nothing approach.
The chance approach.
The affective approach.
The rational approach.

We then consider them in relation to a total approach, which meets the five criteria previously discussed. Finally, we specify approaches in terms of the five purposeful activities.

Table 3-1 lists a number of problem-solving approaches. Their use is a function of cultural values, historical circumstances, and individual temperament. All are variations or combinations of the four basic approaches.

The Do-Nothing Approach

Although the label sounds pejorative, there are many adherents to this approach. It is characterized by the belief that human beings cannot or should not control events; either because fate is capricious or a god will provide. Jesus's injunction to be "as the lilies of the field" is an example of this philosophy. There were (and are) great civilizations that did not encourage problem solving because, in their view, grief, famine, flood, and other events of this world are petty discomforts on the way to the glorious hereafter.

Proponents of this approach are not limited to those of religious persuasion. There is a genuine moral dilemma associated with the decision actively to en-

Table 3-1   Some Problem-Solving Approaches

Fatalism
Contingency methods
Conceptual to scientific to solution modeling
Systems analysis
Gestalt-cognitive
Heuristics
Bounded rationality
MBO—management by objectives
Experimentation
Trial and error
Measurements
Mathematical modeling
Flip a coin
Appeal to higher authority
Political
Contextual reasoning
Analogies and metaphors
Discuss with others, dialectical process
Information processing
Analysis of facts
Organizational development
Logico-positivist
Rational actor
Scenario testing

gage in problem solving. "Many conscientious persons have become concerned with the plight of their less fortunate neighbors. . . . Is it possible that there is an immoral aspect of these devoted and sincere people? Is it immoral for one man to decide what is good for another? . . . Perhaps there is an immorality that originates from a desire to steer the ship of state for the good of all."[3] Without making a claim to definitiveness, this book assumes that it is right to seek solutions actively, both because Western society places a high premium on doing so, and because the overall societal values (Chapter Two) require it for their achievement. These values form the standard for judging results, as well as an ethical framework for a problem-solving approach. Problem solvers cannot assume they are value free:[4] without such a framework of societal values, they may achieve results, but not necessarily beneficial ones.

The Chance Approach

To speculate a bit, it is probable that earliest humans found solutions primarily by chance. Some set of fortuitous circumstances were understood by astute observers, a process that engendered useful solutions like agriculture or controlled fire. The underlying principle or mindset of the chance approach is that the accidental dominates human endeavors. "History is full of momentary trifles . . . the accident which kills or preserves some figure of destiny . . . or a sudden idea that results in some potent invention."[5]

Its methodological implications go in two very different directions. One kind of chance approach relies on flashes of insight or stumbling by chance on the right answer, Einstein's "finding without seeking." In practice, this is close to an affective approach. The second kind is more like a rational approach. It focuses on the constant intervention of accident and surprise in human affairs. Expecting the unexpected leads to an open-ended and flexible approach to problems. Contingency planning is a good example. It recognizes that new discoveries and changing political and social climates create new situations, thus problem solving must continuously adapt to new opportunities and constraints.

The Affective Approach

Emotions, feelings, intuitions and hunches are the ingredients of affective reasoning. Affective problem solvers tend to do whatever comes spontaneously to mind rather than follow a preestablished approach structure. The mindset and methods of an affective approach differ from person to person and are difficult to define. However, certain patterns can be described.

Affectively oriented persons are often unable to explain how they arrived at a conclusion. This may be because the process is too complex and fluid to verbalize.[6]

The elements of this process include free association, analogy transfers, insight, intuition and finding unusual connections among bits of information ordinarily considered unrelated. For example, the chemist who discovered the molecular structure of benzene did so when, upon seeing an ancient symbol of a snake with its tail in its mouth, he intuitively sensed that the structure was a closed carbon ring.[7]

Often the affective thinker relates information via nonverbal internal visualizations outside the scope of language. Albert Einstein wrote, "Words or language do not seem to play a role in my mechanism of thought. The psychical entities . . . are certain more or less clear images which be voluntarily reproduced and combined."[8]

The affective approach can lead to innovative creative solutions. It does however exhibit certain difficulties.

1 It may not be particularly effective for the systematic detailing of solutions necessary for implementation. Implementation may also be hindered by the mutual frustration an affective approach may create in groups. A person using the approach cannot explain how the solution was arrived at, so others may condemn the solution as unreasonable or irrational.

2 The criteria for weighting factors of importance in making decisions may be random and fluctuate wildly. This poses certain dangers. Consider for instance the problems if the postman used an affective approach for delivering the mail, some days relying on names, on others coordinating the stamp pattern with a particular house's architectural design.

3 The affective approach can become very elitist, and the existence of no standardized criteria precludes checks and balances. Charismatic but unscrupulous leaders can use affective approaches in manipulative and dangerous ways.

The Rational Approach

The rational approach appeared explicitly about four hundred years ago. It is not by chance that this coincides with the rise of science. The need for reliable generalizations called for methods neither chance nor affective approaches provided. The success of the rational approach in science was so phenomenal that all other fields of human endeavor (purposeful activities) adapted it, to the almost total exclusion of any other.

Linearity, objectivity, structured decision making and systematic logical processes are the hallmarks of the rational approach. Several themes are basic to it.

Positivism

The conviction that science can solve all problems, indeed is the only way to solve problems, pervades the rational approach. "If we can get to the moon, we ought to be able to end poverty," illustrates recent generic versions of this persistent theme, also known as the technological fix. This absolutism is a carry-over from earlier times when only vociferous advocacy of positivism could counteract prevailing cosmic and faith-based approaches.

Reductionism

Rational approaches are characterized by explicit methodologies. Every methodology begins with information compilation and division of the problem into smaller units. Solve the small problems and supposedly the large one is also solved. The data sought is quantitative and objective "hard data." The existence of nonquantifiable subjective information is not denied but simply relegated to the category of unimportant externals.

The Cult of the Expert

Experts who specialize in data collection arise in almost all fields. Only the expert possessing the information is in a position to arrive at quality solutions. As experts they are presumed to be unobtrusive and value free. And despite the objections raised by physical as well as social scientists, the process of data collection is assumed to have no influence on the phenomena being measured. Experts are a result of the specialization penchant prevalent in the United States. The cult of the expert leads to a limited perspective on problems, functional fixedness, defensiveness on the part of the people for whom an expert's solutions are addressed and a host of other difficulties detailed in Chapters Four and Five.

Determinism

The rational approach assumes that once the facts are asembled and the data analyzed one solution will emerge on which "all reasonable" people can agree. Once this solution is found, presumably the problem evaporates and the solution will always be appropriate. How firmly this determinism is adhered to varies widely, but it is everywhere in evidence. Architects build buildings as if today's needs will be those of the future, managers assume the personnel practices of 25 years ago are applicable today, and urban planners rely on snapshots of the future extrapolated from the past. This is a dangerous practice; after all, who in the 1960s or even 1970s would have predicted the energy crisis and its multiple effects on every sector of society?

There are a number of overlapping variations of the rational approach; looking at some of them will clarify these basic themes.

The research approach epitomizes rationalism. The steps in the approach are described slightly differently in different fields of science. A common version is: (1) identify the specific concern, (2) collect data, (3) analyze it by reducing it to manageable measurable components, (4) establish the hypothesis, (5) verify the hypothesis, and (6) adopt it. This same process characterizes almost all contemporary problem solving approaches.

Systems approaches though widely touted are difficult to define. A search of the literature produced this definition of limited usefulness: "A system is a portion of the world which at a given time can be char-

acterized by a given state, together with a set of rules that permit the deduction of the state from partial information."[9] The question arises, "What about other portions of the world?" Systems analysis focuses on that portion that can be represented by a mathematical model and for that reason systems analysis has been condemned as "intrinsically unsuitable" for all but minor problems.[10]

Measurement approaches begin by quantifying the topic of concern, then manipulating the measurements to mirror "reality." It is assumed that if measurements are abundant and accurate, a solution will naturally follow. What is to be done about nonquantifiable human concerns, for instance, is not the concern of measurement approaches. Unfortunately everything of importance can't be measured, to the detriment of this method's solutions, nor can "all the facts" be obtained.

Application of techniques (modeling, regression analysis, statistics, sampling) is a variant of the measurement approach. It assumes that the knowledge generated by applying several techniques to a problem will lead to solutions. Sometimes applying a technique is deemed to *be* the solution, for example management by objectives in federal agencies.

In addition, there are *single method* problem-solving approaches. Their advocates often claim universal appropriateness for their particular method. One example is the Diamond Model. It begins with problem recognition, proceeds by conceptualization to development of a conceptual model, then by modeling processes to develop a scientific model, and then by "model solving" to arrive at a solution. The final step is implementation of the solution in the problem situation.[11]

The rational approach, while it is very useful in developing generalizations and doing research, is not necessarily appropriate for other purposeful activities. Its ubiquity is not justified. There are serious limits to its effectiveness in generating solutions for contemporary problems.[12]

TOWARD A TOTAL APPROACH

None of the four approaches described can by itself meet the criteria for a problem-solving approach set forth earlier. Chance and affective approaches are haphazard and not fully operationalizable. Chance approaches tend to be fatalistic or merely reactive. Affective approaches, though often creative, cannot assume solution implementation. And rational approaches, which emphasize experts, measurements, and techniques, are not rooted in the human purposes, perceptions, and needs, which are the foundation of good solutions.

What is called for is a synthesis of the best in all approaches, recognizing that each is a legitimate expression of human knowledge and experience. Given the overriding dominance of the rational approach, particularly in educational curricula, it may be wise to speak more specifically to the nature of this legitimacy from a philosophical and scientific perspective.

Any approach's adherents assume that their pattern of reasoning, what they know and how they know it, is "true." This truth forms the underlying mindset of their approach. Clearly, many challenges exist to any assumption of truth. The most obvious one is that there are so many brands, each with its own enthusiastic advocates. None of these "truths" can be definitively proved or disproved. Even among rational approaches, there are uniquely different ontologies (natures of reality views) and epistemologies (perceptions of knowledge), as expressed by several well-known philosophers:[13]

Leibniz—formal, impersonal rules and procedures, data, mathematical.

Locke—experiential, collect data, relatively informal.

Kant—examine idealistic alternatives, seek speculative possibilities, use different representations and premises.

Singer—broad view, anything is subject to change, interdisciplinary, purposeful behavior.

Hegel—conflictual views, argumentation, dialectical processes.

And the list of sets of assumptions challenging the hegemony of strictly rational approaches is endless. It includes a variety of religions, and psychological and philosophical disciplines. To ask which among them should form the basis of a problem-solving approach is an unanswerable query. Yet each suggests different principles and modes of action.

Consequently, it behooves the problem solver to take a relatively pragmatic perspective in choosing a problem-solving approach—to borrow freely from all rather than be limited solely to a rational one. The necessity of enlarging the parameters of the rational approach is clear: "We must replace all narrowly formal conceptions of rationality by a broader functional one. This need involve no rejection of rational inquiry, rather it involves a reanalysis of the nature and content of rationality."[14]

This philosophical perspective has been given scientific credibility by recent left/right brain discoveries in neurophysiology. There appear to be "two modes of thinking, verbal and nonverbal, represented rather separately in the left and right brain respectively."[15] The left hemisphere "appears to operate in a logical, analytical and computer-like fashion. Its language is inadequate to the complex synthesis achieved by the right."[16] The forebrain combines both into decision making.

Several taxonomies of parallel ways of knowing have been developed on the basis of these discoveries. One of these is particularly interesting because it coincides almost exactly with the difference between affective and rational approaches:[17]

Left	Right
Intellectual	Intuitive
Convergent	Divergent
Digital	Analogical
Propositional	Imaginative
Linear	Nonlinear
Rational	Affective
Sequential	Multiple
Analytical	Holistic
Objective	Subjective

Given these philosophical and scientific perspectives as well as the obvious fact that human beings use all *three* approaches (the chance, the affective, and the rational) it would seem that new integrated approaches are called for. In response to this need a number of total approaches have been suggested, including heuristics, bounded rationality, gestalt, cognitive, and "doubting and believing" games. The difficulty with most of them is that they do not go far enough (e.g., bounded rationality still emphasizes quantifiable measurements), or they are operationalized only for very small problem-solving situations, such as laboratory-administered puzzle tests. One exception is the concept of "doubting and believing games," each of which incorporates the idea of a method for finding solutions or uncovering "truth."

The *doubting* game approach to problem solving emphasizes arguing and a rigid reductive rationality method: problem definition, problem analysis, presentation and evaluation of alternatives, and solution detailing. Doubting forces one to poke holes in ideas, tear apart assertions, probe continually, and be analytical. The "doubting" game view of rationality makes a person feel "rigorous, disciplined and tough minded; and if he refrains from playing the doubting game he feels unintellectual, irrational, and sloppy."[18]

The *believing* game creates an entirely different mindset. In it, a person believes all assertions; to refrain from doubting is the first rule. "By believing an assertion we can see farther into it. But this is only possible by inhibiting the doubting game. If we had started to doubt we would have found so many holes in the premise we would have abandoned it.''

The games are interrelated and each contains elements of the other. But although they are complementary, that is, problem solving requires both, they cannot be played simultaneously. To do so "can only result in more muddling." This points to an important aspect of a total approach. Although it must be a synthesis of all approaches, the elements emphasized will depend on the purposes and objectives of the particular problem-solving situation. For example, careful development of generalizations in research requires an emphasis on the doubting game. But planning and design, as we will show later, requires the believing game in order to engender "breakthrough" solutions.

The Factors in a Total Approach

The first question in developing a total approach is What are the factors in such an approach and how are they to be made operational? Human perceptions constitute the most likely source of answers, particularly those of individuals who have previously exhibited successful solution-finding behavior. Many studies have explored what good professional problem solvers do. They serve as the basis for enumerating the factors of a total approach. Although determining all the factors in a total approach is impossible, if we review the factors of the various approaches coupled with the results of practitioner and research studies the following five factors emerge:

1 Pursuing a strategy.
2 Specifying and presenting the solution.
3 Involving people from the real world.
4 Using information and knowledge.
5 Arranging for continual change and improvement.

Pursuing a Strategy

A strategy is a modus operandi; it is a "way followed . . .in accordance with principles" or a process.[19] The function of a strategy is to guide a person or group in achieving a purposeful activity. It is a time-based "road map" that identifies how one proceeds—what one does today, tomorrow, and the next day—over time until an implemented solution takes place. A strategy involves looping and iterative activities, and even signals when it is useful to begin at a different phase or step than the "first" one listed.

All strategies have a common base expressed in the ends-means tree: Generate alternative means to achieve an end, then make a decision to select one al-

ternative, which now becomes the end; generate alternative means ("how to do it") to the new end (what to do and why), then make a decision which now becomes a new end, and so on. A strategy involves sequential steps or phases that identify for what ends alternatives should be developed, and determine what criteria are needed to make each decision. Thus, the strategy for approaching each purposeful activity is expected to be unique.

Specifying and Presenting the Solution

Prescribing the format of the result expected for each purposeful activity enables its specifications to be understood by peers, superiors, subordinates, and, when necessary, the appropriate "public." This format is a solution framework that identifies what factors, properties, and attributes and their interrelationships should be included in specifying a solution.

The systems concept is often put forward as the desired format structure, because a system includes all related attributes of a solution. But a research solution, a planning solution, operating, evaluation and learning solutions so obviously differ that they may require different systems frameworks. Specifying a solution largely reflects the rational approach, as this approach requires orderly and comprehensive detailing.

Involving People

Because problem solving takes place in the context of human desires for change, a total approach must address individual perception and group interactions. The numbers and types of people involved will depend on the type of problem and the number of persons affected. How to cope with a wide array of human concerns within the pursuit of the time-based strategy is the focus of the factor of involving people. When people are involved continuously from the beginning of a project the prospects for solution acceptance and utilization increase dramatically.

People in the client's world should be given continual opportunity to participate and interact throughout the course of a solution-finding effort. Whether or not they do so depends on personal predilections. Types of participation can range from consultative to supportive, joint, bargaining, or complete self-determination. Participation is also influenced by other conditions: the phase or step in the strategy at which the effort is located; the level, work skills, or the type of group process that might obtain effective results from the person-hours involved; and the physical environment within which involvement takes place.

In setting up project teams or planning interactions with clients or organizations, the personality types involved (hard-data–oriented versus intuition-structured, thinking versus feeling, etc.) should be considered. Various disciplinary or interdisciplinary modes of thinking and personal types of control mechanisms also influence how participation is structured.

Involving people is in large part a reflection of affective approaches. It recognizes that feelings, perceptions, and subjective data are an essential part of developing and implementing solutions.

Using Information and Knowledge

Information and knowledge regarding any problem come from many sources (studies, experiences, literature), each with a wide range of potential utility. But the importance of this information and knowledge for a particular problem is likely to change in content, meaning, and amount as solution finding proceeds. The reason for using such information is to predict the future status of the phenomenon or the consequences of deliberate actions and changes.

Much knowledge and information takes the form of models based on past and existing conditions. The mere act of compiling data is a critical warning flag about the capability of the model for prediction. Predicting the occurrence or performance of a *single* case from an aggregation is very difficult (except for the extremely physical phenomena, e.g., yield strength of a steel bar, electron flow in a circuit). A compilation describes and sometimes explains, but seldom predicts adequately. It may have *statistical* significance, but it very often has no *practical* significance.

Using any such information and knowledge will be different for effective accomplishment of each purposeful activity. Research and learning, for example, depend largely on current and past information because achieving these purposeful activities involves adding to, modifying, or creating new categories for existing information. But just knowing the information does not carry with it the ability to use it for, say, prediction and detailing. Knowledge and information by themselves are not power.

The factor of using knowledge and information is a combination of rational, affective, and chance approaches. Its format, organization, storage, and retrieval are largely rational. Its meaning, acceptance, and influence are largely affective. Its availability and potential interactions are usually by chance. Achieving any purposeful activity requires information and knowledge, but each approach uses them differently, depending on the other factors of pursuing a strategy, specifying a solution, and involving people.

Arranging for Continual Change and Improvement

Change is inevitable and any solution, however satisfactory it may be currently, must anticipate and respond to it. The question is *how* this change and improvement is to be carried out. Doing so avoids future shock, which is likely to occur when people are not actively prepared for and pursuing change. Change for change's sake alone is foolish, but the underlying reason for arranging to search for change and improvement in solutions is stability.

Arranging for change requires policies that stimulate and motivate searches for improvements, policies regarding the organizational location and structures for such search efforts, and periodic planned betterment of satisfactory solutions. It also requires techniques of audit and evaluation as well as techniques to monitor changing environmental opportunities and constraints. Arranging for a continuing search has elements of all three approaches, chance, affective, and rational. Chance approaches seek contingency and monitoring methods to respond effectively to disruptive occurrences as well as unusual opportunities. Affective aspects relate to the attitudinal setting, feelings, and commitment of the organization to the major values and objectives for bettering conditions. Rational approaches provide systematic techniques for search efforts, evaluation, and monitoring. A total approach integrates these perspectives to generate valid and appropriate amounts of information, broadly based decisions about what needs to be done, and an ever growing commitment to achieving organizational and societal objectives.

Specifying the Five-Factor Approach for Each Purposeful Activity

A total approach incorporates the five factors just described. But each purposeful activity, because its ends and values are different, requires a different mindset and method of inquiry for each factor if an approach is to be operational.

For example, let's consider the doubting and believing games in terms of the mindset required by specific purposeful activities. Developing generalizations requires detachment, objectivity, tough, piercing questioning, rigid methodology, and challenging old dogma as well as new ideas. This assures that new theories are based on evidence, and that the status quo is not summarily rejected. On occasion a researcher may pursue a believing game when "revolutionary results" suggest a new theory is emerging.[20]

Operating and evaluating likewise require similar doubting-game dialectics. Maintaining a smoothly operating bus system, for example, necessitates anticipation of where difficulties may arise. Evaluation without doubting and probing would be sheer "window dressing." Of course smaller problems occur within these purposeful activities for which the believing game may be more appropriate.

Table 3-2 Operating and Supervising Approach*

Pursuing an Operating Strategy	Specifying and Presenting Solutions† (entries are illustrative only)	Involving People (entries are illustrative only)	Using Information and Knowledge (entries are illustrative only)	Arranging for Continuing Change and Improvement (entries are illustrative only)
1 Clarify the fundamental purposeful activity involved by determining the purpose of solution-finding for the problem. If this is not operating and supervising, proceed to the appropriate approach.	Classification of fundamental purposeful activities	Decision makers; people directly involved in operating the system	Purpose hierarchy, organizational policies, long-range plan	Assess organizational change readiness
2 Gain familiarity with (learn) the system's objectives and norms (V)	Function, values, and measures of performance of the system	Managers; people operating the system; customers or clients; experts to update standards and analyze financial data	Definition of needed measurement categories; utility measures, accounting systems, work measurement, production standards, financial analysis, group process techniques, knowledge related to learning and establishing priorities	Select the appropriate type and level of continuing change and improvement arrangements (e.g., long-range planning process)
3 Obtain the needed operating resources (trained people, equipment, staff etc.); use staffing and maintenance processes	Specifications for personnel, operating equipment, operating instructions, computer software, models, and so on	Managers, resource controllers, people in the system, experts in investment planning and organizational development	Organization theory, investment analysis, available information aids, methods for setting priorities, small group conference processes	Establish in-house arrangements to search for operating improvements, position rotation, merit evaluation, objectives program (MBO), and so on: visitors and consultants to review managerial skills and developments; seminars, discussion groups, collateral organization, and so on
4 Obtain the needed inputs (materials, information, people)—organizing process	Specifications for inputs: nature; audience; desired characteristics; quantity, time, detailed quantitative specifications; quality and cost control, means of assuring a reliable supply; relationship to suppliers and other users; plans for obtaining needed inputs in the future	Managers; people responsible for procuring inputs (e.g., purchasing dept.) and those with first-hand knowledge of the effectiveness of different inputs (e.g., production personnel); to analyze trade-offs and forecast costs of supplies	Engineering knowledge; information about suppliers, resources, trade-offs and costs; forecasting techniques; group conference processes; special-purpose group techniques such as future-creating workshops	Establish external arrangements to search for operating improvements: courses, conferences, community service, intercompany exchanges, and so on
5 Establish appropriate measures and reporting systems for key control factors (V, II, VI)	Information processing specifications; report formats tailored to the intended functions and situations	Managers, resource controllers, people involved in measurement (e.g., accountants); experts to establish measures and set up models	Measurement systems, designed for the actual needs and conditions (all measurement techniques may be considered)	Plan definite times to review the information systems for control, reliance, and effectiveness
6 Establish performance expectations for the people operating the systems, and establish corresponding monitoring, evaluation, and research systems (VIII)	Personnel policies; specifications for organizational development programs; MBO contracts and performance reports	Managers; people for whom the objectives and measures are being established; people needed to design and implement the ongoing measurement and reward systems (personnel or organizational development dept.)	Objectives define results, not processes or specific outputs; simple objective measurement and flexibility represent competing demands requiring compromise	Objectives should be reviewed on a definite schedule
7 Operate the system; leading and motivating processes (II, III, VIII)	Process for transforming inputs into outputs; planned interactions with personnel to provide leadership and motivation; second-level purposeful activities	Managers and supervisors; work groups; formal and informal communication networks among staff; possible involvement of experts in modeling, decision analysis, and organizational development and incentive systems	Information and knowledge from psychology and organizational behavior theory; organizational structure, information systems, financial, and cost accounting; operating plans; decision theory; models of operations; group process techniques	Establish policies for a management improvement program: foster attitudes toward improving operating skills; institutionalize management games, personnel consulting, evaluation, guidance

Table 3-2 *(Continued)*

Pursuing an Operating Strategy	Specifying and Presenting Solutions† (entries are illustrative only)	Involving People (entries are illustrative only)	Using Information and Knowledge (entries are illustrative only)	Arranging for Continuing Change and Improvement (entries are illustrative only)
8 Measure operating performance and outcomes; compare to 2 or 6 (II, V)	Similar to input requirements. Fundamental nature of outputs; desired characteristics; production schedule, tolerance specifications, quality and cost control, production contingency plans; relationship to customers and competitors; long-range production plans; process for testing outputs against specifications	Managers, staff; experts in measurement, evaluation, utility assessment	Decision rules; cost accounting; production schedules; quality control data; qualitative assessment of outputs; feedback from customers or clients	Periodically review and assess arrangements for continuing change and improvement (Use the evaluation approach)
9 Return to 7 if no significant difference in 8. Otherwise find causes and take corrective action, or return to steps 1, 2, 3, or 4 (V, IV, I)	Causal hypotheses and validation criteria (cf. research approach), in a form accommodating the need for prompt action; classification of fundamental purposeful activities	Managers, people involved in the system	Various substrategies for diagnosing operating problems; classification of purposeful activities; group process techniques; second-level purposeful activities, especially creativity (IV)	Use the P&D approach to plan improvement in the continuing change and improvement arrangements. Seek creative courses of action prior to possible discrepancies

* Roman numerals are explained in Table 3-9.
† The system matrix solution framework developed in Chapters Nine and Thirteen can be used to prescribe the types of specifications and detail needed for this factor.

The believing game-mindset is most effective for creating or restructuring a situation-specific solution, planning and design, and for learning a skill or field of knowledge. P&D, to illustrate, needs the believing game's commitment to projection, willingness to explore what is new, flexibility, subjective involvement, mode of deep experiencing, dedication to searching for how an idea could work, determination of how to be larger and more encompassing, working with other people, and listening to and incorporating ideas of others. This helps to generate creative and unusual ideas.

Learning is also aided by the believing game, which enables humans to change or add to their existing knowledge base. Continually believing that information can be learned is likely to result in far greater retention and synthesis. Certain problems or phases occurring within one of these purposeful activities may need the doubting game. Selecting a recommended solution from among several alternatives in a P&D project is a case in point.

Tables 3-2 through 3-6 show how the five factors can be operationalized for the purposeful activities of operating and supervising, planning and design, evaluation, research, and learning. Table 3-7 summarizes them and illustrates the basic differences among the approaches.

No claim to completeness or accuracy is made for these tables, since much more could be written about each of the total approaches. The tables are meant to formalize the basic concept that the approach to a problem varies according to the purposeful result sought. Several comments are applicable to all the approaches described.

1 There is no firm agreement among practitioners or theorists of a particular purposeful activity on what is recorded in Tables 3-2 through 3-6. The methods recorded there summarize my review of the literature and my own experiences in using all of them. (Additional evidence for the P&D approach in Table 3-3 will be provided in the rest of the book). Furthermore, continuing changes in all factors of a purposeful activity will occur as research and empirical evidence accumulates.

2 The approaches were selected with the aid of several criteria developed from the values and needs discussed in Chapter Two. Table 3-8 lists the ones used.

3 The approaches in Tables 3-2 through 3-6 are arranged to convey that all factors are just describers of an integrated holistic view. That is, involvement with people, using knowledge and information, specifying the solution framework, and arranging for continuing change and improvement are integrally linked to the pursuit of the strategy over time. Looping and jumping among the phases of the

Table 3-3 Planning and Design Approach*

Pursuing a Planning and Design Strategy	Specifying and Presenting Solutions (entries are illustrative only)	Involving People (entries are illustrative only)	Using Information and Knowledge (entries are illustrative only)	Arranging for Continuing Change and Improvement (entries are illustrative only)
1 Clarify the fundamental purposeful activity involved by determining the purpose of solution-finding for the problem; if this is not P&D, proceed to the appropriate approach	Purpose hierarchy for the problem-solving system	Decisionmakers and eventual implementers	Purpose-clarification techniques; categorization of purposeful activities	Increasing capability for identifying problems and appropriate purposeful activities
2 Design the P&D solution finding structure	P&D system specifications	Intensive involvement of decisionmakers and people closely affected by the P&D	P&D theory; information systems; organizational structures; budgeting and scheduling techniques	Developing continual support structures; building an environment of change readiness
3 Clarify the purpose and objectives of the solution that is being sought	Purpose hierarchy; functional components; measures of effectiveness for the solution	Intensive and extensive involvement of managers, implementers, and users or clients; often involves people working in the existing system, if any	Purpose clarification techniques: couplet comparison technique; purpose hierarchy and networks; group process techniques	Movement toward larger purpose levels; provision for redirection of purpose over time and in response to the environment
4 Generate solution ideas (IV)	Large number of "uncensored" ideas; low-level of organization and evaluation	Same as 3, plus possible involvement of more specialized experts in relevant areas	Idea generation techniques: brainstorming, word associations, Synectics, nominal group process	Ideas not currently feasible for implementation become candidates for R&D and future reconsideration
5 Synthesize solution candidates, identify regularity conditions, and define feasible target	Systems matrix; hierarchical organization of ideas; morphological groupings and categorization formats	Intensive involvement of the principal planning team and appropriate experts; extensive feedback on proposals	Regularity concept; categorization techniques; prioritization	Develop both short-range possibilities and long-range targets; include adaptive specifications in solutions. Use participation in the P&D to develop organizational P&D capability
6 Select and detail the solution (I)	Evaluation of solution candidates; detailed specifications for selected solution; risk assessments	Managers, implementers, users/clients; prospective operators of solution	Simulation and estimation methods; decision theory; use target solution as guide; irregularities	Schedule planned improvement of the solution; develop longer-range plans addressing larger purpose levels
7 Gain final approval for the solution, and install it	Specifications for the presentation and installation/transition systems; design of report formats; presentations; advertising promotion	Decision makers; implementers: build on the base of support developed in earlier strategy steps	Organizational behavior concepts; graphics; marketing concepts	Build support for the ongoing P&D process, and establish appropriate organizational structures

* Roman numerals are explained in Table 3-9.

strategy are to be expected, thus signifying that all factors "jump" and "loop" with the strategy. It is not unusual for a problem-solving effort in Phase 3 to find that a part of Phase 1 needs to be redone, or that parts of Phase 4 need to be done before all of Phase 2 is complete. Nor does a project necessarily start with Phase 1. Starting with Phase 5 of the operating approach would not be unusual, with Phases 2 or 3 following.

4 Each factor varies in its importance at different times in an approach and from one purposeful activity to another. Involving people, for example, is usually more important in all phases of P&D than of research. Or the standards of specifying a solu-

tion are often more important in research than in operating. Or using current information and knowledge is more important at the beginning of evaluation than later.

5 Determining which purposeful activity and approach are to be considered can be aided by asking several questions noted in Chapter Two: what is the nature of the uneasiness, the need not being satisfied, the result really being sought, the expectations of the manager, the purposes to be achieved, or the values that best express the benefits sought? What does the group or manager consider important? By arraying the responses in a hierarchy of smaller to larger purposes as per-

Table 3-4 Evaluation Approach*

Pursuing an Evaluation Strategy	Specifying and Presenting Solutions (entries are illustrative only)	Involving People (entries are illustrative only)	Using Information and Knowledge (entries are illustrative only)	Arranging for Continuing Change and Improvement (entries are illustrative only)
1 Clarify the fundamental purposeful activity involved by determining the purpose of solution-finding for the problem; if this is not evaluation, proceed to the appropriate approach	Classification of purposeful activities	People initiating and conducting the evaluation (client, funding sponsor, regulator, manager, professional staff)	Purpose hierarchy, measures of effectiveness for the purposed project; analyses of the organization, market, or constituency, to identify the users	Personnel interested in assessing past performance. Possible opportunity to disseminate widely in the organization what is working well
2 Clearly identify the intended users of the evaluation outcome; determine the purpose perspective, point of view, intended use of the evaluation	What is to be evaluated? Why? Who will use the results? What is their value set? How are the results to be used?	Client or sponsor, professional staff, boundary spanners, users of the evaluation outcome	Information characterizing the viewpoints and concerns of these users	Assess the possibilities for ongoing evaluation and information flow arrangements; develop appropriate continuing or periodic evaluation. Develop ongoing evaluation policies
3 Identify the relevant values, objectives, and goals and their priorities (V); establish appropriate measurement scales	Six dimensions of purpose: fundamental, values (Chapter Two), measures (utility models, benefits vs. costs), control, interface (side effects), and future; goals can be specified by qualitative standards of reference or by levels on measurement scales	Users of the evaluation outcome (or representatives of the users); professionals both as facilitators and as modelers	Interview techniques; group processes (e.g., nominal group process) methodology for opinion polls and Delphi interactions; techniques for eliciting and clarifying values and objectives; multiattribute utility theory	Provide continuing arrangements for identifying changes in values, objectives and goals, and making necessary changes in the scales of measurement
4 Develop methods for obtaining measurements from the system under evaluation; proxy measures may be necessary	A system matrix (see Chapter Nine) to specify the elements and dimensions of the measurement system; frank characterization of strengths and limitations of the measurements	Managers, people involved in the system under evaluation, professionals as facilitators and experts	Financial and cost accounting systems, decision support systems, statistical techniques (regression, time series, ANOVA, etc.), related performance measurement techniques	Wherever practical, set up measurement systems that can be operated by the users of the evaluation
5 Implement the measurement system	(Designed in step 4)	(Combined with 4)	(Highly dependent on the content area and the selected method of evaluation)	Set up continuing arrangements for upgrading the skills of participants in evaluation and bringing in new information and knowledge; develop user capabilities, rather than provide only temporary service
6 Analyze measurements; compare current and previous data on same and competing systems, and with performance measures (3) (alternately, use the P&D approach to design a feasible ideal target system to use as a comparison standard); assess the significance of different findings (V)	Summary measures of overall performance and validity; details regarding important areas of strength and weakness that were observed (V)	Managers, staff, experts	Historical performance data, information about competing systems; techniques for summarizing and presenting information; methods for establishing appropriate priorities among possible areas of concern	Periodically evaluate the evaluation process against its own objectives; identify significant problems and determine causes
7 Determine causes for problems identified in (6); interpret data	Causal hypotheses and validation criteria (see research approach)	Professionals, people involved in the system under evaluation	Research methodology, to develop and test causal hypotheses	(Combined with 6)
8 Determine conclusions and recommendations based on the results of (7); use conclusions as part of operation and supervision, or initiate restructuring of the system (P&D)	Presentation format is tailored to its intended use (e.g., input to ongoing operation and supervision, or proposal for P&D)	Users of the evaluation outcome; professionals as facilitators and experts	Classification of purposeful activities; group process techniques; second-level purposeful activities	Use the results of evaluating the evaluation systems either to make operating adjustments or to replan future evaluations

* Roman numerals are explained in Table 3-9.

Table 3-5 Research Approach*

Pursuing a Research Strategy	Specifying and Presenting Solutions (entries are illustrative only)	Involving People (entries are illustrative only)	Using Information and Knowledge (entries are illustrative only)	Arranging for Continuing Change and Improvement (entries are illustrative only)
1 Clarify the fundamental purposeful activity involved by determining the purpose of solution-finding for the problem; if this is not research, proceed to the appropriate approach	Classification of fundamental activities	People initiating and conducting the proposed research (principal investigators, institution, funding agencies); input from the larger research community on the general "research agendas" in various areas and disciplines; curiosity of a person; the modes of thinking needed here are concrete/reflective, and people who operate well in this mode may play an important role	Purpose hierarchy; research objectives; estimated value and impact of different types of results, decision techniques	Identify larger purposes needing research; research to develop better generalizations about effective approaches to different purposeful activities. Initiate P&D to improve research efforts
2 Identify the phenomenon of interest or area of uncertainty where relationships are desired (V)	Areas of knowledge to be organized into new theories; recurring phenomena to be modeled and predicted; requirements of information for P&D	(Combined with step 1)	(Combined with step 1)	Develop a long-range research agenda
3 Assimilate information about the phenomenon (see Learning Approach)	Design of literature review; information in the mind of the investigators: analytic and intuitive understanding of data relationships, conceptual frameworks, and different perspectives on the information (see Learning Approach)	Input from people who have experience with the area or phenomenon; experts in information search methods (reference librarians, information systems experts); the mode of thinking primarily abstract/reflective	Recorded information, observation, and conversation with knowledgeable people; indexing resources include computerized bibliographies and conventional library research methods and materials	Use the Learning Approach to develop a program of continuing learning, in relation to (2) above
4 Formulate general hypotheses or causes that might explain the phenomenon or solve the problem (IV, VI)	Causal and statistical relationships, structural models and taxonomies, quantitative and qualitative representations; idea generation should not be artificially constrained by format	Primarily the people conducting the research, but possibly also editors, technicians, research analysts; abstract/reflective modes of thinking	Modeling techniques (VI), idea generation techniques (IV), analysis, existing theories, different conceptual frameworks	Seek unifying higher-order generalizations to organize large bodies of information effectively
5 Determine operational implications of the hypotheses, and devise appropriate verification tests (see Planning and Design Approach)	After this step the hypotheses are publicly verifiable—hence they are phrased in terms of clear operational definitions, with all relevant assumptions made explicit; verification criteria indicate clearly how the hypotheses could be refuted by data and what new observations they predict ("if-then" format)	Experts in the design and analysis of relevant experiments and tests; abstract/active modes of thinking	Statistical and deterministic models, experimental design theory; existing theory about the phenomenon or area of interest (use several resources rather than assuming one is best); hypotheses that conflict with current knowledge need close scrutiny, but not automatic rejection: conflicting "facts" may be incorrect	Map out possible implications for future research
6 Accept the hypothesis or cause that most effectively explains the relevant phenomena and predicts new results; if none of them prove adequate, return to step 3 or 4 (see Evaluation Approach)	Effective explanations are supported by verifiable data and replicable results, and are fruitful in predicting new information; other solution criteria: structural integrity, efficiency, credibility, relevance, and flexibility; communication of findings via professional journals, conferences, and so on	Interaction with a larger research community; dissemination of results is primarily a concrete/active activity	Develop the interactions of the new generalization with larger bodies of theory	Use the new results as the starting point for further investigations; modify (2) above in light of the findings

* Roman numerals are explained in Table 3-9.

Table 3-6 Learning Approach*

Pursuing a Learning Strategy	Specifying and Presenting Solutions (entries are illustrative only)	Involving People (entries are illustrative only)	Using Information and Knowledge (entries are illustrative only)	Arranging for Continuing Change and Improvement (entries are illustrative only)
1 Clarify the fundamental purposeful activity involved by determining the purpose of solution-finding for the problem; if this is not learning, proceed to the appropriate approach	Classification of purposeful activities	Participation in the situation that motivated the activity (misperception is likely if the main motivation comes from participants other than the intended learner)	Purpose hierarchy, management theory (to identify other candidates for the fundamental purposeful activity)	Identify long-range purposes that involve learning
2 Select the basic type(s) of learning that will achieve the purpose selected in step 1 (see next column)	Specify one or more of the following: acquire specific skills; become familiar with a body of data; acquire new concepts and perspectives; learn to relate concepts and experience in new ways; develop one's ability to synthesize new concepts and perceptions	Learner, in consultation with persons knowledgeable about the task at hand, and with experts in the area of learning	Learning theory; information about the problem locus	Focus on "learning to learn": develop abilities to synthesize new concepts, to apply concepts to many specific needs and situations, and to make effective use of educational resources; flexible long-range plan for learning particular skills and conceptual disciplines
3 Define objectives appropriate to the purpose selected in (1) and the learning categories selected in (2)	Cognitive, affective, and/or psychomotor learning objectives, e.g., develop drawing skill (psychomotor, VIII), appreciation of different drawing styles (cognitive/affective); learn concepts in an area of cultural history (cognitive), develop a sense of ownership of one's cultural heritage (affective)	Learner, experts, teachers, managers, guidance counsellors, audiovisual specialists, and so on	Learning theory; information about particular disciplines of study; accumulated teaching and learning experience, which may not yet be incorporated into an organized body of theory	Periodically review short-range objectives in relation to larger purposes; define long-term learning objectives, including affective ones (e.g., overcome aversions, develop confidence, develop appreciation of viewpoints and perspectives)
4 Plan a sequence of learning activities, including provision for assessment of the achievement of the objectives defined in (3) (IV, V, VIII)	Formal studies and degree programs; learning contracts; reading, practice (VIII), and consultation; agendas for informal discussion groups	(Combined with 3)	Information about various disciplines, skills and learning strategies; available programs of study; recommended curricula and other published learning guides; techniques for measuring performance; guidelines for educational processes related to particular objectives	Develop a flexible long-range learning plan. Provide for *qualitative* assessment of achievement of objectives, particularly where simple measures are inappropriate
5 Implement the learning plan (II, VII, VIIII)	The primary solution framework is the resulting cognitive, affective, and psychomotor skill structure of the learner; system matrix (Chapters Nine and Thirteen) may be effective to represent topic, area, or skill about which learning is to take place	Learner and resource people (teachers, consultants, librarians, etc.); group processes can include lectures, interacting discussions, role playing, gaming and simulation, and dialectical processes	Informational resources: books and journals, audio and video tapes, film, radio, and television programming, computerized information-search systems, learning curves, direct experience, games, computer-aided instruction software, the content of formal courses, and resources for indexing and interrelating information	Periodically revise learning plans, to incorporate changing needs, interests, resources, and conditions

* Roman numerals are explained in Table 3-9.

ceived by the group or client, there is an excellent probability that the "right" purposeful approach will be selected. They will have a chance to use their own criteria in selection, including such personal and political ones as assessing "whose ox may be gored," frequency of occurrence of difficulty, and personal factors—in context. Of course, identifying one approach is the starting point, for several purposeful activities may be involved *over time* with the same problem.

6 Each approach uses many techniques, models, and tools (Appendix A). Common for all of them is the

Table 3-7 Summary and Comparison of Different Approaches to Different Purposeful Activities

Purposeful Activities	Intertwined Factors of a Total Approach				
	Pursuing the Strategy	Specifying Solution	Involving People	Using Information	Arranging for Change
Operating and supervising (Table 3-2)	Learn objective and norms of the system Obtain resources and measures of systems performance Lead, motivate, control and correct operational processes	Performance objectives Specifications for inputs, equipment, personnel, and information systems Operating policies Personnel policies Specifications for the sequence of operations	Active manager direction together with clients, employees, and others Experts to analyze resource trade-offs, plan sequence, design communication, coordination, and measurement systems	Measurement and information systems Organization theory Engineering and marketing knowledge Financial analysis Timely and well focused information about current operations within overall plan of operations	Establish long-range planning to improve the system Obtain resources for continuing improvement of operations (consultants, in-house seminars, personnel development and management improvement programs, courses, conferences, etc.) Develop change attitudes
Planning and design (Table 3-3)	Select purpose(s) to be achieved from hierarchy(ies) Develop feasible ideal solution target for regularity conditions Detail solutions to achieve purpose(s) for all conditions	Purpose hierarchy and dimensions of selected purpose(s) List of ideal and possible solutions Specify solution with eight elements and six dimensions of system matrix	Decisionmakers, users, implementers, and others affected by the solution in defining the purpose, generating ideas, and selecting the solution Professionals used mainly as process coordinators, with other "expert" roles used in response to specific needs	P&D theory and techniques guide process Other information is gathered only if relevant to achieving the P&D purpose in specific setting	Build adaptation into solutions Periodic replanning Develop organizational support for ongoing improvement of satisfactory systems rather than crisis correction
Evaluation (Table 3-4)	Identify evaluation users' purposes and perspective Establish or reconfirm values and objectives Measure performance Interpret the results	Definition of users Descriptions and operational scales for their values and objectives Specifications for measurement procedures Measurement data and interpretation	Users define perspective Clients clarify and operationalize values and measures Professionals measure Users, clients, and influentials analyze and interpret with professionals	Techniques for clarifying and operationalizing objectives, gathering measurement data and analyzing measurement results	Develop ongoing evaluation arrangements Build evaluation into new systems Provide adaptability to changing values, objectives, and reference groups Upgrade participants' evaluation skills Periodically evaluate the evaluation system against *its* objectives and make necessary changes
Research (Table 3-5)	Review background about area of research Formulate general hypothesis Determine operational implications of the hypothesis Devise tests Verify or refute the generalization	Definition of the subject area Investigator perspectives Causal or statistical hypothesis Statements of assumptions and implications to test Empirical results	Investigators and resource people (sources of background information) Experts for design of experiments A larger professional community shapes the research agenda and interprets results	Background resources ("the literature") Techniques for developing models and designing experiments Existing theories Information about the subject area is used comprehensively, because the sequence of discovery is guided by its empirical results, in unpredictable directions	Develop a long-range research agenda Seek unifying higher-order generalizations Use the results of the present study as the starting point for further investigations
Learning (Table 3-6)	Decide on intended information or skill Determine level to attain Implement learning activities Assess information or skill acquisition	Forms of information, concepts, or new applications of ideas Improved ability to form new concepts Choices of cognitive, affective and psychomotor objectives Stated sequence of learning Internalized results within personal "maps"	Learner is primary participant with resource people (teachers, consultants, librarians, etc.) to assist	Learning theory Information about particular areas of study Existing techniques and strategies for different types of study Recommended curricula Varieties of previous experiences and learning Accumulated experience of resource people Information recorded and indexed in various forms	Long-range focus on "learning to learn" Periodically review short-range objectives in relation to larger purposes Identify major affective goals such as overcoming learning aversions Revise learning plans to adapt to changing needs

Table 3-8 Criteria Used to Select Content of Approaches

(a) The effectiveness of the approach in achieving the desired results of the specific purposeful activity

(b) Potential in fostering creativity and innovativeness

(c) Ability to decrease the time spent on converging on the results (specific *how to* methods)

(d) Effectiveness in utilizing all resources (time, money, people, energy)

(e) Clarity in identifying points at which critical decisions are needed

(f) The ease with which people at all levels are involved

(g) Ease of learning the approach

(h) Probability of leading to implementable solutions

(i) Reliability or reproducibility of results

(j) Capability for easy monitoring of approach

(k) Adaptability to and flexibility for different circumstances

(l) Ability to consider related societal and environmental factors

(m) Appropriateness for all sizes, types, and sponsors of problems (purposeful activities)

(n) Opportunities to minimize (balance costs of getting data with costs of inadequate accuracy and precision) and effectively utilize the kind and quantity of data collected

(o) Capability of minimizing the uncertainty level in decisions

---

development of a timeline of major events and personal assignments, work program, or schedule. None of these is reviewed here. The remainder of this book does review them for P&D, and the organization of a volume on each of the other purposeful activities could be similar to that of this book.

7 Secondary purposeful activities are needed in each primary one. Strategies for the secondary ones are listed in Table 3-9.

Some comments about the approaches in Tables 3-2 through 3-6 (and summarized in Table 3-7) will provide specific insights on each.

The Operating and Supervising Approach *(Table 3-2)*

Maintaining a "good" system is the primary objective of this purposeful activity. This is the responsibility of administration or management. The literature suggests many approaches to operating and supervising: expectancy theory; leadership and motivation; contingency theory; human relations; management by results, communications, objectives, performance measures, allocation, exceptions, or forecasting, or so on;

conflict resolution; systems theory; and so on. Many approaches are algorithmic (very specific steps or procedures to follow) in nature (e.g., when to reorder materials, how to schedule work hours, what sample size to choose). The management literature does not however, establish different approaches for the different types of problems or purposeful activities it identifies, such as planning, organizing, operating, and controlling. Table 3-2 synthesizes these different ideas into the five factors, and treats the ideas in the literature as if they applied only to operating and supervising purposes.

The Planning and Design Approach *(Table 3-3)*

An equally large number of P&D approaches are proposed in the literature. However, Table 3-3 represents a synthesis of what "outstanding" P&D professionals do and how research on human perceptions can apply successfully. Most of the P&D methodological literature suggests other methods and ideas, but Chapter Five explains why the approaches of respected P&D professionals and different interpretations of research form the basis for the remainder of the book.

Evaluation Approach *(Table 3-4)*

Evaluation is a relatively recent arrival on the *formal* purposeful activity scene, yet is developing an extensive literature. Evaluation approaches are illustrated by efforts in technology assessment, appraisal paradigms, audit trails, ombudsman offices, and accountability. Business audits are an early form of evaluation. Most evaluation ideas relate to the values and objectives identified at the time a system or solution was installed: at that time, measures of performance or people's impressions about the performance of the system, artifact, or service program are obtained to serve as the base for assessment of achievement. Some methods contain long lists of questions (not necessarily divided into the factors in a total approach) or revolve around experiments or pilot projects. Rationalism seems to govern most approaches, although affective considerations are increasingly voiced.[21]

The Research Approach *(Table 3-5)*

Various specific methodologies (e.g., experimental, philosophical, theoretical, longitudinal, action, synthesis, taxonomical) can be a part of the approach shown in Table 3-5. This is not totally surprising when you consider the various outcomes expected from the purposeful activity: generalizations, previously unknown relationships, causes, and forecasts and predictions. Even though objectivity is a supposed attribute of the research strategies and of "science" in

Table 3-9   Strategies for Secondary Purposeful Activities

I   To make a decision (in any stage, phase, or step in an approach)

1 Establish measures of effectiveness (scales of value or criteria) related to the *purpose* of the decision

2 Establish the weighting or importance of each

3 Determine decision rules that will be followed

4 Measure the amount of each criterion present in all alternatives being considered and estimate the probability, if necessary, of the alternative being workable and implementable on the basis of the criterion

5 Combine by multiplication the measure, weighting, and probability of each criterion for each alternative

6 Select alternative based on decision rule

II To maintain a standard of achievement (control)

1 Identify key factors in the system (see values and measures dimensions) that must be controlled in order to achieve the intended overall result

2 Specify the basis for establishing performance standards for each key factor (forecasts, budgets, standard costs, turnover ratios, evaluation by clients, delays)

3 Define the information—the accounting records, operating data, on-site studies, statistics—that must be accumulated to measure status and performance

4 Establish a reporting structure and sequence that identifies performance in each control area, signals trends, relates causes and effects, and identifies results by responsibility under the plan of organization

5 Compare measurements obtained with desired values, to determine significant variances

6 Take action to correct significant variances, on the basis of available alternatives or by returning to one of the fundamental purposeful activities

III To resolve a conflict

1 Each party develop a purpose hierarchy, starting with conflict topic, and seek agreement on selected level and related goals

2 Each party develop many ideal solutions to achieve selected purpose (IV)

3 Each party develop feasible ideal system target

4 Develop agreement for common target (I)

5 Additional negotiation on how close settlement can come to target (expand resources, stimulation of people, alter positions, etc.)

6 Implement settlement

IV To develop creative ideas

1 Select stimulators (checklists, creativity principles, hierarchy of purposes, analogies, morphological box, etc.) related broadly to purpose for which creative ideas are sought

2 Follow bisociation concept (see Chapter Twelve) of mentally forcing the plane for purpose to intersect with the plane of stimulator idea

3 Use regularity concept (more frequently occurring or important conditions) to stimulate the mind by focusing on only one condition

4 Involve all levels of personnel affected by the ideas to be developed

5 Stress freewheeling, no-criticism, piggybacking, effective group processes, quantity of ideas, and involvement of people (see Chapter Twelve)

6 Break creativity activity into two or more sessions (hibernation or brain resting)

V To establish priorities

1 Determine purpose and goals that priority list will help individual or group to achieve

2 List present and future activities that need to be done

3 Identify the vital few activities that are most important (ranking, couplet, matched pair, Pareto's emphasis curve, etc.) (see Appendix A)

VI To make a model of a phenomenon

1 Break down the phenomenon into simpler ones

2 Establish a statement of model objectives

3 Seek analogies

4 Consider a specific case (with quantifiable values if possible)

5 Establish symbols

6 Record the obvious

7 Enrich factors and abstractions, simplify all features

VII To practice or exercise a skill

1 Determine the attribute or skill in which proficiency is desired

2 Establish overall objectives to be attained

3 Set up ten to twelve time intervals and establish the proportion of the objectives to be attained at each time point (a progress curve)

4 Repeat desired activity (including known corrections)

5 Measure performance (II)

6 Take steps to change if performance is unsatisfactory (lessons, reduce or increase pace, get observer)

VIII To focus and motivate individual efforts

1 Develop performance measures and objectives for the function(s) to be achieved and output(s) to be produced*

Table 3-9 *(Continued)*

2 Design and install methods for the individual and the organization to monitor performance with these measured performance.

3 Establish a system of rewards meaningful to, and understandable by, the employees on the basis of measured performance

4 Provide the resources needed to accomplish the objectives

5 Reward performance on the basis of formal organizational objectives; allow for rewards based on higher-level objectives not included in the formal measurement system; rewards should be timely, and the incentive system should emphasize reward over punishment

* In many cases, the people for whom the objectives are being set participate actively in these steps.

general, the other factors demonstrate their relativity and even prejudicial aspects. Subjectivity, or at least culturally conditioned ideas, form the basis of this as well as all the other approaches. After all, research problems are always defined subjectively.

The Learning Approach *(Table 3-6)*

The theory of learning is really in its infancy, even though humans have always been learners. It is currently believed that cognitive, affective, and psychomotor skills are involved in learning. The available principles are mostly summarized in Table 3-6 and are stated in a way to help accommodate a variety of learning styles.

The five-factor approach for each purposeful activity can be expected to promote continual change and improvement. But the approach ideas already available lay the groundwork for better solution finding and implementation. The five-factor approaches encourage

exploration of alternatives and flexibility. They create an atmosphere of openness and interaction among people, and enable the individuals involved to become better problem solvers in all spheres of their lives. Selecting the appropriate purposeful activity helps to avoid the difficulties expressed in the old adage that "organizations waste more time and money on doing the wrong things efficiently than they ever could on trying to do the right things, even if inefficiently." Determining which purposeful activity is involved improves effectiveness and performance by using an approach that focuses on doing the right things before trying to do things right.

SUMMARY

An approach is composed of principles and modes of action. It creates a mindset and methodologies for problem solving. There are numerous problem-solving approaches, but they are variations on four basic ones: do-nothing, chance, affective, and rational. Do-nothing can be dismissed because this book assumes humans do want to solve their problems.

(1) The chance approach focuses on the importance of the accidental in problem solving and life in general. (2) Affective approaches stress intuition, insight, feelings, and divergent thinking. (3) Rational approaches are characterized by linear, systematic, methodical processes. Each has merit, and serious flaws. Some are more applicable to specific human purposeful activities than others.

A total approach synthesizes them into five factors integrated along a time line: pursuing a strategy, specifying and presenting the solution, involving people, using information and knowledge, and arranging for continuing change and improvement.

This basic structure is then specified for and adapted to each purposeful activity.

CHAPTER FOUR

The Purposeful Activity of Planning and Design

P&D is the label assigned to the purposeful activity of creating or restructuring a situation-specific solution. This chapter explores the nature of P&D—who does it, what they do, and what are the characteristics of P&D problems and solutions. It describes the three objectives of P&D which constitute a common bond unifying diverse professions, and dilemmas in P&D that thwart the realization of objectives.

Professionals tend to assume that "planning" and "design" are different. In point of fact they seek similar ends. What may differ among projects, rather than between the two concepts, is their scale, scope, complexity, specificity, and time horizons. Table 4-1 illustrates this overlapping relationship by placing some characteristics of planning and design efforts on a series of continua.

There are many perspectives concerning precisely what it is that planners and designers do. From most perspectives, P&D is viewed as an end in itself. It is assumed, incorrectly, that theorists and practitioners always comprehend and consider P&D in relationship to other human purposeful activities and values.

Table 4-2 presents a number of these perspectives. A common theme unifies these diverse descriptions: P&D is a set of actions (problem formulation, solution generation, implementation, and so on) that create or restructure a situation-specific system to achieve desired results. They produce decisions affecting the future. Such actions are prompted by unsolved prob-

lems, unmet needs and aspirations, or existing systems requiring change or improvement.

How can we characterize P&D results? One way would be to call these results "artificials" and describe them as human-produced objects that have properties based on images of how things ought to be in order to achieve human values and goals.[1]

We have chosen, for simplicity's sake, to call the results of P&D *solutions*, although *artificial, holon*,[2] or *system* might be equally appropriate. P&D solutions may be physical artifacts, operating procedures, or policies. Table 4-3 suggests the range of P&D solutions.

In using the term *solution*, several stages of the results are implied, including the model or design and its *implemented* condition. *Solution* will be used in the same spirit as many other labels in this text, with the emphasis not on the word itself but on the set of ideas it is meant to convey.

Characteristics of P&D Problems and Solutions

Anything that the human mind can identify as needing a new or restructured situation-specific solution becomes the source or locus of a substantive P&D problem. "Anything" can be physical, social, organizational, conceptual, local or global in nature. "Needing" is, of course, in the eyes of the beholder. Poisonous snakes, for example, pose a safety prob-

Table 4-1   Frequently Used Descriptions of Planning and Design*

Planning	Design
Larger scope	Smaller scope
Open-ended	Specific
Low potential to model the solution accurately	High potential to model the solution accurately
Continuing process over time	Limited to a short time period
Ends are variable	Ends are given
Abstract/social	Physical/individual
Program-oriented	Project-oriented
Deals with future needs	Deals with immediate needs
Mixed technical and non-technical	Technical
Longer time horizon (over 3 years)	Shorter time horizon (< 3 yrs)
Time- and process-oriented	Space- and artifact-oriented
Innovative	Allocative
Larger number of people affected	Smaller number of people affected
Higher risk associated with decisions	Lower risk associated with decisions
Policy and strategic organizational levels	Tactical and operational organizational levels
Fewer well-defined outcomes	More well-defined outcomes

* Each line of description represents the two opposite perspectives on a continuum.

lem in Dallas, but are the solution to the rat problem in Malaysia.

Problems can vary in size and scope, ranging from the need for a national health policy to a need for a "better mousetrap." The emerging awareness that preparing for the future will by necessity be interdisciplinary and even global in nature has significantly expanded the sources and loci of P&D problems.

Urban planners, for example, fifty years ago could control land use at the city level; now diminishing resources and urban sprawl require a county, regional, and national focus.

Values and objectives associated with bettering the human condition also foster "needs" and thus P&D. Dislike of hard work and desire for leisure, for instance, have generated literally thousands of P&D created "labor-saving" devices over many centuries.

There are as many P&D solutions as there are problems. They can be of any size and scope, varying

Table 4-2   Examples of Perspectives on and Characterizations of P&D

P&D IS

1 A process

2 A process for determining appropriate future action through a sequence of choices

3 Rationalism or systems analysis

4 Selectively applying science and technology to attain an end result

5 Advanced or strategic decision making

6 The link between knowledge and organized action

7 Bringing about or guidance of change, or improvement, whether in quantitative terms (growth or diminution), qualitative alterations, or both

8 Creating models and forecasting, most often mathematical or statistical models in computer simulation

9 Applying dynamic systems principles, such as causality, probability, vitality (maintaining continuous life), coordination, and creativity (E. Jantsch, *Design for Evolution*, New York: George Braziller, 1975)

10 Social systems design, from ecological and "whole" systems (e.g., law, ekistics, macroeconomics) to arranging technical and human resources in formal organizations (e.g., organizational development)

11 A philosophical synthesis of social process knowledge, whether called incrementalism, psychology, societal guidance, organization behavior, learning systems, political science or experimental evolution

12 The preparation of plans for long-term concepts, medium-term programs, and short-range operations

13 Current decision making with future alternatives (opportunities and threats) as the guides

14 Specifying and simulating a desired future and identifying methods of reaching it

15 A philosophy and attitude for contemplating and acting on the future

16 Disaster avoidance by revealing future opportunities and threats

17 Characterized as involving a data structure, a set of operators to apply to variables, a set of objectives, and constraints to achieve a goal, and a procedure to generate a set of solutions

18 "An elegant balance of the need to act and the need to reflect" (C. W. Churchman, "The Case Against Planning," *Design Methods and Theories*, Vol. 12, Nos. 3/4, September–December, 1978, p. 170)

in resource commitment, complexity, and time horizons. Size and scope refer to the number of components and people required. National health insurance is clearly larger in size and scope than a design for a patient health care unit. Resource commitments concern the amounts of money, time, person-hours, and

Table 4-3 Various Names for P&D Outcomes

Artifact	Plan
Curriculum	Program resolution
Design	Public policy
Drawings	Recommendation
Equipment	Reply
Equipment request	Set of operating procedures
Feasibility study	Staffing pattern
Guidance advice	Statement
Information system	System
Institution	Target
Organization structure	Tool
Piece of legislation	Work methods

Table 4-4 Characteristics of Different Levels of P&D

Level	Characteristics
Policy	Statements of purposes and objectives, guidelines for specific actions and plans at other levels (5 to 7)*
Strategical	Broad plans or courses of action that represent a means of accomplishing a particular purpose within the policy guidelines (3 to 5)*
Tactical	Specific plans or designs that are usually the implementation, transition, and inter-communication links between strategic plans and operational designs (1 to 3)*
Operational	Detailed designs that prescribe specific actions of specific people at specific points in time (0 to 1)*

* Relative time spans of discretion. A company board of directors may do P&D on a basis of 5 to 7 years, top management 3 to 5 years, middle management 1 to 3 years, and first-line people 0 to 1 years. What the board considers operational P&D, the first-line supervisor will consider policies of 5 to 7 months, the foreman 3 to 5 months, the lead person 1 to 3 months, and the worker 0 to 1 months. A homemaker may consider food policies on a 5- to 7-week basis, the family shopping trip on a 3- to 5-week basis, the fill-in shopping 1 to 3 weeks, and daily meal schedule 0 to 1 week.

types of personnel a solution requires. Complexity and time horizons vary with the problem's purposes, scale, scope, and implementation environment.[3] A company's product development plan may have a six- or seven-year time horizon, for example. An actual product program may be obsolete in two years.

All of these factors reflect the level at which P&D is carried out. These levels may be geographical—home, neighborhood, state, region, nation, the world. More commonly these levels are described as those of policies, strategies, tactics, and operations. Policies are clearly larger in size and scope than tactics. Table 4-4 suggests the characteristics of each level.

Who Does P&D?

One way of classifying P&D practitioners is by the outcomes listed in Table 4-2; another is by problem locus. One could simply list professions whose primary concern or principle of commonality is creating or restructuring situation-specific solutions. Table 4-5 lists over 30. The number is growing rapidly because of both new problems and new technologies, requiring people with special knowledge and skills to transform knowledge into workable solutions.[3] In addition, the societal penchant for specialization unfortunately will tend to increase the number.

Nonprofessionals also engage in a good deal of P&D in personal, family, or organizational situations. Although everyone engages in P&D, the P&D professions emerged because people began to recognize that certain groups who specialized in the collective behavior of creating or restructuring solutions could be more effective than they themselves in achieving improved levels of societal values (Figure 2-2). Early practitioners also promoted the idea that they could be more effective than "lay" people in accomplishing so-

cial goals. Thus, the sine qua non of P&D is to achieve certain objectives and goals that "better" the four values all humans seek (Chapter 2). Table 2-4 described a variety of P&D values, which can be summarized in terms of the following three objectives.

The first objective of P&D is *to maximize the effectiveness of recommended solutions.* There are many definitions of what characterizes an effective solution, ranging from Plato's cardinal virtues of comprehensiveness, economy, practicality, and ethicality to "shared values and flexibility."[4]

Other descriptions frequently encountered are reliability, adaptability, environmental and social soundness, pluralistic element, client satisfaction, high benefit/cost ratio, efficiency, and simplicity. Chapters 13 and 15 provide further insight into effective solutions. All P&D professions have their own criteria for defining effective solutions, but all agree that fulfilling them is the first requirement of good P&D.

The second objective of P&D is *to maximize the likelihood of implemented solutions.* Effective results in the real world are basic to P&D. Failure to implement effective solutions is *prima facie* evidence that something went awry in the P&D process. It has been suggested that effective solutions are the product of

Table 4-5   Illustrative List of P&D Professions*

Ad hoc planning (task force, commission, team, committee, etc.)	Helping professions (social work, personal counseling, psychological therapy, etc.)
Agricultural planning‡	Human factors design†
Applied behavioral science†	Industrial design
Appropriate or intermediate technology	Industrial relations‡
Architecture	Information systems
Area development	Interior design/space planning
Business and corporate planning	Landscape architecture
Career and guidance counseling	Land-use planning
Commercial art/graphic design	Law
Communication design	Long range planning
Community planning	Management science/operations research‡
Development planning	Manufacturing planning
Educational Planning	Organizational development/design
Energy utilization planning†	Policy analysis/planning
Engineering systems design (all branches)†	Product design
Environmental design	Productivity improvement and services‡
Facilities planning	Quality of work life design
Government planning (e.g., defense,† health care, federal paperwork,‡ transportation, space,† law enforcement,‡ parks†)	Safety and accident prevention‡
	System analysis/design
	Technology transfer
Health care delivery planning	Urban and regional planning

* Some P&D fields are oriented to highly individualistic, situation-specific, artistic, and esthetic needs: arts and crafts designer, graphic artist, musical composer, novelist, portrait painter, and sculptor.
† Professions that depend on and may contain a good deal of the research purposeful activity.
‡ Professions that often include a good deal of the operating and supervising purposeful activity.

the *quality of solution* × *implementation*. Even if the solution quality is 100, nonimplementation (0) produces a 0 measure of solution effectiveness.

The third objective of P&D is *to maximize the effectiveness of P&D resources*. It is conceivable that with unlimited amounts of time and money many problems could be solved. But it is highly unlikely that any organization would commit itself to such vast expenditures. Limits on time and money imposed by the real world demand maximizing the synergy, effectiveness, and efficiency of P&D practitioners. This constitutes the work ethic of P&D,[5] this is expected of P&D professionals in return for the problem-solving responsibility delegated to them.

These objectives unify the diverse P&D professions. They create a common bond. Unfortunately, failure to achieve them constitutes a common predicament.

The existence of these maximization objectives immediately identifies the root cause of the dilemmas in P&D. Such objectives require a rigorous theory incorporating techniques for triple (global) maximization of the objectives, quantitative methods for identifying

trade-offs within and among them, and scientific measurement of factors necessary to trade-offs in maximization efforts. Clearly, we do not even begin to have such a theory. P&D is so complex, the human factors so difficult, maybe impossible, to quantify, that the probability of ever having such a theory is infinitesimal.

Nevertheless, the need to create and restructure effective situation-specific solutions remains. The P&D professions have proliferated and prospered on the assumption that they uniquely fulfill that need, by virtue of their experience and expertise. How justifiable is that assumption? An assessment of how successfully the P&D professions are accomplishing these three objectives suggests that a number of predicaments beset P&D. Even a casual perusal of P&D literature substantiates this.

Predicaments in P&D

A common lament concerns the absence "of strategies for planning that work."[6] Resolving these difficulties is what the remainder of this book addresses.

A brief overview of the history of P&D clarifies the current predicaments. Over several centuries a number of different P&D professions emerged from earlier crafts.[7] Each had its own jealously guarded techniques and standards. In the nineteenth century, the P&D professions wholeheartedly embraced both scientific knowledge and the research method. The professions viewed themselves as "applied sciences." The assumption was made that the research method, tremendously successful in generating scientific knowledge, was equally applicable to P&D. Equally pervasive was the notion that scientific discovery preceded P&D innovations. Ironically, historical case studies have proved this assumption incorrect.[8] P&D denied its own rich heritage and became the stepchild of the sciences.

At first, adoption of the research method made sense, largely because problems were "definable, understandable and consensual."[9] Indeed the results were spectacular. Streets were laid out, roads paved, homes built, dread diseases eliminated, indoor plumbing installed, and hospitals and schools built to serve every locale. But by the mid-twentieth century, neither science nor P&D could promise ever rosier futures. Hiroshima, environmental disaster, diminishing resources, and exploding populations inaugurated an era of infinitely more complex and unmanageable problems, problems that are not "definable, understandable nor consensual." Conflict resolution, implementation in highly politicized environments, and multiple impacts pose difficulties less amenable to the research method. Postindustrial society that deals mainly with information and services poses similar difficulties. As the substantive problems have multiplied, so too have the methodological.

Methodological difficulties facing P&D professionals are in large part a function of current theories and techniques. But they also arise out of the P&D environment and the nature of P&D itself. The problems with which P&D must cope are complex and mutually interdependent. How does anyone, including a P&D professional, "handle" something that does not exist? Definitive formulation of "the problem" is often impossible. A professional must deal with anticipated, not exact, futures and has limited opportunity to test solutions.[10] Furthermore, solution implementation occurs in an environment largely out of the P&D professional's direct control. The P&D milieu is one of stress, uncertainty, and conflict,[11] exacerbated by conventional P&D approaches.

From this milieu and historical tendencies to specialization and scientism come many of the predicaments of P&D. Because these dilemmas undermine realization of P&D's three objectives, they have an effect on all of the P&D professions. They include the following:

Absence of an Agreed-upon General Theory

P&D theories range from all-inclusive rational models to piecemeal incremental ones. Models that purport to be all-encompassing fail to account for irrational, logical, and political realities and limited P&D resources. Mathematical models and instrumental rationality ignore the complexity of the real world. Incrementalism accepts "satisficing" rather than striving for optimal solutions. Developing tomorrow's solutions should not be done with today's assumptions. Much more will be said about assumptions and models in Chapter Five. For now it is enough to note that all of them:

- Lack a prescriptive methodology operationalizing all aspects of the P&D purposeful activity.
- Concentrate on solution finding, not implementation, strategies.
- Fail to incorporate psychological and behavioral realities into theory or technique.

The Quality of P&D Solutions Is Declining

Articles like "What Ever Happened to the American Dream," "Why Things Don't Work Anymore," and "Engineering Failure and Technological Overkill in Developing Countries" are representative of a vast literature detailing the failure of newly proposed or installed solutions to even minimally achieve user objectives. High technology just will not "solve all our problems." The decline characterizes P&D solutions on every level, from gadgets to health systems, from trade balances to literacy of high school students. The reasons are myriad and include:

- Classification of problems in terms of techniques rather than ends or purposes.
- Transferring of solutions without reference to situation-specific needs and resources.
- Concentration on physical structures and activities rather than policies or systems.
- The assumption that only piecemeal, symptomatic solutions can be implemented.

This last leads to solutions that are sectoral or disciplinary (suboptimized) rather than comprehensive, and to solutions that are merely reactive rather than innovative guides for the future. Current solutions also reflect, to their detriment, the absence of useful techniques for trend monitoring and futures forecasting. In addition, solutions lack flexibility and adaptiveness. Several theorists have commented on the tendency of

P&D to result in the erection of huge bureaucracies and physical infrastructures that cannot be scrapped if proved ineffective.[12]

P&D Role Definitions are Limiting and Often Self-defeating

P&D personnel are encouraged to be elite experts, concentrating on techniques and analysis rather than on purposes and results to be obtained. Much evidence points to the ineffectiveness of such "elite experts," because so much time and effort is required to "sell" their solutions to clients.[13] Often, solutions are rejected because clients have a completely different perception of the problem, and divergent purposes. Even if accepted, implementation may be impossible because implementers have a financial or emotional investment in not changing, don't understand the solution, or reject it precisely because it "wasn't invented here."[14]

Education of P&D professionals reflects these role characterizations, perpetuating the difficulties. In far too many programs, improved analysis techniques are taught, as if a mathematical formulation can be depended upon to produce solutions with merits so obvious that implementation is automatic. In addition, our culture is biased towards the arts and sciences in education, leaving P&D to data collection and model building.

P&D students are not taught to be implementers. Implementation of changes requires intervention in the client's world. Even the designer of a gear to fit on a transmission shaft is intervening by seeking implementation of a design, however small the adopting organization may be. Successful intervention entails a number of P&D roles other than that of expert: mediator, facilitator, coordinator, advocate, and activist, to name a few (see Chapter Fourteen). Besides almost never being included in educational programs, this concept of multiple professional roles is also ignored in most of the literature. Those theorists who do argue for the facilitator/intervener fail to operationalize their exhortations.[15] It is little wonder that excellent P&D professionals sometimes proclaim they must discard the P&D approaches taught in their educational programs.[16]

P&D Professions are Generally Viewed in a Less Than Favorable Light

Some P&D professions are viewed favorably, others not. But a general mistrust tinges comments about, and actions taken regarding P&D. There is a literal societal rejection of P&D in its broader perspectives. "We avoid that very act of consideration, otherwise known as 'planning.' While strong emotions and proper skepticism surround the term 'national planning' we do need some imaginative inventing."[17] Even the terms *planning* and *design* are often avoided in describing groups whose role is really P&D. The Council of Economic Advisers prefers not to be called a group of planners. "Just at the time in history when technological development seems to require the highest levels of responsible bureaucratic management and thoughtful, systematic planning, the public is in full rebellion against government at all levels, including the bureaucracies that determine the public good. Planning threatens the democratic tradition, not because planning is undemocratic, but because the bureaucratic elites who manage planning are undemocratic. . . . Democratic planning is a process of conflict which is not always rational; it depends upon the belief that public intuition is the ultimate, and perhaps even the best, judge—an assertion, by the way, made by Aristotle several thousand years ago."[18]

P&D professionals contribute to this unfavorable perspective by their limited role definitions. Experts produce solutions to meet *their* perception of people's needs. Often, planners appear to consider their work satisfactory if they generate masses of statistical analysis or sophisticated models. P&D professionals assume that quantitative models are the answer to real-world uncertainty and instability.

P&D professionals are even sometimes accused of focusing on "toy" problems rather than real ones.[19] One "expert" took a company's real need to improve performance in a plant and turned it into the *toy* need to measure accurately the time taken for worker activities. As a result of his diligence with measurements a prolonged strike occurred.[20] It is small wonder that administrators, politicians, and "just folks" are less than enthusiastic about P&D at all levels. Of course, some lack of commitment will always be present, but P&D methodologies should not reinforce it.

While active dislike of P&D poses problems, equally detrimental is the tendency of many organizations to accept "window dressing" reports and analysis as sufficient outcome of P&D. P&D personnel are used as a "show group," demonstrating how modern and advanced the organization is. Great pride is exhibited in elegant mathematical models or information systems, but no effort is made to actually use them.

P&D Is Faced with and Contributes to a Huge Data Overload

The vast amount of information and knowledge generated by the many P&D-related disciplines threatens to overwhelm professionals and decision makers alike. The practitioner contributes to the chaos with an endless stream of memos and reports, which usually remain unread. Because the likelihood is great that new information will continue to be generated at a high rate, overload will always be present. Clearly, not everything done and reported is valuable to a specific P&D professional, but even accessing necessary information is difficult. Computerized data bases still leave much to be desired. This is discussed further in Chapter Fifteen.

The P&D Professions Are Poorly Interrelated

Each profession tends to begin with a restricted focus and to become narrower over time. This narrow specialization is assumed "to buttress the profession's greater claim on society for more respect and autonomy than that accorded other occupations."[21] Jealously guarded techniques and training standards assure professional claims on authority. The result is poor P&D solutions—not only because many problems transcend disciplinary boundaries and require joint solutions and perspectives, but also because theories and techniques are not shared. The social planner and engineer, for example, have much to contribute to each other, but rarely cross paths. And when they do, as in the design of a hospital's computerized medical records system, the results are likely to be disastrous. The engineer assumes his system is so good everyone will automatically use it. The sociologist, more familiar with the human factor, downplays the importance of technology.

The current absence of theoretical and educational linkages prevents the P&D professions from coming together under a common P&D umbrella, as the sciences and humanities each have done. The results have negative effects on P&D education and P&D solutions. It means the professions have no basis for interdisciplinary activities (examples would be a task force on urban problems and solutions, or a new product development committee), because they do not speak the same language. "The same youngster who noticed the emperor had no clothes may now be asking, 'What is all your technology for?' "[22]

SUMMARY

Planners and designers seek similar ends. Their primary function is to create and restructure situation-specific solutions. The three objectives of this purposeful activity are: to maximize the effectiveness of recommended solutions; to maximize the likelihood of implemented solutions; and to maximize the effectiveness of P&D resources. These common objectives unify over thirty diverse P&D professions. These professions also experience problems in achieving the objectives because of a number of P&D predicaments: absence of an agreed-upon theory of P&D; the declining quality of P&D solutions; limiting and self-defeating P&D role definitions; the less-than-favorable image of the P&D professions; the fact that P&D is faced with and contributes to a huge data overload; and the poor relationships among the P&D professions.

CHAPTER FIVE

Approaches to Achieving Planning and Design Purposes

This chapter explores the basis for the total P&D approach outlined in Chapter Three. First conventional approaches are described and their poor record in achieving P&D objectives or resolving the predicaments in P&D are considered. A discussion follows of the human realities, behaviors, and perceptions that must form the foundation of a total P&D approach, if effective solutions are to be created and implemented.

Table 5-1 lists a number of approaches currently used by diverse P&D professions. Almost all are variations on the research, systems analysis or rational model; they reflect the methodological hold of scientism on P&D discussed in Chapter Four.

The pervasiveness of scientism in P&D should not be surprising. Most American institutions, particularly the educational system, reflect it. Consider your own education from primary school upward. When a question or problem is posed you are expected to collect *all* the relevant data, analyze it by breaking it down into discrete components, determine where the problem lies, and find the answer. As a result, any problem almost automatically elicits a "research strategy" response.

Although there are minor variations in the "research strategy," in terms of interactions, decision-making processes and so on, the basics of the conventional P&D approach can be summarized as follows:

1 *Define the Problem* Analysis of what appears to have signaled the need for P&D, get the facts, observe the situation, subdivide, partition, break down, reduce the problem to its discrete components, factor, and otherwise gather information.

2 *Formulate the Problem* Find out "what's wrong," identify the difficulty, ask what is going on, whose fault is it, and otherwise probe for problem information.

3 *Explore Alternatives* Find out how to correct what's wrong, seek ideas to eliminate difficulties, use creativity techniques, and otherwise seek solutions for the troubles.

4 *Select Solution* Use decision-making processes, such as decision trees, behavioral decision making, "satisficing" or selecting the first alternative that appears to work, utility and value theory, and statistical decision processes.

5 *Detail the Solution* Assemble the facts into specifications.

6 *Implement the Solution* Many of the conventional strategies do not include this step, presumably because the P&D professionals assume that some other group—politicians, decision makers, or officers of organizations—will "obviously" implement the good suggestions.

Table 5-1 Some Conventional P&D Approaches
(Mainly Strategies)

I   Architecture

Massive briefing (collect all information that in any way *might* be useful)

Select key features

Synthesize a solution

Detail the solution

II   Business planning*

Evaluation of environmental trends

Determination of opportunities and threats

Establishment of corporate philosophy

Setting of corporate objectives

Generation, evaluation, and choice of strategic alternatives

Portfolio balancing of alternatives

III   Engineering design

Problem identification

Problem definition

Studies

Proposed alternative solutions

Evaluation and decision

Implementation

IV   Machine and hardware systems design

Establish problem area

Determine exactly the nature of the problem

Collect pertinent information

Break down and study information

Assemble the analyzed information into various configurations

Study the merits of each possible solution and select one

Sell the chosen solution

V   Organizational development

Diagnose social system

Set boundaries of analysis

Specify design objectives

Choose a scientific model

Develop questionnaire

Analyze data

Select a design

Implement selected design

Evaluate change

VI   Personal counseling

Describe problem

Analyze factors

Search for causes

Develop alternatives to avoid causes

Select desired alternatives

Test some desired alternatives

Implement behavior change

VII   Planning and Programming

Record current approach

Identify problems

Discover core of problems

Evaluate alternatives

Choose new plan

VIII   Systems engineering and analysis

Identification of major problem determinants

Development of causal submodels

Development of predictive macromodel

Development of subsystem/subproblem interfaces

Development of subproblem-solving instruments

Carry out empirical validation exercises

Develop macrosystem model

IX   Policy analysis

Problem formulation

Issue analysis

Issue filtration

Final assessment

* Strategic, operations, capability, and development planning illustrate similar phrases.

The steps of the strategy seem reasonable enough if the rest of each paragraph remains unread. They might even conceivably fit all of the strategies for the five purposeful activities (Chapter Three). But it is precisely this breadth and generality of the italicized steps that constitutes a major shortcoming of conventional strategies. They describe, but do not operationalize, the fundamental steps in the P&D process. With conventional strategies the questions remain: "How is a problem formulated?" "How are creative solutions generated?," "How is implementation to be assured?"

The set of descriptions following the italicized strategy steps summarize what most P&D literature suggests. It is in relation to these descriptions that the five factors of this P&D approach differ from conventional ones. These differences include:

1 Focusing first on purposes, asking "What is it we want to accomplish?" and "What is the function of the changes we seek?", rather than focusing on extensive data collection to determine "What's wrong?"

2 Integration of the "worlds" of the professional and the client from the beginning of the project through genuine group interaction, in which the P&D pro-

fessional assumes roles other than that of "expert."

3 Use of a solution framework to systematically specify, document, and present the solution.

4 Taking steps to insure implementation throughout a project rather than only at the end.

5 Prescription of methods and techniques for problem identification, solution generation, solution specification implementation and evaluation, and continuing improvement.

In addition, conventional strategies are preoccupied with data collection; the other factors in a total approach are either ignored, incompletely integrated or perceived in an entirely different context. In conventional approaches, *specifying and presenting a solution* is seldom addressed because techniques used in analysis are assumed to be sufficient. Vague references are made to the necessity of a systems viewpoint but without a prescription for doing so. *Involving people,* although it is increasingly advocated, is considered independent of strategy, and the crucial question of precisely how and when people are to be involved is neglected. *Using information and knowledge,* exhalted under the rubric of *analysis,* places data collection and measurement at the heart of an effort, rather than viewing them from an effectiveness perspective. *Arranging for continuing change and improvement* if considered at all, is not systematically integrated into the P&D process.

Aside from failure to operationalize the P&D process, or to integrate the various factors in the process systematically over time, a number of other criticisms are directed toward conventional P&D. An extensive P&D literature details them. Some of this literature has been referred to in Chapter Four, and it will be briefly summarized in terms of the following categories:

Theoretical appraisals of solution quality.

Theoretical appraisals of solution implementation.

The impact of the cult of the expert on solution quality and implementation.

Empirical evidence corroborating theoretical appraisals.

This brief critique should not be construed as a total rejection of the conventional approach. The history of the rational approach in P&D, as described in Chapter Three, has been marked by splendid successes and innovative ideas, from the industrial revolution through the work of Frederick Taylor to systems and policy analysis. Many of these techniques and models should be an integral part of a total approach to P&D.

My main concern is simply with the tendency of conventional approaches to focus on data and techniques rather than the needs and purposes of the people and organizations P&D is meant to serve.

Theoretical Appraisals of Solution Quality

A number of concerns have been expressed regarding the quality of solutions reached by conventional P&D (Chapter Four). This is due, in large part, to poor problem formulation.

1 Conventional approaches fail to elicit effective solutions because they do not ask the right kinds of questions, thus problems are improperly formulated. "Approaches to social problems have proved inadequate. A major obstacle is that problems are conceptualized in ways that do not facilitate solutions. What is done about a problem depends on how it is defined. The way a societal problem is defined determines the focus, the techniques of intervention, and the criteria for evaluation. The way a problem is defined also determines not only what is done about it but what is not done about it."[1]

Lewis Mumford traces these difficulties in problem formulation to the extension of the scientific viewpoint to society as a whole. Scientism is inappropriate because it deals quantitatively with inherently qualitative problems. A systems engineer notes, "The *principle of incompatibility* describes the intrinsic unsuitability of the conventional quantitative techniques . . . for dealing with complex real-life social problems."[2]

2 Problems are poorly formulated because in the attempt to reduce everything to discrete analyzable components, multiple impacts and interrelationships are ignored. A pollution problem, for example may appear solved when in fact all interactions have not been considered. The solution may simply have transferred pollution from one source (air pollution from a power plant) to another (higher lake temperatures).

The tendency to narrow the scope of a problem by breaking it down results in focusing very quickly on solutions before the problem has been fully understood or formulated.[3]

3 The conventional approach forces the professional to define problems only in terms of immediate projects—the assumption, for example, that a highway exists merely to move traffic. The changes in demand, patterns of emigration, and industrial sprawl are not considered. Such "myopic planning is capable of causing intolerable damage. Ways must be found to move toward multipurpose planning that recognizes the full spectrum of human needs."[4]

Appraisals of Solution Implementation

Conventional approaches also have a poor track record in terms of solution implementation. Installation and use of solutions is clearly crucial; without it P&D is futile.

Because conventional approaches stress solution finding, implementation becomes the client world's "problem." Theorists who do emphasize implementation assume that solution quality must necessarily suffer the more the solution attempts to "satisfice" the client's world's multiple demands and values. And even these theorists suggest that the P&D professional remains an objective expert, uninvolved in implementation.

Implementation of solutions requires that the people involved with and affected by a P&D effort modify their attitudes and behaviors at the start of the project in the direction of those required by the solution. Not client size, nor the cost, complexity, or technological level of the solution constitute an exception to this assertion. Such change demands genuine sustained interaction with people in the client world during the entire P&D effort. Unfortunately, conventional P&D tends to view these people as obstacles and barriers to be overcome. The professional as "expert," feels that "they" cannot possibly use or comprehend sophisticated P&D tools. Often, the P&D professional must call on other "human relations" experts to keep troublesome human components from "lousing up" brilliant solutions, and public relations "experts" to "sell" the solution.

The failure of conventional approaches to deal effectively with the client world stems in part from these unstated assumptions:

1 Analysis is the start of every project; huge amounts of information must be collected; the P&D experts must find out what's wrong and who's to blame.
2 The P&D professional is an objective expert whose main task is defining the problem, and finding solutions; implementation is "someone else's" problem.
3 Techniques and models are critical determinants of solutions.
4 "Objective analysis" leads to a rational solution that all reasonable people will accept and implement *ipso facto*, regardless of different perceptions between client and "expert."

An extreme example of where these assumptions lead comes from a situation in which an "expert" was brought in to improve educational performance in a school system. He said, "I view things analytically. . . . Keep emotion out. You don't have to love the guy next to you. Teachers can hate me and still get kids to learn." One teacher remarked, not surprisingly, "There is no way a man with that attitude can succeed in this school."[5]

The Cult of the Expert Undermines Solution Quality and Implementation

Conventional approaches encourage the P&D professional to don the mantle of "expert." This creates a false sense of infallibility, encourages the research strategy, and alienates the client world, thwarting solution implementation. "The technological model dominates the contemporary imagination. . . . We assume that we can predict the social and political future as accurately as we can predict an eclipse of the sun. This certitude underlies the cult of the expert. It can be the source of infinite trouble."[6]

The notion that the P&D professional is an "expert" is reflected in and encouraged by educational programs that are little more than catalogues of techniques. "In view of the key role of [P&D] in professional activity, it is ironic that . . . the natural sciences have almost driven [P&D concepts] from the . . . curricula. Engineering schools have become schools of physics and mathematics; medical schools . . . biological science; business schools . . . finite mathematics; . . . Natural sciences are concerned with how things are . . . . [P&D], on the other hand, is concerned with how things ought to be."[7]

The "real-world" clients of P&D professionals have become increasingly vociferous in criticizing this elitist perspective. Some of the reasons why business has become less enchanted with the techniques of operations research and management science are: "Excessive data requirements, long response time, and invalid assumptions. . . . Implementation problems include: the lack of user participation, the temptation to fit the problem to the model, and the temptation to change the user's definition of the problem."[8]

Urban and regional planners have been equally castigated by their citizen constituencies for elitism and insensitivity. As a result, the urban planning profession has been wracked since the 1960s by heated arguments between advocates for rational "objective" planning models and those for radical participatory ones.[9]

Empirical Evidence

Clearly, conventional approaches encounter a number of difficulties in achieving the P&D objectives.

Nevertheless, the research strategy is advocated by most P&D professions, as indicated in Table 5-1. Interestingly, though, there is no empirical evidence to justify it. It has simply been assumed that this strategy is appropriate to P&D.[10] Ironically, there is a good deal of empirical evidence suggesting otherwise. For example, a comparison of three planning procedures involving health planning showed that the purpose-based approach produced better results than the conventional ones.[11] In another case involving environmental design, the purpose approach took less time than conventional ones to produce results of comparable quality.[12] A survey of nearly 50 manufacturing companies indicated that purpose approaches involving people at all levels produced twice as much yearly cost-control savings per staff member than conventional approaches.[13]

In one case study, an engineer in a large multiplant, multiwarehouse organization used conventional P&D to develop a proposal for a $40,000 expenditure for a piece of automatic equipment on the problem-plagued loading dock. All calculations indicated it would pay for itself in less than one year. His recommendation, based on drawings, statistics, and analyses of the current loading dock procedures, just assumed that the loading dock was needed. The vice president's staff, however, followed the purpose-based approach in reviewing the proposal, and recognized that the warehouse should be sold because a superior, completely different form of product distribution could be developed.[14] A number of other case studies, in Appendix B and in Chapter One, further illustrate the effectiveness of a purpose-oriented, five-factor approach to P&D.

Indeed, much of the impetus toward developing a five-factor purpose-based approach to P&D has come from these case histories as well as from studies of what P&D professionals who have been judged outstanding by their peers do. The professionals do not appear to follow conventional approaches. One volunteered during an interview that he had to consciously throw away the approach he had been taught at the university. All agreed that conventional approaches did not operationalize P&D, or facilitate interpersonal processes requisite to implementation. Others suggested the need to be both creative and practical, as well as to know when it is rational to be irrational; these criteria are not met by conventional strategies.[15]

TOWARD A NEW APPROACH TO P&D

Unfortunately this necessarily brief analysis focusing on the research strategy gives short shrift to a number of other approaches to P&D developed in the last twenty years. The difficulty with most of these new approaches (disjointed incrementalism, mixed scanning, and advocacy) is that they do not fundamentally question the research strategy per se, but modify it, presumably to make it workable. To the extent that they focus on factors other than analysis, solution finding, or new P&D roles, they still fail to operationalize the approaches.

Other prescriptive models have emerged in response to the need for operationalization. For example, the nominal group technique (see Chapter Fourteen), represents a major advance in how a group of people meeting to do P&D can be more productive. Generally, however, such advances apply to only one aspect of a P&D effort, such as decision making, solution acceptance, idea generation, or data collection.

What is needed, therefore, is an integrated and synergetic approach to P&D, both descriptive and prescriptive, which focuses on solution quality, solution implementation, and effective use of P&D resources. This will be the task of Parts Two and Three of this book. Part One establishes the background for such an approach by defining problems, examining solution approaches, developing P&D maximization objectives, and indicating how and why conventional P&D approaches fail to achieve them. What remains is to demonstrate that a new approach needs to be grounded in the realities, behaviors, and perceptions of "real world" individuals involved in a P&D effort. Chapter Six puts these realities in a time frame.

Grounding P&D in Human Realities

The P&D professional, as already noted, needs to interact continually with the client's world if solutions are to be installed and used. The interaction will be greatly facilitated if P&D professionals are aware of the characteristics, limitations, and capabilities of the individuals and groups with which they must work. The following generalizations come from an extensive psychological and behavioral literature. Many of them are so obvious that they are considered "common sense"; others should be approached gingerly. Their message, though, is crystal clear: Each group and every individual is recognized as unique. Certainly these generalizations should not be used dogmatically or manipulatively. They are presented in the spirit that P&D is done by and for human beings, and that understanding human realities will lead to more effective P&D. Incorporating these understandings into an integrated P&D approach enables P&D professionals to avoid the self defeating behaviors, such as the cult of the expert, that undermine effective solution generation and implementation. Table 17-1 reviews several of the following generalizations in relation to how conventional and total P&D approaches cope with them.

1 *The people involved in a specific situation know more about it than outside experts.* The mental perspective, cognitive maps, personal constructs, and frames of reference of an individual usually correspond successfully to the realities of a situation because of the months and years spent involved with them. No amount of data collection or model building can ever capture all this wisdom and knowledge. Often it is simpler, cheaper and more effective to get information from these individuals than to mount extensive data collection campaigns.[16] Urging people to participate in P&D efforts stems from this reality. Of course, experts are needed on occasion to effectively synthesize information, stimulate ideas, evaluate alternatives, and update technology.

2 *The long-term information capacity of people is good, the short-term capacity is poor.* When people have had enough time and experience to deal with a body of information, they develop an intuitive and conceptual indexing framework for it. This well-indexed information is available in the minds of the people at a specific problem locus, and this is another reason why local people can be so important as information sources in the beginning of a project. However, in the short term people are "poor information aggregators." People deluged by information select and retain only a small fraction: "six to seven chunks."[17] Because conventional P&D generates huge amounts of data and analysis, usually at the beginning of projects, most people, including experts, cannot understand it, let alone use it. Frantic efforts to sort out information leave little time available to find effective solutions.

3 *People are likely to accept a problem as stated.* This tendency significantly increases the probability of working on the wrong problem, thus arriving at poor or no results.[18] Individuals tend to quickly classify problems and leap to solutions rather than carefully question purposes and assumptions. The result is that changes occur in the specified problem area, when in fact a more effective solution may result from a change of focus or solution level.[19]

4 *Functional fixedness afflicts almost everyone.* People are inhibited about using an object, system, or policy for any purpose or function other than its original one. Innovation and creativity are the victims. Conventional P&D intensifies this tendency by emphasizing data collection and breaking a problem down into discrete components. This may result in a functional stereotyping that obscures judgment and interferes with creativity.

5 *An individual's decision making is constrained by the rules and regulations of the organization and the position held by the person.* Most people have a don't-rock-the-boat point of view, and select the least risky alternative. It has been shown, for example, that the likelihood of a manager accepting a solution exceeding the usual monetary cost a manager can approve is virtually nil.[20] And this holds true even if the incremental savings of the alternative may be many times greater than the incremental cost of another one. Relatively poor decisions result from this risk-taking aversion; "satisficing" and patching up are encouraged.

6 *People are defensive when confronted with information implying something is wrong with their performance.* Even the most open and flexible people will react to "explain" their position. Conscious effort is required to fight this impulse. Imagine how much additional defensiveness occurs if the motivation for information collection, as in much conventional P&D, is to find out who is at fault or what's wrong. Defensiveness can become a major barrier to change. People concentrate on exonerating or defending themselves rather than on determining "what ought to be" and finding appropriate solutions.

7 *A P&D project is expected to produce one correct solution.* The educational system and scientism foster the attitude that there is always one right solution. Everyone is expected to follow the same rules or system. Often, a solution is designed to meet the worst possible conditions, regardless of how infrequently they occur. For example, federal travel reimbursement forms are long and complicated. They are designed that way, so it is said, to prevent from cheating the 5% who might do so. Nevertheless, everyone is required to spend an inordinate amount of time on the forms, and an expensive bureaucracy is necessary to process them. All this time and expense is part of a single solution that wastes the energy of the honest and probably doesn't even catch cheaters. Conventional P&D tends to submerge individual differences rather than respond to individual needs. A new approach would focus on multichanneled solutions, designed for both regularly and irregularly occurring conditions. For example, why not have simplified travel expense forms and sample audits, or special credit cards, or "exception forms" to reimburse expenses above a set per diem amount, or a combination of these?

8 *People dislike being manipulated and treated paternalistically.* P&D professionals tend to be technicians and experts with a detached perspective on their clients. These inverted priorities, focusing on techniques, not people, easily lead to "We will take care of you" and "We know what is best for you" attitudes.

More alarming is that such attitudes can lead to a sort of Skinnerian or mechanistic behavioral modification of clients by the P&D experts who justify their actions on the basis that they are for the client's own good. Such attitudes diminish client interest in solving problems and may lead to resistance, even subversion. The converse of this is that people respond positively to genuine good will.

An attempt to manipulate people into doing something about a situation with "gloom and doom" forecasts often results in people simply tuning out. They don't want to hear so much bad news. People should dislike and fear paternalism and any manipulation and P&D approaches that perpetrate them.

9 *The time horizon of most people is short.* People are often so absorbed in the *now* that they seldom consider the future. The time horizon of the politician tends to be the next election, of the manager, the year-end earnings statement. Engineers often assume that the imperatives of technology supersede long-term considerations. Conventional P&D is often caught between two extremes, proposing incremental patch-up solutions with short time horizons and instant results, or long-run utopias that sit on the bookshelf. A new approach should provide for long-run guidelines but effective incremental short-run steps to achieve them.

10 *People experience conflicts in selecting solutions.* Faced with making a decision, many people experience hesitation, vacillation, and signs of psychological stress.[21] People are afraid to make mistakes and to commit themselves, which severely constrains acceptance of creative and innovative solutions.

11 *People tend to reject for themselves solutions "not invented here"* (the NIH factor). People may admire, frequently with high praise, something new, but note that "their" situation is different. Attempting to overcome the NIH factor conflicts with other realities and is usually ineffective: P&D experts sometimes try to get the people to believe the solution or idea is theirs (manipulation?), give the people extra money or incentives to adopt the idea (bribe?), set up "education" sessions to convince them of the benefits (indoctrination?), and so on. Dependency on experts in conventional P&D approaches may produce "good" solutions that are rejected simply because people have an NIH perspective. Proposing what someone else developed may produce a feeling of being patronized.

Exhortations promoting the "outside" solution are usually wasted effort. Conventional P&D often places the blame for nonacceptance on the real world's functional fixedness or resistance to change. Such resistance may simply be a rejection of manipulation. A new approach should focus on group development of unique solutions designed to fit the specific circumstances of each client group. When *they* discover they can use a machine (or form or component) someone else developed, they will be delighted to save their own time and effort by adopting it.

12 *People's behavior makes sense to them.* A person acts consistently with a personal, internal view of what is appropriate and what is personally important. Thus, behavior almost always satisfies perceived needs and can be considered justifiable by the person. Actions reflect internal translations of external and internal stimuli into what the individual believes makes sense. Conventional approaches tend to be confrontational and to demand explanations of why so-and-so is acting irrationally. Practitioners assume that once their data and analysis are available, everyone will agree that they are fair and mirror reality. The usual result is that those negatively affected by it immediately object and defend themselves. A new approach should avoid this trap by incorporating participants' "realities" into the understanding of a problem situation and focusing on purposes rather than data collection and blame.

13 *Each person displays a preferred method of understanding reality.* Individuals have different operating styles. In making decisions people vary in how much data they want, whether they rely on intuition, gut feeling or logic, doubting or believing game, and the way they arrive at conclusions.[22] One typology characterizing these personality differences categorizes persons in terms of how they become aware of situations. If they rely on specific empirical data they are called sensation (S) types, if they rely on internal or gestalt data they are identified as intuitive (N) types. Ways of arriving at conclusions are classified as T (logical thinking) or F (feeling). Individuals are various combinations of these types, such as intuitive-thinking (NT) or sensation-feeling (SF). Each of these types has a unique way of perceiving and acting on the world; a combination of all types results in a holistic picture of reality. For anyone selecting and working with groups, a combination of types may result in horrendous conflict, but if properly coordinated may arrive at solutions that are both creative and practical. Conventional P&D all too often attempts to mold people into one "correct" solution rather than capitalizing on the potentials and talents inherent in diversity.

14 *Each person's interest or commitment to any issue or change is different.* Every individual has a unique profile regarding achievement desires, creativity, political attitudes, values, psychological needs, converging-diverging mindset, and so on, as well as a unique personality profile in terms of style, openness, concern for others, and so forth. It is with these multiple profiles that a professional dealing with a client group must work. Because each person's perceptions about a P&D effort are different, new approaches must stress purpose clarification, continuous interaction throughout an effort, and multichanneled solutions to meet individual needs and expectations.

Group Realities

Many of the preceding generalizations are applicable to groups, although group realities tend to be more complex. Groups are not simply the sum of many individual's profiles. They have their own unique chemistry, resulting from a myriad of individual reactions and interactions. Chapter Fourteen and Appendix A provide background and references regarding group interactions and techniques to facilitate them. Some characteristics of groups are presented with the same caution as previous generalizations:

- People in groups play different information processing roles: instigator, listener, court jester, nice guy.[23]
- Sometimes the loudest and most frequent speaker dominates a group to the detriment of the group effort.
- People in groups respond to messages they agree with and tune out information they don't agree with.[24]
- Groups tend to take risks only in the direction of the average pregroup disposition.[25] Group-think can result, negatively affecting solution quality.

In any group, there is always enough information so that, through careful selection and manipulation, *any* position can be supported.[26]

Group interaction is further complicated by the characteristics of the organization (company, city, etc.) from which these groups are drawn. The following statements suggest some of these characteristics. Again, one must proceed with caution because organizations differ significantly as a function of the number of employees, budget, purpose, history, management attitudes, political perspective, decision-making processes, and so on. Each environment in which P&D is attempted is thus unique and may be different next year from now (Chapter Sixteen).

1 *A high degree of inertia afflicts organizations with regards to change.* Inertia is a consequence of self-protection. Self-protection results in reduced risk-taking and a concentration on self maintenance.

Government executives, for example, often display maintenance rather than task-oriented behavior. They occupy themselves with averting potential political threats rather than with government effectiveness.[27] Fear of risk taking means that organizations do not consider fundamental changes "because usually there are circumstances which preclude them from doing anything very different from what they are already doing."[28] Self-protection also leads to organizational overstructuring. Government and business share this tendency. One example is the dramatic drop in the ratio of armed service personnel to admirals and generals since World War II. The result is that many managers each protect his or her own fiefdom, making real change highly unlikely. Indeed such managers may even be the source of problems, but uprooting them is next to impossible.[29]

Surely, then, the actions of conventional P&D strategies retard efforts to overcome inertia, maintenance behavior, fear of risk taking, and self-protection. Even individuals who may not instinctively have these proclivities are forced to adopt them when they are confronted by a P&D professional following conventional strategies.

2 *Organizations tend to hire people similar to those already there.* This influence often reduces the opportunity to obtain competing creative ideas, and establishes similar risk-taking propensities as already exist in the organization, either aversion to or affinity for. Such ingrown tendencies lead to avoidance of the real problems as if they didn't exist, rather than attempts to solve them. The organization's purposes become narrowly defined as a result. Conventional P&D then compounds this narrow perspective by analyzing and subdividing an already limited problem-as-stated.

An organization's past performance tends to indicate future actions. This is certainly to be encouraged if the organization has the breadth, diversity, creativity, and other features requisite to continuous improvement. Unfortunately, this is not often the case. Although organizations pay lip service to the need for creative, resourceful employees, in actual fact the incentive structure and "tribal ways," as one consultant put it, reward standardized thinking and conformity.

3 *A lack of effective communication plagues organizations.* A number of factors thwart effective communication. They include rigid authoritarian decision structures, lack of formal and informal channels for employee input, and myths of organizational policies and performance.[30] The results are personnel grapevines, rumor mills, divided loyalties, and often seething resentments. P&D professionals need to be concerned about the communications environment and other "readiness factors" (Chapter Sixteen) when starting a project. Otherwise the P&D effort may be disrupted by hidden agendas and personal rivalries.

SUMMARY OF PART ONE

Problems have a values dimension and a substantive dimension. Problems are best defined in the context of seven purposeful activities. P&D is one of them, and must be linked operationally to four others: operating and supervising, research, evaluation, and learning. The remaining two, self-preservation and leisure, are almost always converted into one of the other five.

Finding solutions for problems defined in terms of the purposeful activities requires a total approach that is currently described in terms of five factors: pursuing a strategy, specifying and presenting the solution, involving people, using information and knowledge, and arranging for continuing change and improvement.

The five-factor approach incorporates rational, affective, and chance processes. The concept of a five-factor approach is adapted to the development of unique steps and processes for each purposeful activity.

P&D is the major activity of over thirty P&D professions. It is also pursued by everyone at various points in their lives.

P&D has three objectives: To maximize the effectiveness of recommended solutions; to maximize the likelihood of solution implementation; and to maximize the effectiveness of the resources allocated to the P&D effort.

P&D is beset by many problems including declining solution quality, failure to achieve implementation, data overload, and a poor public image.

A theory of P&D is needed. It should be content-free, that is, not structured around the substantive content and methodologies of any specific P&D profession.

A total P&D approach must also include operational methods. Specific "How-to-do-it's" must be flexible enough to handle the specific purposes of each problem situation.

A P&D approach should incorporate real-life human realities, perceptions, and behaviors, which are necessary to solution generation and implementation.

Thus, P&D professionals cannot simply be expert model builders, measurers, and designers. They must also be facilitators, moving individuals and groups from identified purposes to implemented solutions.

The importance of techniques, models, and data collection is not denied, merely placed in the perspective of the entire P&D effort.

There is hope that the difficult situations faced by P&D professionals can be alleviated with a five-factor, total approach that differs significantly from conventional approaches.

PART TWO

Foundations for Planning and Design

TOWARD A THEORY OF P&D

A theory is "a formulation of apparent relationships or underlying principles which has been verified to some degree."[1] A theory has six parts: concepts that apply to past, present, and future dimensions of the phenomena; arrangement of these concepts into categories; hypotheses that indicate the effects of certain treatments or actions; definitions and measures of various units, parameters, and variables; operational linkages and testability of the various concepts, parameters, and variables; and organization of definitions, concepts, and linkages into higher order premises.[2]

A complete theory within the context established in Part One would include two parts: theory *of* P&D; and theory, information, and knowledge *in* P&D. The former includes basic axioms, propositions, and principles of P&D. This is the substance of Part Two. The latter includes the basic methods for operationalizing or converting to practice a theory *of* P&D; it forms the subject of Part Three.

The axioms, propositions, and principles of a theory *of* P&D lead to normative descriptions of how people and organizations *ought to act* to be more effective and efficient. They are similarly needed for the operational aspects of *how to act* more effectively and efficiently.

Such a theoretical framework provides other significant advantages to P&D. It permits comparative and experimental research to test hypotheses, and provides a common conceptual scheme by which significant analytical comparisons among case studies can be made.[3] It also sets the stage for development of a discipline of P&D, because epistemology, history, sociology, ethnography, taxonomy, metrology, and other fields will have a framework on which to focus.[4]

AXIOMS, PROPOSITIONS, AND PRINCIPLES

Every human act is influenced by natural conditions: humans have two hands, gravity holds objects on the surface of the earth, a day has periods of light and dark. Every human act is also influenced by mental assumptions, internalized to the point where they give basic direction to reasoning, decisions, and statements.

The assumptions about the place of P&D in the real world described in Part One are now extended by what I will call *axioms*. Other terms could be used—logical truths, givens, maxims, basic principles, deductions, or postulates. An axiom is a self-evident or accepted concept that people find valid as stated. The axioms and their related corollaries stated here are specifically aimed at P&D, and, although some may be equally useful for other purposeful activities, only P&D applications will be discussed here.

Although assumptions and axioms have a ring of certainty, "the developing relationship between Human Ideas and a Natural World, neither of which is invariant, means we should expect to find variable epistemic relationships between a variable Man and a variable Nature."[5]

An axiom initially may not appear acceptable or completely "true." For example, Axiom 3, "Everything is a system," may be questioned at an extreme point: Is God a system? Acceptability of "truth" for all conditions, even theoretical ones, is not as important for P&D as applicability of the concept.[6] Thus, a statement called an axiom may not fit all extreme conditions, but still be valid over the entire range of interest, in this case, for the P&D purposeful activity. Similarly, the four-dimensional space-time relationships of relativistic physics or the intuitive higher consciousness and otherworldliness of Eastern mysticism may raise extreme-point questions about the immutability of time (Axiom 1). Yet the axiom is "true" for all P&D efforts that seek real-world implemented solutions.

Chapter Six introduces two axioms. One, time must be the basis for understanding any phenomenon. Two, humans vary the purposeful activities they perform at different points in time, on the basis of their perceptions and sense of realities.

Chapter Seven presents axioms establishing a system context. Axiom 3 says that everything is a system. Axiom 4 puts every system into one or more hierarchical and lattice arrays. In other words, each system is always related to other systems. Axiom 5 identifies three existence conditions of a system—conceptual, satisfactory, or unsatisfactory—that are time-related.

Chapter Eight addresses the unique suitability of a solution to its setting. Models and techniques used to represent a solution are also unique and are *not* the solution itself. Axiom 6 demonstrates the fallibility of models by means of the language and semantics concept that "words are *not* things." Axiom 7 continues this non-Aristotelian or probabilistic base by proclaiming that "identity is never found in this world." The stability of this axiom is challenged by a corollary about the lack of certainty about anything.

Chapter Nine utilizes many of the ideas contained in Part I and the first seven axioms to establish Axiom 8. It defines the word *system* in a prescriptive framework as a guide to specifying solutions, in terms of eight elements each detailed in six dimensions or properties.

Chapter Ten uses each of the axioms to formulate eight propositions that describe how P&D is carried out. The propositions join the axioms in establishing the basic principles of P&D, also presented in Chapter Ten. The specific P&D operational methods in Part Three flow from these axioms, propositions, and principles.

CHAPTER SIX

The Immutable Timeline: Axioms 1 and 2

Time is irreversible. It cannot be slowed or accelerated. It is an excellent illustration of infinity. Time *is*. It represents simplicity in being, yet vast mysteriousness in its infinity. Cosmic time, through space-time, discontinuities, quarks, or whatever, are simple once astronomers and physicists discover the relationships. But humans will not plan or design changes in terms of cosmic time. The grand concept of chronological time is the only basis for understanding P&D.

"Time has no divisions to mark its passage. . . . It is only we mortals who ring bells and fire off pistols."[1] Humans define time quantities (hours, minutes, seconds). We refer to concurrency or simultaneity of *activities* or *events* during a period of or at a point in time. We develop quantitative measures allocating blocks of time to an activity, and seek ever more accurate measures of each block. We seek its statistical variances, sequencing, changes, adaptabilities, natural cycles (half-life, circadian), and interdependencies. We seek predictions of conditions, activities, and events in terms of some future time horizon, "a boundary which moves back as we move toward it and separates the foreseeable from the unforeseeable."[2] With these and other sophisticated "attributes," the simple basis and the resulting profound implications of time appear to be forgotten if not ignored:

Axiom 1   A continuous (rather than discrete) timeline is the fundamental basis for understanding the past, present, or future of any phenomenon.   The immutability of

time is surely undeniable. The implications about time as the basis of understanding a phenomenon can be explained with Figure 6-1.

Item A in Figure 6-1 is a timeline representing the chronological passage of time. B arbitrarily locates the present (second, minute, hour, day, week, month, or whatever unit), which automatically defines the past and the future. The units used to subdivide time determine what constitutes a short or long time horizon. This afternoon's weather forecast might consider three days a medium time horizon, this quarter's budget in a manufacturing company might consider five years long range, this year's futurist projection might consider biological research in the year 2000 as middle range, and to today's hospital census, 30 days might be short range.

The matrix (or any other desired modeling format, such as a formula, picture, prose, poetry, drawing, or graph) at C is a symbolic representation of the conditions of the phenomenon of interest (e.g. food sources, construction methods, political structure) at a previous point of time. D similarly represents current and E future or proposed conditions. Other matrices (or desired models) could be developed at any other points (F and G, for example) to describe the phenomenon's status at those particular times.

Each phenomenon description thus far is static (H). Information about past conditions of the phenomenon comes from various sources (I), depending on the particular time scale. Most descriptions represent a lim-

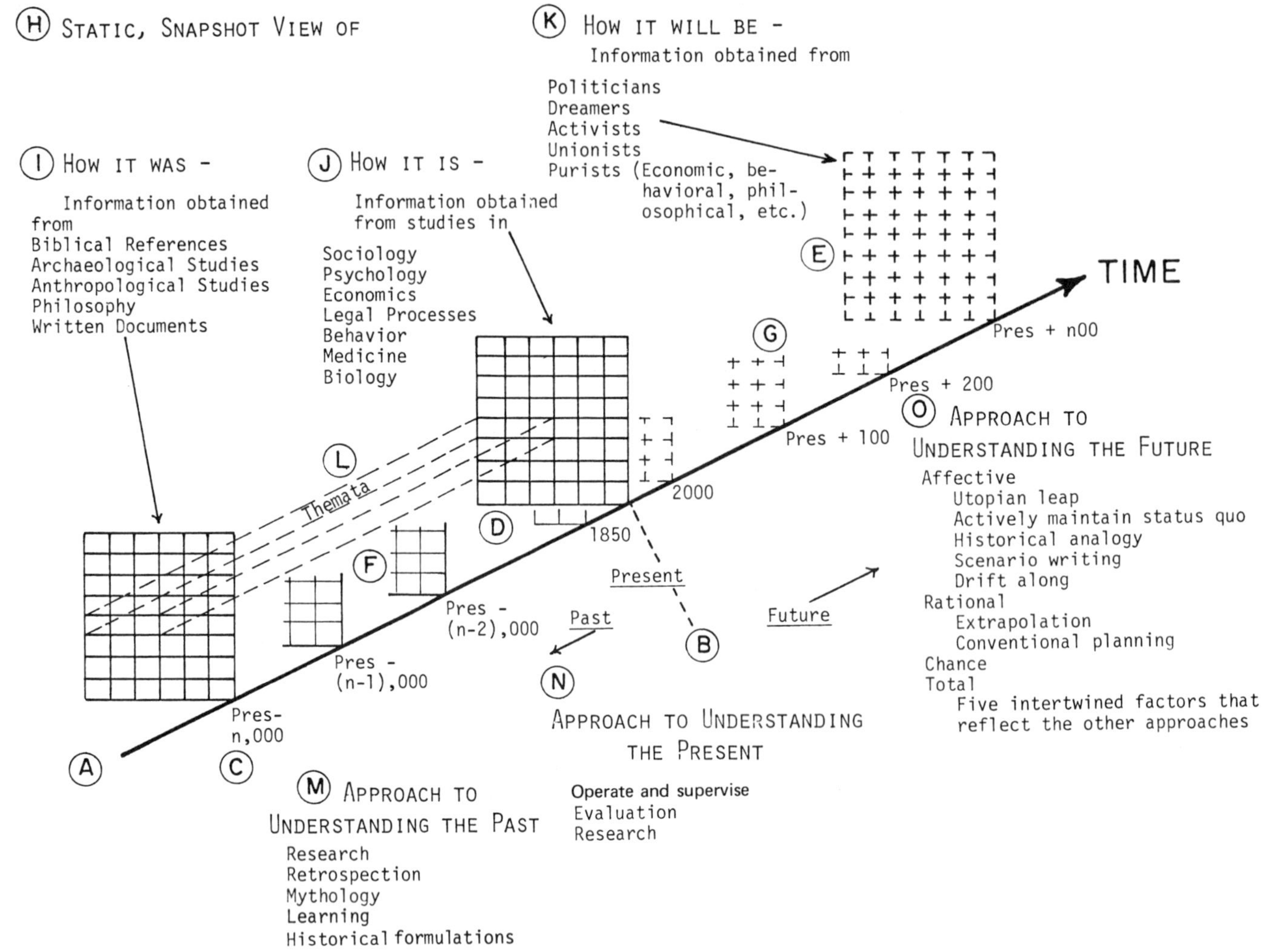

(H) STATIC, SNAPSHOT VIEW OF

(K) HOW IT WILL BE –
Information obtained from
Politicians
Dreamers
Activists
Unionists
Purists (Economic, be-
  havioral, phil-
  osophical, etc.)

(I) HOW IT WAS –
Information obtained
from
Biblical References
Archaeological Studies
Anthropological Studies
Philosophy
Written Documents

(J) HOW IT IS –
Information obtained
from studies in
Sociology
Psychology
Economics
Legal Processes
Behavior
Medicine
Biology

(E)

TIME

(G)

Pres + n00

Pres + 200

Pres + 100

2000

1850

(L) Themata

(D)

(F)

Present

(A) (C)

Pres -
(n-2),000

Past

Future

(B)

(N)

Pres -
(n-1),000

Pres-n,000

APPROACH TO UNDERSTANDING
THE PRESENT

Operate and supervise
Evaluation
Research

(M) APPROACH TO
UNDERSTANDING THE PAST
Research
Retrospection
Mythology
Learning
Historical formulations

(O) APPROACH TO
UNDERSTANDING THE FUTURE
Affective
  Utopian leap
  Actively maintain status quo
  Historical analogy
  Scenario writing
  Drift along
Rational
  Extrapolation
  Conventional planning
Chance
Total
  Five intertwined factors that
  reflect the other approaches

Figure 6-1 The timeline basis for understanding change.

ited perspective about the phenomenon for a block of time, a scrapbook of several snapshots, thus omitting knowledge already available about that point of time, but not considered pertinent to the description of interest. Names or labels are associated with the blocks of time as if the people then had no daily chronological concerns: Dark ages, middle ages, Industrial Revolution, and so forth. We even become nostalgic about the scrapbook and its snapshots. Other sources (J) usually lead to static descriptions of the present, while others (K) typically lead to predictions of static conditions at a point of time in the future. Names are assigned to the blocks of time represented by such snapshots or scenarios of the future as if the condition will emerge as a fait accompli and people between now and then will have no daily chronological concerns. Some of these names are postindustrial society, electronic communications age, ecological humanism, Marxist communism. Some descriptions

escape the static view by developing a themata or historical time perspective about a particular issue (farm implements, science, heritage of an organization), set of issues (civil liberties and political forms), impact of a "great man" (L).

Everything is speculative after the present, irrespective of the firmness and certainty people assign to the prediction or snapshot of conditions or outcomes.[3] Much more certainty can be ascribed to short-range projections (e.g., number of heart attacks per 100,000 population next year) than to those with long time horizons. The degree of confidence associated with a prediction for the future thus depends on the time horizon involved, the phenomenon of concern, the perception of the frequency with which changes occur (when the length of time for which current specifications are valid diminishes, time seems to be accelerated), and the degree to which the phenomenon is embedded within something else that is staying mostly the same.[4] Any change in the future obviously arises from some aspects of the past and present, and these ties, even if they are below the threshold of awareness, are the major ingredients of these factors for assessing confidence.

Static snapshots of a particular phenomenon in the future are seldom appropriate for finding workable solutions, despite the tendency people and organizations have for fixing on them. Most often, the snapshots are assumed to be "right," offering little to support the view and conclusions of their creators except the latter's exhortations. Even explaining the snapshot in terms of its larger "whole" is omitted. In addition, individuals and organizations are usually presumed to know *how* to move from the snapshot of what exists today to the scenario of tomorrow's desired solution. In most cases, this is not known, greatly decreasing the probability that the solution will ever be realized.[5]

Why little confidence should be placed in these assumptions, and thus in any snapshots, is explained by recognizing several reasoning flaws: (1) those predicting the snapshot adopt a posture of *selling* a "right" solution rather than solving a problem; (2) society, organizations, or individuals cannot agree on which snapshot to move toward because so many solutions are being "sold" as the answer; (3) little thought is devoted to working with people within their realities in moving toward a better future; (4) reaching the status described by a snapshot is assumed *now* to be sufficient, and thus the proposed solution omits its own continuing change and improvement; and (5) previous snapshots of, say, over three-year futures have a dismal record. The 1940s version of the American dream began to sour even in the 1960s. The prediction in the 1950s of full automation for our factories by the 1970s is patently wrong. The 1960 futurist snapshots of the last third of the century contained nothing about the energy crisis or the equal rights movement. The 1970 projections reveal little if any understanding of the impact of inflation already greatly reshaping circumstances in the 1980s. The big problems of any year (e.g., in the 1950s, education for so many children, Russian and Chinese monolithic communism) for which optimistic or pessimistic projections are prepared, either disappear, are transformed into another concern, or are resolved much differently than the projections may have intimated. Merely proclaiming that a solution could be technologically achieved (e.g., a computer kitchen in the year 2000) does not mean it should be done.

Moreover, snapshot protagonists or futurists appear to justify their actions by the fact that historians usually select a particular block of time or singular events in the past for their snapshots. That is, describing food distribution around 1000 B.C. is really someone's selectively defined snapshot of interest. Therefore, the reasoning goes, why not just select any future point for a prediction (2000 is a favorite, as if that year has particular magic)? Furthermore, a snapshot of the past creates the impression that conditions existed as described for the block of time (years, decades, months, etc.) and then suddenly jumped to the conditions of the next snapshot, say from 1000 B.C. to 250 B.C. In reality, the phenomenon was dynamic in the real world; it progressively changed (by plan or not) from year to year (month to month, etc.). "Fixed concepts may be extracted by our thought from mobile reality; but there are no means of reconstructing the mobility of the real with fixed concepts."[6]

Thus, understanding the future and achieving *implementation* of effective and innovative solutions require more than just snapshots. We must continue to imagine the future and dream, but change is occurring on a day-to-day basis and can be ignored, resisted, or guided. A timeline perspective of change is needed to guide change toward positive workable results. A tomorrow, a next week, a next month should not and cannot be ignored by believing that the present can be automatically converted at some time into an available snapshot of the future. A major danger in such a belief stems from the inability of the many specialists doing future projections (e.g., health, manufacturing, education, transportation) to incorporate even closely related ideas. For example, "Many proposed solutions to the energy dilemma—liquid-metal fast-breeder reactors, fusion reactors, or some form of solar energy—have about them a curiously static quality. Not only are they seen by their enthusiasts as total solutions, which is itself a presumptive notion, but also they seem to be advanced as if a decision could be made now or soon about the most economical, clean, and safe way to provide energy for the next 1000 years. . . . On the contrary, we can expect that all kinds of unpredictable dynamic developments will occur during the next 25 years, let alone the next 1000. . . . Faced with various and changing notions of unacceptability, with ignorance and the knowledge that tomorrow probably will not resemble yesterday, it is imperative that we not freeze our future options. . . . We must have a plan that can . . . be adjusted frequently."[7]

The other assumption—that society knows *how* to move to a futurist's snapshot—is likewise untenable if one considers information overload, functional fixedness, and other human realities discussed in Chapter Five. The assumption creates a "sense of anguish that accompanies change."[8] An individual, however unique, is the result of many influences and perceptions that interrelate with all the systems in society.

Holding on to this "structure of meaning" appears natural, but the "structure" must be modified if solutions are to be used. The challenge of obtaining a change is not just knowing the history of, say, food distribution (as valuable and interesting as it is), nor understanding and thoroughly diagnosing what food distribution is now, nor even having a clear picture of how food distribution ought to be arranged in the future. It is instead the approach followed in developing a revised "structure of meaning" and implementing effective changes within a time framework that considers the background and realities of the people involved. Their behavior must change as a result of their altered perception of the situation.

This axiom interestingly shows that the timeline approach is also as crucial to studying food distribution in the past as it is to changing it in the future. The approach to understanding the past (M on Figure 6-1) is stymied by the impossibility of reversing the timeline. The approach reinforces present-day interpretations of or lessons to be learned about incompletely reported previous events. ("Lessons are all so one-dimensional and unambiguous and slick. . . ."[9]) Research is the usual approach to developing snapshot generalizations of the past. Learning is also an approach for those seeking to acquire the knowledge of already available understandings of the past. Retrospective stories or scenarios, legends, and mythological reports are techniques to aid in learning.

Understanding the present (N) can likewise involve several approaches. Research about the present is the most frequently considered approach, but it too produces snapshots, all too frequently of a present that has meanwhile become the past by the time they are completed. Evaluation is an approach that compares present results with previous desires and objectives, thus approximating a snapshot of the present. It also often includes action suggestions that presumably will produce greater conformity with past objectives (which may be obsolete). Operating and supervising approaches maintain present activities to achieve objectives set in the past, while hopefully creating a change of climate to accommodate future activities and objectives.

The approach (O) for understanding and changing the future of a phenomenon is well covered in Part One. The need for a different P&D approach is underscored again when the various approaches noted at (O) and their relationship to the timeline are considered. Who in 1945 would have extrapolated, for example, telephone signal transmission into a laser beam in flexible glass cable in 1980? Who wants to rely on the utopian leap technologist who insists on doing something simply because it can be done, or on the vision-

ary or dictator, benevolent or otherwise? And those who actively seek to avoid an improvement just because there is some risk ignore the often greater risks of not changing. Who wants just to drift along into whatever develops from the many pressures of these other futurists?

Axiom 2   Humans perform purposeful activities that influence and are influenced by the time-variant objectives and goals they seek to attain.   This axiom puts purposeful activities and values (Chapter Two) into a timeline framework. Individual and group realities, described in Chapter Five, also fit into the timeline framework because their importance and presence have an inherent tendency to change over time. What society was willing to accept as "minimum" living conditions a relatively short 50 or 60 years ago is intolerable today. Television, telephones, and automobiles, for example, were not considered "essential" even 30 years ago. Few if any deletions occur, and more complex items often replace existing items. Consider how city dwellers replaced the horse with the automobile in the early 1900s. Cars got rid of the mess and horrible smell of horse excrement all over the streets. Now, automobile pollution has led to the creation of additional objectives and goals that increase the complexity threshold beyond those of today and 60 years ago. The car problem is serious, but no one even proposes a return to horses.

The timeline version of human objectives is often portrayed in a life-cycle perspective attributed to almost all products, solutions, and systems: Creation, development, growth, decay, and death. The last part, death, can also reflect modifications of or additions to what previously was considered a good solution or set of human objectives. For example, the addition of pollution control and safety equipment to the automobile develops a "new" solution from the "death" of the old version of the automobile. A life cycle also contains smaller cyclic waves of emphasis and quiescence. Pollution control on automobiles was initially pushed as a "new" solution and was an actively emphasized societal objective in the early 1970s. It entered a quiescent period in the late 1970s. It will receive additional small cyclic waves of emphasis once or twice more before another significant "solution" supplants it (battery-operated cars, solar power).

At the individual level, people continually update their objectives (increase the levels they seek to pursue in their hierarchy of needs) and vary their purposes to fit their motivations (meeting economic needs may call for an operate-and-supervise purposeful activity, whereas satisfying social/warmth needs may require a research or evaluation purposeful activity). What may initiate the perception of a problem and establishment of a P&D project at B in Figure 6-1 may be changed at Pres +10 by human nature, normal changes, external disturbances, and internal power and organizational shifts. This also means that there are no either/or solutions or snapshot conditions. A work organization is not all democratic or all autocratic, an information system not all computerized or all manual. Solutions, like problems (Chapter Two), are rooted in people.

Human goals vary as well with age. Obtaining fashionable clothes for a person at age 20 may seem quite silly as a goal to a 60 year old. The high-income goal of a 30 year old is supplanted by the high pension one of the 55 year old. Personnel managers, insurance companies, and advertising agencies, for example, use the "life-span development" concept or the "watermelon theory" to trace from conception to death the "growth, progress, and ultimate decline of that long, strong thread of individual identity that somehow retains its stability and self-awareness as it moves through nonstop change.... At any given point in this continuity, a human life may be seen as being the accumulated result of all that has happened in its past and as already having a certain directional thrust that is suggested by its proposed future."[10] Nine threads form the connections between conception and death. Five threads are biological (cardiovascular, central nervous system, musculoskeletal, endocrine, and skin) and four psychosocial (cognitive, personality, social, and ekistic, meaning "human settlements development"). The "point representing 'Now' in a person's life-span . . . is a . . . slice through the entire watermelon.... Further, we may even be able to predict something about that person's future—though of course the future is modifiable, as the past is not."

A person goes through five overlapping eras (childhood, adolescence to age 22, early adulthood to 45, middle adulthood to 65, and over 65) wherein the transitions are often times of crisis between the stable life structures developed in each era.[11] All nine threads of life-span development are affected in each era. Thus, the large uncertainties or discontinuities a person seeks to avoid differ in nature from one time period to another, causing individual and group realities to fluctuate in intensities. Variety is a desirable feature of life that many people seek, but they prefer small uncertainties. "How we think affects what we believe, . . . what we believe is the key to how we feel, and . . . how we feel determines how we act."[12] Change to a more desirable state of existence from what exists—change in the form of a generalization, systems solution, operating policy, learning procedure, or evaluation method—builds from this axiom.

The values of humans may be the least variable part of their realities and beliefs. Those values that persist over a long period are said to be "enduring beliefs. [There are] two major categories of values. . . ; namely, instrumental values (defined as modes of conduct such as honesty, competence, courage, self-actualization, and responsibility) and terminal values (defined as end-states of existence such as inner harmony, freedom, and equality)."[13] Making changes among people with firmly rooted values requires the timeline axioms as the basis for understanding how perceptions can be moved toward "the availability [and] desirability of a mutually acceptable solution, . . . cooperation rather than competition, . . . [and] the views of others as legitimate statements of their position. . . ."[14]

A summary of these two axioms in terms of all purposeful activities is provided by the rough scheme shown in Figure 6-2. The timeline is the column on the left. The next column depicts real-world organization activities (manufacturing company, hospital, government agency, city, bank). A problem is perceived and recognized and a decision is made regarding which purposeful activity is involved (more on this critical decision in Chapters Ten and Twelve). The approach of the particular purposeful activity is then followed, as indicated in the third column.

In the meantime, disturbances, new knowledge, and normal operating changes are occurring in the real world, which is performing a variety of purposeful activities. These continuing occurrences have some bearing on the problem previously identified and affect the perceptions and behavior of the people in the organization. If the purposeful activity (P&D) world works on its own, as so often happens,[15] then the people there are having their perceptions changed regarding the problem assigned to them and are obtaining insights into and enthusiasms for solutions that are not shared by the real-world people.

When a solution is then recommended to the real-world people, the stage is set for the solution's rejection. The organizational people also have a different perception of the problem than when it was set up, and they lack a "feel" for the solution that those following the approach developed. Those following the purposeful activity approach lack an understanding of the subtle day-by-day changes that influence the real world, and their perception of a solution may no longer concern what is now viewed as the problem by the organization. Is it any wonder that so much conflict and nonadoption of recommendations occur at this point?

The timeline axioms identify how this impasse can be minimized or eliminated. The purposeful activity world must be continually interrelating with the real world, day by day, week by week, and so on. This al-

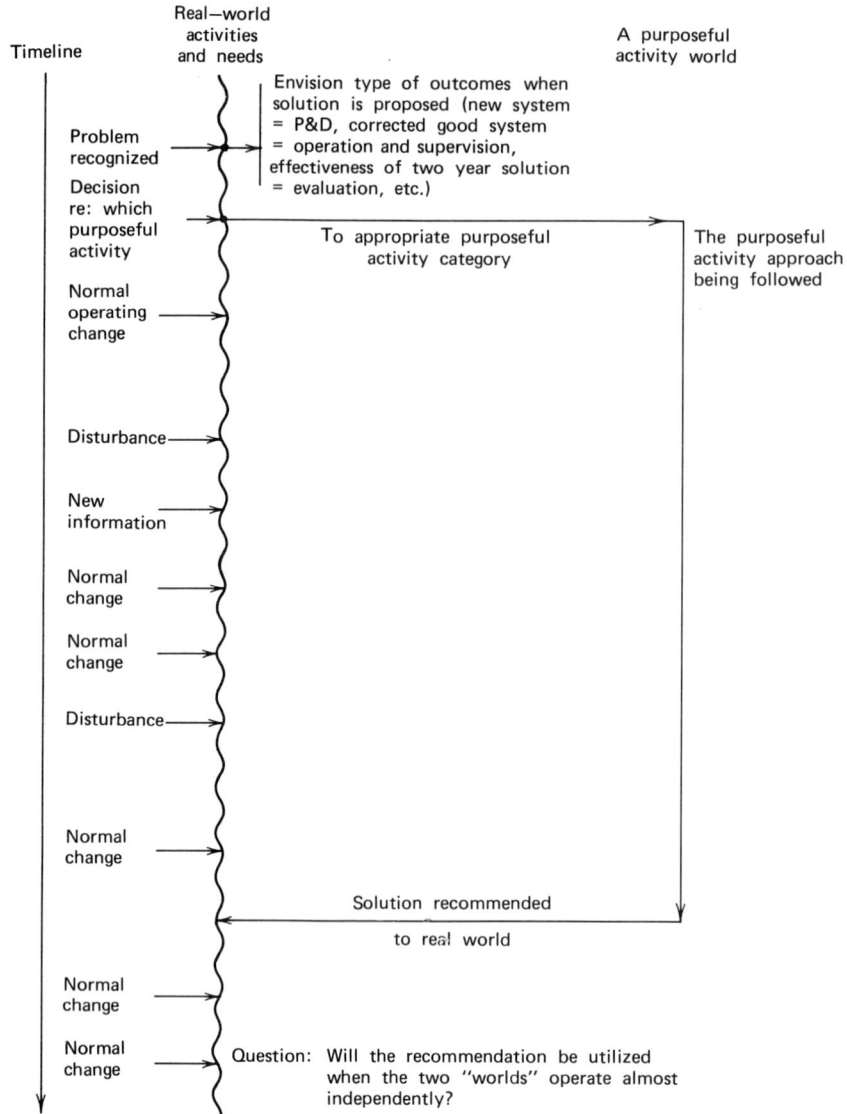

Figure 6-2 The timeline relationship between real and purposeful activity worlds. Purposeful activities include operate and supervise, plan and design, evaluate, develop generalizations or learn.

lows the perceptions and behavior of those in each world to be modified and adjusted to accommodate the realities and knowledge of the other. Such positive behavior can change values, as sociologists and anthropologists are demonstrating. Adherence to the timeline axioms increases significantly the probability that it will take less time to arrive at the implementation of a recommendation, and that more recommendations will actually be put to use. Figure 6-2 is expanded for P&D in Chapter Ten.

SUMMARY

Time is the basis of the initial axioms.

Axiom 1   A continuous (rather than discrete) timeline is the fundamental basis for understanding the past, present, or future of any phenomenon.

Axiom 2   Humans perform purposeful activities that influence and are influenced by the time-variant objectives and goals they seek to attain.

CHAPTER SEVEN

The System Context: Axioms 3, 4, and 5

The word *system* enjoys wide professional and generic use, most often without a broad or generalizable definition, but still reflecting utility and need of the word. Regardless of its specific use, however, the important idea about the concept of a system is holism, the big picture of components and synergetic interrelationships together. The axioms and the approach to finding solutions should provide at least a context for the idea of *system*. Axioms 3, 4, and 5 provide that context. Axiom 8 in Chapter Nine will supply a more specific definition aimed at P&D.

The concept of a system is not a reality so identified in the world. Humans abstract reality and organize representations called systems. The reality is "unaware" of the system construct, although the human ability to think of system images can and does eventually impact on the reality. Yet it will never be possible to have an agreed-upon system definition, theory, or view (see Chapter Five and Axiom 6). The need for a holistic perspective of reasoning can concurrently acknowledge the futility of focusing on *a* technique or *a* definition or *a* single sense of orderliness. Orderliness was an early criterion for advocating a systems view, but it is obviously uncharacteristic of most real entities, so much so that the idea of a *mess* is replacing that of *system*.[1] Yet holism, breadth, openness, interrelationships, control, humanism, and even untidiness are central to the *contextual* setting needed for effective P&D. Thus, the systems view or context of this Chapter differs from the relatively inadequate "sys-tems approach" discussed in Chapter Five. And it will not simplistically proclaim that society is a system of which a model can be made, thus solving the world's problems.

This chapter seeks only to put some P&D utility into the word *system*. Utility is surely not achieved by appending the word "system" to activities people would understand without the added word (e.g., production *system*, accounting *system*, railway *system*, health care delivery *system*, education *system*, banking *system*.)

This chapter will also show that a systems context is only a *part* of P&D, not the whole of it. This continues the theme of the book: Real human problems must be the focus of solution-finding efforts, not the systems references that focus on a specific set of techniques, generalizations (systems theory depends on isomorphism and analogy), or mathematics (analytical congruence and quantitative structure). Most of the literature on systems describes analytical classifications and taxonomies (e.g., closed versus open, hardware versus software, living versus nonliving, stable versus unstable, job versus organization, simple versus cybernetic control, abstract versus concrete, linear versus variety decreasing). Some describe preferred operational characteristics of systems (e.g., adaptive, optimal redundancy, freedom, growth of individuals, complete information transmission, stable). A reason often given for such schemes is to provide a "teach-able" set of concepts. This assumes that the learner then knows *how* to use the ideas, and the description of, say, a living organism (system) can automatically lead to mapping out a P&D solution. Describing an entity called a system may be sufficient for other purposeful activities, but is far from what is needed for P&D.

Prescriptiveness is the criterion that sets out particular but generalized elements and attributes for which specifications are sought to solve the specific P&D problem, such as controllability, measurability, process methods, and output design.

Universality is a criterion needed to achieve usefulness in the wide variety of P&D professions.

Understandability is a critical criterion if implementation is to take place. The people affected by the recommendation must perceive the meaning of the specifications and relationships if implementation is to be achieved. The following axioms meet a beginning level of these criteria.

Axiom 3   Everything is a system.

This applies to natural and living systems[2] (particles, atoms, molecules, crystals, organelles, cells, tissues, organs, etc.). These systems are hardly relevant to a P&D approach *per se*, so the focus will be on human-made systems (artificials).

The major reason for and advantage of this axiom is to be able to *call* everything a system. This avoids the usual semantic hairsplitting between what is and what is not a system: Does it have two or more parts that are interconnected? Is it a collection of entities with related attributes? Is it complex and large scale, automatic and involving computers? Must it be force-fitted to the terms of description of systems—linearity, open loops, complexity, and so on?

This axiom avoids negative or non-P&D-oriented definitions that have little utility, such as the one that says a system cannot have any parts that change! Every solution found by P&D is a system; each class or level of any taxonomy of systems is a system; and each approach to or operation on an entity (research, operate, monitor, improve, control, observe, evaluate, learn) is a system. The locus of any problem (Chapter 2) is also a system. Even the "ad-hoc collection of methods for managing [the American] society"[3] is a system, irrespective of how disjointed and dysfunctional it may be. Perhaps the only "thing" that might conceivably not be a system is time. The measurement of time, on the other hand, is clearly a system.

Axiom 4   Each system is part of at least one hierarchy of systems.

A hierarchy is a set of ordered levels organized in terms of a structural differential.[4] Natural as well as artificial systems can be considered in terms of hierarchies based on a differential. Complexity is one example.[5] Other differentials may be: authority (organizational hierarchy), type of inspection (control hierarchy), abstraction levels (semantic hierarchy) or knowledge competency (learning hierarchy). "Intelligence requires passing from level to level in the [semantic] hierarchy."[6]

The illustrations of structural differentials appear to result in single-channel hierarchical levels, as needed in computer data base management systems, where each system can be part of only one larger system. But some hierarchies may involve multiple and interconnecting channels. Axiom 4 includes both types as well as multichanneled hierarchies, in which a system may well be part of several larger systems (an intersection of streets with a stop light control could be part of the larger hierarchy levels of vehicular movement and pedestrian movement). In effect, almost everything is interconnected.

Corollary 4a   Each system is part of at least one larger system.

The street intersection illustration points this out. In addition, several other interpretations clarify some terms used in other systems literature. (a) All systems are open; there is no such thing as a closed system. Even the classical closed-system illustration of heating a house with a thermostatic control must be part of a larger system, thus negating the very idea of a closed system. (b) "There is no such thing as an object in isolation."[7] (c) No problem exists in isolation. (d) Every system has an inside-out perspective. (e) Every problem is part of a larger problem.

This corollary implies infinitely larger hierarchical levels (something is larger than the universe, for example). Actual hierarchies go so far beyond the range of any human concern (who will ever be asked to plan a new universe?) that the corollary holds for all possible human P&D interests. Not that identifying the hierarchy for all problems or systems is easy. For example, what is the larger system of which the purposeful activity of "develop generalizations" is a part? Curiosity, intuitive interest, or a drive to know or to explore? What are these a part of? But these are far beyond any possible level at which P&D efforts can be employed.

The systems theory literature contains many illustrations of the single-channel-type hierarchy. These serve only as illustrations of hierarchies, though not necessarily ones useful for P&D.

One classification model of levels is (1) static or *framework* structure; (2) simple dynamics, or *clockworks,* with predetermined motions; (3) control and cybernetic self-regulation, or *thermostats*; (4) self-maintaining *cells* that are alive; (5) the *plant* world; (6) the *animal* of mobility, teleological behavior, and self-awareness; (7) *human* level of language and symbols; (8) *organizations* of humans; and (9) *transcendental* systems of ultimates and unknowables.

A second illustration starts with particles, then proceeds to atoms, molecules, crystals, organelles, cells, tissues, organs, organisms, groups, organizations, societies, supranational systems, planets, solar systems, galaxies, and so forth.[8]

The last illustration "is a way of modelling a society . . . as a series of Chinese boxes. Every box is a viable system containing a viable system; every box is contained within a viable system. Continuity is given by the boxiness of the boxes, rather than by their explicit contents—for, as we heard, recursion regards the collections as being all alike, but not identical, for the purpose in hand."[9]

Every system, wherever in the hierarchy it is, will have to adapt to its bigger system. It will have to help attain the measures of effectiveness of its larger system. This is the "composition" principle of coordinating and integrating one level with bigger levels. The President of the United States, irrespective of how often the position is called the most powerful in the world, is a level in a hierarchy that is part of and must adapt to the bigger levels. The janitor's job in the White House is in exactly the same hierarchical set of perspectives, albeit at a different level.

Good P&D will seek to expand the boundary of a system as much as possible to provide a large solution space. One way to do this is to focus on bigger levels in a hierarchy, say, from technical and resource to direct effect and social impact levels. Determining which level(s) in the hierarchy(ies) of larger systems should be selected depends on the purposes and values discussed in Chapters Eleven and Twelve.

Corollary 4b *Each system is composed of smaller systems.* This corollary says that any system can be partitioned and decomposed, an outside-in perspective. This is done often to develop manageable and comprehensible units. Smaller systems, although aligned in a hierarchy, may still have many interactions and exchanges of information.[10] The measures of effectiveness of each smaller system must match and contribute to those of its larger system or systems, which do impose boundaries on the smaller levels. But the larger system cannot be described or accounted for by only the performances (additive or multiplicative) of the smaller systems. The large system almost always has characteristics its smaller systems cannot

attain. These characteristics are the essential attributes of the large system.

Infinitely small systems are a logical consequence of this corollary. Each of the over 100 particles in the nucleus of an atom has smaller units, for example, and so on. Yet such minuteness of systems is an extreme point beyond the range of interest of any P&D project. This corollary is thus operational for P&D ends.

Taxonomical arrays are a frequently used decomposition technique. Plants, animals, rocks, geographical features, chemicals, and evolutionary development are illustrations of areas where taxonomies are used frequently. Nineteen subsystems are suggested for each hierarchical level: reproducer, boundary, matter-energy processors (ingestor, distributor, converter, producer, storage, extruder, moter, supporter), and information processors (input transducer, channel net, decoder, associator, memory, decider, encoder, output transducer).[11]

This corollary is the basis for almost everyone's comments about the complexity of real-world problems and systems. Every problem and system *can* be divided into smaller ones, thus portraying ever increasing complexity. Whether or not this should be done in a project is a major topic in Chapters Eleven and Twelve.

Corollary 4c *Each system exists parallel to other systems.* Several views can be taken of the word *other*. The first concerns functional systems that exist at the "same" or horizontal level (e.g., manufacturing, marketing, and finance in a company; or social welfare, parks and recreation, transportation in a city).

A second view concerns vertical interrelationships, purposes, and information flow that are parallel. Policies regarding personnel selection, training, and evaluation constitute a system parallel to one regarding equipment maintenance. Sales order information processing is a system in parallel to purchasing and materials management.

Similarity and resemblance constitute a third view. Cities of 100,000 population are similar and have some resemblance one to another rather than being identical and congruent. Four hundred-bed hospitals, 600-pupil elementary schools, plants manufacturing 60 cars per hour, and so on, are similarly parallel systems that have few if any *needed* interrelationships and information flow except as voluntarily agreed to.

Problems also exist parallel to others. Clearly separable systems or problems rarely occur in the real world. A semilattice array is almost always a better portrayal of all these corollaries than is a tree or pyramid. A complete or perfect lattice of interrelationships among all the systems or problems is unlikely, whereas showing the needed or important connectedness of systems or problems produces a semilattice. This explains why a specific system or problem can be part of more than one hierarchy.

Parallelism of problems can create complex interrelationships called messes: "A mess is a system . . . of problems. . . . A problem is an ultimate element abstracted from a mess. . . . Problems . . . do not exist in isolation, although we isolate them conceptually."[12] A mess might embody all three corollaries, but vertical and horizontal structure are likely to be obscured. A mess is just more likely to lack clearly defined boundaries, but major vertical and horizontal centrality, and the thrust or aim of each system or problem can still be found in most cases. Part Three addresses *how* this can be done.

The continuing time perspective of Axiom 1 means that the hierarchies of parallel systems and problems change. What may be a problem or system now may not be one tomorrow, the rates of change in each one vary over time, and where no problem exists today may be the locus of one tomorrow.

Axiom 5 Each system at any point in time can be identified in one of three conditions of existence: future, satisfactory, or unsatisfactory. Future existence obviously means the real-world system is nonexistent, but is being developed or planned. As soon as a human conceives an idea or need—policy, object, political structure, combinations, etc.—it is in a future existence condition. An idea often results from the knowledge-push concept and a need from the market-pull view. Another illustration is the one-time system for constructing a building, moving, a political campaign, approval of a recommendation, or setting up a task force.

Any single or multiattribute criterion (see values and objectives in Chapter Two) may be used to measure a satisfactory condition. Once a minimum or threshold level of the criterion is defined, satisfactory or unsatisfactory conditions at a particular point in time are identified. "Satisfactory" often means stable, homeostatic, profitable, cost-justified, adaptive, and market-leading. Positive or better-than-expected performances based on the desired norms usually identify a system as satisfactory. "Unsatisfactory" has the opposite set of characteristics—unstable, problem-ridden, unprofitable, costly, nonadaptive, and market-lagging—but also connotes crisis conditions that are "value- or life-threatening" (going bankrupt, agency funding stopped, possible loss of an election, wrath of citizens on an issue, or any type of natural disaster). External conditions (new emission stan-

dards, minimum levels of insulation, competition, poor reading ability of high school graduates, etc.) may generate another determinant of an unsatisfactory situation.

In one sense all systems are unsatisfactory because more progress along the spiral values can always be sought by challenging outworn decisions. Similarly, certain characteristics of a system mean that an unsatisfactory condition always exists. For example, no system ever becomes completely an "ideal-seeking system . . . which, on attainment of any of its goals or objectives, then seeks another goal and objective which more closely approximates its ideal. . . . An ideal-seeking system is necessarily purposeful, but not all purposeful entities are ideal-seeking . . . It has been repeatedly observed that 'without ideals man's life is purposeless.'"[13] The idea that all systems are unsatisfactory adds weight to the need to consider a planned betterment review of every solution.

Considering what happens to each condition of existence *as time goes on* gives rise to some other interpretations.

First, many claim that the future will repeat the past. Surely, the rate of changes and improvements will remain high. What is nonexistent today will be satisfactory tomorrow, and what is satisfactory today will be unsatisfactory tomorrow. The repetition of physical history—rotation of the earth, sunspots, tides—is a desirable future based on the past, but this falls outside the range of P&D concerns. Humans *have* always sought betterment, and significant change has occurred (communications, transportation, social welfare). P&D embodies the past in a future by always considering all three conditions of existence.

Second, the often seriously stated assumption that if something is working well, it should be left alone, must be countered. Assuming that a satisfactory condition will always stay that way flies in the face of the first interpretation. Good P&D seeks to maintain satisfactory levels by arranging for continuing changes and improvements.

Third, cyclic behavior concerns well-known expectancies of periodic oscillations around the basic performance and trend levels. If the periodicity is fairly long, one may conclude that the system is in satisfactory condition if the performance at that point in time exceeds expected levels, and in an unsatisfactory one if performance is below expected levels.

Fourth, a system's life cycle starts with an idea, concept, need, or invention, then is followed by initiation, development or refinement, successful attainment, maturity, decay, and death. Not much is known about *predicting* the parts or phases of a specific life cycle of a system, such as its time of existence, rate of

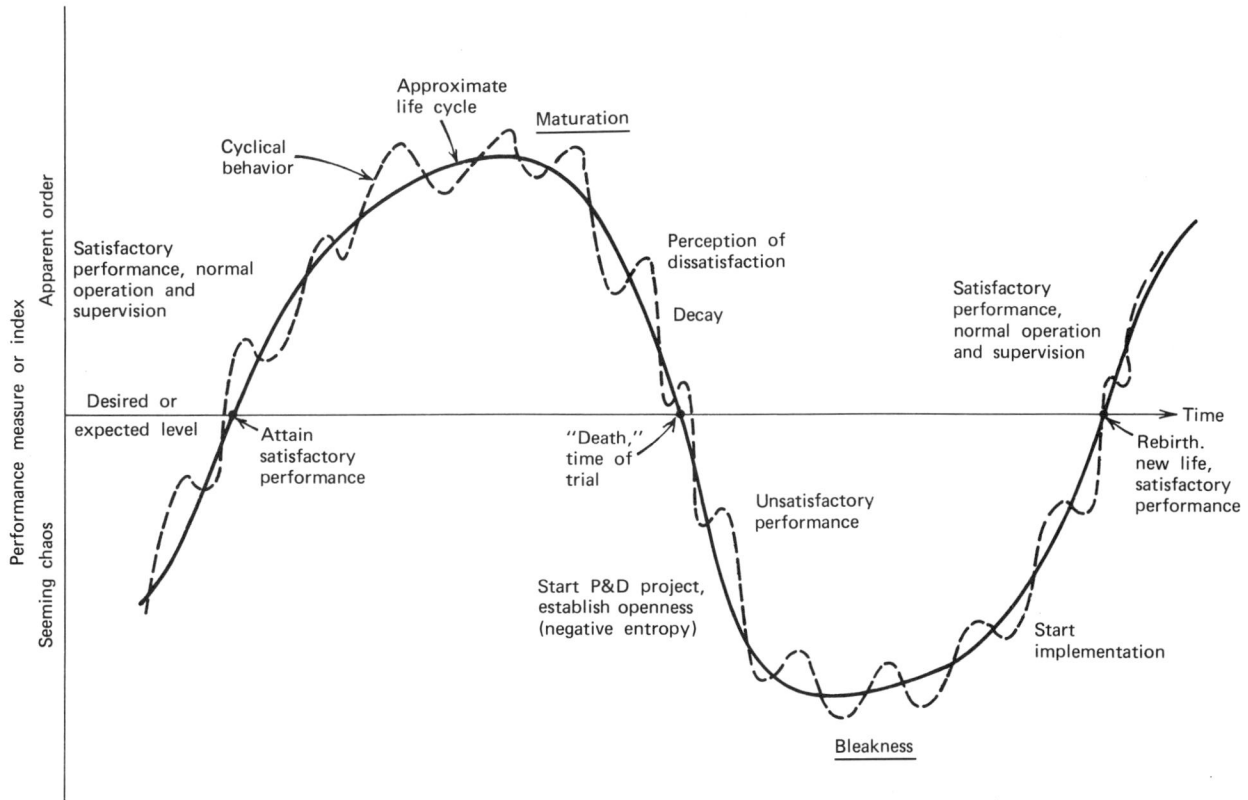

Figure 7-1 Some aspects of usual cyclic behavior and life cycle of a system. Maturation is a good time to begin a betterment P&D project, which is one way of reducing the severity of the cycle. This is a representation of the marketing principle, ''The best time to start development of a new product is at the peak of success of the old one.'' This chart was prepared by W. J. Walkoe.

change from one stage to another, heights of performance, point of maturation, and so on. Cyclic behavior during a life cycle is most noticeable at maturation, but it is also present, although frequently masked, during other parts of the cycle. Satisfactory conditions are usually thought to exist as growth occurs up to and including maturation, although this is far from certain. Many unsatisfactory conditions may exist during growth, just as decay and death stages may occur in well-planned satisfactory stages. Figure 7-1 portrays one illustrative scheme interrelating cyclic behavior and the life cycle.

Fifth, the validity of the axiom holds over long periods of time. A table or a painting, for example, can be considered in satisfactory existence now. They will, however, deteriorate into unsatisfactory physical existence over a very long period of time. In addition, the attitudes of people toward, say, a building, its environmental context, and the motivations leading to its construction could vary over a much shorter time period back and forth between satisfactory and unsatisfactory conditions. Such interpretations reinforce

the time perspective of this axiom. Classifying the condition of a system *today* is no assurance of what it will be after even a short period of time. Arranging for continuing change and improvement can influence in desired directions the performance of a system (Figure 7-1).

Corollary 5a A system tends toward unsatisfactory existence. Physical and social research has established that both natural and organizational entities tend toward disorganization, at least in terms of the measures that define unsatisfactory existence. (Although ''things [may] tend to become more orderly if they are left to themselves,''[14] the orderliness could most likely occur at unsatisfactory existence levels.) The second law of thermodynamics deals with this unsatisfactory existence concept as it relates to gases and uses the term *entropy*. Energy and effort (negative entropy) are required to avoid this tendency toward disorganization in both natural and organizational entities. A satisfactory organization should use energy and effort to seek changes for the better. Conversely, some quite satisfactory *organizational structures* have survived by seeking new opportunities for achievement when their original purpose was accomplished (the Tuberculosis Association changed its focus to lung diseases, the March-of-Dimes shifted its emphasis from polio to birth defects).

Applying energy (negative entropy) will by itself start to change things and tend to make everything around less stable. The immediate results appear to replace order by chaos (Figure 7-1), which is painful if energy infusion is pursued ineptly. Good operating and supervising approaches are one mode of coping. Knowing that the tendency to disorganization exists should stimulate P&D people to provide negative entropy at the appropriate time, especially in planned betterment conditions at the peak of success of what exists (see Figure 7-1). "One way of mishandling a problem is to behave as if it did not exist, [or to treat it with] terrible simplification. . . . [There are two consequences,] acknowledgment is [considered] madness or badness; and . . . the problem . . . [is] compounded through its mishandling."[15]

SUMMARY

The holistic perspective engendered by the word "system" coupled with its wide generic usage lead to establishing three criteria that a definition for purposes of P&D must meet: prescriptiveness, universality, and understandability. The axioms and corollaries here are *about* systems, with a definition of the word still to come, in Axiom 8.

Axiom 3   Everything is a system.

Axiom 4   Each system is part of at least one hierarchy of systems.

Corollary 4a   Each system is part of at least one larger system.

Corollary 4b   Each system is composed of smaller systems.

Corollary 4c   Each system exists parallel to other systems.

Axiom 5   Each system at any point in time can be identified in one of three conditions of existence: future, satisfactory, or unsatisfactory.

Corollary 5a   A system tends toward unsatisfactory existence.

CHAPTER EIGHT

The Unique
Solution Concept:
Axioms 6 and 7

These two axioms provide critical guides that concern the *specific* organization or setting. Individual and organizational reality conditions (Chapter Five) with which P&D must cope can occur in a huge number of possible combinations, enough at least to realize that each P&D situation is different. Even in one organization with many P&D efforts, each will be different.

The individuality of each project explains why P&D should first seek a unique solution rather than try to transfer a successful solution from elsewhere. If the specific group during P&D discovers that an available solution is likely to be effective, that is the time to detail the transfer. Some sort of discovery process is needed, even when a solution is to be transferred throughout a large organization or community.

Uniqueness also means that one standard or stock answer or procedure is unlikely to fit the many reality conditions in a situation. Governments, in their efforts to appear fair and equitable, often impose on everyone regulations and procedures whose real result is often opposite to the desired purpose. One example is the multipage set of restrictions for more than 650 cities and counties in using their Community Development Block grants for housing rehabilitation, road paving, health care, and other services. As one city administrator put it, "Such regulations mean 'you're going to blow it.' We're all different." Uniqueness here re-

quires multiple-channel solutions that would be much more effective and less expensive to operate than the restrictions mandate.

Another example of ignoring the uniqueness idea is the federal government's use of a single set of maximum sizes and specifications for all hospitals in the country without differentiation regarding location. These regulations force almost all hospitals to seek exceptions so that they can meet the specific needs of the areas they serve. Many other methods, such as incentives, policies, and guides, could be used to minimize capital and operating expenses while permitting local flexibility.

These axioms will thus express a set of beliefs different than those imbedded in conventional P&D approaches. Conventional beliefs and approaches are almost completely based on Aristotelian elementalistic reasoning. Aristotelian reasoning is based on rigid dichotomies; this thinking is characterized by statements that something *is* or it *is not*; definitions that disregard undefined terms; attributions to one cause of results that are due to many; and "sharp division[s] between] . . . 'emotions' and 'intellect.' "[1] Such rigidity is not an appropriate foundation for P&D. Non-Aristotelian reasoning, making use of many alternatives, multiple differentiations (Axiom 4) and values, the logic of uncertainties, probabilities of events, and individuality of conditions is better suited to achieving the objectives of P&D.

Axiom 6 A word is only a representation of a reality, not the real thing. The word *word* has many semantic constructs here: model, description, abstraction, a number or measure, definition, specification, concept, map, report, sign, image, equation, symbol, and so on. Even gestures and bodily movements are representations, often of moods, feelings, and emotions. These all represent substitutions for the reality.

The meaning and implications of "word" are many. "A map is NOT the territory it stands for; words are NOT things. . . . Words never say ALL about anything. . . . Maps of maps, maps of maps of maps, and so on, can be made indefinitely, with or without relationship to a territory. . . . The meanings of words are NOT in the words; they are in US. . . . Contexts determine meaning: I like fish. (Cooked, edible fish.) He caught a fish. (Live fish.) You poor fish! (Not fish at all.) To fish for compliments. (To seek.)"[2] Put in another way, there is no absolute truth with words (or numbers, models, descriptions, etc.).

Even the idea of reality is a perception that is impossible to speak about or describe with words. "'Reality' . . . concerns 'opinions' about the meaning and value attributed to the phenomenon in question. This is a far cry from the simplistic but widespread assumption that there is an objective reality, somewhere 'out there.' . . . Anything is real only to the extent that it conforms to a *definition* of reality—and those definitions are legion. To employ a useful oversimplification: real *is* what a sufficiently large number of people have agreed to *call* real—except that this fact is usually forgotten; the agreed-upon definition is reified (that is, made into a 'thing' in its own right) and is eventually experienced as that objective reality."[3]

Thus, a number of different words (maps, abstractions, definitions) can fit a specific "reality." Each one could be considered "right" or at least valid for the specific purposes and criteria of utility. One possible relationship among the various words about a reality is the idea of a hierarchy of words. Semanticists have put "word" in a "process of abstracting" or method of setting up a hierarchical "ladder of abstraction. . . . The object of our experience . . . is not the 'thing in itself,' *but an interaction between our nervous systems (with all their imperfections) and something outside them.* . . . When we say . . . that 'Bessie is a cow,' we are only noting the process—Bessie's resemblances to other 'cows' *and ignoring differences.* What is more, we are leaping a huge chasm: from the dynamic process—Bessie, a whirl of electro-chemico-neural eventfulness, to a relatively static 'idea,' 'concept,' or *word*, 'cow.'"[4]

Figure 8-1 shows a typical "abstraction ladder."

"As [the figure] illustrates, the 'object' we see is an abstraction of the lowest level, but it is still an abstraction, since it leaves out characteristics of the process that is the real Bessie. The *word* 'Bessie' (cow_1), is the lowest *verbal* level of abstraction, leaving out further characteristics—the differences between Bessie yesterday and Bessie today, between Bessie today and Bessie tomorrow—and selecting only the similarities. The word 'cow' selects only the similarities between Bessie (cow_1), Daisy (cow_2), Rosie (cow_3), and so on, and therefore leaves out still more about Bessie."

Several different "ladders" could have been constructed after reaching the word "cow." For example, a biological track could have been followed, or a nutritional, evolutionary, sociological or societal, or religious one (in India), or so on.

Semantics and understanding language build on non-Aristotelian basics: "Beware of the word 'is,' which, when not simply used as an auxiliary verb (he is coming), can crystallize misevaluations: The grass *is* green. (But what about the part our nervous system plays? . . .) Mr. Miller *is* a[n atheist]. (Beware of confusing levels of abstraction. . . .) Business *is* business. (A directive . . .) . . . There is danger of ignoring alternative ways of classifying, as well as of ignoring the fact that everything is in process of change. . . .

"cow_1 is *not* cow_2, cow_2 is *not* cow_3, . . . $Smith_{1949}$ is not $Smith_{1950}$, $Smith_{1950}$ is not $Smith_{1951}$. . . . The word 'cow' . . . calls up in our minds the features that this 'cow' has *in common* with other 'cows.' The index number, however, reminds us that this one is *different*; . . . it reminds us of the *characteristics left out* in the process of abstracting."[5]

Corollary 6a Models are incomplete representations of real-life phenomena. "Model" could be substituted for "word" in Axiom 6. A corollary on "models" (or techniques, analytical tools, charts, equations, etc.) is needed because of the overwhelming reliance on models and techniques in conventional P&D approaches. Models and modeling alone do not solve problems. A detailed model (analysis, technique, etc.) is developed when its incremental benefits exceed the judgment and experience of real-world people.

Models do have benefits that might help in a total P&D approach:

1 Manipulation of relevant solution parameters, variables, conditions, and assumptions to assess the impact of a change without affecting an actual system.

2 Predicting specifications and performances (e.g., costs, interactions, time, yields).

3 Identifying critical factors, qualities, or attributes.

Start reading from the bottom UP

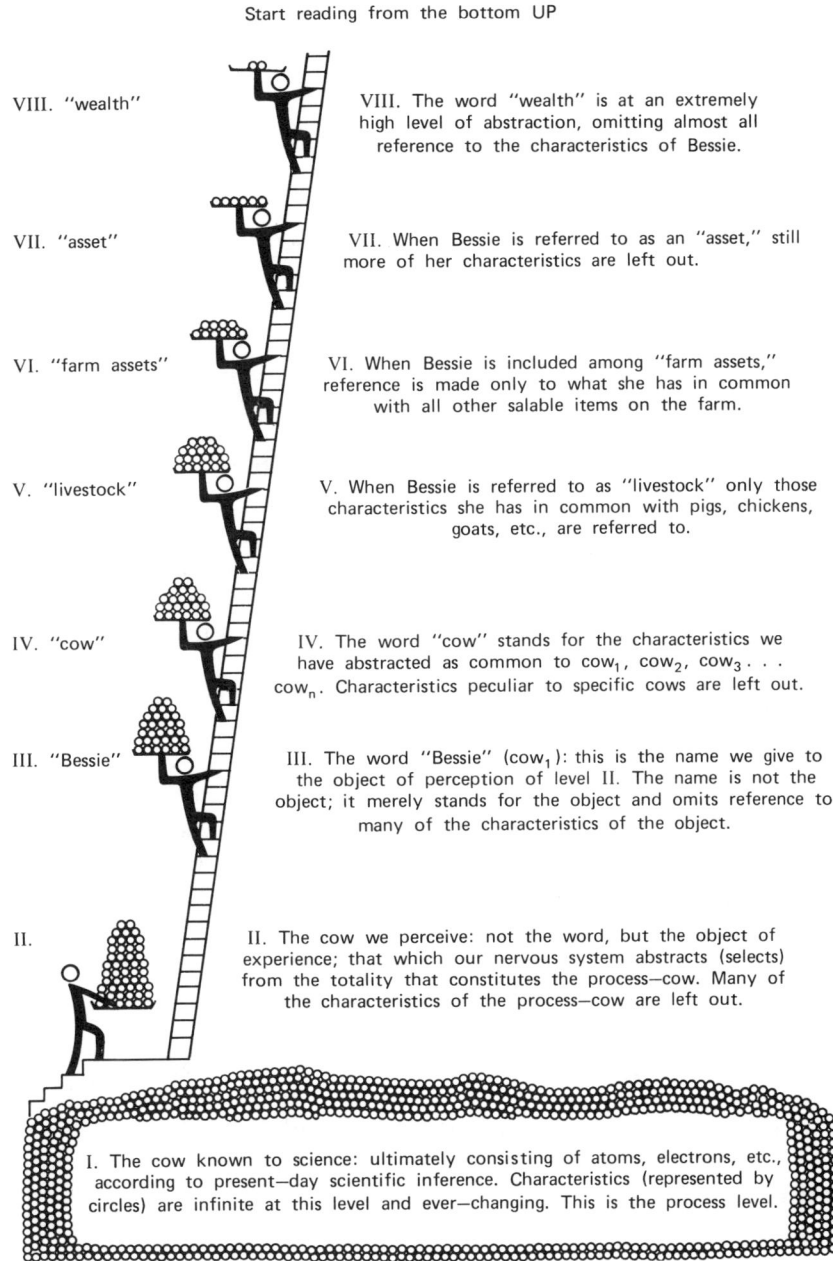

VIII. "wealth"

VIII. The word "wealth" is at an extremely high level of abstraction, omitting almost all reference to the characteristics of Bessie.

VII. "asset"

VII. When Bessie is referred to as an "asset," still more of her characteristics are left out.

VI. "farm assets"

VI. When Bessie is included among "farm assets," reference is made only to what she has in common with all other salable items on the farm.

V. "livestock"

V. When Bessie is referred to as "livestock" only those characteristics she has in common with pigs, chickens, goats, etc., are referred to.

IV. "cow"

IV. The word "cow" stands for the characteristics we have abstracted as common to cow_1, cow_2, cow_3 . . . cow_n. Characteristics peculiar to specific cows are left out.

III. "Bessie"

III. The word "Bessie" (cow_1): this is the name we give to the object of perception of level II. The name is not the object; it merely stands for the object and omits reference to many of the characteristics of the object.

II.

II. The cow we perceive: not the word, but the object of experience; that which our nervous system abstracts (selects) from the totality that constitutes the process—cow. Many of the characteristics of the process—cow are left out.

I. The cow known to science: ultimately consisting of atoms, electrons, etc., according to present—day scientific inference. Characteristics (represented by circles) are infinite at this level and ever—changing. This is the process level.

Figure 8-1 Abstraction ladder. From S. I. Hayakawa, *Language in Thought and Action*, London: Allen & Unwin, 1952; reproduced with permission.

4 Assisting the thinking process by organizing, recording, and stimulating thought and visualizations. Knowing statistics, for example, makes a person cognizant of sample-size phenomena and appropriate significance of data without necessarily modeling or calculating anything.

5 Facilitating communications. An excellent idea has no intrinsic value if it is not communicated.

6 Controlling P&D activities. A model of the solution sequence also prepares an organizational unit to determine if and how well the steps in the solution are being performed.

7 Educating and training.

8 Systematizing knowledge.

Criteria for determining whether or not an available model or a special one is desirable for a particular situation are relevance for the specific purpose; notation of relationships among factors; minimum complexity; ability to understand and communicate the model; ability to manipulate system and smaller system components; ability to obtain benefits almost anywhere during the modeling if sufficient answers are achieved; flexibility; predictive or forecasting potential; ease of checking the model with information from the real situation; accuracy and sensitivity; potential control usefulness; and cost of developing or using a model.

A model can have a format that is mathematical, statistical, physical, physical analog, graphic, economic, schematic, descriptive, or any combination. An extremely large number of specific models are drawn from these nine general types. Chapter Fifteen discusses how they aid P&D.

Although their advantages show their possible use in P&D, dangers and limitations lurk in their use: "Measurements and equations [in effect, models] are supposed to sharpen thinking, but in my observation, they more often tend to make the thinking noncausal and fuzzy. They tend to become the object of scientific manipulation instead of auxiliary tests of crucial inferences."[6] Models too often become objects of affection, being used even when descriptive prose would be better. Some difficulties with models are so severe that one assessment is "that model building is neither necessary nor sufficient . . . in the sense . . . where optimization techniques are central."[7] Some of the more important limitations and dangers of "models" are the following:

1   *Incompleteness.*   The only model that can ever be the same as real life is real life itself.

2   *Assumption That the Model Is the System.*   "The [system] will be identified with a model for it, so that the objects with which the model is concerned . . . will be supposed actually to be the same as the [system]. To these [systems] will then be attributed properties which belong to the objects of a model but which are irrelevant. . . . The price of the employment of models is eternal vigilance."[8] Conclusions about the model of perceived reality are assumed to apply to the real world (A. N. Whitehead's fallacy of misplaced concreteness). A linear programming formulation, for example, is "a model of allocation," not "the allocation."

3   *Assumption That the System has the Same Subdivision Characteristics as the Model.*   Because the components or imaginary divisions of the model are easily manipulated, it is often assumed that the system can likewise be easily manipulated. The danger lies in "transferring the logical necessity of some of the features of the chosen model onto the [system], and thus . . . supposing, wrongly, that the [system], or parts of the [system] have a logical necessity which is in fact fictitious."[9]

4   *Errors.*   Accuracy and precision are almost never as high as people would like. Interpretations must always take account of many errors. This is discussed further in the section on Corollary 7a.

5   *Wrong Viewpoint.*   The modeler's perspective or world-view (rationalist, existentialist, idealist, affective, phenomenologist, hypothetico-deductivist) may not have any relationship at all to the real-life situation. The chemist models a tree, for example, in terms of basic elements and molecules; a forester in terms of cost, number of board-feet, and method for removing it; a botanist as one or more points in a taxonomy of trees; a poet as a descriptive word-picture; an artist models a tree with a lyrical expression of colors and forms.

6   *Identification of What Is to be Modeled.*   So many phenomena are present in even the simplest projects that a selection of one or more is needed. What is a model to one person may be a real-life phenomenon to another. In addition, a model does not enable prediction of what may be emerging attributes and properties.

7   *Consideration of Only a Limited Number and Certain Types of Models.*   Mathematical models are often assumed to be the only type worthy of consideration. But a designer who assumes this errs as much as the designer who assumes that no mathematical models are needed for effective design.

8   *Emphasis on Applying Techniques.*   All projects can overcome most of this tendency by always identifying the purpose of and need for information the technique would provide. Typical information needs are the need to determine structural and qualitative factors in the phenomenon, to identify numerical values of model variables, to establish relationships among variables, or to determine degree or magnitude of relationships.

9   *Communications Gaps.*   The more detailed a model, the more likely it is that the decision maker or manager will not be able to understand it.

10   *Modeling Mindset.*   Every observation by a person who has this mindset is translated into a solution model. An occasional parts shortage is translated into an inventory control model, an absence at a bridge party into a scheduling board, a "pick-up" Frisbee game into a desire to organize a sports league model. This danger of models is similar to the "technological imperative" discussed in Chapter Five.

"While mathematical models . . . can be constructed, the computations derived from these models are of extremely limited use for analyzing the current economic and social situation, and are of even more limited use for predicting the[ir] future . . . conditions. . . . Model building around systems with the many variables of social and economic conditions is an exercise in unreality, particularly when the inability to obtain meaningful measurements of many of these variables is considered."[10]

Whatever the type of model—linear or nonlinear, discrete or continuous, open or closed, segmented or differentiated, lumped parameter or nonlumped, deterministic or stochastic, visual or descriptive, hierarchical or nonhierarchical, and so on—classifying problems with a model type or using models to start conventional approaches can lead to great difficulty. The dichotomies fostered by models encourage Aristotelian reasoning, which is acknowledged to be "indulging in oversimplification. But such is the way of science."[11] Science, of course, is not what is always needed (Chapters Four and Five). The isomorphism based on model types and analytical congruence also becomes a key tenet in using models to solve problems:"what matters is whether [a system] is linear or non-linear, . . . etc. . . . It is the mathematical structure . . . that is of interest to a system theorist."[12] Furthermore, models are never representative of neutral data as conventional wisdom claims. Lastly, problems to work on may be selected solely on the basis of initial perceptions of whether or not a model is available rather than on the problems' actual importance.

Corollary 6b *A solution on paper is not the desired change or implementation.* A solution on paper is a model. It is a snapshot abstraction of a hoped-for real-life world. The solution on paper may be "brilliant," but, unless changes toward implementing the solution occur, the results of the P&D efforts, and hence the methods themselves, are poor.

Not understanding this corollary may have led to the rejection of an architectural proposal for a civic auditorium in a city with a quarter million population. Four and a half million dollars were available to this city from a 1958 bond issue and a prestigious architect was retained. His solution was "brilliant": a proposal for a beautiful building on a very scenic site, which included three-dimensional models to display relationships, and so on. But it would have cost nearly twice the allotted amount. In 1980, the city finally opened a civic auditorium that in *no way* related to the earlier proposal in location, style, size, cost, type, and so forth.

Irrespective of how many awards the original proposal may have accumulated as an art object, for imaginative design, an illustration of good fit with its setting, and so on, it is extremely poor P&D: It could

not be implemented. The desired features could have been incorporated in a plan roughly within the cost limits, which would result in implementation.

Just as many proposed solutions are in reaction to what is called a technology fix (witness the growth of the moderating intermediate or appropriate technology movements), so it is that an artistic or scientific or esthetic fix can be accused of leading to nonimplemented solutions. It is simply insufficient to assume that an image (model, picture, drawing) of a solution is all that a P&D professional is required to produce. Furthermore, optimizing a model or solution on paper is not the same as optimizing the reality. Technique, or model fixation, or mental stuckness, is manifested when the professional keeps arguing that the paper solution "is right" or that the model "says what happened can't occur, so something else is to blame."

Axiom 7 *No two situations or things are identical.* There is no case where "all other conditions being equal" ever exists. Although "close" can occur, each P&D project must be considered to be unique. Isomorphisms, analogies, and analytical congruence are interesting research and modeling constructs, but are anathema to reaching P&D objectives if used as suggested in conventional approaches. Two hospitals or models of them with "identical" characteristics (number of beds, population served, services offered, ownership, percentage of market, and so on) are plainly not identical—if nothing else, the people are always different. Axiom 6 can thus be extended to "No word ever has exactly the same meaning twice,"[13] or to Heraclitus' "truth" that no organism or stimulus is ever twice the same.

Corollary 7a *There is no such thing as certainty in the future.* Probabilists recognize this as a fundamental concept and others usually agree intuitively after a very few illustrations. Even Axiom 7 has a finite probability very slightly above zero of being wrong ("never say never"). This corollary, too, retains an extremely small probability of being wrong, just as the probability of the sun not rising tomorrow is extremely small, rather than zero.

In addition, the generalization portrayed by the mean value of a probability distribution represents only a measure of the aggregation of data describing past conditions and activities. At best, it should be reported with its range of values and various probabilities or odds of occurring. The "law" described by the mean value and probability distribution (or by a correlation regression) can never predict *the* value of a future specific performance or occurrence of another individual case, either in or out of the original sample used to generate the distribution.

The old canard about "the exception proves the rule" says that exceptions are a part of the distribution, but the "rule" reflects only the average or other selected value.

The principle of uncertainty[14] in physics is another way of explaining this corollary. It is impossible to state simultaneously the position and the momentum of an object (particle, nucleus, molecule, etc). Measuring one of them affects the conditions of the others. Quantum physics tells us that matter is in continual motion. If even basic matter is subject to uncertainty, then the corollary is essentially applicable as a beginning premise for all P&D. Many other complexities (e.g., advancing technology, human realities) provide almost by themselves sufficient evidence of uncertainty and unpredictability.

Therefore, all P&D (and other purposeful activity) efforts will contain errors or discrepancies between what is projected and what actually occurs. "Mistakes" from carelessness or ignorance are secondary sources of error which are not the focus of what follows. Three types of errors are defined in statistics: (1) the probability of accepting a value or projection when it should be rejected, (2) of rejecting it when it should be accepted, and (3) of isolating or working on the wrong problem. A fourth type of error is the probability of developing a good solution for the right problem at the wrong time. A fifth type of error involves a set of factors so interactive (students in a classroom, a company in the money markets, patients in a hospital nursing unit) that the number of errors would be very large if one looked inside the whole system. Many errors are submerged when the whole system is treated as a "black box." That is, only the results of the whole system are the focus, not the components. Other errors occur through overcompensation of corrections to oscillations, cycles or periodicity, discontinuous or step changes, or drifts in performance.

The measurement process is also a major source of error. All measuring instruments or methods to ascertain the quality of an attribute of a phenomenon produce errors as a result of the interactions of the attribute(s) being measured, the inadequacy of the definition of the attribute(s), the individual(s) doing the measurement, and the specific measuring method. The error occurs whether the instrument is a micrometer with one-millionth of an inch accuracy for measuring steel bars or a questionnaire for obtaining expert opinion. After a certain point of accuracy and precision has been reached, marginal increments in effort and cost to get more measures return very little in reducing errors and *may* be ineffective.

Some basic ideas about measurements may help establish guides for effectively attaining the P&D purposes at hand with whatever accuracy or precision is needed:

1 Increasing the amount of, emphasizing, or improving measurements in P&D projects may lead to some short-term benefits, especially if the extant measurements are few in number and poor in quality.

2 Long-term emphasis on accuracy and increased amounts of measurements as a means of "seeing" where trouble exists usually produce poor results. The measures focus inward and are often arbitrarily assigned, there is a tendency to ignore as unimportant problems for which measures are not available, and problems where measures are difficult if not impossible to obtain are avoided and said not even to exist.

3 Measurement is primary to scientists for developing theories, but is secondary to P&D professionals for finding solutions. Our society has seriously erred in mimicking for all problems the scientists' need for accurate measurements. It has adopted only the first part of Lord Kelvin's maxim: "When you can measure what you are speaking about, and express it in numbers, you know something about it." The second part, which is ignored, shows that Kelvin's interests, however, were in science. It promotes measurements for the advancement of scientific knowledge through the luxury of ignoring whatever cannot be measured.

4 A measurement focus leads to rejection of useful ideas from other fields (behavioral sciences, philosophy, political science), the omission of which, interestingly, is not measured as a cost by the measurement devotees.

5 Most measurement techniques do not take advantage of available statistical technology that might minimize misconceptions and reduce the amount of data collected.

6 Measurement is used as a threat and as an excuse because it often overawes people, which eventually causes them to avoid, divert, and fight it. Often, when one set of measures does not work, the experts claim that it is the fault of the measures, not of the expert, and all that is needed is better measures.

Predictions are obviously influenced by these types of errors, some more than others. Hard sciences, such as physics and chemistry, have a high degree of accuracy and precision (yet still exhibit uncertainty), geology and biology have less, and sociology and political science have the least. None are able to project the emergence of new attributes and properties. Prediction capability regarding a phenomenon varies over time, just as the occurrence of a predicted event may not have the same impact when it actually occurs as was originally projected.

This corollary and Axiom 6 together explain why any number used in P&D must always be associated with a reality that is described in words. Because both word meanings and measurement techniques are variable, the number is subject to many interpretations. For example, what does "zero" mean? "When people speak of zero they apparently mean different things. . . . In the case of scientific analysis, zero has changed. A few years ago analytical methods might have indicated the absence of a particular chemical in a test sample. Today, with better analytical methods, that same sample would show the particular chemical present; we no longer have the zero we had a few years ago."[15]

Corollary 7b *A solution for a specific problem in one organization differs from the solution for a similar problem in another organization.* People, their performances, and their objectives (Axiom 2) in one organization cannot be the same as in the second (Axiom 7). Some characteristics and factors in a solution may have the same numerical values, such as minimum level professional competency, or the same model of a machine. The realities of individuals and groups (Chapter Five) explain why actual competency and machine performance turns even similar solution specifications into interesting but meaningless data.

The principle of equifinality (more than one solution would be acceptable) is another way of stating this corollary. It also shows that insistence on one solution as the best is wrong. It is probably only "better" than others for the particular organization at that point in time. Yet many solutions are "sold" and promoted with great zeal by people or groups who have made an emotional commitment to that solution. This is one illustration of misplaced commitment.

On the larger scale, organizations, cities, and even countries need unique, situation-specific solutions. Although food and health care are needed everywhere, for example, the U.S. solution or the modes of training physicians in the United States should not be assumed to be applicable to India or even Canada. An individualization program in one high school is not the same as in another. Even large global issues, such as food supply, are far more likely than not to be solved within individual national (or allied) political units than by global exhortations and "solutions." Conditions which occur most frequently or are most critical in each situation are different, thus requiring different solutions. Solutions should still be sought at the

biggest *possible* level in the hierarchy of related systems (Corollary 4a). There is every reason to decry fragmentation of national and international efforts at solving food, energy, water, population, and similar messes, and a focus on the big scene or mess must concurrently be maintained.

The word *possible* is crucial. Moving toward a *better* situation is to be preferred to no movement at all because some will not adopt the one utopian or dream snapshot proposed by the experts (such as the fish protein concentrate "solution" to the world food problem pushed in the 1960s). "Possible" incorporates the realities of people and groups, the timeline axiom, the variabilities of human interests (Axiom 2), and the ideas of continuing change and improvement of the solution.

Nor is it helpful to categorize problems in terms of availability of a solution, technological level, a specified level of computer involvement, etc. "Transplanted designs arouse rejection mechanisms that thwart implementation":[16] the not-invented-here (NIH) syndrome (Chapter Five). It is true that there is no reason to reinvent the wheel, but the organization needs to determine if a wheel is really needed before including one in a solution. Adapting an existing solution (computer software, factory layout, quality circles, curriculum) from elsewhere very often becomes more difficult, time-consuming and wasteful than starting afresh. One reason is that news about a solution focuses on what's good; what's bad or how many factors are interrelated isn't mentioned. Even technological solutions (nuclear energy, biomedical devices and protheses, desalination, resource recovery from refuse, automatic vehicle identification, synthetic fuels, etc.[17]) that are "proven" effective and demonstrated widely should not be assumed to be the solution or technology to be transferred every time a "similar" problem is faced elsewhere. Unfortunately, a person "faced with the choice between the [seeming] complexity [of P&D] and the [apparently] simpler [adoption of an existing solution is likely to choose the latter]."[18] When someone proposes the adoption of a solution, say, quality circles, ask "If the answer is quality circles, then what is the question?"

On the other hand, the idea of *knowledge* dissemination (seminars, articles, movies) is crucial, for people everywhere should *know* about alternatives if they are to be effective in P&D. Their initiative at the specific location will generate the market for the solution by "reinventing" the idea if indeed there is a demand for it. Technology thus learned can stimulate a need or desire that becomes a P&D problem on which to work (Chapter Two).

Each solution will be different also because of dissimilar resource allocation perspectives, such as the organization's current allocation policies, the rationale and values used to set them up, the future prospects for obtaining resources, and the past "injustices" and overall history of arriving at allocations.

Corollary 7c   An analogy cannot prove that a premise should be accepted.   A frequent ploy in debates, discussions, and some P&D efforts is to assert that an idea or point is "proven" or "better" when an analogy is presented on its behalf from another field. Analogies provide interesting *illustrations* of the assertion or predication, and even stimulate creativity, but they hardly ever "prove" a point or "justify" a proposed solution. All one has to do to understand why this is so is to substitute "word" or "model" or "identical conditions" for "analogy." An analogy is incomplete, an abstraction of a different real-life phenomenon, a reference of interest for another purpose, and most often downright dangerous for P&D in a specific situation. One analogy that has hampered the field is the unstated assumption that what constitutes good research methods and approaches are therefore good for P&D[19] (Chapters Four and Five).

The dangers of the analogy and the assumption that a solution from elsewhere will work well in a given situation concern projects of all sizes, from the design of a gear to the selection of loading dock equipment, to setting national policies regarding forest pest management and inaugurating national health insurance. Analogies encourage the view that the grass is greener on the other side. If they can land a man on the moon, then we should be able to have a day-care center for inner city parents. If law courts can resolve legal conflicts, then a science court can use the adversary process to resolve conflicts on technical issues. "We might say that the objectives are admirable but the methods [of analogy] misguided. . . . These initiatives generally come from those whose experience with the law is limited."[20] If other organizations use measured allowed times for jobs in the hospital radiology department as a means of increasing productivity, then our hospital needs the measurement program, even though our productivity is 45% higher than the average.

An analogy as a literary device can summon up an image, provide understanding of a situation, and play on the inherent beauty or relevance of the metaphor or cadence of words. It is not meant to prove that a runner, for example, *is* a gazelle or is literally running at the gazelle's speed or is built muscularly like a gazelle. It illustrates, provides color, creates mental images, and otherwise enlivens reading or discussion. Anyone lapsing into offering an analogy as proof is forgetting a huge number of characteristics about the current situation. It is easy to demolish an analogy offered as proof by using the axioms and corollaries in this chapter. It is even easier by showing how the analogy differs from the specific situation in terms of system elements and dimensions (see Chapter Nine). I hope no one ever has to waste time in such exercises.

SUMMARY

Unique solutions are sought by P&D because the solution must fit situation-specific conditions. A solution being recommended *now* may therefore not represent apparent great innovativeness or unusual creativity, but doing P&D for uniqueness focuses on the specific situation implementation, even though adopting the innovative or creative ideas may be delayed somewhat. The axioms and corollaries that support this perspective are the following:

Axiom 6   A word is only a representation of a reality, not the real thing.

Corollary 6a   Models are incomplete representations of real-life phenomena.

Corollary 6b   A solution on paper is not the desired change or implementation.

Axiom 7   No two situations or things are identical.

Corollary 7a   There is no such thing as certainty in the future.

Corollary 7b   A solution for a specific problem in one organization differs from the solution for a similar problem in another organization.

Corollary 7c   An analogy cannot prove that a premise should be accepted.

CHAPTER NINE

Defining the Word
System: Axiom 8

Axioms 3, 4, and 5, outlining a systems context, provide a holistic perspective, a weltanschauung, for P&D even without defining the word itself.

Yet the word *system* is used so often that it needs a definition. First, boundaries implied in a definition focus attention on key concepts. A framework or "ballpark" idea, even if loosely constructed, gives people involved in P&D an opportunity to have similar levels of understanding. Second, the framework can guide questioning and development of P&D criteria and specifications for a particular project. Third, it encourages sharpness of specification of even nontechnical solutions. This, in turn, provides a basis for good assessment of the consequences of certain design assertions. Fourth, it serves as a checklist for purposeful activities (e.g., operate and supervise, evaluate) which determine initially what is happening now. Finally, readers should know what is meant each and every time the word is used.

These advantages are heightened when the three major criteria (Chapter Seven) for assessing a definition are maximized: prescriptiveness, universality, and understandability. *Prescriptiveness* establishes in advance those characteristics, controls, properties, interfaces, and attributes for which solution specifications must be considered. This criterion provides some assurance of completeness and ability to assess operationality and consequences. *Universality* concerns the applicability of the definition to any possible P&D project, wide open or highly con-strained, large or small, or highly futuristic or mainly current in interest. *Understandability* includes comprehensibility and flexibility in adapting various "words" to fit the ideas and concepts for use in a specific organization. For now, Axiom 8 is a definition of the word *system* that appears to do all of this:

Axiom 8   A system processes inputs into outputs that achieve and satisfy a purpose or purposes through the use of human, physical and information resources in a sociological and physical environment. Systems can vary in size (Axiom 4). Thus, bigger levels in the hierarchy of systems (Corollary 4a) incorporate smaller systems, which are subsystems or components (Corollary 4b).

Because a hierarchy is often a size-based order of systems, with no superior-inferior relationship implied, a vertical channel of systems can be extended for the area of interest. Each system (a white rectangle on Figure 9-1) shows the related horizontal or parallel systems, either within or outside the organizational unit. System levels do not always correspond with organizational divisions (Corollary 4a).

Each system is thus a complex set of interrelated elements. The basic set defines the broad purpose and values of the larger entity or organizational unit within which the system does or will exist. Each system achieves an end. Thus, the purpose, function, or result sought from a system is the first element, and each system has at least one purpose.

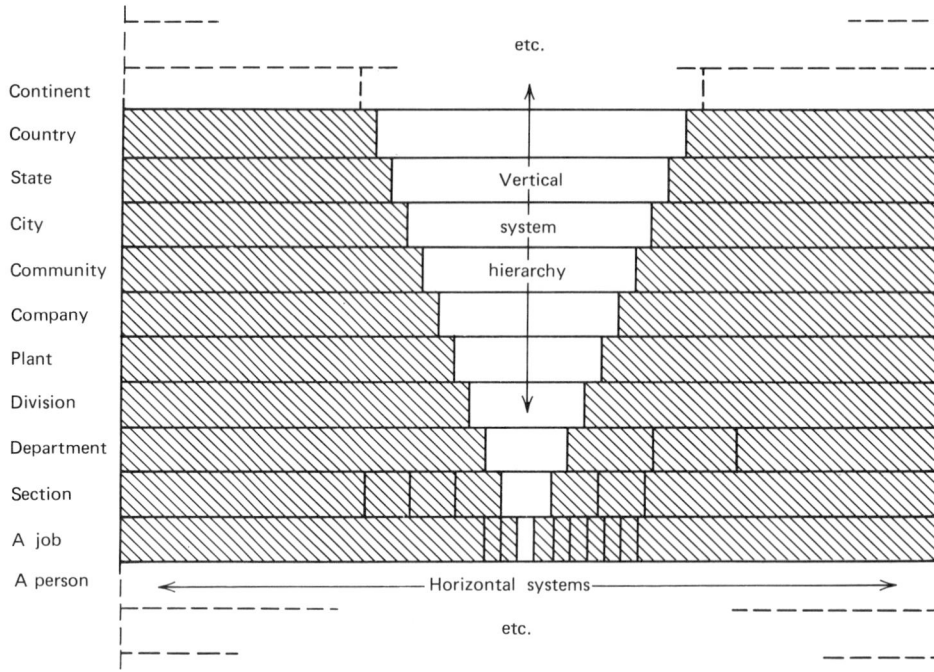

Figure 9-1 Levels in the system hierarchy.

Each system receives physical, informational, and/or human items from smaller, larger, and parallel systems to process into a desired state that will achieve its purpose. Therefore, every system has inputs.

Each system provides physical, informational, and/or human items or services to its smaller, larger, and horizontal systems. These outcomes represent the means whereby the purposes of the system are achieved. Therefore, each system has outputs.

Similarly, five other elements can be developed from Axiom 8: sequence, environment, human agents, physical catalysts, and information aids. The words used for the names of elements are unimportant and can vary, whereas the *ideas* represented by each are critical.

SYSTEM ELEMENTS

1 *Purpose* The mission, aim, need, primary concern, or function of or results sought from a system. The purpose is the contribution made to or necessary for a larger system in the hierarchy(ies). A purpose is *what* the system is to accomplish, with no emphasis on *how* it is to be accomplished.

2 *Inputs* Any physical items, information, and/or human beings on which work, conversion, or processing takes place to arrive at the output(s). *Physical*

items could be coils of steel, powdered plastic, money (the actual currency and coins), the mark-sense punch card, the sales order form, and so on. *Information* could be bank account balance (printed on piece of paper), whereabouts of the president (secretary's explanation), number of toasters ordered (sales order form), amount of production on machine 472 (orientation of iron particles on a magnetic tape), history of the conflicts between key managers (perceptions in minds of people), etc. *Human beings* relevant in this context could be sick people entering a hospital, a housewife shopping at a grocery store, a family wanting house plans, a student attending a college, an overweight person visiting a reducing salon, etc.

A combination input is the return of previous outputs of the system. For example, a large system for manufacturing airplanes includes the reentry of each airplane for major periodic maintenance. A patient may reenter a hospital after having been discharged. User information about product performance serves as new input to the product design system.

Every system requires at least two of the three types of input. A manufacturing system, for example, will require information about alloy, tensile and yield strengths, gauge, and width to accompany the physical input of a coil of steel. A patient entering the system of a hospital represents human (previous medical history and symptoms), and physical (personal belongings) information inputs. A system which is a board of directors meeting needs inputs of information and humans.

3 *Outputs* Desired (and undesired) physical items, information, humans and/or services (response, event, policy, reaction, safety level, correction, etc.) which result from working on or converting inputs. Desired outputs achieve the selected and bigger purposes by adding net value to the inputs. Undesired outputs include such things as dislocations, pollutants, scrap, and trash, for which provisions must be included in the system specifications. Outputs also include substantive properties, performance, and physical or chemical characteristics of the output when actually being used. For example, the dynamic characteristics (cornering, power pickup, shock absorption ability, or acceleration) of an automobile output are a part of output itself.

4 *Sequence* The conversion, work, process, transformation, or order and cycle of steps or events by which the inputs become the outputs. The basic steps are the essential "unit operations" or identifiable changes in the state of the inputs which lead to their transformation into outputs. Additional steps include causal bonds, movement, storage, meeting, decision, and control, which enable the unit operations to take place. Parallel channels for processing different inputs are often included, along with various connective points to interrelate the channels.

5 *Environment* The physical and sociological (psychological, legal, political, economic) factors or ambience (as the French call it) within which the other elements are to operate. These are always changing. Many are usually outside the influence of the system itself, yet others can be modified or specified for the system. Physical or "climatic" factors include temperature, humidity, noise, dirt, light, colors of machines and walls, and so forth. Ecological physical factors "outside" the system include spatial aspects, accessibility, and shapes and relationships in the design of the physical facilities and equipment.

Sociological factors include the state of technology within which the organizational unit operates, the cultural and historical determinants of attitudes, and the society's economic conditions. More specific factors concern the attitudes of the managerial and supervisory personnel, morale and "reality" disposition of working forces (see Chapter Five), the operating controls and rules for personnel, and the social interactions and communications of the people involved. Sociological environment forms the larger context of externalities which "own" or "set the stage" for the system. The Japanese, for example, do not build factories or plants with an entrance on the northeast side, the devil's gate. The managerial style and organiza-

tional structure sets another environmental factor: autocratic, paternalistic, bureaucratic, permissive, diplomatic, or democratic.

6 *Human Agents* Human beings on differentiated levels who are aids in the steps of the sequence, without becoming part of the outputs. Human agent activities or methods to aid in the sequence include the whole range of human capabilities: talking, writing, expending energy in manipulating controls and/or changing input items, reasoning, performing dexterous tasks, decision making, evaluating, learning, creativity, and acting as a diligent monitoring and sensing device. Human beings are either inputs and outputs (patients in a hospital), or human agents (nurses). Overlap exists in most cases, for example, as patients can be human agents aiding other patients, and nurses can be inputs into the cafeteria system.

7 *Physical Catalysts* Physical resources that are aids in the steps of the sequence without becoming part of the outputs. Typical items are chalkboards, machines, vehicles, chairs, computers, filing cabinets, energy, buildings, tools, jigs, automatic devices, paper, lubricating oil, projector, desks, self-measuring sensors, and pallets. A chicken on an egg farm is a physical catalyst. Each of these illustrative items could be a physical catalyst in one system, or input or output in another system. A computer, for example, may be a physical catalyst in an accounts payable system, an input in a maintenance system, and an output in a production system.

8 *Information Aids* Knowledge and data resources that help in the steps of the sequence, without becoming part of the outputs. Computer programming instructions, equipment operating manuals, maintenance instructions, standard operating procedures for human agents, and policy manuals are typical information aids. These may also be inputs and outputs in other systems. On occasion, an expert consultant, media advisor, or corporate legal advisor could embody the role of this element.

Illustration

Even a physical object, such as a table, can be described in terms of system elements. *Purpose*—to locate objects at a particular height; *inputs*—objects; *outputs*—objects maintained in position; *sequence*—dynamic equilibrium between upward forces of the table and downward forces of the objects, and the changes, however subtle, in table strength and object forces and conditions as time elapses; *environment*—physical (dry or damp, etc.) and sociological (careful or careless family, etc.); *human agents*—person to dust or polish; *physical catalysts*—wood, metal, furniture polish, and configuration of table; and *information aids*—yield and shear strengths of table materials, abrasive characteristics of objects.

Any physical object, information item, or human being can be a different element in different systems. A table, thus, could be the output of a manufacturing system, an input into a sales system, or a physical catalyst in a hotel system.

A Model of Any System

One interesting visualization, representational model, or abstraction of any system is a hopper, shown in Figure 9-2. A large one can conveniently contain small hoppers. Each large dot or group of dots in Figure 9-2 represents a smaller system level. A hopper can be "placed" around each dot or group to show how the eight system elements apply to it. The hopper of Figure 9-2 can also be included in larger hoppers, which would thus include horizontal or parallel hoppers.

The numbering of system elements from one to eight reflects the general order in which the elements are designed. A great deal of iteration, jumping, and parallel detailing occur in a real P&D effort. Nevertheless, purpose is almost always designed, specified, or assumed before the other seven elements

are, inputs usually before the other six, and so forth. The order is hardly ever followed because, for example, a project team or leader must know that certain physical catalysts (7) are available for processing plastics into tensile struts for a dishwasher before plastic inputs (2) and outputs (3) can be specified.

The relationships among the various elements may take different forms: necessary, complementary, redundant, or contradictory. The physical catalysts in a specific system, for example, may take on a necessary relationship to the sequence, but they may be only complementary to the output. Flexibility also means that more than one element name can be used in a specific setting. Two or more elements could be drawn from the environment element, the human agent element might be divided into types (professional, political, support, etc.), physical catalysts could be split, and so on.

Corollary 8a   Each element can be specified or detailed in terms of dimensions, properties, or attributes. Models are always incomplete, and the "hopper" is no exception. Form or structure needs to be added to the elements for completeness. *Dimensions*, the word in this corollary used mainly from here on, provide significant operationality to the elements with minimal redundancy.

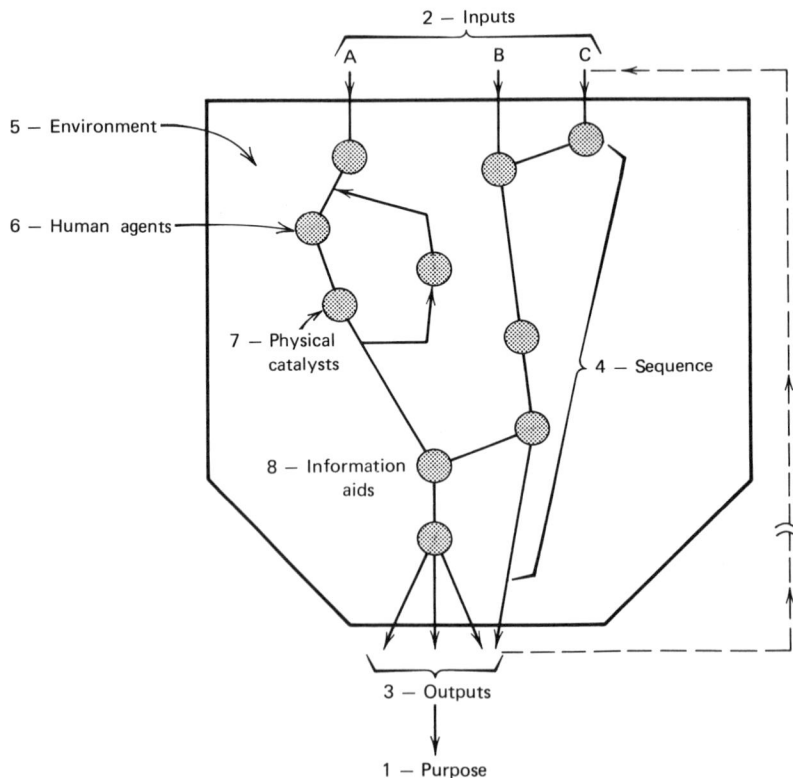

Figure 9-2 Model of any system.

Six dimensions can specify the precise conditions for each element in a specific situation: (1) fundamental existence characteristics; (2) values, beliefs and desires; (3) measures to assess accomplishment of fundamental and value dimensions; (4) control or dynamic methods of ensuring achievement of fundamental, values, and measures specifications; (5) interface relationships of fundamental, values, measures, and control specifications with other systems and other elements in its system; and (6) future existence or desired changes and improvements that can be foreseen in fundamental, values, measures, control, and interface specifications.

The number of dimensions is not fixed, for some can be divided into two or more attributes. Measures, for example, could be listed as an objective dimension and a goals dimension, as described in Chapter Two.

SYSTEM DIMENSIONS

1 *Fundamental* This dimension must exist or no others can be specified. It is the identity or context of a system. Also referred to as the existence, real-life, or manifestation dimension, it concerns tangible, overt, observable, physical, and/or basic structural characteristics. It includes the basic "what-who-how-where" specifications, along with associated quality levels. It states specifically the intensity, degree to which the specific condition is distinguishable from others, and/or the operation of each element.

Determining the specific fundamental attributes is what the P&D approach seeks to accomplish, so that the conditions thus identified can be implemented. Many terms describe the specific numbers, descriptions, drawings, and so on, including specifications, parameters, variables, estimates, relationships, properties, characteristics, and identifications.

2 *Values* This is the situation-specific form of the values part of Chapter Two. It also embodies and enlarges on the "satisfy" part of Axiom 8 by stating both the solution values and the human values (disposition to behave in certain ways).

Motivating beliefs, human expectations, global desires, ethics, equity, and moral concerns can be *ascribed in some form to each element*. The most global values are likely candidates for the purpose element. Other descriptions concern how people and organizations "feel" about desirable results in specifying each element: preferences, basic (unyielding?) or important assumptions (e.g., democratic society), concern with societal life and civil liberties, disposition to a behavior, pleasures, productivity, justice, concern with in-

dividual life, relevance, sensitivities, preferred modes of conduct, involvement of others, essential beliefs, sentiments, convenience, human dignity, willingness to shape societal acts and conscience, emphases on successes rather than failures and wrongs, comprehensiveness, safety, and cultural or esthetic properties. Values could thus be said to capture the "standards" that a solution is expected to continue.

Perhaps the most important benefit of the values dimension for each element is the forced review of what the value standards are and how they need to be part of the solution and the decisions in selecting the solution. "On all sides, one sees evidence today of cop-out realism—ostensible efforts to be sensible in dealing with things as they are but that turn out to be a shucking of responsibility. . . . It is now possible to assess the effect of [the] legalization [of off-track betting and the numbers game]. . . . New York State itself has become a predator in a way that the Mafia could never hope to match. . . . Millions of dollars are being spent by New York State on lavish advertising on television, on radio, on buses, and on billboards. At least the Mafia was never able publicly to glorify and extol gambling with taxpayer money . . . [Also consider the] cop-out realism [in] dealing with cigarette-smoking by teenagers and pre-teenagers. Special rooms are now being set aside for students who want to smoke. . . . The effect of [the] supposedly 'realistic' policy is to convert a ban into a benediction. By sanctioning that which [people] deplore, they become part of the problem they had the obligation to meet . . . The function of [value] standards is not to serve as the basis for mindless repressive measures but to give emphasis to the realities of human experience."[1]

3 *Measures* Measures change the values dimensions into particular objectives and operational goals. They embody the "achieve" part of Axiom 8, and concern how much and when, including what is needed to overcome entropy (Corollary 5a). Measures in general concern effectiveness, time, performance, cost and other factors of importance concerning the fundamental specifications. They are indicators of the success of the eventual solution. They include any associated confidence limits.

The word *objectives* identifies the specific categories, units, verifiable indicators, scales, factors of merit, criteria or parameters that are considered the important measures. Forecasts, financial matters and quantitative factors are almost always included. They should conform to what people consider useful for attaining the values and fundamental dimensions, but should also be clear, capable of being measured, reproducible, unequivocal in interpretation, and as accurate as needed. Some typical measures are cost per month, time per service or output per hour, reject rate, reliability life, expense ratio, and profit per year.

Goals assign specific amounts and time and/or cost factors to each objective. Assume that one value is "Improve safety record in the department." An objective might be "decrease accidents," and a goal "reduce monthly accident rate by 30% within a year." Here is another illustration: the value is to improve manpower services; *one* objective of several is to increase placements of disadvantaged people; *one* goal of several would be to increase by 25% per year the number of disadvantaged placements. No number of objectives or goals will ever capture exactly what is meant by the specific values. In addition, some goals will be set by external groups, such as the standards or threshold levels defined by the Bureau of Standards, Underwriters Laboratory, Environmental Protection Agency, Consumer Product Safety Commission, and American National Standards Institute.

4 *Control* Control comprises methods for ensuring that the fundamental, measures, and even value specifications are maintained as desired (at or within limits around a specified condition) during the operation of the system. Dynamic control of each specification involves (a) making measurements of the performance of the specification as the solution or system is in operation, (b) comparing the actual measurements to the desired specification, and (c) taking actions to correct significant deviations if necessary, through human corrections, automated response, advance modifications of equipment, or by changing a desired specification, or planning and designing an overall improvement. A significant deviation between performance and desired specification is interpreted as meaning that the error of taking action when none is really needed is minimal compared to the error of *not* taking action when it should be taken.

All three parts of the control dimension may be carried out within the system itself, or any one or more may become the responsibility of another system or group. Government regulations illustrate one form of external measurement, comparison, and/or corrective action. Licensing, accrediting, peer review, receiving room inspection, customer surveys and complaints, board of directors review, and outside auditing firms are also possible outside controls. Cost control, waste control, internal audits, and productivity improvement programs illustrate major efforts that may be designed into a solution or activated after implementation. On the other hand, all three parts of the control dimension may be an integral part of the fundamental and measures dimensions of a particular element. For example, a part produced by a machine may be inspected by the operator, or inspection may be done automatically.

The effectiveness of corrective action is judged by measuring the extent to which actual performance recovers to the desired specification level. Correction is measured by stability, as when the significant differential disappears as elapsed time increases; accuracy, or closeness of recovery to desired specification; lag time, or speed of response to the action; and performance oscillations as the control-reaction-control-reaction cycles take place.

5 *Interface* The interface constitutes the relationships of the fundamental, values, measures, and control specifications to other elements and to other systems. Some illustrations of interfaces are inspection of materials received from a vendor, the impact of a changed grading system on parents, shared services with other hospitals, and government reporting regulations related to personnel actions. Illustrations of intrasystem interfaces are process control interactions with human agents, physical catalysts, and information aids; information systems relationships among inputs, humans, physical catalysts, and information aids. Some of these cause difficulties with element specifications, and vice versa.

Interface dimension specifications help in the avoidance of difficulties in getting a system to operate well by anticipating and assessing consequences of negative and hostile interactions. What additional or how much less work will result for other systems? What costs will the other system incur? Can the other system be modified to let this system be implemented, or even to have the other system take advantage of the ideas? Perhaps a substitute or add-on "technological shortcut" might be located by such searching for interfaces. What possible disturbances and forces from other systems (lobbying, special interest groups, oil embargo, supreme court decision) will impact on this system (delay service, increase cost)? Can a model (differential equation) express the interrelationships of the factors or variables? How does the P&D professional or team interact with managers/administrators, users/clients/customers, people working in the current system, and so on? Are there cause-effect research results describing how one factor (element or dimension) changes as another varies?[2]

6 *Future* Anticipated changes in each specification of the other five dimensions at one or more points of time in the future. The future dimension defines the growth, learning rate (evolution, homeostatis) or decay of the specifications. Forecasts of all types (e.g., social attitudes, costs, weather, population) express possible "future" specifications. Also included are specifications on how the specific element dimension is to get to the anticipated stage (a transfer function). The

Dimensions

Elements	Fundamental: Basic or Physical, Characteristics— What, How, Where, or Who	Values: Motivating Beliefs, Global Desires, Ethics, Moral Matters	Measures: Objectives (Criteria, Merit and Worth Factors), Goals (How Much, When, Rates, Performance Specifications	Control: How to Evaluate and Modify Element or System as It Operates	Interface: Relation of All Dimensions to Other Systems or Elements	Future: Planned Changes and Research Needs for All Dimensions
Purpose: mission, aim, need, primary concern, focus						
Inputs: people, things, information to start the sequence						
Outputs: desired (achieves purpose) and undesired outcomes from sequence						
Sequence: steps for processing inputs, flow, layout, unit operations						
Environment: physical and attitudinal, organization, setting, etc.						
Human agents: skills, personnel, responsibilities, rewards, ect.						
Physical catalysts: equipment, facilities, etc.						
Information aids: books, instructions, etc.						

Figure 9-3 Solution framework (system matrix). *Agents*, *catalysts*, and *aids* help process inputs into outputs without becoming part of outputs.

89

arrival at the desired stage may be planned (obsolescence or gradual termination), may be due to learning and duration, or may require a new P&D effort. Sunset laws and zero-based budgeting illustrate two broad ideas for describing *how* arrival at the future point might be accomplished.

Combining this corollary with Axiom 8 forms the system matrix or morphological box of Figure 9-3. It represents the prescriptive, universal, and understandable definition of the word *system*. Different words can be used to represent the same ideas as the elements and dimensions. One version in policy making, for example, uses these elements: purpose-relevant reference system, inputs, outputs, structure and process, and operating, information, and human communication requirements. These are detailed by the following dimensions: physical, values, measures criteria, analysis procedures, elemental interfaces, model interfaces, systems interfaces, and anticipated changes.

Another version of the system matrix is shown in Figure 9-4 to portray the time component aspects of the future dimension. The lines denoting the cells in Figures 9-3 and 9-4 are *not* firm divisions, for there are both overlapping and interrelationships among the cells. Each cell, rather, connotes the major thrust of the element/dimension intersections.

The representational matrix provides an orderly way of denoting all possible types of information to consider in specifying a system. Not all elements or dimensions need to be specified in a particular system. Nor is it necessary to have the same amount of information in each cell. The amount can range from an empty set to some large, almost infinite number of models or sets of data. Similar or identical accuracy is not required for the information in each cell. The system matrix is very seldom, if ever, used in exactly this form as a basis for recording information needed in designing a system. (Chapter Thirteen and Table 13-3 especially, illustrate the type of specification that could fit into each cell.)

The questions raised by probing what specifications should be developed for each cell are almost all-inclusive. They number far more than the usually suggested who, what, why, where, when, and how. They are also much more specific than the usual questions because more than the 48 questions the matrix appears to suggest are available. In addition to the 16 fundamental and values dimension questions, there are *at least* 16 measures dimension questions about the fundamental and values specifications, 24 control dimension questions, 32 interface, and 40 future, or a total of at least 128.

Corollary 8b   *Each element and dimension of a system is a system.*   This combination of Axioms 3 and 8 and Corollary 8a is illustrated by Figure 9-5. Picture a system matrix B behind the output element of, say,

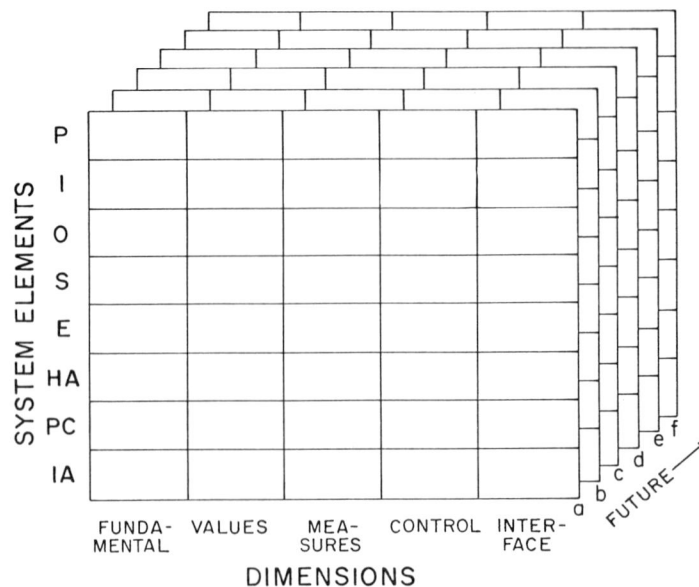

Figure 9-4   Another form of the solution grid. Overlap and interrelationships exist among the cells.

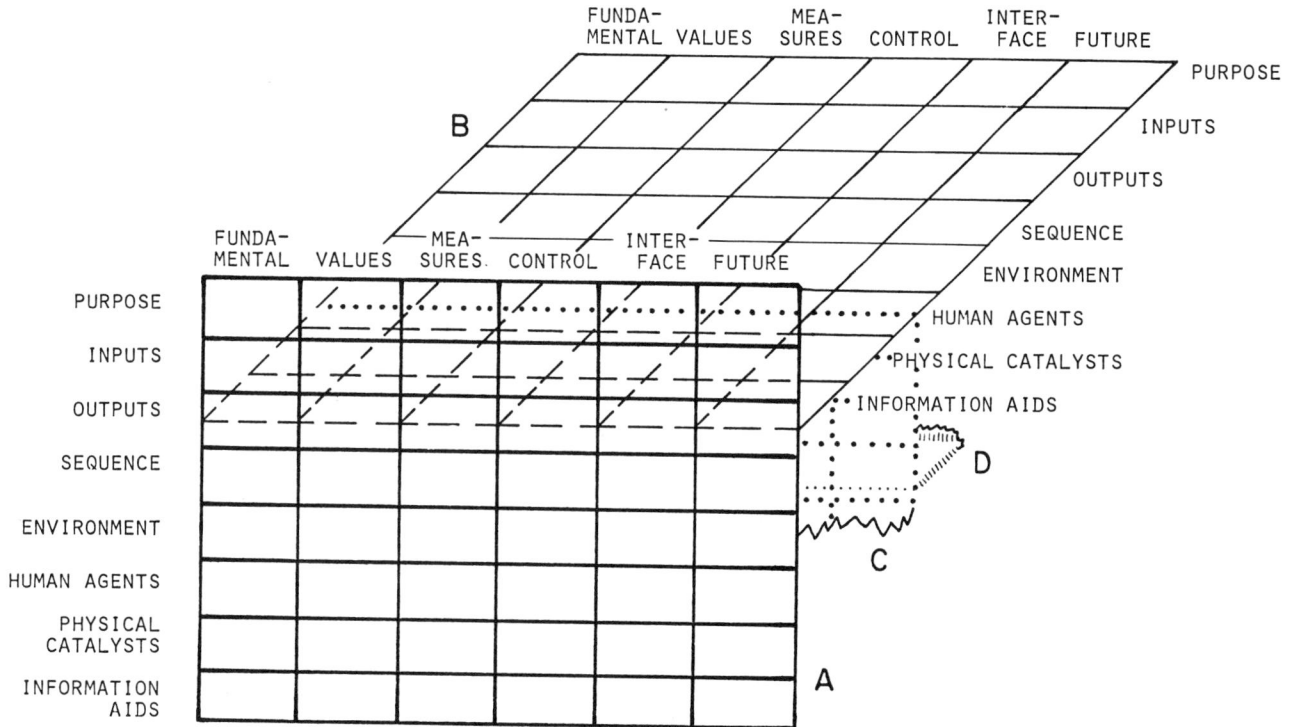

Figure 9-5 A system view of each element.

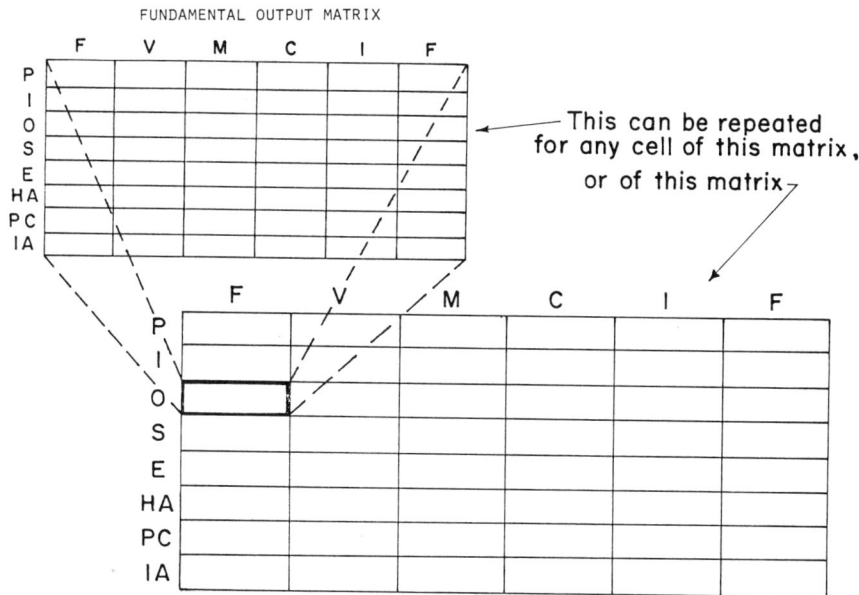

Figure 9-6 A system view of each system matrix cell.

a planning system matrix A. C and D illustrate this corollary further. Or consider a matrix behind the control dimension. Such a control system view illustrates how evaluation and control systems are secondary to a primary system.

A system view of an element could be continued ad infinitum, like the picture of a woman on a box of cleanser holding a box of the cleanser with a picture of a woman holding a box of cleanser with a picture of a woman holding a box of cleanser with a picture . . . An actual project illustrates how Figure 9-5 can structure the interrelationships: The national economy of a country is system A, the transportation system would be B behind the sequence element, the highway system C beneath the physical catalyst element of B, a road system D behind the output element of C.

Corollary 8c   *Each cell of a system matrix is a system.*
This combination of Axiom 3 with Axiom 8 and Corollary 8a is illustrated by Figure 9-6.

    Figures 9-5 and 9-6 demonstrate that infinite numbers of system matrices can be conceptually projected "forward" or "backward" in space from any reference system matrix. This is theoretically correct, thus providing "complete" prescriptiveness, universality, and understandability. In practice, only a few (three or so) matrices in one direction or the other are all that are encountered. These figures provide operational methods, however, for a project of any complexity to consider simultaneous P&D of interdependent units as a means of avoiding the weak links in the whole system.

SUMMARY

Three criteria—prescriptiveness, universality, understandability—guide the sorting process among the very large number of definitions of the word "system." The synthesis of the various perspectives in terms of the criteria leads to this axiom and its corollaries, which fit within the system context of Chapter Seven.

Axiom 8   *A system processes inputs into outputs that achieve and satisfy a purpose or purposes through the use of human, physical and information resources in a sociological and physical environment.*

Corollary 8a   *Each element can be specified or detailed in terms of dimensions, properties, or attributes.*

Corollary 8b   *Each element and dimension of a system is a system.*

Corollary 8c   *Each cell of a system matrix is a system.*

CHAPTER TEN

P&D Propositions

This chapter builds on the definition of *problem,* human purposeful activities and realities, and axioms and corollaries to explain a basic reference structure for a specific P&D approach (PDA). Establishing a clear, precise, and relatively formal set of propositions as the reference structure improves the likelihood of best satisfying the criteria for a good approach (Chapters Three and Five). Not everyone will agree to the truth of these propositions. It is hoped that their meaning will be understood as a basis for investigating the resulting approach.

The theory of P&D set forth in Parts One and Two, including these propositions, moves educational and professional endeavors closer to a desired structure of planning and design sciences. A P&D science would enable professionals and others to use most effectively the fields of natural and social sciences, each with its own structured formalities of knowledge and inferences. A P&D professional can thus be much more effective than at present as a facilitator of change in any organizational context or public arena.

Another benefit of a complete theory of P&D is the base it provides for developing operational principles and ground rules to serve as continual mental stimulators throughout all P&D efforts. Such a set of P&D principles is presented at the end of this chapter.

These propositions, in effect, are the link between the "P&D science" of Parts One and Two and the operational methods of Part Three. They address how P&D ought to be considered so that, when P&D is in action in the real world, the objectives of P&D can more effectively be attained.

Proposition 1 *P&D efforts take place along a timeline parallel with the real-world entity in which the problem or need emerges.* Figure 10-1 builds on Figure 6-2 to start what will become the PDA scenario depicting a flexible and synergistic flow of holistic actions and behavior. The overall timeline is at the far left. Next is the client's or organization's day-to-day or "real" world (including the larger organization, community, markets, and constituencies) as it continues to operate over time. An individual doing personal P&D can also be the client or reality (domestic, parental, professional, etc.). The individual, like a client or organization, has other purposeful activities going on throughout and beyond the P&D effort. The client or organization, however large or small, is the source of decisions regarding acceptance and implementation of the solution. Human and organizational realities (Chapter Five) also emphasize that, even though they must be justified by bringing benefits to the organization, decisions are made by humans who consider benefits to themselves! Thus, *each project is a unique application* for the situation-specific conditions, although the P&D scenario generally describes what is to be done in all cases.

Of course, a problem seldom appears as suddenly as the dot indicated by "1" would imply, except for the date for reinitiating cyclical P&D. Any decision at one point is necessarily tied to many past events and present levels of consciousness. Some dissatisfactions, desires, poor performances, or uncertainties usually build up to the point where the client (a group or person who can take action on recommendations)

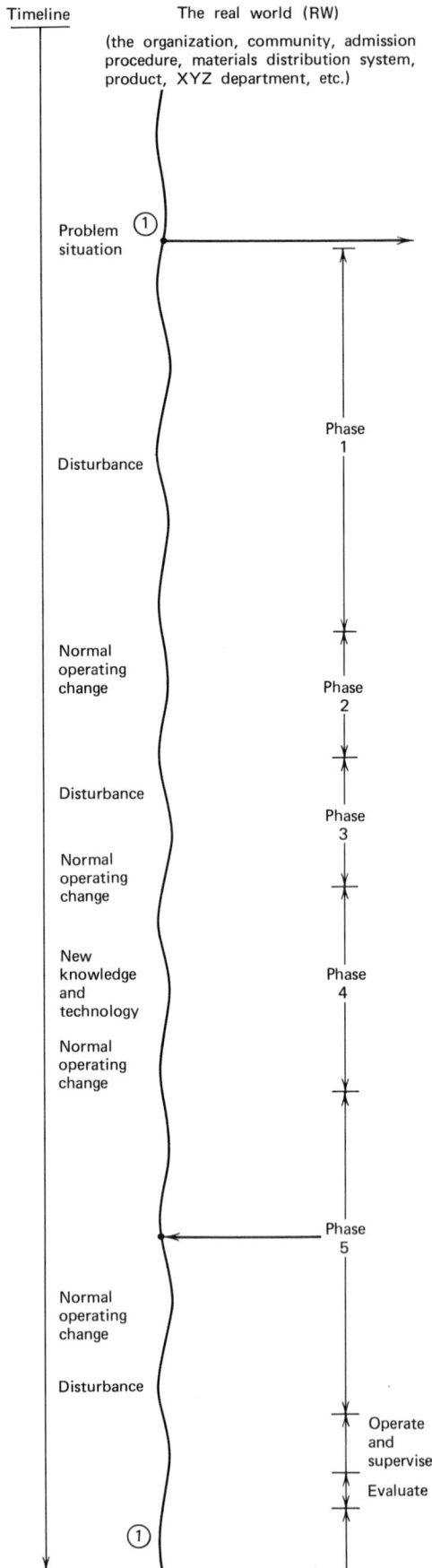

Timeline   The real world (RW)

(the organization, community, admission procedure, materials distribution system, product, XYZ department, etc.)

Problem situation ①

Disturbance

Phase 1

Normal operating change

Phase 2

Disturbance

Phase 3

Normal operating change

New knowledge and technology

Phase 4

Normal operating change

Phase 5

Normal operating change

Disturbance

Operate and supervise

Evaluate

①

decides something needs to be done to create or restructure a situation-specific solution. A "presort" usually takes place to ascertain if the noncyclical problem is really P&D, or if another purposeful activity may be involved for which another timeline scenario should be used (Chapter Three).

The *conventional* P&D scenario takes the problem or cyclical update into the P&D world to be worked on by some process phases (five are shown in Figure 10-1). The P&D experts collect large amounts of data with which to work as they design in isolation from the client. Contact with the client and other people occurs on a discrete, disjointed, out of context basis, occasionally related to data needs. Get the sales statistics! Fit the situation into a taxonomy! Determine the number of abandoned houses! Clients almost immediately develop defenses and skepticism about the efforts which often leads them to provide biased or tainted data they feel puts them in a favorable light. As P&D goes on, the P&D world gets a firmer commitment to its perceptions and assumptions regarding the client's decision to engage in P&D. But later perceptions are usually different than those the P&D expert had at the start. The P&D experts begin to develop "innovative" solutions as their perspective, assumptions, and knowledge begin to diverge from those of the client.

Corollary Proposition 1a *The real-world entity changes along the timeline and is thus different at various points in time after the parallel P&D effort begins.* The client's perceptions, priorities, and understanding of the problem start to change almost immediately after the P&D effort begins. The influences which cause this are noted in Figure 10-1 as "disturbance," "normal operating change," or "new knowledge and technology." The problem itself may be changing, or its importance may diminish or increase, or other entities may "move" unpredictably. Most of these changes initially are imperceptible, but they still alter the individuals' awareness of the organization or community. As more changes occur, the client's world itself becomes different, and the perception of a project's scope and context can be dramatically modified.

The P&D world then "presents" the recommended solution to the client or organization (near the end of Phase 4 or start of Phase 5). At this point many P&D solutions fail. The P&D and the client worlds each have greatly modified their perceptions of the problem, but almost inevitably in different directions. The "problem" has not stayed fixed. The client so often

Figure 10-1 The planning and design scenario—first perspective.

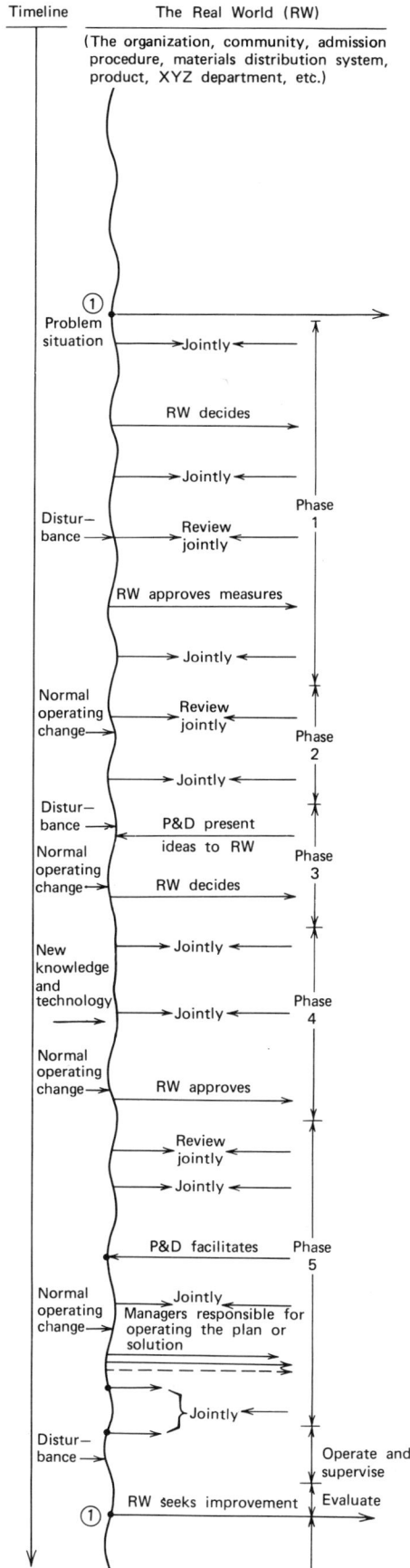

Timeline	The Real World (RW)	
	(The organization, community, admission procedure, materials distribution system, product, XYZ department, etc.)	
① Problem situation	→Jointly←	
	RW decides	
	→Jointly←	
Disturbance →	Review jointly ←	Phase 1
	RW approves measures	
	→Jointly←	
Normal operating change →	Review jointly	Phase 2
	→Jointly←	
Disturbance →	P&D present ideas to RW	Phase 3
Normal operating change →	RW decides	
	→Jointly←	
New knowledge and technology →	→Jointly←	Phase 4
	→Jointly←	
Normal operating change →	RW approves	
	Review jointly	
	→Jointly←	
	P&D facilitates	Phase 5
Normal operating change →	Jointly / Managers responsible for operating the plan or solution	
	}Jointly←	
Disturbance →		Operate and supervise
①	RW seeks improvement	Evaluate

Figure 10-2 The planning and design scenario—second perspective.

rejects what the P&D professionals propose because the premises underlying how each views the proposal at that point are just too divergent. The solution finally adopted, if any, is far too often a compromise that neither side particularly likes. Lack of creativity, unachieved purposes, defensiveness, unmet or barely met objectives, hostility, and unneeded procedures often characterize the results.

Although this scenario appears to apply to large projects, similar changes in perception occur with conventional P&D on "small" projects. The reasons for major differences in perspective also explain why an attempt to transfer or adapt a solution from one situation to another needs a great deal of caution if the far too frequent failures are to be avoided. No two situations are really alike (Axiom 7).

Corollary Proposition 1b *P&D must adapt to and provide opportunities for real-world consideration of various process steps and appropriate interim and recommended solutions.* Figure 10-2 portrays the frequent interactions needed between the client and P&D worlds at every step and phase. Each world keeps "testing" ideas, measures, objectives, and expectations by these jointly related exchanges. Organizational, technological, political, and group learning is thus a continuing content- and methods-rich process for both. Such interactions are needed even if a project team includes people from the client world. The latter quickly become "P&D" people as the project proceeds to modify their perceptions with a P&D orientation. Thus, there is a continuing need to keep the perspectives of both worlds in contact almost up to the immediate moment. The major responsibility for continually seeking interaction falls to the P&D professionals. "Interpersonal influences may be the major factor shaping beliefs and behavior."[1] Both sides are reflecting "future responsive societal learning"[2] in the very broadest sense. A continuing opportunity to keep changing the perspectives of both real-world and P&D people exists because of several features. These include real-world involvement in decisions that guide P&D, joint activities to review P&D steps before proceeding to the next one, communications to keep P&D informed of real-world disturbances and normal operating changes, and P&D information sharing to keep the real-world people abreast of new technology and knowledge. This also helps to schedule milestones or major events as a means of ensuring that decisions are made in a timely fashion to fit real-world needs.

These ideas are summarized by the old professional

dictum for successful implementation of change: "Get in bed with the manager" (or the real world, in PDA terms).

Sharing perceptions and developing understanding are greatly aided if the project is guided by a more effective P&D strategy or pattern of thought than is generally followed (Chapter Five). Such a strategy as currently developed is portrayed in Figure 10-3. Its process essentially deals with purposes, the most effective solution or target for achieving the "regular" conditions of the selected needed purpose, and then a recommended solution for implementation that stays as close as possible to the target while incorporating the exceptions. The iterative and flexible nature of an actual effort are not shown. Iteration is needed because, as time goes along, the P&D effort may at the *then* current levels of perception, have to repeat phases or steps appearing earlier in the strategy. Flexibility is needed because a project may develop ideas at "7," say, before measures of effectiveness at "5."

The reasoning process of the PDA strategy is summarized by the phases on Figure 10-3:

1 Develop a purpose hierarchy (an array from small to large wherein each larger purpose describes the purpose of its predecessor) from which is selected the purpose(s) the solution should achieve. Measures of effectiveness incorporating the outcome expectations of the client, so that successful achievement of the purpose can later be assessed, are identified for the *selected* level.

2 Generate ideas, it is hoped creative and ideal ones, that might achieve the selected and bigger purposes in the hierarchy.

3 Group and shape the ideas into major alternatives, from which a feasible ideal solution target is selected. An ideal solution target or "blueprint" considers only the regularity conditions (factors that occur with the greatest frequency or are considered most important).

4 Detail the workable solution or policy that incorporates all necessary irregularities and exceptions, while staying as close as possible to the target.

5 Implement the workable solution, while using purposes and the target as guides for all the minor decisions needed during implementation and in creating a continuing change and improvement attitude.

These same strategy ideas are also used to develop the P&D system or planning structure (2 on Figure 10-3), which carries out work on the project. This step also establishes, especially for complex projects, an overall protocol of P&D project stages (needs assessment, feasibility study, preliminary design) and adjustments of the strategy to fit each stage of the protocol (e.g., develop ideal alternatives before finishing purposes, do several steps concurrently with different groups rather than sequentially). Step 2 is one of the major keys to developing and implementing successful P&D solutions.

Corollary Proposition 1c   P&D includes the incorporation of proposed plans and designs into operating activities. Plans and designs, by themselves, are insufficient as P&D outcomes.   Usual P&D outcomes, such as drawings for a building, flow diagrams for an information system, counseling plan of action for an individual, proposed legislation, layouts for a factory, and a systems model for national pest management, are far from the end point of P&D. These are only snapshots of a desired future (Chapter Six). To translate such proposals into action, the P&D world must follow through to the building itself actually built, the information system operating, the individual person taking steps to change or to move toward implementation, the law in operation, the factory operating effectively, and a coordinator of the national pest management system in place.

Successful change requires people at all levels to modify their actions and behavior, whether a small or large amount, from what existed at the start of the project. The interactions with P&D over time significantly increase the probability that the real-world commitment will lead to successful use of the solution. Implementation involves changing the behavior of real-world people from the state of their initially perceived need through approval, installation, and use of a solution to a state of continuing search for its improvement.

Figure 10-4 completes the P&D scenario to show how the unpredictability of installation and use can be greatly reduced and the process of implementation greatly enhanced. Figure 10-4 illustrates how all five factors or features of P&D (Chapter Three) fit a configuration that emphasizes that all are an integrated whole at each point in time. At each step in the P&D strategy P&D personnel consider and incorporate the needed portions of all factors at that point in time, rather than occasionally thinking, "We ought to get some people involved" or "We should use systems thinking." Setting up measures of effectiveness ("5" in the strategy, Figure 10-4), for example, is done by incorporating pertinent values, measures and control dimensions of concern into the framework for *specifying and presenting the solution;* by *involving concerned people* who are part of the real world by

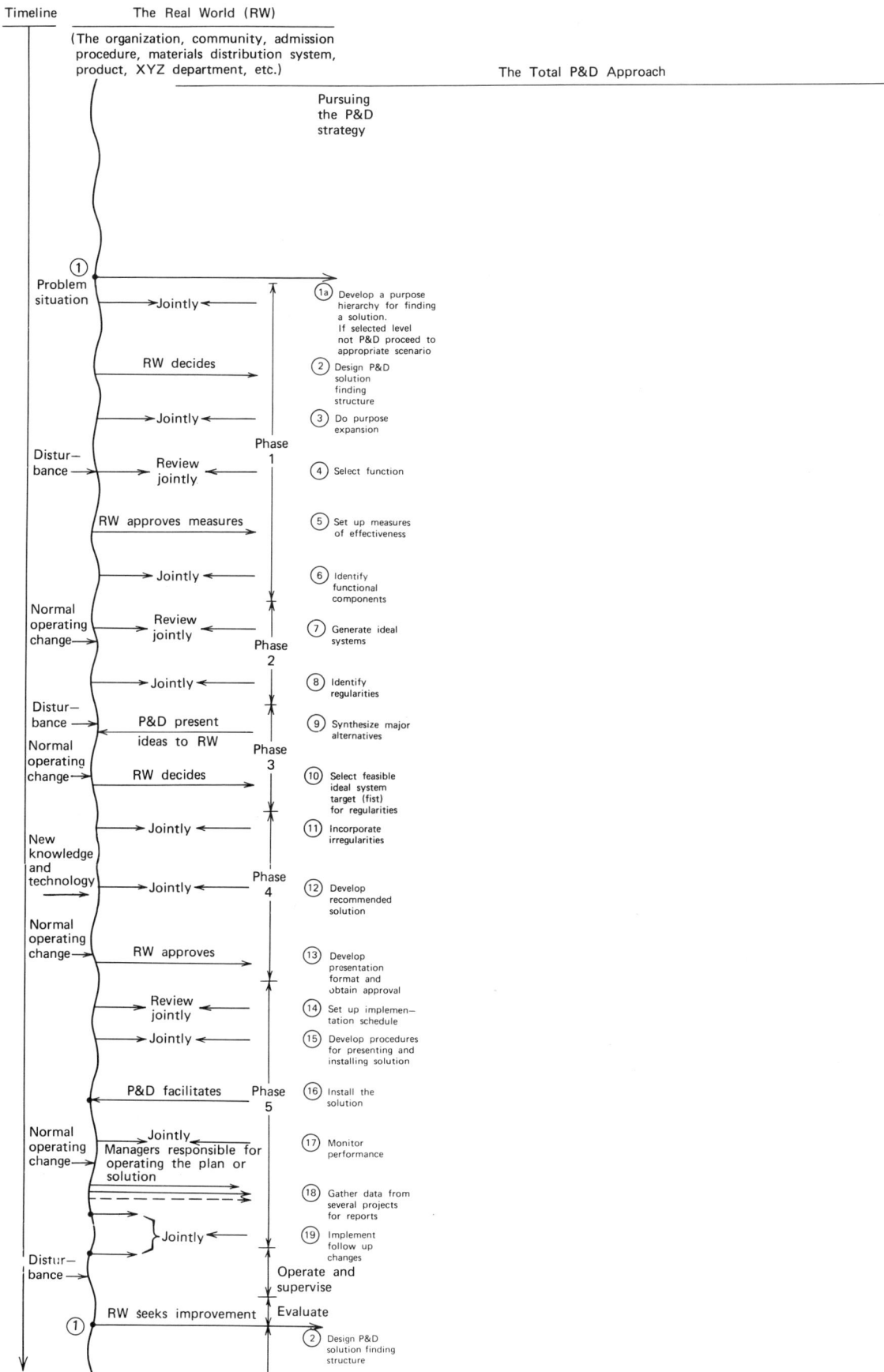

Figure 10-3 The planning and design scenario—third perspective.

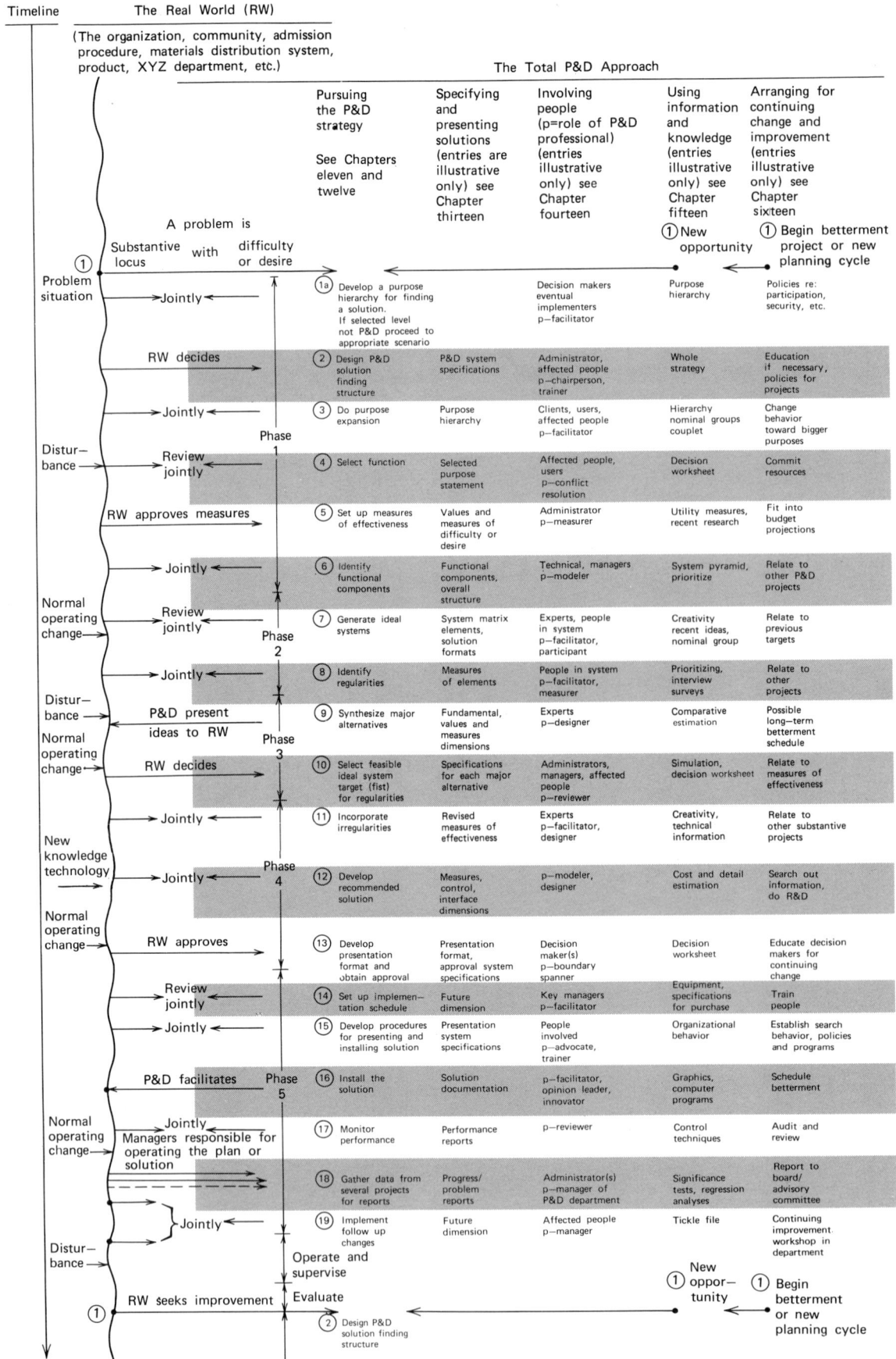

Figure 10-4 The planning and design scenario—complete.

The Real World (RW) (The organization, community, admission procedure, materials distribution system, product, XYZ department, etc.)

The Total P&D Approach

Top-right entries:
- Using information and knowledge: ① New opportunity
- Arranging for continuing change and improvement: ① Begin betterment project or new planning cycle

A problem is Substantive locus with difficulty or desire

Timeline / RW	Step (Pursuing the P&D strategy — See Chapters eleven and twelve)	Specifying and presenting solutions (entries are illustrative only) see Chapter thirteen	Involving people (p=role of P&D professional) (entries illustrative only) see Chapter fourteen	Using information and knowledge (entries illustrative only) see Chapter fifteen	Arranging for continuing change and improvement (entries illustrative only) see Chapter sixteen
Problem situation — ① / Jointly	1a. Develop a purpose hierarchy for finding a solution. If selected level not P&D proceed to appropriate scenario		Decision makers eventual implementers p–facilitator	Purpose hierarchy	Policies re: participation, security, etc.
RW decides	2. Design P&D solution finding structure	P&D system specifications	Administrator, affected people p–chairperson, trainer	Whole strategy	Education if necessary, policies for projects
Jointly	3. Do purpose expansion	Purpose hierarchy	Clients, users, affected people p–facilitator	Hierarchy nominal groups couplet	Change behavior toward bigger purposes
Disturbance — Review jointly — Phase 1	4. Select function	Selected purpose statement	Affected people, users p–conflict resolution	Decision worksheet	Commit resources
RW approves measures	5. Set up measures of effectiveness	Values and measures of difficulty or desire	Administrator p–measurer	Utility measures, recent research	Fit into budget projections
Jointly	6. Identify functional components	Functional components, overall structure	Technical, managers p–modeler	System pyramid, prioritize	Relate to other P&D projects
Normal operating change — Review jointly — Phase 2	7. Generate ideal systems	System matrix elements, solution formats	Experts, people in system p–facilitator, participant	Creativity recent ideas, nominal group	Relate to previous targets
Jointly	8. Identify regularities	Measures of elements	People in system p–facilitator, measurer	Prioritizing, interview surveys	Relate to other projects
Disturbance — P&D present ideas to RW — Phase 3	9. Synthesize major alternatives	Fundamental, values and measures dimensions	Experts p–designer	Comparative estimation	Possible long–term betterment schedule
Normal operating change — RW decides	10. Select feasible ideal system target (fist) for regularities	Specifications for each major alternative	Administrators, managers, affected people p–reviewer	Simulation, decision worksheet	Relate to measures of effectiveness
Jointly	11. Incorporate irregularities	Revised measures of effectiveness	Experts p–facilitator, designer	Creativity, technical information	Relate to other substantive projects
New knowledge technology — Jointly — Phase 4	12. Develop recommended solution	Measures, control, interface dimensions	p–modeler, designer	Cost and detail estimation	Search out information, do R&D
Normal operating change — RW approves	13. Develop presentation format and obtain approval	Presentation format, approval system specifications	Decision maker(s) p–boundary spanner	Decision worksheet	Educate decision makers for continuing change
Review jointly	14. Set up implementation schedule	Future dimension	Key managers p–facilitator	Equipment, specifications for purchase	Train people
Jointly	15. Develop procedures for presenting and installing solution	Presentation system specifications	People involved p–advocate, trainer	Organizational behavior	Establish search behavior, policies and programs
P&D facilitates — Phase 5	16. Install the solution	Solution documentation	p–facilitator, opinion leader, innovator	Graphics, computer programs	Schedule betterment
Normal operating change — Jointly — Managers responsible for operating the plan or solution	17. Monitor performance	Performance reports	p–reviewer	Control techniques	Audit and review
	18. Gather data from several projects for reports	Progress/problem reports	Administrator(s) p–manager of P&D department	Significance tests, regression analyses	Report to board/advisory committee
Jointly	19. Implement follow up changes	Future dimension	Affected people p–manager	Tickle file	Continuing improvement workshop in department

Operate and supervise

Disturbance — RW seeks improvement — Evaluate — ①

New opportunity ① — Begin betterment or new planning cycle ①

2. Design P&D solution finding structure

Figure 10-4 The planning and design scenario—complete.

means of effective group and individual process techniques within effective meeting or operating conditions that draw on the appropriate role of the P&D professional; by identifying and *using knowledge and information* needed from both the range of P&D techniques and the knowledge base reflective of the particular content area where the P&D is taking place; and by *arranging for continuing change and improvement* in the eventual recommended solution through incorporating now available organization units, policies, and activities.

Figure 10-4 thus illustrates how the process view of implementation starts at the very beginning of a project. Doing this reduces the possibility that an installation could become only a symbolic change rather than an integral part of operating and supervising activities. The P&D scenario portrays the holistic complexity of moving day by day, week by week, and month by month *from the beginning of a project*. The five factors now describing the holism of P&D work together synergistically within the basic timeline premises.

Corollary Proposition 1d *Successful P&D develops supporting links with the real-world entity's valued elements of the past and present.* Even the most radical changes need a strong base of values to "support" the people involved. More frequent and more innovative (radical) changes will occur when people are able to maintain mentally the continuity of their values. Involvement at all points on the timeline then produces behavior that could lead to changes in values that people want. This corollary proposition summarizes what the timeline scenario depends on: The perceptions and understandings of people are the beginning of and the necessary concomitant to all P&D efforts. It also explains again why each project, organization, community, and country is unique: Each has a different background and value set. Efforts at diffusion, for example, of a "good" policy, system, or artifact are likely to be ineffectual unless each site develops its own "solution."

Proposition 2 *P&D is a purposeful activity humans want to engage in.* Each person does seek to better the effectiveness of life, enhance individual human values, and reduce environmental uncertainties. Human behavior results from a "fundamental drive to grow and transform."[3] P&D can improve the quality and quantity of solutions while committing fewer resources to P&D problem solving than would intuitive processes alone to reach comparable results.

P&D is the prime human activity for coping with the uncertainties of the future, and the greater the uncertainty, the greater the need for P&D. Interrelating all the purposeful activities gives P&D a much better opportunity to "actively seek to extend the choices [humans] can make, not to dictate them . . . [P&D] should be premised on those properties of [humans] and their institutions that enable them to actively adapt to their environments."[4]

The approach followed to cope with human and organizational realities must therefore exert a positive influence on the very people who, while wanting the changes P&D brings about, want the P&D world to know that what they, the real-world people, do makes sense to themselves. This helps to explain the need for a holistic approach that changes perceptions and behavior of both worlds. Getting this done is a major reason why all types of approaches (rational, affective, and chance) are incorporated into total P&D scenario.

Because humans want to engage in P&D, P&D professionals will need to play roles in addition to that of expert. No P&D expert can become a real-world person in most projects, and this makes even the most mechanical P&D effort a human and political one. Differences in opinion and concerns must be resolved, and no analytical techniques or models alone can do this. P&D people serve a real world that, in its infinite, transient, changing, affective, and chance circumstances, wants implemented changes.

Proposition 3 *P&D is a system.* Even the loosest, most incomplete, most decentralized, or most unorganized and "irrational" processes for creating or restructuring situation-specific solutions can be labeled a P&D system.

Proposition 4 *P&D is part of at least one hierarchy of purposes.* Because P&D is a human purposeful activity, it is very likely to be part of several other purposes. One should plan a learning effort, or evaluation, and so on. A P&D department in an organization should be involved with every other department, so that each department's purpose hierarchy(ies) would contain P&D. These interrelated purposes illustrate why a semilattice arrangement can describe the several hierarchies involved.

Corollary Proposition 4a *P&D at any level is open and a part of a larger system (division, organization, city company, etc.).* The effect of this corollary is to ensure that P&D objectives of smaller systems are always related to its objectives of larger units. P&D is open because it always seeks to move into new arenas and exchange ideas and effort with others and the environment, while still bringing order to the process of change. It represents crucial effort or energy needed to overcome the entropy or chaos that would otherwise occur (Chapter Seven). Treating P&D as part of larger "life" focuses on guiding the inevitable changes in a healthy way. This creates involvement in and acceptance of change rather than waiting for and then resisting it.

Corollary Proposition 4b *P&D is composed of smaller P&D levels.* Five interpretations, if not more, are possible. The first concerns the scope of P&D. One version identifies levels of components: conceptual or policy, strategic, tactical and operational. Another version lists "operations (forecasting, performance objectives, growth directions), strategic (environmental trends, opportunities, philosophy), development (new projects), and capability (evaluation, future, priorities)."[5] Where a person is located in an organization influences the "words" associated with each level. *Strategic* P&D for a Board of Directors (the means to achieve their selected policies) usually represents *conceptual* P&D for top management. *Strategic* for top management often means *conceptual* for the product design office, for example. A bank teller does *conceptual* planning, which the department head considers *strategic,* the manager *tactical,* and the division management *operational.*

The second interpretation concerns smaller parts of a more formal P&D system—statistical analysis, information processing, duplication services, etc. The third revolves around whatever project teams that may be set up for functional components. The fourth relates to the subdivisions in P&D professional societies and associations, where different techniques/disciplines determine the substructure. The fifth puts P&D responsibility with *every person* on every job (methods of operationalizing this are described in Chapter Sixteen).

Corollary Proposition 4c *P&D parallels other organizational activities and purposes as well as other internal and external P&D.* Also part of the parallelism is the range of interdepartmental and coordinating mechanisms and linkages that keeps the organization in operation, through information exchanges, logistics, decision-making allocation, and the like.

Proposition 5 *P&D as part of its larger system (e.g., in a company) at any point in time can be in one of three conditions of existence—future, satisfactory, or unsatisfactory.* Future existence means no organized, formal, or conscious P&D effort exists. Every time a project is about to be started means that P&D is in the condition of future existence. One can thus seek an "original" design of a P&D system or approach. Satisfactory existence is identified by several mea-

sures (see Axiom 5). This P&D status should be challenged to obtain possible improvements by both a scheduled betterment design as well as continual "normal" changes over time. Unsatisfactory existence occurs when the measures established for P&D effectiveness fall below the minimum desired or threshold levels. Correction design is needed.

These definitions are likely to change. What comprises satisfactory performance today will be different tomorrow. Today's establishment may treat the status quo as satisfactory or as the level of stability. Present-day youth may treat a constant rate of change as stability, while tomorrow's generation may define stability as a constant increasing rate of change.

Corollary Proposition 5a *P&D tends toward unsatisfactory existence.* P&D personnel may perform usual activities (e.g., make a model or forecast sales, manipulate financial ratios, collect traffic data, fill in personal data forms in counseling sessions) regardless of the indications that conditions have changed or new needs have emerged. The activities at one time may have been successful in improving the P&D effort, but even unfavorable measures of the operating systems (e.g., the company, downtown area, high school, hospital) tend to trigger only a response of doing more of the same—more measurements, more accuracy, fine-tuning the mathematical model, more analysis of the problems, more rapid computer processing of data, and so on.

Many measures of real-world systems indicate serious malaise that present P&D efforts are not effectively addressing. Consider the poor condition of societal factors—rates of productivity improvement are nearly zero, energy utilization efficiency is low, rates of technological and product innovations are decreasing, the level of national R&D expenditures per capita is going down, costs per patient day in hospital are very high, capital investment as a percentage of the gross national product is down, the number of product complaints per capita is increasing, achievement levels of high school students are falling, willingness to work overtime to fix a malfunction that shuts down a plant is decreasing, and so on. These certainly indicate that P&D efforts are not very effective in these areas. Negative entropy is needed to overcome this tendency in P&D just as it is needed in any system.

Another reason for frequently reviewing P&D is that people involved in P&D have changes in interest, promotions in the organization, changes from one location to another, or little to contribute after certain phases or stages, all of which minimize their P&D effectiveness. Replanning a P&D effort ought to be scheduled every 8 to 12 months, especially for longer-term P&D projects or P&D systems continually in operation.

Proposition 6 *A planned P&D effort is not the same as effective P&D.* Too often, P&D is portrayed as an activity involving many models, data, or grand structures, thus "showing" others how advanced the field is. This is often a far cry from the needed operational and continuing real world endeavor that produces valuable utilized solutions.

Words are seriously misused in P&D. Many people may well have a reasonable word definition of the objectives and goals of P&D, but they must understand that only what they then *do* is accomplishing the objectives. For example, if an organization needs to increase production in response to increased sales, following up by assigning the words "plant expansion" to the P&D efforts is a serious misrepresentation of the need. If the federal government funds an expanded five-year program to cope with forest pests that defoliate and kill trees, following up by assigning the words "do research and development" to the efforts is a serious misinterpretation of needs and P&D benefits. If a manager assigns a problem to the "appropriate" technique specialist (e.g., measurement, computers), the follow-up should be based on what may be the most important problem rather than on the technique specialty available. Labeling a problem with a solution-type phrase (plant expansion problem, research and development problem) is a manifestation of poor word usage, model substitution, and problem solving on paper rather than real problem solving.

Similarly, inappropriate word usage in P&D can conjure up inappropriate ideas in the minds of people. Saying that P&D has good intentions in doing "fact-finding" or "analyzing the assumptions" or "just trying to be sure you are working on the right problem" is far from sufficient. The phrases give people a poor mental picture of P&D. Such phrases suggest observers watching people, digging through files, interviewing aggressively, gathering intelligence, launching a frontal assault on waste or costs or poor operation, and otherwise exhibiting expert and authoritarian postures. Probably compounding the difficulties is the fact that these mental impressions stem from the military usage of the words planning and design, the first social activity that adopted them. There is a subconscious image of rigidity, structure, order, toughness, control, and even a garrison mentality that emerges when such expressions and metaphors are used.

Various words could be associated with each effective P&D idea. Each organization should agree on its own words to associate with each idea. Even so, effective actions must follow, for agreed-upon words are insufficient.

Proposition 7 *The structure of a P&D effort operating satisfactorily in one setting should not be transferred to another effort or organization.* The second organization should design its own P&D arrangements or system. Openness in seeking creativeness in the second P&D system is preserved this way. If P&D components, structure, models, and techniques found to be necessary are already available in other P&D efforts, they should then be used. A P&D professional should learn about new ideas (both the bad and the good aspects of an idea) as a means of keeping mentally alert for stimulating all P&D efforts. This permits the use of the already invented "wheel" only after making certain it is a "wheel" that is needed. Developing situation-specific P&D arrangements overcomes one of the most ineffective assumptions of conventional approaches: An organizational pattern for P&D efforts that is working well somewhere else (e.g., quality circles, productivity improvement program, corporate planning) can be transferred directly to another organization.[6] Organizations pay a high price for trying to adopt the simple idea of a direct transfer.

Starting a P&D project by immediately designing the P&D structure or system is an excellent way of getting all those involved to establish a common understanding about the project area as well as the operational approach. This helps to establish a consistency of premises within the P&D effort where all will be operating. The time required for the design of the P&D structure will vary according to the previous background of those involved; if many have had P&D experience, less time will be needed. Any P&D effort will evoke complex and not totally predictable behavior. Such conditions can best be handled by designing the P&D project using PDA itself. In addition, designing the P&D arrangements for every project gives the organization the chance to keep abreast of, take advantage of, and adapt to disturbances and normal operating changes. This proposition is so important that Figure 10-4 already shows it as an operating part of the P&D strategy (item 2).

Proposition 8 *A P&D system processes inputs into outputs of implemented plans, designs, or solutions that achieve and satisfy a P&D purpose through the use of human, physical, and information resources in a social and physical environment.* Table 10-1 summarizes in a system matrix format the many ideas that constitute the meanings and theory of P&D. Each cell

Table 10-1 The P&D System Model*†

Element	Dimensions					
	Fundamental	Values	Measures	Control	Interface	Future
Purpose	(1) Hierarchy of P&D functions (part of larger system) Continuum of activities Conceptual, satisfactory, or unsatisfactory existence of PS Functional components of selected PS purpose Example: integrate needs, develop policies, forecast, design, develop backup personnel, establish frame of reference	(2) Satisfy client Enhance P&D profession Motivation for P&D Improve return on investment Increase number of alternatives generated Improve integration of plans, yet encourage unit planning Improve communications Improve capabilities	(3) Measures, goals, objectives of P&D (benefit/cost, internal "profits," number of projects per year, etc.) Complexity levels Time horizon milestones Allocation of money for P&D Political satisfactions	(4) Management and control of purpose (*who* should do it) Stockholder's evaluation Accountability Access delays Recycle projects Questionnaire to ascertain perceived values Factors to determine if project should be stopped	(5) Concurrent PS project purposes Control of related PS Other organizations Other systems in this oganization Time-based changes	(6) Future projects Future functions Betterment of PS purposes and dimensions Coordination of PSs
Inputs	(7) Sources and forecasts of needs, environment, information (cognitive), technology Consumer, user—change attitudes, values (affective) Roles of people involved Stakeholder's interests Categories of info (e.g., historical, extrapolates) Combination human/ information (scenarios, etc.) Forcing conditions (weather, capabilities, food, etc.) Performance evaluation Stimulus to act Competition for sales, finance, labor, etc. Physical (paper, tapes, etc.)	(8) Explore people's assumptions Improve communication among management Increase forecasting accuracy and precision only as needed Involve those who influence implementation Culture base People have abilities Committed sponsor or client Consider ecosystem functioning Keep interest in nonquantitative factors	(9) Priority setting Frequency of information update, sampling Meeting frequency Budget (money) available When involve people Quality of information, uncertainty Certainty, ignorance Market share Cyclical behavior and position Number of people to be "moved" along timeline to implementation Specify accuracy and precision of data about past	(10) Budgetary timing Measures of adequacy of information, criteria to evaluate outputs Replication of information Peer and expert audit Error correction of forecasts and other information (who should do it) Negotiation processes (who) Get backup replacements for people Design control with PDA	(11) New technologies Dual input-human role linkages Impact of laws, politics, economics, etc. Level of commitment to change (degree of dissatisfaction) Previous relationship of people in organization Computer entries	(12) Advance scanning of developing technology Predictions of needs Betterment of information Improved selection of people Futuristic speculations Check obsolescence levels

102

Table 10-1 *(Continued)*

Element	Fundamental	Values	Measures	Control	Interface	Future
			Dimensions			
Outputs	(13) Results (installed plans, policies, designs, systems, etc.) Recommended solutions (missions, requirements, scenarios, program statement, investment scheme, etc.) Documentation of P&D process Arrangement for continuing change Three/five-year target solution Feasible ideal target Supporting documents Characteristics (complexity, technology level, etc.) Attitudes and acceptance of consumers (users) System matrix of recommended solution Commitment to action	(14) Verifiable, reliable Be able to adapt to changing times with long- and medium-range plans Comprehensiveness of plans leading to implementation Resolve conflicts Seek appropriate technologies Effectiveness of solution Effectiveness of PS Timeliness of outputs Appropriateness of technology Potentiality of implementation (people are prepared, clear communications, use ability of people in system) Avoid information overload Avoid unintended outputs	(15) Time deadline(s) of PS Total cost and projection (cash flow, etc.) Contingency level, risks, sensitivities, etc. Criteria to measure effect of solution (values, implementability, behavior, adaptive, satisfice, technological level) Scheduled time to update target and recommended solutions Accuracy and precision of specifications Ecosystem impact Organizational impact (turnover, risks, etc.) PS effectiveness	(16) Evaluation of solution(s) Evaluation of PS objectives (who) Evaluate time delays and cost overruns (who) Include accountability Interviews and questionnaires evaluating outcomes Design control with PDA	(17) Implementation methods (road map) Impact assessment Acceptability among users, citizens, customers, etc. Diffusion of innovations Leadership commitment Interrelationship model (costs, resource availability, return on investment, market share, etc.) Negotiation with external parties Environmental impact	(18) Feasible ideal system target Contemplative ideal system (needing R&D) Financial projections Futures snapshot Betterment schedule
Sequence	(19) Protocol of stages (iterative) Strategy or phases within each stage (iterative) Purpose-design (see Chapter Twelve) Information system Decision making processes (criteria, rules, screening, etc.) Direction of thinking Methods for coping with turbulence Methods of working with operators as solution becomes operational	(20) Communicate with all concerned Schedule effectively to keep meetings as few as possible Provide for catharsis as well as opening up activities Use PS resources and human inputs effectively Practice believing game Do most for regularities	(21) Time over which P&D is to take place (scheduling timeline) Milestones Cost of protocol and strategy (PS and allocation) Effect of strategy (flexibility, participation, minimize errors etc.) Simulation data Lead times for P&D, product or service development, market reaction, etc.	(22) Network of milestones Assess consequences (who) Assess dynamic homeostasis of PS (who do it) Assess flexibility (who) Investigation of delays, interrupts (who) Recycle stages, phases, routines PS management system Questionnaires to determine effectiveness of PS sequence	(23) Joint efforts with other PS Change principles Create negative entropy People in P&D problem area Monitor "uncertainty" conditions (who) Relate to human inputs Computer interaction Organizational attitude toward creativity Organizational decision processes Effective information ties between input and output	(24) P&D in other organizations Timeline schedule for planned betterment Investigate contemplative solutions R and D efforts to improve PS (see Chapter Seventeen)

Table 10-1 *(Continued)*

	Dimensions					
Element	Fundamental	Values	Measures	Control	Interface	Future
Environment	(25) Internal attitudes and physical conditions of PS Internal organizational setting and climate Legitimization External attitudes, politics, uncertainties Labor contracts Group contracts Legislation Judicial decisions Power structure and decision links and rules PS organization structure Federal and state regulations (safety, taxes, pollution, etc.)	(26) Minimize "costs" of nature's services Cooperative premises Try to get others P&D conscious Country or organization culture Be aware of threats to organization Human needs and societal values (Chapter Two) Reward policies	(27) Frequency of PS team meetings Frequency of external environmental update Commitment levels Innovativeness Usual time frame of organization "Strengths" of attitudes Demographics, economics, markets, opinions, etc. Financial condition of organization	(28) Frequency of PS team reviews for Decision Makers, Resource Controllers (who do it) "Impossibility" of control of external Political assessment and delays Evaluate impact of PS on internal environment Check awareness of environment info (who) Regulatory processes	(29) Other organizations in similar fields Bureaucracy (internal and external) Interdisciplinary personnel on PS Negotiation stances Review with every element Foster creativity in protocol and strategy Relate to PS purposes Labor relations Lifestyles	(30) Economic, social, political trends and "natural" switches Search for environmental influences Forecasting updates Coming events of importance
Human Agents	(31) Team membership, leadership, collaboration Support personnel Personality types, education, intelligence, creativity, proactive or reactive, etc. Program/project relevant skills Forecasting personnel needs (role differentiation; measurer, modeller, designer, facilitator, etc.) Team membership	(32) Seek to give P&D skills to real world people Have wide repertory of political skills Ability to motivate others to participate Concern for all four spiral values Job security policies Intelligence, leadership, creativity, propensity for risk, education, etc. Varied backgrounds Update HAs Job satisfaction Relate to political context	(33) Total time involved in/out of meetings Rates of pay Performance measures (number of projects, client and peer reviews, etc.) Adaptability Number of people to be coordinated Collaboration amounts among HAs Number of HAs needed	(34) Motivation Performance review and evaluation (who) Retraining (who) External Self-evaluation Rotation of people to stimulate others Management skills Human resource accounting (who) Human input evaluation	(35) Regular roles of people involved Dual role as inputs Input-sequence related to information systems Job security Audit and review (see Chapter Sixteen) Human input evaluation (with environment and inputs) Computers and information systems Education in and outside the organization	(36) Facilitator, modeler, measurer, etc. States of consciousness Continuing education Real skill improvement
Physical Catalysts	(37) Computers, graphics, storage, etc. Videophones Closed circuit TV Visual aids Physical facilities, direct aids in meetings, etc. (Column E, Table 14-2).	(38) Inexpensive and quick processing Utilize effectively Personal "space" Avoid underestimation of costs	(39) On-line timing capability Costs Maintenance schedule Attitudes toward facilities Cost accounting for payoffs.	(40) Constraints on accessibility Utilization Location of decision making Maintenance schedules (who)	(41) Other systems using resources Computerization while encourage human information Ties with other equipment Social and group techniques to use PC effectively	(42) New computer generations Facilitative information terminals Speech inputs to computers Biochemical memory Holographic filing

Table 10-1 *(Continued)*

Element	Dimensions					
	Fundamental	Values	Measures	Control	Interface	Future
Information Aids	(43) Information coding and systems Programs for computer Configurations of information Operating instructions, criteria, etc., for other cells Simulation languages Technical reports References on disciplines (e.g., handbooks) Books on models, techniques, etc.	(44) Have enough minutes to provide audit trail of P&D Improve decision making techniques Policy on data transformation Confidentiality when needed Avoid loss of data integrity Cope with shifts of usurpation of "power" or information	(45) Frequency of program update Accuracy, precision, accessibility, timeliness, etc. Timeliness Completeness Costs of preparing and maintaining	(46) Audit and review of IS activity (who) Security of information External-internal audits (who) Ability to cope with exceptions "Power" over information control allocated (to whom)	(47) IS developments in other organizations IS developments in other departments of this organization Uncertainty, substitutability, workflow pervasiveness and contingencies Quality of interactions Effect of information is based on user Links with external data sources	(48) Interactive, on-line IS Multiyear projections Protection of human values Technological developments Test if serve purpose New heuristics

* PS = P&D system.

† See Appendix A for list of techniques and models that help abstract and accomplish the function of each cell.

contains P&D concepts, theories, empirical evidence, and limiting conditions. The dividing lines between cells in Table 10-1 are fuzzy, for an aspect, facet, or disciplinary topic in a cell may well be pertinent to one or more others and will appear there as well.

The purpose element, cell (1), does not attempt to state what *the* fundamental function of P&D is. A theory of P&D should provide complete latitude to the specific situation in setting its own purposes. Therefore, all types of functions are possible, including describe, collect, display, project, diversify, coordinate, analyze, acquire, map, train, develop resources, distribute, survey, forecast, simulate, change direction of organization, chart, compare, measure, control, develop target plans, detect, model, integrate, revise, communicate, assess, specify, report, examine, decide, estimate, select, support, index, test, expand, print out, and interface. Developing a hierarchy of purposes is thus crucial for P&D, regardless of where the group or individual starts.

Every P&D system will not require a specification based on each aspect or even each cell. Instead, the terms used in the system matrix are stimuli to be turned into questions or terms of reference for setting up the specific P&D system for, say, orthodontists planning the future of the profession, a nondenominational church designing its purpose and structure, or a corporation setting up a long-range planning program.

The entries in each cell have many more ramifications than can be shown in Table 10-1. Tech-

niques and models are available for each cell to aid in abstracting the aspects or answering the questions and in designing the specific P&D system for a specific situation. Appendix A contains a listing by cell number of the techniques and models in this knowledge and information base in P&D.

A teacher who plans a course for the semester, a husband and wife designing their kitchen layout, and a family planning a vacation could all theoretically develop a P&D system whose output is the course plan, the house layout, or the vacation plan. This is seldom done, nor should it be in most cases, yet the concepts of Table 10-1 and the techniques and models listed by cells in Appendix A can be helpful for the individual in thinking through the P&D approach.

An actual P&D system should use words of the particular field in place of the element and dimension names given here. A corporate planning system needs different words than does a regional mental health planning agency. An architect, for example, changed the "environment" element to "shelter creating conditions, accessibility conditions, and attitudinal conditions." A health-planning agency may change "inputs" into "health conditions, policies and programs, and community/citizen characteristics." The whole P&D system, when in operation, becomes the project management structure.

Corollary Proposition 8a *Each element and dimension of the P&D system can be treated as a system.* This gives special meaning to Figure 9-5. System matrix A there can now be assumed to be the P&D system. Then matrix B represents the solution, plan, design, artificial, or system which the P&D system is expected to develop and implement. Matrices C and D simply illustrate the added detail that might be provided for the various elements of the output matrix B. Additional detail about any P&D system element or dimension could similarly be shown.

Corollary Proposition 8b   Each cell of the P&D system matrix can be treated as a system. Although this proposition is seldom used, it is needed on occasion, for example, in one large product manufacturing system which needed details for the control dimension of outputs.

Corollary 8c   The elements and dimensions of a P&D system are interdependent. A change in one cell can bring about changes in other cells. This interdependency also extends to the cells of the system (solution, plan, etc.) which will be the product or output of P&D (matrix B in Figure 9-5). Identifying the existence of these two systems allows P&D efforts to properly place models and information in one or the other or, in some cases, in both matrices.

The interdependency among cells is so strong in some cases that some relatively common themes seem to tie together several of them in all P&D systems. The theme of evaluation of P&D efforts, for example, portrays the interdependency of most measures and control cells. Other examples include financing and budgeting of P&D efforts, plan documentation and presentation, decision support information systems, technology assessment, group processes, and many others.

SOME INTERPRETATIONS OF THE PROPOSITIONS

The propositions identify a wide variety of desirable attributes of P&D. They provide a significant basis for reducing the complexity image of P&D while synergistically incorporating the range of facets. They provide a complete picture of P&D. They portray how all P&D professions, most of which are listed in Chapter Four, can be similarly described in the terms of a theory of P&D. They portray how all cultures can do P&D more effectively through the timeline scenario. They give a cohesive basis for education in a P&D profession.

Many relatively formal or structured planning and design activities (e.g., corporate planning, engineering design, health planning) are defined in terms of a

theory or two, a technique or model, or a set of numerical values or ratios: Program budgeting, thermodynamic laws, top-down organizational goal setting, computer simulations, financial goals and status, systems analysis and modeling, monthly profit-and-loss statements, forecasting, resource allocation, sectoral development, scenario writing, pro forma quarterly operating statements, and on and on. Almost all are needed on occasion in effective P&D, but each one is obviously not P&D, as defined by these propositions. The economic, analytical, and quantitative aspects are usually overemphasized, turning most models into "toy" perceptions of real problems,[7] so that the right questions, problems, or alternatives are ignored.

Unfortunately, the organizations that most need more "formal" P&D are driven away from it. The heavy emphasis on quantitative techniques, extensive models, exhortations to "write it down," the latest computer technology, and other formal devices are frightening to all but the largest organizations. This also creates conservativism in P&D, a tendency to continue or merely extrapolate from what was done in the past. Suggesting that "formal" P&D ought to become the discipline of policy analysis[8] is supposed to add qualitative, political, creative thinking, futuristic and overall organizational change factors as the basis of considering alternatives. But will a change in name really accomplish anything? If current P&D lacks concern with policies or is concerned only with one alternative will policy analysis reverse this?

It must be admitted that a number of factors also mitigate against ever implementing an effective operational theory of P&D as proposed in this set of propositions (as the Chapter Five realities attest): (a) People consider environmental factors to be so uncertain that they see no short-term let alone long-term advantages to P&D; (b) present activities, if at least moderately successful, are a known source of satisfactions not to be exchanged for the unknown; (c) assuring that the organization (department, unit, division, etc.) remains in existence consumes so much of the effort of its people that they fail to see the advantages of long-term planning; (d) developing solutions as an outcome of P&D requires resources and top level commitment that are often claimed to detract from handling current crises; (e) the philosophy, however flexible, theoretically sound, and comprehensive, that supports P&D for an organization or professional practice can never be free of conflict with the numerous mindsets of the individuals involved; (f) the cultural bias against P&D on a scale larger than organizational and community levels is quite extensive; and (g) continual P&D, which good theory and practice show is essential, is difficult

Table 10-2 Principles of P&D

1 Each organization and project is unique. Don't initiate P&D by trying to install a solution from somewhere else. (Strategy, Involving people, Search for change*—1,7)†

2 Think PURPOSE. Think purpose hierarchy. Continually ask "For what purpose/function," or "What is to be accomplished." (Strategy, Solution framework—4,6)

3 Aim toward what the solution would be if you could start fresh, rather than starting with what presently exists. (Strategy, Involving people—4,5,6,7)

4 Develop many alternatives (as ideal as possible) and keep them as options for as long as possible before selecting one. (Strategy, Involving people—2,5)

5 Develop a feasible ideal TARGET for regularities to serve as a guide for continual changes. (Strategy, Involving people, Search for change—5,6,7)

6 Don't worry about everything at once. Treat regularities before irregularities. Separate activities that have different purposes. (Strategy, Involving people, Using knowledge—1,4,7)

7 Treat each problem as a system, regardless of size, including the "problem" of setting up the solution-finding structure. (Solution framework, Using knowledge—3,4,5,8)

8 Gather information only when necessary to answer specific question. Avoid redundancy. (Involving people, Using knowledge—6)

9 Develop solutions that fit users/clients/customers. These are likely to be pluralistic and multichanneled while using appropriate (low, intermediate, high) technology. (Solution framework, Involving people, Using knowledge, Search for change—1)

10 Give affected people the continual OPPORTUNITY to be involved in P&D. (Involving people, Search for change—2)

11 Specify only the minimum number of critical details and controls. Give some flexibility to people operating the system. (Solution framework, Involving people, Using knowledge—2)

12 Set up a schedule for change and improvement when implementing a solution. (Search for change—5,8)

---

* Words in parentheses refer to the factors in the whole P&D approach.
† Numerals in parentheses refer to related axioms and propositions.

for people, even top executives, to appreciate when the pleasures of the first few successfully implemented solutions create the "comfortable shoes one hates to discard." In addition, the process orientation of P&D holds dangers such as difficult communications of policies, hidden agendas, lack of specific early plans people can "attack," lack of definitive or "expert" guidance and objectives, difficulty in educating people about process, and falling into an incrementalist mode without an early "great" target.

Just suggesting these propositions as a better theory of P&D should create more effective P&D efforts everywhere. More people may do P&D if a good premise is established that goes far beyond dealing only with greater data accuracy, precision, modeling capability, quantities of data, and speed of information processing. The value of current techniques and concepts is retained and made more useful because confusion about them is minimized.

The commonly accepted idea that "planning is important, plans are unimportant" is given operational meaning by P&D systems that produce plans as one output. Yet P&D explicitly recognizes that the outputs that really count are *results* in the form of implemented changes and solutions. The ideas within each cell provide insight into the major "levers" that must be manipulated to arrive at changes.

The full background of assumptions, axioms, and propositions can be distilled into some principles or ground rules that a P&D professional should keep in mind when doing P&D. They represent the image that appears best to aim at in dealing with the real world. They are summarized in Table 10-2. Most of them follow directly from the background factors in a total P&D approach (Chapters Three and Five) and the axioms and propositions. These sources are noted in Table 10-2. For example, Principle 2, on purposes and hierarchies, is supported by the idea of different purposeful activities, the need to pursue a strategy, the elements of a system matrix, and Axioms and Propositions 4 (hierarchies) and 6 (meanings and levels of words).

The purpose of Part Three is to demonstrate *how* the principles and the supporting evidence are used in P&D efforts.

SUMMARY

An operational theory of P&D is structured through the propositions that derive from the assumptions set forth in Part I and the axioms. The three major results are the timeline scenario (Figure 10-4), the P&D system matrix representation (Table 10-1) of the structure to be specified for each P&D project and arrangement, and a set of principles that can guide any P&D effort (Table 10-2).

The axioms, propositions, and principles are listed in Chapter One to provide a single reference.

PART THREE

Making the P&D Approach Operational

A theory *of* P&D is now in place. It contains concepts about the nature of problems, human purposeful activities, the assumptions about approaches to solving problems, realities of people, axioms, propositions, and principles. Part Three explicates *how* to do P&D based on this foundation. *How* to do it will introduce many specific techniques and theories *in* P&D, based on the five factors of the total approach: pursuing the P&D strategy, specifying and presenting the solution, involving people, using information and knowledge, and arranging for continual change and improvement.

Developing a situation-specific P&D system is itself a P&D project in which all five features come into play. This iterativeness and pervasiveness of the thinking inherent in the total P&D approach and scenario (Figure 10-4) explain the heavy emphasis the five features and scenario receive in this book. The Chapters in Part Three concern the highly integrated factors of the theory of P&D even though each one addresses separate features of the scenario.

Chapter Eleven concerns the cornerstone of a total approach, pursuing the P&D strategy, or the modus operandi. It provides the direction of action, pattern of thinking, or process for proceeding along the timeline in a P&D effort. The purpose-design orientation copes with the realities of individuals and groups (Chapter Five).

Chapter Twelve provides operational details for extensive use of the strategy. The whole array of protocol stages, phases, and steps are explained to show

how various organizational/community/environmental factors are interrelated synergetically to accomplish the objectives of P&D.

Chapter Thirteen explores various formats in which a recommended solution can be specified and presented as part of the overall drive toward greater assurance of implementation. Although the system matrix is the primary model because of its prescriptiveness and gestalt character, many other forms emerge from it or expand greatly on parts of it. Many names or words are representative of these forms: drawings, contingency plans, five-year corporate plan, master plans, budgets, layouts, policy structure, course outline, funding proposal, and so forth. And all of these may occur with varying time horizons and at all levels: conceptual, strategic, tactical, operational, and project.

Chapter Fourteen sorts out the ramifications of involving various types of people, such as clients, users, customers, leaders, decision makers, influential people, workers, technical experts, managers, and others. Their roles in P&D are reviewed briefly. How such a variety of people can be interrelated with the strategy along the timeline is described in terms of the organizational style, the types of effective individual and group process techniques for involvement, and the conditions under which meetings are held. The many roles of the P&D professional in the total approach are reviewed.

Chapter Fifteen presents some different premises

about using information and knowledge. Three types are identified: information and knowledge *of* P&D, *in* P&D, and *in* the locus content area of the project. Features and characteristics of information and knowledge are described to serve as a basis for understanding how they are transmitted and used in P&D efforts. Factors considered include their structure, stability, incompatibility, indeterminancy, and criteria for utilization. Specifically noted is the idea that tapping the vast knowledge reservoir of people is frequently more beneficial than "hard" data for achieving P&D objectives.

Chapter Sixteen grounds P&D operational concepts in the warp and woof of the organization itself. Arranging for continual change and improvement is presented as a program idea for all purposeful activities, although P&D continues as the focus. A continual *search* for improvement is what is required; change for change's sake is foolish. Several facets of a program that searches for change are management policies to foster interest and locate such a program, education of others in P&D and change ideas, task force or guiding group, type of systems research and exploratory developments, and audit and control mechanisms. Determining the particular specifications for these features in a specific organization is itself a P&D project.

Chapter Seventeen identifies progress to date and benefits that PDA (Planning and Design Approach)

provides for the P&D professions and the individual professional. The impact of these ideas on the problems of P&D (Chapter Four) and the education of P&D professionals is reviewed. Yet the P&D system and timeline approach, to be true to its own assumptions and premises, *must* search continually for change and improvement of the P&D approach. Areas where improvements ought to be sought initially are suggested. Speculations about how PDA might be fruitfully tried for metaproblems are summarized.

Appendix A lists many techniques P&D professionals might use, organized according to the P&D purposes they may accomplish, and by the cells in the P&D system matrix they aid (Table 10-1). References for many techniques are included.

Appendix B presents case histories of PDA in actual projects. The values that pervade all of the operational ideas and methods in Part Three are to achieve greater effectiveness, attain a better quality of life, enhance human dignity, and encourage individual betterment (Figure 2-2). They represent the essence of the democratic society for which P&D is seeking solutions. Democracy does not come "easy—or orderly or cheap or controllable or risk-proof or free."[1] The role of P&D is to help society become a bit easier, more orderly, more worthwhile, more controllable (or at least more capable of directing its future), less risky, and less expensive.

CHAPTER ELEVEN

Pursuing
the P&D Strategy

Proposition 9 *A purpose-design strategy or path of reasoning along a timeline significantly increases the probability of maximizing the effectiveness of a recommended solution, the likelihood of its implementation, and the effectiveness of resources used in the P&D effort.*

The PDA strategy (Figure 11-1) provides the skeleton to which the other four features describing a total approach must fit and adhere. Although each other feature is often discussed without particular attention to strategy, each has less than its potential impact if it is tied to the conventional strategy. For example, the benefits of participation are often negated by an unstructured or conventional strategy because such a strategy generates defensiveness among those involved. Or the power of a systems model is turned inward by a conventional strategy because of its essentially descriptive or reductionist emphasis.

The PDA strategy or modus operandi alone produces significantly better results than the conventional strategy. Research with health planners[1] and architects[2] treating the strategy as an independent variable shows that the purpose-design view produced better results, technically, or produced equally good results in less time. A survey of manufacturing companies also showed that strategies beginning with a purpose or function view produced more economic benefits per program staff person than conventional ones.[3] Even with such results, pursuing the PDA strat-

egy should include the positive perspectives of the other four features. The research results simply indicate that, for those P&D situations where mainly the strategy is needed, significantly better results can be obtained with a purpose-design orientation.

This chapter will review the following points:

1 A broad-gauged direction of thinking for P&D, called the believing game.
2 A five-phase basic strategy pattern of reasoning inherent in purpose design.
3 Developing a multistage protocol wherein the basic strategy pattern is used in each stage.
4 A decision model using a 19-step version of the basic strategy pattern.

These points cover the idea of strategy in increasing detail. Thus, the broad view that starts the presentation of strategy will be sufficient for some fields and projects. Chapter Twelve provides many operational details about the five phases.

A broad modus operandi can quite often help a P&D person more than many strategy details. Very few P&D projects, for example, ever proceed in such a way that all stages, phases, and steps exactly follow the order laid out. Iterations will be needed without knowing exactly what step or phase should be repeated. A P&D strategy is an endless process of approximations. Knowing well the broad direction

111

Timeline

The Real World (RW)

(The organization, community, admission procedure, materials distribution system, product, XYZ department, etc.)

The Total P&D Approach

Pursuing the P&D strategy See Chapters eleven and twelve	Specifying and presenting solutions (entries are illustrative only) see Chapter thirteen	Involving people (p=role of P&D professional) (entries illustrative only) see Chapter fourteen	Using information and knowledge (entries illustrative only) see Chapter fifteen	Arranging for continuing change and improvement (entries illustrative only) see Chapter sixteen

① New opportunity   ① Begin betterment project or new planning cycle

A problem is

① Substantive locus with difficulty or desire

Problem situation

→ Jointly ←   (1a) Develop a purpose hierarchy for finding a solution. If selected level not P&D proceed to appropriate scenario

RW decides   ② Design P&D solution finding structure

→ Jointly ←   ③ Do purpose expansion

Distur-bance   Review jointly   Phase 1   ④ Select function

RW approves measures   ⑤ Set up measures of effectiveness

→ Jointly ←   ⑥ Identify functional components

Normal operating change   Review jointly   Phase 2   ⑦ Generate ideal systems

→ Jointly ←   ⑧ Identify regularities

Distur-bance   P&D present ideas to RW   ⑨ Synthesize major alternatives

Normal operating change   RW decides   Phase 3   ⑩ Select feasible ideal system target (fist) for regularities

New knowledge and technology   → Jointly ←   ⑪ Incorporate irregularities

→ Jointly ←   Phase 4   ⑫ Develop recommended solution

Normal operating change   RW approves   ⑬ Develop presentation format and obtain approval

Review jointly   ⑭ Set up implemen-tation schedule

→ Jointly ←   ⑮ Develop procedures for presenting and installing solution

P&D facilitates   Phase 5   ⑯ Install the solution

Normal operating change   Jointly   ⑰ Monitor performance

Managers responsible for operating the plan or solution   ⑱ Gather data from several projects for reports

→ Jointly ←   ⑲ Implement follow up changes

Distur-bance   Operate and supervise

New opportunity   ① Begin betterment or new planning cycle

① RW seeks improvement   Evaluate

② Design P&D solution finding structure

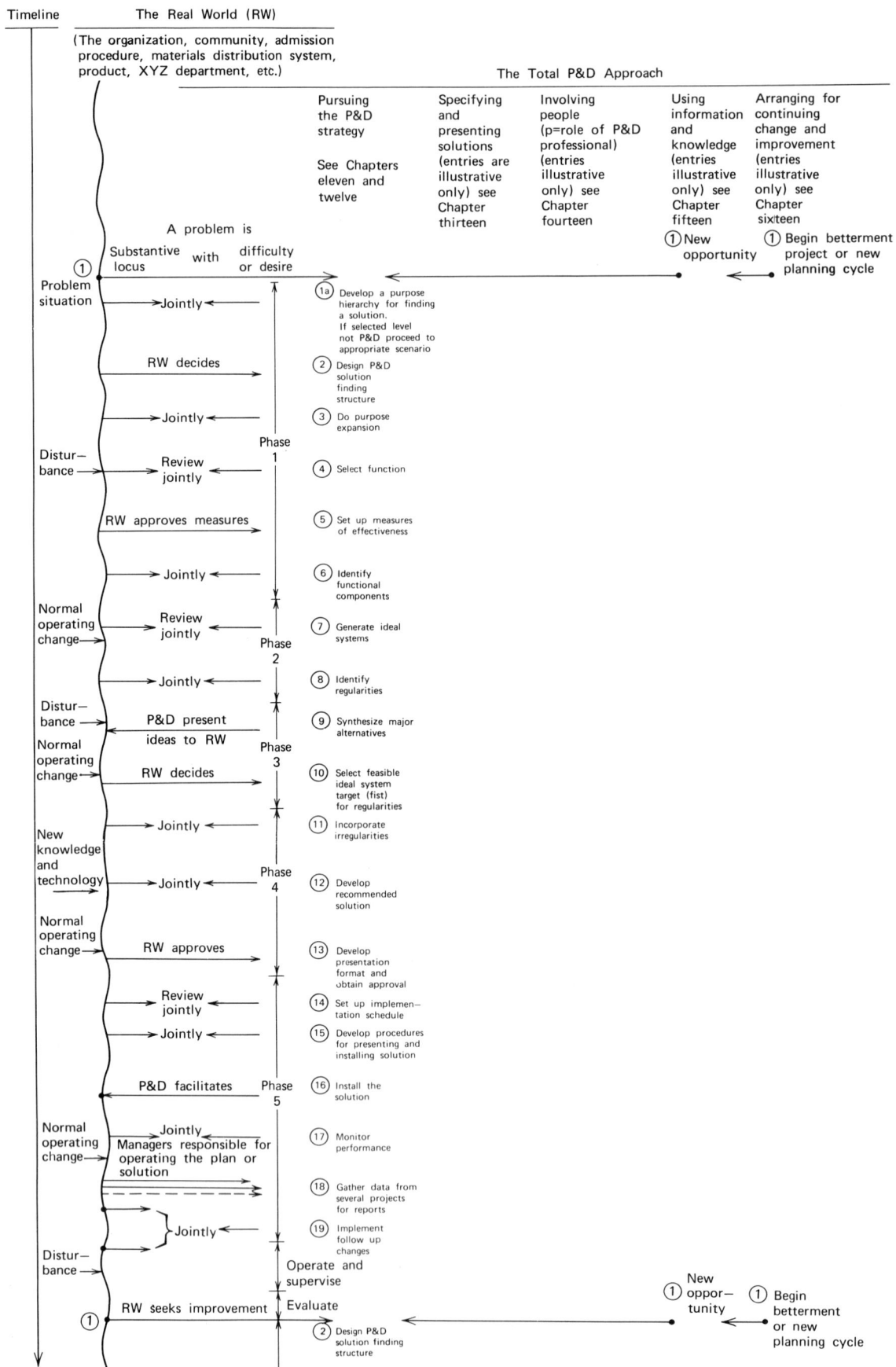

Figure 11-1 The planning and design scenario—feature 1.

112

supplied by the basic strategy pattern can give excellent insight regarding what to do, whereas relying on a dictum that "rule 23 is to be applied after technique M" can be completely inappropriate.

THE BELIEVING GAME DIRECTION

Interaction with real-world people must occur in the PDA scenario, thus identifying a strategy as a dialectical process of posing questions and examining alternative answers in preparation for selecting one that in turn leads to the next question. "Logical" arrangements are supposed to govern a dialectic progression, but what logic or structure or rationality should govern in P&D?

The believing game (Chapter Three) is especially desirable for P&D not only because it provides an effective mode of interacting with real-world groups,

but because . . . it is a way of coming up with right answers. Yet one of the things that must be stressed most as advice for playing the believing game is that you must learn to inhibit your impulse for answers. . . . Trying for an answer is what leads most often to arguments, defensiveness, and possessiveness. ("Did *my* idea or perception turn out to be the right answer?") The itch for closure brings the itch for argument. Playing the believing game means fighting the itch for closure.

In playing, therefore, decide hardheadedly what kind of truth you need and how soon you need it. You'll find that if you answer honestly, you'll need much less than you are in the habit of trying for.

What kind of truth [or solution] do you need? There is a dirtier and a cleaner truth, and the believing game settles much of the time, for the dirtier kind: truth mixed with error. . . . You can benefit from the truth in this mixed dirty bag: if you look at, ponder, and digest all . . . answers—even if you still don't know which is right—you will learn from the right one. . . .

How soon do you need your truth? Many activities . . . could . . . fulfill their goals perfectly if they slow down on generating final answers but speed up the business of making people more perceptive and intelligent. . . . Answers come later: finally comes a reorientation of thinking or perception that makes clear the answer to an issue that was raised much earlier.[4]

Time deadlines are still important. But how one goes about using the amount of time available produces the significant differences in implementable as well as creative answers or solutions. Trying initially *not* to find answers but opening and loosening the setting and exploring what may be very new can be done

regardless of the amount of time available, one hour or one year. Believing that anything is possible is far more likely to produce a breakthrough solution than the doubting or reductionist view.

Nevertheless, the believing game is not played without rules. "The power and fun, . . . the pleasure of a game is in the ritualized process itself, its coherence and structure, rather than in a final goal or content. The release of energy and spirits characteristic of a game also comes from this submission to rules and structure: because one is in a rule-bound structure—because it is not real life—one can let down some of one's guard, and there is a sense of release."[5]

The believing game also has a beneficial impact on coping with individual and group "realities" (Chapter Five):

The believing game . . . is built on the idea that the self cannot be removed: complete objectivity is impossible. Since you can't get away from self-interest, you are given constant practice in trying to get the feel of your own self-interest and to adopt the self-interest of as many other people as possible. Instead of trying to minimize the drawing and estimating models of perception and thinking, the believing game tries to exploit them: you are constantly asked to make the other person's drawing, make the other person's estimate.

The believing game is built on the idea that you can't get away from projection [of yourself to the outside, tending to see things as familiar or not seen at all.] It is the very mechanism for knowing and seeing . . . Dealing with novelty well doesn't mean emptying the mind of past categories—that just makes for stupidity—but rather getting better at building *p*ast categories into new and original arrangements. The believing game is constant practice in getting the mind to see or think what is new, different, alien. The believing game [is] an act of constructing, an act of investment, an act of involvement. . . .

The believing game produces less precision [than the doubting game, but] it does represent a huge advance in precision over undisciplined thinking. And that using the doubting game in the realm where it doesn't work is nothing but undisciplined thinking. . . . The activity of the believing game (trying to share perceptions and experiences) is more likely than the activity of the doubting game (trying to find holes in the other person's view) to keep people willing to talk to each other if the game breaks down.[6]

Playing the believing role about the prospects of purposes and ideal systems, for example, thus provides a likely base for discovering *how* something could work. A comparable perspective is to "be your own enemy, . . . so that the reality of the social system can unfold in a radically different manner. [You can] begin to realize not only what has been left out, but also what the spirit is like. . . . Concentrate on being the political, moral, religious, and aesthetic enemies . . . [to] free [the mind] and explore the larger land of reality."[7]

THE FIVE-PHASE BASIC STRATEGY PATTERN OF REASONING

Grasping the operational capability that the basic purpose-design pattern brings to the believing game can be aided if you follow a case simplified so that only the basic strategy thinking will be dealt with.

Here is the situation:

1 You are the road commissioner for Small County, which matches its name.

2 The position that you now hold is an elected one, by popular vote, every four years.

3 The two main cities in your county are Hubsville and Queen City.

4 The two-lane highway connecting the two main cities is the main county road.

5 The land surrounding and between the two main cities is nominally level—that means practically flat.

6 Obstacle lake, a fairly large and deep body of water, is between the two main cities.

7 The main highway is only half the number of lanes it ought to be to handle the traffic.

8 The main highway is congested with bumper-to-bumper traffic almost all of the time.

9 The campaign promise you made, that just got you elected, was to correct the road situation, at the least possible cost.

10 The road situation is seen in Figure 11-2.

Before illustrating how the PDA strategy would be used, try to think through how you would go about trying to keep your campaign promise (find a solution) in the conventional way. Would you try to measure distances? Or would you just try to draw on Figure 11-2 the lines you think would be the answer? Or draw several sets of lines and experiment with several? Or review carefully with someone else all the facts that are provided? Or ask someone else to help define what additional information you need to collect? Now, back to the case.

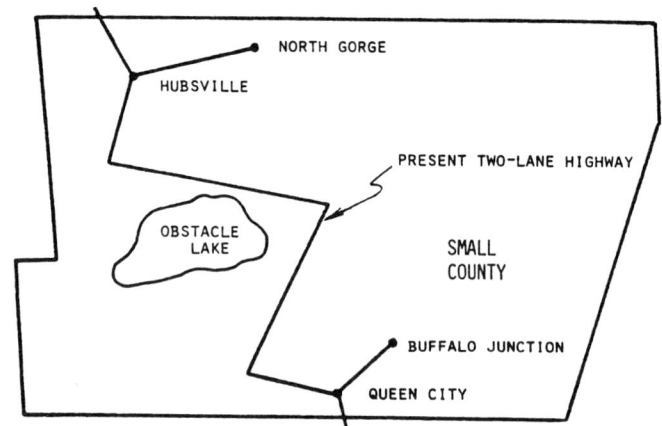

Figure 11-2   Road situation in small county.

First, *determine what ought to be done.*

Q: What are my *values* or motivation?

A: (1) Correct the road situation; (2) do it at the least cost; (3) make it safe.

Q: What project or problem area should I focus on to return the greatest *value*?

A: The main road system between Hubsville and Queen City.

Q: What are the purposes to be achieved with the main road system?

A: Several come to mind—communication link, all-weather surface, more people, and so on.

Q: What is the smallest possible scope of the *purpose* of the main road system?

A: Have an all-weather surface.

Q: What is the purpose of *have an all-weather surface*?

A: Provide a highway.

Q: What is the purpose of *provide a highway*?

A: Have a highway.

Q: What is the purpose of *have a highway*?

A: Permit automobiles and trucks to travel between cities.

Q: What is the purpose of *permit automobiles and trucks to travel between cities*?

A: Allow travel between cities.

Q: What is the purpose of *allow travel between cities*?

A: Facilitate physical movement between cities.

This process would continue beyond this purpose level in practice, but this is far enough for our consideration. The purpose hierarchy developed by answering the questions looks like the following:

To have an all-weather surface

↓

To provide a highway

↓

To have a highway

↓

To permit automobiles and trucks
to travel between cities

↓

To allow travel between cities

↓

To facilitate physical movement
between cities

⋮

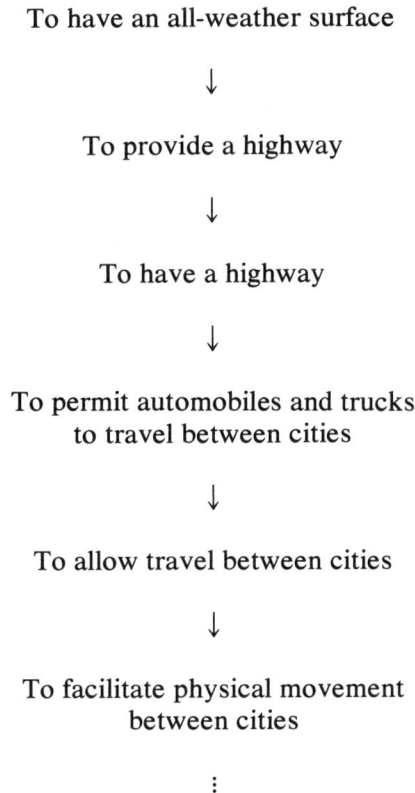

Q: What *level of purpose* should be the focus for which I will develop a solution?

A: Have a highway. (This is totally arbitrary and for this sample project only).

Q: What are the *measures of effectiveness* to determine how well this purpose is achieved?

A: (1) cost of the highway (to be minimized),
   (2) average travel time between Hubsville and Queen City (minimized),
   (3) no slowdowns or delays due to congestion,
   (4) minimum accident/fatality rate, and
   (5) minimum political repercussions.

Phase 1. Determining Purpose That Should Be Achieved   The intent of Phase 1 is to ensure that the P&D efforts seek a solution for the "right" problem, in effect, the right purpose. Rather than just accept the problem as stated, which usually implies technological constraints or a semimandate to adopt what someone *said* was successful in another situation, this phase seeks to enlarge the solution space. This is done by describing several hierarchical levels of ever larger purposes/functions to determine which one should be achieved. The idea of expanding purposes provides a context of functional justification for a problem, a second intent of this phase. It forces continually posing the questions, "What is the purpose of this function,

what does it accomplish?" Manifest purposes expand into latent ones. The hierarchical form of the purposes takes cognizance of the needs and values of the organization, emphasizing that merely stating *a* purpose is insufficient without its relationship to its larger purpose in a hierarchy.

The vital importance of this phase suggests that a wide variety of methods could help it. First, the PDA team or individual could talk with user/client/worker groups to generate a list of perhaps 30 to 50 possible purposes. Several types of questions are fruitful: What need is fulfilled by the system? Who will use the system and for what reason? What mission should the system accomplish? Various techniques (e.g., nominal groups, Delphi procedure, survey questionnaire) are available to stimulate new purpose statements.

Second, start the purpose hierarchy with the most immediate, direct, and unique or smallest-scope function of the problem area as originally presented. If a list of purposes is not developed, start by stating very specifically what the project title means. Expand the first function or statement in small increments into bigger purposes by continually asking what is the purpose of this purpose. Review the statements for a progression of *purposefulness,* not of time or activity. Purpose expansion takes advantage of the opportunity presented by the problem. It helps greatly to eliminate functional fixedness.

Third, establish criteria on the basis of the values and motivations of the organization, for selecting the appropriate purpose level. Some criteria may be potential savings or effectiveness, management desires, project team desires, time limitations, control requirements, and capital limitations. These criteria should reflect why the organization is allocating resources to do the P&D project. A bigger level will tend to be selected if the organization is willing to commit greater resources. The trade-off between bigger and smaller levels involves both pushing for the biggest or most needed level, which may be more extensive and complicated, and formally evaluating all the criteria which may lead to a "safer" or smaller level. The result accomplishes a third intent of this phase: get group agreement and commitment on what the project is to accomplish.

Measures of effectiveness (objectives and goals) for the selected purpose level might now, because of a bigger system level, be significantly different from those originally considered. The importance of those measures becomes apparent when their many uses in the remainder of the strategy are reviewed: (1) idea stimulators in developing broad statements of potential solutions; (2) criteria for selecting the Feasible Ideal

Solution Target (FIST); (3) criteria for selecting the workable, recommended system; and (4) the basis for developing the performance measures for the newly installed operating solution.

Frequent meetings and individual interviews, as indicated in Figure 10-4, should be scheduled with managers, people working with the current system, clients or customers, financial officers, and so on as various parts of this and the remaining phases are thought to be completed. These interchanges are necessary in giving those not on the project team an opportunity to contribute and often "approve" what has been done. The project team can proceed with greater confidence that it is on a track leading to real implementation of significant and innovative changes.

Second, *generate many ideas to achieve the purpose.*

Q: What ideal systems would eliminate the need for the selected level, that is, would achieve a bigger purpose?
A: (1) Piggy-back trucks,
    (2) automated carrier tracks in roadway,
    (3) piggy-back trains.
Q: What are some "best" ways (ideal systems) of achieving the purpose level?
A: (4) A completely *new four-lane* highway in a straight line,
    (5) a new *two-lane* highway in a straight line for one way and *any* existing two-lane highway for the other direction,
    (6) two new lanes, *side by side* with *any* existing two-lane highway,
    (7) require everyone to have four-wheel drive/ dune buggy/land-water vehicle so shoulders on road can be utilized.
Q: What are the *regularity conditions* associated with the purpose?
A: (1) the *area between* Hubsville and Queen City,
    (2) flat land, with *no* obstacles between the cities,
    (3) a highway with two lanes in either direction.

Phase 2. Generate Potential Solution Ideas This phase should free the P&D team or individual of its prejudices and limitations, and should lead toward a desired innovative, yet feasible, solution. This requires that as many creative ideas as possible be developed prior to selecting a solution.

Creativity must sometimes be stimulated in people. Experts are not the only, nor always the best, source of ideas, but they could be involved as stimulators,

detailers, and later evaluators of ideas. Many creativity processes can be used (bisociation, analogies, morphologies, stimulator lists, etc.). Working individually or in groups, people can also create new thoughts by building on the insights provided by the selected and bigger purposes. Ideal systems not tied to achieving needed purposes are almost always useless, and certainly will not facilitate implementation of anything. Sparks of ideas of other people and those that are brought to them help as well, as will concentration on specific elements of a system, such as inputs: How can we ideally combine these two inputs? The measures of effectiveness developed in Phase 1 are also idea stimulators: What is the most ideal way of achieving the selected purpose if only objective n were the measure of effectiveness? What ideal ideas would emerge to accomplish only one regularity condition? What ideal systems for a bigger purpose level would eliminate all or part of the selected function?

The desire is to generate many ideas, not to detail them nor to evaluate or criticize them. Important questions that would have to be answered if an idea were to be used should be noted, but not addressed now.

Regularities are used primarily to help select the target solution. Regularities represent those factors about the selected purpose which are most frequent or important, or "constant" through the time horizon being considered for the purpose. High levels of innovativeness and creativity are possible by developing a target system for regularities. It is very difficult to develop creative ideas that will fit all conditions and factors. People quickly discard ideas that do not "fit" all of them, settling in effect for the worst possible situation as the governing influence in solution finding.

Third, *select a target system for regularities.*

Q: Which of the seven ideas meets best the measures of effectiveness for the regularity conditions?
A: Each idea can be evaluated in terms of each measure (B = best) (as shown at top of page 117).
Q: Is any measure more important than another?
A: Cost would probably govern if other factors in tolerable range.
Q: Which system appears to be a likely target?
A: Idea number 5 should be the target.
Q: Will the target system *work*?
A: Yes, if there is any existing two-lane highway. Since there is, idea 5 will be the target system.

The target system has been defined in Figure 11-3 for the regularity conditions specified.

Idea

Measure	(1) Truck	(2) Road-tracks	(3) Trains	(4) New highway	(5) New two lanes	(6) With old highway	(7) Vehicles
Cost					B+	B	
Travel time				B			
No slow downs		B−	B−	B	B		
Accidents	B	B	B				
Politics					B		

Phase 3. Select a Feasible Ideal Solution Target (FIST) In addition to the selection of the target for regularity conditions, this phase also identifies contemplated but presently infeasible solutions. They are used to stimulate research and development for the period far beyond the time horizon of even the FIST.

The ideas from Phase 2 are reviewed to determine which have potential as a major solution and which are components that may fit into several major solutions. Following this review, more detail is prepared to give each major idea some form, so likely solutions can be evaluated, while an attempt is made to incorporate needed component ideas. This knowledge will allow the ideas to be divided into contemplated and presently feasible systems. Contemplated systems are reviewed with experts to determine eventual feasibility (which may be sooner than the P&D people think) and to set up a continuing change direction for the system. The FIST should be selected from among the feasible solutions for regularity conditions. It represents what we could do if we started all over again for the regularity conditions. It most likely embodies a dominant theme or basic principle or two. The selection is based on the measures of effectiveness developed in Phase 1. They are likely to include cost, reliability, availability, political acceptability, simplicity, and adaptability to future changes.

Fourth, *detail the solution for real life*.

Q: What are the exceptions (*non*regularity conditions)?
A: (1) Obstacle lake,
   (2) New two-lane highway will intersect the existing highway at two points.

Q: How can we incorporate the *Obstacle lake* exception?
A: (1) The target system, but with a *minimal bend* around the lake;
   (2) A smoothly curved two-lane highway, instead of a straight-line highway, to miss the lake;
   (3) A two-lane *bridge* over the lake;
   (4) Drain the lake; and
   (5) Add fill to the lake wide enough for two lanes.

Q: Which one would be the *least cost*?
A: Number 1.

Q: Which one stays *closest to the target*?
A: Number 1.

Q: Will it *work*?
A: Yes, therefore it will be the Obstacle lake solution.

Q: How can we incorporate the *two-point intersection* exception?
A: (1) Have an *overpass/underpass* at each point,
   (2) Have a *traffic light* at each point,
   (3) Have *stop signs* at each point, and
   (4) Arrange routing to eliminate intersections.

Q: Which one stays closest to the target?
A: Number 4.

Q: Will it work?
A: Yes, Figure 11-4 shows the details.

Thus, the target system that suited regularity conditions has been modified to incorporate the exceptions. The recommended solution stays as close as

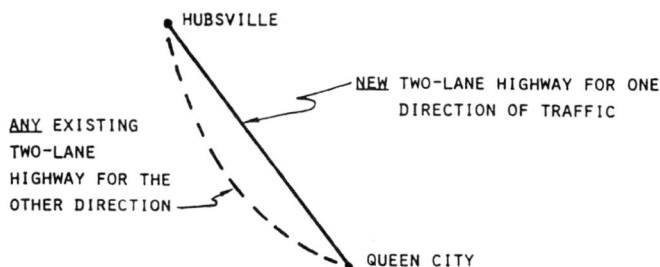

Figure 11-3 The target system for Small County road.

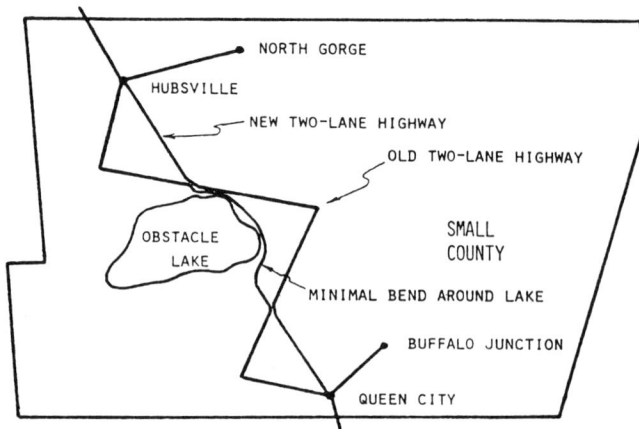

Figure 11-4 New workable system for Small County road.

possible to the target system "way" of having a highway between the two cities.

Phase 4. Develop the Recommended Solution This phase develops a workable solution that stays close to the FIST but incorporates components to handle the necessary exceptions or irregularities. The resulting solution tends to preserve the benefits of the FIST for the regularities while incorporating close to "optimal" components for accommodating the irregularities. Such pluralistic and multichanneled systems do not attempt to force everyone into a single mode of operation.

Several considerations arise in this phase. One is to determine how the irregularities or infrequent demands can be incorporated without drastically altering the target. A simplified application of this same basic strategy pattern is suggested. That is, what is the purpose hierarchy for irregularity *a*? What are some ideal systems? and so forth.

A second consideration is the choice of how and where the FIST is to be modified to cope with the irregularities. An installed solution cannot be all things to all people. If the loss in utility to the primary purposes is greater than the gain for secondary ones, then the modification should not be accepted. It is better, for example, not to include large amounts of data in a computer data base just to satisfy infrequent requests. Adjunct systems, perhaps manual, might better be designed for these secondary requirements. Testing of various ideas is usually done physically, by simulation, through discussions, or using other techniques.

Another consideration often concerns the documentation needed for a solution. Significant detail is needed in some projects so that the various parts of the system can be understood and the workability of the whole can be assured, or to permit bidding to take place. Chapter 13 presents the solution framework as

one proven way of accomplishing these ends. Other projects may only need people's understanding and agreement to proceed.

A fourth important consideration in this phase is to get approval of or agreement to install the recommendation. Applying the basic strategy pattern to the "project" of presenting, getting approval of, or obtaining funding for the recommendation is another illustration of good P&D.

Fifth, *install the workable solution.*

Q: How can I be sure the solution will work?
A: Get independent evaluation, simulate, or otherwise check the details.
Q: What must be done to install the solution?
A: Legal specifications are developed, bids let, contractors hired, and so on.
Q: What follow-up should be arranged?
A: (1) Monitor, install, and actually use, to determine whether performance meets desired measures of effectiveness;
      (2) Schedule review in five years to determine if more of the target system can be installed.

Phase 5. Install the Recommended Solution Nothing in the previous phases *guarantees* that the system will work. Experience alone is insufficient to determine a system's adequacy for achieving the desired purpose, reliability of performance, completeness of specification, and effectiveness and stability in the face of real-life input and operating conditions. The intent of this phase is to intelligently install, adequately measure the performance of, and advisedly plan future changes in the solution.

Testing those specifications, components, or policies that need it is intended to resolve five questions: (a) Will the forms, equipment, and arrangements function as expected? (b) Will irregularities be handled reliably and satisfactorily? (c) Will the output or results satisfactorily meet the needs of the citizen/user/client? (d) Can the human elements needed to operate the system perform satisfactorily? and (e) Will the integrated system do the job as expected under real-life conditions? Answering all these questions is difficult indeed. But these are the types of questions that need to be reviewed in this phase.

The changeover and installation of a solution are P&D projects in themselves, for which the basic strategy pattern can be followed. Training personnel, monitoring installation activities, measuring performances of the newly installed solution, and evaluating whether or not values are being initiated and measures of effectiveness are being met are aspects to include.

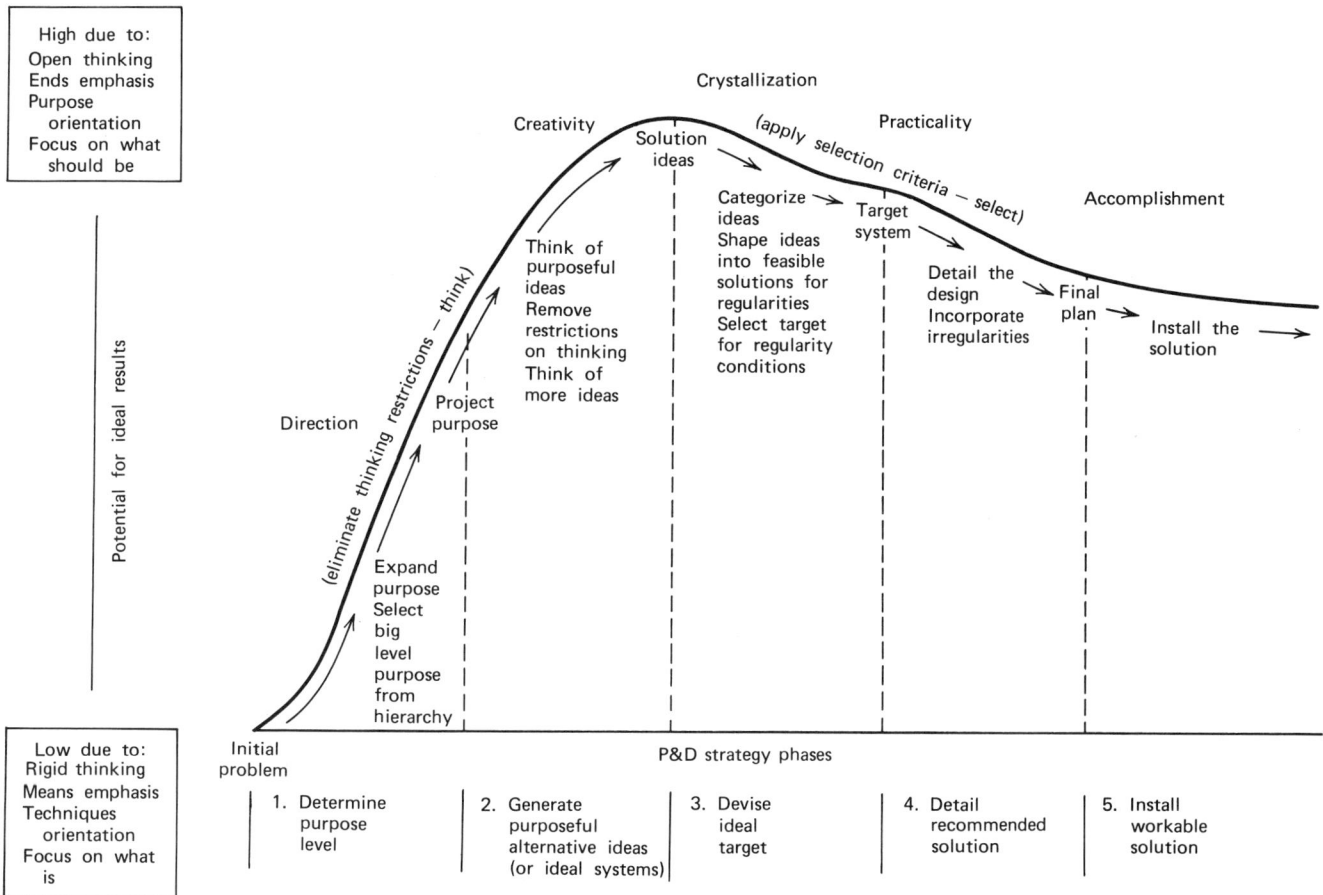

Figure 11-5 Planning and design strategy. Developed by J. C. Thomson, Jr.

Figure 11-5 summarizes the phases of the basic strategy pattern. The abscissa is roughly time-related; real projects require highly variable amounts of time for each phase. (Experience shows 25 to 35% of the time is spent on the first two or three phases and 65 to 75% on the last two or three. Detailing and installation are just more time-consuming.) The curve interrelates the strategy phases, as each one "flows" purposefully to the next. The ordinate reflects the potential for achieving an "ideal" result (creative, great savings, low cost, high level of people commitment, innovative, etc.). The ordinate measures the degree of potential reached for maximizing all the P&D objectives.

In Phase 1, determining the real opportunity offered by a problem involves expanding purposes into a hierarchy, exploring purposeful directions, expanding the solution space, and selecting the biggest purpose/function that the project can seek to achieve. Redefining conceptualizations and transcending current problem formulations are consciously attempted. This process lets beliefs, terms of reference, warrants, and charges to be thoroughly explored to assure the work is proceeding satisfactorily. This is facilitated by

a group. Implementation questions need answering starting in this phase. This phase pushes the project immediately into a level of high potential for ideal results. It is far more likely than conventional strategies to get groups with members in conflict to establish a basic premise through which solutions can be sought jointly. Large systems are handled by developing functional components, each one of which then requires a purpose expansion.

Phase 2 continues this push by utilizing individual and group creativity for what is acknowledged for now to be a needed purpose. As many ideal or "perfect" (in terms of an objective) solutions as possible are developed to widen the choice of alternatives and try to remove any thinking restrictions. The ideas should seek to create a significant difference from current or initially expected levels of performance. If the differential is negligible, the possibilities for action are remote. An ideal solution is a constant guide for continuing change and improvement. This point usually represents the highest potential for ideal results, and the remaining three phases seek to stay as close as possible to this peak.

Phase 3 shapes the ideas into possible major solutions that are developed by playing the believing game: How *can* an idea be made operational? The FIST for regularity conditions, selected at this point, is slightly lower in potential for ideal results because real (regularity) conditions start the crystallization of a possible solution. Yet it represents an excellent blueprint to guide the rest of the project and stimulate future changes even after a solution is installed.

Phase 4 works in the necessary exceptions and irregularities while seeking to maintain the good qualities of the FIST. Why discard the excellent FIST that concerns 60% of the conditions because another 5% cannot fit into it? Conventional approaches would search for one channel or method that would handle both the 60% and the 5%. PDA instead utilizes three or four integrated channels for keeping the recommendation as close as possible to the target for each of the major conditions.

Phase 5 installation keeps the potential for ideal results high by using the purposes, purpose hierarchy, suggestions for ideal solutions, FIST, and regularities in making the many, often minor, decisions that are necessary as a change or installation is under way. Continual interchanges from the start along the timeline between the P&D world and members of the real world make installation a natural action, rather than a sudden change the P&D world imposes. In addition, the information developed through the course of the project lends itself to seeking continuing improvements in and updates of the FIST itself as well as of the installed solution.

Consider, in comparison, how conventional strategies would influence the relationship in Figure 11-5. Gathering data about and analyzing what exists, determining who is at fault, and further probing into the current system greatly restricts or turns negative along the ordinate any chance of a high potential for ideal results. Escaping this trap is almost impossible even with great amounts of effort. Any solution is then usually accepted, an outcome that is hardly conducive to being innovative.

Parenthetically, no amount of recorded information about what the existing system does will ever be equivalent to the knowledge and information base contained in the heads of the people involved (operators, clients, customers, etc., even including prospective users not currently involved). Many strategies *say* that one should be sure the right problem is being worked on without saying how collecting a great deal of data will do this. By using the knowledge of people to develop the purpose hierarchy, generate ideal systems, and so on, the PDA strategy shows *how* this is best accomplished. People will accept changes

they help to generate. This again demonstrates the inextricable intertwining of the five features of a total P&D approach.

The basic pattern of reasoning may, of course, be sufficient in quite a few P&D projects. Several steps within the strategy of Figure 11-1 can be accomplished by the P&D professional alone using the basic pattern. Then, there are some P&D professions that deal with one-on-one problems, where the strategy is the major concern. It is possible to suggest, for example, that individual counseling and/or therapy could follow this basic strategy pattern rather than seek continually to find out what causes the particular behavior. What real evidence is there than one can change a person's behavior once the causes of current behavior are exposed? This is the unstated assumption noted in Chapters Three and Five. What purpose does it serve?

USING THE BASIC PATTERN FOR EACH OF THE MULTISTAGES IN A PROTOCOL

Many P&D problems are, to use the words in Chapter Four, "messes." They involve many hardware/software/people relationships, involve large amounts of time and money, reflect a wide variety of political realities, and so on. Developing a new $120,000,000 medical center or establishing comprehensive forest pest management policies for the northeast quarter of the United States are more complex and involve much more time than counseling a continuing education student. Yet all are P&D problems where the PDA strategy can be used.

The difference in these cases in following the strategy of Figure 11-1 is expressed in the number of iterations or repetitions of the strategy from the start to the completion of the project. Many sequential and parallel repetitions are required for the two "wicked messes" noted above, whereas following the strategy one time usually suffices for the counseling. Also, for comparable projects more repetitions are usually required in not-for-profit organizations than in for-profit organizations. New stages or strategy repetitions can also be set up on an ad hoc basis when the particular complex project hits a snag, as can so often happen.

The most effective way of coping with complex projects, though, is to design a project protocol (milestones, set of stages and levels, work program, and major points for decisions about continuing or stopping the project). This is step 2 in Figure 11-1. The key to doing this step is *plan or design the protocol (in effect, the P&D system) to fit the specific situation.* Proposition 8 is the guide for the P&D system. But most critical is the specific situation—do not adopt the

Table 11-1 Illustrative Protocol Stages
from Various P&D Fields

Engineering Products Needs analysis, feasibility study, preliminary design, detailed design, production, distribution, consumption, and recycling

Education Processes and Packages Awareness of problems and available solutions, commitment to resolving the problem and adopting a solution, changeover process, refinements of solution and implementation, and renewal of commitment to changes

Policy-making Macroplanning Determine level (biosphere, individual resource, regional/composite, localized/individual, impact component), select problem(s), identify knowledge related to problem, develop technical methods, establish political methods, and take action

Systems Engineering Program planning, project planning, system development, production, distribution, consumption, and recycling

Operations Research/Systems Analysis Initial structure of the problem, sensitivity of system objective to subsystem performance, cost effectiveness considerations, and allocation of resources to subsystem activities: three steps in each stage (Do statement, data sources, analytical approach), and four elements in each step (context, cost, absolute effectiveness, and relative effectiveness of sensitivity)

Organizational Planning Policy, strategic, tactical, and operational

Architectural Functional Programming Strategic planning, action planning, project preplanning, select procurement process, project definition, design, detailed construction, contract documents, procurement, construction, space planning and interior design, move in, operation and maintenance, and ongoing evaluation

Multilevel Approach Decompose the problem into subproblems, then into sub-subproblems, and so on; solve the simple problems and recombine into full solution

National Pest Management System (see Appendix B) Plan the P&D system (including the remaining protocol stages) to be put into operation, develop a comprehensive pest management system, plan the approval system, detail design, install recommendations, continuing P&D structured

Planning-Design Continuum Plan long-run direction (coordinative, adaptive, comprehensive) for future needs, propose general action alternatives, design short run specific solutions for current needs, and propose specific time-limited low-risk alternative

Social Systems Design Diagnosis, input analysis and output, implementation, and evaluation

Health planning Needs formulation, project formulation, project proposal, organizing the implementation, control of implementation, and agency(ies) assumption of program

City Planning Plan Preparation Goals; local, regional and national perspectives; alternative futures and review; plan elements; concept sketches and review; priorities for plan components; draft plan and review; sectoral plans; issues and review; master or sketch plan

Medical Procedure or Drug Original idea and modification, knowledge must exist or be developed, funds for experimental work, data to journal, reader response, confirmation, idea enters intellectual sphere of clinicians, initial clinical trial, application to Food and Drug Administration, publication of clinical papers, approval, widespread use, further refinements, public acceptance, continuing search for improvement

stages, levels, or protocols from another project or organizational procedure. Implementation of a solution is especially critical, for the need to change behaviors that will result in adoption must start right at the beginning with the situation-specific people.

On the other hand, there are many protocols and P&D systems that can serve as *examples* of the conceptual arrangements possible when designing the P&D system. Some of the illustrations in Table 11-1 deal with the activity to be performed, some with the nature of the major decision or milestone at each point, others with broad functions, and still others with a combination of all three and even with some of the other purposeful activities (e.g., "production" and "consumption" are operating and supervising functions).

Iteration occurs among the stages and levels in a protocol, just as it does within the steps of the basic strategy pattern. Even if one P&D effort has a protocol similar to another's, each gives stages greater or lesser emphasis and frequency of repetition, and iterates the phases and steps of the basic strategy pattern within a stage quite differently.

Combination protocols and strategies are often portrayed in flow diagrams and information processing models. The P&D timeline scenario is one illustration of this. Other types are path analysis, information process chart, and information resources and handling model. Figure 11-6 shows another version of a P&D approach for manufactured products in a broad information flow format[8] (the box labeled "Design Function" includes no prescriptiveness). Figure 11-6 illustrates the situation that Phase 4 is supposed to achieve: the details of operator instructions, offers to bid, operating specifications, and optimized conditions that relate plant, machines, and humans.

Some protocols and strategies are described to alternate between analysis probing and design synthesis. The initial flow of questions/information is oriented for P&D from design/synthesis to analysis/probing. Information does then flow in the opposite direction when the analysis shows the need for more design. This same initial flow pattern could be said to exist

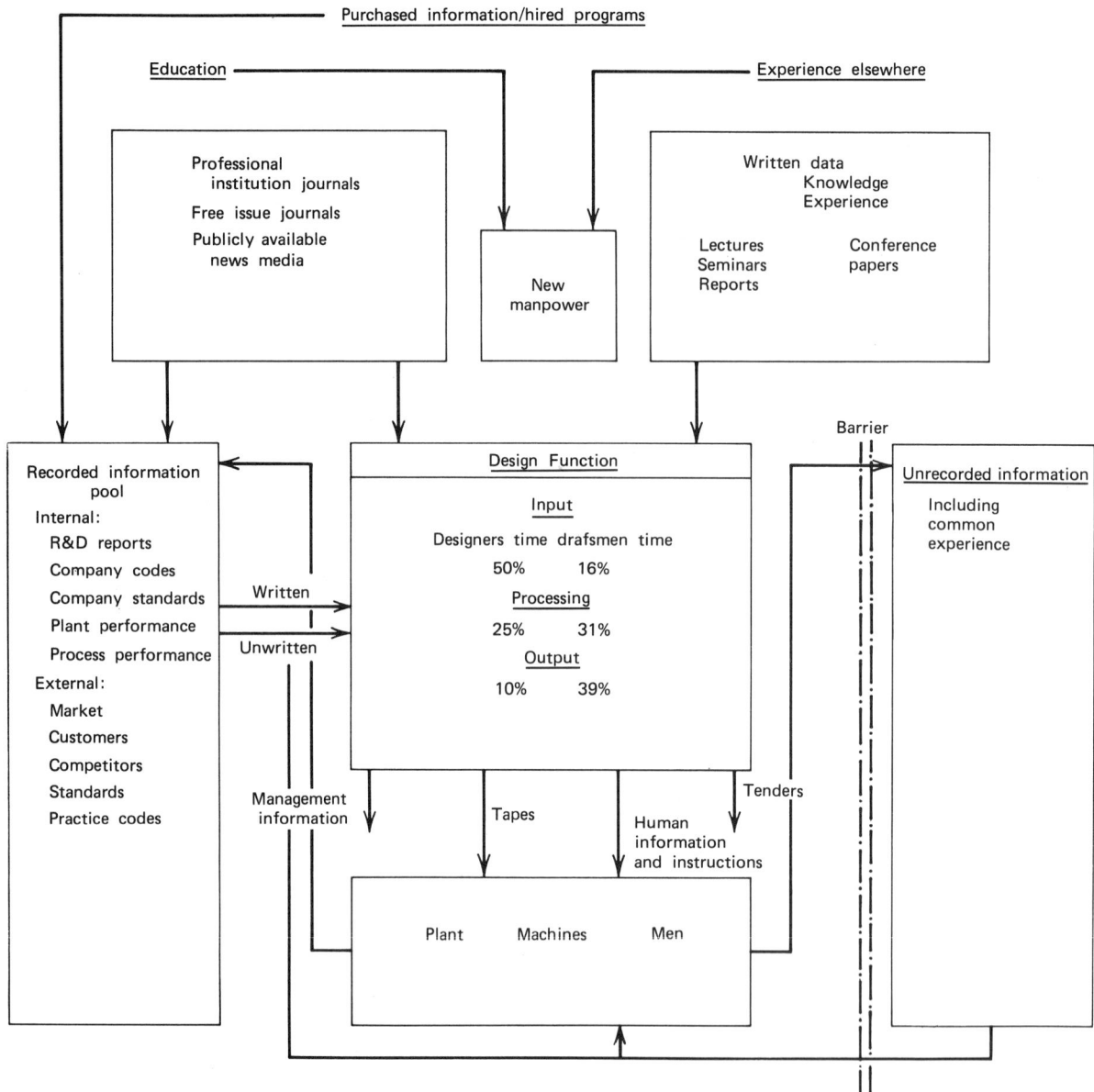

Figure 11-6 Information flows affecting design. In addition to this information, there is a frequently quoted pattern of draftsman time utilization: 35% drawing; 24% away from board; 27% looking up references, reading, clerical; 14% consultation and thought. Reproduced with permission, S. A. Gregory, see footnote 8.

between *create* and *evaluate, ends* and *means, generate alternatives* and *select, designer* and *user,* and even *believing game* and *doubting game.*

Quite critical is *what* each item is concerned with along the timeline: Design and synthesis about *what*? Analysis and probe about *what*? The answers to these questions can be put in the information flow perspective for the basic strategy pattern shown in Figure 11-7.

One of the earliest motivations for developing an information-flow model was to formalize it with an al-

gorithm of bits and "words" for eventual transfer to a computer. By the early 1970s, this "grand vison" of overall computerized schemes "was abandoned because of the impossibility of incorporating the professional reality"[9] of all features into a P&D approach. Many worthwhile computer aids for P&D steps and substeps, however, are described in Chapter Fifteen.

More promising than such models are those dealing with psychological processes, cognitive structuring, and learning. They will probably help in the more minute steps of the strategy (how to transform a list of

Design/synthesis/create
ends/generate alternatives/
designer/believing game
about *what?*

Analysis/adopt/evaluate/
means/select/user/doubting
game to arrive at *what?*

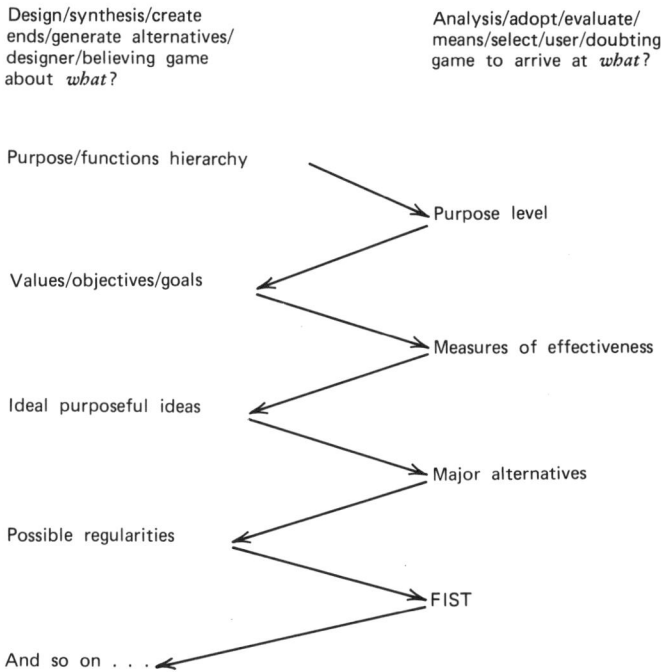

Figure 11-7 Information flow perspective of the basic strategy pattern.

purposes into the initial one starting the hierarchy, how to select the purpose level in the hierarchy).

DECISION MODEL INTEGRATING OTHER STRATEGY VERSIONS

The P&D strategy can be presented as a series of decisions (information flow) that provide additional details about each phase and its steps. A decision-making model is a secondary purposeful activity (Chapter Two) that can now be put into the P&D context.

Decision making is defined in many ways. Some claim it is the whole of problem solving and presents the equivalent of a strategy. Others claim decision making consists of statistical analysis, measurement of costs and benefits, creativity, operations modeling, quantification of subjective judgments and utilities, or participation. All of these ideas are covered at appropriate points in this book. The definition of decision making used here is one of the most frequent: "The theory of decision analysis is designed to help the individual make a choice among a set of *prespecified* alternatives."[10]

A set of *prespecified* alternatives are produced at each step of each strategy phase of each protocol stage. A choice is to be made at each step. This concept is, of course, what leads to the portrayal of the

P&D strategy as a decision model. The selection action itself is aided by many techniques, which are discussed briefly in Chapter Fifteen (also see references in Appendix A).

The definition of decision making addresses two concepts, generating or having alternatives and selecting one. A third idea is necessary to interrelate these two: the organization of the alternatives into usable groupings from which a selection is to be made. Generating alternatives about anything almost always produces helter-skelter ideas, large- and small-scope ideas, some ideas with many unknowns, and other fairly well-detailed ones. Before a choice is made, then, the various ideas need to be organized and shaped into alternative groupings that are somewhat equivalent in detail so that each one can be fairly compared with the others. Just having a list of purposes (generate ideas) is insufficient for deciding what purpose should be achieved (select alternative). Purposes need to be organized and shaped into a hierarchy to display appropriate relationships. Just having a list of ideal system suggestions (generate ideas) is insufficient for deciding which one should be the FIST (select alternative). They need to be organized and shaped into major alternatives to display the merits and "opportunity" of each one.

To put the strategy into a decision-making model thus requires three processes for each step: (1) generate ideas; (2) organize alternatives; and (3) select an alternative. A portrayal of these decision-making processes in relation to the underlying information flow is shown in Figure 11-8. Which particular decision-making task and techniques start the process is, of course, identified by the basic strategy pattern and the steps involved in it.

Thus the steps and phases of the strategy need to be added to Figure 11-8. How many steps to include is not easily answered, for it is possible to continue to subdivide phases into steps, into substeps and so on. A decision is needed at each subdivision but detailing such obscure or minor points in a strategy could cloud the importance of the whole idea. However, a reasonable set of steps in the strategy is shown in Figure 11-1. The nineteen steps there include activities to be performed prior to selection as well as actual decision or selection points. In Figure 11-1, this was done to portray the thought process and direction of reasoning more completely than just selection statements could. Nineteen is not a magical number of steps since, as noted above, there could be 119 or just 9 steps.

Table 11-2 combines the timeline basic strategy pattern and the decision-making process. A particular project will skip some steps, treat others grossly, and

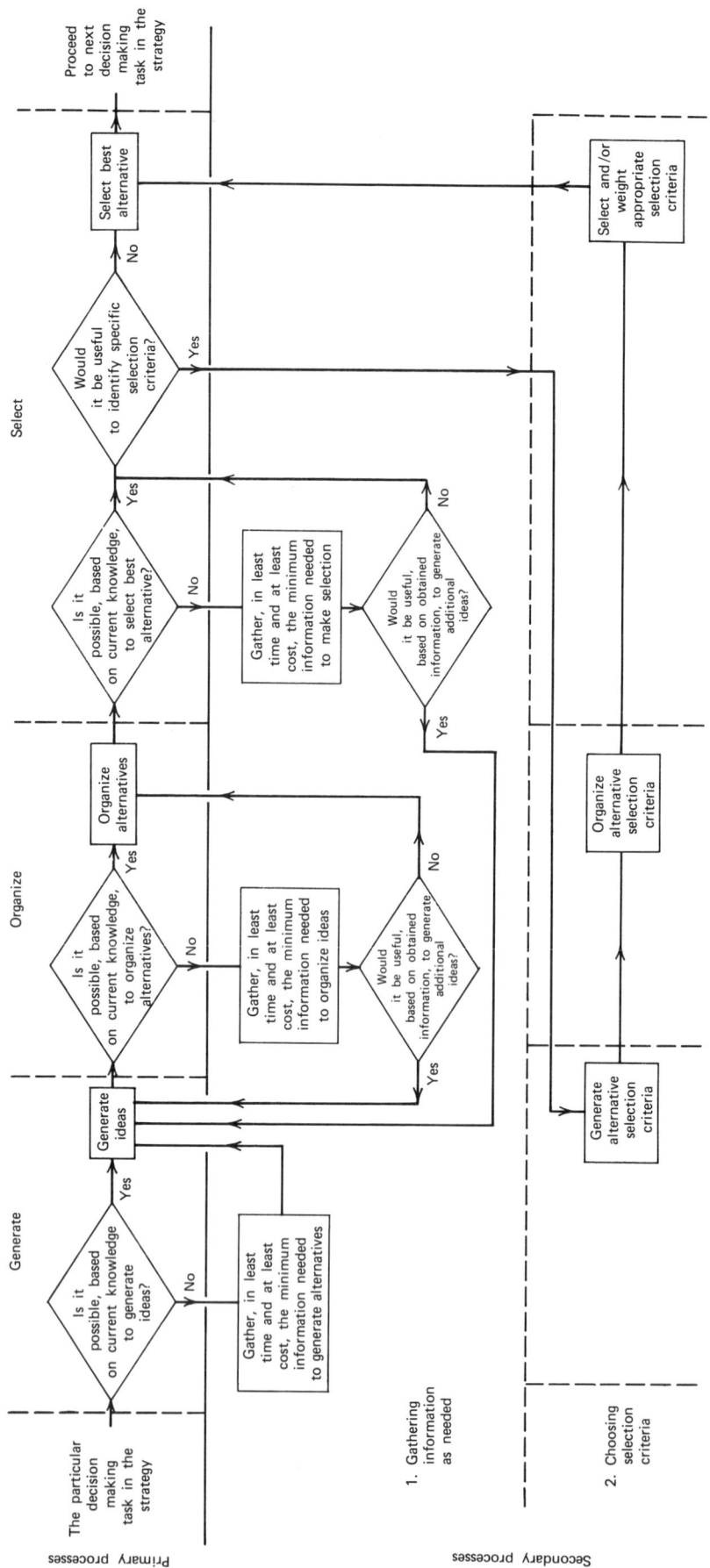

Figure 11-8 Information and decision making processes. Developed by James C. Thomson, Jr.

Table 11-2 Strategy Information Flow and Decision-Making Processes

Illustrative Step Number (Decision-Making Tasks)	Generate ⟵⟶ Ideas about	Organize ⟶ Alternative Groupings of	Select ⟶ "Best" Alternative(s)
1	P&D projects or areas	P&D projects or areas (e.g., noisy, quiet, future)	P&D project or area
2	P&D system structures	P&D system structures (e.g., advisory, task force)	P&D system structure
3	Project protocols	Project protocols (e.g., feasibility, preliminary design, detail design)	Work program, network, P&D stages and milestones
4	Purposes/functions of project topic	Purposes/functions (e.g., pick smallest scope)	Initial purpose/function
5	Purpose/function hierarchies	Purpose/function hierarchies	Purpose hierarchy(ies)
6	Focus purposes	Focus purposes (e.g., criteria to determine likely candidates)	Purpose level
7	Measures of effectiveness	Measures (e.g., values, utilities, preferences)	Set of measures of effectiveness
8	Functional components	Functional trees or system pyramids	Set of functional components (return to step 4 for each functional component)
9	Techniques for stimulating ideal system suggestions	Techniques (e.g., nominal group, stimulator lists)	Creativity techniques
10	Regularity conditions	Regularities (e.g., candidates for various words in the purpose/function level)	Set of regularities
11	Ideal system suggestions	Major ideal system categories (candidates for becoming FIST)	Feasible ideal system target
12	Components for irregularities	Major FIST changes	Set of solutions close to FIST
13	Details for irregularity and exceptions solutions	Components needing detail	Recommended solution
14	Methods for obtaining approval	Methods	Approval system
15	Installation plans and schedules	Installation plans	Installation plans
16	Training and follow-up methods	Methods	Set of training and follow-up specifications
17	Measures of system performance	Measures (relate to step 7)	Set of performance measures system managers can use
18	Reporting methods about meeting expectations on project	Reporting methods	Report method
19	Planned betterment dates and schedules	Betterment dates and schedules	Date and schedule for planned betterment

handle still others in detail. *What* to do *when* is really tied to the timeline scenario (Figure 10-4) that interrelates the strategy with other features and joint activities with real-world people.

SUMMARY

The overall direction of thinking or pattern of reasoning (strategy) that guides the total P&D approach is summarized by Proposition 9.

Proposition 9 *A purpose-design strategy or path of reasoning along a timeline significantly increases the probability of maximizing the effectiveness of a recommended solution, the likelihood of its implementation, and the effectiveness of resources used in the P&D effort.*

P&D projects require a wide variety of specificity regarding the strategy. Several methods of opera-

tionalizing this strategy proposition are presented in ever increasing detail, enabling a P&D professional to select what is appropriate:

1 The assumptions, axioms, and propositions put the reasoning pattern into believing game form.

2 The basic strategy pattern is identified as the following: determine needed purpose, develop many (ideal) ideas or alternatives to achieve the purpose, select a feasible ideal solution target (FIST) for regularity conditions, detail a recommended solution that stays close to the FIST, and install the solution.

3 Most projects will require a series of iterations of the basic strategy pattern for each stage of an overall protocol that can itself be developed by following the basic strategy pattern.

4 Each step (as in Figure 10-4) can be viewed as a decision process of generating alternative ideas for accomplishing the step's purposes, organizing them, and selecting the preferred solution.

CHAPTER TWELVE

Operational Details on Pursuing the P&D Strategy

The details and illustrations in this chapter demonstrate some tools and "tricks" on *how* the PDA strategy is pursued in conjunction with the other features of the total scenario (Figure 10-4). They also show *how* the many descriptions of the P&D process (Table 4-2) are incorporated into the efforts.

Even so, each person doing P&D should probe the purposes of each step to be sure the step is needed in the project. In addition, activities for each step *should* be questioned—ask: Why do it? What ends will I accomplish by doing it? What would I do with that kind of information if I were to have it?

Many techniques and models will be mentioned. For most, only their conceptual essence will be explained. Appendix A provides definitions and references for them.

Each step number does not correspond exactly with those in Figures 10-4 (timeline scenario) or 11-8 (strategy and decision-making process). This chapter concerns operational activities that go beyond the decisions that need to be made. In addition, differences such as these help to show that the strategy should not be considered numerically rigid. Steps may be bypassed, telescoped, or extended. One step does not always follow another in lockstep fashion. It is not too unusual, for example, to find that once a solution-

finding structure (P&D system) is set up, a group starts by developing solutions that might exist (ideal systems) ten years from now if "they could have started all over" (setting up a FIST). They may then return to develop a purpose hierarchy to clarify what purposes the solution ought to achieve. This would also establish the bigger purpose levels as criteria to consider in selecting a target. A strategy is a reminder and merely points out the direction of reasoning along the timeline.

More space is devoted to the initial two or three phases than to the final two. The beginning 25 to 35% of a P&D effort (conceptualization, protocol, etc.) is the most critical in setting the stage for arriving at success. Yet almost all the literature skips over these phases in *operational terms,* which is the focus here. At best, the literature provides exhortations and horror stories about the importance of starting "right." So, even though projects use 65 to 75% of their P&D resources and time on the detailing and installation phases, I will reduce my coverage of them. The usual P&D literature can be used as guidance in these stages because those phases are their major concern anyway. In addition, the last two or three phases become quite technical and locus situation-specific so they could not easily be covered well in a book for all P&D efforts.

Case Histories B9 and B14 in Appendix B are fairly complete reports on the whole strategy, including details about the last two phases.

PHASE 1: DETERMINE NEEDED PURPOSE

A major result of Phase 1 is the identification of the needed purposes for which P&D should seek a solution. This meets the objective of increasing the probability of working on the right problem. Doing very well what ought not to be done at all is obviously undesirable. It is even possible that the approach of another purposeful activity ought to be followed for the problem. Another purpose of this phase is to put the selected purpose(s) in context with its bigger ones. This outcome assures many benefits (greater creativity, criteria for selecting solutions, showing interrelationships, etc.).

Another goal of this phase is to establish the basis for implementation of the recommended solution. This would include setting up a P&D solution finding structure, usually including time milestones and measures of solution success that relate to organizational expectations. Still another purpose is to arrange the utilization of P&D resources most effectively (on parallel P&D activities, doing top priority functional components, seeking additional resources, etc.). In other words, the first phase sets the crucial stage for reaching the basic objectives of P&D.

Table 12-1 lists normal Phase 1 activities. All have flexible boundaries, are performed iteratively if needed, and are not necessarily performed in this order in all projects. Some P&D efforts start with the

Table 12-1   Phase 1: Determine Purpose Level

A	Select P&D project from original, betterment, or correction requirements
B	Set up P&D system structure
C	Expand purposes into hierarchy(ies) and select needed purpose(s)
D	Identify measures of effectiveness for selected purpose(s)
E	Determine functional components (primarily for large or complex systems)
F	Select component(s) if E was needed; return to C

first activity, others with the second (or even third). For example, there may be an existing P&D program with established project priorities that eliminates the need for the first step.

A.   Select P&D Project from Original, Betterment, or Correction Requirements

A P&D project arises from a desire to put an artificial or solution into existence some time in the future (original requirement), to improve a satisfactorily existing solution (betterment requirement), or to correct an unsatisfactorily existing solution (correction requirement). These are the three broad categories (Axiom 5) in which P&D problems can arise (item 1 on the timeline scenario in Figure 11-1). Although many problems appear suddenly or just "walk in the door," many take time to emerge as possibly deserving of P&D attention (Figure 12-1). Note that planned betterment P&D between t_0 and t_1 would be most desir-

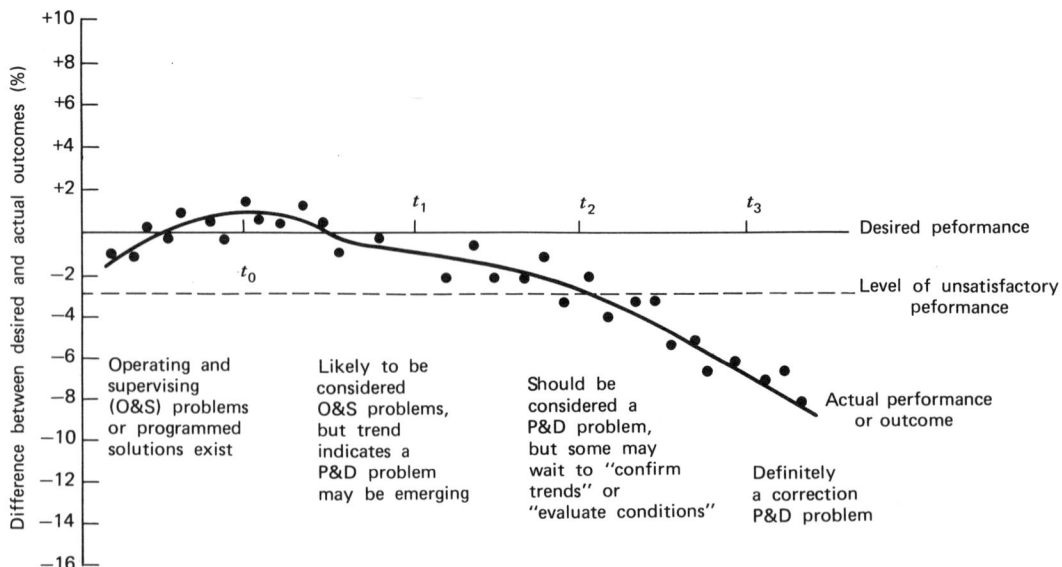

Figure 12-1   Depiction of the emergence of a P&D problem.

able. Other problems that may be quite important may not "walk in" nor be perceived as emerging.

The purposes of this step are therefore to identify all possible P&D projects that may need to be worked on, and to determine which one(s) ought to be the object of a P&D focus *at this time*. A selected P&D focus does not mean that the problem is the "right" one to work on or that P&D is the purposeful activity of concern. For example, a company hired a consultant to plan an expansion of their plant facilities. Rapidly increasing sales had caused serious overcrowding in their available space. The number of shipments per week was falling. The "facilities study group" set up in the company started the next step in the PDA stragegy "design the P&D structure." Within two hours of the first meeting on this step, the group determined that the purpose it should be seeking to achieve was the development of management control systems. Facility expansion planning was a much smaller problem that would be solved much more effectively within the broader context.

What this step does is to get the P&D project or the protocol stage *started*. It starts with the usually poorly structured problem or understood symptoms, as people perceive them, on the basis of the tensions they may feel, in relation to their understanding of the total range of possible problems. What does the client or manager say hurts the most? Is the market "pulling" us or is new information "pushing" us?

Table 12-2 treats this step as a decision-making process, as described in Figure 11-8. The first column in Table 12-2 lists a wide variety of sources and methods for identifying latent as well as manifest problems for which P&D *may* be needed. The second column contains several ways in which the ideas about possible problems can be organized to facilitate selection. The third column presents several choice or prioritization methods. The first two methods in column three illustrate the fact that a P&D problem is on occasion selected "out of the air" without being formally preceded by the other two parts.

Possible problems (or symptoms) that organizations and individuals may identify to start P&D include the following:

Competitors are reducing product prices.
Hospital costs are rising at over three times the inflation rate.
A person perceives that others are getting promoted faster because of better educational background.
Several farmers are worried about a lack of grain storage and handling facilities.
A group of citizens is unhappy about the lower achievement of their children in school.

A city government is concerned with the apparent deterioration (e.g., falling real estate assessments, flight of businesses) of a 200-block area close to the inner city.
A married couple starts to wonder about their constant arguing.
Legislators are receiving complaints about the invasion of privacy in welfare cases.
A theatrical group is concerned with the lack of auditorium facilities.

There are always more opportunities or problems to solve than there are resources, even with participation. Problems flow through an organization, with each one subject to shifting weightings and trade-offs. P&D, even on a continuing basis in an organization, deals with episodic efforts: a project, another year added in a five-year cycle, bimonthly guidance session for a student, a building, a curriculum, a national pest management planning task force. To avoid having to make an intuitive leap in selecting a problem necessitates some sort of constantly revised priority listing based on anticipated benefits and utilization of P&D resources so that scarce available resources can be allocated. Warrants and assignments are likely to change at any time.

Reminder: The problem selected at this point is considered the "problem as given" or the "problem as stated." It may not be the "problem that will be solved," a transformation that will be considered when the next step starts, even for what may now be classified as a "well-defined problem."

B. Set Up a Planning or Design Structure

The "problem as stated" is checked to be sure it is a P&D one. This is most easily done by developing a purpose hierarchy that lists, from smallest to largest, the purposes that the organization or client and P&D professional believe need to be achieved by "searching" for a solution to the problem (1a on the timeline scenario, Figure 11-1). Many specific statements are usually identified (e.g., design system, analyze conditions, develop specification, determine the state of the art). Selecting the purpose level in the hierarchy determines what purposeful activity is involved. If the selected level is related to "create or restructure," then it is most likely P&D. If it isn't, then the appropriate purposeful activity scenario (Chapter Three) should be followed.

The same result might be obtained by proceeding to develop the P&D system for the now-assumed P&D problem. If the selected purpose is not P&D, the group

Table 12-2 Selecting P&D Project(s) (If Needed in Step 1A)*†

Generating Ideas about Possible P&D Problems	Organizing Alternative Problems	Selection of P&D Project(s)
Results sought: List of prospective problems for which P&D may be needed	*Results sought:* a greatly reduced but arranged list of possible P&D projects	*Results sought:* A P&D project or set of projects to which P&D resources are *tentatively* to be allocated*
Methods, Techniques, and Resources to Attain Results*	Methods, Techniques, and Resources to Attain Results*	Methods, Techniques, and Resources to Attain Results* Assigned by someone else (e.g., building request to architect, product design to engineer, student to counselor) or a question or prospective P&D problem is suggested by someone influential Personal selection (e.g., plan a vacation, develop filing system for tax papers, set up continuing education program)

Human perceptions and feelings
  Intuition
  Mood
  Values
  Perceived gaps between present and desired circumstances
  Sense of inequalities
  Sensitivity to needs
  Dissatisfactions
  Curiosity
  Question own role in system
  Drive to search for areas of change
  Expectations
  Critical event(s)
  Exploration of current assumptions
  Motivation
  Desire for the up-to-date
  Desire for benefits (money, time, etc.)
  Tension
  Shame/humility
  ''Where you are in the head''
  Internal pressures
  Frustrations
  Sense of vicious circle
Information aids and stimuli
  Consumer/user needs/complaints
  Budget/profit-loss variances (A)
  Biggest budget allocation
  Index values (productivity, project completion times, quality, utilization, market share, etc.)
  Surveys/studies (activities, opinions, attitudes, technology level, needs, safety etc.) (A)
  Life cycle location (A)
  Leading indicators
  External developments, pressures, trends, innovations, disturbances, etc.
  Time since last P&D effort (quiet system)
	· Group or aggregate prospective problems by activities, workstations, forms, or other basic locus divisions
	
	· Identify the major stakeholders (customers workers, shareholders, top management, directors, citizens, etc.) and group possible problems by which stakeholder(s) will have direct interest
	
	· Organize a seminar for all related people to review needs and start the sort process; other techniques to identify needs include nominal groups, interviews, survey, observation, or review of documents (citizen or customer complaints, budget variances, productivity reprints, etc.)
	
	· Assign which purposeful activity is primary for each possible problem on the list
	
	· Write scenarios of or position papers on possible future conditions, and note which possible problems appear in each scenario or paper
		· Decision worksheet* (A) (C)
		
		· Prioritization‡ (A)
		  (a) among P&D professionals
		  (b) which problems are other purposeful activities
		
		· Quick payoff array‡
		
		· Set broad goals (expectations) and select problem(s) or opportunities that fit each overall goal
		
		· Negotiation among internal (and often external) parties to set priorities or select ''the'' problem
		
		· Do feasibility study(ies) on one or two apparently major problem areas

Table 12-2 (*Continued*)

Generating Ideas about Possible P&D Problems	Organizing Alternative Problems	Selection of P&D Project(s)
Results sought: List of prospective problems for which P&D may be needed	*Results sought:* a greatly reduced but arranged list of possible P&D projects	*Results sought:* A P&D project or set of projects to which P&D resources are *tentatively* to be allocated*

Generating Ideas about Possible P&D Problems	Organizing Alternative Problems	Selection of P&D Project(s)
Methods, Techniques, and Resources to Attain Results* Cost/time on critical path (A) High cost/time/scrap/delays/fatigue/losses/ overtime/turnover/penalties/idle time/accidents/ conflict/absenteeism/work loads/etc. (noisy systems) Control charts (cost, quality, etc.) (A) Planned betterment schedule (quiet system) Competition prices, costs, rate of advertising, etc. Big differences between goals and performance Advanced scanning/preissue problem identification model/information system Review each locus for possible P&D (layout, workplace, form, material, machine, working condition, handling/movement/component/ service, supply, product design, course, etc.) Recently successful projects Cross impact analysis (A) Reconnaissance Other signals, stimuli, search ideas, problem-finding methods Limitations on something are presumed Something is felt to lack efficiency Needs assessment (A) A situation gives concern A conflict or conflicts Intentions meet barriers Vigilance Scouting and reconnaissance A crisis A value/objective/goal cannot be reached A challenge Dramatic value change turns quiescent problem into "noisy" one Yearly planning cycle List noisy systems List quiet systems List nonexisting "systems" or unmet needs Informal group discussions to do above three listings Tap existing information sources Needs for organizational continuity (growth, acquisition, divestiture, management succession, products, services, financing, structure, etc.) Technological breakthrough/discontinuity presents opportunity or problem	Methods, Techniques, and Resources to Attain Results* · Group possible projects by amount (time, cost, satisfaction, etc.) of *opportunity* each represents · Use Pareto Law model to array possible projects by a factor of importance (cost, time delays, waste, etc.) (A) · Arrange a matrix with columns as departments, services, products, etc., and rows as specific values, objectives, goals, etc., and put each possible problem in appropriate cells to identify major groupings · Filter possible projects through a group of people involved with or attached to the organization to establish the major categories (A) (B) · Determine available P&D resources (skills, person-hours, etc.) inside or outside the organization, and list possible projects each person/resource group could handle · Put each possible problem into a five-point scale (high, above average, average, below average, low) for each of two dimensions in a matrix, potential payoff and potential implementability if solution(s) found	Methods, Techniques and Resources to Attain Results* · Have a debate/presentation/ live interchange before a panel of key people (implementation is likely to be influenced by the people) · Compare to available project portfolio · Sequence of reduction sortings into candidate problems, then problem statements, preliminary briefs, problem specifications, and selected one(s)‡ · Client and P&D professional assess situation and *agree*; client has commitment to seeking and implementing a change

Table 12-2 *(Continued)*

Generating Ideas about Possible P&D Problems	Organizing Alternative Problems	Selection of P&D Project(s)
Results sought: List of prospective problems for which P&D may be needed	*Results sought:* a greatly reduced but arranged list of possible P&D projects	*Results sought:* A P&D project or set of projects to which P&D resources are *tentatively* to be allocated*
Methods, Techniques, and Resources to Attain Results* Increasing weighting for one factor may decrease it for another Futures study groups Science fiction literature Societal trends (nonrenewable resources, increasing interdependence, nationalism, self-determination, decreasing productivity, etc.) Calls for action Participatory identification (A) (B) Images Challenge outworn decisions Compliance with policies	Methods, Techniques, and Resources to Attain Results* Establish connectivity or sequential order in which problems may need to be worked on (product design before distribution, citizen needs before equipment purchases, etc.)	Methods, Techniques, and Resources to Attain Results*

* Many items in column 1 may be organized by one or two of the smaller number of items in column 2, and a selection made by one or more of the still smaller number of items in column 3.

† (A) See Appendix A about references for these techniques. (B) See Chapter Fourteen, as well as Appendix A, for additional details about these techniques. (C) See Chapter Fifteen, as well as Appendix A, for additional details.

‡ Criteria typically used for selection decision: Total amount of resources now involved, criticality or sense of urgency, projected need for and importance of outcomes, possible availability of alternative solutions and breakthroughs (long-term implications), number and amounts of current (noisy) or projected (quiet) difficulties, potential resource commitment and flexibility, political and social relevance, potential for feasibility, implementability of a solution, etc. Relationship to other problems, risks if not worked on, time available, potential gains, maintain freedom of choice.

could proceed to set up the solution-finding structure for whatever purposeful activity is involved.

This step now designs the P&D system which, when implemented, will do the P&D work on the selected problem. Both P&D efforts are obviously related because the functions/purposes of the P&D system in a hierarchy must always lead to the functions/purposes of the problem-project.

A P&D system or structure for P&D is similar to project management and control groups used for years in construction and large research efforts. There are several reasons why developing a P&D system represents a rather important breakthrough for P&D: the increasing amounts of money required for many projects; longer time between the start and finish of a P&D effort; greater amounts and sophistication of technology available and usually needed; need to stimulate creativity early in and throughout a project; and the large number of people (citizens, experts, financial officers etc.) involved in most projects.

Some interesting factors can be considered in developing a P&D system.

First, every P&D project, regardless of size or number of times the solution will be used, theoretically needs a P&D system first. Planning a vacation, designing your house, and developing your educational plans could benefit from developing a P&D system. But even though the incremental benefits may seem to be small, "thinking" in P&D system terms leads to considering right at the start many factors necessary for eventual solution utilization. A project with "maximum certainty" of implementing whatever solution is developed (e.g., a vacation, house plans) is not likely to need a P&D system. "Maximum certainty" can be envisioned for a project if a single P&D professional is involved with a "single user, who anticipates using the system for a very definite purpose which can be specified in advance with great precision. Including the person who will maintain it, all other parties affected by the system understand and accept in advance its impact on them. All parties have prior experience with this type of system . . ."[1] As the amount of risk in each of many factors increases, the need also grows for a P&D system. Chapter Sixteen presents eight risk factors concerning eventual implementation with which the P&D system can cope.

Second, a project should not import the P&D structure of another project. This premise applies even for a well-established product design department, corporate planning group, health planning agency, or architectural firm. Although the same P&D system may appear useful over and over, each project should be treated as an *opportunity* to redesign the P&D system. Different people are often involved and they need opportunity to design their own P&D system.

Third, put emphasis on the whole P&D system (Table 10-1), not just, for example, on the protocol (cell 19), controls (cells 4 and 22 as illustrations), input information or forecasts (cell 7), or organization structure (cell 25).

Fourth, a P&D system can be developed for a full program of continuing P&D efforts, for each project within a program, or for independent ad hoc projects.

1 *Who should be involved in planning the P&D system?* The idea is to start a project and group toward being most effective. In general, the key decision makers, resource controllers, influential persons, implementers, people in the field, and adopters are included (see Chapter Fourteen).

2 *Provide time for developing the P&D system.* Organizations differ in their understanding of what P&D is, what P&D skills are, motivation for P&D, climate for change, information base, top executive commitment to P&D, and assignment of P&D responsibilities. A poor level of understanding means more time is needed to develop the P&D system than a good level. Conversely, too much time should not be allocated to this step because people will believe their efforts are being diverted from the "real" problem.

3 *Follow the basic strategy pattern in designing the P&D system.* This allows people to question their assumptions (purposes of the P&D system), express feelings of tension and conflict in a positive way (purpose hierarchy, develop ideal P&D systems, seek a target P&D system for regularity conditions), and generate overall support for the project. In other words, the unfreezing process is started.

4 *Several outcomes are expected from this step.* One outcome sets the terms of reference and measures of effectiveness for the P&D project. Another outcome is a strong mandate for the effort from key decision makers and influentials. A third is the allocation of resources that effectively balances the time/cost trade-off (i.e., accomplishing the same project outcomes in less time usually costs more). A fourth is the appointment of the P&D person to "operate" the P&D system along with the others who form the

design group, project team, task force, commission, blue ribbon committee, or whatever may be selected. A fifth is the completion of the specifications of the P&D system (Table 10-1) for the particular situation (see items 5, 6 and 7 below). Sixth, the PDA scenario, as tailored for implementation, is documented for the specific project.

5 *The protocol, network, or set of stages for the whole project is developed.* As noted in Chapter Eleven, the protocol for a P&D effort is unique. The names of specific departments and people should be used, and the specific proclivities (forms, meeting arrangements, frequency of reporting, etc.) of the decisionmaker(s) should be utilized. A frequent addition to usual *project* protocols is a beginning stage on *organizational* preparation for the P&D efforts. The degree of readiness for change varies from group to group (Chapter Sixteen).

6 *A timeline with milestones to fit the protocol, stages, and phases is set up.* Definitive review points for decision makers and other influentials are included. The milestones express explicitly what results, approvals, and updates the group expects at specific points in time. Milestones are most frequently based on estimates of an activity's start, duration, and access to P&D resources. People and equipment "loading" charts also encourage a realistic focus. Expected jointly performed activities, as shown in the P&D scenario (Figure 10-4) are usually scheduled approximately. A P&D project needs continual assessment to provide the organization with the chance to extend, keep, or reduce the effort's commitments (financial, manpower, time, etc.). The timeline also permits project personnel to control the project with timely corrective actions, watching for key decision points, properly modifying resource commitments, and maintaining and updating schedules. Delays, unexpected snags in development, unusual "people" questions, and so on can easily affect the accuracy and precision of time/cost resource estimates. A bar chart or graph, tree diagram, and/or network with critical path are three techniques (see Appendix A) that are often used to represent a project timeline. Figure 12-2 illustrates one of these for a project in a product design department.

7 *Resources needed to implement the P&D system are estimated.* Commitments are obtained for at least the first several milestones. Cost estimates of a P&D system are based on the project's complexity or organizational technology (variety of problems considered, number of organizational units, prospective number of functional components, etc.), nature of the problem (abstract versus concrete, etc.), documenta-

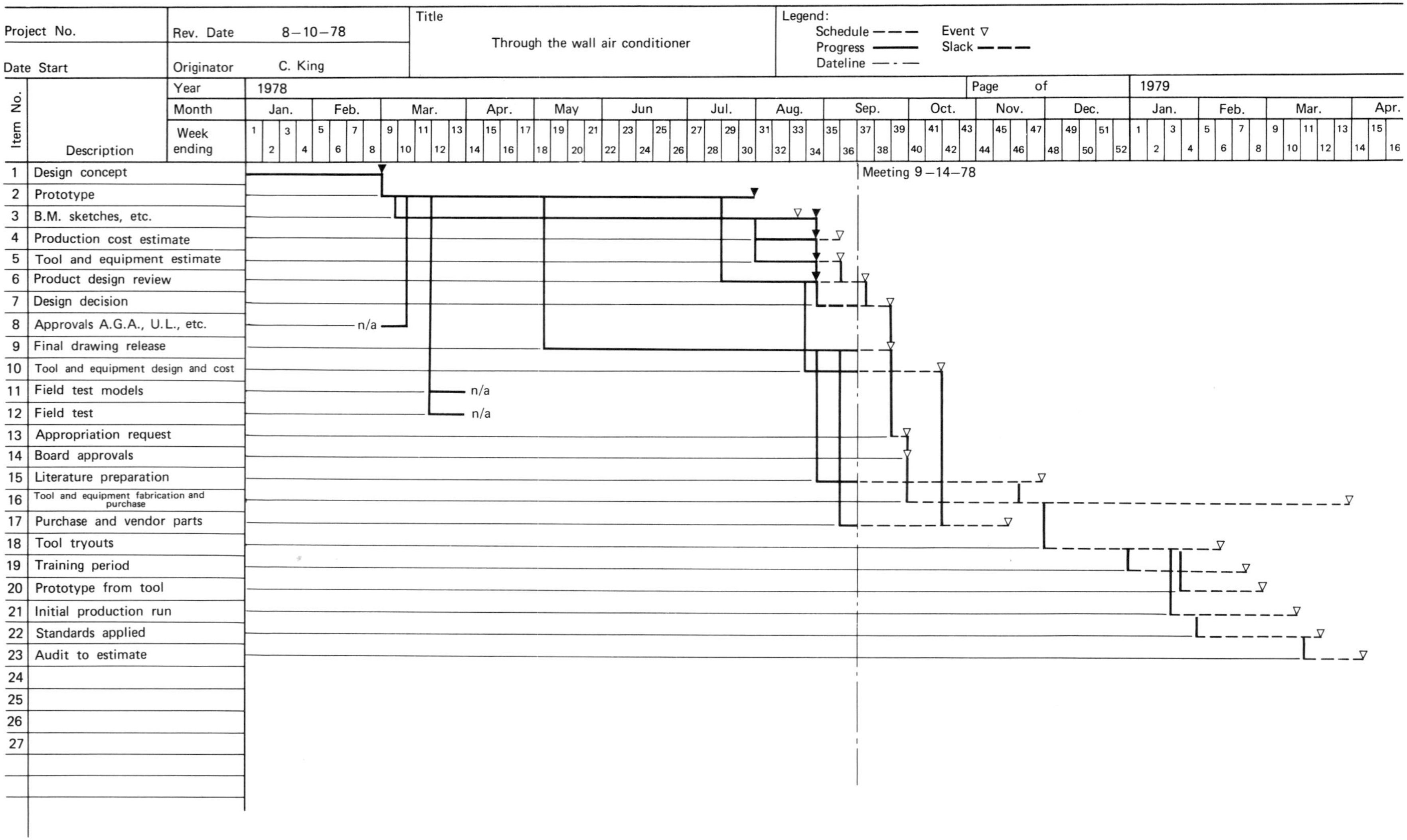

Project No. | Rev. Date 8–10–78 | Title

Date Start | Originator C. King | Through the wall air conditioner

Legend:
Schedule – – –
Progress ▬▬
Dateline — · —
Event ▽
Slack — — —

Page ___ of ___

Item No.	Description
1	Design concept
2	Prototype
3	B.M. sketches, etc.
4	Production cost estimate
5	Tool and equipment estimate
6	Product design review
7	Design decision
8	Approvals A.G.A., U.L., etc.
9	Final drawing release
10	Tool and equipment design and cost
11	Field test models
12	Field test
13	Appropriation request
14	Board approvals
15	Literature preparation
16	Tool and equipment fabrication and purchase
17	Purchase and vendor parts
18	Tool tryouts
19	Training period
20	Prototype from tool
21	Initial production run
22	Standards applied
23	Audit to estimate
24	
25	
26	
27	

Year 1978 — 1979

Months: Jan. Feb. Mar. Apr. May Jun Jul. Aug. Sep. Oct. Nov. Dec. Jan. Feb. Mar. Apr.

Week ending: 1 2 3 4 5 6 7 8 9 10 11 12 13 14 15 16 17 18 19 20 21 22 23 24 25 26 27 28 29 30 31 32 33 34 35 36 37 38 39 40 41 42 43 44 45 46 47 48 49 50 51 52 1 2 3 4 5 6 7 8 9 10 11 12 13 14 15 16

Meeting 9–14–78

n/a

134

Figure 12-2 Project schedule and milestones for a product development.

tion amount and type required at the end of the project, and sectoral location (public sector projects often cost more than the "same" type in private organizations). Changes in resource amounts are quite likely to be needed at several points in a P&D project, and these should be included as milestone reviews on the timeline.

8 *Measures of effectiveness of the P&D effort itself should be established.* In addition to the obvious factors related to the quality of the solution, which will be identified in step 1d, other factors are effective utilization of P&D person-hours, attitudes of the organization's people after contacts with the P&D personnel, motivations to seek continuing change, and so on.

Many advantages accrue when a P&D project is started with a group of decision makers and influentials developing the P&D system itself. Such a group:

- Allows catharsis to take place in a positive vein. Human perceptions, feelings, stresses, tensions, and emotions cause individuals to present their biases and positions. Following the basic strategy pattern regarding the P&D system does not force them to defend their previously stated assumption. A production control expert in the "facilities study group" noted earlier forcefully stated at the beginning of the two-hour meeting that the essential function of the group was to collect detailed information about the magnitude of the production shortfall. Yet he was the person who 15 minutes later labeled that function as very small and helped expand the hierarchy to arrive at the selected level. (Also see case history B1.)

- Expands as far as possible the words and often overly restrictive terms of reference that may be initially stated by client, contract, or other managers.

- Provides people with an illustration of a success with the strategy. Those not previously involved with P&D have an opportunity to try out and learn the strategy in a relatively unrisky situation.

- Incorporates rather "automatically" the policies, legitimization, sense of urgency, commitment to resolve conflicts, technology levels, reward structure, communications channels, and management style of the top people involved.

- Determines forms of intervention that are most likely to succeed. The uniqueness of each situation means a specific set of beneficial actions and behavior can be planned rather than simply occur.

- Establishes commitment among those who must authorize and supervise a project. The "real" client

is very likely to be established. A mandate developed from this process for the opportunity present in the problem is very likely to generate enthusiasm and motivation to proceed.

- Forms the basis for a win-win condition, the belief that a solution can be found. Differences of opinion can be a strength when a preliminary P&D effort is completed. Possible dissonances are surfaced before they become a crisis.

- Starts effectively the implementation process. Commitment of decision makers, methods for coping with natural conflicts and different personality traits and types, and joint activities to cope with uncertainties greatly enhance and promote eventual implementation.

- Promotes confidence in the P&D effort because milestones are review points where cutoff and go-ahead decision responsibilities can be exercised. In addition, including a postproject audit to assess why and how success or failure occurred is easier because the trail of P&D activities is well identified. The P&D system is itself "self-designing" and capable of handling the unexpected.

- Recognizes "politics" as part of any P&D effort. Arriving at an implemented solution means concern about leadership, influence, power, expertise, fiscal control, and so on, right from the start.

- Needs little time to design an initial P&D system. The "facilities study group" did it in just two hours. A day was needed for the gypsy moth pest management system, a project anticipated to take one and a half to two years to complete (see Appendix B). The benefits/costs ratio for the deliberate "delay" in developing a P&D system is thus very high.

C. Expand Purposes into Hierarchy and Select Needed Level

This step has several purposes that are critical to *all* P&D efforts:[2]

- Provide a significantly higher probability of working on the right problem or key issue.

- Change a problem into an opportunity and fresh view (believing game is enhanced). A focus on purposes lets people normally unaware of alternate formulations learn how an expansion view improves the potential benefits of a solution.

- Generate valid information about a specific problem, especially about users' needs and objectives/goals and their commitment to them.

- Explore underlying assumptions, values and beliefs people bring to efforts to resolve the problem. Try out variations in the way the problem and purposes can be framed.
- Expand the solution space within which P&D is to take place (always look for the larger order change).
- Create cohesion among people involved (often called ''goal'' convergence or congruence).
- Give everyone a positive learning experience (e.g., explore several hierarchies about same situation).
- Assess and establish the priorities for allocating P&D resources to the various needs or purposes that surface.
- Establish a well-knit project group (e.g., team building, unfreezing).
- Enable critical comments and barriers to be expressed in a nondamaging form.
- Place any selected (or assigned) function into its purposeful context as a means of enhancing creativity and eventual implementability of a solution.

The operational outcome of this step is the selection of the biggest suitable purpose or function level on which P&D efforts will focus. This process is able to eliminate P&D efforts on the initial problem and instead focus on a far more critical purpose (Appendix B). ''The failures of society and its institutions derive more from their failure to face the right problems than from their failure to solve the problems they face.''[3] The mid-1960s saw, for example, efforts to promote fish protein concentrate as the solution to the world food problem. In addition to the error of selling a solution (Axiom 7), an expansion of the purpose of ''to supply proteins'' would much more likely than not have developed the ''right'' problem. It is easy to state *a* purpose that has the ring of importance and priority, but the hierarchy of purposes is far more crucial in selecting the biggest one that is better. (There is no such thing as the ''right'' problem, just a greater probability that it is right: Axiom 7.)

Therefore, this step is critical for P&D, not just preparatory to it. The hierarchy and selected purpose level are actually specifications of the system being designed (the fundamental dimension of the purpose element, Chapter Nine). The effort of expansion initially seeks a breakthrough on each project, for there is no way of knowing in advance where or when a significant change might occur. Looking for the big purpose and different perspective can increase significantly the probability of the breakthrough solution.[4]

The purpose hierarchy can also clarify meaning and

direction for any protocol stage, phase, or step to avoid treating them as activities that are to be done under all circumstances. Questioning the purpose of the steps involving, for example, regularities, feasible ideal system target, measures of effectiveness, feasibility study, creativity principles, preliminary test, and so forth, is quite likely to produce a lean and effective P&D process.

Purpose has certain characteristics to consider before trying to develop a hierarchy. First, purpose has several parts, as is described in Chapter Two: a mission, aim, primary concern, or need; desired conditions (values, desiderata); objectives (measures, factors); and goals (amounts of the measures). The first part is often called ''function,'' although ''purpose'' is frequently used generically. Table 12-3 illustrates

Table 12-3   Illustrations of Word Distinction
Components of Purpose

Radiology
    Function—to produce x-ray of needed body sections
    Values—improve diagnostic ability, make people well, increase health care quality, provide patient care (higher level function)
    Objectives—number per day, accuracy, cost
    Goals (measurable performance specifications)—30 per day without error
    Example activities: place patient, turn on machine, interpret x-ray

Hospital engineering
    Function—to keep equipment in running condition
    Values—improve equipment efficiency, increase quality capability of hospital, efficient use of resources
    Objectives—percent of machines that are operating
    Goals—95% in running order per week
    Example activities: repair of machines, preventive testing

Personnel department
    Function—to have necessary human resources available
    Values—hire capable personnel, reduce turnover, provide employment
    Objectives—% human resource requirements satisfied
    Goals—90% requirements satisfied
    Example activities: screen, hire, train, fire

Automobile manufacturing company
    Function—to produce vehicles for transporting people and objects
    Values—make a profit, be stylish, have quality dealers, meet energy requirements
    Objectives—earnings per share, return on investment, market share
    Goals—20% improvement in earnings in 1981, 15% in return on investment
    Example activities: purchase, weld, paint

---

these differences, although I will use "function" and "purpose" interchangeably. Some people prefer one, other people the other word.

Second, "a purpose is not less of a purpose when it is vague, or more of a purpose when it is precise and its outcome is vividly anticipated."[5] The degree of precision and clarity a function statement should possess is related to the amount of common understanding all the people have about it. What may appear vague to an outsider or a semantic purist may still elicit common images, root definitions, and perceptions on the part of those doing P&D.

Third, a function statement is composed of an action verb and a subject. The action verb is prescriptive and concerned with the total set of conditions (for example, to provide, to have, to establish), compared to the amount of change or incremental objectives or goals (to increase, to minimize, to reduce). Thus the simplest function statement has two substantive words—"to establish a group."

Fourth, a function statement is specific but nonlimiting. Every added word reduces the possible solution space with a limitation, even though it may appear needed at the time it is formulated. Compare "To establish a project group" with "To establish a well-knit project group." Almost every function or purpose statement has modifiers (like "well-knit"), even though technically they are not really needed. They could appear in other cells of the solution matrix.

Table 12-4 presents various questions and guides to help structure a function statement and develop a hierarchy. The following substeps should help put the guides into perspective for arriving at an array, hierarchy, or semilattice of functions or purposes (used interchangeably from now on).

1 *Generate a List of Possible Functions* One or more techniques can be used. Record *all* suggested functions, preferably on an easel or chalkboard so group members can always see the list. Figure 12-3 illustrates the very first list for an actual project, the "facilities study group" project mentioned before.

Here are some alternative techniques to help generate possible functions and purposes:

- Discuss functions and purposes, brainstorm functions, "mess around" with and talk about purpose ideas.
- Send a questionnaire to various individuals or groups. What functions do customers, clients, or users want achieved? What purposes do the operators/managers perceive as necessary? What need is served by the problem area? What is our business regarding the topic? What functions does

Table 12-4 Structuring Function Statements and Hierarchies

QUESTIONS FOR FUNCTION EXPANSION

1 What are we really trying to do when we perform this function?

2 What higher-level function has caused this function to come into being?

3 Why is it necessary for this function to be performed?

GUIDES FOR DEVELOPING A FUNCTION HIERARCHY

1 Start with the perceived needs of the group or organization.

2 Select the initial statement for the function hierarchy based on its uniqueness to the originating system. One way to start a function expansion is to create a list of many possible functions, and then choose the one with the smallest scope as the starting function. A small function theoretically elicits a fewer number of ideas regarding how it might be accomplished than would a larger or more profound function.

3 Make functions prescriptive and specific but nonlimiting, using only a few words.

4 Write function statements in active verb-noun forms, which implies complete states rather than changes in states.

5 Exclude qualifying adverbs and adjectives from function statements, such as "reduce," "improve," and "increase." Locational modifiers may be needed (e.g., measure temperature *of human body*).

6 Proceed in small rather than large increments (jumps) when expanding functions into a hierarchy.

7 Select statements for the hierarchy from a list of possible functions or generate additional functions as necessary.

8 Make each function statement a bigger level function of the function preceding it and of the originating project, program, or system. (One way is to generate many ideas about the possible next level, and choose the smallest.)

9 Construct the hierarchy in terms of function or purpose rather than sequence of activities or explanations.

10 Choose the most regularly occurring function if more than one are likely candidates for the next bigger level.

11 Relate functions to the organizational unit or audience of concern.

12 Expand functions well beyond any possibility for the selected function level.

13 It should actually be possible to design a means or system that can achieve the selected function without reference to some other need or function.

1   Better procedure/methods for raw material flow (inspection, incoming inventory, how and where stored, primary operations etc.)

2   Determine facilities to meet customer requirements for products and service

3   Determine plant expansion needs

4   Organize work (material) flow

5   Be able to change with the changing times (energy)

6   Provide an environment (envelope) for better flow of material and manpower and arrive at finished state and shipment

7   Determine plant reorganization, facility-wise

8   Establish (or plan) a workable design (system) for the "shop"

9   Determine needs for proper material handling and storage

10 Establish status of parts—current, representative, etc.

11 Look at difficulties throughout shop from start to finish

12 Maximize* production and shipments while developing and implementing item 6 (short-range goal)

13 Utilize* to a greater degree the available computer facilities (potential uses)

14 Same as 7

15 Improve* inventory control

16 Improve* communication among management—up and down

17 Maximize* ROI

18 Determine long- and short-range marketing goals

19 Satisfy our customers

20 Schedule and coordinate production needs closely with sales forecast

21 Reduce* lead times

22 Improve* procedural planning

23 Same as 20

24 Improve* flow of new product changes/releases, etc.

25 Increase* production capacity

26 Create ability to give a good (delivery) shipping date

27 Improve* product quality

28 Improve* forecasting methods

29 Improve* service, repair parts shipping (forecasting, handling, etc.)

30 Be able to change with marketing changes

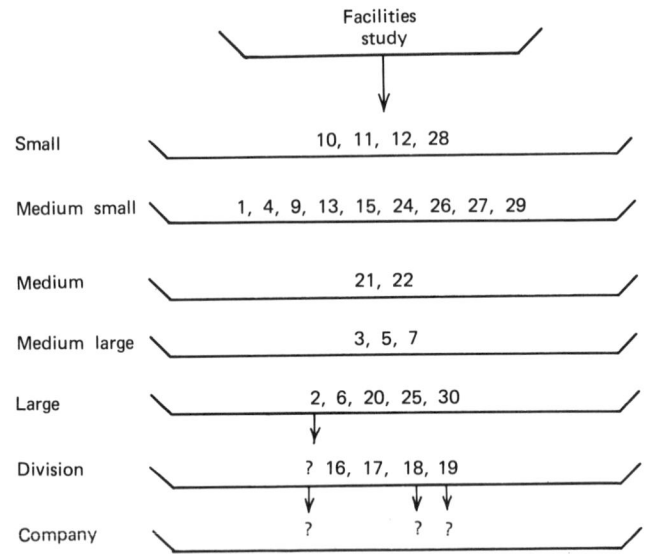

* Guides 4 and 5 in Table 12-4 are "violated" by the verbs marked with an asterisk. However, this list is reproduced as actually developed by a group, and these types of violations almost always occur. The P&D professional with a group goes along *initially* with it because of the purposes of the whole P&D scenario. "Correcting" the group takes place only as needed and when group perceptions can accept them.

Figure 12-3 Possible purposes/functions as actually listed by a facilities study group.

society expect? Stakeholders? What new needs may emerge? What purposes are our sister departments or organizations expecting? What functions are stimulated by competitors? Are there functions stimulated by the advent of a new technology?

- Use the nominal group technique with the initiating statement: "List as many purposes as possible you think ought to be accomplished by [name of system or *area* of problem]." (See Chapter Fourteen.)

- Set up a Delphi technique survey. (See Chapter Fourteen.)

- Have an individual or a group of three or four use an interactive computer terminal that poses various questions on the screen to stimulate purpose re-

sponses, and have the terminal keep track of the responses.

2 *Choose a Small-Scope Purpose as the Beginning of a Hierarchy* A small-scope purpose is unique to the problem, or the most direct or irreducible minimum one (that is, it has the fewest number of ways of being accomplished), even if it seems to be superficial or "inside" of the problem area or system. Actions (telephoning, signing), structuring (arranging, measuring), and tasks (ordering, loading), for example, are smaller than projects, missions, jobs, and careers. It should not represent the purpose of any other system in the broad organizational unit. Some statements may need to be converted from objectives/goals to purposes (e.g., "increase space available" to "have space available," "reduce citizens' complaints about recreation" to "facilitate use of recreational resources," "improve inventory control" to "have inventory controlled"). A small-scope function gives some assurance that peoples' perceptions and understanding of a problem are the start of the P&D effort.

Possible methods for selecting the smallest-scope purpose include:

- Just pick one from the list by consensus action of the group.
- Select likely candidates for smallest (superficial, structural, task) scope function/purpose from the list. Then select one by consensus from the shortened list or by the couplet method.
- Use the couplet method. Compare the first statement with the second. Ask which one is smaller. Is function$_1$ (smaller) the purpose of function$_2$, or is function$_2$ (smaller) the purpose of function$_1$? If we achieve function A would we need B (B is then smaller)?
- Review each one. Classify it as small, medium small, and so on (see Figure 12-3). Then each level can be assigned a summarizing purpose or two, or be expanded into an actual hierarchy or two if more than one channel of purposes seems to be present.
- Put each statement on an index card. The group around a table can move the cards around as it tries to establish a hierarchy.

3 *Expand the Initial Function into a Hierarchy* All of the remaining entries on the list are candidates for describing the purpose of the initial one. But many purpose statements not on the list are also possibilities. Several stimulators can be reviewed to identify possible purpose statements for each successive level (synonyms can also be added e.g., synonyms of "acquire" are "obtain," "collect," "get," "procure," "pick up," "earn," "attain," "capture," and so on):

To acquire	To design	To plan
To accept	To exchange	To prepare
To advise	To exercise	To produce
To analyze	To have____	To promote
To consume	To investigate	To provide
To control	To learn	To research
To cultivate	To manage	To select
To do____	To operate	To sell

More than one purpose/function can usually de-

scribe each successive level. Selecting one can be done with the techniques noted in 2. Then the next level is developed in the same way.

What should be done if two or more purpose statements are equally likely candidates for a particular level? (a) According to guide 10 (Table 12-4), select the one related to conditions that occur most frequently or regularly (70% of the students arrive with high school chemistry credit, so purposes related to previous chemistry preparation are selected instead of those not so related). (b) Guide 11 says, "Pick the purpose that is related to the organizational unit of concern": A railroad company designing a system for an ore-mining company moving materials from the pits to processors selected functions based on ore company needs rather than its own needs, because the system was a marketing effort. (c) Ask, "If we develop a system for purpose$_1$ will we still want one for purpose$_2$?" (d) Do two or more individual function expansions from the point where the question arises, and select the most regular one or the one related to the organizational unit of concern. (e) Do two or more expansions and keep them in a multiple-channel hierarchy or a semilattice array. Continue to expand each one at least three to five levels beyond the point where the channels and connections result in a single hierarchy. Figure 12-4 illustrates a multichanneled expansion.

How can a big jump in expansion be avoided (guide 6)? A group in a manufacturing company, for example, listed "to make tables" as the first function level. Some people then said the next function was "to have objects supported." Others felt this was too big a "jump" because the second one was far outside their organization. A method of avoiding or checking this condition changes each word in the first statement into broader and bigger functions. Thus, "to make tables" might become to *produce* tables, to *have* tables *available,* to *have* tables, to have *flat surfaces* supported in space, to have flat surfaces *parallel* to the floor, and then to have *objects* supported. Large jumps are undesirable because the intermediate purposes are not available for consideration as a possible level to select. The opportunity of working on the right problem may be missed because the smaller purpose is usually selected. In addition, the lack of its succeeding hierarchy reduces the chances of functional stimulators to help generate more creative ideas. After all, more ideas can be developed for accomplishing "to have tables" than for "to make tables."

How do we know if we have the right hierarchy? You can never know, for there is no *right* hierarchy in terms of accuracy and precision. In addition, the first hierarchy is seldom the final one. I personally have never been involved on a P&D project (among hun-

A. Air passenger services

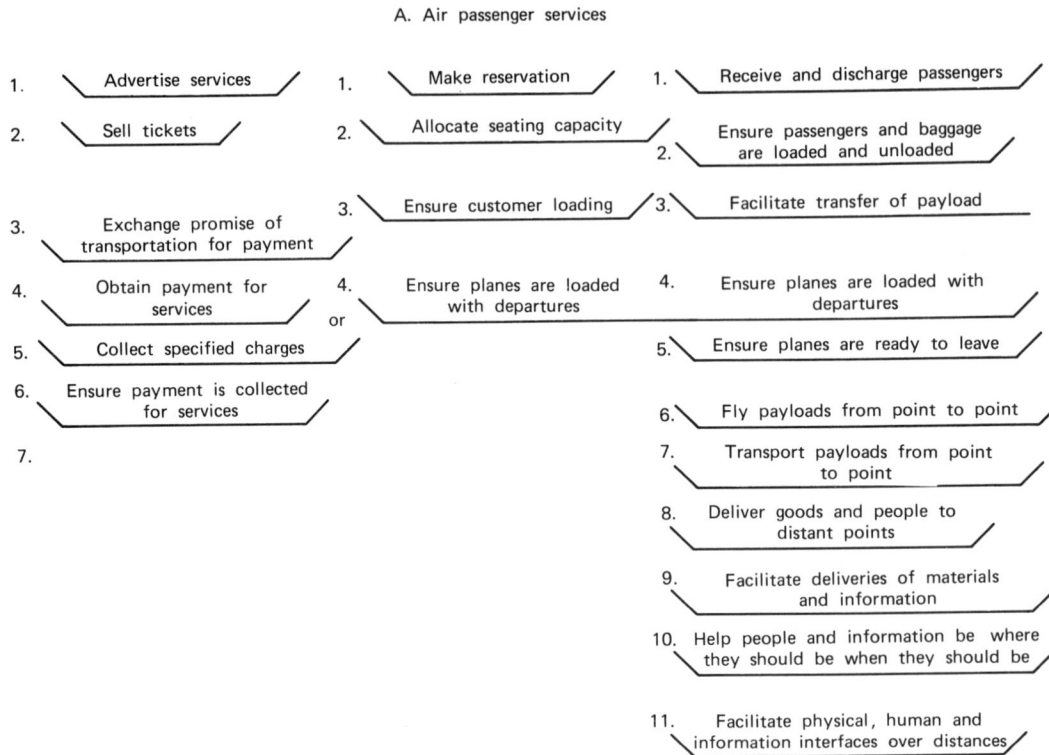

B. Performance appraisal system

To appraise performance
To establish performance
To communicate performance
To inform subordinates and superiors
To provide performance data

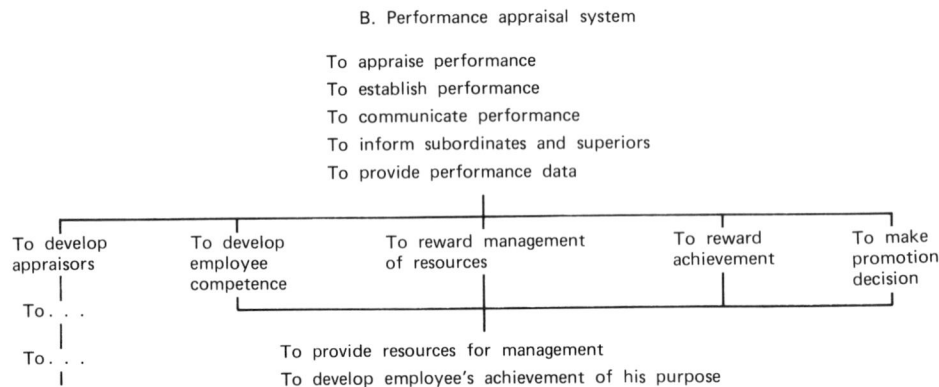

Figure 12-4 Examples of multiple channel hierarchies.

dreds I've worked on) where the first hierarchy remains as the one reported for the project. It is not unusual to develop two or three hierarchies and compare them before selecting the one that captures most of what the people perceive and believe. Instead of seeking *the* right function level and hierarchy, a group should spend a little time discussing the alternatives, but agree to proceed to "see what happens" before deciding what hierarchy or level to use. "Messing around" with hierarchies is an apt way to describe this substep. It gets a group to view purposes from differ-

ent perspectives, during which time mental sets are being expanded and contexts are being worked out.

Figures 12-5 and 12-6 illustrate lists of possible functions and the hierarchies. Chapter One and Appendix B contain other examples.

A group may decide that developing a function hierarchy is not necessary because "everyone knows what the purpose is." If the group is adamant, one or more actions can be considered. (a) Get the group to agree on a statement of the purpose that everyone knows. (This usually convinces them that they do not

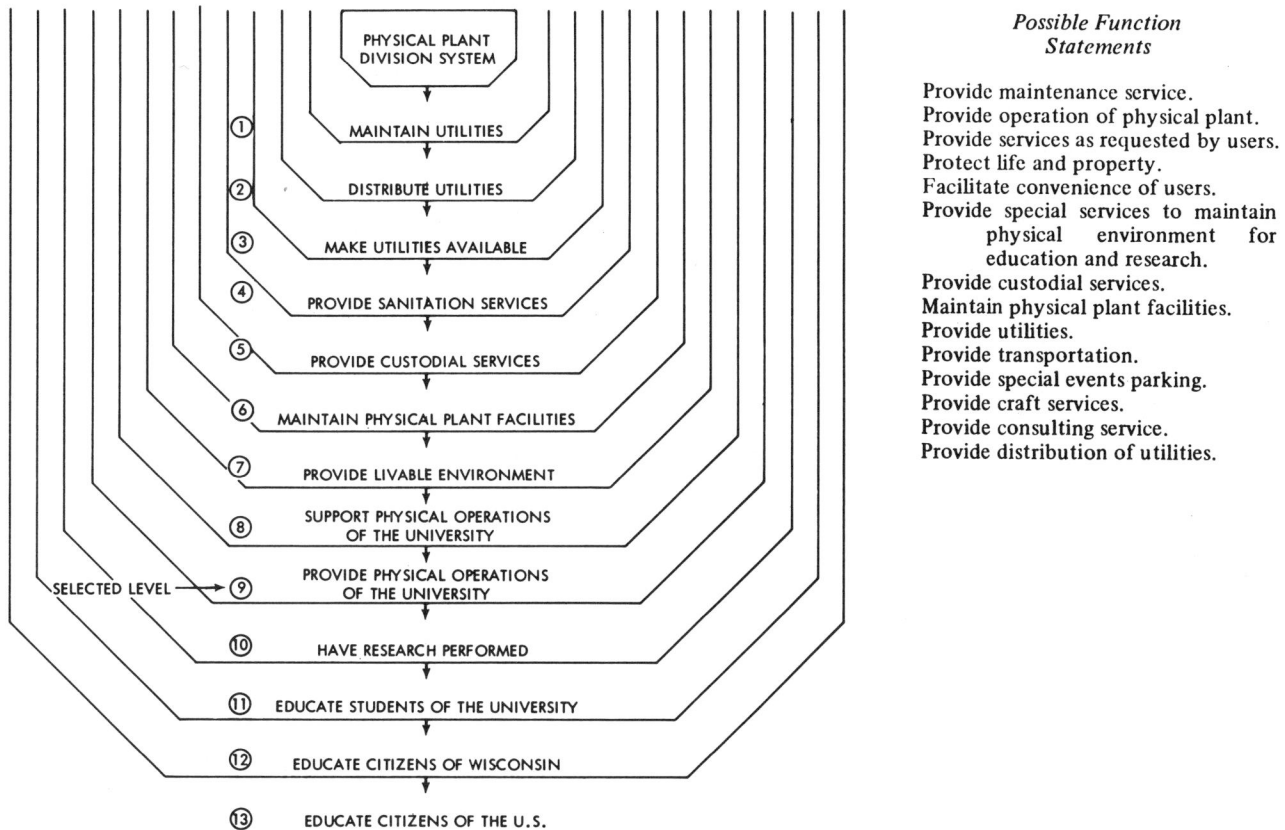

Figure 12-5 Function expansion for physical plant division of a university.

know it.) (b) Develop what they think the system ought to be in five (or one or three) years if they could have "their own way." (c) Identify measures of effectiveness for judging the quality or success of the eventual recommendation for achieving the function "everyone knows." (d) Generate a list of purposes and let staff members bring alternative hierarchies to the next meeting. (e) Determine functional components for the function everyone knows. Any one of these causes a group itself to decide that determining the purposes and a hierarchy is needed first.

4 Set Up Criteria for Selecting the Function Level This substep starts a virtually classical decision-making process. The purpose of setting up criteria is related to organizational needs and "available" P&D resources that tend to limit the purpose that will be selected to one smaller than the biggest. Several techniques can be utilized to generate alternative ideas about criteria—discussions, questionnaires, nominal group, interview, Delphi, and so on (see Appendix A). Organizing them may involve subjective aggregation of like criteria, each member ranking (and/or rating) the top five alternatives before aggregating all of them, setting up a multi-attribute utility model, and so on. Selection of criteria might be done

by voting, aggregating measures, a modified decision worksheet where more than one alternative may be selected, and even trying out (messing around with) a level or two to get the "feel" of several criteria.

Here are some criteria that have been found useful in several, but not all, function selection situations:

• *Potential Benefits* This includes *all* resources and the *whole* system whose function is being considered, costs, human and physical. Does current rate of change influence possibilities of demonstrating benefits? Is there a continuing need for physical or service outcomes?

• *Management Desires* With its intuition and power base, management may well insist that a project should not go beyond a particular function level. Going further might in management's view put the project beyond the capabilities of the organization, any physical realizability or real-world implementation, or beyond the resources that could be made available in creating a system to achieve that function.

• *Political Factors* Who is expressing urgency for change and where are the pressures coming from?

Figure 12-6 Function expansion work sheet. Container is a spool-like receptacle for yarn. Problem statement: reduce costs of container service.

- *Time Limitations* A project to be completed in six months can often involve a bigger function level than one with a time limit of 24 hours.
- *Project Cost*
- *Complexity Associated with the Function Level*
- *Organizational and Jurisdictional Factors* A project in manufacturing might often concern itself with a related function in the sales department, yet some organizational units just do not permit crossing departmental lines.
- *Control Factors* Government, association, or other external controls and regulations may conflict with a particular function level.
- *Capital Factors* Is a particular function likely to lead to a solution that requires large amounts of capital? What is the impact of capital-intensive solutions on flexibility (high capital intensity is relatively inflexible)?
- *Future Resource Needs*
- *Other Factors of Significance in Function Selection* Included here would be relationship to other projects, physical realizability, availability of technology within or even outside the organization, workability, actions of competitors, patent situation, compatibility with company history, liquidity, market position, and adequacy of facilities.

5 *Select the Function Level* Several slightly different procedures may be of help in accomplishing this step.

- *Reverse Steps of Expansion* A group can evaluate each function level, starting at the biggest one, with each of the criteria. If the level is not selected, then the next biggest is reviewed with the criteria, and so on. Or the level which is best for each criterion taken one at a time could be identified and a mean level selected.
- *Decision Worksheet*
- *Delphi Procedure* Outside experts can establish weightings, set up methods of measurement, evaluate functions, and select the function level.
- *Nominal Group Technique* Ratings and rankings can also be established with this technique.
- *Subjective Judgment* Used when the hierarchies are poorly structured or independent criteria are difficult to identify.

Although *one* purpose level is usually sought, it is not at all unusual to have a group agree that two or even three levels will serve as the foci. Quite small increments between levels often lead to a focus on two or three purposes. The group concerned with the hierarchy in Figure 12-5 also decided to focus on the next bigger level, whereas the group involved with the Figure 12-6 project agreed that their focus also comprised the next smaller level.

D. Identify Measures of Effectiveness (M of E)

Factors leading to the selection of this project now combine with the selected purpose level(s) to establish the M of E for evaluating alternative solutions proposed to achieve the purposes. The M of E should also reflect the expectations of the real-world people regarding their initial sense of the problem. They reflect the critical factors the organization believes lead to success.

M of Es are thus not established in a vacuum, nor will they remain in a vacuum. M of Es are shaped by a great deal of preliminary thought and perception as well as subsequent reconsideration and assessment. M of Es were not firmly set up before because there was no assurance that the initial problem would be the one of focus. M of Es should be related specifically to the selected and larger purposes, as well as the initial tensions, desires, and values that led to the problem. The M of E will be subject to continuing modification as later phases give rise, for example, to ideal system suggestions, regularity conditions, and detailed design specifications. These ideas may change some seemingly unimportant M of Es into significant ones, and vice versa. The M of Es could be developed in three levels: At this point in the strategy, to clarify the values (Chapter Two) regarding the selected purpose; after generating ideas in Phase 2, to select the objectives or make the values more specific; prior to selecting the target solution in Phase 3, to set goals.

M of Es stem from the values and motivations of people in an organizational setting. They especially incorporate performance factors the "boss" will use to gauge effectiveness of the recommendations for achieving the purpose. Whether or not a P&D project needs or should have the usual specific goals (e.g., reduce costs by 25% by the end of one year, increase citizen involvement in the city recreational program by 50% within two years, rehabilitate 50 inner-city houses per year for the next four years) depends on the circumstances. They may restrict creative thinking. Should a group ignore ideas that reduce costs by 40% or rehabilitate 70 houses? What is needed can only be determined with a specific project, so objectives/measures (cost per product unit, number of citizens participating per year, number of houses rehabilitated per year) will be the focus here. The important test at this point is whether the objective can be measured now, after the project's conclusion, and at several points along the way.

A measure can be dichotomous (either-or, yes-no, go–no go), continuous (several or many possible values), or threshold continuous (a minimum, either-or level must be attained, and then many values are possible). An alternative that does not contain or achieve a desired dichotomous or threshold factor will be rejected. The number of these factors are usually minimal.

No measure is ever complete, unequivocal, accurate, or precise (Axioms 6 and 7). Therefore, setting up M of Es requires a trade-off among possible objectives that are project-related and those that are related to the eventual recommended solution. Another trade-off occurs when the various M of Es are weighted to establish the importance of each one (as used, for examples in the decision worksheet, Chapter Fifteen and Appendix A).

The following are some desirable characteristics of M of Es. "*Complete*, . . . cover all the important aspects of the problem [function]; *operational*, meaningfully used; . . . *decomposable*, . . . aspects of . . . evaluation . . . can be simplified by breaking . . . into parts; *nonredundant*, . . . [avoid] double counting of impacts; . . . and *minimal* . . . "[6] In addition, everyone concerned should be able to obtain or at least understand the measures and agree that each *directly* mea-

sures achievement of the purposes. That is, a measure should not just *assume* the link to purpose exists (for example, the management-by-objectives technique was selected by the federal government to increase the productivity of the bureaucracy, but the M of E concerned the number of MBO programs installed rather than effective services rendered). M of Es should also provide some assurance that the group can actually influence and control the factors in determining if success is obtained.

Determining the M of E is a decision process, as sketched out in Table 12-5. The second column, organizing alternative measures, may suggest a sequential order of several techniques for coping with the usual large number of possible measures. Sort first by the test of importance, and then divide them into go–no go categories.

Include M of E factors and amounts that would indicate when a project ought to be stopped. Not every P&D project can be expected to be successful. Some signals that the project might have to be abandoned include too much time taken, project is 50% over budget, no solution proposed would result in an improvement of 15% over what exists.

Objectives, goals, and measures are unique to each situation (Axiom 7). Yet, some general goals are often stated for broad categories of organizations or projects. They illustrate the "literature sources" entry in the first column of Table 12-5 and serve the purpose of providing stimulators for a specific project. Some examples of the values, objectives, goals, or measures (some presented in objectives tree form) to serve as stimulators in several fields are included in Table 12-6.

Before finally selecting M of Es, determine whether presently available and continually collected data establish the current levels or amounts of desirable measures. If present levels of a measure cannot be identified, then the P&D group should seriously consider a delay of the P&D effort until such data can be collected and continuing measurement established. (The P&D of such an information system can be a PDA subproject itself.) Measurements to be made at the end of a project need a base point of preproject conditions so that effectiveness of proposed solutions can be gauged. Whether or not productivity, for example, is improved by changes at the end of the strategy can be assessed only if current productivity measures are adequate.

E. Determine Functional Components (Primarily for Large or Complex Systems)

Functional components are virtually independent of each other. Complete independence is not possible;

Table 12-5 Selecting Measures of Effectiveness for Purpose/Function Level (Step 1D)*†

Generating Ideas for Measures of Effectiveness ⟷	Organizing Alternative Measures ⟶	Selection of Set of Measures
Results sought: List of prospective measures of effectiveness to gage possible solutions and eventual success of implemented solution	*Results sought:* Similar and related measures appropriately identified and arranged	*Results sought:* A set of measures hopefully ranked or even weighted to use for evaluating possible and implemented solutions
Methods, Techniques, and Resources to Attain Results*	Methods, Techniques, and Resources to Attain Results*	Methods, Techniques, and Resources to Attain Results*
Stimulators (ask: What M of E does this stimulator suggest in your mind for the selected or bigger function or purpose) Stated values of decision makers Characteristics of good M of E‡ Illustrations in Table 12-6 Checklist of objective ties to purpose hierarchy Client initial charge to P&D individual or group	· Go–no go (discrete—what must be present in a solution or it is automatically out) vs. continuous grouping · Deterministic (a specific amount) or probabilistic (a minimum/maximum desired level with a certain confidence) · Related measures to basic values (safe, low cost, low detail times, etc.) to have several branches	
Review list of purposes from Phase 1C for objectives included therein	· Objectives tree or hierarchy‡ (A) Broad at top to specific at bottom Each smaller level is part of next larger branch level Put branches together into tree	· Prioritization (A)‡ Importance Data availability Prospect of getting data
List factors by which the solution will be judged as satisfactory	· Level of data availability for each possible measurement	· Decision worksheet (A) (C)‡ For purpose/function measures
Determine which suggested restrictions, givens, or limitations, or government regulations are possible M of Es	· Array of measures which could be assigned to each level of the purpose hierarchy‡	· Rate trade-off categories (A) (subjective measures)
Nominal group technique (A) (B)	· Array of measures which are related to each major word of the purpose/function level statement‡	· Must exist vs. measurable-amount categories
Interviews of key individuals (A)	· Trade-off categories‡ Utility vs. measurability	
Literature sources (what others have identified as critical values within which this project solution should fit)—Especially specific fields (information systems, manufacturing company, quality of working life, development, etc.)	Understandability vs. completeness Simple vs. complex Motivation vs. objectivity · Test of importance—would possible solution be altered if factor omitted?	
Questionnaires, Delphi surveys (A)		
Policy statements of organization		
Define performance specifications desired (e.g., portable, adjustable, comfortable for four hours)		

* Many items in column 1 may be organized by one or two of the smaller number of items in column 2, and a selection made by one or more of the still smaller number of items in column 3.

† (A) See Appendix A about references for these techniques. (B) Also see Chapter Fourteen for some details. (C) Also see Chapter Fifteen for some details.

‡ See characteristics or criteria for M of Es in accompanying text.

Table 12-6 Illustrative Stimulators for Developing Measures in Particular Projects

Business Organization Resource utilization (efficiency), innovation/adaptiveness to environment, morale, goal achievement (effectiveness)

Another Version for Business Market share, return on investment, amount of sales, cost reduction expectation, number of customer complaints, material utilization, absenteeism and turnover rates, timing of new product introductions, cost of grievances and industrial disputes, productivity ratios

A Hospital View of Performance Interface relationship (minimize patient delay prior to admission, number of community educational programs, score on community attitudes toward and reputation of hospital), staff and patient satisfactions (comfort level, staff morale, consideration of social as well as medical condition of patient, information supplied to patient and family), efficiency of operation (minimize length of stay, medical staff time utilization, material utilization, cost per service), effectiveness of operation (mortality, morbidity, readmittance numbers, community awareness levels)

Engineering Design Go–no go (physical laws, nature with or without physical laws), societal laws (Constitution, standards of technical associations, codes of communities), safety standards (underwriters' laboratory, insurance companies), resource availability (materials, energy, equipment and/or capital, labor), amount of capital and operating costs (reliability, maintenance, quality), and marketability.

Appropriate or Intermediate Technology Utilization of renewable energy resources, labor intensiveness, use of locally available materials, compatibility with local labor skills, simplicity of installation and maintenance, use of decentralized technologies, satisfaction of local needs, environmental soundness, durability of solution

User Benefits in Environmental and Architectural Design Conformance of user requirements to environmental form on basis of facilitating behavioral needs (overall, functional, operational, stimulus, spatial, and contingent), physiological maintenance (support, climate, hazards, and physical endurance), perceptual maintenance (consonance, operational, and sensory), and social facilitation (territoriality, organizational orientation, convergence, social isolation, and social accommodation)*

Urban planning Economic, environmental, political, and social considerations. Additional stimulators: impact on organizational structure, degree of value agreement, need for coalition development, impact on resource allocation, technical difficulty, and level of environmental stability

---

* D. M. Murtha, *Dimensions of User Benefit: Environment Design Criteria*, Washington, D.C.; American Institute of Architects, 1976.

otherwise the components would not be part of the selected purpose/function level. Functional components permit more effective allocation of P&D time and resources. Concurrent P&D of functional components to reduce overall project time or a sequential priority (similar to a protocol) to use limited resources can be established.

Complexity is a relative matter. Several criteria, such as total cost, number of output items, number of employees, size of area, and number of locations, may be used. A system may be considered large or complex if one person or group would be unable to do P&D alone, or if the cost of and the number of people now involved in or contemplated for the solution are rather high. Limited P&D personnel resources may also indicate that components are required for suitable priority and allocation.

Corollaries 4b (each system is comprised of smaller systems) and 4c (each system exists in parallel with other systems) essentially express the basic terms of reference for this step. Other terms in the literature include multilevel approach, functional programming, element set, entity clustering, hierarchical systems theory, structural modeling, tearing or partitioning, mission slice or product-market, tree diagram, semilattice structure, and decomposition.

Figure 12-7 puts the idea of functional components into the perspective of the purpose hierarchy. If a project starts with the "hopper" shown with an asterisk, purpose/expansion proceeds as shown in compliance with Axioms 3 and 4. Turning Figure 12-7 upside down portrays, with all the dashed lines, a system pyramid that defines the functional components. Figure 12-8 shows the format used in a nurse utilization project.[7] It also contains other notes stating which components need P&D and which will be left as they are. A portrayal of functional components may also show "horizontal" or contextual connections, in effect, a semilattice view. Functional components or *subpurposes* are the critical criteria for developing the type of format shown here, although other factors may define the nodes in the model (objectives, goals, activities, authority relationships, etc.). Several alternative *sets* of functional components may be developed, from which the "best-fitting" set can be selected.

The main reason for functional component identification at this point is to help the project get organized. No firm commitment to the components as part of the solution is intended. The actual solution components will very likely be dynamically developed during the rest of the project.

Table 12-7 provides several questions, guides and suggestions for identifying functional components. They all start with the selected purpose level.

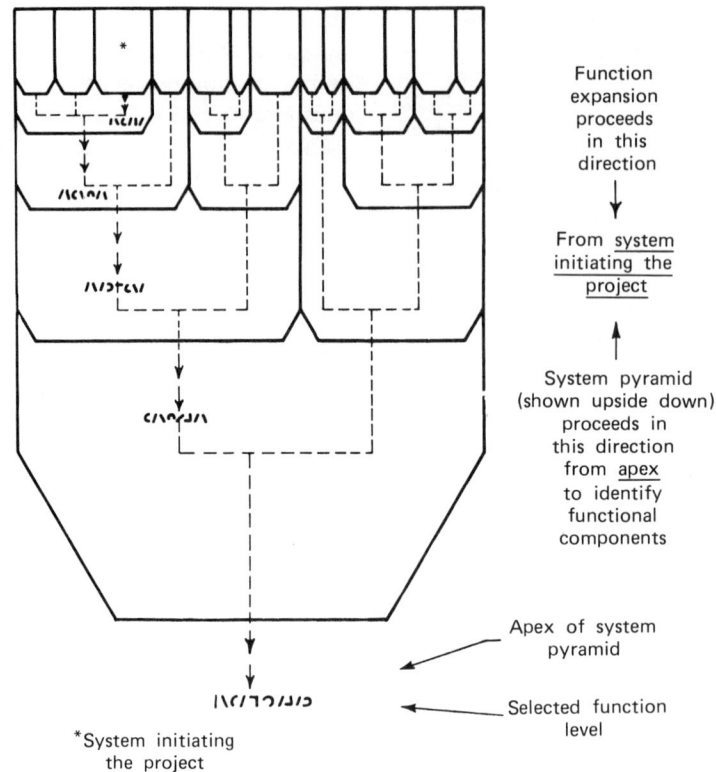

Figure 12-7 Relating function expansion and functional components.

F. Select Component(s) if E Was Needed. Return to C

This step either identifies a functional component for which the remaining phases of the strategy are followed, or concurrently assigns components to individuals or groups for each of which P&D is to be done. The latter situation is most desirable because the overall purpose will be accomplished sooner. Even though each component is the subject of a P&D project, the PDA strategy should be continued for the overall purpose to ensure the best possible "whole system" design and interrelationship of components.

Criteria in addition to those for selecting the function level are needed. One is the availability of P&D personnel, and another is the amount of time available for completing the design of the total system. Given enough P&D personnel, several functional components can be designed concurrently. Conversely, given sufficient time to design a system for the overall function, there may be no reason to have more than one component worked on at a time in priority order. Usual decision-making techniques (Appendix A) are used in making the choice or setting up the priorities.

One or more components are thus identified at this point for continued P&D efforts. To arrive at this juncture usually requires retracing some P&D steps.

First, the P&D structure (step 1B) will often need to be revised in terms of estimates of subgroups, people needed, resources required, and personnel assignments. In addition, cost estimates for doing P&D will most likely have to be reformulated. The overall timeline and milestones will certainly need updating. Teams will need to be set up for each component. Added resource commitments will often be required.

Second, each functional component is approached (step 1c) by developing its purpose hierarchy first. Each component represents an opportunity that should be explored to ensure its purpose is necessary.

Third, measures of effectiveness (step 1d) for each component are probably subfactors or partial measures of the overall set.

Some specific functional components may even require another iteration through steps of Phase 1. A functional component may itself become larger or more complex so that subfunctional components or sub-subpurposes are necessary.

PHASE 2 GENERATE PURPOSEFUL ALTERNATIVE IDEAS (OR IDEAL SYSTEMS)

Knowing the "right" problem or purpose to achieve opens immense possibilities for finding an innovative solution if the action now focuses on what is best or

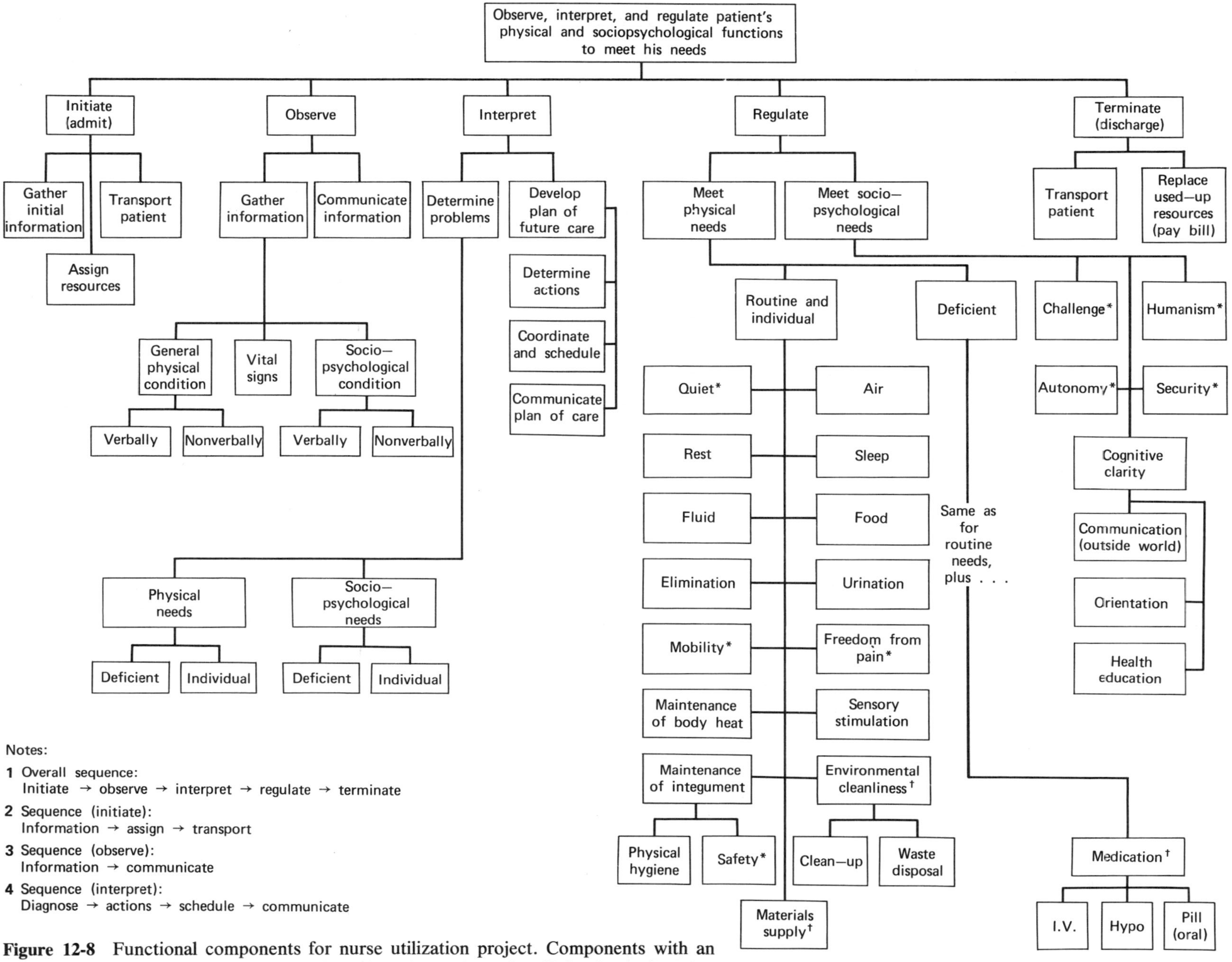

Figure 12-8 Functional components for nurse utilization project. Components with an asterisk will not be specifically designed for unless the needs are insufficiently met by other systems. Components with a dagger are not "logically similar" to the others; however, they are sufficiently important parts of most of the others to be designed more effectively as a separate component.

Notes:

1 Overall sequence:
Initiate → observe → interpret → regulate → terminate

2 Sequence (initiate):
Information → assign → transport

3 Sequence (observe):
Information → communicate

4 Sequence (interpret):
Diagnose → actions → schedule → communicate

Table 12-7 Questions and Guides for Identifying
Subpurposes or Functional Components

· What are the functional components or subpurposes of
———? Insert the selected purpose in the blank space.
The question, with each functional component, is con-
tinually asked.

· What linkages are relatively fixed between the purpose
level and its component subpurposes?

· What minimal number of constants make up the
function/purpose level?

· What minimum set of subpurposes or functional components, when each one is achieved and coordinated with
the others, will effectively have achieved the selected
level?

· What minimal number of subpurposes will be likely to
remain present throughout the time horizon of the purpose level?

· Are possible sets of functional components of similar
scope and significance?

· Is each pair in a level of functional components relatively
independent? Or does one conflict with or overlap the
other?

· What criteria might help align possible function components, equal "size" components, number of people or organizational units per component, minimum numbers of
components?

· Would mathematical decomposition or partitioning be
useful? Some measurable criteria might be cost, saturated
information links, minimal information flow between
clusters (functional components), connectivity, or the
ratio of the number of links at a node to the maximum
number possible, and relational or reachable matrices
based on linkage needs and transitivity conditions (if A
is bigger than B, and B is bigger than C, then A is bigger
than C).

· Can other features such as probability of occurrence and
risk factors help separate components?

· Can questionnaires, Delphi technique, or nominal group
technique be used, especially for systems not yet in existence where subjective opinions are needed?

· Might *function* sampling (instead of activity sampling) of
"stable"-type functions (high likelihood the functions will
remain during the longest possible time horizon of the
project) give "importance" factors to the components? (A
nurse walking, for example, is recorded not as walking,
but as the purpose the nurse seeks to accomplish as a result of the walking, such as administer medicine, record
blood pressure, or obtain a treatment tray.)

most ideal. What is the way of achieving the purpose if
we could start "from scratch"? Dealing with purposeful "best" alternatives immerses those in the
P&D system in ranges of ideas that are quite likely to
produce significant implementable solutions.

Reasons for Seeking "Best" Solutions

First, the concept of an ideal system or solution a
group might utilize if it could start all over again is a
characteristic identified in many studies as critical to
enhancing the innovative process. The ideal system
concept says that the solution to be installed and used
for achieving a necessary purpose should be as close
as possible to the feasible ideal system target (FIST)
for regularity conditions. The ideal will serve as a
longer-term guide to stimulate continuing improvements.

"Ideal" might be defined as perfect, absolute, con-
summate, best, faultless, flawless, pure, unblemished,
choice, quintessential, or prime. Clearly, then, P&D
efforts should strive to reach the best solution with
whatever resources are allocated. Ideals serve as does
a compass on a ship. The compass points the ship toward a desired destination; you may experience
difficulties with the voyage, but there is at least an excellent chance of reaching the desired destination.

A positive way of using the experience and knowledge of people is to ask continually, "What are some
ideal and purposeful solutions from which a target can
be selected?" The target will cause people to seek and
accept changes. Satisfaction with a solution is not a
deterrent to further changes.

The simple representation shown in Figure 12-9
identifies three levels of ideal system. Assume that the
line connecting two equidistant points from the apex
along the legs of the angle defines a performance measure of importance. Three levels of ideal systems can
be described.

Ultimate Ideal System

The apex of the triangle in Figure 12-9 represents zero
cost per unit, no scrap, no energy needs per unit, or
zero time per service (the infinity level). Such ultimate
ideal systems *for a necessary function* cannot be designed and will never be reached. The ultimate ideal
system level represents a limit value. No attempt is
ever made to design an ultimate ideal system because
it is only a conceptual level.

Contemplative Ideal System

Such a "real" solution could not be installed today
until further developments rendered it feasible. Contemplative ideal systems present visionary and utopian

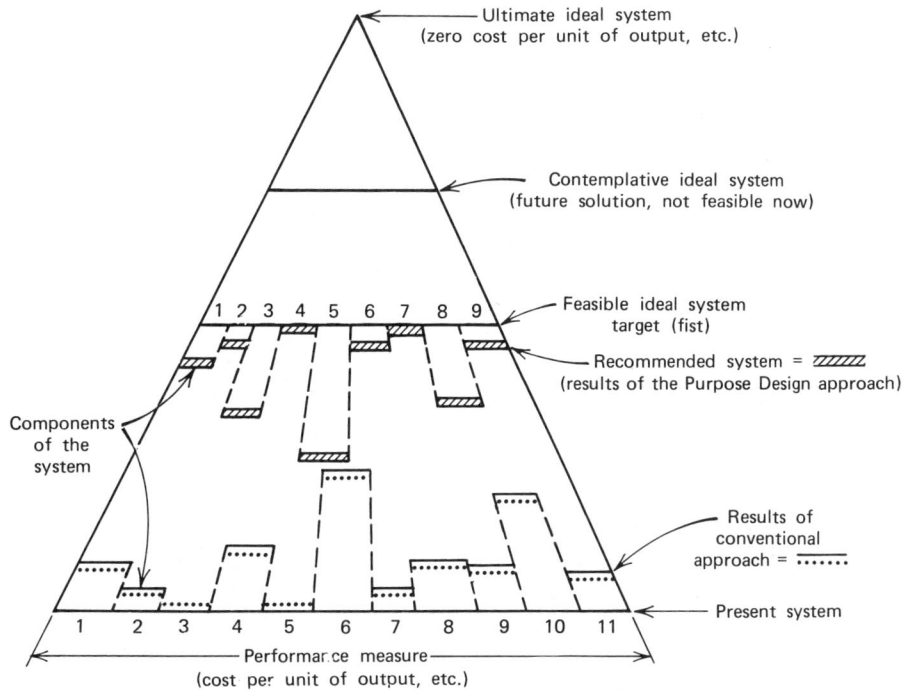

Figure 12-9   Levels of ideal systems for a necessary function.

challenges: How *can* the metal be made to shrink more as it cools? How *can* the product be distributed automatically? How *can* a correspondence curriculum be made to work? How *can* the traffic flow be arranged without any stops? As the result of a contemplative ideal system proposal in a meat processing firm, an entirely new product was suggested, investigated by the company, found feasible to produce, and then marketed successfully.

Feasible Ideal System

Such a system, even automation, could be installed *if* only regularity conditions actually prevailed. For example, the most frequently ordered mechanical pencil out of the, say, 53 styles and 14 colors available may involve only 17% of all sales, but several feasible ideal systems would be designed as if this model constituted 100 percent of the orders.

One of several suggestions is selected as the feasible ideal system target (FIST) to serve as a guide in developing the recommended solution. The FIST line in Figure 12-9 represents one selected from the various ideas. It is assumed to have nine components. Each component has a certain cost per output unit. The need for 14 colors of mechanical pencils in whatever recommended solution is developed instead of one, for example, causes the development of other ideas that would seek to modify FIST component 1 as little as possible. Component 2, when examined, may involve

a capital expenditure far beyond the resources and borrowing capacity of the organization. Therefore, the alternative involves a greater cost per unit than the FIST component, but at a proportion that may be different from component 1. The same examination goes on for each component in the system. Some of the components, such as numbers 4 and 7, are used directly as designed in the FIST. The recommended system then comprises the selected alternative of each component that stays as close as possible to the FIST component.

Second, an effective role for creativity in P&D is defined. Creativity is far too often treated as a separate skill that, once "learned," is the same as problem solving. It is a technique that must fit within the context of a purpose or need. Creativity is needed so much in everything that it should be highly integrated into all parts of all approaches to all purposeful activities (see secondary purposeful activities in Chapters Two and Three).

Thus, all stages, phases, and steps of the protocol and strategy should foster creativity. Purpose expansion, for example, is a creativity process. The believing game fosters creativity. Regularities boost creativity for developing a target solution. The whole P&D timeline scenario fosters creative methods for implementing solutions. Chapters Thirteen to Sixteen concerning the other factors in P&D will benefit from the creative vision of what is best.

Third, developing many alternative ideas, even if not ideal, is far more likely to lead to a creative "best" or "most effective." Trying to "sell a solution" (Corollary 7b) precludes consideration of many ideas that ought to be considered before closure on a recommendation. In addition, discussions and even arguments about ideal systems and targets are preferable dialectical processes to those about who is to blame for a problem or what are the "real" facts about the problem. This carries on the process established with purposes, where many alternatives are generated as well. The timeline scenario of all features likewise fosters deliberative creative search for many alternatives in all steps and phases.

All such alternatives, regardless of how grossly or crudely they may be stated, should remain as long as possible in active consideration as the possible target. This believing game process causes the "best" to emerge. P&D is unable to anticipate in advance if a "breakthrough" creative solution is possible, so developing many creative and ideal alternatives increases markedly the probability of finding a breakthrough if one indeed exists.

Concepts of Idea Generation

Whether called creativity concepts, guides to creativity, methods of developing ideal systems, brainstorming, or concepts of developing innovations, the purpose remains the same: develop *many* ideas for achieving the selected and bigger purposes.

Very little is known about how the brain develops ideas or creative alternatives. Many studies have reported on personality characteristics of those who were creative, organizational conditions that spawned many ideas, group dynamics that fostered creativity, and other topics that report about *past* creative or idea generation situations. But these do not usually offer prescriptions for generating many ideas or being creative, let alone explain *how* creative ideas are generated.

The "bisociation"[8] version of what happens in the human mind when purposeful and creative ideas are forthcoming is probably the most reasonable prescriptive method suitable for Phase 2. Bisociation postulates that ideas occur in the human brain when two thoughts, two concepts, two models, two "things," two abstractions are mentally forced to intersect. Ideas, creative and purposeful, emerge, whether or not the idea can be traced back to the forced relationship. Nor does it make much difference to P&D if an idea can or cannot be related to two specific items.

A prescriptive version of bisociation asks that a

person think of two planes "floating" in space, each one representing one of the two items. Then the forced relationship between the two can be visualized as the line along which the two planes intersect, along which the idea is somehow structured and turned to cognizable form.

One of the planes or items is the selected purpose. Figure 12-10 illustrates the bisociation "planes" as arranged for Phase 2. The secondary plane concerns the concept, or thought, that is forced to intersect with the primary purpose plane. The two planes are "forced" to intersect many times, each time with a different thought item, technique, or concept forming the secondary plane. The forced intersection can thus benefit from different perspectives juxtaposed with the purpose plane. The major items that could comprise the secondary plane are noted in Figure 12-10.

Moving from what the individual mind does to what conditions help a group generate ideas leads to the following suggestions for improving creativity. Most of these are even more effective than the studies indicate if used with this strategy. For example, "avoiding criticism" of an idea is far easier to accomplish when seeking ideal systems for achieving a selected purpose than when trying to eliminate existing "faults." A believing game environment also helps to continually encourage creative ideas. What good is it to develop unusual and innovative ideas when the organizational climate is not willing to try to exploit them? Sug-

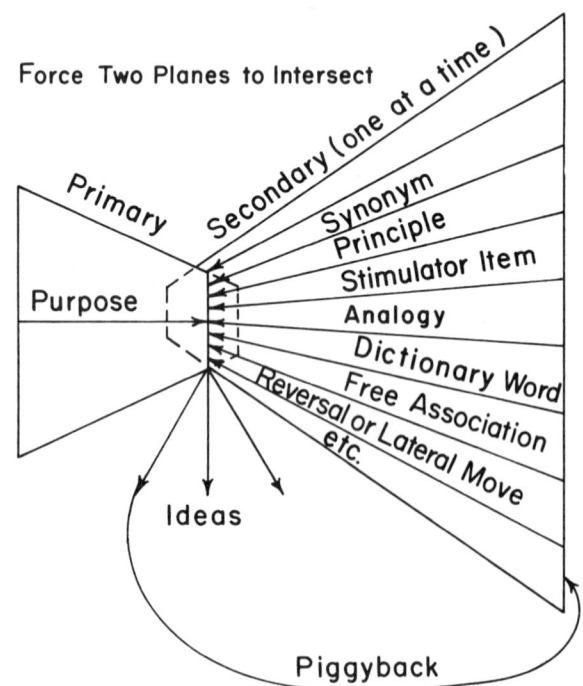

Figure 12-10 Bisociation concept of creativity.

gestions for improving group creativity include the following:

- Criticism is ruled out when ideas are being generated. Judgment and assessment of ideas occur separately, in Phases 3 and 4.
- Freewheeling is encouraged, however wild the individual ideas may appear. Talk in believing game frame of reference. Fantasies are encouraged.
- Different creativity techniques should be used to

Plant layout	Electronics devices	Forms design
Packaging	Job design	Motion economy
Automation	Student learning	Counseling
Computer systems	Appropriate technology	Inventory control
Organization design	Human factors	Warehousing
Office layout	Product design	Ergonomics
Machine and tool engineering	Information handling	Production Processing
Materials handling	Physiological distress	Chemical processing
Instrument design	Anthropometric measurement	Cybernetics
Accident prevention	Production processing	Kitchen arrangements
		Urban planning

suit the different forces that stimulate different people.
- Attempts are made to build upon an idea to combine and improve it. Piggybacking helps. Ask "what if?"
- Organizational openness, trust, and team orientation are encouraged (see Chapters Fourteen and Sixteen).
- Top-level commitment and policies conducive to searching for continuing change and improvement aid creativity (Chapter Sixteen).
- Be persistent to achieve purposes.
- Get participation of other people in applying principles.
- Involve someone not connected with project.
- Consider brain resting.
- Record all ideas.

Techniques to Foster Generation of Purposeful and Ideal Alternatives and Ideas

Figure 12-10 includes only a few of the techniques researchers in the field of creativity propose. Many depend on the evidence that unstructured word lists help people to generate ideas. Some explanation of word lists follows (see Appendix A for references for most of these).

1 *Synonyms* Develop or use a list of words related

(they may even be antonyms) to each major word or phrase in the selected purpose statement (a thesaurus is helpful). Use each one, one at a time, as the secondary plane to intersect with the purpose plane: "How could we possibly achieve (purpose x) by means of (synonym/antonym y)?"

2 *Principles* Almost every P&D profession, content area, or locus of a project has a set of principles that are felt to describe desirable and ideal conditions or solutions. This is a sampling of an almost infinite number of such types of principles:

Other titles are often assigned to such principles: checklists, laws, theories, precepts, maxims, guidelines, ideologies, and postulates. Table 12-8 is a form of principles for developing ideal systems. Another form lists key words that have been found useful: adapt, modify, magnify, minify, rearrange, reverse, substitute, invert, combine, and so on. Principles and other formats are used one at a time as the secondary plane to intersect with the purpose plane: "*How* could we possibly achieve (purpose x) by means of (principle/law/precept/checklist item y)?"

3 *Stimulator Items or Checklists* Each P&D profession or locus/subject area has many specific illustrations of previously successful ideas or solutions that can be turned into stimulators or prods for developing alternative ideas for the specific P&D project. One excellent format for organizing such experiences is the system matrix model (Axiom 8). Table 12-9 shows the arrays that might be put together for just two of the eight elements in a manufacturing setting. Other attribute listings dealing with desired properties or features is another version of a checklist.

4 *Analogy and Metaphor* If an individual or group knows about an innovative solution in a completely different field (personal, direct, symbolic, or fantasy analogy), use it as the basis of the sec-

Table 12-8   Principles for Designing Ideal Systems

1   Eliminate the need for the purpose
2   Specify one low-cost input
3   Specify one low-cost output
4   Put related knowledge/experience/information together when action is needed
5   Use automatic techniques—automation, electronic data processing, and so on
6   Deal with variances at point or origin—adaptive control
7   Utilize 100% of each resource
8   Deal with regularity factors before exceptions
9   Consider only one measure of effectiveness or behavior to be reinforced

ondary plane. Or try to turn what is strange into something familiar or vice versa. Or select a completely different field in which the same type of purpose may be needed and develop alternatives for that field, then use the solution from the second field as the basis for adaptation in the initial field. Synectics is a "problem solving process" that builds on the analogy method. The first version of analogy is the most frequent form of generating ideas: "*How* could we possibly achieve (purpose *x*) by means of (analogy *y*)?"

5 *Dictionary Words*   Thumb through a dictionary and pick out a word at random, then pose the same question: "*How* could we possibly achieve (purpose *x*) by means of (dictionary word *y*)?" This is a lot of fun for any group.

6 *Free Association*   A variant of the dictionary word method, this technique takes any thought, object, or vision that occurs or is observed as the basis of a question. Notes and forms drawn on paper are often used to start a chain of associations that may lead to ideas.

7 *Reversal or Lateral Move*   Sometimes called zig-zag thinking, this method borrows from some of the others. A reversal might look at smaller purposes in the hierarchy as the secondary plane (instead of the "frontal" attack of using larger purposes only), and a lateral move might be an analogy or stimulator item. Both are represented in thinking about how to accomplish the "opposite" purpose, or piggy-backing on another idea and thinking about its "opposite."

8 *Imaging or "Future Perfect Thinking"*   Use of the measures of effectiveness as the secondary plane to visualize what the solution might be if that measure were achieved "completely." Then

use each measure in the same way. Both the measures and the images serve as stimulators to determine how that future might be reached.

9 *Scenario Writing*   This technique can be used at two levels, first to write out the scenes of what is desired, and, second to write out the actions needed (administrative "moves," resource acquisition, possible "games" of people, etc.) to implement the first scenario.

10 *Morphological Analysis*   A morphological matrix, box, tree, or array are other terms that represent the essence of this technique (Appendix A). Various values, dimensions, examples, characteristics, conditions, properties, or attributes of a relatively independent variable become the columns, while the aspects of another variable constitute the rows. Each cell is used as a forced relationship between the two variables to generate ideas. The two variables can be one or more of several sets available in the strategy or the organization: purpose hierarchy and measures of effectiveness, inputs and outputs, regularities and functional components, business strengths and industry attractiveness, levels of people involved and values, product mix and markets served, and so on.

11 *Group Techniques*   Delphi, nominal group, brain writing, telephone conferences, and individual interviews are just some of the techniques (Chapter Fourteen and Appendix A) that are useful in generating ideas, used alone or in conjunction with most of the other techniques. Asking each group member to generate ideas away from a meeting to bring to the group is also quite effective.

12 *Small Groups Focus on Different Purpose Levels*   Set up groups of at least two people. Each group is assigned a purpose statement from the hierarchy, one group the selected level, a second group the next bigger purpose, and so on. Each group is to develop ideas to achieve its assigned purpose, and can use any creativity techniques it desires.

13 *Other Techniques*   Many other techniques are similar to those mentioned here: "What's good about it?", list of aphorisms, spin-off, search and discover (find solutions *out there*), looking at one thing and seeing another, planned ignorance, fantasy exploration, concept transformation, juxtaposition method, advocate method, crossing the senses, are good examples. Lists of slogans or thoughts that are displayed are general stimulators.

Table 12-9 Illustrative Manufacturing Stimulators Based Only on System Elements 2 and 4

STIMULATOR LIST 2: INPUTS

What ideal *input* specifications can you design for the purpose/function by considering:

New material
Scrap
Another material
Packaging
Frill elimination
Standardized parts
Purchased items
Parts manufacturing
Size of part
Positioning devices
No parts redundancy
Received size (length, width, etc.)
Shelf life
Shape
Finish specifications (colors, etc.)
Turn inside out
Product design to eliminate a material
Packing material
Nontangling parts
Weight of parts
Modular construction
Standardized forms
Small parts

Strong material
One-time carbons
Punched cards
Light-gauge material (also heavy-)
Supplier performing additional work
Strict specification of incoming quality
Auxiliary materials (oils, etc.)
Reverse of cause and effect
Number of output components
Quantities shipped
Palletized loads
Quantities packaged
Enlarged parts
Packing rearrangement
Prepack to specifications
Acceptance sampling
Analogy with completely different system
Piggy-backing of one input with another
Programmed instruction
Time to obsolescence
Composite materials
Parts redundancy

STIMULATOR LIST 4: SEQUENCE

What ideal *sequence* specifications can you design for the purpose/function by considering:

Order of performance
Combination jigs
Physical processing technique
People receiving form or report
One operation into two
Rebalance of work
Scrap handling procedure
Lot size
Operation in another department
Performance during machine time on another job
Dispatch of material from central point
Number of steps
New equipment
Two operations into one
Unit loads
Magnetic circular fields (microscopic) or bubbles in
  metal
No controls
Control established sooner or later
New processing techniques (list several)
Real-time response
Services (air, gas, water, etc.)
Sensors
Microfilm
Additional package uses
Sliding, rotating, and fixed parts

No parts redundancy
Electronic devices
Process more than one at a time
Requirements for preceding and succeeding jobs
Continuous flow processing
Handlings
Relocation and rearrangement of operations
Two or more operations
Large quantities
Omission of operations
Number of steps
Resource allocation
Piggy-back of one sequence with another
Reports directly to worker
Department size
Level of decision making
Programmed instruction
Homogeneous activities
Digital control
Parts redundancy
Computer-aided design and manufacturing
Requirements for succeeding jobs
Work while parts are in transit
Reverse order
Steps in best order
Performance after more operations than at present

Table 12-9 *(Continued)*

Alikes and unlikes	Proper point for verification
Location of performance	Number of controls
Training of operator	In-process inventory
Multispindle setups	Direct shipment
Two operations at one place	Location of storage
Material changes (see "input" list)	Analogy with a different system
Combination machinery or equipment	Regenerating answers with logic
Reprocessed scrap	Shipment from storage
Operation(s) on another machine(s)	Span of control
Correct performance or method on previous jobs	Inventory levels
Heuristic decision process	Telemetering
Slack in critical and other parts	Site requirements
Delegation of authority and decision making	Modular construction
Electronic teaching devices	Computer-based education

Parts of Phase 2

Table 12-10 lists suggested actions that can utilize all of the previously noted ideas and techniques. Item 2B, for example, refers to all of the techniques just described. Many of them are used rather than just one or two. The repetition of the phrase "ideal systems" in each of the prods in Table 12-10 should encourage the best of ideas, yet any and all ideas are sought and welcomed in Phase 2.

Each item in Table 12-10 is stated in a form that fits the bisociation concept. Item 2A, for instance, puts the bigger purpose levels into the secondary plane, seeking to force an intersection of it with the primary plane concerning the selected purpose level. Item 2D puts regularity conditions in the secondary plane and Item 2F uses measures of effectiveness. Each part of Phase 2 can be done in any order. They are not listed in any suggested sequence of steps as is done for all of the other phases.

The critical outcome of Phase 2 is a list of as many specific ideas as possible for achieving the selected or bigger purposes in the hierarchy. A *specific* idea is one that does not merely reiterate with similar or other words the stimulator or principle being used. For example, an ideal system for the function of preparing invoices should not be stated as "use electronic data processing"; this merely restates principle 5 (Table 12-8). A specific statement might be: "The customer's order is keypunched on a card which deducts the quantities from the inventory memory, adds them to the computer sales analysis register, and automatically types the combination production order–shipping copy for file, bill of lading–invoice form . . ." When principle reiteration or very general statements occur, the proposer should be asked "What do you mean by that?" or "How can you make that idea work?"

A second outcome, not always attained or necessary, is a list of the questions for which information may need to be collected. Seeking ideal systems is probably the best source of such prospective unknowns about which information is sought. It is virtually certain that all potential sources of knowledge and latest developments will not be known to everyone on the project, even if some of them are "experts" in the field. Not all questions need such a serious information-gathering effort, but the right questions are likely to be asked through this process.

PHASE 3 DEVISE FEASIBLE IDEAL SOLUTION TARGET (FIST)

All of the ideas should be viewed as potentially useful for as long as possible. Yet some decision is required through establishing a target guide or central theme for the development of a recommended solution in Phase 4.

Table 12-11 lists the steps usually considered in Phase 3 to move toward an idealized target solution which is not overly explicit in all details. It does, however, set up a model or portrait for complete specification that occurs in the next phase.

A. Identify Regularities for Target Design

Anyone trying too early to specify the details of a complete solution tends to get bogged down in coping with all the circumstances surrounding any real situation. When this happens they are likely to throw out the new ideas (because they are more difficult to work out) and go back to old ways or "proven" ideas. If this

Table 12-10 Phase 2: Generate Purposeful Alternatives (Ideal Systems)

A   Develop ideal systems that would eliminate the need for selected purpose level. What ideas achieve a bigger level purpose?

B   Develop ideal systems for achieving the selected (and bigger level) purpose by applying creativity processes.

C   Develop ideal systems for achieving the selected (and bigger level) purpose that eliminate the need for any assumed limitation.

D   Develop ideal systems for regularity conditions.

E   Develop ideal systems by reviewing list of purposes from Phase 1 to select suggestions contained therein.

F   Develop ideal systems that must satisfy only one measure of effectiveness, focusing on each one, one at a time, as if it were the only objective.

G   Review the list of ideas generated. For each clearly unachievable idea, develop proposals for the nearest approximation that is close to being feasible.

happens, the creativity of the second phase is lost and even the selected purpose may not be achieved.

The resolution of these difficulties is to develop *initially* a solution that applies *only* to the regularity conditions. The ideas are sorted into a *target* solution which would achieve the purpose only for the most important, regular or usual conditions. Then at a later time exceptions to these "regularities" are incorporated. This lets people assimilate ideas, real-world conditions, and complexities at a rate they can handle.

In effect, this process develops a feasible, workable, usable, and, it is hoped, creative target solution or central theme to fit relatively "ideal" conditions, those defined by the regularity units. Such a target solution often leads to the eventual installation of a multichanneled or pluralistic system that handles the irregularities or exceptions, yet retains most of the benefits of the target solution itself. A pluralistic or multichanneled implemented solution also sets up a continuing change perspective on the part of people in the system. It is easier to change one of the channels when it is fairly well identified than to change a part of the monolithic, single-channel solution that fits all conditions.

A regularity condition is a factor, item, or situation that most frequently occurs, is biggest, heaviest, longest, most critical, or most important. It is expected to remain relatively the same over the long term (perhaps three to five years). It actually can be anything that a group or individual wants it to be. Each regularity condition is considered to exist 100% of the

time for the purpose of developing the target. "Real" regularities are preferable to assumed ones, even though a regularity could reflect an important or critical though less frequently occurring condition. Heart attack patients in an emergency room are a small percentage of all admissions, but are considered the initial regularity condition because of their critical nature.

More than one regularity condition may be put together so that the set is assumed to be the 100% condition. For example, group technology in manufacturing seeks families of similar parts for developing "ideal" systems. A family of parts is a regularity that could be assumed to exist 100% of the time.

Each major word or phrase (verb, subject, modifier) in the selected or bigger purpose level in the hierarchy can serve as the basis for identifying *possible* regularity conditions. Each is reviewed to determine what real-world factors will be constants, basics, or invariabilities even well beyond the time horizon for the project. As an illustration, consider "to ship standard products to dealers." The major words or phrases, are *ship, standard products,* and *dealers.* For the word *ship,* these factors may be listed for consideration as regularity units: mode of shipment, destinations, form and size of shipment, shipping materials, and costs. *Standard products* might include types, styles, sizes, and quantities. *Dealers* may include wholesaler/retailer, size of city, type of dealership, total quantities purchased, and level or maintenance service provided by dealer. (See Appendix B for a wide variety of illustrations.)

In many cases, the units of regularity are tied to words that represent primarily inputs or outputs of the eventual solution. Inputs and outputs deal with larger systems or external environment that are less likely to

Table 12-11 Phase 3: Devise Feasible Ideal Solution Target (FIST)

A   Identify regularities for the target.

B   Separate ideas into major alternatives and incorporate as many component ideas as possible into each alternative.

C   Provide more detail for each major alternative to ensure workability and allow assessment of effectiveness.

D   Identify each major alternative as contemplative or feasible. Review contemplative categories with experts to determine their present feasibility.

E   Select feasible ideal system target (FIST) for regularities by evaluating the major alternatives with measures of effectiveness.

F   Make FIST more ideal and as operational as possible.

G   Save other ideas.

change for the project, however large or small it may be. In other words, identifying conceivable input and output conditions regarding each word of the purpose is another way of suggesting possible regularities.

Another method of identifying regularities relates to the functional components that may have been identified in Phase 1. A purpose level decomposed into a system pyramid establishes conditions from which one or a set of components can be selected as most regular. Similar techniques, such as the relationship chart or interaction matrix (Appendix A), portray frequency or importance of activities which may be viewed as possible regularity units.

Still another method merely selects a distant point in time as the "regularity." This permits people to think in terms of ideal conditions: "How do you think a college of engineering would best be organized 10 years from now?" "What would be an ideal gypsy moth pest management system for the United States five years from now?" "How would the downtown area look four years from now after the urban development project is completed?" Each of these time-based conditions may also require "smaller" regularity decisions, but they are often much easier to make in this context. The most important engineering topics to serve as regularity conditions for 10 years from now are likely to be considered easily because people's personal concerns *now* are not at stake.

No unit should be accepted as a regularity if it in any way limits creativity. For example, although the most frequently occurring mode of shipment *can* be identified (railroads 40%, trucks 35%, air freight 20%, and customer pickup 5%), assuming that railroads are 100% of the conditions may well cut off innovative ideas about air shipments. One way to avoid this trap is to make successive assumptions first that air, then that trucks, and last that customer pick-up constitutes 100% of the shipment conditions.

Thus, regularities are not an end in themselves, but rather a means toward the end of developing a FIST. Even though the concept of regularities represents a significant breakthrough in actually designing "ideal" systems, just listing regularity possibilities does not mean any of them should be used. The list is reviewed to decide which might need further consideration. Some data *might* be collected to get specific values for the regularity units. The question is to determine if precise data would change any conclusion based on estimated data.

Selecting the units for a specific project is often accomplished on a trial-and-error basis. Formal criteria, such as suitability, importance to management, and proportion of cost in the whole system, might be used, but most decisions to utilize a regularity unit are made

on a subjective basis. In addition, the design of ideal systems can easily switch to or from any regularity unit, thus making this a noncritical decision.

If more than one regularity condition is selected, and each becomes the basis of its own FIST, then Phase 4 would seek to combine the best features of all the FISTs.

B. Separate Ideas into Major Alternatives

The quality, type, and degree of utility of each idea in Phase 2 is highly variable. The objective there was simply to generate ideas of any type or scope: minimal improvements over what exists, "wild" ideas, solutions others have used successfully, vague scenarios, custom-made systems, complete and self-explanatory ideas, incomplete kernels of an idea, modifications or adaptations (piggy-back) of what others are doing, or significant creative concepts. More of all types are encouraged even in this phase.

Actually, the search for ideas and alternatives should continue as long as possible. Commitment to any one idea or concept should be avoided until the latest possible moment, approximately step 3E. Creativity is encouraged through competing alternatives. One tactic of possible help is to develop an optimistic and a pessimistic scenario for each alternative. This also helps to overcome the propensity for an organization to develop very early only one solution idea more completely than others.[9] Setting up major alternatives thus encourages avoidance of premature closure on just one idea and simultaneously the forced inclusion of as many good ideas as possible into each of the alternatives being considered.

A *major alternative* is a broad and complete idea that, if implemented, would *in itself* achieve the selected purpose basically for regularity conditions. Major alternatives are relatively mutually exclusive. Only *one* of them is selected as the target for achieving the selected purpose, even though a "small" idea may appear in several of the alternatives. A *major component* may be broad, but it is not a complete solution in itself. It must be combined with others to produce a major alternative, may be part of one or more major alternatives, or combined with other major components in various ways to produce additional major alternatives. Any remaining ideas are *details* that may fit many major alternatives or major components.

Each idea on the list from Phase 2 is reviewed to determine its status: major alternative, component, or detail. Additional ideas are listed as they are thought of or as various components are combined or restructured to form a new alternative or component. If no major alternatives are initially identified, then ideas and components should be put together to form them, the purpose expansion should be redone, creativity techniques should be used again, or the believing game should be "played" while focussing on regularity conditions.

C. Provide More Detail for Each Major Alternative

Each P&D effort will need different degress of detail. All that should be sought is the amount needed to assure the organization that each alternative is workable and to assess sufficiently its performance in terms of the M of E so that all the alternatives can be compared. The stage of the protocol for which the strategy is being applied affects the amount of detail needed. The amount is far less for the feasibility study stage than for the stage of developing construction plans for bidding; for determining marketing policies than for locating warehouses; for the overall degree curriculum than for the fourth unit in Course 345; for determining users' information needs than for the flow process in developing computer programs.

The system matrix (Axiom 8) can guide how each alternative is probed to determine what details are needed. Certain factors (purpose hierarchy, selected function level, M of E, some human agents, etc.) may remain the same for each alternative, but the remaining cells can provide more than enough stimuli for questions whose answers are needed to insure workability and estimate performances.

Other guides are available to help provide the level of detail needed here:

1 Adhere to basic principles, ideal system concept, regularities, and so forth. The question to ask is: How *can* an ideal system be developed from the major alternative idea using this principle?
2 Incorporate some exceptions. The question to ask is: How *can* the "ideal" system alternative stay the same while incorporating this particular exception? One particularly good exception to inquire about concerns the control dimension. These questions are usually detailed after the fundamental parts of the alternative are detailed, but control details often go hand in hand iteratively with fundamental ones, so that workability and effectiveness might be better assessed.
3 Identify significant and sensitive parameters or variables. The level of detail needed in this step should only involve determining whether a system's workability is contemplative or feasible. Parameters, variables, and other M of E can also be reviewed at this point to determine if dynamic considerations ought to be considered in place of the

usual static measures. Each M of E can be used in a series of questions: "How much detail is needed for the effectiveness of alternative 1 on measure A to be assessed?" Then on measure B, and so on. Then the same questions are asked for each of the other major alternatives.

4 Many types of models (Appendix A) could be used to provide details (see the secondary purposeful activity of modeling in Table 3-9). When combined with the system matrix, these techniques and models enable an initial "testing" of the alternative to determine how it would possibly work in a dynamic setting, how it relates to other systems (interface dimension), how it might respond to disturbances, new knowledge, and normal operating changes (Figure 10-4), and what types of organizational consequences might be anticipated.
5 Play the believing game with each major alternative. Believe the first major alternative *is* the FIST, then ask, "What is needed to do to make it work?" Then believe the second major alternative is the FIST and ask the same question. Continue with all of the alternatives.

Other guides useful here can also help in all detailing activities in Phases 4 and 5:

1 Be sure a specification is accomplishing the achievement of the purpose.
2 Specify only the critical minimum amount of detail, and let people in the system add what remains.
3 Include multiple modes of achieving purposes and objectives whenever appropriate.
4 Put information and control requirements at points close to the origin of difficulty and where actions can be taken.
5 Include transitional and changeover specifications.
6 Schedule into the details the effort for planned betterment design.
7 Determine if the specification(s) make sense to readers and users of the solution (especially Phases 4 and 5).
8 Provide complete, operational, decomposable and nonredundant specifications.
9 Relate specifications to performance expectations (costs, time, life cycle, quality of work life, etc.).

Many questions naturally arise as such detailing is underway. Every question should not necessarily lead to an information-gathering project. Instead, each question should first be assessed to determine if answers are needed at this point to achieve the purpose of this step and the Phase (to select a FIST).

Broad and sometimes specific performance characteristics are often needed as effectiveness analyses of each major alternative before it will be possible to select the FIST. Most performance characteristics are the M of Es (e.g., costs, time, technical capability) but may also include other critical operational components (e.g., form of control, social interactions, environmental impact, legal conditions). When the M of Es and operational components are estimated or measured for the amount of their presence in each alternative, the outcome and some operational conditions will be available for selecting the FIST. The values, measures, and control dimensions of the alternative system matrices (hypothetical or actually available) aid in generating specific state variables or performance characteristics to accompany the M of E. The required estimation of particular performance conditions for an alternative and the probabilities of outcomes not conditional on actions taken are accomplished with some of the many available techniques: historical time and cost data, forecasting models, reliability distributions, overhead rates, progress functions, predetermined motion-time data, time series analysis, multiple regression, sensitivity analysis, simulation with or without computers, and many others (see Appendix A).

D.   Identify Each Major Alternative as Contemplative or Feasible

The purpose of this step is to identify the major alternatives from which the FIST is to be selected. Another outcome is a list of ideas for which additional research and development might be started.

A major alternative is contemplative if several of its components do not now appear capable of real-life implementation. It would be considered feasible if current levels of information, development, and technology indicate that all components *for the regularities* apparently are implementable immediately without regard to costs to achieve the purpose.

Changes and additions to the major alternatives are often found in this step. Some weeding out of less effective alternatives takes place, but no urgency exists to omit one yet.

Other criteria for delineating contemplative and feasible alternatives are suggested by those proposed for assessing "the strategic merit of a potentially radical technological innovation . . . [These include] inventive merit . . . to relieve or avoid major constraints inherent in the previous art . . . [sufficient so] that the new constraints were not binding; embodiment merit [to give] physical form to inventive concept [through] substantial additional engineering [that]

minimize dilutions of the value of the inventive concept while maximizing enhancements; operational merit [to determine] the effect of an innovation on a company's existing business practices [where] the more potent the technology in question, the more likely it is that existing business operations will be superseded; [and] market merit [to assess] final demand, not intermediate demand, and total revenue opportunity . . . by price reduction . . . or by an increase in the attractiveness of the product."[10] These criteria will help also set up priorities for allocating research and development resources for trying to change a contemplative idea into an eventual feasible one.

All contemplative alternatives should also be reviewed with experts (e.g., manufacturers and/or their representatives, research and development organizations, federal government information centers, libraries, technicians). They are often in a position to provide good estimates for the timing of a breakthrough that the FIST might need to anticipate. These resources can also provide some estimate of how long it may take to get needed information about feasibility and workability questions.

This step makes it possible for groups with varying amounts of knowledge and ability to be successful in P&D. Someone not knowledgeable in all the latest technology is likely to call a major alternative contemplative when it is really feasible. Reviewing such ideas with experts can ascertain the actual feasibility of each.

E.   Select Feasible Ideal Solution Target (FIST) For Regularities

This step establishes a guiding solution, the FIST, for achieving the function. Even though the FIST is considered workable, economic, beneficial, compatible, and aesthetic (if this is important) for only the regularity conditions, it serves as a beacon for or central theme of what is most desirable during the development of the solution to be recommended for coping with all conditions. A FIST is

1 Workable
2 for only regularity conditions assumed to exist 100% of the time
3 for which it provides the optimum balance among
4 all measures of effectiveness
5 in achieving the selected and bigger functions/ purposes.

It is selected from among the several major alternatives, each of which can be considered a candidate for feasible ideal solution. Each major alternative is usually available to this step as a complete, unified, logical, and internally consistent pattern of relationships, albeit not detailed sufficiently for actual implementation.

Arriving at a FIST is essentially a decision-making process. FIST purposes need two broad amplifications: First, establishing factors about which information is needed in order to make a selection, and second, processes of utilizing the factors in making the selection.

Factors about Which Information Is Needed

The decision worksheet (Chapter Fifteen and Appendix A) states the basic factors: (1) the criteria, scales of value, or measures of effectiveness (step 1D) for judging the merits and demerits of each major alternative; (2) the weighting or importance of each criterion; (3) the methods of measuring the amount of a criterion "possessed" by each alternative, and (4) the specific alternatives to be assessed.

1 On the basis of the dichotomous and threshold measures of effectiveness an alternative will be rejected for further consideration if it does not meet the desired conditions. The continuous criteria use the performance characteristics (step 3C) to assess an alternative (dollars, job satisfaction, time, number of people).

2 Weightings or importance values are usually critical for each of the variable criteria to provide an appropriate method of combining all of the measurements about each alternative. Assigning differential loadings to each criterion is itself a critical measurement activity. It is essentially impossible to do accurately and precisely. Some of the subjective available techniques to help in evaluation include utility theory, subjective judgment, questionnaires, nominal group technique, Delphi technique, and voting (Chapter Fifteen and Appendix A). One quite simple method picks out the least important criterion, to which a weighting of 1 is assigned. Then a numeral is assigned to each other criterion to express how much more important it is (2 times, 5 times, 1½ times) than the least important one.

3 Measuring the amount of a criterion that each alternative contains is often already accomplished when performance characteristics are determined: The alternative will have a capital cost of $15,000; it *does* include ramps for the handicapped; an audit mechanism will operate once a year; four hours will be needed to process the inputs into the outputs; and so on. Other criteria will ordinarily need to be measured at this point: esthetic appeal, capability for continued change, monotony, flexibility, maintainability, safety level, conduciveness of political climate, and so on. Several subjective techniques may be used, all of them variants of utility theory. A simple subjective tool involves a scale from 0 to 100, with 0 representing absolutely none of the criterion or absolutely the worst condition (e.g., infinite costs, no reliability, infinite time, no flexibility), and 100 absolutely all of the criterion or absolutely the best condition (e.g., zero costs, complete reliability, complete flexibility).

The 0-to-100 scale can be used for each criterion in evaluating the alternatives. Start with criterion A, for example, and determine (or ask the group to assess) how much from 0 to 100 of criterion A is present in alternative 1, then in alternative 2, and so on. Then how much of criterion B is in each alternative, and so on. Another form of the question is, what performance from 0 to 100 would we expect from alternative 1 in terms of criterion A?

A more theoretically "correct" method assigns 100 points, say, to each criterion. The 100 points are then divided up among all the alternatives according to each one's expected performance.

When probabilities of occurrence (or utilities of certain external conditions or states of nature) can influence the level of a criterion in an alternative, and data are available about the occurrences, a group can also estimate the probability of each state by means of the 0-to-100 scaling technique. Multiplying the amount (utility, goodness, allocated points) of a criterion present in an alternative by the weighting (and if necessary, by the probability of a state of nature) produces the "numbers" to be utilized in making the selection.

Processes of Utilizing Factors in Selecting the FIST

The decision worksheet puts all of the weightings, measurements, and probabilities together by multiplication in a cell representing the intersection of the criterion row and alternative column. This provides a basis for adding numbers. The alternative with the highest total is supposedly the one to be selected. It presumably represents the solution that most effectively trades off the various criteria and values that are in conflict with each other (e.g., cost and esthetics, practicality and innovation).

Yet that alternative should never be accepted as the FIST on the basis only of this total. Errors and differences in opinion along with uncertainties cause the numerical scores to have wide variability. A change in just a few of the measurements could effect which alternative is selected. When added to the impossibility of ever having *all* of the criteria clearly stated, this variability indicates only the alternative that should start discussions among the people involved until an alternative is finally settled on. In addition, all criteria, weightings, and measures should be reviewed so that everyone is sure of their meanings, because the decision worksheet is a linear reasoning process, whereas combinations of alternatives and components are not directly linear (in other words, additive or multiplicative).

The literature of decision making often refers to the usual process in terms of a mathematical equation or criterion function. If the total points are the dependent variable X, then $X_k = \Sigma_1^n W_i X_{ik}$ explains the description in the previous paragraph, where W_i = weight of criterion X_i, and X_{ik} = the measure of the amount of criterion X_i in alternative k. $W_i X_{ik}$ could be further modified for each of the probabilities about a state of nature or outcome not dependent on the alternatives. Then the X_k are compared to obtain the first approximation of the FIST. The difficulties in developing a completely quantitative selection of the FIST suggests that some simplified techniques might well be as effective.

One is the index or ratio value that divides the measures into two groups: benefit/cost ratio, effectiveness/cost ratio, benefit/risk ratio, and so on. Some factors may not appear to fit into either category and may thus be neglected, but this is not particularly wise.

Another simplified technique is the lexicographic model, which ranks (rates or measures) each alternative on the basis of the most important criterion. Those with the same "highest" desirability value are then measured on the second most important measure of effectiveness. Those with the same score or index value are then measured on the third most important criterion, and so on until only one alternative remains.

The decision tree is another technique for relatively large projects. Each functional component has several possible alternatives, and an alternative selected for one functional component will fit with any alternative selected for another component. Thus, the functional components are relatively independent (e.g., for a new metropolitan mass transit system, the type of buses, form of schedule, personnel selection.) Another decision tree version starts with a project where the sequence of activities is important. How one activity is performed sets up a range of alternatives somewhat different than the range available for another initial activity. Probabilities of the occurrence of certain states of nature could influence the selection of the next activity. Still another version translates the lexicographic model into a visual tree format where each level concerns only one criterion. Probabilities are also easily incorporated and portrayed.

In addition to selecting one FIST for the regularity conditions, some projects in this step might select several FISTS, one for each of the major regularity conditions or relatively independent functional components. This occurs if *each* regularity condition was treated as if it occurred 100% of the time, and ideal systems were developed for each one in Phase 2. Then Phase 4 would combine all of the FISTs into a recommended solution, while staying as close as possible to each FIST.

Multiple FISTs may also be needed when the same project is performed in several locations. A letter I received describes this view:

I have been working with three project teams—one from each of our three main plants. All three were given the same problem—designing a new hog cut [initial processing of hogs in meat-packing company] for each of their respective plants. Our original thought was that we would have a common target system for all three plants. As it worked out, however, we found that a separate target system was required for each of the three plants. Even slight differences in such things as product mix, local specifications, etc., meant that a common target was not practical. On the other hand, it may well be that the differences that eventually showed up in the recommended systems will be blessings in disguise. Because of this we were forced to design a better control and information system that will do a better job of evaluating the performance of the proposed system as well as better information in future systems. Corporate management is very enthusiastic about the proposed systems. The estimated cost reductions and returns on the investments are far better than they expected and even better than I had guaranteed before the project was undertaken.

The FIST or FISTs are somewhat comparable to concepts in other P&D approaches. A "blueprint" is suggested as a guide for formalizing the concepts of a variety of people who seek changes based on their ideological premises. A "sketch plan" is a set of guideline policies or central themes that reflect the "optimum" balance between "what is" and "what ought to be."[11] Even "master plan" might be used if it referred to guides rather than to specific details not to be changed. A FIST differs from these because the strategy and approach does influence their quality. A FIST is purpose, ideal- and regularity-based, whereas the others are usually activity-, current-, and expert-based.

F. Make FIST as Ideal and as Operational as Possible

Two viewpoints explain the first part of this step. The first is simply always to seek an ideal result. Be a thief: Steal what is good from B, C, and D, even though A has been selected. The FIST for regularity conditions should always be viewed, regardless of resources allocated or time available, as constantly subject to being developed to a more "ideal" state. In addition, compromises may have resulted in a "nearest semifeasible solution" or "somewhat creative" level, which should always be considered open to further improvement.

Clues as to how this might be achieved are furnished by the measurements of goodness of the criteria in step 3E. A criterion on which the FIST did not measure well offers a good potential area for making the FIST better. If the capital cost criterion showed that the FIST may involve a high initial expenditure, a better ideal system might be sought to achieve the function with a lower capital expenditure.

The second viewpoint is the recognition that, in a year or two, the FIST itself, irrespective of how valuable it is now, should be developed all over again to take advantage of new knowledge and technology. Avoid associating finality with the FIST. The FIST, like recommended solutions, has to change or stagnation sets in.

Developing a more operational FIST (or set of FISTs) is not always necessary, but it should be actively considered in a project as a means of helping the overall implementation process. Providing greater assurance of workability can go a long way toward getting decision makers and implementers to accept the value of a target guide(s) for aiding the rest of the P&D effort. In addition, being alert to workability and operationality questions can help minimize the delays of decision makers and others in accepting and moving toward the eventual recommendation. Even though regularities are involved, decision makers and others often ask about how the FIST will "actually work," who will be able to do it, when will or could it be done, and from where will the resources be obtained (usually what other organizational areas will be changed or eliminated to provide most of them). Preparing such scenarios in advance helps speed up implementation.

One other consideration may arise, timing of the project. The more innovative the FIST and thus the likely recommendations, the more the client or organization needs to be ready and able to accept it. The PDA timeline scenario addresses this specifically. Yet a deliberate effort may be needed to make certain the real world's perceptions are moved along. This is not a deliberate delay as much as it is reflective anticipation of the needs in the timeline scenario.

G. Save Other Ideas

Retaining all ideal system suggestions, major alternatives, and components may help at a later time in the particular project and in other projects. There is always the possibility that the FIST may be rejected later, and a new target will be needed. Alternatives, if needed, can in Phase 4 be stimulated by review of the file of ideas. A computerized arrangement of key words could be used, or a filing system should be established to keep the various ideal systems categorized by organizational unit, technology involved, components used, and project number.

PHASE 4 DEVELOP AND DETAIL THE RECOMMENDED SOLUTION

The FIST is but a milestone event towards an implemented solution, only a means toward the desired P&D end. It guides short-term activity in developing a recommended solution and long-term activities in making the many small decisions necessary in Phase 5 as installation takes place.

A simple illustration demonstrates the purposes of this phase and the benefits of the FIST-recommended solution relationship. I was helping a men's retail store company develop a warehouse to serve nine stores in one metropolitan area. The group with which I was working had just arrived at a FIST, as shown in the solid lines of Figure 12-11. Its regularity condition was merchandise to be marked with tags for shipment to the stores (60% of the arrivals at the warehouse). The merchandise was unloaded onto the conveyor and proceeded along it until it was ready for loading on trucks for delivery to the stores.

The president of the company walked by the group at about the time the FIST drawing only was on a big sheet of paper on the table. After some explanation of purposes, measures of effectiveness, and ideas explored before arriving at the FIST, the president exclaimed, "But you can't do *that*," pointing to the FIST. "It won't handle the merchandise to be returned to the vendors." In other words, he was immediately willing (as occurs in most conventional P&D) to throw away the solution idea that was "good" for 60% of what occurs because he felt 8% of the needs would not be processed in the same "system." He was displaying the syndrome of "one route" or "one process" for everything.

The group did search very diligently for methods of adjusting the FIST as little as possible so that the irregularities could be included, but found, as the president intuitively noted, that the irregularity of merchandise to be returned to vendors really could not be incorporated into the conveyor concept of the FIST. But that doesn't mean the group discarded the FIST. They developed "FISTs" for the major exception

—————————— CAPITAL LETTERS = FIST for new merchandise to be marked

for 9 stores

------------------ lower case letters = additions to FIST to develop a

recommended solution for all conditions

WAREHOUSE FOR MEN'S CLOTHING RETAILER WITH NINE STORES IN A LARGE CITY

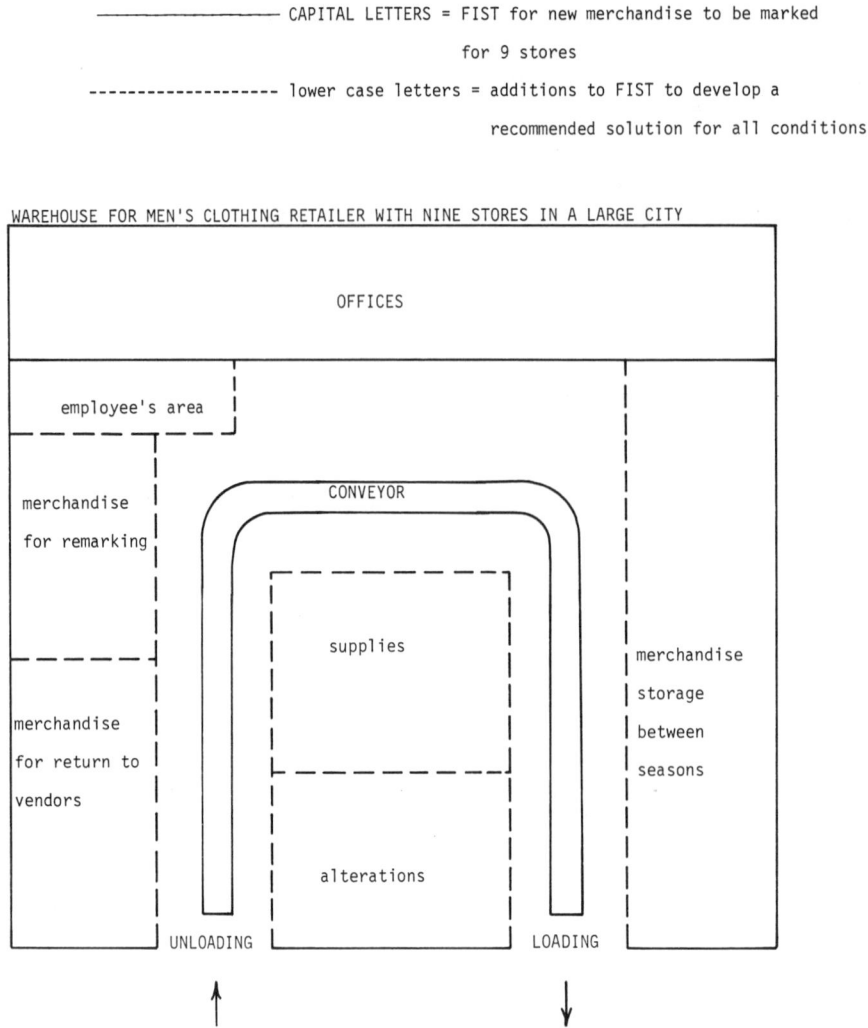

Figure 12-11 An illustration of the FIST and recommended solutions.

conditions, and where compatibility with the major FIST could not be developed, set up a separate channel or "system" for the irregularity. These are shown with dashed lines in Figure 12-11. The trade-offs and effectiveness balancing among the several alternatives showed that the conveyor FIST should be retained in the recommended solution along with the other channels. There was no reason to have one "system" to handle everything.

Thus, the outcome expected in this phase is the set of recommendations that are supposed to constitute the solution to be installed. The recommended solution is developed to stay as close as possible to the FIST, and is very often multichanneled and pluralistic. The steps usually needed and iteratively performed in this phase to arrive at the recommendations are summarized in Table 12-12. Detailing a solution can be an extensive activity, especially since several steps in the phase can each become a P&D project.

Table 12-12 Phase 4: Develop and Detail the Recommended Solution

A Develop alternatives for FIST components that will incorporate needed irregularities, exceptions, and conditions while staying as close as possible to the FIST.

B Estimate performances, outcomes, and consequences of each alternative to assess effectiveness and incorporate possible self-correction methods.

C Select the workable solution that is to be recommended for adoption or for approval.

D Formulate plans to get final approval of the workable solution.

E Develop details of the solution as far as needed to permit its installation or movement to next stage of protocol. Use elements and dimensions of solution framework.

F Review the recommended solution framework with knowledgeable people to assure its implementability.

A. Develop Alternatives for FIST Components

The FIST can be divided into units or components (Axioms 3 and 4). Each unit or component is represented abstractly by means of a particular model or set of specifications. Figure 12-12 illustrates a simple layout with the components identified by letters. Figure 12-13 shows the same type of component division with a simple form process chart.

This step generates as many additional ways as possible each component could be achieved if the irregularities were included where needed. Some components (C in Figure 12-12, for example) may need no alternatives because the FIST component suits all conditions. No alternatives may be found for a component that needs some. In this case, the solution will probably involve multiple methods (as in Figure 12-11), or the project may need to return to a previous phase or step.

There are several ways to find alternative workable solutions for the components that need to incorporate irregular conditions:

1 *Apply the Basic Strategy Pattern* Because each component is a system, ask What is its function? What are ideal systems for achieving this function? Some of the ideas might even improve the FIST component as well as incorporate ways of coping with irregularities.

2 *Adhere to Principles and Special Checklists* Principles and stimulator lists in appropriate fields (e.g., human factors, numerical control, facility planning, job design for older workers, learning, nursing care, group behavior) can prod thought processes for developing alternatives: How could Principle 3 be turned into a way of achieving the purpose of component A that stays as close as possible to its FIST? Special considerations, such as appropriate technology in developing countries, can be incorporated: What is an ideal solution to achieve the purpose of the component with 100% labor or local resources?

3 *Creativity Methods* As reviewed in Phase 2, persist in achieving purposes, freewheeling, talk aloud, involve someone not at all connected with the project, brain resting, etc.

4 *File Ideal Systems Ideas* Other ideal systems ideas on file as well as those recorded at the end of Phase 2 may be helpful.

5 *Get People to Participate* Without any of the other aids, this alone could achieve the purpose of this step.

Figures 12-12 and 12-13 show how there may be various ideas for accomplishing each component. Combinations of ideas for various components give rise to many alternative solutions. Alternative 1 could be A1 + B + C + D1 + E1; alternative 2 could be A2 + B + C + D1 + E1, and so on. Each possible combination of component ideas could be identified (especially if a computer is available) to provide a complete set of alternative solutions for evaluation in step 4C. Such a list could also stimulate additional ideas. Patently unworkable alternatives can be eliminated at this point.

Another perspective for this step was noted in step 3E: Develop a FIST for each of the major regularity sets or for each of the functional components. Each regularity set is considered to exist 100% of the time for which a whole FIST is developed. One project re-

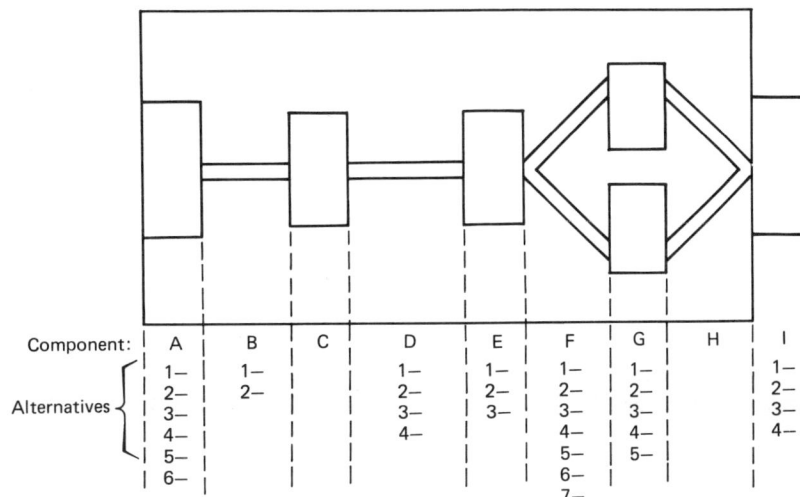

Figure 12-12 Illustrative layout model of a FIST.

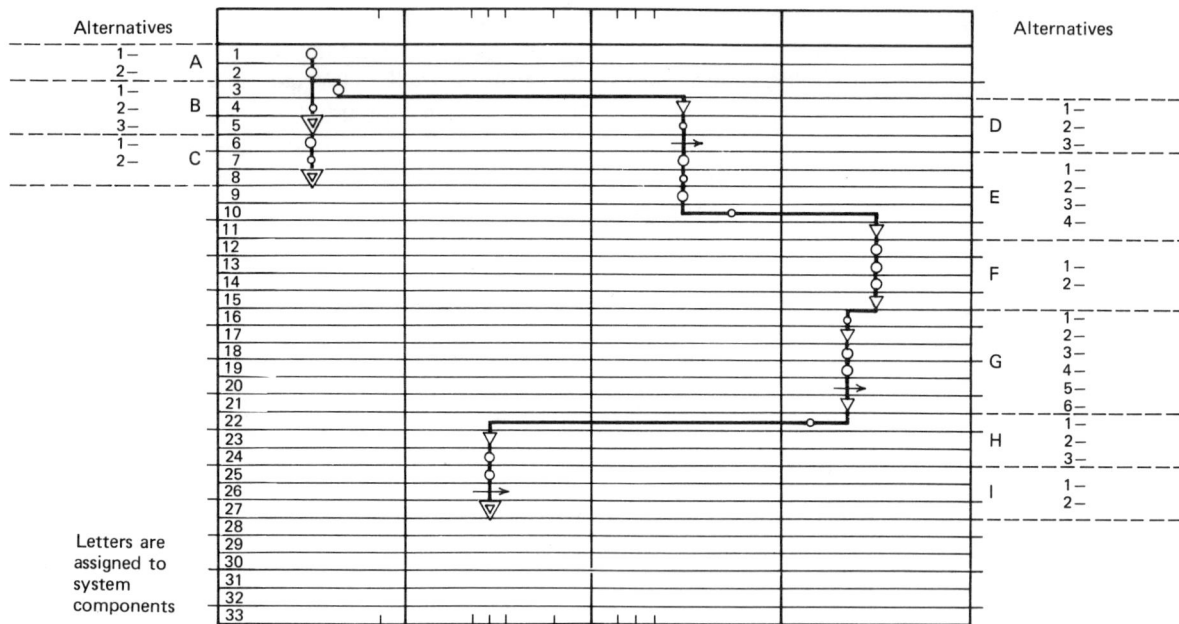

Figure 12-13 Illustrative form process chart of a FIST.

calling military personnel from leave in an emergency, had six functional components, each of which had a separate FIST. Separate FISTs are also helpful in large-scale projects, such as planning a hospital, regional planning of irrigation, or developing a multiproduct marketing program. Such efforts usually involve almost independent functions (in a school: science class, maintenance, sports) or "fundamental" unit operations (see sequence element, Chapter Nine). Some changes are inevitable whenever FISTs are put together. These are also the alternatives sought in this step.

B. Estimate Performances, Outcomes, and Consequences of Each Alternative

Additional detailing of these alternatives should really precede any effort to estimate performances and consequences. This will provide greater assurance that they are workable, suitable, and "proper" (anticipate effects *on* people, cope with undesired outcomes, etc.) before estimates and assessments of utility are obtained. Getting operational details is a procedure already discussed in previous sections, so I will proceed directly to the estimation purposes of this step.

The accuracy and precision of these estimates are likely to be greater than those in step 3E but not as great as the measurements needed in Phase 5 for the eventual operators and supervisors of the system. Several techniques may be considered for developing the estimates. They are listed in the purposes/

functions referencing in Appendix A under the following headings:

Analyze job methods and motions

Appraise/assess investments

Appraise/assess alternative options/plans/policies/ programs

Appraise/assess systems

Collect data and/or information

Describe/establish/measure relationships

Estimate budget and dollar requirements

Evaluate alternatives

Measure errors

Getting the variety of estimates needed—performance, consequences, labor needs, learning and progress curves, reliability, benefits, advantages, cash flow and costs (direct, indirect, capital), time, outcomes—for each alternative to the FIST may be done by comparing what has been needed with similar types of activities or objects, for which historical data are available. But it may quite often require a study or data collection process. The basic strategy pattern can be used to design the needed information/data collection "system." Experience in many projects using the basic strategy pattern for information gathering leads to five ideas:

1 *Keep asking what the purpose/function of the information collection system is* Even if the purpose is necessary when information gathering starts, a group or specialists can easily get sidetracked. Also, continually assess if the specific information or measures being sought must be obtained so accurately.

2 *Seek an ideal system target to guide information collection* At least the principle of zero data collection should always be a guide while information-gathering systems are being developed. Ask if subjective estimates will suffice. Ask if a few measures rather than many will suffice. And so on.

3 *Ascertain the representativeness of the population basis and the sample of data for the function to be achieved* ''Good'' data about the wrong set of conditions or population are useless. The period of time over which sampling data are collected must also represent the desired framework. Starting with an unrepresentative basis can almost never be corrected by any type of prediction or forecasting, the main need in this phase.

4 *Accuracy of data to be collected should reflect only the needs of the decision to be made, not usual statistical presumed confidence levels* This is often a question of sensitivity. What impact will a lack of data or of accuracy have on the decision to be made? If a slight error affects the decision, then greater accuracy or more data are needed. Would the decision be modified if the data were, say, negative? This idea emphasizes the value of roughing out the form of the estimates needed, simulating the values to be obtained, and manipulating the information in a hypothetical fashion to determine the questions where accurate decisions need to be made.

5 *Get people involved in providing estimates as well as in obtaining information* Those involved in the project or real world can help and be helped toward eventual implementation by being a part of this process. Chapter Fifteen reviews some techniques for getting ''good'' measures and data with people.

Organizing information about each alternative in a system matrix format (Axiom 8) is an effective way to identify what estimates and other specifications may be needed. It can also pinpoint where specific trade-off conditions require consideration among the alternatives (greater federal centralization in gypsy moth pest management must be balanced against the need for a fast response time when an infestation occurs) and where more or less measurements may be needed. Some operations research and optimization techniques may be needed within (how many servers will

minimize wait time) or between alternatives (make, buy, or lease) to provide suitable estimations.

C. Select Workable Solution to be Recommended

Step 3E is essentially applicable here. Some differences include M of Es and weightings that reflect all regularity and irregularity conditions, and more accurate measurements of the amount of a criterion present in each alternative.

A frequent difficulty in the selection process is the evaluation of *how well* (effectiveness) each alternative accomplishes the function. For example, the function of one telephone company system is to initiate action when a customer calls requesting service for a telephone. Time and cost were natural M of E, but the intangible effectiveness ingredient determining how well the function was accomplished was the voice image, or pleasantness, the customer experienced when making the call. An alternative may be less costly and take less time, but its coldly efficient performance may destroy a valuable source of information about the company as a whole. A company lending library for nonfiction books may have an automatic system to procure, check out, and return books to achieve least cost and time goals. But the critical factor, determining how well the function is accomplished, may be the enthusiasm a reader may develop by discussing various titles with a knowledgeable librarian.

Psychological and organizational factors are major considerations here, especially when expanded by other terms—social, political, legal, consumer, community, and even technical. Different skills and levels of complexity influence the way people react to an alternative. People tend to view what they are already doing as representative of the highest-level personal capacity. When a possible solution requires greater skill and knowledge, they wonder how they are to achieve the new level, and often reject the suggestion because of this apprehension.

Even though the PDA scenario involves people, the attitudes of some may not always be sympathetic. For example, persons from whom authority and information must be obtained may have personality characteristics that make them difficult to work with. On occasion, the person from whom final approval may have to be obtained was instrumental in setting up the current system, which the alternative would change. A suggestion for change may not agree with the attitude that ''my system is quite outstanding.''

Some consideration beyond the alternative itself must extend to its probable effect on personnel in general. What will the current people do with their extra time? Is more work available? What will happen

Table 12-13 Illustration of an Evaluation Work Sheet Selection of Workable System

System or Operation: Door for Burner (handling)				*Project No.:* C-100 series	
Dept.:				*Date:* Sept., 1960	

	System No. 1, 3, Forklift	System No. 1, 4, 5,	System No. 2*	System No.	System No.
How much installation cost?			Conveyor		
1 New machines	10,000	50 trucks @ $50 =	$20/ft. × 700 = $14,000		
2 New tools Material Labor	—	$2,500	Motors $800		
3 New designs		4-wheel hand trucks			
4 Installation	50		Hangers (200)		
5 Overhead			$2,000		
6 Scrap of machinery, tools, and materials					
7 Misc. (loss of production, wages, etc.)					
8 New cost	10,050		$16,800		
9 Less salvage					
10 Total cost	10,050	2,500	16,800		
(a) Depreciated cost per year	2,010	500	3,360		
How much operating cost?	—	—			
11 Present system Labor Material Machine rate, overhead, and misc.					
12 Total					
13 Proposed system Labor	$3 × 500 hrs. (for door line) = 1,500	$2.50 × 1,000 hrs. = 2,500			
Material Machine rate, overhead, and misc.	$2 × 500 = 1,000	$1.50 × 1,000 hrs. = 1,500	Power $500 Maintenance $300		
14 Total	$2,500	4,000	800		
15 Cost per unit or $ sales	—	—			
16 Expected volume per year					
17 Total operating cost per year	2,500	4,000	800		
18 Present operating cost per year					

Table 12-13 (*Continued*)

19	Gross savings/ year 10 or 10a less cost	$+ \dfrac{2{,}010}{25\% \text{ util.}}$	500	3,360
20	Net savings/ year	Total cost/yr. = $3,000	Total cost/yr. = $4,500	Total cost/yr. = $4,160
21	Rate of return			
22	Hazard factor	Need wider aisles—greater safety problem	Creates poor housekeeping	—
23	Control factor	Flexible	Can cause too much damage to parts through handling	Closer to ideal system target
24	Psychological factor	—	—	—

From G. Nadler, *Work Design: A Systems Concept*, Homewood, Ill., Richard D. Irwin, 1970.
* Selected system.

to workers removed from jobs? Are any important social groupings involved with the change? What effect will local and national economic conditions have on the personnel if the change is made now? Chapters Thirteen through Sixteen are concerned with how most of these questions may be answered.

Judgment and nonquantitative factors usually determine the selection, primarily because so many trade-offs are needed among criteria. For example, choosing an alternative asks which one adds or achieves the greatest amount of the values in Chapter Two with the fewest number of risks (no risk is an impossibility). External factors very often affect the decision (e.g., availability of money, interest rates, personal relationships of the chief executive officer and financial institutions, area wage differentials). The decision worksheet (or specially prepared evaluation worksheet, illustrated in Table 12-13) most often summarizes measurements and weightings of criteria for each alternative.

Many short cuts inevitably occur in utilizing any formal mechanism such as a decision or evaluation worksheet. A whole alternative is likely to be judged in the aggregate as satisfactory or not rather than selectively, in terms of finer measures of the individual factors. Subjectivity per se is not bad, being more useful at certain times even when more accurate and precise measures are available. A total P&D approach needs all modes to be effective in arriving at *implemented* solutions.

Bargaining is another way of selecting a recommended solution. Individuals singly or in small groups represent perspectives or constituencies with differing values. The conflicts can be small (e.g., among people with different responsibilities in one company who must make the decision) or large (between labor and management, between countries, between one "side of the tracks" and the other, between racial groups). A P&D professional group may be quite formal in its analysis of the alternatives, but the bargained solution may combine parts of several previously and newly developed alternatives.

Studies reveal "very little use" in P&D decision situations of the formal methods implied in such techniques as a decision worksheet or multiattribute utility assessment.[12] The typical situation "sees the [professional] presenting his factual analyses of the consequences of various alternatives to the manager, who determines the value trade-offs in his head [or bargains] and thereby makes a choice."

D. Formulate Plans to Get Final Approval

One or more additional approvals of the recommended solution are often needed. Authority to commit the organization is often vested in other people. This occurs when the project involves capital expenditures beyond what the individual, group, or manager can authorize, needs reallocation of limited resources, is rather large and complex, needs external regulatory approval (e.g., health planning, public service commission, environmental impact statement), impacts and interfaces with several departments/constituencies, or will need to be installed in several parallel departments or locations. Approvals are also desirable even if not *really* necessary, as a way of building a coterie of favorably disposed intermediaries throughout the organization. This helps to minimize the risk factors for eventual implementation (Chapter Sixteen).

What is typically needed is approval at as many levels as the organization requires regarding costs and budgets, organizational consequences, or possibility of negative impacts. A recommended solution for an ineffective loading dock in a warehouse, for example, was selected from several alternatives by a P&D project team that included the warehouse supervisor. But the $40,000 expenditure with a payback of eight months required approval of the manager of warehouses and the director of distribution. Then, because 24 warehouse loading docks would each need a comparable capital expenditure, the executive vice-president had to approve it. Parallel as well as hierarchical approvals may be necessary.

Such additional approvals involve people who are not as familiar with the solution, its details, and the competing alternatives from which the solution was selected. In addition, people who think they will be negatively influenced seek protection through negotiation or politicking. Continual joint interaction with real-world people (Figure 10-4) could help overcome this lack of knowledge and understanding so that this step will be much more likely to be accomplished.

Even so, "political" and affective forces, even adroit lobbying within a company as well as in legislative and executive government, are part of gaining approval. *How* a proposal is put together and presented as well as when and who is promoting it are just as critical as what the proposal is all about. Legislators from several states at a conference with educators described efforts of higher education groups to influence legislators about approving some solutions. They used terms suitable for almost all organizations: "Impractical studies delivered months after the due date, ivory tower mentality (elitism), naivete, contempt for 'politics,' and obfuscation in accounting methods." They also expressed a reasoning process they use in allocating tax dollars. The message can be used by any organization, even though the legislator's first need is to get reelected: "What is the overall good of the state [company, association, etc.]? What will be best for my district [department, plant, etc.]? How can I stay on good terms with the politically active [creative, knowledgeable, management, etc.] people in my district? How can I stay on good terms with other influential

people [bankers, suppliers, other executives, etc.]?"[13] Longer-term interests, behavior, premises, policies, and rules loom large in all organizations, and they often can only be marginally affected by the specific approval being sought if it is to be obtained. This is another explanation of the overriding need for joint modification of real-world and P&D perceptions over time.

Some organizations have relatively formal or structured processes through which approvals are to be obtained. This step may not be needed there, but many of the ideas discussed here may aid in a more effective use of the formal process.

The plan for obtaining approvals should be designed for the specific situation following the basic strategy pattern: What is the purpose of the approval plan (final approval, go ahead with next stage, communicate solution to management, set up pilot effort, exploratory test, etc.)? What are some ideal systems for achieving the selected purpose level (report, videotape, personality likes of approver(s), oral presentation, etc.)? What are the regularities? Each report and presentation, even within a well-established process, should also be developed with the basic strategy pattern. Creativity should be encouraged because this is a crucial point in almost all P&D efforts. The plan for getting approvals should, in effect, phrase the proposal in terms of the opportunities available to and the purposes of the organization. This makes it easy for decision makers to say *yes*.

Developing the approval plan may lead to additional needs from a previous phase or step: The proposed solution may need to be clarified; related more closely to the abilities of current and possibly available personnel to carry out the solution if it were installed; integrated more carefully into the organizational behavior and reasoning patterns; matched with the feelings and levels of felt stress and tension; translated into a more thorough installation plan (training, involving others in P&D at local levels, purchasing—see Phase 5); and structured to provide motivational commitment to see the solution through the usually difficult installation and into full operating status.

Several factors appear helpful in considering the documentation or report that is usually needed after a project is completed. It will certainly enable good subsequent reviews and evaluations to be made:

1 Documentation or a report has a rhetorical purpose (inform, stimulate thought, persuade, and induce action) that is different from the technical purpose of the project (design, explore, formulate, solve, etc.).

2 A report is usually addressed to the primary

decision-making and transmitting audience. People or units affected by and who implement recommendations are addressed by reports, if necessary, in Phase 5.

3 A report should address the perspective of the reader, usually from the specific to the general. The basic strategy pattern can summarize what happened in the project in some cases.

4 Redundancy selectively included will allow differing audiences to find what they need.

5 Reports in the form of working papers should be submitted at several points during a project. They help move perceptions of people along the timeline and raise questions at an early point.

6 A report submitted by the project team is better than one submitted by only a P&D professional.

7 Justify the recommended solution in terms of its advantages over what may exist, or over other alternatives that were not selected if nothing now exists. Benefit/cost ratios should be prominently displayed, along with what should be done about any proposed personnel changes—reductions, retraining, severance with high pay, or relocation.

8 A description of the FIST should be included as the target toward which the recommended system is aiming. Betterment dates for the FIST and the solution can be suggested.

9 Explain why the FIST is not being recommended in its entirety. The decision maker(s) may well find that a limitation perceived by project team members or managers really does not exist, thus leading to a better solution. Also, include comments about follow-up on FIST components not now being recommended, and about research projects set up to investigate the contemplative ideal systems.

Getting approval of a proposal almost always involves a comparison of it to other proposals or present activities in the organization or community. A capital expenditure request is one of several, a new federal-state management board is one of several usually political alternatives the agencies have available, and a curriculum proposal is faced with many creative alternatives that the concerned people know about. The resulting, inevitable bargaining or negotiations almost always concern matters of much broader scope and interfaces than the actual proposal itself. An outstanding benefit/cost recommendation may thus become a pawn or chip so that a rejection now may have nothing to do with the intrinsic merits of the proposal, irrespective of how well its benefits and positive features are spelled out and presented orally and in writing. Not all of the reasons decision makers provide to

explain a rejection or request for modification will satisfy a project team, but the people should understand the nature of the negotiation process and why the continual joint relationships with real-world people (Figure 10-4) is so essential, starting even with initial legitimization of and resource commitment to the project.

The process of getting approval illustrates why many P&D projects are aborted at this point. New products, proposed buildings, changed information systems, improved curriculum and education ideas, and proven health care measures are often forgotten from lack of resources, if not outright disapproval. Sanctioning of the proposal should, however, be far more likely when the PDA timeline perspective is utilized.

E. Develop Details of the Solution as Far as Needed

Starting with this step, it is virtually impossible to be specific. Each P&D project is now so different that the discussion will shift from operational details about the steps to listing briefly some of the pertinent functions and outcomes that ought to be considered. A few process ideas will be suggested for getting to the outcome and accomplishing the functions.

This step seeks to develop sufficient details to assure the initial *and continued* workability of the selected and approved solution. A secondary purpose is to try to keep the selected solution as close as possible to the FIST for achieving the purpose.

The system matrix (Chapters Nine and Thirteen) provides a reasonable formulation from which details can be developed. It is a good basis for checking interfaces, consequences, impacts, computer programs and data bases, performance specifications, flows and layouts, and so on. It provides the type of insights needed for a "worst case analysis" of the solution through the measures, and control and interface dimensions of all the elements. It helps to avoid the difficulty of enthusiastic individuals involved in the project forgetting to detail the solution specifics that must be substituted for assumed workability. The future dimension can help find specifications to avoid the usual deterioration and distortions that often afflict solutions (Corollary 5a). It also encourages contingency planning for the solution itself and helps to anticipate questions from managers, installers, and users of the solution.

Detailing often involves careful specification of two areas not usually thought out too well before hand: mechanical and physical items (inputs, outputs, circuitry, environment, automation, physical devices and catalysts) and sequence and human agent elements (work balancing, organizational arrangement, equipment location, software, personnel planning, information-flow aids, estimating training needs). An interaction matrix between needed unit transformation operations (sequence) and technical factors (temperature, noise, chemical reactions) illustrates one technique for detailing. These specifications lead to revisions and details in the budget proposed for the workable solution. The projected budget should be continually updated through these last two phases.

Another outcome started here is the schedule of events needed to put the recommended solution into operation. This is actually a system that could be designed with the basic strategy pattern.

P&D people can use several processes to develop the details. Visualization or what the mind's eye sees is probably most critical. It is a mental image of the solution from which information can be recorded as details. Visualization usually includes "seeing" the interrelationship of the mechanical and physical items within the sequence and with users, people inputs, and/or human agents. Visualizations are frequently recorded by means of models (Appendix A). Most of these techniques help in the analytical and experimental processes of arriving at detail specifications. Table 12-14 lists some of the guides for detailing implied here.

The large number of handbooks on very specific details and performance specifications (on metals, chairs, colors, computers, electricity, machine tools, organizational design) provide a rich resource for this step. So, too, do the large number of techniques (data collection, optimization, sensitivity, economic, systems modeling) reviewed in Appendix A. The purposes to be achieved by detailing a solution aspect are the usual point of entry into such a listing of techniques and models.

When virtually independent or separable functional components are identified as constituting the solution, each one or combination of more than one can be assigned to separate subgroups or individuals as a P&D project in itself. Detailing of each component could, in effect, be another P&D effort of a smaller scope. The regional planning unit that sets up a five-year plan may then organize another group to detail (or do P&D on) the housing component. The invoicing part of accounts receivable may be a separate project, and detailing the gear for an engine transmission is likewise a P&D project.

F.   Review Solution Details with Others to Assure Proposal Workability

Continual closeness to a project can easily cloud the vision or make roadblocks regarding the implementability of the solution harder to discern. In addition, people associated with a project frequently become enthusiastic about their recommendations and many fine design points may be omitted in the surge to install a solution. Such commitment is generally desirable, but in this step assurance is sought that sufficient details are available to enable the solution to operate simply, properly, and effectively while remaining as close as possible to the FIST.

A wide variety of questions arises from general considerations of what constitutes a review as well as from the statements of uncertainty and inquiry raised by the decision maker(s) in the approval step. The following questions are only a sample of all that may need to be asked:

Table 12-14   Guides for Detailing

1   Be sure a specification is accomplishing the achievement of purpose/function
2   Specify only the critical minimum amount of detail, and let people in the system add what remains
3   Include multiple modes of achieving purposes and objectives whenever appropriate
4   Put information and control requirements at points close to the origin of difficulty and where actions can be taken
5   Include transitional and changeover specifications
6   Schedule into the details the effort for planned betterment design
7   Determine if the specification(s) make sense to readers and users of the solution
8   Provide complete, operational, decomposable and nonredundant specifications
9   Relate specifications to performance expectations (costs, time, life cycle, quality of work life, etc.)

1   Can the recommended system be brought closer to the FIST? Can the FIST even be improved? Additional small changes in specifications should be made before installation to avoid the reaction, "Why weren't all the changes installed at the same time?" or "If you don't have time to do it right, when will you have time to do it over?"
2   Are *needed* specifications included in the recommended solution? Will it actually work? P&D Principle 11 is operable here. Perhaps all specifications should not be included so the people working in the system will have some flexibility.
3   What components and subsystems need testing? What type of testing would be effective?
4   Should priorities be set up or redone for the next

stages of the protocol? What effort over the next five years should be allocated to the major P&D projects? Which components of the recommended solution should be installed first?

5 Who should be responsible for actual installation? The following are some useful ideas: Let the P&D project team supervise the installation; set up a more permanent transition management group; give the responsibility to operating and supervising managers *directly* in charge of the solution after installation.

6 Should other organizations, departments, groups, associations, *adopt* the solution, or should they start their own P&D project? The latter is usually preferable, but many large organizations require standardization on certain policies, systems, and the like.

7 What possible conflicts can be anticipated? What actions need to be taken to minimize or eliminate their impact on achieving successful implementation?

8 Have users/customers/clients/recipients/citizens been involved and/or informed, so that reactions can be adequately considered?

9 What sensitivity does the set of specifications have in relation to desired workability? Who should do the review and how might they proceed?

This sampling of review questions indicates that a similar breadth of resources may need to be utilized for effective accomplishment of this step:

a People involved in the operation of the system, but not involved in the P&D. These people may be found at all levels, from top management to supervisory and operating level personnel. They can participate at this point by going over each phase of the strategy as if it were being followed for the first time.

b Workshop groups and project teams. The original P&D group could "review" by approaching the solution as a betterment project.

c Separate review committee. Various personnel, such as foremen, associate administrators, board members, supervisors, workers, and technical staff, although previously consulted, could constitute such a committee.

d Outside audit committee. Consultants could even be used.

e Evaluator with principles and stimulator list items. An internal or external "inspector general" is good, especially when a group has been relatively isolated during P&D.

f Submit the proposal for approval. This is an effective and critical review or "trial balloon," especially with some flexible-minded units, such as health systems agencies and corporate planning departments.

g Have another staff person use the system pyramid to probe the feasibility and workability of all functional components.

The time needed for this step may appear to be delaying the P&D effort. The critical criterion for judging whether or not to formalize this review and how much time to allocate to it is the amount of evidence needed to "move" the perceptions of the real-world people (Figure 10-4) toward accepting the workability and benefits of the recommended solution. Many previous meetings of key decision makers and representatives of constituencies may mean less time is needed in this step. The larger, the more complex or the more people affected by the solution (highway location, computer system, school assignments, social welfare, procedure, etc.), the more likely is the need for a thorough review.

PHASE 5 INSTALL THE WORKABLE SOLUTION

A major precept of PDA is the focus on implementation and continued use of the recommended solution. Implementation is intertwined within the whole timeline and integrity of all five P&D factors (Figure 10-4). Utilizing the mechanics of implementation developed through conventional approaches would most likely be inappropriate, ineffective, and misleading.

A P&D professional should be directly involved with this phase rather than assume that installation is "beneath my dignity as a P&D professional." Involvement is needed even if the organization has a smoothly operating transition procedure to take P&D solutions through the several needed departments or staffs (for a product design: prototype, tooling, sales literature, start-up manufacturing, and production runs; for an educational degree: approvals of college faculty, university peers, administration and board of regents, and then scheduling office). A recommended solution, regardless of how well detailed and documented, will need modifications as the installation proceeds. Installation may slow or stop, even though the difficulties are trivial, unless the P&D person or group keeps abreast of and contributes to the activities. They are far more likely to perceive how the least debilitating modifications can be incorporated into the solution.

Not that everything can be planned and designed to

cope with contingencies, external disturbances and drifts of policy. Personnel difficulties and uncertainties will still emerge. But the continued involvement of P&D people in actual installation is another part of the operational P&D theory that significantly increases the probabilities of effective results (see Chapters Four and Five).

The steps of this phase, as presented in Table 12-15, are far from sequential in performance or operational in details. Many of them occur concurrently, iteration may occur several times, and some steps describe continuing operational activities of the organization. They describe functions and outcomes needed in most P&D situations. The basic strategy pattern is followed to develop the specific installation steps, actions, personnel and organization.

A. Test, Simulate, or Try Out the Solution

Will the proposed solution work and actually achieve the purposes? Nothing in Phase 4 guarantees this. Nor does great amounts of experience answer the question. Therefore, in this step methods are sought to ensure workability, adequacy of achieving the selected purpose, completeness of specifications, effectiveness, stability, and efficiency.

Many additional questions concern the solution and its components: Will the physical equipment perform as designed? Can purchased parts, materials and input information perform as designed? Will people in

Table 12-15   Phase 5: Install the Workable Solution

A   Test, simulate, or try out the solution

B   Set up installation/transition schedule (phase-in and overlap times, etc.)

C   Develop procedures for presenting and "selling" the solution

D   Prepare operational resources (equipment orders, location preparation, job descriptions, department specifications, train or shift personnel, etc.)

E   Install solution (or proceed to next stage of protocol)

F   Provide close monitoring to follow-up on and solve operational problems

G   Establish operational performance measurements to provide operators/managers with norms

H   Evaluate performance of installed solution in terms of current goals, objectives and purposes

I   Establish timeline for planned betterment change of the installed solution

J   Aggregate performance data for all projects to report on P&D professional results

the client or user world provide the information and insights needed as the system operates? Will output items effectively achieve the purpose (avoid an early glamour treatment which so enamors individuals that they fail to recognize that the purpose itself is not achieved, clearly defined, or even necessary ot appropriate for the circumstances)? Can the human agents perform according to the solution specifications?

Finding the answers now, before installation, will permit modifications at the most propitious time. It is not even too late to discover that the solution concept is unworkable.

Testing is a system that can be designed with the PDA. The test system needs purposes, measures of effectiveness, alternatives, regularities, a FIST, and so forth. The following procedures are some of the frequently occurring testing systems:

1   *Experiments*   Use the research approach, especially in betterment projects where some time is available, to *test a hypothesis* on which a key part of the recommendation is based. Will people be able to read the highway signs in the time available? Will workers be motivated by a methods improvement buy-back incentive?

2   *Physical Models*   These are usually *reduced-scale* (sometimes enlarged, as in an atomic model) versions of an actual physical item. A *pilot plant* is a full-scale but less comprehensive version of a process activity. So is an inexpensive *mock-up* of an operation workplace, or the preparation of a *prototype* product. Layout and flow diagrams and *two- and three-dimensional* models are possible substitute test methods. Actual *construction* of only one workplace may be desirable for cases that will require many similar workplaces (e.g., airline reservation positions, maintenance activities, nursing, cashier stations in department stores).

3   *Simulation*   Performed with or without a computer, simulation usually provides estimates of solution performance (the number of individuals, pieces of equipment, or items of inventory). It can explore various configurations (layout of facilities, flow of people and things, mix of products, component specifications). The usual computer-based mathematical or statistical simulation models range from a very specific situation (to define the number of beds in a hospital postanesthesia room) to the economic or system dynamics of whole firms, urban areas, and world growth (see Appendix A). However, symbolic paper-and-pencil

models such as a multiactivity chart can simulate shifts of work among people and machines to "test" various methods.

4 *Make Simple Changes in Existing Systems* A solution involving a slight rearrangement of equipment, tables or workbenches, forms, or methods, may be tested by simply making the changes. The original conditions can be replaced if the procedure does not work.

5 *New Machinery* Tests of expensive machinery would be desirable, but such equipment usually cannot be borrowed. Perhaps a test could be done in the manufacturer's plant. Another "test" is to visit other organizations that have similar equipment. If no equipment test is possible, other techniques, such as simulation, should be utilized.

6 *Scenario Writing* By forcing the preparation of a description of what would happen if the solution were used, a group or individual can "visualize" future conditions. This utilizes experiences, intuitions, and commitments of the people in a form of the believing game.

7 *Negotiation, Role Playing, and Other Behavioral Activities* This is the active form of scenario writing.

8 *Pilot Demonstration or Field Test* This is similar for nonhardware solutions to the physical models, prototype, and pilot plants noted in 2. It is usually limited to a few departments (people, departments, locations, etc.) and period of time.

9 *Optimization and Theoretical Calculations* Similar to computer simulations, optimal conditions for physical items can often be tested on computers (vibration frequencies, material usage, stress concentrations, etc.). This uses, when possible, known theories and principles in physical, mathematical and statistical fields.

10 *Quality Audit* An independent group conducts a review of the proposal (especially solutions that are nontechnical, policy based, or procedural) to assess workability, acceptability, degree of improvement, achievement of performance specifications, ability to interfere satisfactorily with other organizational activities, and so forth. The approach to the evaluation purposeful activity might be fruitfully considered.

11 *No Test Possible* There may be many reasons why a solution cannot be tested: not enough time; a one-time system (e.g., fireworks show); the procedure does not lend itself to testing (e.g., social policies, course curriculum); involves too many people (e.g., urban renewal); and not enough

money. In such cases, "testing" should be considered in step 4F.

B. Set Up Installation/Transition Schedule

More than cold deadlines and due dates are involved. Any actual installation creates disequilibrium, strains, uncertainties, role conflicts, and disruptions to ongoing activities, irrespective of how completely the previous phases have been carried out. Such personal and organizational dysfunctional symptoms may be dealt with in different ways: parallel operation, where the old is operated concurrently with the new to greatly increase the likelihood of operability of the new; phase-in sections or parts from either the beginning or end of the proposed system as a balance between likelihood of operation and total costs; complete installation or "cold turkey" change over a weekend or night (President Jimmy Carter's normalization of diplomatic relations with mainland China in December 1978 was an example of this); and pilot testing the whole solution in one location of several very similar locations.

With each of these installation concepts must go internalized questions that the host organization must answer: What inducements, rewards, or incentives will be used to "move" people not involved with the P&D effort toward acceptance and implementation? How can as many people as possible participate in preparing the schedule? How and by whom will conflicts among various people and groups be resolved? What education in the approach should accompany solution descriptions? How will members of the organization be kept informed on what is occurring, both favorable and unfavorable developments? The next step also addresses these questions.

Setting up an installation schedule means expressing in detail what was general in the original project timeline (as illustrated in Figure 12-2). For many P&D projects (physical or hardware design, moving into a new house) this detailing is most likely all that is needed.

The installation process for most projects, however, is affected by two difficulties. The first is that people at all levels of an organization may play one or more "games," even after they agree that a particular solution is desirable. They delay, if not scuttle, the installation. The second is "that the character and degree of many implementation problems are inherently unpredictable."[14]

Playing games during installation is both a conscious and a subconscious response. It is subconscious to the extent that people react automatically to the changes because of the individual and organizational realities defined in Chapter Five. For example, the "not invented here" factor can surface at almost any time, even with excellent participation by many. This may cause the "massive resistance" game to become operational because several people are very likely not to be completely informed about all of the development details. The games may take several forms: "(1) . . . Massive resistance . . . or refusal or defiance [by those] in a secure enough position to do so, . . . (2) tokenism . . . or an attempt to appear to be contributing . . . publicly [to implementation] while privately conceding only a small ('token') contribution, . . . (3) procrastination in making [a] contribution or substituting a contribution of inferior quality, . . . (4) bureaucrats playing reputation, . . . (5) deflection of goals, . . . (6) not our problem, . . . (7) keeping the peace, . . . and (8) end play"[15] or taking a set of actions that ostensibly achieves the purpose being sought but in a way which "protects" existing perceived power/authority/fiscal control arrangements. Other games take on many forms—strikes, slowdown, high turnover rates, high number of grievances, joining a union, and so on. All such games "[divert] resources, especially money, . . . [deflect] policy goals, . . . [resist] explicit . . . efforts to control behavior administratively, . . . [and dissipate] personal and political energies . . . that might otherwise be channeled into constructive action. . . . [Thus] the three principal perils [are] . . . underachievement of stated objectives, . . . delay, and excessive financial costs."[16]

Delay is the principal peril because the other two are probably its consequence. Delay can, of course, occur as a result of uncontrollable "legitimate" factors: A vendor ships a machine or product late, a price increase or decrease from external sources causes a reassessment, a large number of actors are included in the sequence of approvals or actions needed, or a natural disaster occurs. The delays of concern here stem from organizational, societal, and other human sources. The more games the actors play, the lower is the probability of a successful implementation.[17]

This is the foundation of the second difficulty: Implementation problems are unpredictable. Because delay may be considered synonymous to "perpetual procrastination, . . . effective resistance or obstruction," it takes on a purposive character, resulting in playing games in addition to reflecting a pathology.[18] Thus, an installation schedule needs far more than slack time for natural (external) occurrences of delay. It needs to incorporate appropriate considerations for the whole range of factors that cause delays.

The timeline and work program depicting a realistic time and cost installation schedule are the usual man-ifestations of this step, incorporating the major events, related activities, and person(s) responsible for each activity. A written scenario can also help to interrelate the people and groups that impact on certain activities and influence certain events/decisions. These characteristics can be incorporated in a schedule which is thus likely to be realistic because it considers "the problems of social/entropy (incompetency, variability in the objects of control, and coordination), dilemmas of administration (tokenism, massive resistance, procrastination, monopoly conditions, deterrence, incentives, etc.), diversion of resources, deflection of goals, dissipation of energies, and delays."[19] Time and costs can be allowed to find methods of motivating and inducing people to contribute and of otherwise overcoming the games. At the very least, time for "delays" that are likely to arise can be incorporated. Perhaps an extra event or two could be built into the schedule for negotiations, group actions to provide collective support, revising priorities, instituting better control of installation activities and events, arranging top level support, introducing incentives for cooperative effort, adding efforts to look and listen for delaying activities, appealing to authority, or otherwise "fixing the game."

These factors should not detract from the first need to identify the critical events and activities for the actual installation of the solution. It is very embarrassing and destructive of P&D credibility to do well at the art of game fixing and then have a "technical" failure of the actual solution.

Developing an installation/transition schedule might thus be a sizable P&D project in itself. Treating it as such leads to the major suggestion for "how" to set it up: Follow the PDA approach, or at least the basic strategy pattern, for this step.

C. Develop Procedures for Presenting and "Selling" the Solution

The word "selling" will continue to appear in quotes here because its interpretation at this point differs from that in Axiom and Proposition 7. The meaning here concerns, first, obtaining organizationwide utilization of a solution that could not possibly have involved everyone affected in the original P&D effort. For example, developing a service order system that affects 40% of the 60,000 employees in a telephone company covering five states could not really involve them as the timeline scenario suggests, even when a widely representative (functional and geographical) task force did the P&D. A second meaning concerns transferring a solution found effective in one part of the organization to other departments or locations within the same administrative purview. Some examples include a good inventory control and accounting system in one warehouse of fourteen in a company, and effective policies for screening citizens for heart disease in one county of twelve in a health systems agency. This meaning is often called *process institutionalizing of the solution* or system as soon as its success is established. Reward structures will need to be developed. Both meanings do tread lightly at the fringes of Axiom and Proposition 7, so that care must be exercised to avoid their dangers while achieving the needed purposes of this step.

This step continues step 4D formulation of plans for obtaining approval of the recommended solution. This step now seeks psychological and social commitment and acceptance for implementation.

By this point, a constituency favorable to having the solution installed is probably well formed. Links to the various support services are mostly in place. Even with an internalized search for continuing change and improvement, many projects require commitment to push for adoption of the solution as it is now formulated. This step seeks to organize the constituency and its resources to arrive at the *continuing* sanction of all those who will influence the effectiveness of the implementation.

Now for different people, this step concerns all of the individual and group realities described in Chapter Five. These are *added* to the installation dilemma of an inherent unpredictable character. The new groups of real-world people are at a level of perception that is far different than that of the P&D world or the initial real-world people, who may already be using the solution. In effect, this step seeks to greatly reduce the probability that the "new" people will negatively affect the solution installation. The reactions of the "market" (customers, clients, users, and so forth) to the solution, predicting who will play what "games," and estimating the degree of intensity of commitment to their games all contribute to the uncertainties requiring this step.

Stating the difficulties in this fashion reminds us that this step needs the total P&D approach along the timeline, as depicted in Figure 10-4. Following the basic strategy pattern to do this probably will be concurrent with setting up the installation schedule. This will result in an installation plan that identifies the key actors, changes their perceptions and behavior (in a facilitative and educative fashion it is hoped rather than a coercive one), and retains flexibility even at this stage for changing the solution. If some of the key actors can be identified earlier, they should be involved in developing the installation plan. (Ask each one for their advice on how to go about getting solution A im-

plemented). They can also surface organizational factors that might impede installation. They develop a direct "ownership" of the operating solution, motivating them to assure effective installation.

The plan that reflects the outcome of this step will quite likely contain the names of people to meet, who is responsible in the other departments, what is to be covered, when operational resources should be ready (see next step), timing and assignment of responsibility for actual changes and switch-over, methods for follow-up and monitoring, and so on. A network of events and activities would not be an unexpected form of representing the outcome.

D. Prepare Operational Resources

The virtual impossibility of being prescriptive about this step is illustrated by comparing two widely different solutions. What human, physical, and informational resources need to be prepared (1) for installing (constructing) a $120 million medical center, and (2) for implementing a seventh grader's self-designed plan for studying a required book to read?

People must have the skills, abilities, and other knowledge to be able to actually do the required *installation*. All of the materials, equipment, information, customer/client acceptance and human agents necessary to *operate* the installed solution must be ready before it can be successfully implemented.

The elements and dimensions of the system matrix (Chapter Nine) are a reasonable basis on which to portray the scope of the installation system. The following are only *partial* in number and *suggestive* of this scope:

Inputs Introduce customer/clients/users to new ordering/information/monetary requirements, order new forms, get new material specifications and quality levels, set up bills of material, establish continuing attitude survey of users, prepare patients for new reception and admission procedures, establish line of credit for operating funds, and so on.

Outputs Set up financial accountability methods, measure quality of product/service in users perception, get regulatory clearances for services/products, organize distributors for new advertising campaign, and so on.

Sequence Hire equipment movers to change layout, prepare locations for control information to be obtained, prepare advertising materials, determine optimal allocation methods the supervisor can use, set up methods for tagging these products distinctively, and so on.

Environment Change to new organizational structure, develop the political support for continued operation, set up departmental operating rules, prepare for letters "smoothing" the way, arrange for new organizational design, and so on.

Human Agents Train personnel for new assignment(s), transfer/hire new personnel, set up job descriptions, establish and evaluate performance requirements, train troubleshooters to handle difficulties in the operational condition, obtain professional services needed, and so on.

Physical Catalyst Order new equipment, order refurbishing of tooling, change location of dials on work surface, obtain comparisons of equipment specifications, and so on.

Information Aids Update maintenance manuals, prepare interpretive regulations, set up implementation manuals, reprogram the software for the monitoring activities, and so on.

(Note that almost each one of these items can be considered a small P&D project, where the basic strategy pattern could be used: Design or plan a system to introduce customers to ordering requirements, establish continuing attitude survey, set up financial accountability methods, train personnel, etc.)

The sequence of these activities should be fairly well established by the installation schedule and the procedures for presenting and "selling" the solution. Several items can be occurring concurrently, with layout changes taking priority, for example, over information or system modifications, while both are going on. Both may also be higher priorities than, say, modifying the organization structure or developing new product designs, while some work is still being started on the latter two. Prioritizing and precedence establishing techniques are noted in Appendix A.

Many decisions about and compromises of the recommended solution will be required as preparations and the remaining steps are under way. Refer continuously to the purpose hierarchy, measures of effectiveness, major alternatives and components, regularities, FIST, and other P&D information to aid in making the decisions. These information resources provide choices on the basis of long-term effectiveness and workability.

E. Install Solution. DO IT!

This step starts the transition to and significant overlap with the operating and supervising real world. Installation is influenced by many of the same dynamic factors that affect the other steps of the strategy: "[The

factors] delay it, stop it, restart it. They cause it to speed up, to branch to a new phase, to cycle within one or between two phases . . . [There are] six groups of dynamic factors: *interrupts,* which are caused by environmental forces, *scheduling delays* and *timing delays and speedups . . .* and *feedback delays, comprehension cycles,* and *failure recycles.*"[20]

F. Provide Close Monitoring To Follow-Up

This responsibility is ordinarily taken by the operating and supervising personnel, but the P&D group or professional with an excellent understanding of the solution's purposes, regularities, FIST, and other alternatives, ought to "stay in bed with the manager." This is one way the solution's benefits can be maximized to at least the level proposed in the recommendation. This also establishes a method of trading off long- and short-term considerations effectively. Several concepts put this step in perspective.

Monitoring to provide troubleshooting and follow-up may involve several actions: Schedule definite visits to the areas where the solution is installed until the new solution "habit" is formed; provide a tickle file for periodic reminders that certain project areas must be visited for a check; keep close tabs on the triggers needed to activate contingency plans; set up a technical assistance committee; include all levels of people in checking out solutions in their own and other departments; establish a separate group or designate an individual to follow up on all newly installed solutions; include the new installation for review on the betterment program schedule earlier than usual; or review performance data with the progress function or learning curve techniques.

In addition to time and cost per "unit," other performance data are good monitoring indices: efficiency, productivity, budgetary control ratings, excess direct labor cost ratio, equipment utilization ratio, cumulative failures or failure rate, number of breakdowns, and so on. One point at which it may be desirable, and often profitable, to discontinue follow-up and debugging efforts occurs when the learning curve reaches a plateau or when reliability or other factors reach the desired level and stay relatively constant for a while.

Operating personnel and external clients/users involved in the P&D effort make good monitors. Their enthusiasm for and understanding of the solution help assure implementation. One aspect of follow-up such people can focus on is the appropriate utilization of time or money "saved" from what was being done before, especially in professional (engineers, nurses, architects, etc.) and nonprofit organizations (case workers, teachers, counselors, etc.). If the people and resources are not being channeled into the new or specified activities incorporated in the recommended solution, then the solution benefits are not being realized.

Many of the performance evaluation techniques that might be used in this step—learning curves and progress functions, control charts, index values, and exception reporting, to name a few—are highly interrelated with the performance measures to be developed in the next step. They are also prospects for the operator/managers to use on a continuing basis after the norms are established.

G. Establish Operational Performance Measurements

Step 5E started the transition of the solution to an operational status. This step virtually completes it by providing the norms needed in the operating and supervising purposeful activity.

Every effective organizational entity requires performance measurements and norms. Consider operational requirements for continuously doing the following:

- Adjusting equipment and people needs.
- Estimating when machines and other equipment items need maintenance or replacement.
- Determining how work can be subdivided to achieve a balance of job enlargement, skill utilization, and minimum delay time.
- Establishing the size of a crew for a particular operation.
- Estimating costs for submitting bids for special products or quantities.
- Determining the selling price of to-order products and services.
- Establishing task measures for employees to guide their work performance.
- Obtaining and updating control limits for quality assessment techniques and performance measurements output evaluation.
- Preparing budgets.

Many organizations have some data that could be used as performance measurements (e.g., elemental time standard data, standard costs per machine, historical records). Many norms, however, will need situation-specific data that can be collected as the solution is being implemented. In many cases, estimates developed with the people involved are quite sufficient. The agreement on an estimate is very often all that is needed to create an effective stimulus for accomplishing that level and more.

Performance measurements for the whole solution or its components are based on the M of Es from previous phases. They are expressed in various units: time per output unit, time per element, time per work component, output units per minute (or hour), number of citizens served per week, dollars per transaction, percentage of machine utilization, per capita complaints, productivity index, percentage of material utilization, hours of direct labor, cost per unit, and so on.

Two measures may be paired as a check and a balance. When one gets better, the other should not get worse. Some examples of check-and-balance pairs are percent efficiency and percent downtime; percent weight utilization and number of rejects; percent of direct labor and amount of indirect labor. Picking any set of measures will involve trade-offs among criteria—accuracy compared to understandability, measurability compared to rigidity of conformance to organizational goals, process measures compared to outputs/results modeled.

A performance measure should be expressed as an expected value (mean, mode, minimum, etc.) with its associated variability and confidence levels. Variability limits are psychologically desirable for operators and managers who already know that each performance cycle will not take an exactly identical time (Axiom 7). All parts of the performance measure need updating periodically as part of the operating and supervising purposeful activity.

A performance measure must be associated with a well-defined activity, artifact, or outcome. An individual or group should be able to influence the real-world represented by the measure. It attains greater accuracy and precision (less variability) the greater the specificity of the underlying reality phenomenon to which it is associated. Compare the accuracy and precision of possible performance measures for a regional planning unit in a developing country with that for a winter road-salting program for a northern city in the United States. In addition, the frequency of occurrence of a phenomenon influences accuracy and precision needs. A three-hour performance measure for the activity of preparing a course syllabus once a year can tolerate far greater variance than the number of radios produced in an hour in a factory. Many techniques (Appendix A) are available to collect and organize performance information so that a norm or performance measurement can be established.

Performance measures should be consistent among comparable jobs, tasks, departments, and so on. They need to be congruent with the organization's goals. This means that the measurement processes "program" needs a periodical audit and review. A betterment design project, say, once every year or two, is one way of doing this. A control model based on, for example, number of complaints per week, is another that is based on the control strategy (Table 3-9). A third way is to follow the approach for the evaluation purposeful activity (Table 3-4).

Because a performance measure is always tied to a well-described phenomenon (job, department) there is a tendency to treat the phenomenon as rigid. But good P&D encourages continuing improvements in the phenomenon, even though this affects the performance measures with updating. Several methods may be considered in handling suggested improvements in the system:

Place the idea in the suggestion system.

Let the person or group with improved output continue with the old performance measure for a specified period of time (i.e., earn whatever is possible, if on incentives) before changing the performance measure(s).

Utilize nonfinancial incentives, such as newspaper and other publicity, to provide psychic attention rewards to the individual or group.

Institute a merit increase for the individual.

Determine the effective savings for a specified period of time, such as six months, and pay the operator that amount, then change the performance measure.

Provide a methods incentive. An increase beyond, say 140% performance, means an incentive payment to the operator and a change in allowed times, or performance measures.

Determine if increased frequency of the phenomenon activity signals a need for improving the accuracy and precision of the performance measure.

Performance measurements should motivate people and thus create favorable human attitudes and performance. Three key essentials for doing this are purposes, societal values, and P&D objectives, which should guide establishment and use of performance measures (such measures are never precise—Axiom 7); people should know how the measurements are developed, and they should know as quickly as possible their results as they operate the system or solution.

H. Evaluate Performance of the Installed Solution

A P&D group or professional periodically should assess just how well specific project purposes, general P&D objectives, and overall goals are being attained. This goes beyond the normal daily or weekly reporting (or exception reports) of system performance an or-

ganization would normally have prepared. Goals, objectives, values, and purposes were agreed upon for each project, and a solution was selected to achieve them. How well are they being accomplished, now that a period of time (a year or so) has elapsed? In addition to providing an audit and review function for P&D efforts (Chapter Sixteen), this evaluation may signify when betterment P&D for a project should be set up (see next step) if interim reports about the project indicate no particular difficulties. The results are also likely to be very beneficial to the P&D people in terms of future projects. The PDA approach should lend itself effectively to postinstallation evaluation because the assumptions, hypotheses, principles, and criteria used in the project are quite likely to be recorded and available for relating to the evaluation data.

Critical to the evaluation are the perceptions of operating personnel and clients. The personnel need to "feel comfortable" with the solution and perceive advantages. Clients and top managers want to know that organizational, and thus personal, benefits are accruing through the changed "behavior" of the organizational personnel. Customers should also perceive the benefits and pleasures of a better-quality, lower-priced, or improved timeliness of product or service.

The evaluation approach (Table 3-4) sufficiently describes how this step could be performed.

One factor that may appear often in evaluation is the status of productivity achievement in the solution. Yet productivity for a specific solution/system is best measured by overall performance factors (step 5G) and the bigger purposes in the hierarchy rather than by specific and limited terms. In other words, reducing waste or increasing the number of output units per day or decreasing delays in the specific system assume that overall productivity is being improved. This may not be so if bigger purposes and societal values are not being achieved; increasing the daily number of buggy whips produced is hardly the same as increasing productivity. Productivity measures or indices are really an aggregate concept (see step 5J).

I. Establish Timeline for Planned Betterment Change

Every solution undergoes normal operating changes of even minimal sorts as time goes on (Figure 10-4). Most of these usually represent ideas of individuals to fit their own proclivities (tape down a switch, tape a note of instructions on the file cabinet, organize files differently, build a bookshelf at the back of a desk, etc.). Most of these are the individual's way of making sure the system *works*. Some improve the solution and its operation, while others lead to deteriorating performance and even subversion of the solution. The evaluation step should detect the latter conditions so that a correction P&D effort can be organized to handle the unsatisfactory existence.

The timeline for betterment P&D effort relates primarily to improving a satisfactory solution condition, as gauged by performance compared to norms. The first way of accomplishing this is to be punctual about follow-up on changes that are found to be necessary as the solution is being installed. Delay in getting them incorporated can cause poor habits to form in the operation of the system.

A second way is to schedule short time periods (say, three to six months) for audit and review of performances for the purpose of determining if small changes might move the solution closer to the technically attainable measures noted in step 5G. Operating and supervising personnel are nominally responsible for doing the audit and review. P&D personnel can at least provide continued assistance with all parts of the organization in getting good results.

The third way is to schedule a completely fresh P&D project. This would occur every two, three or more years, but would approach the system as if it didn't exist. This would be done even if all the measurements indicate the solution is completely satisfactory. The best time to develop changes in a system is at the height of its success (Axiom 5). Programmatic aspects are discussed in Chapter Sixteen. The idea is to *search* for a new FIST and recommended solution

to determine if there is enough difference between what exists and the new recommendation to make it worthwhile to install a change.

A fourth way produces an updated FIST, yearly for instance, suitable for year t_2, even as changes are being instituted today to move the installed solution closer to the FIST for year t_1 (see Figure 12-14). A FIST that describes a renovated downtown area in a medium-sized city five years from now should be updated every two or three years to keep abreast of changing community needs, even as the area is now being modified in accordance with the recommended solution derived from the current FIST (also see Case History B1).

A key reason for emphasizing continual changes and betterment scheduling is to provide a "happy but dissatisfied" atmosphere. Attaining an attitude of continual improvement induces the tension psychologists and organizational behavioralists claim needs to exist for arriving at successful changes. Unsatisfactory conditions create their own tensions, so betterment efforts need scheduled events as a start toward building the tensions for a search for change.

J. Aggregate Performance Data from All Projects that Report on P&D Results

If the P&D projects are being performed within one organization or community, a yearly report or summary of P&D activities and results is usually desirable

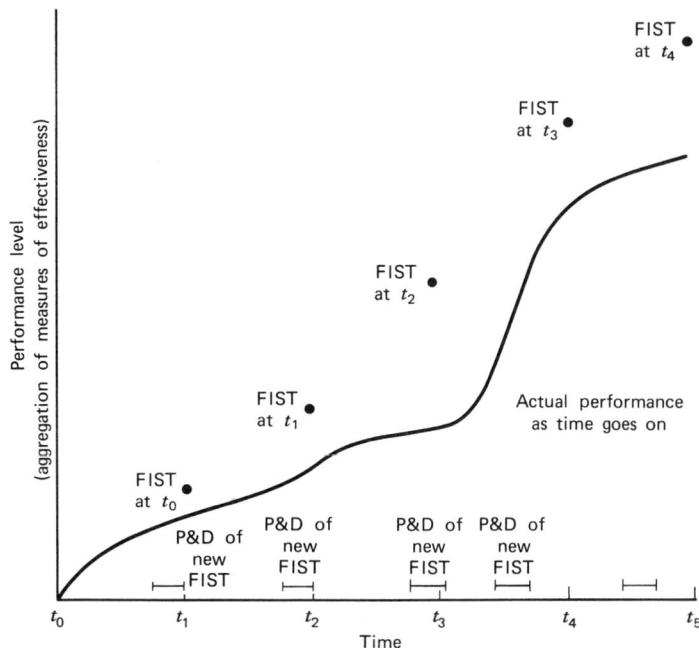

Figure 12-14 Updating the target and bettering the installed solution. Adapted from L. Jakobson, "The Sketch Plan Concept and Its Application to Central Tunisia," Regional Planning and Area Development Project, International Studies and Programs, University of Wisconsin-Madison, November 1980.

to portray the overall effectiveness of the P&D resources. Even if the P&D professional is independent and works for a different client on each project, a yearly recapitulation of overall effectiveness and results would be desirable.

Besides, data are being collected continuously about the performances of various solutions and systems. Why not aggregate them for an overall assessment? Such information brings the organization up to date about the utilization of P&D resources, difficulties with achieving the expected results on newly installed solutions and possible bases for continual betterment changes.

A series of reports can accomplish these ends. Table 12-16 illustrates a monthly version. Graphs are often used for portraying performances and indices because of their easy understandability. Other organizations use motion pictures to portray the various changes of an installation. Bulletin board displays,

monthly or quarterly newsletters, annual conferences or workshops, quarterly capital expenditure recovery reports, and budget review sessions illustrate other ways of portraying and transmitting such aggregated data.

One very commonly sought aggregated measure is the productivity index. Many P&D projects eagerly pursue increased productivity as an objective and a stated goal. Yet it is almost never possible to predict. It is almost always a descriptor of the past. Foremost among the difficulties is the lack of a clear-cut definition of productivity that can serve as a basis for measurement and aggregation. What usually happens then is that several other measures, singly or collectively, are usually *assumed* to be synonymous with productivity, such as time saved, number of shutdowns, waste improvement, total cost of quality control, per capita coverage with allowed times, dollars of cost, reliability, and rate of change in any of these or other

Table 12-16   Industrial Engineering Monthly Report Savings Summary, Short-Run Anticipated (September 15, 1962)*

Project	Savings					Costs		
	Number of People No Longer Needed	Savings in Salaries	Time Made Available for Other Productive Activities	Additional Space Made Available	Other Financial Savings	Equipment	Additional Personnel	Installation
1 Admitting office			Reduced time to admit a patient from 32 min. to 10 min.	Two offices total of 162 sq. ft.		$ 140		
3 Ground floor lab study	2 technicians	$ 5,880		250 sq. ft.				Uncertain
4 MCRC, social service, admitting office layout study				125 sq. ft.		Uncertain		Uncertain
6 Pharmacy study	1 clerk	$ 2,400	Auxiliary . 1,000 Pharmacy . 532 Nurses ... 1,680 Stu. nrs. . . 1,575 Nrs. aide . 709			$4,250		$ 425
7 Printing department					Reduced printing costs	Uncertain		Uncertain
5 Nursing study	To be determined						Uncertain	Uncertain
2 Central sterile supply	3	$ 7,200	Approximately 10,000 hrs.	530 sq. ft.	$11,240	$4,200		$8,500
Totals		$15,480	15,496 hrs.	1,067 sq. ft.	$11,240	$8,590		$8,925

From G. Nadler, *Work Design: A Systems Concept,* Homewood, Ill., Richard D. Irwin, 1970.
* This monthly report shows *anticipated* savings accompanied by the monthly *actual* savings report and the monthly *long-term anticipated* savings report. These other forms are comparable to this illustration.

measures. Some of the groups of data are called *process productivity* or *bounded productivity* (the relationship between actual and total capacity outcomes). All such measures and indices leave much to be desired, but can serve as a comparative historical basis from one point in time to another, say, a year.

Productivity basically refers to creation of wealth or the addition of value to the materials being used. This is done by utilizing human abilities (time, energy, skills, ingenuity) along with tools and equipment to modify the materials. This concept is still applicable on the international comparison level, where total outputs (products and services) available for purchase by others can be divided by the total inputs (labor hours, investments, materials) to give a gross productivity index. This obviously is very difficult for an individual organization to use, and certainly almost impossible to use to highlight the specific effect of P&D projects.

What has emerged as the closest approximation for an organization is a combination of the several factors the people in it or in similar groups identify as constituting desirable performance. One manufacturing company used five factors to incorporate in its added-value idea of productivity: employee performance, money performance, material usage, level of activity, and growth. It then looks to internal contributors to all of these as the manipulable action levers to improve the factors: product development, innovations, marketing, administrative efficiency, and resource (material, equipment, people) utilization. The exact relationship among all these is not established, but knowing what is considered important and obtaining measures of them allows P&D efforts to be keyed to what is sought in the organization.

Some techniques in Appendix A could interrelate or combine the factors (e.g. rate of return on investment, multiattribute utility model, multiple regression), but nothing really significant is available. The information about individual factors remains critical for the organization in considering what actions (approach) to take (purposeful activity to pursue) in increasing productivity (or effectiveness) in step 1A.

SUMMARY

The details about pursuing the PDA strategy for a project are incorporated in the various steps within each of the five phases of the basic strategy pattern. Providing this detail does not mean that the strategy is mechanistic, or that it involves one step always following another in lockstep fashion. Iterativeness and skipping steps are frequent characteristics of how the strategy is used. The steps are listed below:

Phase 1   Determine Purpose Level

A Select P&D project from original, betterment, or correction requirements.
B Set up P&D system structure.
C Expand purposes into hierarchy(ies) and select needed purpose(s).
D Identify measures of effectiveness for selected purpose(s).
E Determine functional components (primarily for large or complex systems).
F Select component(s) if *E* was needed. Return to *C*.

Phase 2   Generate Purposeful Alternatives (Ideal Systems)

A Develop ideal systems that would eliminate the need for selected purpose level. What ideas achieve a bigger-level purpose?
B Develop ideal systems for achieving the selected (and bigger-level) purpose by applying creativity processes.
C Develop ideal systems for achieving the selected (and bigger level) purpose that eliminate the need for any assumed limitation.
D Develop ideal systems for regularity conditions.
E Develop ideal systems by reviewing list of purposes from Phase 1 to select suggestions contained therein.
F Develop ideal systems that must satisfy only one measure of effectiveness focusing on each one, one at a time, as if it were the only objective.
G Review the list of ideas generated. For each clearly unachievable idea, develop proposals for the nearest approximation that is close to being feasible.

Phase 3   Devise Feasible Ideal Solution Target (FIST)

A Identify regularities for the target.
B Separate ideas into major alternatives and incorporate as many component ideas as possible into each alternative.
C Provide more detail for each major alternative to ensure workability and allow assessment of effectiveness.
D Identify each major alternative as contemplative or feasible. Review contemplative categories with experts to determine their present feasibility.
E Select feasible ideal system target (FIST) for regularities by evaluating the major alternatives with measures of effectiveness.

F Make FIST more ideal and as operational as possible.

G Save other ideas.

*Phase 4 Develop and Detail the
Recommended Solution*

A Develop alternatives for FIST components that will incorporate needed irregularities, exceptions, and conditions while staying as close as possible to the FIST.

B Estimate performances, outcomes, and consequences of each alternative to assess effectiveness, incorporate possible self-correction methods.

C Select the workable solution that is to be recommended for adoption or for approval before continuing to next stage of protocol.

D Formulate plans to get final approval of the workable solution.

E Develop details of the solution as far as needed to permit its installation or movement to next stage of protocol. Use elements and dimensions of solution framework.

F Review the recommended solution framework with knowledgeable people to assure its implementability.

Phase 5 Install the Workable Solution

A Test, simulate, or try out the solution.

B Set up installation/transition schedule (phase-in and overlap times, etc.).

C Develop procedures for presenting and "selling" the solution.

D Prepare operational resources (equipment orders, location preparation, job descriptions, department specifications, train or shift personnel, etc.).

E Install solution (or proceed to next stage of protocol).

F Provide close monitoring to follow up on and solve operational problems.

G Establish operational performance measurements to provide operators/managers with norms.

H Evaluate performance of installed solution in terms of current goals, objectives, and purposes.

I Establish timeline for planned betterment change of the installed solution.

J Aggregate performance data for all projects to report on P&D professional results.

CHAPTER 13

Specifying and Presenting P&D Solutions

A P&D-recommended solution needs clear specifications to serve as the basis for presentations to obtain approvals and for eventual installation. If possible, it should be documented also for follow-up, operating and supervising, evaluation, learning and possible research. The format of solutions is thus an ever present feature in all steps of the strategy (Figure 13-1) and even all other purposeful activities.

Solution specifications in P&D projects will vary in details and accuracy. Consider, for example, the difference between the level of detail of specifying vacation plans and the design drawings for a Mars probe. In addition, some P&D solutions (architectural plans, product design, manufacturing system, urban plan, computer system) always need details regardless of size, whereas others (education plan, organizational development, industrial relations, personal counseling) are much less dependent on detailing needs.

Yet the P&D solution specifications for such variety can have the same basic characteristics and definitional framework. That is, any P&D effort should portray the solution with these highly interrelated attributes:

1 Details of the fundamental structure that is to exist when installation and implementation are complete. A structure refers to an arrangement, configuration, organization chart, relationships, or physical portrayal. This attribute describes what the recommended solution should "look like." It also concerns the FIST version of the structure and the adaptive routes that may be pursued in moving toward the FIST from what is installed.

2 The way the structure or solution will operate or flow over time once it is in place. This scenario of how operations will proceed should include steps to improve the whole solution and to update periodically the FIST guide.

3 The major activities and events needed to move from approval of the recommended solution to the condition where the structure and its operation are in place (basically prescribed in Phase 5 of the strategy).

Several simple "solutions" illustrate the meaning of these three attributes:

Vacation Plan (1) The location(s), point(s) of interest, activity(ies) to pursue, mode(s) of transportation, time of occurrence, and so on. (2) When to depart, relationships to previous and future vacations, what to do first and where, second, third, and so on. (3) Contact travel agent(s), write relative(s), get sightseeing literature, and so on.

Timeline

The Real World (RW)

(The organization, community, admission procedure, materials distribution system, product, XYZ department, etc.)

The Total P&D Approach

| Pursuing the P&D strategy — See Chapters eleven and twelve | Specifying and presenting solutions (entries are illustrative only) see Chapter thirteen | Involving people (p=role of P&D professional) (entries illustrative only) see Chapter fourteen | Using information and knowledge (entries illustrative only) see Chapter fifteen | Arranging for continuing change and improvement (entries illustrative only) see Chapter sixteen |

A problem is

Substantive locus with difficulty or desire

① New opportunity   ① Begin betterment project or new planning cycle

① Problem situation

→ Jointly ←

⓵a Develop a purpose hierarchy for finding a solution. If selected level not P&D proceed to appropriate scenario

RW decides → ② Design P&D solution finding structure — P&D system specifications

→ Jointly ← ③ Do purpose expansion — Purpose hierarchy

Phase 1

Distur-bance → Review jointly → ④ Select function — Selected purpose statement

RW approves measures → ⑤ Set up measures of effectiveness — Values and measures of difficulty or desire

→ Jointly ← ⑥ Identify functional components — Functional components, overall structure

Normal operating change

Review jointly → ⑦ Generate ideal systems — System matrix elements, solution formats

Phase 2

→ Jointly ← ⑧ Identify regularities — Measures of elements

Distur-bance → P&D present ideas to RW — ⑨ Synthesize major alternatives — Fundamental, values and measures dimensions

Normal operating change

Phase 3

RW decides → ⑩ Select feasible ideal system target (fist) for regularities — Specifications for each major alternative

→ Jointly ← ⑪ Incorporate irregularities — Revised measures of effectiveness

New knowledge and technology →

→ Jointly ← Phase 4 ⑫ Develop recommended solution — Measures, control, interface dimensions

Normal operating change

RW approves → ⑬ Develop presentation format and obtain approval — Presentation format, approval system specifications

Review jointly → ⑭ Set up implemen-tation schedule — Future dimension

→ Jointly ← ⑮ Develop procedures for presenting and installing solution — Presentation system specifications

P&D facilitates Phase 5 ⑯ Install the solution — Solution documentation

Normal operating change

Jointly

Managers responsible for operating the plan or solution

⑰ Monitor performance — Performance reports

⑱ Gather data from several projects for reports — Progress/problem reports

→ Jointly ← ⑲ Implement follow up changes — Future dimension

Operate and supervise

Distur-bance →

RW seeks improvement — Evaluate

New ① oppor-tunity ① Begin betterment or new planning cycle

① → ② Design P&D solution finding structure

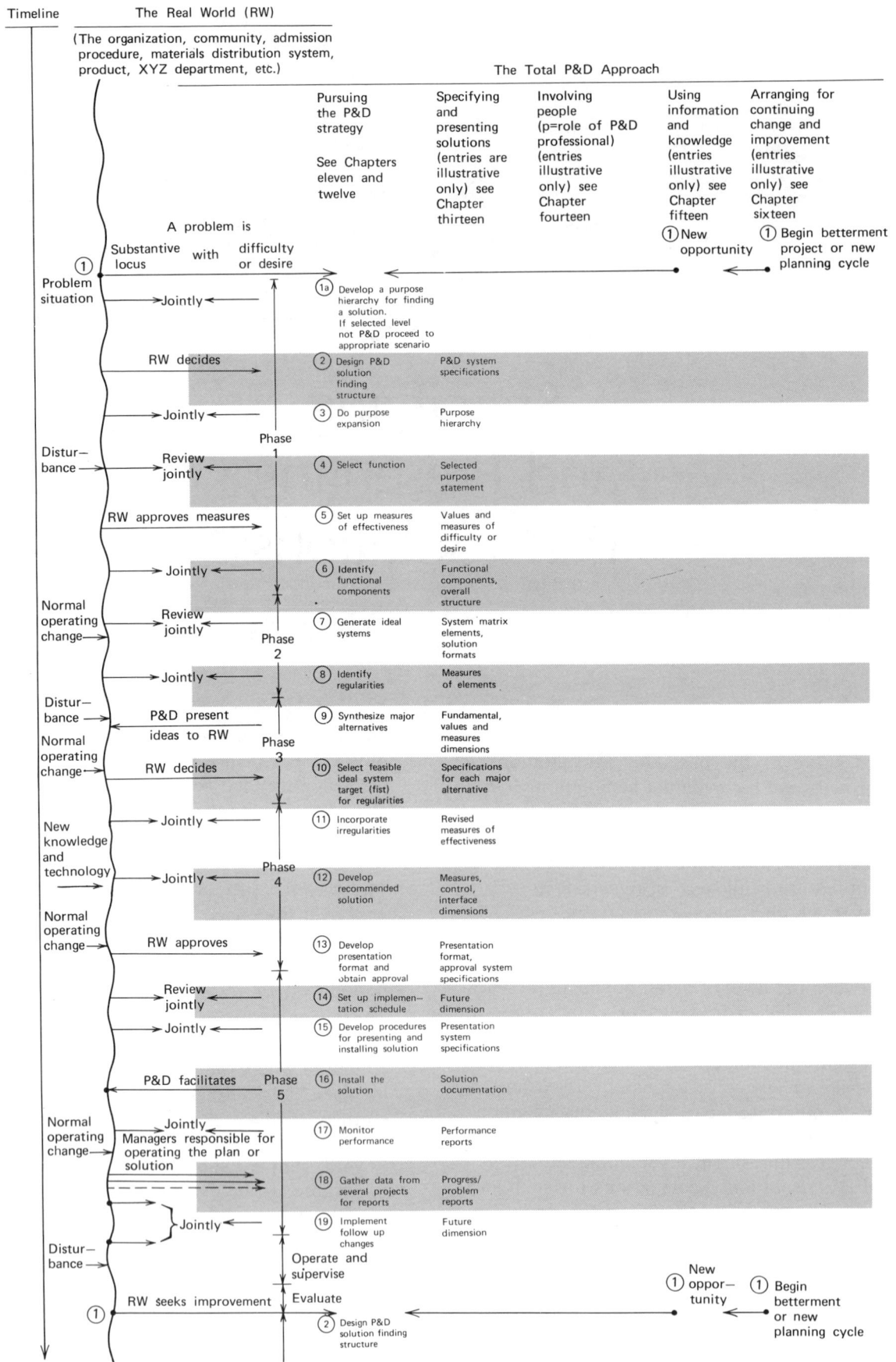

Figure 13-1 The planning and design scenario—feature 2.

184

Mars Probe (1) Master and detailed drawings, three-dimensional mock-ups, launching mechanism details, organization chart of responsibilities for project, calculations of optimal launch dates, data collection, design specifications of data collection devices, and so on. (2) Assignments for monitoring flight, real-time and later batch calculations, correction procedures if needed, and so on. (3) Network of activities and events to arrive at launch time, possible vendors and contractors, programming algorithms, simulation of flight and setdown procedures, and so on.

Annual Corporate Plan (1) Purposes of the company, new product developments, facility improvements, human resource developments, financial status being sought, organizational chart, five-year plan in all categories (FIST), and so on. (2) Appointment of project teams or individuals for one-time efforts (new product, changed organization, etc.), organizational changes for operating and supervising, timing for capital expenditures, arranging bank loans, instituting training programs, and so on. (3) Preparation of monthly budget allocations by cost/profit centers, obtain warranty claims printouts, schedule departmental meetings to review budget implications, and so on.

Developing this arrangement or framework for specifying and presenting a P&D solution would appear to fulfill the prescriptiveness, universality, and understandability criteria noted in Chapters Seven and Nine. Such a solution framework can play a significant role in posing effective questions as the protocol and strategy are being followed. The solution framework becomes a surrogate for the hoped-for real-world conditions, and can also serve as the cohesive basis to capture P&D decisions over time (Figure 10-4).

Documentation is also accomplished with such a framework. Having a framework available throughout the strategy helps organize all the interim reports and documents (e.g., alternative candidates for the FIST, models, information). Thus documentation is provided in varying degrees of "completeness." Such documentation is enhanced with the bigger view of a solution framework that encourages comparisons among, say, each alternative's elements and properties.

The concepts for a solution framework will be presented in this order:

1 The nature of and criteria for a "good" solution framework.
2 Usual solution frameworks.
3 The system matrix perspective.
4 Timeline perspectives of specifying and presenting a P&D solution.

NATURE OF AND CRITERIA FOR A "GOOD" SOLUTION FRAMEWORK

Many factors need to be considered in specifying and presenting a solution, as portrayed by the total PDA scenario. Several key ideas and criteria demonstrate how a prescriptive, universal, and understandable framework is possible for all the P&D application areas.

1 *Prescriptive Assistance While Following the Strategy along the Timeline* The solution framework should contain sufficient specificity to raise critical questions to consider at almost every point in the strategy, yet be flexible enough to cope with large as well as small project areas. It should foster expansiveness and creativity. Several formats raise questions, but in a restrictive and incomplete fashion. For example, one P&D field does raise many questions with its eleven specifically stated subplans that are claimed to be the components of a total plan. But their cut-and-dried nature is relatively restrictive and gives a false sense of security because *how* to probe more deeply into any question or subplan is not reviewed. Their specificity for a particular field also provides little stimulus to creativity.

The format needs simplicity, understandability, and convenience of use so that all those involved in the P&D effort can benefit from it. The cost of using it should be low. Also, it should be reliable in probing the complexity inherent in almost all solutions.

2 *Flexibility of Language* The structure of a good framework will allow quite specific *meanings* to be established, while permitting a wide variety of *words* or phrases for them to fit particular settings. Jargon is the bane of many P&D professionals, creating an aura of expertise that somehow only the professional can dispense. Professional and technical concepts are a definite part of specifying a P&D solution, but separating the root meaning from the specialized words is critical for presenting a solution with understandable words to the large number of people involved in a project. Many technological solutions, for example, require mathematical equations (say, for control processes) to establish basic meanings and relationships, yet graphs, pictures, and descriptive statements (for control processes—measure the outcomes, compare to what is desired, take action if difference is significant) are labels that many can understand. Conversely, a broad policy (a solution) needs many well-established meanings to make up its full specification. This would permit, for example, detailed explanations about implications, constraints on action, or the premises on which forthcoming decisions will be based.

3 *Solution Organization Assistance* Many ideas appear initially in bits and pieces during the P&D process. A solution framework should have the utility of immediacy so that some or many details can be developed to flesh out the idea rather rapidly. Playing the believing game about an idea is greatly aided by a solution framework high on this scale.

4 *Ability to Represent Desired Future Conditions* P&D solutions are usually "contrived responses to anticipated future environments . . . , thus requiring delineation in a manner that facilitates adaptation . . . to the evolving circumstances."[1] Representation and delineation concern both the initial conditions the solution is supposed to become in reality and the continuing processes of change. In addition to such models or surrogates for the "whole" solution, the framework must be flexible enough to incorporate the large number of techniques, analytical tools, charts, equations, and models that are usually needed in P&D (Corollary 6a). Timeline considerations are critical in representing a P&D solution—how to model the processes of making changes, operating the solution, flexible routes of activity, and continuing to improve, all at various levels of detail *during* a P&D project and at its conclusion.

5 *Documentation Capabilities* Some P&D professions require a great deal of documentation (architecture, engineering, urban planning). Subsequent activities—bidding, contracting, performance evaluation—depend greatly on the standardization of organizing intentions about the specific solution. The documentation may even need to include the process leading up to the solution and what is to follow its implementation. Other professions (educational counseling, policy analysis, organizational development) may need less official specification because implementation depends a great deal on what people perceive and understand the solution to be. Some of this documentation also needs to incorporate what transpired to arrive at the recommended solution. Documentation can have a dynamic rather than static perspective, thus allowing it to serve the objectives of P&D rather than to be treated as a chore that someone else imposes ("we need it for the files").

Documentation of the solution itself along with descriptions of the time-related P&D activities produce the equivalent of a case history. (Those involved in the P&D effort may not be interested in subsequent development of case histories of "what did we do to be successful." Their attitude propels them to accept the next P&D challenge rather than dwell on past successes.) Recording timeline activities at the time of generation avoids the need for retroactive reconstruction of what occurred in preparing such documentation.

6 *Detailing Capability* A solution, especially an artifact, needs quite specific details about what is to be done or changed. A solution framework should detail what the basic conditions should be and how they will be maintained in their desired state, how they interrelate with other real-world conditions, and how they may be expected to change after installation. Details about minimum expected performance provide guidance to users.

Each P&D profession needs to escape most of the strictures about a solution framework imposed by its historical precedents. Some "require" too little detail—a set of drawings for a house, a sketch of a jig for a machine, or a new form everyone is to fill out—while others are excessive and, yet, very often incomplete—a business plan with exactly nine subplans, a labor-management negotiated contract, a legal brief, a unit study plan in a fifth grade teacher's curriculum. Comprehensiveness of plans is probably the operational word for describing detailing needs.

7 *Framework for Communication* The entire timeline scenario is based on many joint interactions between the real and P&D worlds (Figure 10-4) as part of many steps of several phases. This continuing communication needs a format for solutions that fits the "world views" of the various recipients. Chapter Five showed how variable this reality is. A P&D professional who proclaims that solution details are too technical for "you people" to understand is in trouble. A good solution framework is a major contributor to communications within the framework of the other scenario features.

8 *Adaptability to Various Needs for Details* The level of specificity of solution details varies from very little at the start of a project to complete at the end. Rough alternatives are developed in Phase 2, conceptual "straw men" and then feasible details are added in Phase 3, and the recommended solution has many details in Phases 4 and 5. Thus, the solution framework needs adaptability through these five levels of detail.

USUAL SOLUTION FRAMEWORKS

P&D activities are centuries old. Successful solutions stemming from P&D surround us. Prior to the installation of a solution someone had the specifications for it in some framework. Reviewing these usual frameworks takes advantage of P&D solution frameworks already available. It also shows how all of the criteria for a "good" solution framework are not sufficiently met with current formats.

One reason that many usual frameworks fall short of meeting all of the criteria for a good framework is that they have emerged from the conventional P&D approaches. The conventional setting that spawned them has given them a patina of limited characteristics. For example, conventional approaches to P&D usually assume that the techniques used for analysis purposes (e.g., subdivision, fact gathering, modelling) are more than sufficient for connoting the solution. If a layout space and flow analysis was done initially, then a layout space and flow model can describe the solution. If a control equation summarized the facts about the present methods, then it can model the solution. One eight-step systems approach uses the first seven steps to analyze the problem with a variety of techniques and models (e.g., Delphi, scenarios, game-based models, Bayesian-type a priori subjective probability models). It then claims the eighth step is to develop the solution model by convergence of these techniques to find "a system model that gradually finds modularity, [or] partitioning giving way to integration."[2] Shades of the unstated assumptions regarding the P&D approach (Chapter Five)!

Here are some usual types of solution frameworks that may be useful at one time or another within the PDA feature of specifying and presenting solutions.

A. Playing by Ear

This label implies little prescriptiveness, but it does partially encourage an integrated view that could encompass the "whole." A gestalt or whole view framework, for example, is "(a) unique and (b) tightly integrated (in the sense that its elements [are] mutually complementary, or *synergistic,* fusing around [some] dominant element of [product or service]). . . . Gestalt [solutions] . . . seem to appear frequently in organizations. . . . They seem to develop at one point in time, generally when the organization is founded. . . . They [also] seem to be associated with single, powerful leaders. Perhaps such a sophisticated integration can be effected only in one mind."[3] Another related phrase is "organism as a whole."

B. Experience

Almost all of the usual successful formats are based on accumulated knowledge or experience. This category concerns the "raw" experience of sorting out what *appeared* satisfactory *in the past.* If engineering drawing (or architectural program statements) seemed

sufficient for the last 25 years, then that is all we need now; if apparently successful policy statements comprised eight factors in the past, then develop all policy statements with eight factors.

Some writers offer suggestions about utilizing primarily experience for a solution framework:

1 *Parts of a Policy Statement* These are suggested "at an intermediate level of abstraction: administrative and financial accountability mechanisms; the willing participation of presumptive beneficiaries or clients; private providers of goods and services such as professional service workers, developers, landholders; clearances or permits by public regulatory agencies or elected officials; innovations in the realm of program conception and design; sources of funds; troubleshooters who iron out difficulties and assist in coordinating the more routine activities of the assembly process; and political support that sustains and protects the assembly process."[4]

2 *Long-Range Plan Formats* Organizations use primarily their experience to establish relatively effective plan formats. The major failing seems to occur because there is no insight about what is being omitted. Table 13-1 illustrates what a hospital trustee proposes as the outline of a plan. Additional items of documentation are readily apparent; maps of the location of other health care facilities, tables of patient origin, formalized relationships with other institutions and agencies, trends of utilization, and so forth.

One corporate planning framework suggests a system pyramid-type set of solution plans starting with the mission plan and operational plan. The former has subplans for organizational development, acquisition and mergers, basic research and P&D, while the latter has subplans for production, marketing, financial, and administration.[5]

Another experiential format concerns levels of automation that are used to describe each unit operation in a sequence: hand tools and manual machines, powered machines, semiautomatic devices, automatic transfer machines, self-measuring and adjusting, and computer control.

3 *Social Systems* One framework proposes these "dimensions: . . . relative advantage, . . . impact on social relations, . . . divisibility . . . (extent of which a change can be implemented on a limited scale), . . . reversibility, . . . complexity, . . . compatibility, . . . communicability, . . . time, . . . risk and uncertainty, . . . commitment, . . . and susceptibility to successive modification"[6]

4 *Engineering Designs* A wide variety of solution frameworks emerge from the many branches of en-

Table 13-1 Outline of a Plan for Hospitals*

Facts about our hospital
  Historical background: founding, major additions, major changes in ownership or in health care role
  Trended statistical data for the past 10 years, showing utilization by major departments, room rates, expenditures, income
  Current medical staff data
  Trade area served (the geographic area and the people who live in it)
  Data on competitive facilities in the area

Trends, and where they appear to be taking us
  Society
  Government
  Medical developments
  Health care
  Competitive plans
  The hospital's own trends projected ahead five years on the assumption of no change
  The hospital's own trends projected ahead five years on the assumption of changes in society, government, medical developments, and health care

The stated role of the hospital (also called the mission statement)
  As it is (or is not) now written
  As it should be written, recognizing all the facts, problems, strengths, and weaknesses we know about
  Compared with the stated role of other nearby institutions

The strengths of the hospital: what we've got to build on in achieving our ambitions in the next 5 to 10 years
  Medical staff
  Nursing staff
  Facilities
  Reputation
  Trade area
  Management
  Board

The issues to be addressed: the problems we must solve if we are to succeed in our mission in the next 5 to 10 years
  Medical staff
  Nursing staff
  Facilities
  Reputation
  Management
  Board
  Relationships with other health care facilities
  Other

Alternative planning solutions for the next 5 to 10 years
  Ideas that might solve the problems
  Each alternative assessed for cost impact
  Each alternative assessed for potential results

Recommended course of action for the next 5 to 10 years: timing and action
  Who will do what, and when
  Who must approve
  What costs will be incurred
  What savings will be made
  What results are expected, and when

* From N.H. McMillan, *Planning for Survival*, Chicago: American Hospital Association, 1978.

gineering. Table 13-2 describes one such format. Other more specific formats often recommended are drawings, mathematical equations, flow diagrams, and so forth. Licensing laws require an engineer to certify the completeness of drawings and the "format" used by the engineer is almost completely experiential. An environmental impact statement represents a partially engineering-based solution format.

5 *Administrative Plans* Pro forma monthly profit and loss statements, cash flow projections, inventory levels, and product sales distributions illustrate some of the many operating formats that may become part of specifying a P&D solution. Four broad elements are proposed by organizational development for a sociotechnical factory design—product design and total process/unit operations, work relationship pattern or structure, variance control process, and work domain structure.[7]

Several health systems agencies (207 over the whole United States mandated to do health planning for their region) produce plans for five years in the future along with yearly plans that specify levels of achievement within certain times for the first priority goals. Thus, the format is a listing of goals with one or more specific objectives for each, none or more subobjectives for each objective, and none or more recommended actions for the objectives. One plan in 1980 had 19 goals, 41 objectives, 11 subobjectives for one objective, and 64 recommended actions for 32 of the objectives.

6 *Dichotomous Formats* Many people tend to describe phenomena or solutions in two categories which are assumed to include all factors. Some illustrations are structure and process, static and dynamic, primary and secondary, and major and bonding. Bonding, for example, includes logistics, funding, and information systems that tie together major ones. A solution framework for a factory expansion may therefore involve a structural or static component (layout, organizational responsibility assignments, product drawings, building program, etc.) as well as a process or dynamic

Table 13-2 An Engineering Design Solution Format*

ASPECTS OF SOLUTIONS

The engineer's objective in solving problems, in getting answers, is to meet the client's or supervisor's needs, and to help himself to do so. He is searching for practical, timely answers to real problems, which, in the cases that concern us, he has never dealt with or solved before. These new problems, we suggest, should be converted by the act of modeling into familiar form and size, leading toward progressively more and more useful and realistic answers as the fidelity of the model iteratively improves in use.

VARIETY OF MODELS

Models are generally classified under three names:

Iconic: It specifically *looks like* the original.
Analog: It specifically *behaves like* the original (obeys the same laws of action).
Symbolic: It compactly and abstractly *represents the principles* of the original.

PURPOSES AND POWER

Iconic
A. Visualize: Enlarge, shrink, emphasize sense of texture and shadow, show aesthetics.
B. Establish relationships: Rank, order, proportion, arrangement. Observe the interactions.
C. Synthesize: Make a whole out of parts.
D. Communicate and record: With self, clients, subordinates.

Analog
A. Simulate performance: Operate in the desired mode and in real or artificial time.
B. Determine numerical results: Check quantitative interactions.
C. Employ various phenomena: Suggest new areas of investigation.
D. Interchange variables and parameters, at will.
E. Use one piece of equipment (analog or digital computer) to solve many varieties of problems.

Symbolic
A. Use maximum generality in attack on problem.
B. Economize effort: Use symbolic shorthand for attributes and operations.
C. Lead to numeric outcomes, to explicit functional relations.
D. Use methods of mathematics geometry, and other logics.
E. Solve many problems economically: Use only pencil and paper.

LAWS INVOLVED

Iconic
A. Scaling ratios: Lines, areas, volumes.
B. Laws of projection, geometry, etc.
C. Rules of seeing: Limitations both by physiology and by dramatic effect.

Analog
A. Equivalence of the differential equations, or other equations of behavior.
B. Dimensional homogeneity.
C. Rules of similitude.

Symbolic
A. Self-consistent axioms and laws of the logic used: Numbers, functions, etc.

LIMITATIONS

Iconic
A. Limited number of variables: 1, 2 or 3 (dimensions).
B. Optimization generally done visually.
C. Limited by the engineer's conceptualizations.

Analog
A. Fidelity of assumptions: Simulation increases probability of correct answers.
B. The range of the specific equipments available.

Symbolic
A. The fidelity of assumptions: Answer must be tested.
B. Solving-power and skills of the engineer or mathematician.

* From T. T. Woodson, *Introduction to Engineering Design*, New York: McGraw-Hill, 1966.

one (flow of activities, development methods for improvement and growth of products, people-production operations, on-line information systems, continuous monitoring, etc.).

7 *Specific Formats* Construction is the installation of a P&D solution. Writing clear specifications for construction represents an even more detailed solution format than what an architect would produce. Specifications are, of course, based on the architect's P&D results. A person skilled in specification writing is primarily operating and supervising an existing notational, code-based, and contracting system rather than performing P&D. Computer programming is another illustration of such specific formating.

8 *Flowcharts and Structural Diagrams* A series of symbols (squares, triangles, etc.) connected with arrows and lines to indicate relationships and direction of actions. This is one of the most common portrayals of solutions, yet it is almost always insufficient in details and scope. It provides a rough and important form of conceptualization.

C. Criteria for a Good Solution

Many fields present checklists that incorporate the "good" features of solutions. A P&D outcome is therefore supposed to state the levels of the features used or, in effect, how much of the criteria are met. Those developing automation P&D solutions, for example, will use criteria for good automation in checking the solution details. Most of the criteria are therefore similar to principles for generating ideas and being creative (Phase 2 in the strategy), and may thus omit factors for assessing workability, interfaces, and flexibility of the solution.

Consider the principles of appropriate or intermediate technology. In broad sweep, these could take the following form:

Develop new policies and programs for science and technology which give greater attention to the basic needs of people.

Emphasize and support the development of technologies which are: In harmony with nature, culturally fitting, provide meaningful employment, are low cost, small scale and which lead to local self-reliance and the dignity of humans as well as their physical comfort.

Consciously redirect technological programs and scientific research toward improving the well-being and autonomy of the lesser advantaged nations, communities and individuals.[8]

Such principles mix measures of effectiveness, values, and stimulators, and should provide some way of prescribing what details a solution should comprise. Here are some other criteria used in designing a freeway through Beverly Hills, California, that do the same thing:

1   Will not increase congestion on already heavily traveled surface streets.
2   Will not visually divide the community.
3   Will not create unsightly structures of any kind.
4   Will not create noise pollution.
5   Will not intensify air pollution problem for local residents.
6   Will not transform the character of the present residential streets. . . .
8   Will significantly reduce travel time for traffic through Beverly Hills.
9   Will be safe for pedestrians and for surface and freeway traffic. . . .
11 Will provide for relocation within the community. . . .
13 Will have convenient access for local residents.
14 Will allow for future load expansion.
16 Will preserve natural or man-made amenities. . . .
17 Will provide functionally designed facilities for interchange among all the various vehicular and pedestrian systems.[9]

Several new P&D fields tend to present criteria with such fervor that the criteria or values are often assumed sufficient for specifying solution details. Some

of these include quality of working life,[10] organizational development, productivity improvement services, development planning, and technology transfer. Each one needs a solution framework in addition to their "good" criteria that can best be used in developing creative suggestions (Phase 2).

Criteria can also be formulated to serve as a protection against forgetting details in a solution framework. They include operational accountability assignments, ability of the solution to absorb disturbances and change, explicitness of the P&D decision processes and the solution's decision rules, relationship of specification to expectations of the organization, absence of technical jargon in communications, ability to identify aspects that achieve the purpose and obtain results, availability of implementation details and deadlines, sources of organizational and social support for the implementation of the solution, and assignment of implementation responsibilities (dependence on just one person for everything is a poor solution specification).

D. Science Basis

Mathematical, statistical, or predictive equations are often considered sufficient as a solution framework. In some of the literature three forms of scientific knowledge are considered sufficient framework: "*Descriptions* are viewed as recounts of what happened in a situation. *Frameworks* represent gross prescriptions for behavior. They can be very broad, as in the Marxian framework for economic behavior, and also very open to varied interpretations, as in the systems approach. *Algorithms* represent specific prescriptions for behavior, down to the level of the [individual action]. Most products of science can be viewed as one or a mix of these three prototypical outputs."[11]

Once one of these forms is available, nothing else is really considered necessary, even for many P&D fields. Some fields, such as policy development and social system design, treat the outputs of certain techniques as being "scientific" and thus a representation of a solution—a procedural network, a Delphi survey, a formal questionnaire, a computer program, utility and preference curves, a forecasting equation and so on.

An interesting possibility for a "scientific" solution framework deals with eight events in a scientific discovery. Prescribing a solution with all eight would entail: (1) scientific context of the event at a given time (or basic content of solution at a point in time); (2) time trajectory of situation leading up to event; (3) personal aspects of activity in which the event is embedded; (4) time trajectory of design activity; (5) psychobiological development of people whose design is being stated; (6) sociological setting, conditions, influence, funding, and evaluation at the time of development; (7) cultural developments outside area of design; and (8) logical analysis of project.[12]

E. Professional Education

Each P&D profession inculcates its students with at least an implicit solution framework. Typically, it is presented without any explanation as "just the way it is done." Most often, some particular concept or set of techniques is presented as *the* modern "all-you-need-to-know" idea: control models, information processing, decision making, networks, computer simulation, building program, operations research models, sketches or line drawings, and so on.

Some professional training in P&D involves specific plan preparation concepts:

1 Statement of the Strategic Business Unit's *Mission* . . .
2 *Key Environmental Assumptions*. . . . opportunities and threats . . .
3 *Key Competitor Assumptions*, . . . strengths and limitations of competitors . . .
4 List of *Constraints* . . .
5 *Objectives* . . . destination of SBU . . . in both qualitative and quantitative terms . . .
6 *Goals* . . . time-based points of measurement . . .
7 *Strategy* . . . course of action the SBU intends to follow . . .
8 *Programs*—development, investment, divestments, etc. . . .
9 Required *Resources* and sources . . .
10 *Contingencies* and associated "what if" contingency plans . . .
11 *SBU Financial Forecast* . . .[13]

Several P&D professions (architecture, furniture design, commercial art) include the esthetic, artistic, and stylistic as part of the solution framework. These are additional criteria that are combined with functional ones for both the solution and the solution framework. An architect who is praised for a work of art ought not to produce a home that leaks and makes people living there uncomfortable. A mural on an inner city library may win a prize but it ought not to cause area residents to destroy it because it represents a slur to their heritage. A home device may be judged esthetically pleasing, but it ought not to cause customers to scrape their fingers when using it.

Reports are another solution framework stressed in professional training. Technical writing and communications provide specific categories that should comprise a report: purpose of report, audience addressed, introduction, recommendations, justifications, explanations, and so on.

Optimization is a major recent emphasis. The solution specification is assumed complete once optimality and sensitivity calculations are available.

Licensing of P&D professionals where required offers interesting solution framework perspectives. Optimization techniques, for example, are far easier to test by means of exams than abilities to interrelate all factors in a total approach. The exams thus influence educational emphases. People providing professional training would quite quickly perceive the need for providing a more complete solution framework if licensing groups would ask, for example, when the examinee *wouldn't* use the answer supplied by the optimization calculations.

F. Questions and Checklists

The factors, concepts or principles in all of the solution frameworks could be put into checklists and questions. This makes them primarily beneficial for creativity stimulators. They lack some flexibility, comprehensiveness, and especially prescriptiveness as ingredients of a solution framework. For example, "What will be the result of the technological change" and "Do we have enough information to answer the previous questions?" hardly identify what solution characteristics are needed.

G. Systems Models

These models provide more specific suggestions regarding formulation of the solution compared to the gestalt and "think whole" exhortations of category A. Systems advocates will treat equations, descriptions, graphic relationships, or algorithms as the solution framework (as per category D). The output specification is sometimes described "as a formal description of the total range of possible performances by the system to be designed, from the possibility of abysmal failure to the possibility of perfect performance."[14]

Another description addresses the solution format question by proposing that a "plan should include several components, though the depth or extent may vary substantially: The assumptions on which the plan is based—the *basis*. The description of the planning unit and its interactions with its environment in the past—*the descriptive scenario*. Identification of the *planning horizon*—that period of time into the future for which effective definition and estimates of event sequences is possible. A *value system design* in which the structured objectives appear. A portrait of the planning unit as envisaged at the planning horizon, incorporating a statement of what is to be retained, what is to be eliminated, what is to be added, and how the new planning unit will be functioning in the future—*the normative scenario*. Methods for moving from the present situation to the desired situation over time, including financial arrangements—*the transition scenario*."[15]

Each solution framework is truly a perspective in the eye of the beholder. The person or group is self-referencing and not objective, for objectivity is what humans bestow on a solution, whereas the reality has no inherent objectivity.[16] An effective solution framework enhances the understanding of people in the real world setting. If "objectivity" is to be "attained," the people involved must internalize, from the beginning to the end of the strategy, the concepts and values that lead to specifying and presenting the recommendations.

THE SYSTEM MATRIX PERSPECTIVE

Strands of good ideas for a solution framework are present in almost all of the previously noted methods. Yet the desired attributes and criteria for a "good" solution framework point to the need for something much more effective. The system matrix appears to offer this opportunity while making use of whatever benefits the other frameworks supply. The remainder of this chapter draws on Chapter Nine concerning the axioms and corollaries defining the word system.

Proposition 10   A universally applicable, prescriptive system matrix is a cost/effective framework for specifying and presenting the needed conditions of a P&D solution.   Several reasons explain the effectiveness of the system matrix as an integrative solution framework. First, it represents an open perspective along at least two continua: Time (Figure 9-4), and level of detail (Figures 9-6 and 9-7). The time continuum shows how the FIST (say, f on Figure 9-4) and recommended solution (a on Figure 9-4) can be time interrelated. Documentation of what is actually implemented might be represented by b or c in Figure 9-4. Figures 9-6 and 9-7 show how infinitely small and large descriptions of any solution can be prepared. Although seldom carried very far on either continuum, the recursive characteristics of the framework can handle real-world complexities. An idea may be transformed from a mental state to informal, formal and reality states.

Second, the ability to conceptualize bigger and smaller specifications, as engendered by the system matrix, captures the reality of non-Aristotelian reasoning (Axioms 6 and 7). The axioms concerning uniqueness reiterate over and over the essential idea of the nonisolationism of any reality, that the world does not objectively have systems to present to us, that we need flexible interpretive methods that consider each level and time as a system in itself. Each recursion of the system matrix is valid irrespective of its decomposition or aggregation representation, or its present or future states of existence. These perspectives greatly minimize the dangers of assuming that one "system" in the eye of *a* beholder is *the* system.

Third, deductions from Axiom 3 (everything is a system) define any solution—plan, design, policy, curriculum, course of action, therapy, program—as a system.

Fourth, the principle of objectification,[17] or making a solution understandable, is advanced significantly. The system matrix and its interpretive extensions both stimulate the need for details and enhance retention of information about the system. There should be far less chance than with usual solution frameworks, for example, of having "cultural, social, economic, and political determinants . . . be finessed by a 'technological fix.'"[18]

Fifth, the large number of questions raised in each cell of the matrix at each time or detail level significantly increases the probability of providing a total version of a solution. Needed parts of a total solution, such as control features, can be designed in advance. All the usual solution frameworks are not discarded but rather enhanced by a broad framework.

Sixth, a system matrix provides a "deliberate" orientation that enables "realization" of solutions, rather than just a "retroactive [view] . . . that the organization wakes up to find itself with."[19] Many solutions, especially public policies, will tend to yield "to an unplanned and unchosen drift in the affairs of society,"[20] yet the system matrix format can embody the developmental drifts of the past (Chapters Six and Nine) while ameliorating the "conflicts of interest" and fostering the embodiment of "shared values" for the future.

Seventh, each cell can encompass all of the various conditions in which a solution specification may be forthcoming: as designed deterministically with or without risk, as designed stochastically with or without risk, as designed for uncertainty, or as a limitation or constraint of any type.

Because the system matrix may represent a "small" (a drill press operation) or "large" (a national health insurance program) solution situation, the entries in the cells in the system matrix and any of its recursive matrices will vary widely in scope and content. Yet some additional insights into the *meaning* of each cell might help in using the system matrix in actual projects. Table 13-3 lists illustrative items and ques-

Table 13-3 Some Illustrative Entries in a System Matrix Solution Framework*

	Fundamental	Values	Measures	Control	Interface	Future
Purpose	(1) Primary concern, aim Purpose hierarchy Priorities of function Mission statement "What business are we in?"	(2) Increase effectiveness and innovativeness Attain better quality of life Enhance human dignity Encourage individual betterment Convert problems to opportunities Assumptions underlying purposes Maximize organizational effectiveness Sensible	(3) Profit (discretionary income) Market share Return on investment Debt-equity ratios Dividends Number of complaints Earnings per share Degree of risk	(4) Stakeholders/board of directors review Review timing for changing plans Profit/loss operating statements Balance sheet Review trigger points to change to contingency plans (22)	(5) External environment (27) Diversification of objectives Mergers/acquisitions prospects Dividend policy Corporate and governmental planning agencies Pragmatic effects of information (43) Organizational myths	(6) Bigger purposeful level in three years Betterment schedule Profit and other measures forecasts for five years Problems/opportunities priorities Status of each specification in cells 1–5 at n, $n+1$, $n+2$ (time periods in the future)
Inputs	(7) Problems, needs Clients, users, etc. Raw materials, parts, etc. Forms, cards, tapes, verbal information Cash, checks Raw data Reports Previous outputs	(8) Minimum loans Frequent changes in needs Customer/user expectations Material efficiency (local, sufficient, etc.) Preferences/utilities	(9) Rate of problems Cost per unit Amount of cash per day Reaction time to order Number of customers Material yield Number of users involved Arrival times Product mix	(10) Incoming inspection control Orders/requests monitoring Invoice/accounts payable control Variance reports Consumer attitude study Data entry control	(11) Relate changed orders/requests to adaptive plans Relate to expectations (30) Planning/design assumptions Market being served Interest/tax rates Info display to users Decision support system (43) Materials suppliers	(12) Different sources of supplies Demographic/population analysis and trends Status of each specification in cells 7–11 at n, $n+1$, $n+2$ (time periods in the future)
Outputs	(13) Policy statements Drawings/products Programs Marketing plans Actual service, conference, class, meeting, etc. Corporate plan (policy, strategic, tactical, operating, structural, contingency) Product diversification plan Models (iconic, analog, symbolic) Transformed information Individual outcomes (study, personal life, relationships, etc.) Reports and memos Environmental impact statements (29) Sketch plan	(14) Quality outcomes Flexible Comprehensive coverage Effective product/service (pluralistic) Pricing/costing policies Interesting/elegant/inspiring/esthetic Simple (one-page report) Appropriate-technology based Satisfy user Difference between desired, undesired (waste), spurious (poor quality), and incidental Equity Products are designed with remanufacturing capability Stylish	(15) Timing of installation or production, priorities Market share Cash flow Break-even quantity Sales per assets, employee Cost per unit Number of on-time deliveries or services Selling costs Sales price Warranty expense Operating margin Dividend payments Product/service mix Occupancy rate User satisfactions Number of beneficiaries (or losers) Amount of incentives to adopt	(16) Credit investigation Monitor warranty requests Final inspection/evaluation Accounts receivable control Reports control Failure rate assessment Sensors for indicators Compliance with instructions Cost control Accident assessment	(17) Market analysis Competitive analysis Product/service reputation Patent condition Relate to expectations (30) Advertising External certification Distributors/retailers/and users Securities Exchange Commission Form 10K Implementation game plan Semantic meaningfulness of information displays (43) Contingency plans (21) Inventory levels (21) Regional integration of services Coalitions of supporters	(18) New product R&D Sales growth New domestic/international markets Availability of new products Projections of old and new products to provide future sales Financial forecasts Dividend projections Maintain freedom of choice for future users (open-endedness) Status of each specification in cells 13–17 at n, $n+1$, $n+2$, (time periods in the future)

193

Table 13-3 (*Continued*)

	Fundamental	Values	Measures	Control	Interface	Future
Sequence	(19) Implementation plan network Set of unit operations Information system Distribution system Scenarios for up and down inputs (orders/requests) Decision processes Storage methods (material, information) Maintenance system Flow pattern	(20) Minimum (optimum) time lag between input and output Be able to handle emergency cases Facilitate normal operating changes Easy communications Use only available resources Meet deadlines Make sense to people Multichanneled capability Avoid controls that are "worse than disease" Minimize energy use	(21) Rate of service, priorities Cost per unit operation Inventory turns Free cash flow Capacity of system Conversion efficiency Distribution costs Specific scheduled updating Schedule of implementation Amount of working capital Budgets (overall cost centers) Storage capacities Productivity ratio In-process time/order Risk probabilities Work hours Vacation schedules	(22) Inventory report and action Budget versus performance Quality control Production control Variance reports Contingency processes Maintenance activities Upside/downside budget with triggering points Accident control Sensors for indicators	(23) Physical catalysts (37 and 39) Communications net Facility layout New product development protocol Seasonal variations Person/machine allocations Integrated logistics support Interaction with user Routinization "What if" questions Accident prevention Internal audits	(24) Future processes Expected free cash flow Feasible ideal solution target Labor skills of future New facilities Target date for new component or product Budget updating Technological forecasting Status of each specification in cells, 19–23 at n, $n + 1$, $n + 2$ (time periods in the future)
Environment	(25) Strategic policies Regulations Competitors Threats and opportunities Labor supply Organization structure Management style/philosophy Union contract Temperature/humidity/noise/dust/light level Technological character of organization	(26) Pleasant Quiet Organizational development Consultative management style Ecological awareness Social accommodation Organizational myths and beliefs (ambience) Organization value type (output, motivation, flexible, image, administrative) Legal conditions and style	(27) Probability of event Risk (+ or −) with event Capital resources Overhead budget/expenses Amount of formalization Lowered level of decision making Social indicators (mobility, info access, political participation, cohesiveness, etc.) Rate of ventilation	(28) Person assigned to monitor events Report to cells 1 and 3 Management depth Standard operating procedures Physical environment controls	(29) Impact on location and vice versa When to reorganize Disturbances Decision processes (19) World conditions Sociopolitical conditions Chamber of Commerce Departmental jurisdiction and linkages Impact statement (13) Wave patterns of enthusiasm	(30) Expected future events and disturbances Futures studies research Transportation improvements Advanced scanning Status of each specification in cells, 25–29 at n, $n + 1$, $n + 2$ (time periods in the future)
Human Agents	(31) Workers, operators, supervisors, etc. Responsibility assignments Technicians, professionals Training program Work grouping Leadership style Skill, power control requirements Group autonomy levels	(32) Good quality of working life (autonomy, decision making) Personal development and growth Individuality within groups Maintain territorial integrity Respect of affective beliefs Civil liberties and rights Reward monetarily to fit good performance Personal values Equitable treatment Safe work conditions	(33) Allowed time per operation Percent idle, delays Accident rate Ratio administrative to "line" personnel Compensation system at all levels Turnover rate Training costs Wage/salary rates Education level Job satisfaction Age distribution Productivity level Liability rates Health status	(34) Productivity comparisons Quality control charts Conflict resolution methods Payroll verification Contingency assignments Personnel policies Bonus triggers Management and person can measure	(35) More productive equipment (7 and 39) Accidents (39) Labor market Wage surveys Professional licensing, regulations and associations Union organization Family leisure, community life Experience levels Boundary spanning Linkages, internal and external Job security Vacation schedules	(36) New professional/technological skills Manpower problems/trends Bureaucratization trends Maintain freedom of choice of methods Status of each specification in cells 31–35 at n, $n + 1$, $n + 2$ (time periods in the future)

Table 13-3 *(Continued)*

	Fundamental	Values	Measures	Control	Interface	Future
Physical Catalysts	(37) Machines/tools Space, physical facility Facility location components Workplaces Desks, chairs, etc. Equipment Computers Power, liquids	(38) Clean, well maintained, safe Secure information Use available physical resources	(39) Capacity per machine Age of each item Percent downtime/utilization Accident rate Capital expenditure budget Depreciation methods Time of access Maintenance cost Memory/CPU capacity	(40) Timeliness of delivery Quality control charts Performance reports	(41) Sequence needs (19 and 21) Location with cells 25 and 27 Accidents (35) Maintenance activities (22) Equipment supplies	(42) New technological breakthroughs Space for expansion Status of each specification in cells 37–41 at n, $n + 1$, $n + 2$ (time periods in the future)
Information Aids	(43) Training manuals Service and maintenance manuals Library sources Equipment references Computer programing languages Physical laws and properties Measurement theories and techniques Syntactic structure of display Decision support system Models (iconic, analog, symbolic) Data bases	(44) Readily available Complete Security	(45) Time response Cost overall & per unit Number/type of inquiries	(46) Security monitoring Transmission control Quality assessment Check in/out	(47) Categories of knowledge Central info banks Linguistic forms Levels of technology Display formats P&D data bases User and human agent satisfactions	(48) Coding research Status of each specification in cells 43–47 at n, $n + 1$, $n + 2$ (time periods in the future)

* Numerals interspersed within a cell refer to other cells.

tions for each cell, many of which reflect solution frameworks presented above.

Each item in each cell can be turned into one or more questions for which details *may* be needed in a specific project. For example, what is the specification or detail, if needed, for the measures of inputs (cell 9) in the solution? Or what is the cost per unit of input material? Or what is the amount of cash input per day? Or what number and when will customers or users arrive? The individual or group decides whether or not something needs to be specified or not, whether or not additional information needs to be collected. Chapter Fifteen presents the concepts of models, techniques, and aids for representing, modeling, and manipulating prospective entries in each cell.

Some experiences with Table 13-3 as a solution framework can be summarized to show another aspect of its great flexibility. A very broadly stated solution may need very rough details about only the fundamental dimensions of purpose, inputs, outputs, and

sequence. This is the *minimum* level of detail. Additional detail may involve physical catalysts and/or human agents and/or information aids and/or any additional dimensions for several of the elements.

The element and dimension names are just words. They represent ideas and meanings that can easily be expressed in terms of other words (technical, scientific, colloquial, jargon) to suit the specific situation (Axiom 6). The order in which the elements and dimensions appear are also changeable to fit, for example, the specific presentation needs (local custom, audience). The system matrix can be easily modified to become an excellent basis for developing the situation-specific solution framework. An architectural project (Case History B9), for example, used nine elements (environment was split), and called the fundamental dimension ''conceptual'' and the values and measures dimensions ''quantitative.'' A Canadian colleague (Alan D. Scharf) uses a ninth element, *financial*, on an optional basis to consolidate monetary and financial specifications now located in various elements. The generic themes the specific people prefer thus shape actual use of elements and dimensions.

A manufacturing company adapted the matrix to incorporate some aspects of the strategy, such as regularities, as shown in Figure 13-2. Each unit operation

is described on a separate sheet in terms of ideas, FIST, or recommended solution.

A timeline version of the sequence element activities is often added to provide sufficient detail and relationships for effectively understanding parallel and prioritized activities. The target system for the gypsy

Unit operation _____   Subunit: _____
Inputs: Main functions: _____   Output: _____

Element	Unit	Physical Regularities	Physical Irregularities	Additional Information (including what might be future of*)
Size, Weight, Shape, Material } *				
From: Handling method* Quantity/run Total weight Frequency				Including safety
Time: Set up operation				Including safety
Space: Operation Storage				
Inspection:				
Facilities: Workplace, Storage } * Tools Utilities Machinery Information sources				Other items Interaction with other work Percentage of utilization
To: Handling method* Quantity/run Total weight Frequency				
Who: Skills, etc.				Including human resource development Quality of working life

Flow chart   Sketched layout

Figure 13-2 Adaptation of system matrix for a manufacturing company.

moth pest management system (Case History B1) was presented in a timeline arrangement of the functional components. Words were modified to fit the group's perceptions. "Functional components" became "elements," "sequence" became "line activities," and so on. A system matrix then was used to describe each "subsystem element" and "line activity."

Management information systems projects can define the word *information* by adapting the elements "physical catalysts" and "information aids." They become *display media* and *attention catalysts* (aspects for understanding and using the information), and values and measures dimensions become *time* (chronology or intervals) and *value* (importance, cost, benefit, and contribution measures). Technology, as a human cultural activity, is distinguished by six aspects or components quite comparable to the system matrix elements.[21]

TIMELINE PERSPECTIVES OF SPECIFYING AND PRESENTING A P&D SOLUTION

As valuable as a solution framework actually is for the static documentation role and portraying the "results" of P&D, knowledge about elements and dimensions is a critical benefit in all steps of the P&D strategy, in conjunction with the other intertwined factors. Perhaps the key benefit stems from the system perspective that can be considered in each step. Appropriate interrelationship questions are raised at all times, not just at the end of a project. The infinity concepts of the system matrix (Figures 9-4 and 9-6) provide at any point the openness to specify quite small or rather conceptual details for review and assessment.

The essential train of thought for specifying and presenting a P&D solution considers the system matrix "empty" with no specifications at the beginning of the strategy. At the end, it is completely "filled in" with all needed specifications. Entries or specifications are added as the strategy steps, phases, and stages are completed and decisions are made, for example, when the purpose level is selected. More than one system matrix may be involved at the same time, as when several major alternatives are being considered before selecting a FIST. Different parts of elements receive differing amounts of emphasis at different times, as when desired outcomes (output element) are considered in Phases 2 and 3 while undesired outcomes are considered in Phases 4 and 5.

Saying that the system matrix is empty at the start is obviously a technicality. Every project is always part of a larger system (Axiom 4), which automatically means some specifications must exist. But because the strategy emphasizes the initial importance of identifying the "right" purpose, determining at the beginning what these larger system specifications are could be a waste of time. They may well be much different when the purpose level is selected. Thus, start with a clean slate, or, operationally, an empty system matrix.

Table 13-4 omits several steps from Chapter 12 so that this concept can be illustrated. The steps can occur in several orders, the values dimensions may be specified before others, etc. The solution framework can also be used as a stimulus to answer questions raised by the strategy: What are possible areas or cells to search in finding regularities? What is meant by alternatives for the FIST? What factors should govern testing? Other formats could be used in the right-hand column of Table 13-4: element-by-element narratives, a description developed with questions from the system matrix as checklist, and so on. A small amount of detail is developed in the first two or three phases. Much more is then incorporated in the last two or three phases. This keeps options open for ever better solution ideas. When the project gets to the FIST or beyond, certain cells require much more detail than others, such as working drawings and specifications for a building in a shopping center system for the fundamental dimension of physical catalysts.

A system matrix on a sheet of paper is almost never used as a repository of solution details because it is far too limited for almost all P&D efforts. It does provide the indexing key and flexibility for referencing where the specifications may be found. Figure 13-3 shows the system matrix array for a statewide natural resources data classification system (the A system). The coding to find the specifications is contained in each cell. The B data entry system is shown as an input to the A system, C as the accounting or control system for the data entry system, and D as the data input control system. Several "system matrices" can detail multichanneled or pluralistic solutions that occur as irregularities considered during Phase 4.

Detailing is making a model of what the solution and its components should be after installation. The secondary purposeful activity (Chapters Two and Three) of making a model is essentially what the feature of specifying and presenting a P&D solution is all about. The whole solution framework is only a model of what is sought, not the actual reality (Axiom 6). Two broad levels of detailing may occur: one for the FIST, which will need continuing updating, and the other for the solution to be installed, which is based on the FIST.

Many techniques, tools, and models are available to help with the process of detailing. One type of

Table 13-4   The Time Interrelationships of the Solution Framework and Strategy

Phase or Step	Expected Outcome	Status of Project Solution Framework (SF) (illustrations of specifications that are developed)
⋮		"EMPTY" SF
1C	Purpose/function/hierarchy and selected level	Fundamental dimension of purpose Some future and interface dimensions of purpose
1D	Measures of effectiveness	Values and measures dimensions of purpose, also some control Some values and measures dimensions of outputs
1E, 1F	Functional components	Several system matrices, one per component Priorities for components in *overall* SF purpose element
2	Ideal systems	Each component matrix and the overall SF repeated as many times as there are ideas. At least start with sketches of possible operational timelines and structures Each matrix with an idea serves as a "straw man"
3A	Regularities	Overall SF with input, output, sequence, or other element entries in fundamental, measure, or control dimensions
3B ⋮	Major alternatives for FIST	One system matrix for each major alternative "straw man" (and for each functional component), each one containing all of the previous specifications. Desired levels preferred.
3E ⋮	Select FIST	SF with broad details for most cells. Desired outputs only.
4A ⋮	Alternatives for FIST components to accommodate irregularities	FIST SF repeated with additional details, one for each alternative
4C ⋮	Selected recommended solution	SF with more specific details. May have separate SF for each multiple channel for irregularities. How to cope with undesirable outputs.
4F ⋮	Test and evaluate recommended solution	SF with still more details, working drawings, and specifications, etc.
5G ⋮	Completed project	SF with documentation details plus future dimension re: betterment review and changeover
		"COMPLETED" SF

model is used to portray the specifications of the solution itself. These include prototype forms that will be needed, cost/price models, engineering drawings of products, flow charts, bills of material, office layout diagrams, and so on. Models and techniques of representing the solution vary a great deal from one P&D field to another. A few of the general types of techniques are included in Appendix A.

The other type of model is used by P&D professionals and groups primarily on a one-time basis to aid the process of arriving at the solution details. Some examples are computer simulation, activity sampling, Delphi, survey of income levels, decision matrix, physical item operational modeling (e.g., heat transfer through a wall), and attitude questionnaire. An activity sampling study, for example, will help decide the location of equipment in the office layout diagram model. A Delphi survey will help decide what items of information to incorporate on the prototype forms. A heat

transfer operational model will help decide what thickness of metal to specify on the engineering product drawings. A computer simulation of surgical patient arrivals and service in a hospital postanesthesia recovery room will help decide how many beds will need to be accommodated in the flow chart and layout diagram.

Other techniques and models that are aids in the process of arriving at solution details may themselves become a continuing part of the solution. Some examples include forecasting models, job descriptions, pro forma profit-and-loss statements, computerized decision support models, and marketing surveys. Because these models are also part of the solution, they should be designed originally with PDA and frequently redesigned or bettered. For example, a six-month moving average sales forecasting model may have been very effective in designing a new system and may have been in operation for the last two years. A betterment de-

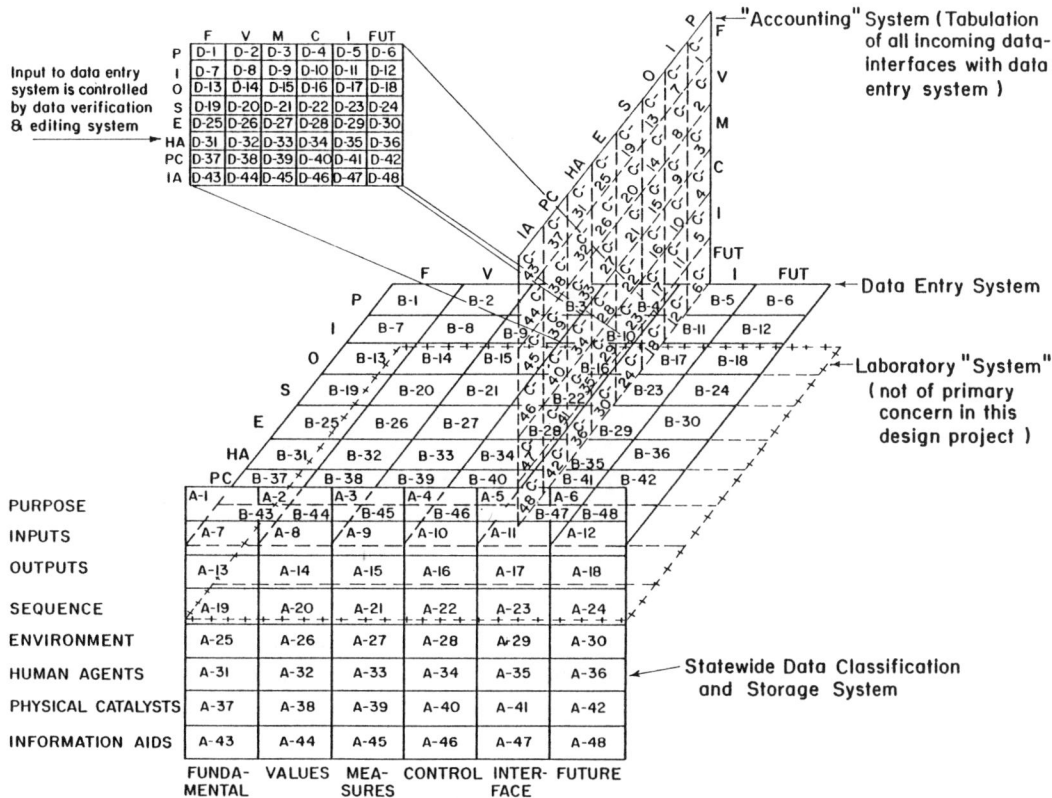

Figure 13-3 Statewide data classification and storage system.

sign should be scheduled every year or so to determine whether the "sales forecasting system" (including data collection, evaluation, storage, etc.) can be improved.

Appendix A lists mainly those techniques and models used in P&D efforts to aid in the process of arriving at solution details. Selecting which model(s) to develop is highly project-specific, but there are some guidelines. First, be sure the purposes of the *model* are necessary. Second, review the criteria in Corollary 6a (Chapter Eight) regarding the selection of model(s) to use. Third, check other items in Table 13-3 for possible concurrent model needs. Fourth, review the purpose/function cross reference in Appendix A to identify possible techniques to use. Fifth, follow the general strategy for modeling a phenomenon, number VI in Table 3-9. Sixth, determine if the resulting model specifications provide a likely effective representation of what will be installed in the real world.

Many "tricks of the trade" or actions flexibly adapt the solution framework and models to the specific scenario situation. All "tricks" could not possibly be reviewed, so a few examples should suffice. The timeline idea is critical for detailing the sequence element. One method for doing this is to get a group to

mentally role-play what would occur over time if the particular idea were in operation. Talk about the flow or order of events describes the series of actions you visualize occurring. Then, mentally consider the structural arrangements needed to get that flow and series of actions to come about—what organizational structure, how many people, what layout, what particular input format, and so on. As the ideas start to emerge, alternatives for the specific part of the sequence can be listed and reviewed for selection as a specification.

Another "trick" or action is to focus on only those elements or dimensions that interest the group. The P&D professional must translate the other elements and dimensions into consequences of or impacts on the major interest. The gypsy moth pest management system planning task force (Case History B1) seemed to focus on outputs—what manual will be available for field people, where will the leading edge of infestation be, how many acres of forest will be sprayed, and so on. The method ties each output focused on by the group to every question generated by the other elements—what necessary and bigger purposes does that output achieve, what ideal (or detailed) inputs does that output need, what effective sequence of activities will produce that output, what internal and external environmental factors can be best arranged within which the output will be maximized, and so on. A project or group that wants to focus on, say, human agents can proceed with similar questions—what necessary and bigger purposes will those human agents help to achieve, what ideal (or detailed) inputs will those human agents work with, and so on.

A third action or "trick" relies on the basic strategy pattern. Specifying a particular detail or presenting a particular solution or component recommendation can be viewed as a P&D project in itself. Take, for example, the presentation of revised measures of effectiveness (step 11) on Figure 13-1 for the "jointly" interactive setting with the real world: What purposes should be achieved with the presentation? What "ideal" alternatives can we think of? Or, specifying the measures, control, and interface dimensions (step 12) on Figure 13-1: What purposes should the specifications of those dimensions achieve? What "ideal" alternatives can be considered to develop the specifications? Or, specifying the details for performance reports (step 17): What purposes should the performance reports achieve?

Integrating System Matrix Ideas and Usual Solution Frameworks

The system matrix owes a great deal to the usual frameworks. They at least structured the idea that certain characteristics are needed as the output of P&D. They also are contributors to the system matrix definitions and the models and techniques used within the matrix. Now the system matrix can suggest ways in which the existing formats can be enhanced so that each is more effective if its use is continued.

Take, for example, the plan format for strategic business units presented previously under "professional education." Table 13-5 assigns as much meaning as possible to each of the major ideas in that plan format. It also lists *some* other possibilities suggested by the system elements and dimensions. The speculative suggestions appear to contribute the advantages of thoroughness, completeness, and utility.

The parts of a policy statement, presented previously, would be enhanced with the same type of suggestions noted in Table 13-5. They might become operational by means of a series of questions: What is the hierarchy of purposes that the policy addresses? What are the various dimensions of inputs, especially information, needed for the policy? What specifically are the fundamental and measures dimensions of outputs? What is the interface between almost all the elements and external and related internal groups? Several other

features of the whole PDA (Figure 10-4)—strategy, interrelationship with the real world, involving people, continuing change and improvement—are involved with those questions rather than just the solution framework. The whole PDA is trying to avoid the simplistic drawing-board or formula-based view of specifying solutions that appears to be the direction of reasoning of even those in political and social sectors.

The system matrix can help specify and present specific solutions, such as process control in a manufacturing company. One way is to incorporate at least the values, measures, and control and interface dimensions of the sequence element portrayed in the model. A second way is to treat the "process control" (sequence control) cell modeled in Figure 13-4 as a system matrix itself—define the six dimensions of purpose of process control, define the six dimensions of inputs to process control, six dimensions of outputs from process control, and so on.

Mathematical models are also frequently presented as *the* P&D solution framework. For example, a paper on selecting which of several products to develop claimed at least two phases: technical (to improve the product), and commercial (to produce and sell it). The uncertainties in each phase were treated in terms of maximization of expected value of return within budget and return/pay-back constraints, and in terms of compound probabilities. Numerical solutions were found with dynamic programming. Yet these aspects concern only the measures and possibly the interface and future dimensions of inputs and outputs. Thus, the mathematical solution framework would be enhanced if all the other cells were included. Computer programs to optimize some performance factor (travel distance, time elapsed, cost) produce a solution model specifying where machines, bins, and other objects ought to be located. They could also be enhanced with insights from the system matrix. In other words, "Be literate before being numerate."

Reports are another favorite "solution framework" for a P&D project. A system matrix is an obvious guide for structuring a report (e.g., a program statement for a new building should specify and present the purposes, inputs, outputs, sequence, environment and remaining elements anticipated for the solution). A system matrix guide would help to avoid these reviewers' criticisms of a report generated by a conventional design project: Sharing arrangements among departments were not resolved, economic trade-offs had not been calculated concerning transfers of workers to new jobs, and departmental work procedures in light of the new centrally controlled truck services were unresolved. One of the best ways of developing a report is to use PDA to design it. This proved exceptionally

Table 13-5 Suggestions Arising from the System Matrix* to Enhance Another Solution Framework

Strategic Business Unit Plan Format	Elements and Dimensions of System Matrix	Some Possible Other Items to Include*

Mission	Purpose
	    Fundamental, values (assumes hierarchy, but not identified)
	Outputs
	    Interface, future
		How control mission
		What future missions or purposes
		How mission relates to other elements

Key environmental assumptions	Environment
	    Fundamental, measures, control, interface
	Outputs
	    Control, interface
		Values of environment
		Future prospects of environment

Key competitor assumptions	Inputs
	    Measures, interface
	Outputs
	    Measures, control, interface
		Specific fundamental inputs
		Values of competitors
		Fundamental outputs, how and future

Constraints	(Government regulations could fit in several cells) Purpose Values	Should avoid, but include only external factors not worth trying to change
Objectives	Purpose Measures, future	Relate to purpose values

Goals	Purpose
	    Measures, future
	Output
	    Measures, future
		Relate to values dimension

Strategy	Sequence Fundamental, values, measures, control	Fundamental, and future dimensions of outputs

Programs	Purpose
	    Interface
	Outputs
	    Interface
		Future outputs
		Interface purpose and outputs

Resources	(Very broad, could include some inputs, human agents, physical catalysts, and information aids)	(See items in parentheses left)
Contingencies, "What if?"	Inputs, outputs, sequence, environment, human agents Fundamental, control	Triggering mechanism

Financial forecast	Purpose
	    Measures, future
	Outputs
	    Output, sequence
		—

OTHER POSSIBLE FACTORS SUGGESTED BY SYSTEM
MATRIX* TO INCLUDE IN PLAN FORMAT

Human agent (workers, managers) development	Technological progression
Compensation schemes	Market prospects
Information systems/flow for decision making	Physical environment changes
Management personnel backup	Management style
Physical facilities projections	New materials to serve as inputs

* See Table 13-3 for specific items that might make up the cells noted here.

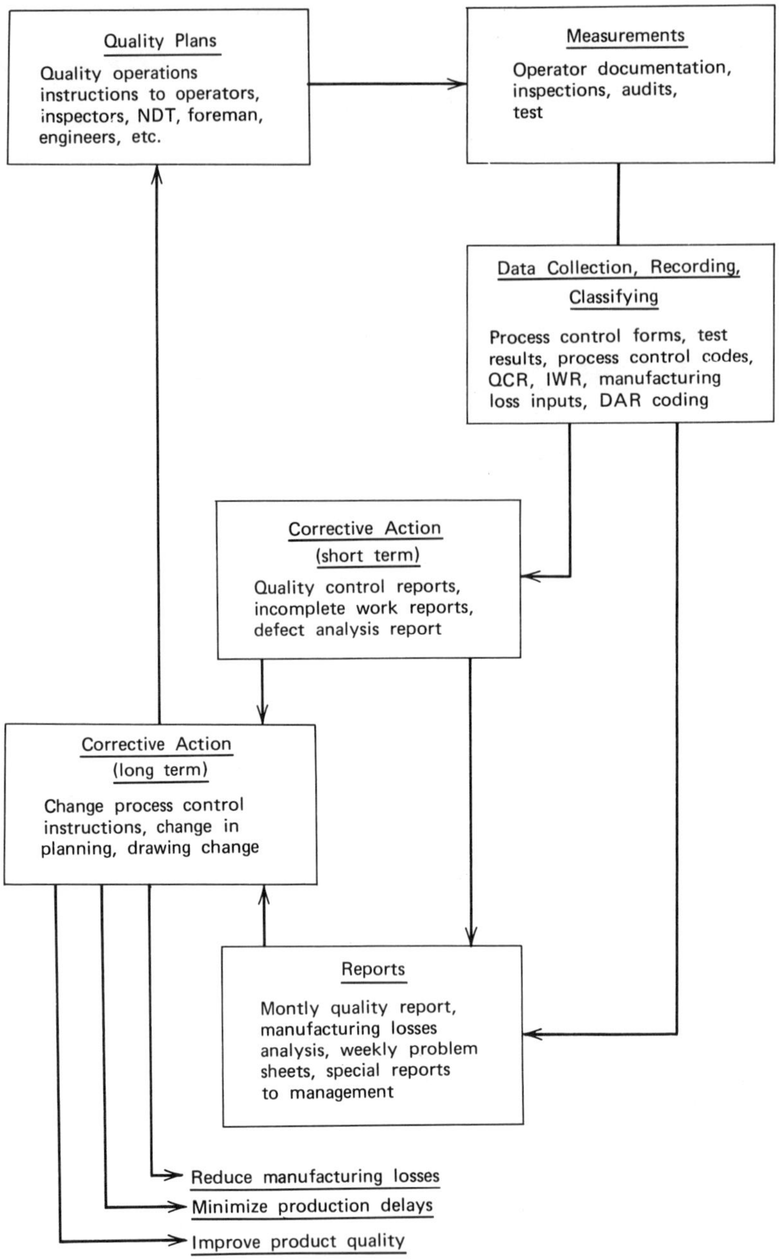

Figure 13-4 Process control system. From D. T. Koenig, "Process Control in a High Technology Impact Heavy Industry Job Shop," Turbine Department, General Electric Company, Schenectady, N.Y., 18 January 1974.

valuable in the gypsy moth pest management system (Case History B1).

Whatever the basis for developing the specifications of a solution (as presented in this Chapter), several outstanding organizations (e.g., Proctor & Gamble, Emerson Electric, United Technologies) require the recommendations to be presented in only one page! Brief reports are indeed powerful.

SUMMARY

Specifying and presenting a P&D solution concerns the formalities of plan making or preparation within the total and holistic PDA timeline scenario. A solution framework is needed to spell out what conditions are to exist when implementation is complete, how the in-place conditions are to operate over time and be improved or updated, and the steps needed to move from approval to intallation and operation.

Criteria for a "good" solution framework include degree of prescriptive assistance while following the strategy, flexibility of the language to fit the situation, assistance in organizing a solution, ability to represent *desired* conditions, documentation capabilities, detailing capability, communication capability, and adaptability to various needs for detail.

Several solution frameworks that stem from conventional approaches include playing by ear, experience (policy statement, long-range plans, social systems, diagrams, etc.), principles that the locus content area considers representative of "good" solutions, science/research format, professional education, questions and checklists, and systems models.

The system matrix (Chapter Nine) is presented as the most likely effective solution framework:

Proposition 10 *A universally applicable, prescriptive system matrix is a cost/effective framework for specifying and presenting the needed conditions of a P&D solution.*

The activities needed to specify and present a solution fit the timeline perspective by considering the system matrix as empty at the beginning of a project and completely "filled in" at the end of the project. Some illustrations showing usual solution frameworks (e.g., corporate planning, policy development, reports) can be enhanced through use of a system matrix perspective.

CHAPTER FOURTEEN

Involving People

Participation, involvement, and cooperation of people in P&D are considered so important that they are like an axiom. Most of the literature treats participation and involvement as ends in themselves, without real consideration of other factors in the intertwined P&D scenario (Figures 10-4 and 14-1). Involvement of people in a conventional P&D strategy, for example, is far from sufficient. Assume that a meeting called for a P&D project starts with the participants being asked to describe the problem, where the difficulties occur, and who is to blame. Will participation and involvement help?

The way participation and involvement are interrelated with pursuing a P&D strategy significantly affects the results obtained. If the group gets started with analyzing the situation, the whole effort can suffer. A P&D game using information cards was used to start a course, and each of the four groups of six graduate students worked independently. The first person to speak in one group said, "It is obvious that the problem is . . ." and the group never recovered from the blinders of this statement. The first person to take action in another group shared the information he got from the card he turned over, and the group shared all subsequent information. The first person in the third group to turn over a card returned it to the stack and did not share the information. No one in that group shared any information from then on. The first person to speak in the fourth group asked, "What are we trying to accomplish?" and then, "What would that accomplish?" This group designed a plan to achieve its selected purpose, and then implemented it. They far outscored the other groups.

A case might thus be developed to show that *how* participation is carried out is as crucial as the actual involvement. Initial actions or statements cast the die. Although the evidence is not complete, it appears that groups lose hope for success and even stop trying if some success is not attained almost immediately.[1] The conventional probing of difficulties is likely to produce a feeling of helplessness, to the detriment of present and future P&D projects. And although hard work and perseverance may occasionally overcome learned helplessness, it will not happen too often. Conversely, with a group starting with purposes, "ideal" solutions, regularities, a target, and so on, their enthusiasm and commitment will probably produce better results and will carry over to other P&D efforts.

Many sections of this book focus on the human basis of P&D. The importance of involving people in P&D is ingrained in the entire approach. It is not a nicety or an extra. It is essential. People are a major source of information and are key in maximizing the utility of their own knowledge. Involvement is the only way of coping with the realities of people and the organization. People are influenced by the group, and an individual or minority can influence the group. Involvement thus calls upon ideas from affective and chance domains in developing the total PDA.

Another reason affective and chance ideas are incorporated in the PDA scenario stems from the multiplicity of "worlds" or "lives" of each person outside the P&D situation. The "real-world" person in a PDA scenario is the organizational one, where the person's livelihood is earned. Other lives or worlds include family, bowling league, church, poker club, children's

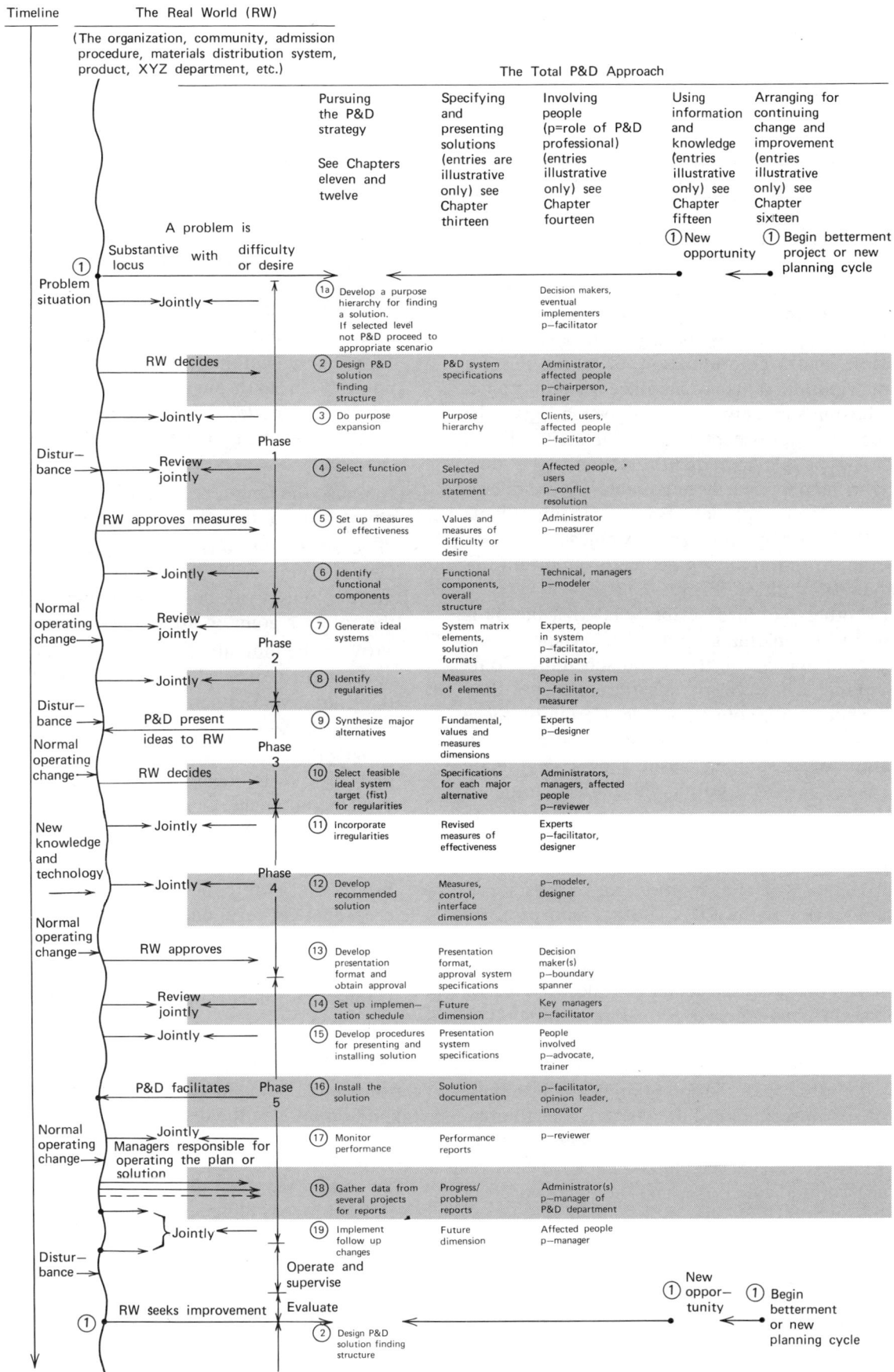

Timeline

The Real World (RW)

(The organization, community, admission procedure, materials distribution system, product, XYZ department, etc.)

The Total P&D Approach

Pursuing the P&D strategy	Specifying and presenting solutions (entries are illustrative only) see	Involving people (p=role of P&D professional) (entries illustrative only) see	Using information and knowledge (entries illustrative only) see	Arranging for continuing change and improvement (entries illustrative only) see
See Chapters eleven and twelve	Chapter thirteen	Chapter fourteen	Chapter fifteen	Chapter sixteen

① New opportunity ① Begin betterment project or new planning cycle

A problem is

① Substantive locus with difficulty or desire

Problem situation

→Jointly→ ①a Develop a purpose hierarchy for finding a solution. If selected level not P&D proceed to appropriate scenario — Decision makers, eventual implementers p—facilitator

RW decides → ② Design P&D solution finding structure — P&D system specifications — Administrator, affected people p—chairperson, trainer

→Jointly← ③ Do purpose expansion — Purpose hierarchy — Clients, users, affected people p—facilitator

Phase 1

Distur-bance

Review jointly ④ Select function — Selected purpose statement — Affected people, users p—conflict resolution

RW approves measures → ⑤ Set up measures of effectiveness — Values and measures of difficulty or desire — Administrator p—measurer

→Jointly← ⑥ Identify functional components — Functional components, overall structure — Technical, managers p—modeler

Normal operating change → Review jointly ⑦ Generate ideal systems — System matrix elements, solution formats — Experts, people in system p—facilitator, participant

Phase 2

→Jointly← ⑧ Identify regularities — Measures of elements — People in system p—facilitator, measurer

Distur-bance — P&D present ideas to RW ⑨ Synthesize major alternatives — Fundamental, values and measures dimensions — Experts p—designer

Normal operating change → RW decides Phase 3 ⑩ Select feasible ideal system target (fist) for regularities — Specifications for each major alternative — Administrators, managers, affected people p—reviewer

→Jointly← ⑪ Incorporate irregularities — Revised measures of effectiveness — Experts p—facilitator, designer

New knowledge and technology → →Jointly← Phase 4 ⑫ Develop recommended solution — Measures, control, interface dimensions — p—modeler, designer

Normal operating change → RW approves ⑬ Develop presentation format and obtain approval — Presentation format, approval system specifications — Decision maker(s) p—boundary spanner

Review jointly ⑭ Set up implemen-tation schedule — Future dimension — Key managers p—facilitator

→Jointly← ⑮ Develop procedures for presenting and installing solution — Presentation system specifications — People involved p—advocate, trainer

P&D facilitates Phase 5 ⑯ Install the solution — Solution documentation — p—facilitator, opinion leader, innovator

Normal operating change → Jointly ⑰ Monitor performance — Performance reports — p—reviewer

Managers responsible for operating the plan or solution

⑱ Gather data from several projects for reports — Progress/problem reports — Administrator(s) p—manager of P&D department

Jointly← ⑲ Implement follow up changes — Future dimension — Affected people p—manager

Operate and supervise

Distur-bance →

RW seeks improvement Evaluate

① New opportunity ① Begin betterment or new planning cycle

② Design P&D solution finding structure

206 Making the P&D Approach Operational

schools, neighborhood association, fishing group, and many others. A P&D effort in one of these other entities involves a different set of dynamics and interpersonal characteristics. Similarly, one person's role and experiences in groups outside the working organization influence perceptions and behaviors there.

It is virtually impossible then to avoid the influence of affective and chance characteristics of all these other spheres on a particular P&D project. No rational approach could possibly consider and incorporate the impact of these other worlds. The P&D projects with the smallest scope, such as the design of a gear for a transmission shaft, determination of a routing for product distribution, a plan of an office layout, or a design of a hospital inventory control system, give the appearance of being susceptible to completely rational analysis. The people ingredients appear to be relatively few in number, easily negotiable, or conducive to acceptance of any solution. But people ingredients there are. Because there are very few clues *in advance* as to whether or not involving people is important, including them from the start is prudent.

Several other words describe what this factor is about—political, diplomatic, practical, sagacious, discreet, artful lobbying, infighting, and scheming. Some of these sound distasteful or unscrupulous, yet they portray the need for involving people. Certainly, these characteristics influence behavior regarding implementation of a solution desired by a legitimate group. It is too late to cry foul when other groups or external individuals use the ideas behind the words to effectively block the plan or implementation. Involving people effectively means interweaving various "political" aspects of the situation, as various steps, phases and stages of the PDA strategy and protocol unfold.

For those who claim all of this is "manipulative," I plead guilty to the positive meaning of the word. Even a conversation between two people is manipulative; each person seeks to convince the other of the merits of a position or the validity of information. Involving people is not done with the intention of being unfair, fraudulent, or unscrupulous. Integrity is the foundation of the concepts here. Although one can use all of the P&D ideas to illegal and unfair ends, just as research, operate and supervise, and the other purposeful activities can be, the idea of involving people has the desired values of society (Chapter Two) as the guiding principles.

Thus, "manipulative" behavior is a double-edged sword. Concerned and affected people can and should have the opportunity to "manipulate" the P&D professional, as Figure 10-4 expresses. And a P&D professional working on a real-world problem these

people want resolved will have to "manipulate" them to modify perceptions and behavior along the timeline. Such open "manipulations" are essential if human and societal ends are to be continually achieved. The frequent exchanges in the P&D approach (Figure 10-4) purposely get people to negotiate and structure their own social sense of reality.

The advantages to the whole P&D endeavor of such interpersonal exchanges thus become fairly clear:

- Significantly increase the likelihood of acceptance and implementation of a solution.
- More likely lead to acceptance of an innovation and possibly breakthrough solution (in other words, minimize functional fixedness, help determine the "right" problem to work on, and foster creative thinking).
- Increase the long-term commitment to assure workability and continued improvement of the solution.
- Give acceptable answers to questions that bother people, such as "why change?" "what's in it for me?," "why work on that problem?," and "how is the solution going to affect me?"
- Provide the individual with insights on how to exert some control over what is to be done, thus avoiding the "not invented here" syndrome.
- Add an important intellectual aspect and source of satisfaction to the work of most people; they learn and use P&D ideas, thus increasing their self-esteem and image.
- Fit changes within the social and cultural values of the organization/community.
- Develop a more cohesive work group and thus decrease longer-term uncertainty and ambiguity.
- Provide greater assurance that the P&D world does not become separated from the real world.
- Generate top-level support for the P&D process and solutions.

Some disadvantages can occur, but the advantages far outweigh them. In addition, several actions can be taken to minimize the disadvantages' effect:

- A person whose specific idea was not adopted may be frustrated and angry. To minimize this, use group process techniques that avoid having an individual become committed early to a specific idea.
- The openness of the P&D strategy may cause some always to seek the biggest solution, thus apparently increasing the project time. This does not actually occur. Actual comparisons on real projects show that the PDA strategy takes less or equivalent time to complete than conventional strategies.

- Involvement may not satisfy *everyone*. Give people the opportunity to take part and keep those who don't informed of progress.
- Some managers feel they are losing control when others get involved in what they consider their province. How to minimize this feeling is discussed in this chapter.

"Involving people" can have broadly differing meanings for different individuals. Each person tends to adopt a certain relationship or posture regarding a specific P&D effort. Similarly, in each P&D project a person may have a different role. An expert on telecommunications in a hospital medical records P&D project may be a user in a payroll system P&D project, a worker in the system of supplying consulting services to organizations, and a resource controller in the library acquisition system. Table 14-1 lists some of the roles of people in the P&D system (Table 10-1).

To explain *how* people in these categories can be effectively involved, the rest of this chapter is divided as follows:

1 Some tenets and principles about involving people in P&D.

Table 14-1 Some Roles of People in the P&D System (Table 10-1)

Inputs People who perceive the problem: Users, clients, consumers, target groups, decision makers, resource controllers and their representatives; activists; lobbyists; those now operating the system.

Outputs Same people as inputs except that they have a solution(s) that is implemented; the whole target or impact group affected by the solution.

Sequence All of the input people following the stages and steps of the P&D strategy: the P&D professional as facilitator; the expert as information resource.

Environment People who have indirect influence—politicians, religious leaders, administrators and managers, community influentials, bankers and financial executives, tax payers.

Human Agents P&D professionals, experts (scientist, statistician, sociologist, thermodynamics expert, political scientist, etc.), boundary spanners, draftpersons, technicians of several types (measurement specialist, interview technician, data analyst, etc.); see the last section of this chapter for more details.

Information Aids Specialists with information ordinarily contained in manuals and standard operating procedures (e.g., training, information systems, documentation, evaluation methods, sources of continuing education, maintenance, payroll).

2 Considerations in arranging the involvement of people.
3 The role of the P&D professional.

The basic theme is summarized thus:

Proposition 11 *Involving people in the P&D system as inputs, outputs, part of the environment, actors in following the P&D strategy, information aids, and human agents can maximize the number and effectiveness of implemented solutions and the effectiveness of utilizing P&D resources.*

SOME TENETS AND PRINCIPLES ABOUT INVOLVING PEOPLE IN P&D

Any prescriptive notions about involving people must start with some basic premises. The first is that the individual and group realities presented in Chapter Five are conditions with which P&D *can* cope. Organizations are already modifying their modes of operating and supervising to take cognizance of new values people seek: self-expression, autonomy, assertiveness, personal freedom, and "doing my own thing."

The second premise is the basic timeline scenario of P&D. A P&D project must start immediately with concerns for implementation, or how to get the solution "utilized" even before the solution is known. The timeline scenario establishes the basis of a behavior-contingent progression for getting there: Get the people concerned to change their perception about and behavior toward the solution by involving those who can make it work.

A third premise is a commitment to the believing game concept. Moving "real-world" people along the timeline to change their perceptions is in effect getting them to "believe" the process and the resulting, usually pluralistic and continually changing, solution. What people (Table 14-1) are supposed to do is change their allegiance to or belief in the familiar, "certain," and "unambiguous" present, however much they themselves agree that it needs to be replaced, to an allegiance to a future state with its uncertainties. This asks people not only to change their minds, but to believe in a state about which nothing is really known.

"An analysis of mind-changing is in order. I use myself as an example. . . . Where I actually *did* change my mind, it strikes me . . . that it was not, in fact, the process of being devastatingly argued against that did it . . . There was always a something else that had to happen. . . . It happens most when the person arguing against me lets up on his guns a little, stops trying to show that I'm an idiot, and in fact shows some glimmer of understanding for why *I* believe what I do believe. He shows a bit of willingness to share *my* perception: then I'm more willing to share his. . . . The believing game helps this mind-changing process more than the doubting game does. Though the believing game is in-taking or incorporatory, nevertheless this taking-in permits a greater letting-go. . . . Letting-go requires an atmosphere of acceptance and trust, and the believing game helps inspire this atmosphere much more than the doubting game does."[2]

What these premises do, then, is to provide a positive framework for establishing tenets and principles on which to base the process of involving people. They identify positive characteristics about people to serve as grounding points that can deal with their "realities" (Chapter Five). Tenets and principles about involving people are discussed below.

A.   People Touched by P&D Efforts and Eventual Results Should Be Given *Continual* Opportunities to Participate

In the best of all worlds, all those who should be involved in a P&D effort would take part and contribute. In reality, few people become involved and fewer still contribute even if they are involved at the appropriate time in a P&D protocol or strategy. Large masses of people in a developing country, for example, are unlikely to "participate" in an industrial development planning project, yet some efforts toward this condition ought to be considered. Similarly, the design of a gear to go on a transmission shaft will not motivate all those affected to take part, yet some efforts toward this condition ought to be considered.

The provision of the continual *opportunity* to take part, to contribute, to keep abreast of the proceedings, is the basic consideration of this tenet. There is no way to predict just who will contribute at what point, and thus all options should remain open. Physicians, for example, find it difficult to attend sessions concerning a hospital P&D project. They are likely to contribute at some time if they receive agenda of meetings, minutes of previous meetings, telephone calls to set up likely meeting times, short questionnaires they could complete on their own, and an interview visit on occasion by one or two group members or P&D professionals. Their perceptions are thus quite likely to change so that implementation is more likely to occur. The P&D professional is responsible for finding the ways of giving people the frequent opportunity to be involved to the extent they want to be.

People do feel that they *can* contribute. If not asked to do so, an individual may feel snubbed. What is worse, people may let negative factors take over their attitude toward the whole P&D project—

apprehensiveness, apparent fear of technology, feelings of insecurity, concern for job security and status, and expressions of personal dissatisfaction could manifest themselves this way. If invited to take part, an individual may elect not to do so, but will have at least had some perceptions modified and contributory desires satisfied. With continuing invitations to participate, a previous decision *not* to take part is not an obstacle to the individual's future contribution. There is no way initially to predict who will take part and when, so keep the *opportunity* available all of the time. All of us know people who do not speak up until the third or fourth meeting while others dry up after the first. When given a freely arranged basis for the exchange of ideas, humans will make informed choices that are conducive to their own development as well as contribute to the larger whole of which they are a part.

B.   People Are the Source of Information

This refers to the contextual situation rather than to the vast number of "facts" (Chapter Fifteen) and the large amount of routine data (orders, inventories, dollars in a budget) available in any organization.

Obtaining the contextual and situation-contingent information when needed in the form desired by the P&D strategy should rely on direct involvement by the relevant people. Inserting an intervening analyst, modeler or measurer to collect data is not only a manifest waste and misdirection of usually scarce P&D resources but a well-nigh impossible task (Axioms 6 and 7). Analysts and measurers *are* needed in some projects and phases, but their usefulness is greatly enhanced when the people involved also perceive the need for the model or data collection (e.g. for purposes, ideal systems, feasible solution targets, regularities). This is the way to benefit from people's long-term memory capabilities (Chapter Five) because all information is more likely than not to emerge in an appropriate context, something an analyst finds practically impossible to control or cause. Much less information needs to be collected. Information *is* needed but "it is right here in the room with us."

Thus, the mental abilities of an individual are not measured solely by level of education or intelligence quotients. Nothing portrays this innate ability of humans to produce appropriate information at the appropriate time better—though unfortunately in a negative way—than the hugely creative reasoning they display to show why a solution or plan developed by others is inappropriate. This rather typical reaction to conventional P&D results is indeed pitiful, in view of the latent pool of combined intelligence, experience, and judgment of people that could lead to individual and societal good.

What this tenet addresses in large part is the "subjective data" everyone knows is *a*, if not *the*, major determinant of decisions. It is valid and obviously influences P&D results. The tenet also recognizes that each person has an individual style both of retaining information and of gathering it from the surroundings and environment.[3]

C. People Can Understand Intricate Techniques and Complex Situations

Some individual realities (Chapter Five) might seem to contradict this tenet: functional fixedness, constrained decision making, and short time horizon, for example. Conventional approaches do exacerbate these, while the basic strategy pattern and total P&D approach move toward mitigating their presence. Rogerian psychology (as empathic counselor for basically "good" people), continuing learning as an organizational and societal imperative, transactional analysis, and the sociotechnical concept of humans as alive, curious, learning, reasoning, evaluating, and "grown-up" in their total lives, not just work, are theories and concepts increasingly supported by evidence.

The burden of responsibility for explaining a new technique, model, or complex idea falls on the P&D professional. There is no reason to claim that "they" (the affected people) cannot really grasp the sophistication, beauty, and elegance, of "my" technique. A satisfactory technique in P&D or in an operating system must have a logically acceptable basis to those involved. Linear programming, for example, *was* explained to a line supervisor who was to make daily decisions using the model, although he had only a grade school education.

Beyond the benefits for a specific project, this tenet leads to many long-term desirable consequences for the work organization and community at large. People who learn new techniques, ideal solution ideas, expanded purposes, and technological advances will be better prepared for future P&D projects and for operating and supervising purposeful activities. The utilization of the basic strategy pattern gives even unskilled people a P&D dimension which will stand them in good stead when they are promoted. People who know the P&D approach are likely to utilize it.

D. P&D Group Meetings and Involvement of Individuals Can Be Productive

Meetings of groups for P&D purposes or individual contacts with P&D professionals do not currently produce the benefits many people expect: they do not produce creative, timely, cost-effective, and implemented results. Some of the reality conditions noted in Chapter Five would seem to militate against the success of involvement and group processes: group inertia regarding changes, organizations hiring people like themselves, using selective information to support a position, and group polarization on prediscussion tendencies.

Other conceptual and research results, however, suggest several methods on *how* this tenet can become operational: "Reading or listening to arguments generally produces less effect than actual participation in discussion, . . . participative discussion has a greater effect than mere information presentation, . . . the [positive] impact of active role playing [is demonstrated] as contrasted with passive exposure; . . . passive learning about the target of an attitude is not sufficient to change the attitude; the subject must actively reformulate, or rehearse, the information he has received in order to internalize an attitude change; . . . [and] our attitudes tend to move toward our behavior. People may feel an increased sense of certainty and conviction after openly committing themselves to the dominant alternative."[4]

Involving people in P&D at individual and group levels must on the one hand foster openness, expansive thinking, creativity, and willingness to change. Then must come some closure, commitment to an initial solution, and willingness to detail. Then additional openness and creativity are needed to find continuing changes and improvement, then commitment to implementing new changes. Different skills and relationships are needed in these seemingly contradictory modes. But the quoted results indicate that each mode can be enhanced, if timing is appropriate. What the group leader or P&D professional does and when in the meetings and personal contacts will determine if this tenet can be met in practice. "The group leader might suppress mention of initial preferences while eliciting relevant arguments. The finding that verbal arguments are more polarized than individually written briefs suggests the usefulness of generating arguments by individual effort; contrary to the popular myth about the great quantity of ideas produced by group brainstorming, most experiments actually reveal that individual production generates the greatest quantity of ideas from a given group of people."[5]

Many techniques (see the next section) enable a P&D professional to cope with frequent group difficulties: uneven distribution of interaction among group members; dominant amount of time and conceptual control of meetings by "high-status" people; limited range of communication in a meeting because people interact primarily with those in close proximity (conventionally those from a peer group) or the same work situation or similar social status; and rejection of views of an unaccepted or "deviant" person or group, even though they are technically worthy of consideration. These techniques produce satisfactions, motivations, and often a sense of autonomy for those involved as well as effective implemented solutions. The basic and detailed strategy patterns (Chapters Eleven and Twelve) are essential parts of realizing these results. For example, all the teachers in a junior high school wanted to plan what the school would become in ten years. Prior to the use of the basic strategy pattern, the group had been polarized because of the fractiousness of several members and arguments revolving around only a particular set of educational packages for adoption.

E. People Enjoy Working and Accepting Responsibility for P&D Projects

Some of the individual and group reality conditions in Chapter Five would seem to explain this tenet: People know the needs, people are defensive about information portraying something is wrong, people dislike being patronized, people exhibit the not-invented-here syndrome, and people's behavior makes sense to them. This tenet is especially supported if the basic strategy pattern is followed.

The PDA strategy is also the major form of explanation about *how* those realities which appear to mitigate this tenet can be managed to allow the tenet to become the reality.

Accepting the Problem as Stated   Purposes, hierarchies, measures of effectiveness, ideal systems, and so on, open up prospects for "finding" the right problem.

Functional Fixedness   Not very likely to remain, for the reason just noted.

Constrained Decision Making   Exposing alternative purposes, purpose hierarchies, various ideal systems, and so on should enlighten any decision maker to change regulations if possible and be more open about "constraints."

Short Time Horizon   What better way to diminish this than by the expansiveness of the timeline, hierarchies, ideal systems, regularities, and so on.

Different Personality Types   Getting together a broad range of decision makers, intermediate managers, engineers, personnel chiefs, and so on to start with Phase 1 brings the different types to focus on the project and to work out differences of understanding. The PDA strategy helped a group containing two federal bureau chiefs from the same agency who had not talked with each other for nearly 10 years. The strategy did not give anyone a real chance to attack anyone else about

blame or fault concerning the problem. The two men at least were willing to communicate regularly because the solution showed each one how each person's work depended on the new system.

Organizational policies reward inimical behavior Designing the P&D system to be put in place to do the P&D of the outputs helps to expose these policies for possible correction. They almost always are not the "givens" or "constraints" we have to live with that most conventional approaches assume.

Most surveys show that 75 to 85% of people in almost all organizations feel they would be able to handle more responsibilities, as "predicted" by the hierarchy of needs (Chapter Two). P&D is one of each person's purposeful activities, and finding a positive approach through which they can be engaged in P&D does generate excitement for many people who work on, for example, manufacturing jobs. One group of workers in a plant were involved in designing a new department for a new product. They felt so positively about one alternative that they challenged the engineering people who favored another to a trial run to decide. Their alternative was shown to be much better. Whether or not one could prove that the engineers' preference was technologically more effective is the wrong question. The workers would now make certain their alternative would work, and in addition, they already know what future changes may occur so that continuing improvement is built in.

F. The Individual Is the Source of P&D Ideas

Whether creative, combinatory, implementation-oriented, or whatever, an idea is the product of a specific mind. A mind may be triggered by a simple word, complex relationship, gentle prod, forceful statement, or random thought. Although group processes may stimulate creativity, they *alone* may stifle the very ingeniousness being sought. Some people do not participate as well as others, yet have tremendous capabilities that need to be tapped. Some individual follow-up may be helpful if the stimulus of the group fails to elicit ideas from any individual.

This tenet seeks to enhance the ability of the individual to be creative. As a matter of fact, the most underdeveloped P&D resource in this country is the people in an organization. Because people enjoy designing rather than the drudgery of analysis of the existing system, they have the opportunity to utilize mental as well as physical skills, perform work that is meaningful, and assume real responsibility. Organizations that fail to utilize the P&D ability of their people to help them meet their own and the organization's

ends are incurring huge costs. Believing well of the
abilities of each fellow being may create the good you
believe in. People who could not read or write participated in many P&D programs where their excellent
abilities were a valuable contribution.

Three other ideas can help put this tenet to work.
The first pertains to enhancing the individual's
"space," so natural abilities will be able to operate
effectively. Each individual's differing ability, personality, information acquisition style, and achievement
motivation can be enhanced if the organization environment and management style permit, encourage,
and reward it. Chapter Sixteen addresses organizational attitudes and their impact on individual performance in P&D and improvement activities in general.

The second idea for making this tenet workable
pertains to the role of the basic strategy pattern. Questions based on purposes, regularities, and target solutions add "positive rationalism" and forward or future orientation for people. These are means to sort
through the huge amount of information that bombards
us all so that people are stimulated by the relevant
items.

The third idea for making available the content of
the individual mind stems from the findings that appropriate group activities can increase the creativity
and productivity of an individual, even the most
superior one, over what the same individual would
generate alone.[6] A group with appropriate techniques
in the PDA strategy provides access to external resources and is likely to "push" on each individual, so
that an alternative is discovered that the individual
alone would not find. An individual can also attain personal goals that only a group can bestow—recognition,
ego stroking, value to the organization, and so on.
Further, the individual can motivate other people and
supply them with well-supported, logical, and consistent information by not conforming to obtain social
approval, or seeking closure before each individual
can contribute. Lastly, a group helps the individual if it
consciously seeks to include, at least on occasion, a
wide range of "experts" or "outsiders"—scientists,
younger/older specialists, technical literature reviews,
manufacturers' representatives, and so on.

G.   People Will Accept and Implement P&D Solutions They Help to Develop

Several features of the timeline process of arriving at
the P&D solution are probably more important than
the solution itself:

1   When people develop a P&D solution, the reality
    that their behavior makes sense to them becomes an

underpinning for their commitment to the resultant
solution. In this view, an individual is acting out of
self-interest by focusing on higher levels of the
hierarchy of needs—security, social, affiliation,
esteem, self-actualization, and cognitive.

2   People affected by a solution will be able to de-
    velop what is best for the circumstances. Good
    P&D facilitation will help a formal or informal
    group to develop a more effective solution than
    would be obtained from unfacilitated meetings or
    the conventional strategy.

3   Involving people in P&D is essential for coping
    with their tendency to reject external solutions as
    "not invented here."

4   People want to be involved in making P&D deci-
    sions that influence their lives. They want to de-
    lineate their own needs, possible solutions, and so
    on. They want to participate in the decision process
    irrespective of how much modification, expansion,
    flexibility, and simplicity/complexity they may in-
    troduce into any other solution from elsewhere as
    they pursue their own solution. People may well
    accept a decrease in flexibility in their personal
    work activities, but perceive greater control
    through the decision process that established that
    decrease in flexibility. Workers, for example, are
    leery if someone else "humanizes" their work.

This tenet also creates a difficulty in getting people
involved. As more people participate, individual
"control" decreases, uncertainties of quality of results
increases, and "responsible" people "lose" control.
A manager, for example, trades off loss of control with
increased commitment of people and likelihood of implemented change.

H.   A Person's Perceptions and Value System Generally Change with Age and Reflect the Time of Reaching Adulthood

The state or condition today of any previous tenet for
any one individual or group is no assurance of what it
will be a year from now. The political world reflects
this: Consider the changes in the meaning of the word
liberal since the '60s. In foreign policy, it has gone
from an activist, interventionist, and militaristic stance
to one of noninvolvement; in social policy, from equal
treatment of each individual regardless of creed or race
to use of quotas to determine treatment of race/creed
groups; in fiscal policy, from big government spending
to a "balanced budget."

The roles people play, and their personality types,
social interaction abilities, implosive/explosive reactions, and intellectual maturity and understanding also

cause differences over time in modes of involvement and perceptions. This existentialist or phenomenologist view is basically equivalent to a timeline explanation of real-world relationships. Who is feeling "in" or "out" of the group, who is "up" or "down," who likes to "schmooze" (tell jokes, talk with friends, long lunches)[7] or to "stick to the job," who is continuing to learn or not, who is "ignored" or "listened to," or who feels others are friends or not are time-variant factors that affect people involvement. The watermelon theory of life-span development (Chapter Six) explains many of these factors, and puts some names on "points" at which wisdom is gained and perceptions and values modified—family person, first-time homeowner, midlife crisis, empty nest, second job, and so on.

The era in which a person enters mature adulthood has an interesting impact on behavior. It sets up differentials between the managers/administrators/older adults and those, say, 20 years younger. Child psychologists know fairly well that the development of a human fits a certain pattern: 1 to 7 years is imprinting; 8 to 13, intense role modeling and locking in gut level values (e.g., with hero-worship); 14 to 20, socialization and value programming; and over 21, any significant emotional event (broken marriage, a war, a book) may shift some of the set conditions. For example, in 1980 people who are in their sixties had value programming during the depression of the 1930s; those in their fifties in 1980 had value programming in World War II, with its anger and commitment to win; those in their forties had value programming in the 1950s with that decade's affluence and overindulgence, and those in their thirties had this programming in the 1960s and were influenced by television, the space race, Vietnam, and the civil rights movement. The world views of these generations are thus much different. Each will perceive current trends, such as the growth in the 1970s of calculators, computers, and electronic games, in terms of their life-span development process. There is no right or wrong, good or bad. The tenet tells us of a factor that the PDA timeline scenario can fortunately cope with: what people believe and perceive.

This principle should help to avoid classifying a person or group once and for all by means of a static set of relationships. In addition, criteria for good group members (or good managers or good politicians or whatever) will almost always change from project to project, even from stage to stage in one project. Social homogeneity may be desirable in one case, and it may be anathema in another. Value conformity, levels of power, opportunistic perspectives, creative ability, courage, morality, and cognitive style can likewise require variability in representation in P&D efforts.

The major role of all the tenets leads to a positive basis for involving people that copes with the realities of humans and groups (Chapter Five).

CONSIDERATIONS IN ARRANGING THE INVOLVEMENT OF PEOPLE

How to do it is the theme of this section. It is insufficient, however utilitarian, to depend solely on exhortations to get people involved. Not that psychologists would completely dispute the motivational effects on performance of such statements. There is a great deal of truth to the notion that if people are treated as if they have intelligence and a desire to accept responsibility, they will respond in this fashion. If the P&D professional *thinks* and *acts* as if a person has real ability, the person will consistently do better than previously thought possible, even though a person may initially have come prepared to protect "turf" or search for maximum personal return. "If we are going to err about human possibilities, then for God's sake let us err on the generous side."[8]

Some specific activities or methods to involve people can be suggested based on these important motivational beliefs:

a   Ask questions. The questions can be about where you are in the steps of the basic strategy pattern. These are nonthreatening.
b   An informal "team" could operate during, say, a usual lunch grouping, an organizational athletic meeting, or a community's weekly service club meeting. Such groups have many other purposes and activities, yet the meeting represents an opportunity for asking positive and nondominating questions.
c   Set up a one-time meeting with people who might have constituted a good long-term project team had it been possible to get one established. One meeting of about 35 people was called to develop a statewide plan for getting school districts to set up a balanced unified learning approach demonstrating the relationship between ecological systems and human systems. Staff people were able to carry on with small group meetings and individual interviews.
d   Similar to c is the one-time meeting to plan the P&D system with the basic strategy pattern (Chapters Eleven and Twelve), as illustrated in Case History B1.

The following five considerations (Table 14-2) appear at this time to capture the relevant factors re-

Table 14-2 Interrelated Ideas about Involving People in P&D*

A. Approach Activities along Timeline	B. Level of Organization Participation	C. Roles of Input People	D. Group Processes†	E. Meeting Conditions
Obtain mandate (commitment)	None	Consumer, purchaser, or user	Interacting	Office
Develop overall pro-gram of change and improvement	Persuasive autocracy	Impacted group	Lecture	Conference room
Train others in P&D approach	Consultative	Client	Nominal	Classroom
Develop P&D system Level	Reactive control	Owner	Opinion poll‡	Workplace
Policy	Bargaining	Expert (scientist, en-gineer, computer, statistical, etc.).	Questionnaires‡	Table arrangement (round, oval, U, V, etc.)
Strategic	Participatory control	Person now working in system	Charette	Location—on or off site
Tactical	Joint determination	Citizen	Shared participation	Paper, pencils, easel, chalkboard, etc.
Operational	Supportive	Lobbyist	Delphi‡	Space zone per person (2–4 foot minimum)
Protocol stages	Permanent work-groups	Manager (first level, middle, top)	Leveling re: likes and dislikes	Name tags
Project priorities and selection	Complete (self-determination)	Opinion leader	We agree	Place cards
Determine values, criteria, etc. for deci-sion making		Judicial volunteer	Honoraria‡	Lighting
Personnel assignments		Decision maker, source of power (re-source controller, politician, board member, etc.)	Telecommunications‡ (CCTV, interactive cable, satellite, phone, computer)	Temperature
Phase 1 (Purpose)		Representative of con-stituency	Interviews of indi-viduals in group‡	Ventilation
Phase 2 (Ideas)		Activist, intellectual	Role playing	Noise level
Phase 3 (FIST)		Personal qualities—autocratic/participative/permissive, personal-ity, etc.	Computer graphics	Group arrangement (random, alphabetical, organized mixing)
Phase 4 (Solution)		Group size (seven ± two)	Game or simulation	
Phase 5 (Install)			Brain writing	
Obtaining approval			Short conference	
Develop support for solution			Referendum‡	
Obtain feedback on status			Public hearing	
Conflict resolution			Drop-in center	
Move to another pur-poseful activity (see Table 3-7)			Future-creating work-shop	
			Debate	
			Team building	
			Sensitivity training	
			Arbitration, mediation	
			Huddling	
			Media-based ballot-ing‡	
			Decision worksheet	
			Multiattribute utility assessment	
			Estimate silently—talk—estimate	
			Dialectical argumen-tation	
			Think aloud‡	

* On the basis of P&D approach activities (Column A) and the level of participation in the organization (Column B), *one or more* items are selected from each of the other three columns. Some research and applications evidence is available to guide selections (see text).

† Most techniques are listed by purpose in Appendix A.

‡ Techniques that do not require a group to actually gather together for meetings.

garding *how* to get people involved. All five are not necessarily important in every specific situation (i.e., it is not necessary to be overly concerned about meeting conditions if individual interviews in people's offices are the group process).

A.   Approach Activity along the Timeline

The stage or step of the protocol/strategy for the project or continuing effort is the major factor in arranging for people involvement. Put another way, the purpose or function to be achieved by the step is the crucial determinant of who, when, and how to involve people.

This consideration thus represents timeline scenario perspectives. Different groups of skills, influence, and knowledge can be expected to be needed at various steps. Consider, for example, the purposes and needs of Phase 1 in the strategy (purposes to be achieved) and of Phase 4 (detailing).

People's interest and concern also change (Axiom 2). Some people in the real world who were interested initially may not be as involved later as they perceive, for instance, that they are not threatened by the project which may have motivated them initially to take part. The converse is also true. Furthermore, people transfer jobs or terminate or new people are hired as the project proceeds.

The project itself will experience difficulties not linked directly to a specific step. Each step is not necessarily completed before the next one starts. Even being at step $n + 4$ does not mean that everyone is clear on or agrees to step $n + 1$. Projects almost inevitably have one or two "muddles" that occur along the way. A muddle or midproject panic can happen in several ways: Some project team members or real-world people "say they think the whole project is a waste of time; [important people] get into an embarrassing argument in the middle of a meeting; a previously uncommunicative and uncommitted [person] suddenly starts crusading for a cause you thought had been killed off, . . . meetings are getting unruly; . . . there is a general moroseness and a sinking feeling that the [organization] is going down the tubes unless [the P&D project] does something about it; there is a general understanding that the big ideas that surfaced in the first few meetings were naive, even childlike."[9]

These events can mean several things. A previous step was not sufficiently completed to permit progress in this step. New information from external sources (such as a new legislative bill, oil embargo, politician's decision) casts some doubts on decisions in previous steps. A technological innovation is announced that reduces (or enhances) the validity of a currently ac-

cepted FIST or recommendation. In some cases, the muddle causes greater concentration on the difficulties. This may be good because "the mixing of good minds, different backgrounds, solid facts, and intelligent guesses about the future [portends] the point at which you are about to make a big breakthrough."[10]

A return to a previous step or renewed diligence regarding the current step are probably reasonable courses of action. New people may be needed, or some may drop out for a step or two, or additional resources (human agents, money), time, or political support may be needed. Another course of action is to redesign the P&D system or protocol.

Column A in Table 14-2 includes items from other scenario features (e.g., program of change and improvement, develop support for the solution), and excludes the internal steps of the phases. This helps portray the range of purposes that can help identify whom to involve. A more complete Column A would be the timeline of actual stages and steps developed for the specific project. The static generalizations in the literature about the relatively constant group of people to involve in projects should be viewed very skeptically because the purposes of the many steps are so varied.

B.   Level of Organizational Participation

Trying to get many people involved in a P&D project can backfire if the organization, for example, has a pattern of authoritarian processes and style. This is not to say some simpler participation methods could not be used (see specific methods **a** and **b** above), but rather that determining the types of people and how they will become involved is going to depend on the levels of participation and involvement extant in the organization. It is difficult to imagine, for example, how workers and first-line supervisors in an autocratic-type organization will ever get involved in meetings to design a new manufacturing facility.

Identifying the level of organizational participation is not necessarily easy. Some measures of this are managerial style, organizational climate, readiness for change, or level of involvement (as discussed in Chapter Sixteen). Column B lists overlapping levels or styles on the general scale, from no participative climate to completely participative climate.

A particular level that "describes" an organization is at the very best a generalization that incorporates information on the behavior and morale of individual people, each of whom is different and possibly in conflict with others, in terms of style, objectives and values (Axiom 7 and its corollaries). No statement of an organizational level is a predictor of the specific style or participatory character of a given division, group, project team, and so forth. In addition, time-variant characteristics impinge on a selected level. A person, department, and surrounding circumstances may well change over time in one direction or the other (e.g., the owner/entrepreneur relatively autocratic style gives way to collaborative management). Furthermore, the purposes and objectives of an organization are not directly correlated with its participatory style or that of its subunits. One hospital does not have the same level of participation as another with supposedly identical size and services. One tool-and-die department does not operate with the same managerial style as another. Nor will one project team or permanent P&D group operate with identical levels of participation at all times.

The following are brief descriptions of the participation levels in Column B.

None Participation and involvement do not occur. People express surprise if the "boss" asks them a P&D-type question. People are paid to "work," not "think." Decisions are made by the managers and their staffs, including P&D professionals who consider the manager's role to consist of making decisions to "send down." Workers, customers, clients, etc. (in Column C) and interviews, worker attitude surveys, referenda, etc. (in Column D) are unlikely to be considered with this level.

Persuasive Autocracy Some recognition that an effort of "selling" the project or the solution is considered and incorporated "if there is time and money."

Consultative Responsible managers ask others many questions and seek to obtain as many ideas as possible. Yet establishing criteria, weightings, and details is left entirely to managers.

Reactive Control Assuming that the current solutions or systems are basically satisfactory, the organizations do get others involved with measuring, comparing, and assessing the performance in relation to what is desired. Citizens groups, regulatory boards, peer review, and so on, are means whereby participation is obtained. Policy formulation matters only occasionally arise along with operational and control matters.

Bargaining More adversarial or at least structured formal involvement is built into normal operations. Stereotypic views of this level usually consider only interacting group meetings as the group process (Column D), but many others could be used.

Anticipatory Control The organization consciously scans the horizon to become aware of possible future occurrences. Large groups can get involved through

reporting intelligence that could indicate developments. They could also develop alternatives for responding and "controlling" the future.

Joint Determination Relatively continuous interchanges of ideas between those charged with the responsibilities for operating a system and those working in the system. Although decisions are usually joint, a mandate or agreement usually does not exist. This means management operates in this style because *we* think it is desirable while workers have no assurance of its continuation. Many other stakeholders also may not be included in the participatory effort.

Supportive Collaborative efforts are likely to be more formalized, with some decision responsibilities spelled out (e.g., advisory group, citizens' commissions).

Permanent Workgroups Regularly meeting employees and managers (usually during working hours) seek to solve all types of problems that emerge in any area of concern. Illustrations include productivity or quality circles of 8 to 15 people in each department of a plant, boards of visitors, health planning agencies, improvement committees (see Chapter Sixteen), and so forth.

Complete Self-determination is carried out by joint worker/management board of directors, or several joint groups share key decision-making responsibility (budgets, new products, acquisition/divestiture, personnel policies and practices, etc.).

The related continuum of participation in planning in a country starts with little if any participation, if only the central government does the planning. Other markers on the continuum would be ministerial or sector participation, regional governors, city/town heads, community leaders, and all citizens.

Some explanation is needed about the frequently used word *group* (any two or more people set up to meet informally or formally) in relationship to a P&D question or assignment. A group is not always needed in P&D, but these characteristics of groups should be considered whenever a project is organized (i.e., the P&D system is designed):

Purposes and Objectives of a Group P&D level involved (policy, strategic, tactical, operational), clear, valid, flexible, capable of changing, internally or externally developed, measures of effectiveness for group activity.

Source of Legitimization and Reporting (Purpose and Inputs) Degree of support, ability to terminate or extend, degree of autonomy, to whom is group responsible.

Membership (Inputs) Relation to P&D level (policy, etc.), how each became member of group (appointed, self-interest, etc.), degree of leadership each seeks to exert, relationships with other members and appointing individual or selecting group.

Procedures and Participation Patterns (Sequence) Communication modes, positions of individuals (executives, workers, mixed, etc.), formal and informal operating methods, format of real-world interchanges (see Figure 10-4), openness and permissiveness (see Column B, Table 14-2), ability to act as a unit, nonverbal methods of communication.

Atmosphere and Cohesion (Environment) Freedom and friendliness, frankness of discussions, willingness to speak up, ability to operate effectively as a team, operation under crisis, commitment to purpose.

Timeline Commitments (Measures of Sequence) Interrelationship of all aspects into a time schedule, standards of group operation (on time, rules of order, etc.), cost of P&D, external audit control of group.

Subdivision Modes of Organization (Environment) Functional components, issue-based, persons interested in the specific arrangement, coordination mechanism among subdivisions.

Leader or Facilitator (Human Agents) Degree of control, P&D professional as facilitator with member as chairman (depends somewhat on P&D level involved), source of decision making.

Physical Resources Available Computer terminals, condition of physical meeting facilities.

Information Resources Available Library and data base facilities, expert-knowledge persons, accessibility.[11]

A *permanent* P&D group (group for product development, curriculum design, long-range corporate or regional planning) needs some other characteristics: team-building skills, contingency decision methods for switching roles on occasion, and modes of interrelating with other organizational groups charged with operating and supervising responsibilities (e.g., executive office of the company president, academic dean's council, employees' work group on production problems, hospital administrative council). Ad hoc task or temporary groups can be set up within an organization or to reflect community or cross-organization needs. They enable an organization to react fairly quickly to new needs or to obtain a relatively independent P&D effort. They can often perform without disturbing normal operating and supervising responsibilities and regular activities.

Either type of group can provide a greater variety

of perceptions and reasoning patterns, creativity views, and communication channels. "Ownership" of the solution is promoted to help ensure acceptance and implementation. Better-quality solutions with fewer errors are developed. New "leaders" or managers are given a chance to "try out" as chairperson of a group, and individuals are able to assess their own interests in a wider variety of settings.

There are disadvantages to groups: Conformity may be socially advanced for lower-quality solutions by even powerful minorities. The risky-shift phenomenon may infect a group. Some groups tend to settle too quickly on a solution. Some avoid even high-quality ideas once a tentative solution has been accepted. Individual goals and "hidden agenda" may push toward "winning" in the group rather than toward a better solution. Self-prominence may motivate some rather than organizational benefits. Some disagreements on project or substantive topics may lead to personal animosities that manifest themselves in attack, silence, or resignation. Some different techniques (Column D) may be used if the group is geographically dispersed with insufficient funds for people to travel to a meeting.

C. People to Involve

The variety of people who ought to be involved, in terms of their roles and positions, is almost always large, whether or not they are in the group per se. Some should be included in the whole project, most at various points in time (Column A). In addition, many people in and outside of the organization may have an interface relationship with the project area. They may need to accept the solution, change behavior, bargain for scarce resources, understand the solution, authorize a loan, and so on. *Whom* to involve is thus very critical. *How much* to involve them is also critical, up to and including "getting in bed with them."

Each human is involved in several activities each and every day—work, transportation, parental, religious, social, civic, marriage, and so forth. Each one involves roles and produces problems with different purposes. Each activity has an impact on the others. To assume that a factory worker, for example, will deal with an organizational P&D project on its "objective" merits only without considering the other personal roles is foolish.

Column C refers to the roles a person plays in relation to a specific P&D project. The same person is very likely to play another role in other P&D purposeful activity projects in the same day or week. Even a person's percent of time in each category will vary over time. Today's expert may be tomorrow's manager, today's activist tomorrow's politician, today's worker tomorrow's union leader.

In general, the variety of roles and skills needed for a P&D project should be identified before individuals are considered. Then, the various possible roles of each individual should be listed to determine where a person could be utilized in more than one role and where other roles of the person potentially conflict with the needs of the effort. A person selected for a "citizen" or "consumer" role in a health care planning council may not be effective because a job assignment concerns selling medical supplies. Even a "small" project will need several roles, all of which need to be blended over time.

A person now working in the system is a "craftsperson" at the job, however mundane (janitor) or esoteric

personal qualities is certainly desirable in a group to provide broad perspectives and balanced views.

People who are to fulfill these roles may themselves have different characteristics, irrespective of their "personal qualities." A person with experience may be a desirable participant, regardless of personal qualities. Some will be—must be—clients needing the service, owners, or a concerned manager commissioning the project. Some will be selected by "outsiders," such as the chamber of commerce and the citywide labor organization selecting their representatives to a mayor's task force. They cannot be omitted, irrespective of imbalance or lack of experience. This real world gives greater poignancy to the concepts embodied in the timeline scenario (Figure 10-4). Obviously, though, there are desirable characteristics that should guide the selection of people if there is a choice:

Communicative	Flexible	Experience
Cope with information	Motivated	Good image of P&D
Persistent	Good judgment	Intelligent
Abstract/reality compatibility	Sensitive	Respected in usual role
Good interpersonal skills	Values the problem locus	Willing to work
Opportunity seeking	Aware of need for P&D	Willing to listen
Willing to do share of work	Willing to express views	Persuasive
Civil to others	Credible	Respected by peers
		Productive
		Tolerate ambiguities

(cooker of electronic computer chips). They contribute quite effectively because thoughts about purposes and ideal systems have most likely crossed their minds many times. Such a person has often contributed ideas that would, if implemented, eliminate the person's job. With a focus on effective *implemented* solutions, such involvement becomes an essential of good P&D.

The modern-day expert is considered the possessor of arcane, abstruse, and esoteric knowledge that can overwhelm the nonexpert, irrespective of its veracity. Discussions tend to shift from the users' perspectives to those of the experts. The P&D strategy is thus crucial because following it can keep the breadth of alternative options open as long as possible before arriving at closure.

Most of the roles listed in Column C are self-explanatory. A comment or two may be needed regarding the entry "Personal Qualities—Autocratic/Participative/Permissive, Personality, etc." People at any level have different styles or "amounts" of realities (Chapter Five). None of them is easy to identify for a specific individual, but some "show" up more easily than others. A mixture of amounts of these

Still, the major criterion for selecting people should always be improving the probability of arriving at an effective (and innovative) implemented solution while effectively using *all* P&D resources. This almost always means that "social homogeneity as a selection criterion . . . [and] social conformity as a standard for conduct"[12] are *inappropriate* for a good P&D group.

Several guides identified in many research and experiential projects can help a P&D professional and an organization in putting together a "good" P&D group when this is possible. Because membership in many groups cannot be set up on the basis of "good" guides, adaptations may need to be made in the strategy, group techniques, information used, continuing change concepts, and so on.

Group Size Seven plus or minus two is advised. More than 11 or 13 tends to restrict interchange because people do not listen, hide and do not speak, form small coalitions, or make speeches. Aggressiveness of a few predominates, the chance for consensus and a quality solution decreases. Fewer than five is usually too small for adequate representation and dynamics.

Groups with odd-numbered membership promote productivity, avoid coalitions, and generally result in effective outcomes.

Name of group Many are possible, but local conditions and word meanings (Axiom 6) should govern. Some frequently used terms include *project team*, *task team*, *task force*, *design group*, *venture team*, *P&D committee*, *P&D circle*, *planning group*, *action group*, *commission*, *committee*, *planning unit*, and *"X-system" planning team*.

Representation All roles, key actors, and skills regarding the real-world locus and values should be present. Convergent and divergent thinkers, bureaucrats and freethinkers, all should be included. Heterogeneity is to be sought, for this increases the information base collectively available in the minds of the people. It also increases the creativity and number of ideas as well as the likelihood of eventual acceptance of a solution. It may cause some problems in communications because of jargon and may force limits on the space in which a solution might be found. Some difficulties may arise because of people of different status being in the group (e.g., top management, technical staff, line managers, workers in locus area). Several of the group process and meeting ideas can ameliorate these difficulties, helping the group to learn together while aiming toward a solution.

Longevity People should be sought for ad hoc groups who are likely to stay with the organization through installation.

Commitment and Cohesiveness The position held by a person might very well indicate that the incumbent ought to be included. But if the person is not interested or has no philosophical *commitment* regarding "doing something" to find solutions, then why include that individual?

Expansion and Contraction A core group may be selected for service throughout the project or for the permanent P&D function. The members would seek content area experts to add, say, in Phase 2, decision makers in Phase 3, technical people for detailing in Phase 4, and operating people for installation in Phase 5. A permanent group (e.g., corporate planning committee, hospital long-range planning committee) would operate in the same way, expanding and contracting as needed. Involving such people can also include sending them meeting minutes, a core member informing them occasionally in person, listing them in a Delphi set of questionnaires (Appendix A), sending them a regular newsletter, and/or interviewing them on a regular basis. Another version of expansion occurs when several other groups are needed for each of the functional components developed in Step 1F. The core or

overall P&D group continues to coordinate the other groups. The functional component groups proceed to do P&D until their work is integrated into the overall plans, or they may stay in existence until installation is complete.

In other words, groups are dynamic and need constant change. A P&D group itself could well be replanned every year or so. Many people get new positions or assignments that significantly influence their effectiveness and interest. Others may just lose or change interest as certain steps or phases are completed. A method should be set up for replacing such people and bringing in new people.

Actually selecting the people is a decision-making process (Chapters Eleven, Twelve, Fifteen, and Appendix A). The following are some general criteria:

- Fit the level of P&D involved. Even though a company worker might be involved with policy-level formulation, perhaps a representative of workers would fit better.

- People internal to the organization who feel the "tension" or difficulties (Chapter Two) are likely to be motivated to seek a solution.

- Original, betterment, or correction needs.

- People usually external to the system who form a pressure group (of consumers, clients, etc.) urging changes.

- Nature of the project. This may vary over time, starting with, say, a correction design need, but becoming bigger through purpose expansion.

- Time available for the P&D effort. Less time may mean more people.

- Importance of convincing others before implementation can take place. A large decentralized organization where a solution influences many may require more people with geographic links.

- Stakeholder representation. Several considerations illustrate this: who pays for the project, who will gain (lose) financially from a solution, who affects implementation, and so on.

- Importance of the quality of the solution. Higher-quality solutions need broader sets of experts and knowledgeable people.

- Range and credibility of skills available internally and externally.

- Leadership abilities of possible chairman and/or P&D professional.

- Variety of affective human characteristics: ego involvement, individual and social aspirations, propensity for risk and for conflict, attitudes toward change, personality type, political and value sets, and so on.

- Ability to recognize the need for changing the group membership. For example, if the selected level in the purpose hierarchy is bigger than initially expected, the members should be willing to drop out and/or ask others to be involved. Furthermore, the need for various human abilities decline (knowledge, technical skill) or grow (estimation, communication) as the strategy phases proceed.
- Person(s) who know where information can be found or inexpensively obtained.
- Amount of resources available for the P&D staff and other support for the group efforts.
- Widely distributed influentials.
- Accord with legislative mandates.

Identifying likely candidates can often be accomplished by asking five or more people in key positions in the organization (community, region, P&D locus, etc.) to nominate people who satisfy these criteria. A person's name appearing on, say, 30 to 50% of the lists, is a likely member of the group. This technique also communicates the need to and establishes a resource for ideas in key people.

A chairperson is often named in advance. This selection is critical. The chairperson must keep a group "moving" in coping with the almost inevitable short timeline for the effort. The chairperson should be neutral regarding what solution may emerge, and ensure that all ideas are aired, even when personal predilections are challenged. Too often, group members feel they are being coopted into accepting what the chairperson has already decided. This should not be the case for a P&D effort. Calling a group together to design a presentation, training, or orientation system for a previously developed P&D solution is a legitimate activity (strategy Phases 4 and 5, Chapter Twelve). A good chairperson would also learn something about the background and interests of each P&D group member before the first meeting.

Other criteria for selecting a chairperson include the ability to keep the group from tangential issues; understanding when to suggest consultants, experts, aides, or sounding boards; ability to gauge which questions, components or aspects are critical; ability to be given status and mandate support; capabilities as a communicator (listener, speaker, enthusiasm); understanding of rules (for running meetings, yet capable of "bending" the rules when the group senses it needs to do so); and a sense of humor.

The P&D professional is often a staff person to the chairperson and group, very often conducting significant portions of meetings so that the various strategy steps and techniques are utilized effectively. On some occasions (see Case History B1), the P&D professional is the pseudochairperson, setting up the meeting agenda (always in consultation with the key people who collectively might constitute the equivalent of a chairperson) and generally conducting the meetings on behalf of the group. The roles of a P&D professional are the subject of the concluding section of this chapter.

D. Group Processes and Techniques

A group is arranged to achieve certain aims, and it should do so in the most effective manner possible. Several overall ideas are therefore germane.

First, having a group does not necessarily mean that meetings will be held. Several techniques (Delphi, opinion polling, telephone conference, interactive TV/computer processes) let groups "meet" without the meetings.

Second, one or more of the Column D group process techniques can be used individually or together in a meeting. Several may be used sequentially (e.g., nominal group for purposes, brain writing for ideal systems, gaming for major alternatives). In addition, each technique, as described in most of the literature, must be adapted to fit the PDA scenario. Almost all are presented in conventional terms, for example, to probe for problems or difficulties or barriers, instead of purposes or ideal systems or regularities.

Third, the techniques can "mix or match" with one another and with various groupings of people. The nominal group technique, for example, would divide a large group of, say, 40 people into four groups of 10 people each. Assignment to each small group is usually random. However, the small groups could be organized by roles (users, politicians, operators/workers of current systems, etc.) if each role-type feels its point of view must be sharpened. Or they could be organized by personality type (sensation-thinkers, intuition-feeling, sensation-feeling, etc.) if a variety of ideas for a step is desired. In general, though, coalition formation (e.g. users, politicians) should be avoided; getting a diverse group to work together is, after all, a key objective for P&D.

Fourth, a technique is always insufficient unto itself. It must be tied firmly to the other considerations shown on Table 14-2. The question to ask or the purpose to be achieved is often far more important than the technique. Using a nominal group technique to elicit assumptions concerning how to convert reading research results into classroom instructional procedures is virtually certain to elicit many statements about a wide variety of *present* conditions of reading instruction. Asking the group instead to determine purposes/functions of reading instructional procedures is far more likely to get the group to identify what really needs to be accomplished in hierarchical terms and how these might be creatively achieved. Good group techniques by themselves will not necessarily be effective, just as participation by itself is not effective without concern for *how* the questions are posed.

Many techniques and models *not* included in column D could be used in group modes. Some are discussed in Chapter Twelve: couplet method, purpose hierarchy construction, regularity development, and solution framework. Others in Appendix A (interpretive structural modeling, activity matrix, utility assessment, scenario writing) could also become the basis of a group process.

Many techniques are interwoven into the strategy being followed along the timeline. For example, a nominal group might be used to develop a list of purposes, an interactive discussion (normal open interchange) with the couplet method to select the smallest scope statement to start the hierarchy, and a completely interactive discussion to do the expansion, all in the first meeting. Then a partial nominal group (silent generation of rankings) to select the purpose level and shared participation to generate measures of effectiveness might constitute the second meeting. Interviews with individuals to generate possible ideal systems would precede a third meeting, which would involve an interacting group discussion of the interview results to add more ideas. And so on.

Using a group and "having a meeting" thus require serious consideration about "*how* to do it." In addition to the techniques in Column D, there are some additional guides for conducting good meetings. For example, one set of ideas says that there are six aspects of a group meeting: communications, role of each member, leadership and authority, group needs and aspirations, decision process, and intergroup issues.[13]

Summarizing and adapting all these ideas for P&D purposes results in the following guidelines for the leader (group chairman or P&D professional):

- Stick to a previously distributed agenda where topics are purpose oriented. Many research projects show structured group activities are far more effective and take no more time than unstructured groups.
- Err toward covering a little too much on an agenda for the available time rather than too little. Parkinson's Law does seem to hold: the work expands to fit the time available. An attitude of parsimony does tend to prevail even though all may not be accomplished.
- State on the agenda how long the meeting will last.
- Within each agenda topic, control only the process, not the content. Be a gatekeeper: give everyone a chance to contribute by a leader-arranged round-robin process, call on nonspeakers, use techniques that assure everyone's participation (e.g. nominal group, brain writing), and statement of meeting rules of order (Robert's *Rules of Order* are *not* usually good for P&D groups).
- Start with statement of expectation of achievements by end of meeting.
- Inform group of developments since last meeting. Use displays. Individuals responsible for interim activities should inform others of progress.
- Summarize what the meeting has accomplished, what is to be done and by whom before next meeting, and what the next meeting will concern.
- Use majority voting only as last resort when differences are pronounced enough so that consensus is not really possible. Use the telephone to get information.
- Be enthusiastic about the group's work if you expect the group to be interested and enthusiastic.
- Put any P&D decision that narrowly achieved a majority on the agenda for the next meeting as a means of surfacing new information, obtaining ideas from experts and persons with other roles in the organization, heeding warnings of moral and ethical consequences, and getting greater group concurrence.
- Reiterate as needed the overall strategy and total approach within which the meeting's agenda topics fit so as to reinforce the holistic perspective as a basis for P&D decisions. "Listen with your *whole* being." Because continued practice of the approach will reinforce behavior patterns of individuals for other projects, emphasize purposes/functions for all deliberations and decisions. Check and recapitulate to assure broad understanding among members.
- Avoid spending too much time on a conspicuous idea or the first alternative, and look for other alternatives and broadening information. Avoid the dangers of "groupthink" pressures toward conformity and uniformity.
- If possible, have someone other than a group member take minutes, to be circulated before the next agenda is distributed. Record ideas initially in the way an individual states them.
- Avoid handing out material at the meeting not pre-

viously reviewed by the group. This may be difficult to adhere to because the nature of P&D causes new information to appear at short notice.

- Adhere to time limits and set up future activities on a timeline basis.

- Maintain some flexibility so informality is not cut off when group members seem to need it for building openness, creativity, and trust. Discussion can be encouraged if a hot topic arises affecting the P&D project, even outside the agenda or from outside the group. Avoid self-censorship.

- Maintain a positive tone: rephrase ideas positively, offer one or more interpretations, cut off name-calling, establish civility and respect among members irrespective of differing viewpoints.

- Recognize that each group is different. Some start as a collection of individuals, an affiliative group from the same organization, supporters of a movement, or class or level of worker. Each should design its own "system."

- If status (organizational level, experience, power, reputation) is highly variable, talk with the high-status people before the meeting to get expressions of willingness to have equality of treatment in the group (advocate first-name basis for everyone; avoid introduction of any status symbols such as "expert" or "doctor"; avoid criticism of ideas during idea generation steps; seat people at random or alphabetically rather than by position or representation).

- Conflicts that arise should be put into a win-win form that aids rather than disrupts the P&D process. Creativity can emerge from conflicting viewpoints. For example, move to bigger level purposes in the hierarchy, get each person to express the other person's position so it is acceptable to the other one, focus on achieving the purpose and the P&D results rather than on defeating a person, give all people all information to avoid coalition formation, and take a little more time rather than moving directly to voting. Table 3-9 contains a strategy for conflict resolution (number III) that might also help in P&D groups because it seeks to *design* a solution to the conflict.

- Refer to supporting evidence for the axioms and propositions if a person promotes early on *the* solution the P&D group *should* support, emphasize the difference between believing and doubting games, remind the group that purposes come before solutions, and so on.

- Be alert for problems and difficulties. Some people may act bored, attendance may be low, some people may attack the chairman (self-interest is al-

ways present in individuals), time always seems to run out, there is a lack of team skills and respect, facilities are not good, people have mistaken expectations, people think material presented is too complex, and so on. One difficulty that has arisen in PDA projects is the frustration a person or two on occasion feels about *not* being able to install the FIST right away. Referring them to the continuing change factor and getting them involved in installation actions may help alleviate this "interesting" development.

- Wait at least three seconds after completing a question, even if there is complete silence, before saying anything else at all. Continued talking or only a short delay after asking a question minimizes greatly the likelihood of responses.

- Be neutral in responding to member's ideas. Avoid saying, "OK," "good," "great idea," "fine," and so on. Additional questioning and probing stimulates more and better response because people do not become subconsciously smug and satisfied as they would with the complimentary words.

Overall perspectives about how information and techniques might be generally utilized are presented in Chapter Fifteen.

E. Meeting Conditions

More often than not, conditions surrounding a meeting do make a difference. One hospital, for example, had just been refused a request by the state for a rate increase. A program to reduce costs and increase productivity while maintaining good quality of care was necessary. Two or three people from five different constituencies were asking to attend a meeting to initiate the program: Trustees, administration, medical and nursing staff, union, and former patients. The board chairman was meeting chairman. Three of my colleagues were invited to discuss how the program could get started.

Several seemingly trivial decisions had to be made regarding the meeting conditions. Where should it be held? A corner of the cafeteria was selected because it represented "neutral" turf. What seating arrangement should be set up? A large square was formed from several tables so people could sit on all four sides in a nonconfrontational mode. How should people be identified during the meeting? Name place cards, 6 by 9 inches and printed on both sides in advance of the meeting, would be placed in wooden blocks in front of each person. How should seating be arranged around the table? If nothing were done in advance, it is virtually certain that the three union representatives would sit together, three trustees together, and so on. Coalition formation would be encouraged too early. Instead, the name place cards were set up on the tables in advance so that all representations were mixed. Other meeting conditions and features were also considered and incorporated—reduce noise by using sliding partitions, optimize amount of light by setting tables near the window, and keep temperature at 70 to 72 degrees to encourage staying awake.

Some research suggests certain wall colors and textures as being soothing or stimulating. Physical appearances can also convey stillness or inertia rather than a P&D desired movement and stimulation. The amount of space per person should also be sufficient for the purpose of the meeting.

Column E contains many items, from which several are almost always selected. Some items are always present (amount of light, heat, noise, ventilation, etc.), and their inclusion in Column E conveys only the need to check these factors prior to a meeting. What seating would avoid mixing smokers and nonsmokers? Ventilation (none is a poor condition), for example, should be checked to determine whether some can be provided, or whether drafts can be avoided.

Utilizing the Five Considerations of Table 14-2

Most desirable would be information on which categories of Columns C, D, and E should be selected for the project's status (Column A) and the organizational participation level (Column B). Figure 14-2 illustrates such a possible set of relationships. If such relationships were available for each step of a project, most of

the human parts of a P&D system (Table 10-1) could be quite thoroughly developed. In actuality, such a level of knowledge will not be available for some time. Yet portraying the form of the desired structure, such as Figure 14-2, does show how Table 14-2 can be used to provide guides for effectively involving people.

But for many, even most, organizational situations (companies, city or federal departments) and almost all P&D projects in nonorganizational settings (regional planning, architecture, development planning, policy analysis), complete freedom in setting up and running a P&D group doesn't exist. What is to be done if 19 people are and must be involved? What if several executives in a group just do not like the "childish" silent recording parts of the nominal group process? What type of P&D group will be organized if top management is not very open and runs things fairly autocratically? There is no way for the guides (and the concept of Figure 14-2) to predict exactly what is needed. Table 14-2 thus presents only stimuli for developing the people involvement in the P&D system and for adapting actual P&D activities to specific circumstances as the project progresses.

The payoff for considering the Table 14-2 guides as the P&D strategy unfolds can be immense. It will be difficult to sidetrack a solution when it is developed by and/or known to many individuals and influential opinion leaders beyond the decision makers and those "in power." Legitimacy for a solution is developed when many partake in its development. Successful implementation occurs when "a large number of people collaborate to invent solutions that are their own making and which have their own endorsement."[14]

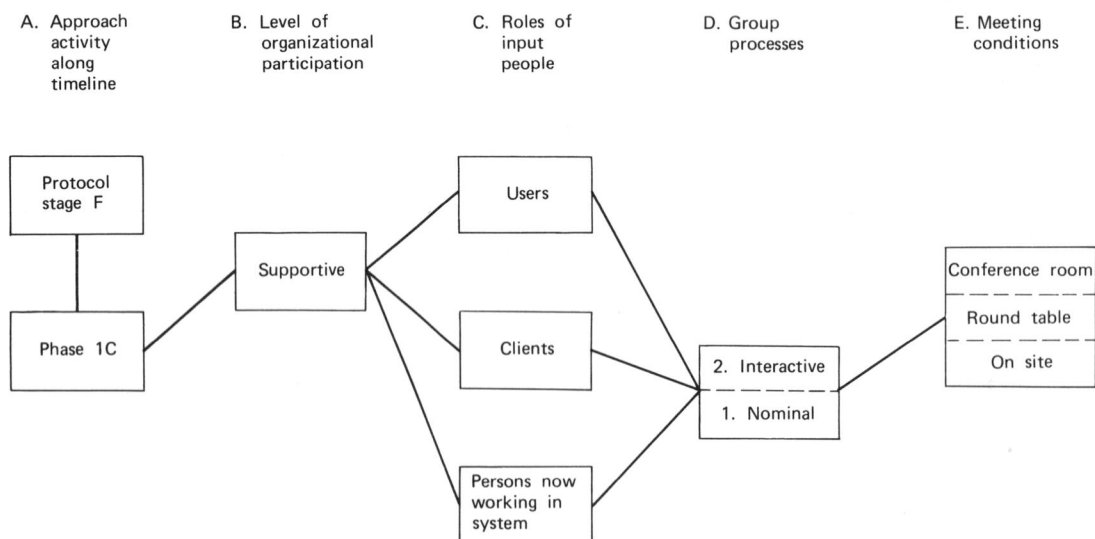

Figure 14-2 Possible utilization (illustration) of integrated ideas about involving people in P&D (based on Table 14-2).

Especially significant is to keep those in the real world "jointly" interactive with whatever group or individual is responsible for the project. Those in a P&D group, even part-time from the same real world, become part of the P&D world for that project and become afflicted with the P&D equivalent of the Hawthorne halo effect, which can blind people into believing that only their idea is good. The rest of the real world is not so affected and needs jointly to be involved.

THE ROLE OF THE P&D PROFESSIONAL

A critical link in the factor of involving people is the person(s) who takes on the mantle of P&D professional seeking to achieve the three P&D objectives. Although the phrase *P&D professional* is used throughout, everything that follows is also applicable to the person who coordinates or chairs a P&D effort (a person who designs a personal residence, a vice-president assigned to be committee chairperson to develop a new manufacturing facility, a business leader who serves as chairman of the governor's commission on education, a mathematics faculty member who coordinates a new curriculum design committee).

A P&D professional is a human agent who is expected to play several roles in the P&D system for intervening in a problem where an implemented situation-specific purposeful solution is sought.

This view gives a P&D professional the perspective of a change agent. A *change agent* is a person who aids or serves as a catalyst to the real-world entity in creating or restructuring a situation-specific solution that is implemented to correct an unsatisfactory system, better a satisfactory one, or meet a currently unmet need (Axiom 5). *Change agent* for P&D purposes is thus almost synonymous with *human agent* in the P&D system. Most of the literature about change agents assumes change of any sort is good, an assumption not made by P&D. Another word, *interventionist*, has the same connotations as *change agent*.

The change agent's, P&D system human agent's, or "interventionist's primary tasks are to generate valid information, to help the client system make informed and responsible choices, and to develop internal commitment to these choices. . . . [Working on] a client system with these three criteria in mind tends to create the conditions which will minimize intentional or unintentional client manipulation of the interventionist or vice versa. . . . If and when pressures mount against [obtaining valid information, for example, the interventionist] must ask the clients to discuss . . . leaving the system. Similarly, if the key power

people within the client system begin to ask for private meetings to make decisions about aspects of the program; if they call meetings with subordinates which are loaded against informed and responsible choice (through lack of time or pressure to make decisions); or if they request that data be withheld from subordinates, the interventionist may again wonder [about continuing work] within the client system."[15]

A P&D professional is not simply a neutralist when intervening. There is a moral value implied that proclaims a motivation for and a belief in finding solutions (Chapter Two). The professional P&D human agent does become an advocate of employing a holistic P&D approach to seek and implement a solution. It is an advocacy of process rather than of content. In all cases, ethical behavior by the P&D professional is assumed (see Chapters Two, Four, and Five). "Politically oriented planners have a more liberal interpretation of what is ethical than the most technically oriented ones, with a third group—high on both the technical and political dimensions—falling in the middle. . . . [Perceived] role, political views, attitude towards agency, and propensity to express values . . . [explain] why some . . . think differently than others about what is ethical."[16]

What are the specific roles the P&D professional might adopt when stepping into a P&D project or program? Several roles are needed at different points during a P&D effort. In all cases, the three objectives of P&D are the measures that attest to professional performance in playing the roles and blending them effectively over time.

Table 14-3 lists most of the different types of roles a P&D professional may need to adopt. None is a "pure" role, because their boundaries are not clear. More than one may need to occur together at one time: Designer/expert/modeler for developing a house plan; boundary spanner/facilitator/project manager/trainer for a patient admission and health records system in a hospital; or measurer/participant/advocate for a productivity improvement program in a company. Which role(s) a P&D professional is to play will also depend on the real-world group. For example, *facilitator* roles may be associated with users, or *advocacy* with resource controllers. A P&D project may start in Phase 1a with the P&D professional in the role of an advisor/consultant, then Phase 1b as advisor/facilitator/(planning system) expert, followed by Phase 1c as facilitator, Phase 1d as measurer/facilitator/expert, and so on. Figures 10-4 and 14-1 show some possible roles that might accompany various strategy steps.

Current practice of certain P&D professions tends to emphasize just a few of the P&D roles and functions in Table 14-3. An architect, for example, tends to focus

Table 14-3 The Several Possible Roles of a P&D Professional

R&F Number	Role and Function	Characteristics	When Used on Strategy Timeline	Others Involved (RW = real world)	Advantages (A) and Disadvantages (D)
1	*Advisor/consultant* Be available as needed by others for clarification of other roles, interpretation of data, review, etc.	Listen well, be observant to clues (body language), simplify, summarize, get others involved. Can be short- or long-term. Assess leverage points in process. (See R&Fs 10 and 11.) All three require persuasive methods.	In any stage, phase, or step. Often informal, between meetings. When person/client needs sounding board/advice/"independent" view/reinforcement "strokes."	As needed, usually content expert, measurer, modeler, other P&D team members.	A: Separate means-ends, identify real issues, motivate, provide leads and sources, evaluation and feedback. D: Inconclusive, no action role, implementation not included.
2	*Advocate/adversary/ activist/lobbyist* Promote actively (a) a particular party or position, (b) a solution or outcome, or (c) a process or approach (e.g. P&D) for finding a solution.	(a) Could be narrow, emotional, no empathy. (b) If work with P&D project for a time could well present FIST or recommended solution. Seek to answer selling questions: Why should I listen, what is it, who says so, what's in it for me, why should I do it now. (c) Prepare plans that document why approach recommended is better. (See R&F 18.)	(a) It is to be hoped never as a partisan representative. Often in a debating situation. (b) Phases 3, 4, and 5 of project if presenting group-developed solution. (c) Throughout a P&D project, especially steps 1a, 1c, and 1f.	(a) Almost any one who will listen, especially decision makers, visible persons and groups. (b) Decision makers, technicians to prepare materials, influentials, resource controllers, public hearings. (c) Everyone in P&D effort or who can interface with it. Usually involves poor, dispossessed people.	A: (a&b) Commitment, convincing evidence of support. (c) Same, plus getting people to cooperate on "noncontroversial" matters. D: (a) Extremism, offensive to some. (b) dogmatic, means-oriented rather than purpose/need oriented. Technological imperative. (c) Too much emphasis on process as replacement for solutions ("keep at it, we'll get an answer")
3	*Analyst* Separate a whole into parts and interactions, and examine them to explore for insight and characteristics.	Inward looking. Reductionist. Often done with hope that something significant appears. Necessary prior to measuring. (See R&F 15.)	With any part of strategy needing measurements or identification of factors that should be measured (e.g., measures of effectiveness, regularities, performance specifications).	Often done alone with subsequent approval of group or decision makers. Some initial ideas come from group and then analyzed for factors. Experts may be needed.	A: Emphasizes "hardness" of measures. Useful for developing specifications for measures and control dimensions of solution framework. D: Hard data "needs" may distract P&D effort, may cause people to forget that nothing can be completely analyzed or measured.
4	*Boundary spanner* Bridge the information/style/ interest gaps between P&D user/clients/ adopters. Serve as integrator or link to explain ideas to, say, physicians about computers and computer specialists about health care and physician needs.	Large-scale complex projects often create huge differentials of understanding between P&D group and those who operate the client system. Role requires values and understanding of real world as well as technical P&D skills. "Schmoozing" ability helps. (See R&Fs 27, 33, and 36.)	Can start early in project so purposes are reviewed early, measures of effectiveness, etc. are being tested early rather than waiting until recommendation is ready. Definitely needed if large, complex project in Phases 3, 4, and 5 of most protocol stages.	Negotiating/integration/ bargaining nature will involve any type (managers, workers, union representatives, government regulators, etc.). Stage-setting through "behind the scenes" discussions to obtain commitment of influentials and resource controllers.	A: Identify relevant actors in implementation, cope with the "games" they are likely to play in several steps, increase probability of implementing effective solution. Develop interface dimensions. D: Specific skills needed poorly defined, effectiveness of role difficult to measure, person may not be viewed as a P&D professional.
5	*Catalyst/motivator* Provide stimulus and skill availability to a group or individual.	Pose critical questions. Provide assurance to group that the process is likely to lead to a solution. (See also R&Fs 1, 10, 11, 12, 14, 16, and 20.)	In any stage, phase or step. Catharsis especially valuable at beginning of purposes questioning.	As needed. See also R&F 12. Useful for individual on "sink or swim" assignment.	A: Keep project going during times of stress and muddles. Put performance information (including poor results) to group into motivating frame. D: Passive role if professional does not interact with the people involved.

Table 14-3 (*Continued*)

R&F Number	Role and Function	Characteristics	When Used on Strategy Timeline	Others Involved (RW = real world)	Advantages (A) and Disadvantages (D)
6	*Chairperson* Be responsible for a P&D project and facilitate the P&D team/group/task force.	Follow the Guides for Group Leader given in this chapter. Large projects usually need a project manager (R&F 21). See R&F 10, especially control process, not content. Mandate/charter/legitimation must be clear. Often serves as an arbitrator/parliamentarian.	The chairperson should follow the parts of the protocol and strategy (e.g., purpose hierarchy, regularities) before meetings to gain insight into types of questions to ask group, then discard all the work before meeting.	Often plays other roles, especially participant (see R&F 20) if an ad hoc P&D group (e.g., faculty curriculum, new plant building). Play role impartially even if have preferences. May need some stage setting. (See R&F 4.)	A: P&D approach likely to follow completely, increased probability of implemented and innovative solution. D: Possible conflict of interest among various roles.
7	*Decision maker* Select a preference from among alternative possibilities for topic of concern.	Usually a role for less important matters (e.g., functional component array, regularity conditions) than for key topic (purpose, measures, solution). (See R&F 9.)	All parts of the protocol and strategy, but key decisions should be labeled "tentative" to permit other P&D activities to proceed.	Must relate to resource controllers, influentials, etc., even if P&D professional concerned with project for personal reasons.	A: Efforts can continue in face of lack of top decision makers. D: No impartiality possible, may reduce group involvement and commitment.
8	*The Designer/Planner* Produce the solution specifications and serve as advocate of the solution through the implementation.	Individual (or firm) proceeds "on its own" in creativity, measurement, modeling, etc. Capabilities can be mobilized within agreed-on time and cost estimates after assignment. Power turned over to *the* designer who *tells* the client what is "best" available solution (e.g., real estate development, land-use planning, guidance counselor, architect, fund raising).	Whole responsibility taken on and strategy set by *the* designer, who is involved in almost all steps. The individual's plans, biases, experiences, and education have significant impact that may not relate to user's/client's/customer's needs.	Selling the solution becomes the mode of operation. People involved may be none of those selected by *the* designer. *The* designer may preclude people involvement: "My houses aren't shaped for clients' needs." Power can be used as aid in influencing rather than ordering others.	A: Useful when size, scope, technological arena, etc. are well delineated so that output (e.g., computer program, component, form design) fits solution. D: violates several axioms and propositions, promotes elitism, creates client dependency, technological fix often permitted, usually huge amounts of irrelevant data collection, and "error of the third kind" (working on wrong problem) very likely to occur.
9	*Expert* Provide high level of knowledge, skill and experience in a specific content/topic area of application with or without comparable capabilities in the P&D approach.	Highly competent source of information about subject (e.g., transportation, computers, mathematics) and related techniques, research, costs, exemplary practices, and people. Capable of evaluating data "accuracy" in subject, structuring decision models in field, estimating time/costs for data collection/research in field, teaching topics to others, etc. (See R&Fs 3, 8, 15, 17, 25.) Experts may exude aura of certainty, based on "knowledge specialist" image.	Phase 2 in developing ideas, Phase 3 in identifying regularities, sorting ideas into major alternatives, selecting FIST, and Phases 4 and 5 in detailing and installing actual changes. Tends to analyze/model/measure in terms of expertise.	If project is group- or manager-controlled, all people in task force, etc. will be involved. If expert left alone, will tend to not involve people, except if expertise is in the P&D approach. (See R&F 10.)	A: Wide range of knowledge available for any project. Necessary as *resources*. Can raise many questions that help detailing and lead to technological feasibility. D: Ineffective results if "expert" uses conventional P&D method. Analysis and measures may be irrelevant (wrong problem). Accuracy of measures and techniques often an end in themselves. Expert might discourage or intimidate people.

Table 14-3 (*Continued*)

R&F Number	Role and Function	Characteristics	When Used on Strategy Timeline	Others Involved (RW = real world)	Advantages (A) and Disadvantages (D)
10	*Facilitator/coordinator* Provide P&D approach (all five factors) guidance and structure to a P&D group.	Develop meeting agenda and minutes with chairperson; be well versed in most other R&Fs, and know when to use them; promote free and informed choice; utilize minimal but valid information; establish and maintain timeline of activities; utilize effective group techniques in and out of meetings; be enthusiastic if you expect the group to be the same. (See R&F 6.) "Read" audience or group and gauge reactions so techniques and questions can be selected. Follow Guides for Group Leaders in this chapter. Often requires R&F 2 as advocate for the P&D approach.	Keep the group moving toward results by maintaining steady progress along the strategy timeline without controlling the context. Must call on other personal R&F abilities when needed (modeler in Phases 3 and 4, expert in Phase 2, etc.) as well as get other P&D professionals for certain R&Fs. Always seek to learn new ideas, technology, concepts so all phases and steps are performed effectively with latest ideas and techniques.	Provide setting for equitable participation. Motivation of group overcomes entropy among RW people, share and teach process knowledge (demystify the facilitator's "expertise"), effective use of "power" of process control. Integration of P&D staff specialists (statistician, modeler, computer programmer, attitude survey measurer, plant facility designer). Jog people's minds, search for hidden agenda among key people to identify major issues. Some stage setting (R&F 4).	A: Supplies environment conducive to participation and learning, permits enthusiasm for the process without early commitment to content solution, adaptability of strategy and facilitative R&F likely to get people involved to change their perceptions along the strategy timeline. D: Process facilitation is difficult, person must convert personal ideas into stimulus questions; sometimes difficult to obtain equitable participation if "power" and opinion leaders or experts are in group with persons less accustomed to such meetings.
11	*Helping professional* Combine empathy for a person (or small group) with knowledge, skill and experience in guiding the individual or group to a resolution of personal/group difficulties.	Many helping professions have each a wide variety of techniques and information sets for developing purposeful solutions with the client, individual or group (see Chapter Four)	Gets individual to develop list of purposes, values, objectives, and goals, to create own list of ideas how to achieve purposes and goals, and so on. Helps group with conflicts to work together (R&F 10).	Individual for whom self-reliance, autonomy, and self-help are sought. Group may want sympathetic ears without criticism, or someone to challenge assumptions.	A: Lets person resolve personal difficulties, develop confidence and self-discipline. D: P&D professional may be viewed as expert dispensing answers. Role is better suited to other purposeful activities.
12	*Information resource person* Be familiar with the categorization and availability status of data related to field of P&D effort.	Familiarity with very broad range of data, references, and sources puts this R&F close to a modern librarian (i.e., knowledgeable about computer search centers, *futures* information, computerized design consortia, etc.). Passive by quoting information and history. Active if combined with R&Fs 1, 5, and 9.	Information sources potentially useful in every step and phase. P&D profession is tied to information base (e.g., in business, may be forecasting, environmental scanning, capability status, financial models, etc.), an organization may have specialists/experts in each topic.	Does not necessarily deal with range of people, but with specific person transmitting requests for information.	A: Wide range of information usually needed, especially regarding futures and advanced R&D. D: Key words as source of categorizing information are often removed from project purpose/need. May not translate into P&D usefulness. Limits the role of the P&D professionals.
13	*Innovator/inventor* Seek to produce a creative/unique/advanced technology solution and advocate its use all the way through implementation.	See R&F 8, which is virtually the same. Major difference: This R&F encourages hard-driving, committed person who usually seeks a physical end item. "Utopian" conceptualizations.	Not often related to strategy because of fierce independence of this ilk. The P&D strategy here is able to offer this P&D person some help. Could be an aid in Phase 2.	Almost none at all, but very demanding when others get involved. Needs supportive policies in rest of organization.	A: Need creativity often, and inventor type with many ideas often stimulates others as well. D: No assurances of implementation focus on purpose. Solutions often need to be sold.

Table 14-3 (*Continued*)

R&F Number	Role and Function	Characteristics	When Used on Strategy Timeline	Others Involved (RW = real world)	Advantages (A) and Disadvantages (D)
14	*Manager of improvement search program* Operate and supervise the program for continuing search for change and improvement in the organization (see Chapter Sixteen).	Take action on redesign of solution on betterment schedule. Audit organization performances to identify potential P&D problems. Search for new P&D opportunities. Suggest and promote project topics which appear to have room for improvement. Evaluate past projects to assess success.	Whole continuing change and improvement program impacts on the P&D strategy in each project. Assignments to P&D staff for specific projects would usually involve specifying the P&D strategy.	Active interchange with managers and executives of operating units. They aid in setting project priorities. Get charter and "political" commitment from executives/decision makers for projects and overall P&D objectives. (See R&F 4.)	A: Can incorporate almost all of the other R&Fs. Highly desirable in any formal organization. Helps follow through on future dimensions of solution framework. D: Must avoid bureaucratization into a measurer/modeler/expert department.
15	*Measurer* Obtain data and facts about existing conditions. Usually a "quantitative determinist."	Measurements needed to gauge effectiveness of changes. Measurer in conventional approaches assumes that, given "all" the data in most accurate and precise form (attitudes, costs, waste, mobility, etc.), solution emerges "easily." Should be familiar with many types of measurements (from subjective judgments and easy-to-apply indices to sophisticated statistical and technical instruments).	May be needed in any phase or step, but most likely in Phases 1 (measures of effectiveness), 3 (selecting FIST), 4 (selecting recommended solution), and 5 (evaluating performance of installed solution). Need for timeliness of measurements almost always precludes "completeness" or high accuracy and precision. (See Chapter Eight, Axiom 7.)	Objects being measured—strength of beam, interarrival time of orders, toxicity of liquid, capacity of machine, etc.—represent little measurement problem. Humans being measured should almost always be informed about the measurements and their purposes. Strategy and group should identify when measurements really needed.	A: Needed to gauge performance and progress toward values, objectives, and goals. Often required to obtain valid information. D: Data collected even when not needed, often because measurements of any type are assumed "good." (See R&F 3.) Accuracy and precision of data sought as "good" in themselves.
16	*Mediator* Serve to conciliate different perspectives of two or more parties in a P&D effort, especially when conflicts arise.	Aid parties (each with one or more persons) to exchange and understand information by putting each side's views into acceptable language for all. Rephrase own ideas so not appear to promote them. May on occasion be an arbitrator.	Any time in strategy when disagreement appears to be insoluble. Main technique: rephrase ideas to generate understanding. Follow strategy on point of conflict—what purpose trying to achieve, how do it ideally, etc.	All parties in conflicting situation or even power struggle. Stage setting with individual parties will require behind-the-scenes preparation to make mediation effective. (See R&F 4.)	A: Resolve points that would disrupt the P&D project. Almost always needed because conflicts are always going to occur. D: Project will drift with wasted time and effort if this is the major R&F.
17	*Modeler* Produce abstraction (see Chapter Eight, Axiom 6) of existing or desired phenomenon.	Mathematical, statistical, graphical, schematic (flow, network), pictorial, or descriptive models are usual. Systems, management science, operations research, computer simulations, modeling often considered "modern." A modeler usually considers that the model knowledge confers power on the individual.	May be needed in any Phase or step, but most likely in Phases 3 (shaping major alternative), 4b (detailing the recommended solution), and 5a (test and try out solution). No model is ever complete, and it ought to be as simple as possible. A model should fit the needs. It is always a means to an end. (See R&F 15.)	Too often, others involved are fellow modelers who form a knowledge elite. Those in the P&D project and RW should understand *what* the model is trying to do. Modeler must remember that a model does represent value assessments.	A: Must have some abstraction of solution if it is to be implemented. (See Chapter Thirteen.) D: Assumptions rarely checked because model rather than purpose becomes the focus. Elegance of model is too often viewed as the "good," valuable in itself because it demonstrates superior knowledge and relationships.

Table 14-3 (*Continued*)

R&F Number	Role and Function	Characteristics	When Used on Strategy Timeline	Others Involved (RW = real world)	Advantages (A) and Disadvantages (D)
18	*Opinion leader* Seek to influence others regarding their contribution to P&D or the efficacy of a P&D solution however it was developed.	Previous success and good judgment provide this R&F with legitimization in the eyes of others. This person lets project develop in general form and can convince others if personally convinced. Sees real pressure to change to new solution and enjoys the process (see R&F 2).	Tends to be an overall R&F. Person could serve as chairman, facilitator, boundary spanner, etc. (see R&Fs 4, 6, 10), because likely to get along with people better than specific field related P&D professional.	Involves many others, especially key decision makers, resource controllers, other influentials, those who could impact on implementability, etc. "Politically" oriented selection of people to involve. May set up groups to create "political" voice. Needs some work behind scenes (R&F 4).	A: Implementation likely to occur irrespective of creativity of solution. All perspectives likely to be included. D: This R&F almost impossible to train for, because creativity is usually sacrificed even before it has a chance to be used. P&D effectiveness left solely in hands of the very unusual person.
19	*Organizer/promoter* Develop a need, a plan or design to meet it, and a program to get the solution adopted/ sold/used.	A combination of R&Fs 2, 7, 8, 13, and 18. If P&D professional has the ideas and need, may then operate as per R&Fs 6, 10, 20, and 21.	Whole protocol needs to be set up by P&D professional. Other R&Fs used with phases and steps of each stage.	All those indicated in the R&Fs noted in "characteristics" column.	A: Commitment is outstanding. Creativity is enhanced. Motivation stays high. Many good decisions if person is outstanding (Sol Hurok, Thomas Alva Edison). D: All semblance of impartiality is gone. Decision making limited to individual.
20	*Participant/collaborator* Provide input occasionally as group member in the P&D system based on normal citizen or organizational knowledge.	The P&D professional can contribute on basis of educational specialty, value structure, culture, ethics, performance of other purposeful activities, etc. Know when and how to be participant without being threatening (e.g., one project with five team members had facilitator take part in a nominal group exercise).	Needs and goals in Phase 1, ideas for solutions in Phase 2, experience for regularities in Phase 3 as well as utilities and interests in selecting a FIST, etc. Language used in each step must fit RW humans so that jargon does not overwhelm them.	All those on team. P&D system matrix (Table 10-1) enables all individuals to sort out which element role being played (input or human agents) and when. A politician, for example, can be an advocate, input, and facilitator at different points. Collaboration is far more critical than artificially maintaining role distinctions.	A: A P&D professional does have ideas and perspectives that should be considered in a P&D project. D: P&D professional is tempted to manipulate the other P&D R&Fs in a way that maximizes the participant role contribution.
21	*Project manager* Operate and supervise and continuously evaluate the usually large-scale and complex P&D system.	Match project objectives with those of end result sought. Assure match with P&D project area of concern. Set up schedule and control mechanisms for alerts about difficulties, conduct audits periodically, arrange for other resources (people, experts, computer programs, and heuristics). Contingency planning. Market project with clients, prepare proposal including costs, bill and collect, and maintaining continuous contact with clients.	Phase 1B, especially timeline and whole P&D system. Resource allocation. Supervise others doing all stages, phases, and steps elsewhere (work programming and packages, controls, level of detail, scheduling, costs, etc.). Determine time/cost/risk tradeoffs as project goes on. Plays many roles throughout project, especially R&Fs 1, 2, 4, 5, 6, 7, 10, 12, 16, 18, 23, 24, and 25.	Use collateral teams (with regular assignments) or matrix organization. Develop team skills. Establish authority, power, and influence relationships with charter for project. Status review with managers/administrators. Continual assessment of P&D team and individual performances attempting to generate synergy, not just individual skill luminescence.	A: Full-time assignment of a person to the P&D effort increases likelihood of successful implementation. Person has time to be responsible. Costs and time likely to be controlled. D: Difficult to remove an ineffectual person.

Table 14-3 (*Continued*)

R&F Number	Role and Function	Characteristics	When Used on Strategy Timeline	Others Involved (RW = real world)	Advantages (A) and Disadvantages (D)
22	*Researcher* Seek to develop a generalization about a particular phenomenon of concern in the P&D project or overall efforts.	Some details of basic relationships are to be specified—what percent of incoming merchandise agrees with purchase orders, what is a good measure of severity of burns, how does the percent downtime of equipment vary with capital cost, what is correlation between egg-mass sampling in the fall and amount of gypsy moth defoliation in the next summer, and so on? Can be any type of research—library search, experimental. (See Chapter Seventeen.)	Can occur in any step, but most likely in Phases 3 and 4 as regularities, selections, and detailing occur. Purposes of and reasons for seeking generalization should continually be explored as research goes on to improve quality of generalization. (See R&Fs 3, 9, 15, and 17.)	One person usually does the research. If generalization concerns people performances or characteristics (e.g., attitudes, needs, morale), then all precautions regarding human subjects need to be followed.	A: A formal research methodology (see Chapter Three) increases the reliability, validity, and usefulness of the generalization. Reduces uncertainties and risks regarding certain detailing and conceptual decisions. D: Research methodology is so familiar that the rest of the project could slip over into following it.
23	*Reviewer/evaluator/critic* Assess the phenomenon (a plan, a previously implemented solution, process being followed etc.) in terms of its adherence to desired values, objectives, and goals.	Audit plans of various units to determine consistency of formats. Examine the phenomenon in terms of inclusion of all elements and dimensions. Have another group do project again or concurrently independent of the first group. Aid a group in following the P&D approach by providing comments on their activities. Design experiments, sampling, etc.	Can be done at any step, or after implementation is considered complete. Most critical reviews (purpose level, regularity conditions, criteria for selecting FIST and recommended solution, etc.) are performed with the real-world people. Should be done after ideas regarding steps are freely developed.	The review/evaluation system ought to be designed with the P&D approach by involving the people who are to be affected by the data produced by the assessment. They must have confidence in the data and information produced.	A: Provides basic information for identifying learning needs, personnel replacement, actions to keep the P&D effort moving effectively, and to revise solution concepts and details. D: Can cut off creativity if done in overly negative fashion, or timed prematurely.
24	*Surrogate* Present views of others not attending a meeting.	Express ideas previously given to professional—"The mayor's views are . . ." "The president said that . . ."	At any meeting or presentation. Any phase or step may be involved.	Others to whom the statements are made and who presumably need the information.	A: Needed information that might be omitted is available. D: Possible misinterpretation of original ideas. P&D professional may be compromised if presented poorly.
25	*Trainer/educator* Have people involved learn the skills and knowledge of the P&D approach.	Provide opportunity for group members and managers to learn *how* to do effective P&D. Do as the project proceeds, or by special seminars or courses, by one-on-one training, or through a regular part of orientation activities. Arrange for some technical training as needed in a content area (e.g., types of telecommunication equipment, sources for individually programmed instruction, characteristics of computers).	Education may occur anywhere in the strategy, especially as people ask for certain information or knowledge. A seminar on PDA usually occurs during Phase 1B or when a group starts Phase 1C. Each training/education experience should be designed by applying the strategy. All training/ education should provide not only technical skills but the contextual framework as well.	Those in the P&D project, plus any others who would appreciate the opportunity to learn PDA or other topics. Depending on prospective supervisory and managerial needs, the opportunity for seminars and other educational experiences should be widely available to develop capabilities in P&D.	A: Gives each person an understanding of *why* as well as *how* PDA works. Helps in the human resources development efforts of an organization. D: A tendency toward more teaching than doing P&D very often arises, on the assumption that learning is always good (studies show high performers do not take more adult/extension/ postgraduate courses than low performers).

Table 14-3 (*Continued*)

R&F Number	Role and Function	Characteristics	When Used on Strategy Timeline	Others Involved (RW = real world)	Advantages (A) and Disadvantages (D)
26	*Arbitrator* See R&Fs 7, 9, 14, 16, and 21.				
27	*Bargainer* See R&Fs 4, 5, and 16.				
28	*Challenger* See R&Fs 3, 12, 16, and 23.				
29	*Conflict resolver* See R&Fs 1, 4, 11, and 16.				
30	*Consultant* See R&F 1.				
31	*Coordinator* See R&F 10.				
32	*Data gatherer* See R&Fs 3, 12, 15, 17, and 22.				
33	*Integrator* See R&Fs 4, 10, 14, 21, and 25.				
34	*Lobbyist* See R&F 2.				
35	*Motivator* See R&F 5.				
36	*Negotiator* See R&Fs 4, 5, 10, and 16.				

on *the* "designer" (Role and Function 8), an operations researcher on "analyst" and "modeler" (R&Fs 3 and 17), a productivity improvement specialist on "expert" and "measurer" (R&Fs 9 and 15), and a social worker on "expert," "helper," and "mediator" (R&Fs 9, 11, and 16).

All roles and functions *may* be needed by any single P&D professional. A major R&F is that of facilitator (R&F 10), while other important ones tend to be information resource person (12) at almost any time, expert (9) when P&D systems are being developed, and measurer (15), modeler (17), and reviewer (23), when detailing a system in Phase 4 and evaluating performances in Phase 5.

A facilitator role does not mean that a P&D professional should not be highly prepared in a specific problem area or locus (e.g., architecture, engineering, manufacturing, regional studies). The practice of such necessary P&D specialties should take place within the broader setting of different R&Fs in a total P&D approach. This role expansion should be an important ingredient in avoiding the commonly used pejorative label "specialist." In addition to changing roles as needed in a scenario, the P&D professional must call in others who have particular role capabilities, includ-

ing a variety of experts in the specific locus content area. Even though a person may be more comfortable with certain roles than with others, P&D professionals should gain skills in different ones to add to their repertoire.

The personal characteristics, responses and roles of the user, people working in the system, or customer, hereinafter called *client,* also change over the time of the project. The client must be willing initially to commit the organization to the P&D project in steps 1a and 1b, to certain measures of effectiveness in step 1d, and so on. Other responses and roles of the client, as organized roughly along the timeline of Figure 10-4, include:

- Willingness to express dissatisfaction, sense of difficulties, and initial interpretation of data as a basis of stating that a problem exists
- Provide situation-specific content expertise
- Provide top level commitment to P&D
- Make requested information available
- Make timely decisions regarding the P&D system
- Designate key persons to participate in the P&D system

- Allocate resources for P&D
- Be open regarding purposes, hierarchy, and measures of effectiveness
- Provide priority ratings on measures of effectiveness

In other words, clients must recognize that effective P&D depends as much on them as it does on the P&D professional. When a P&D professional, for example, is allowed to proceed on a solution that is artistic or esthetic, but not very well related to effective and functional performance (an architect designing a house with a column in the middle of a bedroom, a computer systems engineer designing an information system with 75% more data output than needed just because it is available, an urban and regional planner determining the policies and allocation the developing country ought to make in its agriculture sector), it is just as much a result of the client's ineptness in fulfilling client roles as it is a result of the elitism of the P&D professional.

This leads to a review of the personal characteristics of a P&D professional, for arrogance and elitism are hardly desirable ones. Of course, artistry, esthetics, and beauty that reflect the creativity of the P&D professional can be features of any solution as long as it still effectively achieves the purposes clients seek. Any description of desirable P&D professional characteristics is therefore not a limit on innovativeness and new thinking on the part of the professional, but rather an expansion of the probabilities that the creativeness will be adopted and implemented! Table 14-4 lists such desirable performance characteristics.

Another way of arranging these characteristics deals with traits and qualifications to be sought in hiring a P&D professional (Table 14-5). These features should be examined with candidates and even explored with prospective entrants to a specific P&D education program. The person who possesses such features will quite obviously be able to develop the desired performance characteristics (Table 14-4).

A dynamic characteristic of P&D efforts concerns *how* the P&D professional should cope with the minute-by-minute, hour-by-hour actions in groups and behaviors of clients. Clients and groups will express various sentiments colored by their levels of reality conditions (Chapter Five) at various times. For the lack of a well-timed, positive psychological stroke for an individual a P&D project may be lost.

Always asking about purposes and functions instead of activities and who is at fault will in itself help a great deal in the minute-by-minute, hour-by-hour interactions of the P&D professionals and clients. Another effective process for the P&D professional to

Table 14-4 Desirable Performance Characteristics of a P&D Professional in Most Roles and Functions*

1 Provide *process* direction but let the people involved determine the specific *content* of purposes, solution ideas, regularities
2 Practice diplomatic and negotiative conflict resolution skills to combat three main sources of human difficulties: Self-interest, projecting your thoughts and values onto someone else, and lack of precision of thought
3 Remain alert to needs, in order to build an effective team
4 Share the "magic" of process directions so the people involved can later operate effectively on their own
5 Exhibit intelligent dedication and high mental energy in search of innovative yet effective solutions
6 Communicate clearly and persuasively in oral, written, visual, and graphic forms; present material coherently in educational format
7 Ask questions (what are your purposes, goals, or so on) rather than give answers
8 Exhibit the behavior you want people to adopt (*telling* others to learn new techniques while you don't keep up to date will not lead to learning behavior)
9 Treat all solutions as the beginning of continuing changes
10 Be aware of many alternative process techniques, good practices in content field, experts and sources of organized knowledge, models and techniques, and of when they might be used, as the audience or group is "read" to gage its needs
11 Practice creativity and imaginative thinking in most steps before treating it as routine P&D
12 Be aware of personal values, biases, strengths, and limitations (ask for help when needed), and respect and reflect those of others
13 Remember that the P&D perceptions of real-world people (users, politicians, etc.) must be moved over time from the beginning if successful implementation is to occur
14 Conduct meetings and decision sessions that allow for free and informed choice in an interdisciplinary setting
15 Help to develop organizational commitment to the search for and implementation of effective solutions
16 Be able to relate to other P&D projects, organizational needs, managers, and outside resources
17 Persevere in the face of obstacles and muddles. Good P&D overcomes discouragement and continues on to new efforts, even when a specific project is not successful
18 Maintain a perception of the *whole*; seek to synthesize parts and large amounts of information into a cohesive whole
19 Provide performance information to and accept it from others
20 Be able to "communicate" with computer systems

* A P&D professional is not necessarily full-time or internal to an organization.

Table 14-5 Traits and Qualifications to Seek
in Hiring a P&D Professional

1 Has technical knowledge of content field and P&D approaches

2 Is conversant with full range of tools, practical to sophisticated

3 Has sufficient credentials to gain respect of others

4 Is concerned with P&D administrative matters and details

5 Has experience in working with interdisciplinary groups and individuals

6 Is not self-centered, aloof, or autocratic, and understands common social courtesies

7 Is alert and eager while being knowledgeable about likely real-world constraints

8 Has good personal character

9 Displays willingness to take advice, admit mistakes, and not rely on dignity and status

10 Is poised, patient and good sport

11 Takes timely action on personnel matters

12 Shows political acumen regarding time to change a previous agreement, understanding "hidden" agenda, and interpersonal relationships

practice is called *transactional analysis,* where a transaction "consists of a stimulus by one person (the Agent) and a response by another (the Respondent). The response, in turn, becomes a new stimulus for the first person to respond to."[17] A transaction thus describes the behavior of people. "Behavior is best understood if examined in terms of ego states."[18] Three ego states or "coherent systems of thought and feeling manifested by corresponding patterns of behavior,"[19] are identified as the Parent, the Adult, and the Child. The Parent ego state is mainly made up of behavior copied from parents or authority figures. "It is simply a constant and sometimes arbitrary basis for decisions, the repository of traditions and values, and as such it is important to the survival of children and civilizations. . . . The Parent . . . is not a completely fixated ego state since it can change over time. Thus a person's experiences can add to or subtract from his Parent's repertoire of behavior."[20]

The Parent ego state is divided into the Nurturing (*permissive* and *protective*) Parent and the Critical (*prejudicial*) Parent. These two subdivisions of Parent are each divided into OK and Not-OK parts: "When a person is in his OK Nurturing Parent, his voice will usually be warm, comforting, nurturing, and his facial expression and bodily posture relaxed, open and accepting."[21]

The Not-OK Nurturing Parent, however, is over-

protective, enveloping, engulfing. The things done by a person acting in his or her Not-OK Nurturing Parent are negative in that they do not increase the self-esteem of the person to whom they are given; they weaken it. The terms "OK" and "Not-OK" relate to existential positions. It is especially important that a P&D professional should not 'come on' as a Not-OK Nurturing Parent.

"The OK Critical Parent criticizes constructively, both when the criticisms are directed internally, at oneself, and externally, at others. . . . The Not-OK Critical Parent criticizes out of need to 'put down' or 'discount' others. These criticisms are usually unjustified, and are often projections of problems or defects onto others."[22]

"The Adult ego state appraises its environment and calculates its possibilities and probabilities. The Adult deals with facts and options."[23] "The Adult is the problem solver. Rational and objective, it provides clear thinking and analysis—fundamental skills in managing people, . . . an objective consideration of Parent and Child feelings, attitudes, possible prejudices."[24]

The Child ego state is based on the premise that "each person carries within himself a little boy or a little girl, who feels, thinks, acts, talks, and responds just the way he or she did when he or she was a child of a certain age."[25] Two aspects of the Child ego state are the Free (or Natural) Child and the Adapted Child. In

Table 14-6 Ego-State Contributions to Behavior*

What the Parent Does	What the Adult Does	What the Child Does
Nurtures	Processes information	Invents
Criticizes	Takes objective action	Expresses curiosity
Restricts	Thinks, then acts	Acts on impulse
Judges	Organizes	Acts selfishly
Blames	Plans	Loves
Encourages	Solves problems	Imagines/brainstorms
Supports	Estimates risks	Acts belligerently
	Ferrets out assumptions	Complains
Source: the relationship between you and your parents	*Source:* the emergence of independent thinking in early life and its subsequent development	*Source:* the best and the worst of your young self

* From C. Albano, *Transactional Analysis on the Job*, New York: American Management Associations, 1974.

turn, the Adapted Child may be either Compliant or Rebellious.

In the healthy person all three of the ego states, Parent, Adult, and Child, are available for use and there is a continuous process of checking and counter-checking between them, shifting from one ego state to another. Table 14-6 summarizes the ego state contributors to behavior.

With proper training and practice, a P&D professional would be able to recognize, by visual and verbal signals as shown in Table 14-7, various ego states of participants and know what to expect. People use a great deal of imagery through gestures and metaphors. Just as important, P&D personnel would be able to monitor the appropriateness of their own ego state behavior. They would know, for example, when their Rebellious Child had been "hooked" by a participant's Critical Parent, or when they were "coming on" from the wrong ego state for giving permission and protection for the group's Free Child to be creative, and were instead actually stimulating the member's Not-OK Rebellious Child.

The concept of strokes is a unit of recognition. By our giving strokes to others we show, and they perceive, our recognition of their existence. Strokes may be verbal or non-verbal, and may be negative as well as positive. Also, strokes may be either unconditional or conditional.

There are four basic categories of strokes: (1) *Positive unconditional* strokes, such as "I like your attendance just for your being present." (2) *Positive conditional* strokes, such as "I will appreciate your presence if you do this well." (3) *Negative conditional* strokes, as when someone says "If you do that I will not respect you." (4) *Negative unconditional* strokes like "I can't stand the sight of you."

"The best strokes are positive unconditional and positive conditional; that is, recognition for being and recognition for doing. The worst strokes are negative unconditional strokes. However, the most terrible thing of all is to get no strokes. This situation is intolerable, and when it occurs people often set up situations so that they get negative strokes, because negative strokes are better than no strokes."[26]

Table 14-7 Indicators of Ego States

	Body Language and Gestures	Expressions	Vocal Tone
Parent indicators	Looking down over rim of glasses. Pointing an accusing finger. Hands on hip, the head leaning or straining forward. Patting on the back.	"You should . . . you ought . . . you must . . ." "Why don't you . . ." "Stay loose" "Be cool" "Don't tell me . . ." "You disappoint me." "You always . . ." "Poor thing . . ." "I'll protect you."	Harsh Judgmental Soothing Indignant Commanding Comforting
Adult indicators	A straight, relaxed stance. Slightly tilted head. Appearance of active listening. Regular eye contact. Confident appearance.	The offer of alternatives and options. Use of the five W's† in questioning. We and ours, not I and my. "Aha, I see" "I see your point" "I recognize . . ." "How do you feel about . . . ?"	Relaxed Assertive Somewhat deliberative Self-assertive
Child indicators	Forlorn appearance. Drooping shoulders. Withdrawal. Pursed lips. Scowling. Skipping. Hugging. Twinkle in eyes.	"I want . . ." "I wish . . ." "Wow." "I should . . ." "If only . . ." "Did I do okay?" "One of these days . . ." "It's not fair . . ." "It's not my fault." "Oh boy!"	Appealing Complaining Nagging Indignant Cheerful Protesting Grumbling Mumbling Sullen

* From C. Albano, *Transactional Analysis on the Job*, New York: American Management Associations, 1974.
† What, when, where, who, why.

Much of the stroking done in our culture is verbal. "Stroking words have stroking value only when they are invested with the emotion they are intended to express. . . . Words are dependable sources of strokes only when the sound of the voice, the facial expression, and the body language are consonant."[27]

Perhaps the most common form of negative stroking is in the "discount"—putting down a person: "When one person discounts another he acts as if what *he* feels is more important than what the other person feels, says or does; hence he does not really pay attention to what the other person wants—that is, he 'discounts' him."[28]

Discounts can be given from one person to another or a person can discount himself, privately or for the benefit of spectators. Often people use self-discounting as a means of "hooking" the Nurturing Parent of others and thus try to establish rescue relationships. In this way they attempt to get strokes from others. For example, one person may say "I can't do anything right" (self-discounting inviting rescue). If the second person is hooked and responds by saying "That's not true, sure you can," a rescue has begun. A better response would have been for the second person to stay in his or her Adult ego state (and not shift to the Nurturing Parent) and try to hook the first person's Adult by asking that he or she logically explain what was meant by the statement. In this way discounting is stopped and rescue is avoided. . . .

The concept of strokes is thus quite useful to the P&D professional. First, it would enable P&D personnel to more effectively assess and plan for the involvement of people. Keeping the need for strokes and the goal of minimizing discounts in mind can be useful in determining who is to be involved and how the involvement should take place.

Second, it would be valuable for P&D personnel to be aware of strokes and their effects so that they could monitor and improve their own stroking behavior (by giving more strokes and minimizing discounts) and, at the same time, guide the behavior of the participants in the same way. . . . The minute-by-minute, hour-by-hour progress of a meeting with a group or individual can thus be improved. The P&D professional . . . must gauge [personal] statements and strokes to maximize group or meeting results. The professional must also recognize the need to change ego states, over time as various steps are the focus. For example, the P&D professional may need a Nurturing Parent state . . . in describing the advantages of designing a P&D system, an Adult state when getting a group to determine a purpose hierarchy, and a Free Child state when developing ideal systems.

Finally, an awareness of the concept of strokes would enable P&D personnel to facilitate the design of better stroking mechanisms into the target and recommended solutions. For example, chains of authority, communication channels, reporting procedures, and reporting mechanisms are, in a very real way, stroking mechanisms which can provide both positive and negative strokes.[29]

Thus, the roles and behaviors of the P&D professional demonstrate *how* the practitioner adapts minute-by-minute and project-by-project with different kinds of clients who also have time-variant needs and behaviors. For many P&D efforts—the architect with a home owner, engineer with a product designer, a computer systems planner with a user, a curriculum designer with a faculty group—these role and behavior ideas are sufficient.

On the other hand, many projects are too large for just one professional to handle: A new manufacturing plant, nursing home quality care assessment, income distribution policy for a developing country, long-range planning for public television—are examples. The introduction of a staff of P&D professionals means that role assignments will be needed. This raises many additional questions of appropriate organization roles, functions, and characteristics to effectively utilize the resources. The questions will be raised and answered in Chapter Sixteen on the organization structure of the P&D system. But the behavioral processes will now need to be practiced among P&D staff members themselves.

A P&D project or continuing effort should produce "human" people from the inside of the project as well as in the solution. A significant, cogent argument could even be provided that the "humans" are the real outputs sought from any system or solution, irrespective of the actual outputs of buildings, forms, products, information—any solution—proclaimed to be the primary focus.

And that is a suitable reason for involving people in all P&D projects and efforts.

SUMMARY

The real world (client, organization, decision makers, users, customers, workers in the system, etc.), the P&D professionals and other experts, and those selected or elected from the real world to serve on the task force or special group are the three relevant broad people classifications. Complicating the involvement of any group is the multiplicity of "worlds" in which each person lives (family, religion, recreation, etc.). Affective and even chance factors are consequently usually critical in people involvement.

Proposition 11   Involving people in the P&D system as inputs, outputs, part of the environment, actors in following the P&D strategy, information aids, and human agents can maximize the number and effectiveness of implemented solutions and the effectiveness of utilizing P&D resources.

Several assumptions support this proposition and also provide a basis for dealing with the realities of individuals and groups presented in Chapter Five. (A) People should be given continual *opportunities* to participate. (B) People are the source of information. (C) People can understand intricate techniques and complex situations. (D) P&D group meetings can be productive. (E) People enjoy working on and accepting responsibility for P&D projects. (F) The individual is the source of P&D ideas. (G) People accept and implement P&D solutions they help to develop. (H) Perceptions and values of people change with age and time of reaching adulthood.

Arranging the actual involvement of people involves knowing where in the approach activities along the timeline the project happens to be, the amount of participation already extant in the organization, types and roles of people that ought to be involved, the group processes and techniques that produce effective results, and the meeting conditions that aid the group in being effective.

The P&D professional blends different roles and serves different functions as the P&D activities proceed along the timeline. At various points, the needed role may be that of experimenter, mediator, analyst, facilitator, modeler, *the* designer, measurer, and so on. The professional must especially "read" the ego states of an individual, whether alone or as a member of a group, in order to respond appropriately. The "adult-to-adult" state is most often needed, although the professional may occasionally need to adopt a child or a parent state to best move a group along the timeline.

CHAPTER FIFTEEN

Using Information and Knowledge

Information and knowledge are the medium of exchange in P&D. They form the basis of today's P&D formulation of actions to take tomorrow.

Information refers to present and past compilations of "hard" (physical) and "soft" (social, political) generalizations about nature. *Knowledge* refers to human understanding of and mental interconnections between past and present information and the ability to imagine, speculate about, and envision a future. *Wisdom* is also intertwined with information and knowledge (to provide inner insight about how information and knowledge are generated and endowed with content and character), the intellectual forms of understanding human nature, and the appreciation of the interior self. Wisdom, in a sense, is the subject of the whole book, but information and knowledge is the thrust of this chapter (Figure 15-1).

Now, there are huge amounts of information and knowledge (I&K) "out there." Some of it is modern and sophisticated, some is intermediate or "tried and true," some is in subject content areas or disciplines (thermodynamics, paleontology, properties of material, English grammar, anatomy, etc.), and some is speculative. I&K that will be needed for a particular P&D project is determined by following the total approach. The total approach deals with what the whole problem *needs* in the way of information and knowledge, not just arbitrarily defined technological, human, or intellectual I&K. Policy makers in Congress and federal agencies, for example, treat "technology" as

information and knowledge sufficient unto itself. Yet a "technological policy" regarding developing countries that claims intermediate technology should be used instead of capital-intensive concepts misses the point about the need for situation-specific solutions. It may be far better to focus on products or industrial firms of any level of technology as long as they increase total employment (e.g., transistor radios and devices involve many jobs in marketing, distribution, service, uses).[1] Similarly, Congress may not be getting what it needs from the Office of Technology Assessment[2] because the focus on "technology" I&K may be a distraction from the real focus of a plan/design/solution and its implications.

Many different arrangements of the seemingly infinite amounts of information are proposed by librarians, communications specialists, educational researchers, information systems experts, and others: (a) Various disciplines and subdisciplines that comprise university departments is one. (b) The classification schema in a large encyclopedia is another, and the special taxonomy in any field or even large discipline (philosophy, history) is typical. (c) Some people propose the main ideas of Western civilization[3] as another basis (other criteria to define the word *main* would produce another listing). (d) Figure 15-2 shows three major yet interrelated bodies of knowledge: humanities, science, and design.[4] (e) Professional and technological education, especially engineering, is described this way:[5]

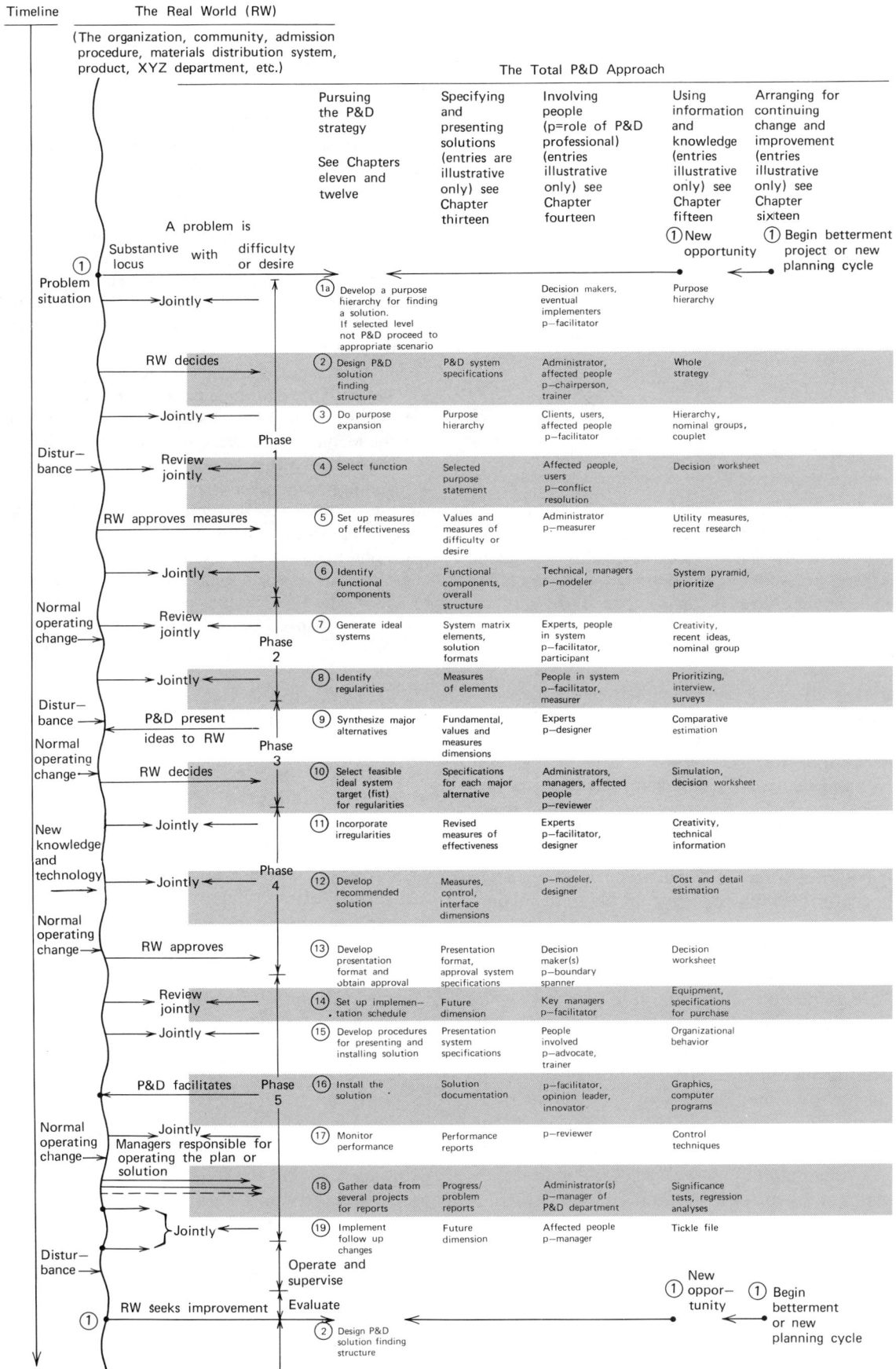

Figure 15-1 The planning and design scenario—feature 4.

Timeline | The Real World (RW)

(The organization, community, admission procedure, materials distribution system, product, XYZ department, etc.)

The Total P&D Approach

#	Pursuing the P&D strategy (See Chapters eleven and twelve)	Specifying and presenting solutions (entries are illustrative only) see Chapter thirteen	Involving people (p=role of P&D professional) (entries illustrative only) see Chapter fourteen	Using information and knowledge (entries illustrative only) see Chapter fifteen	Arranging for continuing change and improvement (entries illustrative only) see Chapter sixteen
				1 New opportunity	1 Begin betterment project or new planning cycle
1a	Develop a purpose hierarchy for finding a solution. If selected level not P&D proceed to appropriate scenario		Decision makers, eventual implementers p-facilitator	Purpose hierarchy	
2	Design P&D solution finding structure	P&D system specifications	Administrator, affected people p-chairperson, trainer	Whole strategy	
3	Do purpose expansion	Purpose hierarchy	Clients, users, affected people p-facilitator	Hierarchy, nominal groups, couplet	
4	Select function	Selected purpose statement	Affected people, users p-conflict resolution	Decision worksheet	
5	Set up measures of effectiveness	Values and measures of difficulty or desire	Administrator p-measurer	Utility measures, recent research	
6	Identify functional components	Functional components, overall structure	Technical, managers p-modeler	System pyramid, prioritize	
7	Generate ideal systems	System matrix elements, solution formats	Experts, people in system p-facilitator, participant	Creativity, recent ideas, nominal group	
8	Identify regularities	Measures of elements	People in system p-facilitator, measurer	Prioritizing, interview, surveys	
9	Synthesize major alternatives	Fundamental, values and measures dimensions	Experts p-designer	Comparative estimation	
10	Select feasible ideal system target (fist) for regularities	Specifications for each major alternative	Administrators, managers, affected people p-reviewer	Simulation, decision worksheet	
11	Incorporate irregularities	Revised measures of effectiveness	Experts p-facilitator, designer	Creativity, technical information	
12	Develop recommended solution	Measures, control, interface dimensions	p-modeler, designer	Cost and detail estimation	
13	Develop presentation format and obtain approval	Presentation format, approval system specifications	Decision maker(s) p-boundary spanner	Decision worksheet	
14	Set up implementation schedule	Future dimension	Key managers p-facilitator	Equipment, specifications for purchase	
15	Develop procedures for presenting and installing solution	Presentation system specifications	People involved p-advocate, trainer	Organizational behavior	
16	Install the solution	Solution documentation	p-facilitator, opinion leader, innovator	Graphics, computer programs	
17	Monitor performance	Performance reports	p-reviewer	Control techniques	
18	Gather data from several projects for reports	Progress/problem reports	Administrator(s) p-manager of P&D department	Significance tests, regression analyses	
19	Implement follow up changes	Future dimension	Affected people p-manager	Tickle file	

Timeline / Real World annotations (left side):

- ① Problem situation — A problem is: Substantive locus, with difficulty or desire — Jointly
- RW decides
- Jointly
- Disturbance — Review jointly
- RW approves measures
- Jointly — Phase 1
- Normal operating change — Review jointly — Phase 2
- Jointly
- Disturbance — P&D present ideas to RW — Phase 3
- Normal operating change — RW decides
- New knowledge and technology — Jointly
- Jointly — Phase 4
- Normal operating change — RW approves
- Review jointly
- Jointly
- P&D facilitates — Phase 5
- Normal operating change — Jointly — Managers responsible for operating the plan or solution
- Jointly — Implement follow up changes
- Operate and supervise
- Disturbance — Evaluate
- ① RW seeks improvement — ② Design P&D solution finding structure

Bottom right: New opportunity / ① Begin betterment or new planning cycle

Figure 15-1 The planning and design scenario—feature 4.

237

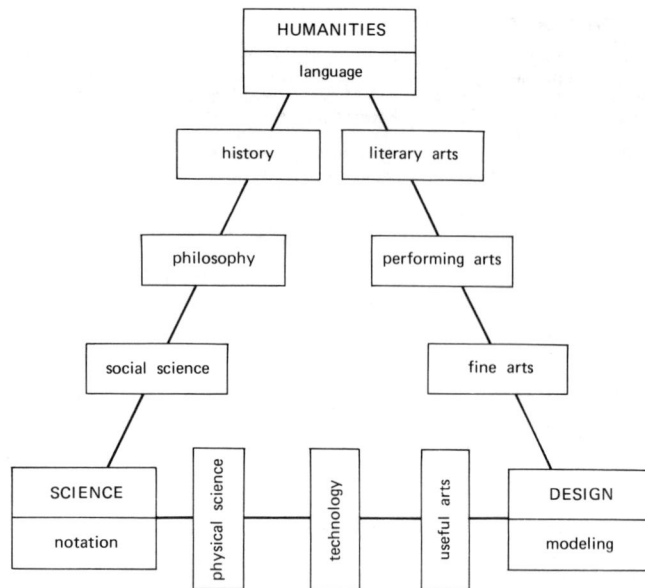

Figure 15-2 The relationships among three areas of human knowledge. From B. Archer, K. Baynes, and R. Langdon, *Design in General Education*, London: Department of Design Research, Royal College of Art, October 1976, Part 1.

You began by studying . . . subjects [that] end in the syllable ICS [or LOGY]. They emphasize the log*ic*; . . . scientif*ic*, . . . analy*tic* . . . [mathematics, physics, electronics, geology, sociology]. The end effort is to know . . . Departments [are] concerned with planning, designing, analyzing, manufacturing, specifying, evaluating, testing, scheduling, managing. . . . It is an ING world, a world concerned with do*ing* . . . Then . . . there is the TION world, the functions and institutions of society: transportation, habitation, nutrition, energy production, energy distribution, communication, recreation, education.

(f) Fifteen nonexhaustive and pluralistic types of synthesis are reviewed, including as examples "generalizing over instances, . . . creation of theory, . . . normal science, . . . emergence of a paradigm, . . . semantic, . . . assessment, [and] assemblages."[6]

One can thus imagine the large number of such arrays, based on an organization's or individual's biases and perceptions. None are "wrong," for what one perceives as reasonable may well be fine for that person's needs. Yet all suffer from their single-channeled arrays with few if any networks or lattice-type connections.

Almost all of these are established with the basic but implied assumption that, once organized and available, people will know *how* to use the I&K. This is often stated as "The key to progress is knowledge." This premise is only partially correct, and is made on the assumption that an individual can be "better" by

knowing more. In reality, the expression would be better stated as "The key to progress is knowing *how* to use knowledge." Both the approach to finding solutions *and* the knowledge are needed. Knowledge alone is insufficient. Even "advanced" or science-based fields need much more than knowledge.

The production of integrated circuits and microprocessors (the heart of the new generation of computer electronics) starts with the design of a desired set of circuits. The design, it is true, ultimately derives from . . . "pure" knowledge. But the designing itself is laboriously done by engineers. . . . These designs are photographically reduced and reproduced by means of a pattern generator that creates a master mask. . . . Yet both the pattern generator and the photorepeater are themselves manufactured singly by skilled craftsmen working in a manner not much different than that of the medieval clock-maker in effort, attention to metal-working precision, and solitary pride. [And] who are considerd among the most valued workers in the integrated circuit industry? The handful of people who run the "ovens" that "cook" the chips and microprocessors. They are almost regarded as alchemists, possessing arcane skills that cannot be transmitted by observation or learned by university study. . . . Conditions *have* changed. We *are* more dependent on knowledge than before. But we ought not exaggerate that dependence.[7]

This leads to the first reason for delving specifically into the topic of using information and knowledge: Merely knowing a body of knowledge or set of theories is insufficient for effective P&D. This is a specific form of general finding that shows nonutilization of information and knowledge to be extensive. Three theories are offered from research on knowledge utilization to explain this:[8] The producers of the knowledge inhibit utilization through narrow views, biases, quantitative orientation, nonuser orientation, and inappropriate data and methods; the prospective user is constrained because the need for quick, concise, and simplified information can seldom be met by producers; and each side has mismatches due to terminology differences, reward structures, values, methodologies, and standard of significance. Knowledge, for P&D purposes, can only be considered "good" if it is successful in influencing P&D decisions.

The second reason for the PDA scenario feature of using I&K is that the huge amount of I&K causes current specialists in a P&D field to overlook almost all I&K in related fields. This results in plans/designs/solutions that may be incomplete or, most likely, concern the wrong problem. The difficulties in P&D (Chapter Five) could arise not so much because we have insufficient *specific* I&K, but *because* there is just too much all together.

The information monsoon in which we live [leads to] a downright bias against "knowing" anything. . . . The search to "learn more" is pursued as an evasion of . . . taking action. . . . The national greed for information has destroyed our ability to make use of it. There is simply so much of this seeming "evidence" floating around—statistics, reports, the rest—that if you cannot find some to prove a perception, no matter how strong or logical or certain it may be, you might as well give up. "There is no evidence that," . . . the opposing argument will go, and you are cooked . . . [We live with] the principles of a forced scientific experimentalism. Sooner or later, I have no doubt of it, we are all going to die of terminal . . . science.[9]

The constantly accelerating accretion of knowledge, therefore, may not always be counted as good. Can circumstances change so as to devalue the net worth of new knowledge? . . . Institutions . . . devote much energy and effort and talent to the advancement of science. . . . In so doing we apply essentially only one criterion—that it be good science as science—that the work be imaginative, skillfully done, in the forefront of the field. Is that, as we approach the end of the twentiety century, enough? . . . The basic tactic . . . is analysis [and it] has worked splendidly. To answer my question, however, the focus must not be inward but outward, not narrowed but broadened.[10]

The huge amount of I&K already available is not an argument to stop generating new information and urging people to learn and know more. On the contrary, we always should search for and develop new information. Chapter Seventeen will propose, however, that the most important type of I&K concerns the gaps in the P&D operational theory so that research and technology data also continually being generated might be more effectively utilized. It is essential that we continue such work because "the technology base counts for a great deal in terms of national security, competitiveness in trade, and expectations for economic growth. It could make a big difference if the base were found to be softening over time, rather than firming up."[11]

The third reason for concern about using I&K is that it is not organized for utility in P&D. I&K is almost always presented in the form of generalizations from research, taxonomies from learning, comparisons from evaluation, or experiences from operating and supervising. A generalization that aggregates I&K cannot predict the performance or condition for a specific situation (Corollary 7a). A taxonomy is a human perception imposed on an unaware real-world phenomena that often has no relevance to what a solution ought to be (Corollary 6a). A comparison shows the effectiveness of a system which very seldom has relevance to another specific P&D instance (Corollary 7b). An experience (e.g., case history) regarding an operating and supervising problem often demonstrates a management style that is not likely to have direct

utility in another P&D situation (Corollary 7b). All of these forms of information are valuable for a P&D professional to learn, but they must be revised into a different format for effective use in P&D.

The literature on "high level" *learning* emphasizes the skill and ability to actually use the I&K without saying *how*. Nor are other levels of learning (in-depth knowledge about the concept or phenomenon, or knowledge about where information is available—experts, libraries, computer data base, etc.) usually put into a form for use in P&D. Neither is there any indication of *how* various gradations of the I&K might fit various steps of the protocol and strategy. A person may possess the greatest level of knowledge/information, but that does not mean the level should be used. For example, a sophisticated technique may provide much more accurate and precise—and costly—data than could ever be utilized in a project, and thus should probably not be used most of the time.

Thus, I&K availability is not at all the same as I&K arranged for and used in all or even most P&D situations. Conversely, it is not very likely that I&K will ever be arranged "suitably." I&K is basically in minds, not what is recorded. Humans are at the base of I&K. Any I&K item is always in a contextual setting and cannot be tossed about like a brick. The meaning of the brick to you is different than it is to me.[12] (This is one of the reasons the development of artificial intelligence is experiencing great difficulty: The world is not described by enumerating its atoms.) In addition, such human variability carries over to *how* people would and could use any arrangement of I&K. Some people, for example, are dominated by the right-hemisphere brain (imager, gestaltism, intuition, artistic, conceptual, holism, and overall problem solving). Others are left-hemisphere–dominated (speech skills, mathematics, formalisms, analysis, and step-by-step problem solving). Then imagine the infinite number of combinations that could and do exist. This partly explains several of the realities (Chapter Five) of human psychology.

Thus, there should be more than one way in which I&K is available. A P&D professional should learn about, for example, the needs and interests of citizens in a community through a priority listing of topics with percentages of times citizens noted the topic (a generalization), a comparison with what citizens said they needed in prior years (an evaluation), a set of measures expressing degree of dissatisfaction with present solutions and their management for meeting those needs (an operating and supervising form), and number of purposes the citizens would like to achieve to interrelate and satisfy the needs and values (P&D). Why assume that just formulating a generalization is sufficient or that repeating the generalization many times and in many places is a satisfactory information transfer?

The transfer of I&K suffers from the above problems, especially the lack of an approach to create or restructure a situation-specific solution. Most efforts at technology transfer take the form of technical briefs, for example, which try to "sell" the solution or technology for use somewhere else (violates Corollary 7b). The record of such transfer or spin-off attempts, at least in the federal government, is very poor.[13] Even the active attempts of the National Aeronautical and Space Agency to transfer technology by searching for likely specific *applications* (as compared to passive circulation of reports) was only marginally more successful than the passive approach because a P&D solution that *might* use the information in another location is still a matter of considering a total approach—the people are always different, organizational settings are always different, the wrong problem is being addressed, and so forth.[14]

Acknowledging the seeming paradox (simultaneously, an information monsoon, and each item of I&K is perceived differently) actually provides some philosophical support for trying to organize I&K in a way that facilitates using it in P&D. P&D effectiveness suffers now in addition to its use of conventional approaches because using I&K in the form usually available is time-consuming, debilitating, and conducive of errors. The seeming intractability of the I&K dilemma indicates that a contextual setting with all the P&D factors could possibly improve its use.

Three categories of I&K seem to be discernible: (a) I&K *of* P&D, (b) I&K *in* P&D, and (c) I&K *in* the locus content area.

The overall emphasis of this book (especially Parts One and Two) is on **I&K *of* P&D**. This emphasis puts the various P&D factors into a total context. Comments about one of the five factors must be subsumed within all of them. Parts One and Two provide an attitudinal referent conducive to accomplishing implementation of change. I&K *of* P&D involves topics that describe major parts of an educational program for almost every P&D professional as well as sets the stage for P&D operational aspects:

Axiology: goodness or value in [P&D] phenomena, with special regard to the relations between technical, economic, moral and aesthetic values;

Philosophy: language of discourse on [P&D] moral principles, [processes governing thought, and metaphysics];

Epistemology: Nature and validity of ways of knowing, believing and feeling in [P&D];

History: what is the case, and how things came to be the way they are, in the [P&D] area;

Pedagogy: principles and practice of education and the [P&D] area.[15]

I&K *of* P&D thus deals with the interrelationship of P&D to society as a whole (Chapters Two through Ten). In addition to this content, these topics establish the "mind-set" of *practitioners* of P&D, a critical factor in appropriate use of I&K.

Most P&D-specific studies, techniques, algorithms and models fit the catagory of **I&K *in* P&D**, regardless of the problem locus. A study, for example, dealing with heuristic decision rules under uncertainty to reallocate resources to activities displayed in a critical path network will usually produce results useful to a P&D professional's work, whatever the field—construction, computer information system, research project, patient admission system in a hospital, regional planning in a developing country, and so on. All of the techniques and models in Chapters Eleven through Fourteen—purpose expansion, identifying regularity conditions, Delphi, system pyramid, nominal groups, system matrix—are also in this category. They are generally useful in all P&D projects.

A P&D professional in a specific field should have skills in, have detailed knowledge about, or know where to get information about almost all of these theories, models, and techniques. An extraordinarily large number of them are available (see Appendix A). Quite a few journals report primarily on I&K *in* P&D, such as *Journal of the American Planning Association, Behavioral Science, Decision Sciences, Design Methods and Theory, Design Studies, Industrial Engineering, Journal of Applied Systems Analysis, Long Range Planning, Management Sciences, Networks, Operations Research,* and *Policy Sciences.* Appendix A lists other reference sources for specific techniques and models.

"Technique after model after study after technique" could be listed within the category of I&K *in* P&D. The P&D system matrix represents a reasonable format within which to place most techniques and models useful *in* P&D. They could be added to the basic P&D system (Table 10-1), as illustrated in Appendix A.

I&K *in* P&D also includes topics that describe other major parts of an educational program for almost every P&D professional and also sets the stage for P&D *operational* aspects:

Praxiology: [efficient action within P&D] techniques, skills and judgment applied in a given area]

Language: vocabulary, syntax and media for recording, devising, assessing and expressing [P&D] ideas; . . .

Taxonomy: classification of [P&D] phenomena; [and]

Metrology: measurement of [P&D] phenomena, with special emphasis on the means for ordering or comparing non-quantifiable phenomena.[16]

I&K *in* P&D is intimately tied to the strategy followed on the project. A different set of techniques and models will be needed for step 1c than for 3a. Figures 15-1 and 10-4 portray the variability. Also affecting the techniques and models used are the needs for specifying and presenting a solution and for involving people in the same step.

I&K in the locus content area refers to the specific bodies of knowledge pertinent to the realm of the particular P&D project. Architecture needs technology much different than design of pest management systems; the same is true for electronic controls versus commercial art, urban and regional planning versus personal counseling, and agricultural planning versus interior design. Yet these apparent opposites are not always separated in a real P&D project, simply because there is no way to know in advance just what bodies of knowledge will be needed. Progress on the project may identify several locus content areas not initially identified for the problem the real world presented to the P&D world. Very seldom does it occur that only one content area is needed in pursuing the PDA strategy toward an implemented solution.

A large number of taxonomies, information structures, disciplinary categories, data formats, problem provinces, and so on are proposed and available to present I&K *in* the locus content areas. Consider the six provinces of "Basic needs in people: science, economics, language, art, religion, and politics."[17] Then there are the 12 technologies into which audiovisual resources are placed for purposes of academic courses on technology and society: arts, foods, mineral resources, energy, communication/information/education, automation/mechanization/work, population/life/health, defense, construction/housing, space/transportation, environment, and history of technology.[18] Or one could find over 40 state problem areas or topics for which reporting services are available, or even a listing of 2653 "distinct and widespread problems . . . present or emerging in the world today"[19] for which large bodies of knowledge are available. Lastly, there are the thousands of references about *classes* of devices and equipment with many specific items and producers within each class (e.g., computers, automobiles, materials handling equipment, men's clothing, plate glass).

Another caveat emerges: Do not depend on any one synthesis or categorization of I&K. Overlaps exist in any single array and certainly among them. The delineation and delimiting of I&K should remain open as long as possible. Transdisciplinarity of I&K is the regularity in P&D. Most critical for identifying and selecting the specific I&K in a locus content area is the set of decisions and needs developed in pursuing the P&D strategy.[20]

To provide additional insight into using I&K *in* P&D and I&K *in* the locus content areas, the rest of this chapter will present:

- The proposition associated with the feature of using information and knowledge.
- Characteristics of I&K.
- Transmittal of information.
- I&K *in* locus content areas.
- I&K *in* P&D.
- P&D timeline perspectives of using I&K.

Appendix A summarizes many techniques and models *in* P&D, some of which are mentioned in this chapter.

PROPOSITION FOR USING INFORMATION AND KNOWLEDGE

Proposition 12. Knowledge, information, and models aggregate data that can be used cost-effectively in P&D if each aggregation includes statements about its relative inability to predict an occurrence or performance value of a future specific instance or case, emphasizes the importance of its integration with the other four P&D factors, and is presented with accuracy and precision values to reflect past and present conditions.

Relative inability to predict reflects primarily the impact of Axiom 7 and related corollaries. The generalization from any research effort or aggregation of data (e.g., attitudes of workers in a factory, salaries of engineers five and more years after graduation) will not predict the attitude of a specific worker today or what the salary of today's new engineer will be five years from now. Neither can generalizations about physical phenomena predict the specific number, for example, of pounds of pressure per square inch at which a single steel column in a building will collapse.

Yes, prediction and projections are necessary in P&D, but almost all would reflect the uncertainties Axiom 7 addresses if the ambiguities of the generalization and aggregation were included. Prediction alone is insufficient; importance is just as critical.[21]

Figure 15-3 illustrates this. The solid line portrays a typical generalization from surveys about engineers'

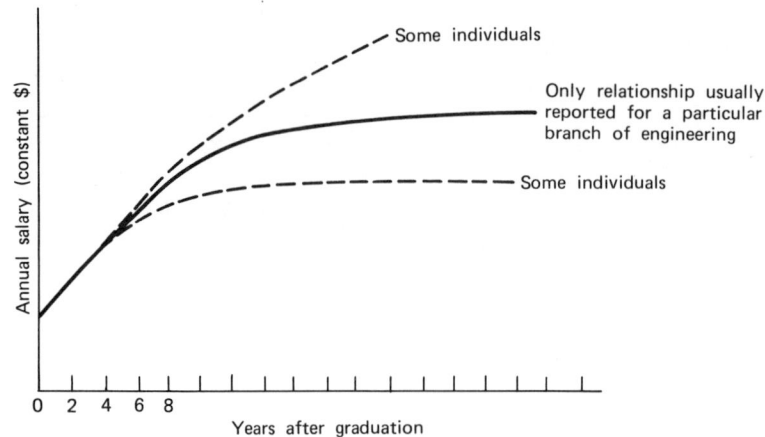

Figure 15-3 One generalization result of salary surveys of engineers.

salaries. The results usually include tabular lists per year of upper and lower quartiles to reflect the wide variability of the raw data aggregated into the solid line. Yet I have heard of two recent references to the solid line in two different P&D situations (projecting career potentials in a company and establishing the plan for division of merit raise money in a university faculty) where the interpretations clearly ignored this lack of ability to predict. The former case involved people who said there was no need to worry about the quality of engineers who were hired because the solid line ''showed engineers peter out eight to ten years after they are hired anyway.'' The latter case involved a faculty member who said raises should be allocated on a dollar basis per performance merit unit (rather than on a percentage of current salary or other combinations) because the solid line ''showed that this reduction of the gap between senior and junior people should be built into our allocation.''

Without commenting about the alternatives being discussed, the use of the solid line generalization was wholly inappropriate. It does not provide a good basis for predicting the individual case or specific plan. Note the two dashed lines in Figure 15-3. Surely, some engineers follow the upper one and others follow the lower one. The engineers in one company could be those around the upper line and engineers in another company could be those around the lower line. Hiring better engineers is likely to produce more of the upper lines because they will not ''peter out.'' Faculty members are likely to be more productive continuously if the upper line is available rather than the assumption being made that the solid line is ''built in.''

The *relative inability to predict* also suggests that P&D need not look so far in the future. The 20-year master plan for developing a community or industrial area or even the five-year economic plan updated once

every five years are dinosaurs in P&D. Community development plans should include no more than a three- to five-year target horizon *as long as a continuing P&D effort is concurrently set up* to change the target plan every year or so.

The timeline perspective is critical because it recognizes that real world updating of even the best plans is necessary. Portraying even ''smaller'' phenomena on a timeline can also make them reflect the real world much more effectively. Control theory is an example. It is almost always presented in the feedback loop form shown in Figure 15-4. Yet the model is a mixed metaphor. Time for the processing system moves from left to right, but the control ''feedback'' goes ''backward in time,'' an obvious impossibility (Axiom 1). Control ideas should be presented in only a timeline frame of reference, as Figure 15-5 demonstrates. In addition to helping P&D, the formulation along a timeline is a far better portrayal of the control generalization. The feedback loop presentation is static at best, very misleading at worst. An adjustment or change from a control process cannot ''return'' to correct what has already been processed. It can only do something about what is to be worked on in the future (see a in Figure 15-5). Even ''automatic'' control devices operate in this timeline frame (see b in Figure 15-5). The static feedback loop is also incapable of showing the response time, such as is differentiated in Figure 15-5. The same feedback loop of Figure 15-4 would be presented as a model of both a and b in Figure 15-5, thus producing critical distortions in understanding. The lack of prescriptiveness (Figure 15-4) can be quite devastating. The whole P&D scenario with its five features will be modeled in Chapter Seventeen on a timeline comparable to Figure 15-5 to illuminate its range of benefits. (The word *feedback* does fit the interchange among people who represent

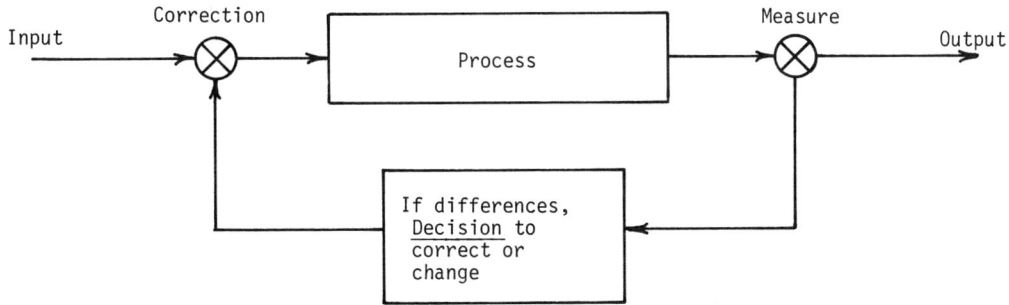

Figure 15-4   Typical static control feedback.

information resources seeking updating of information levels.)

Large amounts of information do not necessarily increase the ability to predict. One well-known reason for this is the statistical square-root relationship between increased confidence in the data and the increase in number of observations. Doubling the sample size, say from 25 to 50, only increases the confidence (or reduces the variability) in a relationship of $\sqrt{25}$ to $\sqrt{50}$, or approximately five to seven instead of one to two. Another reason is that understanding *what* is needed from a prediction will be far more effective in using I&K than any assumed large number of observations, studies, reports, and so on. In other words,

practical significance is as important as statistical significance. This is one of the major premises for changing a prevalent view in many P&D fields that condones seemingly endless requests for "more information." Somehow, people assume that greater precision will automatically improve predictability. But "the compulsive drive for ever more precision in information may be neurotic, if the increased precision means very little in relation to the way of improving the validity of the model."[22] Predicting a specific instance will almost never be possible. Thus the probable minimal incremental improvement in predictive ability needs to be traded off with the large initial and incremental costs of gathering a large amount of data.

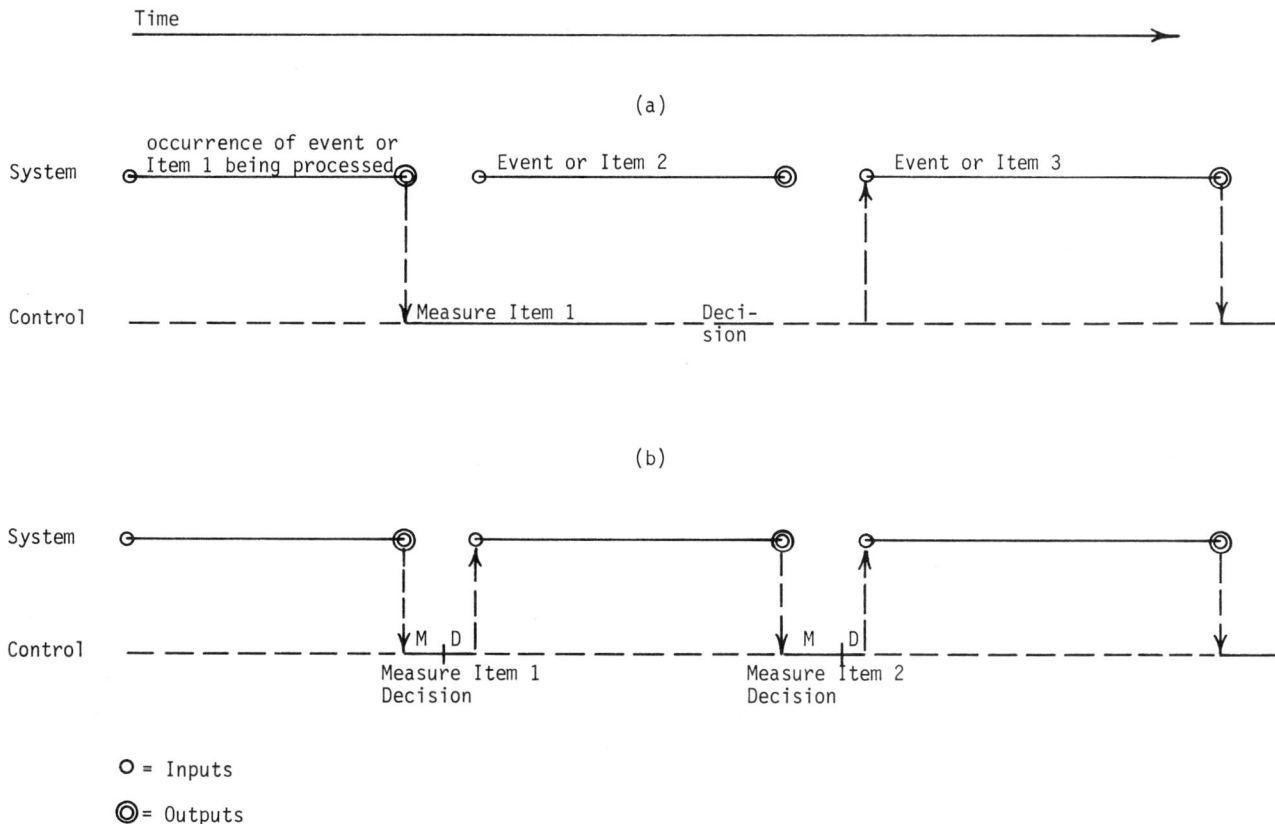

Figure 15-5   Timeline version of control.

Importance of its integration with the other four P&D factors is a reminder that the theory *of* P&D governs the use of I&K. This should put to rest the usual presumption that I&K has a life of its own in P&D. Far too often, a technique becomes a seeming imperative, whereby certain criteria are proclaimed to identify *all* of the situations where the *technique* is usable, and therefore it must always be used: Activity sampling must start a utilization improvement project, a needs analysis must precede a curriculum plan, a sketch is necessary before beginning an architectural project, accounting principles must be the guides for corporate planning, and so on. These are just not true, not even part of the time. They are I&K-based, rather than PDA-based.

In addition, keeping the costs of and time spent on collecting data and information relatively low is highly dependent on the other factors. So much I&K resides in the minds of the people concerned with the locus (Chapter Fourteen) that huge costs and long periods of time would be involved in trying to "get" or record a very small portion of it. Then there would be little assurance that what information is needed would actually become available. Involving people directly within the whole P&D scenario is using the most powerful "computers" ever devised—the brains of people—to sort and select I&K pertinent to the purposes of the project.

Accuracy and precision values to reflect past and present conditions addresses a need to improve current conditions about presenting I&K. Surprisingly, most I&K does *not* include indicators of accuracy and precision. When it does, the indicators of accuracy and precision are often ignored in interpreting and using the I&K item. A 50% response to a questionnaire (with 95% confidence) showing a preference for the color blue for a bedroom will make the generalization a bit more meaningful than a 35% plurality response at 68% confidence. Such accuracy and precision should always accompany the specific I&K, even though neither one can predict an actual preference in a specific case. At least this type of data gives a P&D professional an opportunity to gauge the degree of assertiveness to exhibit regarding a solution proposal. Routinely including accuracy and precision as part of all I&K improves the chances for its use. In addition, I&K with the same accuracy and precision may have a "meaning" and sensitivity in one phase that is different in another phase of the strategy. What is stable in one may be unstable later. What is incompatible in one may be compatible in another, and so on.

With formidable amounts of I&K becoming available every day, a P&D professional needs to keep up with it somehow. Continuing and recurrent education of all sorts (courses, seminars, journals, television,

correspondence) will grow as the professional seeks to learn new I&K as well as the improved accuracy and precision of "old" I&K.

CHARACTERISTICS OF I&K

Everything is fluid and changing in nature (Axioms 1, 6, and 7). So too is I&K itself. A myth of science (people can observe and model identically the same event or phenomenon when each person has the "same" frame of reference, concept structure, emotions, personal values, and training) has long been exploded and dismissed in discussions of physical as well as social realities. Epistemological studies show the shift from the view of I&K generation as the search for "truth" to the view of it as the development of functional models that serve a purpose now and will be changed or modified in time. What is "factual" I&K is inextricably entwined with human perceptions of its framing at particular points in time.

So too it is unlikely that what follows can be treated as definitive "characteristics." As I&K changes in amount and content, so will any listing of characteristics.

A. Structure

Humans continually seek to put the vast amount of I&K into taxonomical or categorical forms as a reference source, whether for P&D, other purposeful activities, or for any particular locus content area. The following criteria categories about structure are helpful for using I&K to achieve P&D purposes:

Raw Data

Observations, measurements, specific incidents, research calculations, interviews, questionnaire returns, exemplary practices, and so forth. "No data are truly 'raw.' Every record [of an event or object is] subjected to editing and transformation either by man or by his instruments."[23]

Descriptive

Extractions from and embellishments on raw data, organized sets of elements and dimensions, equations, research results, analysis results, explanatory, summary, "factual," "understanding" and so forth. A description of any phenomenon should include its particular perspective, value set, or assumptions.

Comparative

Evaluative, criteria-based descriptions and relationships, policies compared to actions, index values, abstraction or pattern compared to reality or matter ("shape of an ocean wave as contrasted to the water that composes it, . . . shapes of letters on this page as contrasted to the ink and paper . . .[24]), survey of literature, evaluations of I&K in one project or program compared to others (e.g., methods for dynamic control of projects, tests on emissions of auto engines), technological solutions or equipment available for certain problems (e.g., pump water, remove metal, count units, make scientific calculations), and so forth.

Predictive

A wide variety of formats (models, equations, mapping, graphs, monographs, path analysis, charts, scenarios, etc.) to calculate or arrive at the amount or condition of a "dependent" variable(s), given the amount or condition of one or more "independent" variables. The data for the independent variables are aggregated from several instances, so that the amount of the dependent variable is an estimate of an aggregate, not a good prediction of an individual case (Axiom 7). Cause-and-effect relationships, extrapolations, "recurring regularities,"[25] useful estimates or statements about the future, forecasting and sensitivity when identical conditions are assumed, anticipated responses when the conditions are changed, and so forth.

Normative

Consequences of a prediction, thus identifying factors that need to be "changed" if the desired prediction is to occur. This puts purposeful and human concerns at the fore. Available evidence (data, descriptions, comparisons, predictions) thus needs exploration concerning its solidity, finality, practical significance, sensitivity, consensus among experts, and amount of contradictory evidence. Many techniques seek to provide normative insights: contingency-based games, technology assessment, risk analysis, life-cycle costing, worst-case analysis, computer simulation, sensitivity analysis, and scenario writing. A normative structure is difficult to obtain except in some physical situations (Axioms 6 and 7).

Presumptive

Experience and wisdom are often the only data base "structure" available. Hardly a structure in the formal sense (rationality), presumptive I&K illustrates that affective and even chance aspects influence "hard" areas, such as data and information. Other words also explain this category: speculation, heuristics, guess and test, theorizing, intuition, hunches, and feeling. It deals with human concerns. Although this I&K "structure" is least likely to be *sought* while doing P&D, it is probably most widely *used*. A predictive or normative insight, for example, may be needed to de-

termine how downhill skiers will respond to the new safety program regulations, but even after one or more user surveys, someone or a group will *presume* a set of responses. Unfortunately, most presumptions at the broad or societal levels tend to be "false bad news,"[26] a condition to consider in P&D and to be guarded against as a regularity.

Although predictive and normative structures are preferred for P&D, very little I&K is so arranged. Descriptive and comparative structures, along with P&D-initiated collection of raw data, are usually converted into usefulness by presumptive structures. Useful I&K in predictive and normative forms is most often related to physical phenomena (e.g., concrete that dries under conditions x, y, and z will exhibit characteristics a and b, accelerating a car from 0 to 60 miles per hour in 8 seconds instead of 12 seconds will triple pollutant emissions, double the tire-tread usage, halve the oil life, and so on).

B. Stability

I&K that seemed certain yesterday is not as likely to be certain today (Axiom 7). Even the "hardest" of sciences, physics, today incorporates variability rather than determinism into its generalizations. Physicists also recognize that their personal perceptions influence the "reality" for which the generalizations are being sought. Some people claim that every culture has a different "science" or approach to developing generalizations or "truths" that are related to its values, especially in any area beyond the very "hard" sciences. Evidence is accumulating that, within a given culture as well, human and societal factors, such as psychological types (Chapter Five), result in different types of scientists ("analytical scientist, concept theorist, particular humanist, conceptual humanist") who produce different views of reality or phenomena.[27]

A rough idea about the stability of I&K might be obtained by using a scale from 0 to 100. A specific item of any structure may then be assigned a point on the scale, with 0 measuring absolutely no stability and 100 absolutely complete stability. Nothing is likely to be assigned a 0 or a 100, but items nearly 100 would be very useful for many years (e.g., $f = ma$, activity-sampling technique, break-even model, osmosis method of plant feeding) and those near 0 hardly useful at all (using last year's high, mean, and low temperatures for tomorrow's date to predict tomorrow's temperatures, fashion, survey responses of teenagers in Los Angeles or Chicago, number of remote infestations per year of gypsy moth defoliation). Or ask people to give odds on a bet they would make on how stable the I&K item is.

Still another way of describing stability is to combine the perceived P&D utility notion with relative variability or stochastic nature of the I&K item. *Stable* or *static* I&K is unchanging for very long periods of time whether deterministically based (mathematical constants, such as *pi* and *e*) or stochastically (physical constants, human volume–surface area ratio, and BTU efficiency of natural gas). *Dynamic* I&K shows cycles of the measures in some regular fashion deterministically (alternating current) or stochastically (temperature of humans). *Kinematic* I&K concerns motion paths of objects which can be relatively deterministic (rotation of earth around sun, crankshaft connection to piston rod in an internal combustion engine) or stochastic (hand movement in an assembly operation, flight path of airplanes between New York and Atlanta). *Chance* can mean only stochastic conditions surrounding the event (time between eruptions of a volcano, amount of earth movement in a quake, location of pot-holes in a street).

C. Incompatibility

Certain I&K may be highly suitable for one P&D project and not for a similar one (Corollaries 7b and 7c). A study about the effectiveness of teaching reading in elementary schools may have little impact in one specific school and major impact in another. A simulation model to determine the number of beds in the post anesthesia recovery room of one hospital may be incompatible with the decision-making process in a second hospital.

Incompatibility is particularly relevant to the form in which I&K is packaged for others to learn and supposedly apply. Once an I&K topic is found to have utility or relevance in several fields or problems, it is assumed to be compatible with all fields. Consider these illustrations:

Is it necessary to teach integral calculus just so we can point to a probability density function and show that the area under the curve is equal to 1.0000? I think that we have prostituted everything that we want to teach in the name of rigor.[28]

Precise quantitative analyses of the behavior of humanistic systems are not likely to have much relevance to the real-world societal, political, economic and other types of problems which involve humans whether as individuals or in groups.[29]

I would like to ask some questions and suggest some reasons for believing that systems engineering, systems analysis, and Management, as practiced, are likely to be part of the problem, and indeed causative agents.[30]

Some investigations report on surveys concerning the usage of certain I&K, techniques or sets of them. "Despite substantial commitment to forecasting and the existence of a wide range of techniques, many companies do not feel they are getting their money's worth."[31]

One idea to transmit I&K in a compatible form that does not necessarily tie it to the discipline from which it may have emerged uses five questions that help teachers unpack knowledge:

1 What is (are) the *telling question(s)*? (topic, superordinate propositions)
2 What are the *key concepts*?
3 What *methods of inquiry* (procedural commitments) are used?
4 What are the major *knowledge claims*?
5 What are the *value claims*? . . .

The telling questions should have some generic meaning to the learner and should be relatable to concepts already present in the cognitive structure of the learner.[32]

Another idea increasing compatibility is to describe each I&K item or especially a technique in several ways. The first way is in terms of the results of using the technique. Several techniques or models can give output that are similar or identical. The second way is in terms of the inputs that serve as the starting point for using the technique. The third is in terms of the purpose(s) the techniques or model serves. The fourth type of description is in terms of special characteristics, and the fifth describes references for details of the technique.

Another idea is shown in Appendix A. Techniques and models are listed by purposes and by cells of the P&D system matrix. The P&D professional is thus very likely to select a more appropriate technique and thus reduce incompatibility.

D. Indeterminacy

Words, signs, symbols, and language used to identify I&K are indeed characteristics that positively or negatively affect its utilization. Social and esthetic I&K could be overlooked, for example, if a P&D project labels itself as a chemical treatment effort.

"True" words to assign to I&K items and techniques are almost never going to be available. The P&D system is one form of such words (Table 10-1), as are the names for the many techniques used in the P&D system. As one other illustration, consider this "systems" array or "map." It is organized into four columns of analysis types—"deterministic, moderately stochastic, severely stochastic, indeterminate"—with four rows of identification with an entry for each analysis type: *"Analytical bases*—positivism, inductivism, deductivism, heuristic; *Instrumental bases*—optimization, extrapolative/projective, game-based, metatheoretical; *Administrative modalities*—finite-state, servo-cybernetic, stochastic-state, heuristic; [and] *Cognitive bases*—traditional engineering, decision-making, policy-setting (normative system-building), system architecture approach to complex problem-solving."[33]

As valuable as key word searches are in computerized information retrieval systems, everyone using them has had the experience of feeling that something is missing or wondering what other key words could "truly" express what one is seeking. The retrieval systems compound the indeterminacy by limiting the number of key word phrases that can be entered. Thus, research into signing and notational languages that can be associated with meaning—semiotics—seeks to find more effective and cost-efficient labels for I&K.[34]

Incommensurability is another form of indeterminacy. It concerns "disagreement on the structure and organization of the [I&K item]—on what it *should* mean and on what would count as pertinent evidence for its [support]."[35]

E. Amount

Determining the amount of data, observations, and information for a particular step involves considerations of quality, accuracy, precision, purposes, and the tie with other characteristics. More is not always good, even if accuracy and precision are improved. These two factors may not have much bearing at all on the purposes needed for the step. Consider these ideas that can help explain and determine the "amount" for a P&D step:

I&K is Subjective

Stability and incompatibility characteristics B and C above support this idea. Axioms 6 and 7 and related corollaries proclaim its verity. Yet some other comments are noteworthy.

An I&K item is a system (Axiom 3). It is part of a larger set of I&K and it can be divided into smaller items of I&K (Axiom 4), ad infinitum. An I&K item must always be interpreted in terms of its context, explicit or assumed. Even when the context is explicit, so many hedges and interrelationships become apparent that the I&K is irretrievably subjective. Add the incompleteness of any representation (Corollary 6a) or

the data collection measurement errors (Chapter Five), and subjectivity becomes evident, so much so that I am amazed at the numerous references to and university courses on "Failure to Implement Quantitative Models," "How to Sell Operations Research Techniques" and "Implementing Mathematical Models." All treat the data, I&K, or model as "true" or correct and thus it must be "sold," violating Corollary 7b as well as ignoring the subjectivity of I&K. They focus on the wrong question. Achieving the needed purpose is crucial. The model, data, or I&K are often irrelevant to doing this.

Yet I&K, data, and models are necessary in P&D. So the real question is "What use can the group members or individual make of the specific I&K?" The average height of workers in the plant is subjective, even if every one is measured. But the project team may have great confidence in the number, and thus make it useful. Using a scale of 0 (absolutely not useful) to 100 (positively useful) would let people express what they *perceive* to be usable. No guarantees accompany such perceptions, for many can attest to the difficulties that arose when "objectivity" and "accurate" representations were inappropriate. In addition, developing an I&K model of any phenomenon is subject to the "eye of the beholder" symptom (see Chapters 4, 5, 6, 8, and 10). That is, in the case of I&K *in* P&D, a model may be developed from a rationalist perspective and it will differ from one from an idealist, empiricist, deductivist, phenomenologist, or dialecticist perspective.

In general, subjectivity is greatest at the level of I&K *of* P&D, less at the level of I&K *in* P&D (Appendix A), and least at the level of I&K *in* some locus content areas. People are less likely to consider subjective the data about the amperage requirements for a 200-watt bulb (I&K *in* locus content area) than they are about the site location recommendation from a linear programming model or a corporate structure of an organizational development study (I&K *in* P&D). Other locus content areas are still quite subjective. Sears, Roebuck and Co. changed their merchandising policies when several "sharp" MBAs "proved" with a computer model that higher-priced merchandise would increase their profits. The change was quite unsuccessful ("We lost our shirt."). Avoiding subjectivity in such I&K is impossible.

More I&K is Not Necessarily Better

Because people have been "fooled" many times by the subjectivity of data, they tend to assume that more data, measurements, and I&K are better, as if "good" I&K were always available. Many steps in P&D need more and better I&K (e.g., Phases 3, 4, and 5), but the purposes to be achieved are always defined at the beginning of every step, so that only needed I&K is generated. It is simply the arbitrariness of the dictum "the more I&K the better" for *all P&D situations* that needs to be exposed and disposed of here.

Consider but one example of the poverty of this dictum.[36] A manufacturing company went public in 1969, the best profit year since the company was established in 1935. Current sales are about $80 million. But in 1970, 1971, and 1972 the company sustained significant losses even as 15 to 20% yearly gains in sales were recorded. The president of the company, an engineer by training, repeatedly said he could not cut costs or improve profits because the measurements were poor and he could not believe the basic data: poor I&K in inventory (a million-dollar write-off at the end of 1971), poor and untimely measurements in accounting, the increasing age of accounts receivable because of inaccurate data on the amount of delay time, and so on. He claimed for three years that, as he obtained better measurements, the loss picture would change to profit. He was removed as president in April 1973. The new president and a committee of the board focused on purposes and objectives while using their judgment with the available data to "turn the company around." Every year through 1980 has been better than the last, while the company has maintained their well-established good personnel and community policies.

There is no question that some lack of I&K or measurements did create some difficulties in the president's decision-making process. But every organization has more than enough data on hand for almost all purposes. Making a profit in that company, as in any company, needs to be based on being productivity-minded, being savings-oriented, and having a profit attitude. The plea for accuracy in measurement is a perpetual and non-ending problem. That problem should be worked on by the researchers, but it should not distract attention from a focus on organizational purposes and objectives.

Measurements especially must always be secondary to achieving real-world purposes and goals. The folly of a primary emphasis on measurement is illustrated by Robert McNamara and his colleagues, who rushed

toward the quantification of concepts even though the variables may be imprecisely defined and the necessary data unavailable. . . . The dangers of premature quantification . . . are best described . . . in the following statement: "The first step is to measure whatever can be easily measured. This is okay as far as it goes. The second step is to disregard that which can't be easily measured or give it an arbitrary quantitative value. This is artificial and misleading. The third step

is to presume what can't be measured easily really isn't important. This is blindness. The fourth step is to say that what can't be easily measured really doesn't exist. This is suicide."[37]

Finally, all the I&K about a phenomenon cannot ever be obtained, even though large amounts of money are allocated over a long period of time to acquire "a really complete set of information." Such metaphors are completely devoid of any sense of reality. In addition, people involved in P&D really can't absorb all the I&K, even if it were obtained (Chapter Five). Thus, the trade-offs must be considered. Does the usually very small increase in perception and understanding regarding the P&D effort justify the large costs of and even continuing organizational negativism (from, say, "defensive" reactions) resulting from obtaining great amounts of I&K?

Purpose and Need Should Dictate Amounts, Type, and Accuracy of I&K Obtained

Whenever someone proposes a study, data collection, building a model, a library search, running an experiment, developing mathematical relationships, writing a report, conducting a survey, a computerized information system, measuring performance, or any other I&K-related activity, the purpose and its hierarchy ought to be developed for each proposal. In effect, each one seeks to create or restructure a situation-specific system or solution. As might be expected, doing this eliminates much unneeded generation of I&K.

The long-term issue to P&D professionals is comparable to the pollution and ecology issues being thrust at engineers by society in general—a P&D professional may create initial good but look how they created such a poor environment. Emphasizing I&K collection, modeling, and measurement is creating organizational and societal pollution through the preparation of many unneeded and unread documents, perpetuation of an elitist view of P&D, insistence that "our" measurements are correct and "fair," arbitrariness, dehumanization, and so on. P&D professionals must seek better overall results, not just a result that happens to produce P&D pollution.

The P&D tie to the real world (timeline scenario of Figure 10-4) reinforces this point. One *can* carry out each proposal to obtain I&K. One *can* be very smart about the techniques, models, etc., and yet be quite stupid in knowing why and when to use them and the resulting I&K.

It is not a new phenomenon, of course. The French have had for several centuries, a category labelled *"les idiots savants"* . . . [These are] rational people who manage to reason themselves free of all connections with common sense—that basic apprehension of reality that permits us to distinguish real questions from unreal ones, real possibilities from unreal ones. . . . We are being inundated by academic research—once again, based on fabulously complicated statistical techniques—that "proves" [something] ought not to happen, according to their theories—and so it can't be happening.[38]

Surveys and questionnaires are especially suspect techniques for data and information collection, which are often used by such people. "The statistical techniques for selecting samples and analyzing data are well developed. 'But the questions themselves are unbelievably naive and primitive [in most surveys]'. . . . Many of the questions are worded so that either their meanings are ambiguous or . . . the issues are prejudiced, [leading to] undue emphasis . . . on relatively unimportant issues when the analyses are reported."[39]

If those concerned are unable to meet to do P&D for I&K purposes, the P&D professional and related small group, if any, should visit with the manager, worker, legislator, financial controller, office supervisor, factory foreman, consumers, etc., to explore what "rumor mills" imply are "good" measures or data to obtain for achieving the purposes and needs. After generating some commitment or ownership among prospective users, the data and information can be collected by means of any of the many techniques and models available (Appendix A). Some documentation or audit trail may be necessary for later phases of the strategy or in actual installation to guide decisions at that point.

All of this means that developing I&K is subject to the basic concepts of this book. To paraphrase, be literate in purpose, not necessarily numerate. These ideas do change rather dramatically the type, amount and accuracy of information utilized in a P&D project. One experiment,[40] for example, dealt with student architects using three different strategies on three problems. Those following a conventional P&D strategy used mainly problem details and analysis data. Those following a purpose-design strategy used mainly solution-oriented information. The latter also took less time than those using other strategies to arrive at essentially similar quality results.

Get People Affected to Contribute to and Assess Adequacy of I&K

The subjectivity of I&K shows why this theme is significant. All people observe differently. So people with different views are much more likely than a professional measurer and modeler to work out a consensus or agree to the collection of "hard" data to resolve differences. They will have a perspective about the relationship between the purpose to be achieved with the data and the subjectivity and distortions of the data.

Experts are needed to supplement the usual I&K *in locus* content areas (heat transfer, infection symptoms, predators of pests, psychology of learning, political theory of legislation, etc.,) and *in* P&D (multiattribute utility theory, nominal group technique, discrete simulation, computer logic, etc.). When the people involved recognize their own need, experts are received well.

Use the methods preferred by sources of I&K. If a telephone call is preferred, do it. If a written request is "required" or bargaining is the style, however time-consuming it may be, following the methods will probably be most suitable for *this* project.

Review any I&K that is collected with the affected people before it is released, to assess its soundness and representativeness. Get their interpretations and suggestions.

Ask for and try to develop visual means of portraying I&K. A graph, a chart, a picture, a list, or other types of representation are good for both eliciting new I&K and reviewing what has been collected. People will almost always be able to state a preferred format or two rather than just accept "0.78 is the correlation" or "the linear programming allocation to minimize distance traveled is . . ." or "the computer information system must. . . ."

Provide Documentation of Proposed Solutions, not Necessarily of all Parts of the Approach

Another reason (besides the conventional strategy) frequently given for collecting a great deal of I&K *about what exists* is that it is necessary for documenting the project. This is just not the case. What I&K is needed is fairly complete documentation of the solution being recommended and installed. Explaining and justifying the recommendations supplies more than sufficient identification of what exists and perhaps even about how the P&D approach was used. Documenting the latter two items would be desirable for students at a later time, for example, to study the project in preparing a case history. This is hardly a reason why an organization should do it (I personally would benefit if it were done because one course I teach involves students preparing case histories of successfully implemented solutions). But organizations should not be in the business of documenting all I&K about what existed before the successful implementation.

Besides, if meetings, group and design activities were performed as suggested in Chapter Fourteen (with agenda and minutes), sufficient documentation will exist. Such notes *as the project is proceeding* usually supply an excellent audit trail for the P&D process as well as for the solution flow. Other forms of presenting the solution can be included—slide/tape, closed-circuit TV, computer display, movies, and so on.

Measurement Instruments and the Formats into Which I&K Is Placed Vary in Effectiveness

Format includes model, tool, and technique that structure the data collection process. Measuring the heights of students in a class can result in a format (mean and standard deviation) that is accorded a high degree of effectiveness by most people. But using queuing theory as a format for modeling interarrival times of student reports leaves much to be desired (a cannon to kill a fly). Conversely, a yardstick with one-eighth inch markings is far more effective as a "measurement instrument" than only using an object of known length (11-inch side of a sheet of paper).

A precise measuring instrument or a highly validated technique or model will usually require less data, but lack of precision or validity does not mean an equivalent increase in or sensitivity of data to be collected. Each physical measuring device and most mathematical models include indicators of precision, accuracy, and/or validity, which permit fairly good estimates of appropriate or optimum amount of data to collect. Many instruments (attitude survey, cost estimate) and formats (benefit/cost model, heuristic computer simulation) do not have "satisfactory" evaluations comparable to those in the physical world.

Evaluating instruments, formats, techniques, and models useful in P&D can involve several methods. The first evaluation method is empirical. Determine the difference between what the instrument produced and the measures (even subjective) that were previously considered satisfactory. Determine the percent difference from the earlier base, and aggregate the percentage differences into mean and variance data.

A second method is experimental. Use subjects to develop, for example, layouts for a variety of problems and compare their average results (handling costs, time to arrive at solution) with those produced by one or more computer layout algorithms. A panel of experts could make a blind assessment or grading of the layouts.[41]

A third method uses criteria that permit each instrument to be evaluated individually. Some criteria prepared initially for evaluating situation-specific models appear useful, as shown in Table 15-1.

A fourth method draws on a paradigm used to evaluate a case study of a model.

The urban dynamics model was examined from three points

Table 15-1 Criteria for Evaluating Models*

Criteria		Describer
1	Relevancy	Does the model describe the policy context?†
2	Distortion	Is there a bias between the model and reference system?
3	Structural integrity	Is the model design based on internally consistent principles?
4	Reproducibility	What is the model's "track record" for replicating historical data?
5	Tractability	Is the model easily utilized?
6	Accessibility	Are the model's input and output familiar and intelligible?
7	Flexibility	Is the model design capable of undergoing change?
8	Common sense	Are the model's forecasted results offensive to basic intuition?
9	Credibility	Is there consonance between the model builder and the policymakers?
10	Efficiency	What are the costs associated with operating the model?

* From O. P. Hall, Jr., "A Policy Model Appraisal Paradigm," *Policy Sciences*, Vol. 6, No. 2, June 1975, pp. 185–195.
† Author's note: This is a vague question, not keyed to necessary purposes and hierarchy.

of view. First, the model's policy perspective was analyzed to determine what policy problems the model purports to deal with. Second, the adequacy of the model's theoretical support was examined. In this in-principle examination, the basic question was: How well are the supporting theory and concepts of the model buttressed by relevant research? Third, the model's capability to deal with policy problems in-practice was explored to determine how well the model as a whole tied together theory, assumptions, and data to deal with real-world policy problems.

The model's policy perspective [was examined by] a comparative analysis . . . of what urban dynamics and [15] other urban simulation models offer from a policy-making point of view. . . . The comparative analysis concluded that urban dynamics provides a perspective for the study of urban policy problems different from that of previously developed models. . . . The in-principle examination . . . reviewed and evaluated prior research related to the model [on the basis of] seven research tasks. . . . Serious deficiencies were found in the supporting research for the model. . . .

The in-practice examination . . . tested the capability of the model to represent a specific city [Washington, D.C.] and to deal with an actual policy problem [housing], for that city. The in-practice examination emphatically refuted the idea that the urban dynamics model has utility as a tool for policy studies related to a specific urban area.[42]

A final method would be after the fact, to assess the utility of the instrument/format to the key decision makers/administrators. Several factors could be considered: "complexity of system being modelled, saliency of policy area addressed, organizational relationship of modelling effort to policymakers, and quality of modelling staff; all suggest practical measures that can reduce the gap between models and policymakers."[43]

The "amount" characteristic seeks to keep collected (recorded, studied, etc.) and modeled I&K to a minimum for progress toward an effective and innovative implemented solution. The "beauty" of all the data and models that might be generated is superfluous. Achieving this minimum, however, depends on at least two other factors:

The amount of I&K already available in the organization for usual operating and supervising purposes. An organization that does not have, for example, data on costs, time, and outputs per hour operation of a milling machine (or computer or farmspraying airplane) is hard put to estimate (if needed) the costs of a possible P&D alternative using the equipment. A lot of data would then be collected during the project. Such data should be available just to operate and supervise existing systems. Or an organization that does not ordinarily or systematically learn about new technology or techniques or governmental actions will need to collect at various points during a P&D project much more I&K than those which do.

The organizational climate that encourages or discourages people to contribute the vast amount of I&K available in their minds. The attitudes and style of management greatly influence the retrievability of this I&K. One utility company, for example, decided that the work of constructing steel tower transmission lines was insufficiently productive.

Therefore, an extensive work measurement program was instituted . . . and a massive quantitative time data base was . . . available. . . . The time values were invariably tighter than those which had previously been used based on historical data. This resulted at first in bitter opposition to the use of measured data and all the usual sabotage attempts against such a program were evident. . . . [The management, however,] adopted the attitude of saying to the people concerned that while the measurements taken would not be forced upon them, the concept [purpose] of establishing and making commitments to [results] would not be abandoned. . . . [The workers themselves set] what they considered to be reasonable, realistic and attainable targets, . . . and they felt the need to justify their performance. . . . Gradually the target time per assignment became increasingly tighter, to the extent that now a frequent reason given for non-use of the measured day data bank is that the times are too loose.

Even in this illustration, much less data would have been collected and a potentially explosive situation avoided if management had treated the initial problem as a P&D project (to focus on purpose and involvement much earlier). Fortunately, a good management attitude existed. Imagine what would have happened if the initial measurements were treated as accurate or if management had had the attitude that it was their right to establish measures.

TRANSMITTAL OF INFORMATION

For non-project-specific I&K to have any utility at all, it must be conveniently available to almost everyone. No one person can "know" all the I&K, and providing accessibility and transmittability is not an easy matter. Consider as an example the I&K needs in the design of computer hardware only. New I&K areas in addition to physics, electrical engineering, heat transfer, materials sciences, and structures, are becoming relevant. In the field of chemistry, "a biological crystal computer [is being developed] out of something like DNA, which has a genetic memory of 10^{10} bits of information and is programmed to rebuild itself from its own chemical storage to accomodate new experiences." In the field of pattern recognition, work is being done "to develop visual processing and speech inputs that can lead to computers that provide access to incredibly wide worlds of information, along with instructions on how to best use this information in a particular circumstance."[44]

How does I&K that is made available influence its use or nonuse, and how does the need of the user influence how the I&K should be made available? Several factors in the overall scheme of establishing channels for transmitting P&D-related I&K are reviewed briefly to answer these questions:

a Generation The sources of I&K are numerous—basic research, R&D activities, exemplary practices, raw data about operations, analytical or extracted summaries, and the files of an organization. What constitutes the source of I&K depends on the level or point of perspective. A scientific paper is the "end" for a researcher, but may be one of several "raw data" items for a P&D professional and may not be of any concern at all to the manager. Journals and magazines are the usual first point of transmittal of I&K generated at any source.[45]

b Data Bases These are compilations of related discipline-specific I&K, regardless of how generated. The major difficulty involves developing a hierarchical or structural format or taxonomy that portrays all of the interconnections among the items. Extracting summaries and developing syntheses (principles, models, performance rates, etc.) of the data are thus crucial for setting up a data base, but portraying all the interconnections in any realm at all is almost impossible. Almost all data bases therefore require some sort of search intermediary, a person who knows how to interact with the usual online computer base when a particular need or purpose is identified. A data base facilitates the sharing of data, provides timely data, and is relatively easy to update. Most data bases incorporate I&K *in* specific content areas, sometimes in a format to help P&D in a very specific field.[46]

A significant "data base" is people. The managers, technical personnel, researchers, analysts, secretaries, vendors, and librarians are excellent data bases.

c Information Systems This term has many meanings, just as the term *production systems* would. Many information systems can exist in an organization. Many are now computer-based, but many are and will remain manual. Computer-based systems usually involve I&K that is synthesized from several sources, usually as a data "production" system. An information system involves users who want certain types of I&K, usually right away, in normal work activities. A certain form of presentation is usually desired. Information systems usually involve quite formal authorization requirements and confidentiality protections.

Topics of concern are wide ranging: finance, production performance, inventory levels, payrolls, citizen attitudes, medical records, marketing, personnel, computer aided manufacturing, order analysis, warranties, R&D, follow-up on impact of treatment on patients, competitive intelligence, and so forth. The possible manipulations of I&K differ in complexity: retrieve an item or two of data, manipulate several I&K items, present results of calculations and aggregations, produce hard "copy" (checks, invoices, sales reports, etc.), estimate times/costs/operating characteristics of several proposed alternatives, propose some alternative solutions within a preset (usually quite constrained) frame of reference,[47] and so forth.

A whole range of information-handling and word-processing devices are becoming available to help automate information systems, such as text handling systems, intelligent typewriters, interactive terminals, electronic mail, teleconferencing, graphics terminals.

d Decision Support Systems Estimating characteristics of alternatives and proposing some solutions,

making decisions in relatively standard situations, developing specifications for different sizes of transformers ordered, and issuing titles and licenses for a state motor vehicle department are decision support systems (DSS). Large amounts of I&K and short time response are involved. Graphics, small terminals, individual microcomputers, "natural" interactive inquiry capabilities, and tie-ins to cable TV and telephone satellite communications are technical advances used in DSS. The user/P&D professional/decision maker's insights, style, and judgments are integral, shaping the types of predictive guidelines to include, the nature of questions posed, and the resulting communications output. A DSS accommodates the individual's or small group's assumptions and "myths" about how the specific organization "works."[48] A variety of data bases is usually available to be used as a basis for increasing the scope of questions that might be raised. A DSS is also organized to monitor the user/decision maker to suggest update needs. Figure 15-6 illustrates how a decision support system can portray the information flows and interconnections with other data sources in an organization.

e Artificial Intelligence (AI) This research seeks to discover and understand the basic processes of "intelligent behavior." Applications focus on developing computer systems to display this behavior in specific situations (diagnosis, synthesis of a particular area of physical research, mathematical theorem proving, etc.). AI has the potential for stating a problem-solving method, primarily a total search of a well-defined solution space, for representing facts, actions, and judgmental conditions so other components of the AI system can use them, and for perceiving useful I&K from spoken and written natural languages. An early development may be a system that handles some of the secondary purposeful activities (see Chapter Four). Since these occur frequently during a P&D project, they are excellent AI candidates to *help transmit* I&K (computer-*aided* design), but hardly to do P&D. Currently, quite minimal associations and causal and physical phenomena are incorporated in decision tree, algorithmic, search, and heuristic computer programs. Significant advances will be slow to occur, if they occur at all, because of the inability to treat I&K in its total context. I&K items are not bricks.

f Internalizing I&K Transmitting I&K should develop people's abilities so they can use the I&K "regularly." Actual use of I&K learned by rote is highly unlikely to take place in "a form similar to that in which it was presented for learning." Meaningful

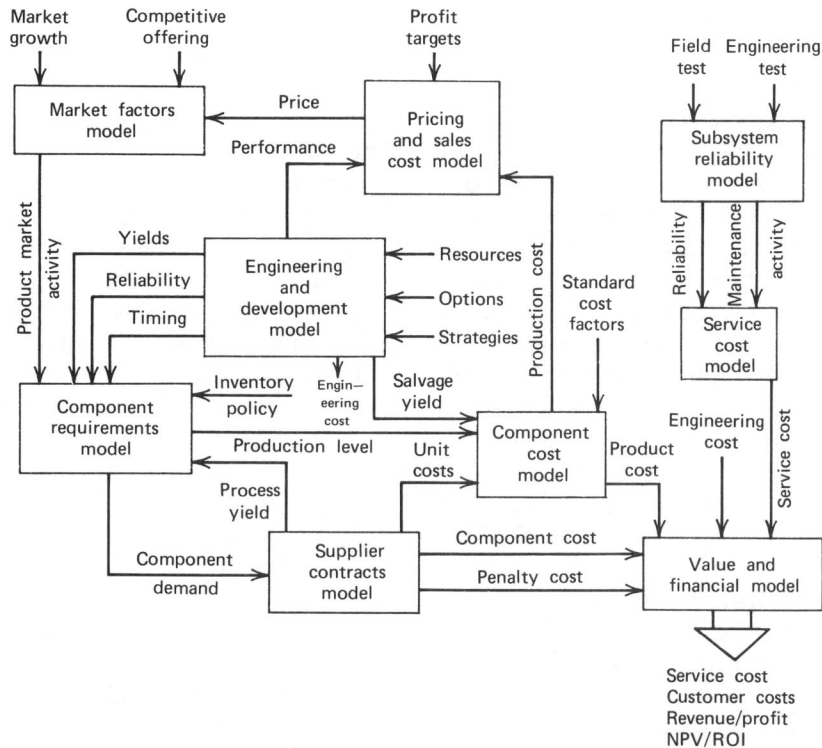

Figure 15-6 Information flow relationships for new product planning. From R. G. Hudson, J. C. Chambers, and R. G. Johnston, "New Product Planning Decisions under Uncertainty," *Interfaces*, Vol. 8, No. 1 (Part 2), November 1977, p. 90.

learning, or forming linkages of the new I&K to one or more elements of a person's conceptual framework, is likely to enable a person to explore possible uses. Rote learning, although needed on occasion, seldom motivates the "affective responses associated with learning."[49]

Letting the P&D approach raise the questions for which I&K is needed establishes the mental associations to which I&K is much more likely to be linked. Each person also has a particular learning style that can help determine what form is better. Thus, various types of learning/teaching materials may be necessary for transmitting I&K "internally"—workbooks, lecture courses, abstract of reports, newsletters, discussion/problem-oriented course, retrieval systems, conferences, executive summaries, seminars, briefing sessions, programmed learning, interactive simulation, field trips, press reports, technical reports, direct mailings, informal telephone calls, slides, movies, television, phonographs, tapes, or reading and problem assignments from journals, reports, testimony, and books. Emphasizing the relationship of P&D need to the I&K that is internalized is advantageous: "Education with inert ideas is not only useless: it is, above all things, harmful, . . . [a] horrible burden . . ."[50]

g P&D of Situation-Specific Transmittal Channels Several Axioms and Propositions pertain here: each I&K transmittal situation is unique; do not attempt to transfer a solution from somewhere else; and real-world people must have their perceptions change through constant interaction with P&D personnel. These apply mainly to items (c), (d), (e), and even (f), just discussed. Items (a) and (b) are very often national or regional resources. Using PDA for each specific situation provides many opportunities to question people's assumptions by means of the purpose expansion, to be creative in Phase 2, and so on. This helps to determine if the I&K is really needed, to let people learn, to minimize the risks of poor effects on the entity affected by the P&D results, and to maximize the benefit/cost and degree of satisfaction among those involved.

Surveys of people seeking specific I&K *in* locus content areas show that informality is likely to be preferred. For example, "ten different ways of getting information about new materials and possibilities for their use were listed [by] respondents . . . in order of perceived value to them: . . . colleagues, conferences, exhibitions, government information services, internal company channels, journals, newspapers, patent specifications, television, visiting representatives from other companies."[51]

I&K *IN* LOCUS CONTENT AREAS

First, a warning about this section is necessary. The amount of I&K *in* locus content areas is so huge that even classifying it is an almost impossible task (consider the great difficulties in the Library of Congress schema). Also, having access to all I&K items that would fit into an assumed perfect classification *is* impossible (consider the enormous number of studies, reports and projects in individual companies, agencies, and organizations, which are available somewhere "out there".) People in P&D must recognize that I&K *in* locus content areas constitutes the overwhelming bulk of all I&K, and there is no way all of it can fit easily into or be characterized by any structure.

I&K *in* each locus content area at a particular point in time is under the influence of and being assaulted by several factors. First is the continual attempt to find information, techniques, theories and models that are parsimonious (simple, economical, fewer but broader generalizations, etc.). Second is the evolutionary nature of I&K. Even "hard" data or "facts" about stainless steel, for example, may be inappropriate tomorrow. Third is that nothing more should be expected from a given item than what is stated. Analogous ideas, predictions, and extrapolations are human acts, not part of the item. Fourth is the contextual nature of any item. No I&K item is free of a value base or set of metaphysical assumptions.

Ways of Connoting I&K *in* Locus Content Areas

What is a locus content area? Different P&D professions (architecture, civil engineering, career guidance), technologies (food, energy, defense, construction/housing), nontechnical fields (literature, history, culture, semantics, art), similar and combination fields (e.g., "the Scholar's Market lists 847 journals of literary history and criticism alone, . . . half of them founded since 1960"[52]), and so on. Consider a very small sampling of journals from the 700-page, 8½- by 11-inch, small-type listing of volumes of the library at the University of Wisconsin at Madison: *The Journal of Cuneiform Studies, Medieval Scandinavia, The 14th Century English Mystics Newsletter, The Germanic Review, History of Education Quarterly, Journal of Medieval and Renaissance Studies, Mathematics of Operations Research, A/E Concepts in Wood Design, Datamation, Rheology, Machine Design, Footnotes to the Future, Bytes, Cybernetics and Control, Journal of Architectural Research, Educational Technology* . . .

There are so many ways of describing I&K *in* locus content areas that Table 15-2 serves only as an initial stimulator of possible sources a P&D group might review. The enormity of the amounts of I&K *in* locus content areas should literally overwhelm a person, since it is patently obvious that no one person can know everything.

Emphasizing the enormity of I&K *in* locus content areas serves two purposes. First, a person can always learn about new techniques/theories/models/information, and should keep alert about the wide range of available I&K. This will provide insight into where details could be obtained from resources and experts. Second, all fields, disciplines, substantive matters, or content areas are potential contributors to a particular project. The more one keeps away from classifying a project as "just" structures, or "just" transportation, or "just" mathematical programming, or "just" rural development, the more one will be able to consider diverse bodies of knowledge as potential sources of creative ideas and details.

In what form can the particular I&K *in* a particular locus content area be found? Everyone is familiar with several of the usual and overlapping modes:

Checklists	Models
Principles	Theories
Data bases	Proceedings of conferences
Journals	
Textbooks	Fact Sheets
Microfiche or holofiche (holofiche contains 200,000 times as much information as the same volume of punched cards)	Research project paper
	Taxonomies or typologies
	Newsletter of abstracts
	Computer storage
	Library reference desk
	Experts

Availability of I&K *in* Locus Content Areas

The I&K *in* a specific locus content area may be difficult to locate. Some I&K may appear in the very large number of specialized handbooks, magazines, (*Iron Age, Datamation*), and newspapers (*Women's Wear Daily*). There are also many generally little-known sources for obtaining needed I&K.

Fortunately, agencies and organizations seek constantly to disseminate, diffuse, and interpret the I&K they develop. Most government agencies awarding grants require some dissemination procedures. Some of the sources from which I&K of all types might be obtained are listed in Table 15-3.

The interest is so great in making I&K available as quickly and completely as possible that organizations

Table 15-2 A Few Ways of Describing I&K *in* Locus
Content Areas

1 List of journals and publications (see text, and Table
15-3)
2 Basic disciplines
(a) See Figure 15-2
(b) Literature, history, culture, semantics, art
(c) Mathematics, science, philosophy, history,
humanities
(d) Professional fields
3 Subdivisions of basic disciplines
Example: mathematics: calculus, statistics, topography,
etc.
4 Subdivisions of each P&D profession (see Table 4-5)
5 Specific topics not wholly in a discipline or subdivision
(a) Organization de-   (i) Paints
velopment   (j) Welfare recipients
(b) Colonic diseases   (k) Abilities of twins
(c) Academically   (l) Parasite control
gifted students   (m) Steel
(d) Appropriate   (n) Flowers
technology   (o) Tax laws
(e) Logic chips   (p) Roofing
(f) Single-parent   (q) Arithmetic ability
families   (r) Advanced technol-
(g) Space capsules   ogy*
(h) Moon rocks   And so on
6 Synthesis of disciplines to focus on specific area or problem
(a) Improve reading ability of children, not just cognition or phonics research
(b) Develop long-range plans for public television, not
just past programming and citizen's interest
(c) Design a gear for a drive shaft, not just mechanics of
forces and materials, but also lubrication, manufacturing process, and group technology
(d) Improve the quality of working life, not just results
of worker production experiments, economics of
supply of materials, replacement patterns of customers, etc.
7 Categories in specific organizations:
Budget, equipment performance capabilities, standard
costs, market patterns, personnel attitudes, contingency
events, competition, political environment, management
style
8 Department of Labor *Dictionary of Occupational Titles*
(3rd ed., 1965), 21,741 in all
9 Taxonomies (a tree structure or system pyramid)
(a) *Illustration:* Environmental policy and management, subtopics of ecosystems, resources, environmental deterioration, elements of ecomanagement, and social bases for ecomanagement† or the
three initial categories (and subcategories) of access
(b) *Illustration:* Impact of buildings on the health and
lives of people: Researchers (monitoring, retrieval,
processing, service), practitioners, (translation, dissemination, service) and systems planners (aug-
mentations, synthesis, and management)

* See, for example, *Science*, Vol. 208, May 23, 1980.
† J. Mayda, "Lawyers and Ecomanagement," *Louisiana
Law Review*, Vol. 34, No. 5, 1974.

publish compilations of other publications in certain
fields. One service publishes a *Science Citation Index*
and set of *Current Contents* (listings of the tables of
content of journals in a particular field such as social or
biological sciences). Another publishes a newsletter
reviewing available I&K on a topic (e.g., types of
computers in use in various countries of the world).

Given the need for I&K *in* a specific locus content
area, a person can take another form of action. Three
to five letters or calls to people in libraries, universities, research labs, government agencies, companies,
and the like should provide fairly rapid convergence on
the major sources to contact or explore.

Comments about I&K *in* Locus Content Areas

New I&K in *Locus Content Areas*
Is Being Developed Daily

Researchers, managers, workers, and "backroom"
inventors (e.g., the person who developed the 84-
miles-per-gallon auto engine demonstrated in 1979) are
just a few of the generators of I&K. Many P&D projects and techniques also produce new I&K *in* a locus
content area (Appendix B). An activity sampling
study, for example, for determining the percent of time
nurses spend on achieving certain functions will produce previously unavailable I&K *in* the locus content
area of nursing and patient care units of that hospital.
There is so much new I&K *in* locus content areas that
it is not unusual to have clients/users/customers ask a
P&D professional about a development before the
professional has even heard about it.

Any Content Area May Be Needed in a P&D Project

Do not decide too early in a project that it needs, say,
only materials-handling I&K. A project should remain
very flexible regarding posssible I&K sources, especially through Phases 1, 2, and 3 of the strategy. This
is not completely possible; for example, an architect
is not likely to be retained for a computer information
system project that will call on the I&K *in* social welfare work.

Value-free "Facts" Are a Myth

The so-called "fact" of I&K emerges from a contextual and value-laden perspective. If a few of the conditions or metaphysical assumptions could be changed, a
different interpretation of the "fact" would emerge.
This concept is so fundamental to all I&K that even a
basic or "hard" content area (for example, yield
strength of a certain grade of steel) requires the P&D
professional to use hefty "factors of safety" to overcome the contextual I&K item.

Table 15-3 Some Sources of I&K *in* Locus Content Areas

NASA (National Aeronautics and Space Administration) Industrial Applications Centers—Universities of Connecticut, Pittsburgh, Indiana, New Mexico, and Southern California; Research Triangle Park, North Carolina

OECD (Organization for Economic Cooperation and Development)—Publications office; various books and periodicals on 17 world economy and related subjects

NTIS (National Technical Information Service of the U.S. Dept. of Commerce)—Abstracts, newsletters reporting government-sponsored research and development, reported in 26 different weekly issues, in topic areas such as agriculture and food, building industry technology, chemistry, electrotechnology, medicine and biology, natural resources and earth sciences, physics, and transportation

ERIC Centers (Education Research and Information Centers)—At several universities, each one for a particular I&K field (e.g. higher education, counselling and personnel services, languages and linguistics)

National Library of Medicine—Several automated information retrieval systems for medical care; characterized as ''electronic handbooks''

NSF Centers (National Science Foundation)—For specific technological areas (materials, thermodynamics, controls) and particular models/techniques: chemical engineering models at University of Houston, Design Research Center at Carnegie-Mellon University, mathematics education processes at Education Development Center in Newton, Massachusetts, continuing education in specific engineering topics through Project PROCEED at Massachusetts Institute of Technology

Professional societies and trade associations—Business/trade periodicals: *Wall Street Journal, Journal of Comparative Psychology, Investment Surveys, Medical Economics, Printer's Inc., Management Science, Industrial Marketing,* annual reports and so on.

Intensive computer and heuristic models—Human skeletal movements, finite analysis for structures, for example

U.S. Patent Office

Information synthesis and data files—e.g., The World Future Society has a *Guide to Information Sources* as well as listings of books, cassettes, games, and learning materials in *The Future: A Catalog of Resources*; The Research and Development Interpretation Service of the National Institute of Education publishes synthesis volumes such as *Research within Reach: For Reading Educators*; The National Center for Health Services Research publishes *Announcement*, a bimonthly journal on its research activities; private firms publish newsletters on specific technological subjects

Other government agencies—Trade with China in Department of Commerce, wind machine technology in Department of Energy, Bill Status Office in U.S. Congress, cost-of-living information, locations for retirement, and conservation policies at Department of Interior

Table 15-3 *(Continued)*

Handbooks, thesaurus on particular topics (hopefully *user-*oriented), looseleaf notebooks on specific topics such as taxes, and so on

Specific organization or company computer-aided design data bases (e.g., highway and bridge, water treatment, building structures, automated assembly, electronic layout)

Proceedings of conferences and seminars of all professional societies, research agencies, universities, thinktanks, and so on

Vendors

Customers

Consultants, technical staff, research and development department

Unpublished reports in the organization

Great Care Must Be Exercised in Using Any Item of I&K in a Locus Content Area as a Predictor

Most of the mistakes in P&D occur here. P&D may neglect opportunities because the ''facts'' say it can't be done, or decide on an inappropriate action because of what the ''facts'' predict. This is not to say one should not search for I&K that others may claim are indicators (if not predictors) of the future: resources for the 1980s, consumer attitudes in the 1980s, innovation management to grow from within, the future of lasers in manufacturing computer control of inventories, and so on. Learning about these I&K items is good but they are certainly not predictors of what a *particular* solution ought to concern (Axiom 7).

Many Experts on I&K in a Particular Locus Content Area Will Need to Be Consulted in Relation to any P&D Project

The emphasis is on *consulted*. They have available in their heads a set of specific items of I&K *in* a particular locus content area, organized within their context and value set which may not at all coincide with the needs of the P&D project. The expert may even be aware of these limitations, but use this knowledge of imperfection to justify a personal interpretation: After all, the I&K is imperfect, so trust me as an expert to know what to do.

I&K in Interdisciplinary Content Areas Is Relatively Unavailable

Nor is it likely to become available in reasonable form very soon. For example, I&K available in many content areas (group processes, curriculum structure, topic content, learning styles of children, teaching methods) might be involved in the P&D of a program for academically motivated students, but the content areas' interactions or interdisciplinary relationships may be unknown. Perhaps that is why P&D is a major purposeful activity. Developing solutions depends on getting people to perceive what needs to be done.

I&K in Locus Content Areas Is, to a Great Extent, in the Heads of People

Many people in an organization keep abreast of developments in their fields, and will often know about new I&K. An expert may still be needed for detailing. What the people know may be better because it will most likely be contextually interrelated rather than just an item of I&K.

I&K in Locus Content Areas is Almost Always in the Wrong Form for Use in P&D

Its structure is usually descriptive or comparative rather than predictive or normative, its stability static rather than dynamic. It may be difficult to communicate, may not fit exactly in the current schema in people's minds, may not be "try-able," may lack divisibility, meaning that parts cannot be applied one at a time, and it may not have achieved the relative advantage of reaching a level of maturity suitable for the prospective user.[53] Most I&K in locus content areas will not be in a form suitable for use in P&D because those who develop I&K are researchers whose purpose is not P&D. They assume that, once an item of I&K is available, its application is easy (the unstated assumption). Every P&D professional should restate each I&K item in a locus content area that might be applicable or useful to provide some indication of the consequences of utilizing it in a design specification.

I&K IN PLANNING AND DESIGN

Each P&D profession revolves around I&K in P&D it has found useful in the past. Articles typically refine I&K previously available—relax a mathematical constraint, increase precision or sensitivity, change the viewpoint from which modeling is done, improve accuracy or robustness, add a different symbol for further details, sharpen a measuring device, change the form of a question or two for an interview or in a questionnaire, and so on. The I&K item is often presented as if the technique or model alone is all that is needed in a P&D effort. (This assumption has gone so far that people are now doing research on and investigating why the models are not being implemented.

They fail to ask the basic question, should the model or technique have even been used at all?)

The total P&D approach governs when, why, how, by whom, where, and if a technique/model/piece of information in P&D should be used. Little space need be devoted to assessing the worth of one technique versus that of another (a current thrust of much literature) because even an imprecise technique is likely to be worthwhile in several circumstances. Research to develop more accurate and precise techniques/models is, of course, desirable to make these techniques and models more readily available.

Table 10-1 presented a panorama of the P&D system to indicate the range of actions and decisions that are needed in a total approach. Appendix A presents a range of techniques/models in P&D that can aid in the actions and decisions. They are also listed in the appropriate cells describing the P&D system. The question of how, for example, to select people for inputs to P&D, is partially answered by selecting one or more of the techniques listed in the appropriate cells for the input element. Or it is possible to review the list of purposes to identify techniques that may appear reasonable.

Anyone perusing the techniques/models in Appendix A is likely to discover that one or two "favorite" techniques are not included. Just add them. No claim for inclusiveness is made for Appendix A. It only tries to cover a wide range of possibilities to make one aware of potentialities.

Comments about I&K in P&D

A few major comments about this topic are in order because Appendix A only records techniques and models without commentary regarding using the I&K in P&D efforts.

I&K in P&D Helps in the Many Decision-Making Steps of the Strategy

Figure 11-9 shows 19 steps. Each step involves three parts to make a decision. Different techniques, models, and information in P&D can aid each part. The technique useful in generating alternative purposes may not be as effective as another for generating alternative regularity conditions. A tool for organizing alternative project protocols may not be as desirable as another for organizing alternative components needing details. And a model for selecting the best alternative purpose level may not be as effective as another for selecting the best alternative installation plans. More than one technique/model/tool is available for each part of each step (see Appendix A).

Most of the I&K Needed in P&D Relate to the Secondary Purposeful Activities

Table 3-9 details the strategy for each of them. The secondary purposeful activities recur throughout a P&D project, relying, interestingly, on the various roles of a P&D professional (Chapter Fourteen). For example, *maintain a standard* requires a measurer's role and techniques, *resolve a conflict* requires a negotiator's role and tools, *develop creative ideas* requires a stimulator's role and skills, and so on.

Simple Techniques/Models Are Likely to Be All That Are Needed

Parsimonious tools are likely to be understood and appreciated by those affected by P&D. For the few times something more complex is needed (e.g., computer simulation, control methods, statistical sampling, questionnaire, forecasts, performance measurements), the techniques should be explained in terms of the assumptions underlying its use (purpose, results, methods, etc.). This allows everyone to put its conclusions or specifications into proper perspective. Such understanding, rather than its "beauty" to the professional, will aid toward eventual implementation. The incremental benefits of a model or technique should be assessed against the benefits of using judgment and experience.

Since decision-making techniques are most frequently used, I usually offer a simple explanation to a group based on the decision worksheet of Figure 15-7. It does not deal with probabilities of occurrence nor with future states of nature. Go–no go and threshold criteria are evaluated previously, and only combination criteria beyond threshold levels are included, along with continuous ones. Chapter Twelve reviewed scaling methods for determining pay offs or cost of a criterion for an alternative. Questions about more complex risks, costs, dependency of the criteria on each other, trade-offs and probabilities will require additional sophistication.[54] For example, each alternative column could be divided into several subcolumns to reflect different probabilities or risks. Other decision tools could be used, such as optimization modeling, multiattribute utility assessment, Bayesian combination of judgments, decision trees, or simulation.

An even simpler decision process stems from "per-

Table 15-4 Questions for Evaluating Each Possible Course of Action*

1 Does the course of action you plan to follow seem logical and reasonable? Never mind what anyone else has to say. Does it make sense to you? If it does, it is probably right.

2 Does it pass the test of sportsmanship? In other words, if everyone followed this same course of action, would the results be beneficial for all?

3 Where will your plan of action lead? How will it affect others? What will it do to you?

4 Will you think well of yourself when you look back at what you have done?

5 Try to separate yourself from the problem. Pretend, for one moment, it is the problem of the person you most admire. Ask yourself how that person would handle it.

6 Hold up the final decision to the glaring light of publicity. Would you want your family and friends to know what you have done? The decisions we make in the hope that no one will find out are usually wrong.

* Distilled version of Harry Emerson Fosdick's six-point test for telling right from wrong. The author of distilled questions is unknown.

Scales of value (criteria) (Those that remain after "no-go" and below threshold level ones are eliminated)

		Alternatives						
	Weight	1	2	3	4	5	6	7
1	3							
2	1							
3	2							
4	1½							
5	4							
6	1							
	Total							

Figure 15-7 Decision worksheet.

sonal help'' prescriptions. Table 15-4 illustrates one of these. The questions are adaptable to a P&D situation and allow each alternative to be assessed on its own merits. Simple techniques are good because many decision makers are happier with descriptive rather than numerical assessments of judgments, measurements, probabilities, and utilities. Setting up word scales is simpler and can be translated into a numerical scale if more detail is necessary or calculations need to be made. For example, the word scale of *not at all likely to occur, not very likely to occur, not likely, may be as likely as not, likely, very likely,* and *almost always likely* may be very easy for a person to use. It can be translated *if needed* into numerical values of 10, 25, 40, 50, 60, 75, and 90.

Computer Technology Is Providing Significant Assistance

Computers (and programmable calculators) make available a wide range of aids for I&K *in* P&D:

Layouts and space representations
Computer-aided drafting
Partitioning
Micro and Macrosimulations
Risk and cost compilations
Computer graphics and visualizations
Digitizing photographs
Automated data path design
Mathematical programming
Network formulation and review

Design verification (with standards) and documentation
Interfaces with data bases for I&K *in* content areas (e.g., engineering, architecture)
Interactive displays, graphics, routings, and scheduling
Fault-tree assessment
Hierarchical modeling
Project control management and scheduling
Three-dimensional representation of motions of human limbs as various actions take place and forces are applied.

Many specialized computer aids are developed within these categories for specific fields or locus content areas: linear programming in chemical processing, partitioning in building physical systems, optimization of electronic circuits, simulation of power system networks, cost minimization of transformer design specifications, fault-tree assessment of nuclear control structures, and hierarchical modelling of urban spaces. Many computer-aided design techniques are interactive, to allow people involved with the projects to take some part in the technical aspects of developing P&D specifications. Quite valuable to a project is the rather quick response to the ''what if'' type of questions many people ask.

The key words are *aids* and *assistance*. Even for the areas mentioned above, computerization is often viewed as a mixed blessing at best and downright debilitating at worst.[55]

I&K in P&D Serves as a Communication Mechanism within the P&D World and between Real-World People and P&D People

Communications within the P&D world are far too often concerned with impressing professional colleagues, causing unnecessary and complicated techniques to be used. Simple tools are better for both professional exchanges and for exchanges between RW and P&D worlds. Technical needs constitute the basic criterion for deciding whether or not to use complex techniques; the elitist view of professionals is not a good criterion, for it can destroy good opportunities for communicating, explaining, and helping to seek effective *and* implemented solutions. I&K *in* P&D should help all to ask questions, provide listening capability, exchange interpretations, activate creativity, initiate catharsis, and otherwise orchestrate and facilitate the flow of the total P&D approach—which is the essence of communication.

Purpose and Need within the Total P&D Approach Dictate What Amount, Type, and Accuracy of I&K in P&D to Obtain

A project would need to be well into Phase 3 or even 4 of the strategy before many frequently touted techniques/models *in* P&D might even be considered. Claiming, for example, that ''deterministic (fully determined . . . system behavior), moderate stochastic, severely stochastic (ill-defined . . . qualitative alternatives), and indeterminate (no causal relationships or heuristic)''[56] are archetypes of models sets in motion far too many restraining forces on a project. Even ''deterministic'' models do not remove uncertainties, whether they are conceptual or result from other factors in PDA. Field and laboratory studies are verifying the complex web of issues and factors that impact on technique usefulness.[57] The plausibility of accomplishing a purpose and need governs what kind of I&K *in* P&D is useful.

P&D TIMELINE PERSPECTIVES OF USING I&K

How to get a P&D effort from the inception of a project to the desired result while effectively utilizing all types of I&K is the role of the total P&D scenario. One objective of the scenario is to increase the probability that the people affected by the solution will support the recommendations because the I&K is believable, even though uncertainty or risk will still be associated with the I&K. Some timeline views of I&K ranging roughly over a comparatively short to a long time span include the items in the following discussion.

A. The Timeline Proposition (Figure 10-4) for Structuring a Theory of P&D for a Specific Effort

I&K needs will differ depending on the protocol stage and strategy step at which the project is located. Just review each of the I&K items listed for each step in Figure 15-1. As brilliant as a computer simulation model may be for Phase 3 in a project, it is not necessarily what is needed for Phases 4 and 5. As illuminating as a purpose hierarchy may be in leading a group to selecting the "right" problem in Phase 1, it is not what is needed for generating creative ideas in Phase 2 or selecting regularities in Phase 3. As necessary as the latest research on reading (or thermodynamics or electronics) may be in evaluating alternatives in Phase 4, many other I&K items *in* the locus content areas are critical in other phases.

In addition, the other four PDA factors and the broad concepts in the real world play a role in deciding what I&K is used at each step. The people involved, the organizational style and structure, the political and social milieu, and the number of open or nonspecified cells in the solution framework influence the choice. A particular manager, for example, may prefer questionnaire responses to interview responses in operating and supervising, and this is likely to carry over to P&D.

Chapter Twelve provides another theme. Focus on the purposes of the step, on what needs to be accomplished, and not on the technique or model or technology. The question is more important than the answer. Technology may be part of an answer, but avoid being hung up on *the* technological answer. The technology of fiber optics, for example, may be very promising, but it should not be the only technology to consider in developing possible solution ideas in Phase 2 of the P&D strategy.

A variety of I&K is needed at each step in almost all cases. The requisite variety can almost always be obtained by agreeing on what purpose the I&K is to achieve, getting started with a data collection technique or model building, and involving people and their ideas right away on the I&K purposes. This will also minimize the amount of formal data collection and provide greater assurance that whatever techniques/models are being used will be changed and adapted over time to fit up-to-date project needs. This can avoid the frequent embarrassment of completing a big data collection or model-building project that initially appeared to be needed but was found unnecessary after only 20 to 30% of the work was completed. Merely maintaining momentum should not be the reason for completing an I&K effort. Minimizing costs and time of information gathering is a continuing objective in the P&D timeline scenario. Acquiring "new" I&K is not necessarily beneficial,[58] as the PDA scenario portrays, and most decision makers do not seek new channels of I&K.[59]

B. The Timeline for the Transfer of I&K from Its Initial Development to its P&D Understanding and Use

It takes time for the huge amounts of I&K *in* a locus content area to find its way from, say, research through synthesis, diffusion and dissemination, normative guidelines, and demonstrations, to its use in P&D efforts and obtaining real world impacts and results. Several "filters" impose the criteria of feasibility, economics, motivation, incentives, history and psychology on the I&K. A technique or I&K item also tends to follow a life cycle similar to products: concept or idea, birth, growth or fad, leveling off, and decline or death. The cycle's length is highly variable. Some I&K items just don't make it.

The same time factors apply to I&K developed *in* or *of* P&D by case histories, raw and extracted data, or records of exemplary practices. The recursive nature of pursuing the P&D strategy also causes recursiveness in using I&K, so that necessary I&K should be adaptive. Because the passage of time is the key underpinning of recursion, new techniques can also be utilized later.

The timeline for transfer of I&K helps to explain why the development of "ideal" systems in Phase 2 of the P&D strategy is so valuable. When people are encouraged to be creative, they become willing to *search for* new I&K as opposed to waiting passively for it. The search is thus shortened when an approach to I&K is made from the users' side as portrayed, for instance, in a system matrix of the desired "ideal." This also takes advantage of the human proclivity to enjoy asking questions as they see it rather than being forced into someone else's data/information query format.

The I&K transfer timeline is also affected by the capacity of an organization to absorb and utilize it. A company processing basic metals has limited capacity to deal with laser beam technology, a developing country has limited or nonexistent resources that can exploit any but the most basic methods of farm management, and the small rural town in the United States has only minimal capability to adopt urban mass transportation ideas. "[In a] developing countr[y] [this] has led . . . to . . . appropriate technology, which has come to mean technology that is smaller in scale, more labor-intensive, more subject to local mastery, repair, and control, and more in ecological and cultural harmony with its surroundings than the technology that would likely be used in an analogous situation in the North. . . ."[60]

Countries and states as well as organizations exhibit different capacities to absorb and utilize I&K. For example, "in many areas, . . . there exist certain 'bellwether' jurisdictions consistently years ahead of all others. . . . Sweden is a particularly consistent and striking example of such a 'precursor' nation . . . in terms of experimentation with, and implementation of, public policy . . . in the domain of attitudinal and value changes. . . . Innovative diffusion . . . domestically [shows the same pattern by states]."[61]

C. The Timeline of People Committed to Finding/Forcing a Use of a Specific I&K Item

All types of I&K result from human invention or perception. How fast humans use I&K and how much of it they use are time-based phenomena.

Almost all P&D projects require a strong and committed sponsor, but this timeline perspective starts much in advance of obtaining such a commitment. Someone must be committed to a set of values seeking creation or restructuring of solutions, or to adoption of a particular solution, or to the knowledge-push perspective of a key principle *in* a locus content area (e.g., health care availability for all, powder metallurgy). By force of will, political position, persuasiveness, monetary backing, and/or aggressiveness, such a person can shorten the timeline to implemented solution. Such people, however, almost always believe the time for acceptance was too long.

What the person is committed to provides no intrinsic assurance that it is "good" or desirable (is the marketing effort to sell new appliance frills worthwhile?). It may be a result of the technological imperative (we know we can build space colonies for 100,000 people, so let's do it now). The technological imperative ("use our advanced farming methods") has already been shown to be a very poor practice in developing countries. The timeline can be shortened by commitment—and if a "good" is involved, it is worthwhile finding such a sponsor. Interestingly, the P&D approach could be followed to develop a system that "pushes" such a commitment, for PDA is far more likely than other approaches to show if the commitment is misplaced. An important test of the utility of (or misplaced confidence in) any I&K item is to put it into one or more other formats. Numerical mean and standard deviation values, for example, might be charted as a distribution "to see what it looks like," treated as a scenario description, and evaluated by examining the sensitivity of a cost prediction to the mean plus one standard deviation.

D. The Timeline of an Evolutionary Scale Dealing with Utility and Replacement of I&K Items

Everything about I&K is subject to human frailties: errors, cognition, learning without knowing, and evolution especially. Thus, one key aspect of using I&K *of* P&D, *in* P&D, and *in* locus content areas is that over "longer" periods of time (maybe every ten or so years), changes in all three categories will occur. Life-cycle stages (Chapters Seven, Ten, and Twelve) and format preferences affect I&K as well as the systems that process the I&K.[62]

I&K errors *in* locus content areas do occur now, and are due to omission, commission, or lack of understanding or perspective. But one does not know when an error exists. Consider the problem as stated for scientists and engineers, and one can grasp the magnitude of the problem for all the P&D professions: "Unfortunately, the . . . literature contains many erroneous values. Few scientists or engineers seem to have given much thought to the magnitude of the problem, and some probably regard every numerical entry in a handbook as revealed truth. Yet anyone who has had to seek a particular number in the literature and searched out a dozen or more reports, only to end up with a set of widely disparate values, comes to realize that a substantial intellectual effort and a considerable background in the field are needed to arrive at reliable figures."[63] If errors occur in what might be called such "hard" I&K *in* locus content areas, think of the even larger errors regarding I&K *in* other content areas, *in* P&D and *of* P&D (see Chapter Seventeen).

Cognition deals with the human's control of the mental processes. Individuals deal with a huge bombardment of stimuli, and the exercise of choice and integration of I&K provides a mechanism for coping. A human handles new I&K better or worse than others dependent on what I&K has already been learned by the individual. Association with previous referrents allows the new I&K to be retained. Another factor concerns "temporal integration [or] time-binding [for] integrating stimuli over time, ranging in scope from milliseconds to decades."[64] Consciously seeking new I&K that the human knows will be available in the next year or two and that a P&D project identifies as necessary is the best way of dealing with the inevitable changes in I&K.

I&K itself has an evolutionary scale. Any I&K items, "like individuals, have their histories, and are just as incapable of withstanding the ravages of time as are individuals."[65] The evolutionary process is obviously related to how and when humans change the currently established I&K. This process has many names—relearning, transitory learning, experimenting, paradigm shift—but the concept of evolution to a "higher" form, to match the biological idea, is basically sufficient to explain that any effective P&D professional thirty years from now will just naturally be operating at a bigger cognitive level than today or at least with a different I&K base. In addition, P&D professionals need to encourage changes in the education of new P&D professionals to fit continually changing I&K and to help students "push" the evolutionary process. Chapter Seventeen also discusses how education of P&D professionals needs drastic changes to accommodate what is already known and what will occur in the future in the use of I&K *of* P&D, *in* P&D, and *in* locus content areas.

SUMMARY

The huge amount of information and data available is overwhelming people, irrespective of the large number of attempts to classify, categorize, or otherwise synthesize all of it. Yet most information and knowledge (I&K) are poorly arranged for P&D usage. I&K can be put into three P&D groupings: I&K *of* P&D, I&K *in* P&D, and I&K *in* the locus content areas.

Proposition 12 *Knowledge, information, and models aggregate data that can be used cost-effectively in P&D if each aggregation includes statements about its relative inability to predict an occurrence or performance value of a future specific instance or case, emphasizes the importance of its integration with the other four P&D factors, and is presented with accuracy and precision values to reflect past and present conditions.*

I&K can be described in terms of characteristics: (A) Structure (raw data, descriptive, comparative, predictive, normative, presumptive); (B) stability; (C) incompatibility; (D) indeterminacy; (E) amount (in view of subjectivity, more is not necessarily better, purpose to be achieved, people affected should contribute I&K, documentation, and effectiveness of measurement formats).

Several representations are available to describe modes of transmitting I&K: source of generation, data bases, information systems, decision support systems, artificial intelligence, internalizing I&K, and using P&D to develop a situation-specific transmittal.

I&K *in* locus content areas is so huge in amount that classifying it is an almost impossible task. A locus content area is any disciplinary field, body of knowledge, or real-world concern of P&D. Many special compilations and retrieval systems are available in almost all locus content areas.

I&K needs and utilization vary with the step of the strategy. In addition, I&K itself will be different according to different stages of developing the timeline theory *of* P&D, different stages of its transfer from development to use, the interests of the people involved, and the evolutionary scale of utilization, utility, and replacement.

CHAPTER SIXTEEN

Arranging for Continuing Change and Improvement

P&D reflects human interest in changing and improving the social and physical conditions under which we live.

That raises a question: If humans have such a drive for bettering their lives and values, why is a separate factor on arranging for continuing change and improvement (ACCI) identified in the total P&D approach? Several reasons appear germane. First, a conflict arises between the long-term desire and willingness to better their values (ask anyone if they would like a specific improvement and they almost always say yes), and the short-term reluctance expressed by human realities (Chapter Five) to actually change. Continuing progress needs conscious arrangements. Second, the rate at which changes are implemented *by others* is increasing. Human control of the timing, structure, and beneficiaries of implementing changes needs conscious arrangements. People are willing to adopt changes they themselves help to develop. Third, whereas *future shock* denotes the impact of change on people when they are unaware of the location (the particular system or portion of life) and the timing of the change, conscious arrangements for the search for possible improvements provides understanding of what changes might occur so that future changes are no longer a shock. Fourth, although many ideas are available for plenty of changes, conscious arrangements to search for continuing change and improvement in a specific setting adds some assurance that an implemented change serves a "real" purpose and does better the conditions. Change for the sake of change alone is foolish.

The relationship between real-world and P&D-world people (Figure 16-1) illustrates the close interaction of ACCI in P&D with operating and supervising. The effectiveness of ACCI in P&D is, in effect, inextricably interwoven with the continuing change and improvement orientation of the organization regarding the other purposeful activities. If many "normal operating changes" occur, a favorable continuing change and improvement attitude prevails in operating and supervising the organization. If "new knowledge and technology" is viewed with excitement and as a possible opportunity, a favorable improvement attitude prevails toward learning in the organization. If research and development budget allocations continue to be made in poor as well as in good times, a favorable attitude prevails toward seeking new generalizations in the organization. If a disturbance elicits a prompt and steady unfurling of already prepared contingency plans or new solutions, a favorable attitude toward continuing change and improvement prevails in the organization.

Conversely, a good P&D effort in ACCI can be a

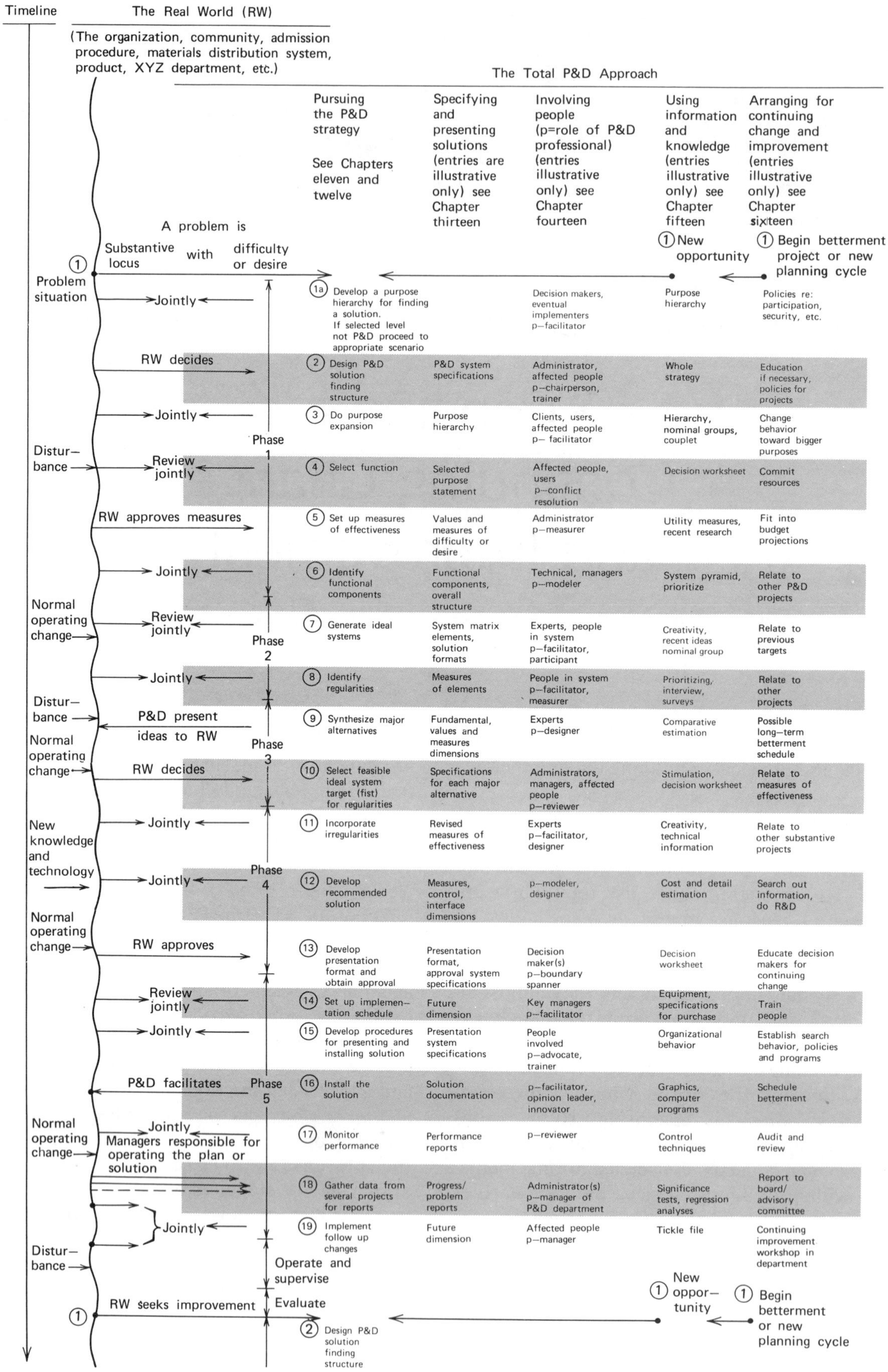

Figure 16-1 The planning and design scenario—feature 5.

Timeline | The Real World (RW)

(The organization, community, admission procedure, materials distribution system, product, XYZ department, etc.)

The Total P&D Approach

Step	The Real World (RW)	Pursuing the P&D strategy (See Chapters eleven and twelve)	Specifying and presenting solutions (entries are illustrative only) see Chapter thirteen	Involving people (p=role of P&D professional) (entries illustrative only) see Chapter fourteen	Using information and knowledge (entries illustrative only) see Chapter fifteen	Arranging for continuing change and improvement (entries illustrative only) see Chapter sixteen
① Problem situation	A problem is Substantive locus with difficulty or desire				① New opportunity	① Begin betterment project or new planning cycle
1a	Jointly	Develop a purpose hierarchy for finding a solution. If selected level not P&D proceed to appropriate scenario		Decision makers, eventual implementers p—facilitator	Purpose hierarchy	Policies re: participation, security, etc.
2	RW decides	Design P&D solution finding structure	P&D system specifications	Administrator, affected people p—chairperson, trainer	Whole strategy	Education if necessary, policies for projects
3	Jointly	Do purpose expansion	Purpose hierarchy	Clients, users, affected people p—facilitator	Hierarchy, nominal groups, couplet	Change behavior toward bigger purposes
4	Review jointly	Select function	Selected purpose statement	Affected people, users p—conflict resolution	Decision worksheet	Commit resources
5	RW approves measures	Set up measures of effectiveness	Values and measures of difficulty or desire	Administrator p—measurer	Utility measures, recent research	Fit into budget projections
6	Jointly	Identify functional components	Functional components, overall structure	Technical, managers p—modeler	System pyramid, prioritize	Relate to other P&D projects
7	Review jointly	Generate ideal systems	System matrix elements, solution formats	Experts, people in system p—facilitator, participant	Creativity, recent ideas nominal group	Relate to previous targets
8	Jointly	Identify regularities	Measures of elements	People in system p—facilitator, measurer	Prioritizing, interview, surveys	Relate to other projects
9	P&D present ideas to RW	Synthesize major alternatives	Fundamental, values and measures dimensions	Experts p—designer	Comparative estimation	Possible long-term betterment schedule
10	RW decides	Select feasible ideal system target (fist) for regularities	Specifications for each major alternative	Administrators, managers, affected people p—reviewer	Stimulation, decision worksheet	Relate to measures of effectiveness
11	Jointly	Incorporate irregularities	Revised measures of effectiveness	Experts p—facilitator, designer	Creativity, technical information	Relate to other substantive projects
12	Jointly	Develop recommended solution	Measures, control, interface dimensions	p—modeler, designer	Cost and detail estimation	Search out information, do R&D
13	RW approves	Develop presentation format and obtain approval	Presentation format, approval system specifications	Decision maker(s) p—boundary spanner	Decision worksheet	Educate decision makers for continuing change
14	Review jointly	Set up implementation schedule	Future dimension	Key managers p—facilitator	Equipment, specifications for purchase	Train people
15	Jointly	Develop procedures for presenting and installing solution	Presentation system specifications	People involved p—advocate, trainer	Organizational behavior	Establish search behavior, policies and programs
16	P&D facilitates	Install the solution	Solution documentation	p—facilitator, opinion leader, innovator	Graphics, computer programs	Schedule betterment
17	Jointly / Managers responsible for operating the plan or solution	Monitor performance	Performance reports	p—reviewer	Control techniques	Audit and review
18	Gather data from several projects for reports	Progress/problem reports	Administrator(s) p—manager of P&D department	Significance tests, regression analyses	Report to board/advisory committee
19	Jointly	Implement follow up changes	Future dimension	Affected people p—manager	Tickle file	Continuing improvement workshop in department

Phase 1, Phase 2, Phase 3, Phase 4, Phase 5

Timeline labels: Problem situation — Disturbance — Normal operating change — Disturbance — Normal operating change — New knowledge and technology — Normal operating change — Normal operating change — Normal operating change — Disturbance

Operate and supervise
Evaluate

① RW seeks improvement — ① New opportunity — ① Begin betterment or new planning cycle

② Design P&D solution finding structure

264

positive influence for getting the whole organization to ceaselessly question and adapt if it does not now exhibit this desirable characteristic.[1] The search for continuing changes emphasizes the inability to have perfect solutions and the desirability of using imperfections as opportunities for both stability and viability. ACCI concerns planning change in the implemented change. This concept should not be "added" after a solution is installed. It is insufficient at that time to say "we will just have to watch that solution and see if changes may appear." Developing a plan or solution that has the capability of self-modification is a major objective of P&D.

ACCI impacts on what some P&D solutions ought to "look like." They should initially state, for example, only essential specifications and let many of the details be determined by the people doing the work. This also improves the quality of involvement, keeps specification options open as long as possible, and makes implemented solutions more flexible.

Many organizations embody some aspects of ACCI in a long-range planning process. The most common version in corporations and other large-scale complex entities (e.g., university, public television, health planning agency) involves a five-year plan. A new fifth year is added each year while the coming year's plan is converted to a monthly operating budget and the plan for the second year to a quarterly budget. Long-range planning is generally credited with *some* early anticipation of difficulties, *some* worthwhile contingency action plans if environmental disturbances or fluctuations occur, and the development of *some* creative avenues of action (e.g., a new product, a new health care service, a new public TV programming idea). The word *some* is emphasized because much long-range planning focusses only on dollars, ratios, and measurements rather than on specific directions to pursue and actions to take. Other concepts about ACCI such as improving attitudes and setting policies regarding change for a specific project can therefore significantly improve long-range planning.

Several studies indicate that searching and ACCI pay off. Organizations with long-range planning, for example, seem better situated than those without to withstand bad times (but they appear to be less adept at taking advantage of opportunities to do better in good times). Most reports on failures to implement changes indicate the organization showed no pre- or postinstallation concerns for future changes that may occur or be sought regarding the solution. Changes in the environment almost surely indicate that organizations need to change. For example, they need to cope with the higher educational levels of new employees, diversity of work force, interests, technological changes, union contracts, government regulations, and

attractiveness of other activities besides work.[2] Mostly, though, ACCI provides assurance about the continued workability of a solution. It is a kind of insurance for success. It becomes a self-fulfilling condition by providing insights for the coming direction of the solution or organization.

This chapter will present the following ideas about arranging for continuing change and improvement:

- PDA concepts already presented that support ACCI and facilitate continual search, change theory, and ACCI.
- A proposition that concerns ACCI.
- ACCI based on specific betterment changes in each recommended solution.
- ACCI based on the daily practice of favorable behaviors.
- ACCI based on organization policies promoting search for change.
- ACCI based on an institutionalized program.
- Timeline perspectives about the factor of ACCI in the P&D approach.

CONCEPTS ALREADY PRESENTED THAT SUPPORT ACCI AND FACILITATE CONTINUAL SEARCH

The total P&D approach portrays the intertwined nature of the five factors. Yet emphasizing only one of the factors may not necessarily help the other four. An organization can be highly oriented toward the search for change and improvement because of, for example, the charismatic exhortations of the top executive or administrator, yet use very ineffective methods within the other four factors. Going to the other extreme, ACCI could become almost automatic or a minimal afterthought if all of the other factors are utilized to their fullest extent.

Even though ACCI *ideas* are emphasized throughout PDA, some possible negative factors from "reality" can influence ACCI. Nothing can be considered completely effective, certainly not the rather grand idea of people always searching for change. A few of the negative influences will be explored to put them in a perspective, which should enable a P&D professional to cope with them.

A. Level of Attainment in Spiral Set of Values Is Already Satisfactory

Recent literature about limits to growth and restricted resource availability suggests society has sufficiently progressed to satisfactory levels of each of the four basic values. At the same time, the ills facing our society are obvious over and over—lack of productivity improvement in all sectors, deteriorating environment, eroding human rights, poor education, and many others. I see no reason to belabor this point when Chapters Two and Four describe so many problems which society and each organization face. Even if one were to assume "satisfactory" overall levels of values had been reached, an assumption with which I obviously do not agree, a huge number of P&D needs remain just to adequately readjust solutions to provide better equity. Chapter Two portrayed the unevenness of attainment of each value that creates the dynamic search and tension for continuing improvement in each. "Progress" along the spiral of values will always be expected by one or more segments of society.

A P&D professional can also contribute in several ways to constructively creating or inducing tensions for ACCI. First, initiate the planned betterment arrangements set up in Phase 5 (Chapter Twelve) of the strategy (punctual follow-up on installation changes, frequent audits of the performance of a new solution, scheduled P&D of a whole new solution, redesign FIST every *n* years to keep it three or so years ahead of what is being changed now).

Second, develop systems to supply people with operating information and performance evaluations. People can be asked about the type, form, and frequency of information with which they would like "to keep score" about current performance (notice that this is a P&D project in itself). The data can also point out undesired differentials and possible new needs that create a tension to search for change and improvement.

Third, translate the conflicts that occur naturally in any organization into prospective P&D problems. Most organizations are moving away from the idea that conflicts ought to be neutralized or swept under the rug, and are now admitting that conflicts exist and should be allowed to surface. Some conflicts concern operating and supervising what all agree is a good system. But if conflicts concern the structure of the artificial itself, a win-win position will far more likely occur if a P&D project is set up for it.

B.   Realities of People and Organizations Inhibit ACCI

Complaints about individuals' narcissism, concern for instant gratification, and limited range of knowledge appear to doom ACCI. So too do complaints about the growing bureaucratization, lack of productivity concerns, and negative impacts of government regulations on organizations. Add the realities reviewed in Chapter 5, and the obstacles seem insurmountable.

At the same time, people are willing to take a greater role in decision making and gain the benefits of programs in quality of working life. A P&D professional can accept the position neither of insurmountable obstacles nor of willingness to participate when coping with the huge number of seemingly intractable problems. Neither position can predict specifically what any organizational unit will do when arranging for change. An effort to do something is necessary, for if no attempt is made, then it is certain that nothing will occur.

The P&D professional can build on this contention by using the knowledge about individual realities. First, because levels of the realities change as people leave and enter the organization, working with the personnel department may help employ people—given that potential employees are equal in job-related factors—with "less" functional fixedness, single solution orientation, or defensiveness.

Second, the P&D professional can help managers to view ordinary operating problems in a more positive fashion. Perhaps the question may be turned from "What can I do to motivate people?" to "What purpose (and hierarchy) am I trying to accomplish?" A purpose orientation will help a manager view a situation from the other persons' points of view and listen to their changing rather than fixed needs (Axiom 2).

Third, P&D professionals must practice the P&D principles they preach. Role models are established by actions, not by words. People will live up or down to the expectations they perceive are being communicated indirectly (body language, nonverbal communications, word choice). These may be opposite to what is being *said*. People will not take part in P&D the manager says is "good" for them if the manager then autocratically excludes them from operating and supervising decisions.

C.   Entropy and Inertia Are Difficult to Overcome

Inertia is the tendency of any private or government bureaucracy to feel that its current systems are the only way their work can be done. Changes almost never occur except when a crisis arises or new personnel join the organization. Entropy is the natural tendency of any organized structure to become disorganized. Even an initially successful solution may, after a few years, succumb to a form of personal inertia. A plant with a highly acclaimed quality of work life program faced "indifference and outright hostility from some [of its] mangers, [and the system] has been eroding steadily. [The program] came squarely up against the company's bureaucracy. . . . The basic reason was power. . . . People like stable states. *This system has to be changing or it will die. . . . Concerted effort* [must be] made to evolve the organization."³ [Emphasis added.]

Two conditions help explain this malaise, inertia, and entropy. One is the apparent sharp change in attitudes people are exhibiting toward work and in what they value in life. Most organizations, though, continue to maintain roughly the same style and policies the people were at one time willing to accept as givens. The resulting alienation and desire for immediate self-gratification thus feed the unwillingness of the employees to be creative and to seek structural changes. The second condition is the use of conventional P&D approaches. They feed the inertia and prevent real visions of the future by focusing on details about what exists. This often leads to the question, "Why try planning?" which fosters entropy.

What is the P&D professional to do? First, the initialization of efforts could take the form of developing the abilities and positive attitudes of middle, if not all, managers. Then they could help design the "systems" that could eliminate or minimize the very obstacles the management may have created. The preparation of "modern" organizational policies might be a suitable start, dealing with, for instance, salary for all instead of hourly wages; reward systems that support desired creativity, initiative, and resourcefulness, rather than conformity; variable work hours or flexi-time; and common service facilities (cafeteria lounge) for all.

Second, develop ACCI efforts with the specific organization irrespective of how far removed it may appear to be from the "perfect" program. Getting started today in some even minimal way bodes well for the probability that additional movement toward desired levels of continuing change and improvement will take place tomorrow. The people in the organization are far more likely than not to treat the effort as their own if they help design it with the P&D strategy (Chapters Eleven and Twelve).

These suggestions are small defense against this negative influence, which is one of the most insidious of all. At the very best, these P&D efforts have only a slight chance of success. Some additional techniques and concepts noted further on will help, but no combination can "promise a rose garden."

D. Systems and Problems Are Too Complex for P&D

A variant of inertia, this form of defeatism is highly related to what conventional P&D does to people: The vast amount of detail overwhelms them and creates a patina of complexity. Real-world problems are indeed complex, but the benefits of applying the PDA to them are far greater than the cost and risks of *not* tackling

them. P&D is necessary for the continued existence of any organization, especially private corporations.

The P&D professional can seek to overcome this influence by diligent and careful planning of the P&D system (Chapter Ten) that will be put into operation to do the P&D of the complex system. Some additional actions are:

- Consider the various ramifications of the system matrix (Chapter Nine), such as the view of an element as a system matrix itself, as a means of coping personally with the complexity. Once the system matrix is understood by you, the professional, the means of explaining it and working with others is far more likely to emerge.

- Diligent attention to all cells of the system matrix should enable a group to answer key questions that emerge in complex systems: Who will be affected by the solution? What interfaces need to be considered? What people will need special concern, training, interviews, etc. in the P&D implementation? Where will ACCI be incorporated? Simple as well as complex systems still need to look toward connectivity, a central concern that is common to all of P&D for putting pieces together.⁴

- Determining what purposeful activity is being dealt with at each step of a project and using the appropriate total approach for it should provide additional assurance that the most effective available ideas are being used. Perhaps the learning approach is needed to educate one or another groups, or the research approach to develop a generalization that the solution may need, or a formal decision-making strategy to weave through all of the many complexities.

- Identify within the cells of both the P&D system and the complex system being designed those factors that may provide risks in eventual implementation efforts. Rough assessments of the probability of occurrence of each risk factor will give some semblance of priorities to the P&D group. Some of the factors are "non-existent or unwilling users; multiple users; . . : disappearing users, implementors, or maintainers; inability to specify purpose or usage pattern in advance; inability to predict and cushion impact in all parties; lack or loss of support; lack of experience with similar systems; technical problems and cost/effectiveness issues."⁵ Almost all are, because of their complexity, likely to occur. Thus, it pays to design carefully the P&D system for each project and especially the approach to each of the major risk areas.

In relation to all the negative influences, the P&D professional and group must above all, "believe" and remain flexible. Real world people and organizations are not perfect, and they display reluctance to face problems in bad times and exploit opportunities in good times. No guarantees for success accompany any P&D effort (Chapters Four and Five), and some projects will not be successful.

- Strive to attain momentum toward the feasible ideal P&D system target.
- Keep abreast of normal operating changes in the real world, especially as people depart and enter.
- Give people who will work in the complex system opportunities for flexibility once the skills and basic unit operations are specified during the P&D efforts.
- Practice diligently the frequent joint interaction efforts with the real-world as noted in the Figure 16-1 P&D scenario, especially when complex P&D almost always involves a separate and often isolated-at-headquarters project team.

CHANGE THEORY AND ACCI

Another way of portraying ACCI is to put the ideas and principles into a format suggested by change theorists (see Chapter Fourteen). Change has certain characteristics:

Realistic advantage [or] unique benefit[s]; *impact in social relations*; *divisibility* [or] extent to which a change can be implemented on a limited scale . . . at the trial stage of adoption; *reversibility* [or] the ease with which the status quo ante can be established if a change . . . is later rejected; *complexity* [or] the degree of difficulty in using and understanding a change, [distinguishing] between complexity-in-use and complexity-in-understanding; *compatibility . . . with the situation in which it is to be used*; *communicability* [or] the ease with which information . . . can be disseminated; *time* [or] optimal speed with which a change is introduced [which means] the most appropriate rate of change may not correspond to the maximum rate of change possible; [and] *other dimensions* [such as] risk and uncertainty, . . . commitment . . . [and] susceptibility to successive modification.[6]

Change theory is often presented in terms of three sequential steps: recognition of some disequilibrium or unfreezing of attitudes and perceptions, development of the specific recommendations, and the emergence of a new equilibrium or refreezing. Unfreezing can be further defined in PDA terms to include identifying the felt need or desire in values, scouting for problems or loci, establishing a P&D system relating a professional and the real-world client, and developing mutual commitment to the "right" purpose. Developing and

modifying solutions includes creativity, evaluating alternatives, developing a FIST and a recommendation, and testing it. Refreezing is different in PDA which is concerned with the installation, evaluation, and utilization of the recommendations within a context of searching for continuing change and improvement. Why encourage with refreezing the very mental attitude and human behavior that is to be undone when the almost certain continuing search for change is started?

The three steps of change theory stimulated a reorganization of the P&D principles of Table 10-2 into the basis presented in Table 16-1.

Getting Started

A large number of stimuli are available to get a project under way (see Chapter Twelve) or to start ACCI. Some potential sources of stimuli can be found by scouting around to find a focus whether physical or abstract (e.g., policy, information); identifying appropriate entry point(s); relating the felt-need or pain or desire to operational P&D; motivating individuals to seek "reinvention for us" of a new generalization or someone else's good solution; developing or understanding tensions for P&D change or improvement; seeking the action levers in the organization/community; obtaining a committed client who gives a mandate and will do something about later installation and operation; and working out the jointly convergent actions between the real-world client/group/organization and the P&D professional or world.

Developing Specific P&D Recommendations

This section of Table 16-1 captures many of the ideas of the P&D approach as a whole. Principle 6 concerns the basic approach idea, while the others deal with specific aspects.

Principle 7, for example, notes that even the most seemingly simple project requires fairly considerable P&D skills and that maximum effectiveness of results is not likely to be attained on all projects. But *movement* toward P&D objectives is what is desired. Any positive change should be acknowledged, for its success might motivate other parts of the organization to get started, and can serve as the basis of ACCI to help the project itself later.

Success is a difficult word to define because it is so dependent on the situation-specific conditions. ACCI efforts next year, as an illustration, may be very dependent on the first success level, irrespective of how much or little it may be. Success might thus be measured by the degree of agreement reached by the group

Table 16-1 Some P&D Principles Leading to Implementation and Continuing Improvement

GETTING STARTED

1 A unique P&D system or structure (P&D project team or continuing change program, interview, meeting, etc.) is needed for each organization (department, company, city, etc.)

2 Each project for a P&D problem is treated as a unique and complete effort irrespective of its seeming similarity to others inside or outside the organization (the people are always different, so reinvention may be desirable to create ownership on their part)

3 Words are adapted to the meaning and usage in the organization rather than jargon being forced on the organization (ideas are important, and many words can convey each one)

4 The perceived needs or tensions of the organization must form the starting point of any program or project. Any change in this perception should stem from following the P&D timeline approach to expand the thinking and solution space of the involved people

5 A client or group committed to installation and follow-up as well as to P&D should be identified very early or the P&D effort may not be worth starting

DEVELOPING SPECIFIC P&D RECOMMENDATIONS

6 Follow the five phases of the strategy (purposes, ideal systems, target for regularities, recommendation that incorporates irregularities, installation) integrated continuously along the timeline with the solution framework, involving people, using information and knowledge, and arranging for continuing change and improvement

7 Any successful P&D effort, however small, should be acknowledged because no organization has a perfect P&D program nor a project an ideal completion record, and one success encourages others

8 Use a systems matrix perspective on all projects, irrespective of size, as a basis of generating a syndrome of successful holistic thinking

9 A P&D professional should exhibit with groups and individuals the behavior he/she recommends they adopt (others are not likely to practice participation if the professional merely lectures *about* participation)

10 Milestones should be established for the program and all projects, ensuring that priorities for information and activities are established

11 Recommendations should always be justified. Information in terms of prospective measurements of *results* must be available about the current status of the system at the beginning of an effort (base line data)

IMPLEMENTATION OF A SOLUTION WITHIN CONTEXT OF CONTINUING SEARCH FOR CHANGE

12 An organization should focus attention on all three conditions of solutions—nonexistence, satisfactory exis-

tence, and unsatisfactory existence—for which it should allocate resources for original. planned betterment, and correction P&D efforts

13 Implementation of a solution is a system that can be planned and designed, and the most effective implementation system must literally start at the very beginning of the P&D effort

14 Involving people in a continuing search for change through ideas of expansion, ideal systems, regularities, and target system guides provides many of the satisfactions from work itself that people seek

15 Achieving all four societal and organizational values (achieve greater effectiveness, attain better quality of life, enhance human dignity and encourage individual betterment) is always so dynamically uneven that redressing the balance requires a continuing search for change and improvement

to adopt and use the solution, the length of time the solution is in use, the improved attitudes and process skill of those involved, the commitment to ACCI, and the perceptible improvement in output or performance factors.

Principle 11 is quite logical in concept and seemingly obvious in practice. But it addresses a factor first discussed in Chapter Twelve, Phase 1e (measures of effectiveness). Many people forget that measures of effectiveness need to be identified in Phase 1, or they assume that it will be easy to reconstruct the information later. First of all, this is very difficult to do. Second, people will not always agree with calculations made for their area of work. Third, even if everyone agreed on content, Chapter Fifteen showed how accuracy and precision are very difficult and costly to obtain. A comparison of product cost estimating illustrates how difficult this may be:

A set of costs, revenue, and other required data were presented to a group of technically oriented cost accountants with the request that they calculate product cost and profit. The model data pertained to a company in an industry familiar to the entire group. In *every* instance, *everyone* doing this exercise produced a *different* cost and profit for the same product selling price! What seems simple and straightforward turns out to have several interpretations.[7]

Implementation of Solution within Context of Continuing Search for Change

As noted before, success of a P&D solution is multi-faceted. Many P&D efforts fall short of meeting *all* the criteria, but no one criterion is sufficient by itself.

An implemented P&D solution is supposed to change what people do or what exists, that is, change the systems people will be operating and supervising. But a change in a situation involves its growth or diminution (usually quantitative), alteration (usually qualitative), coming into being or passing away, or effective arrangement in place. Thus, successful implementation initially refers to *measurable* growth or diminution, alteration, existence, or arrangement, or *perceived human beliefs* that one of these has been accomplished. All the measurements in the world that "show" a successful change has been made are worthless if the people in the situation do not believe it, even if they are forced presently to use it. They ususaly find many ways of demonstrating their attitude, most of which erode the benefits of P&D and militate against ACCI.

Implementation is thus affected by many variables, which is a reason for including Principle 13 in the list. Reviewing the following variables [8] found to influence implementation should clearly demonstrate why implementation must start at the *beginning* of a P&D project or program: level of "political" influence; degree of participation (see Column B, Table 14-2); degree of commitment of client/customer/user; magnitude of change involved in the solution; personality type and cognitive style of decision maker(s); risk-taking propensities of organization; perception of need for P&D; reward structure or incentives; skill enhancement, promotions, and so on for those involved in making the changes; availability of resources (technical skills, money, management support, etc.); and amount of information made available to others throughout the P&D process.

A PROPOSITION THAT CONCERNS ARRANGING FOR CONTINUING CHANGE AND IMPROVEMENT

Effectively searching and arranging for continuing change and improvement in an organization is highly likely to identify many kinds of potential problems, which will then be sorted into different purposeful activities. Yet many P&D solutions will be installed for an individual or small group (a single-family house, a plan of personal education). The proposition concerned with ACCI must meld these two disparate perspectives. The following is offered as most reasonable at the time of writing (mid-1980):

Proposition 13 An implemented P&D change can be considered complete only when the solution includes a closely interwoven set of future specifications, just as the human units where the changes occur should con- *tinually search for improvements in all current systems and for solutions to meet new needs.*

Future specifications implies establishing in advance a wide range of potential actions that might later improve the solution currently being implemented. The specifications refer to the future dimension of one or more elements in the system matrix formulation of the solution. It can include time-phased installation of solution parts that fit irregularity conditions or add FIST components, arrival of equipment, transfer or promotion of people, introduction of new products or services, and retraining of people to obtain new skills. It might even designate when the current FIST ought to be completely redesigned for the next period of time. The gypsy moth pest management system solution (Case History B1), for example, started with a 1983 target system, which is to be designed again from scratch in 1981 for the time period ending in 1985. A five-year corporate plan revises its fifth-year target system every year.

The actual installation thus reflects the "manifest" part of the solution, while the future specifications reflect the "latent" part. Both together are the solution, not one or the other. Such a "complete" solution is a logical consequence of the conceptual support and modes of ACCI reviewed in Table 16-1.

Human units means starting with the individual and extending to successively larger groupings or associations of people (similar to the levels in Figure 9-1). The larger units are presumably better in ACCI, but countervailing forces push in the opposite direction. Local and regional governance are preferred for many needs and functions. Single-issue political groups, as a matter of fact, are springing up so fast that their diverse lobbying efforts are immobilizing state legislators and Congress. Narcissism and the desire for immediate gratification lead people to focus on the individual, to the exculsion of others. The single technique is assumed to be able to solve all problems. The deterioration of a sense of national feeling is changing the degree of influence of larger groups (labor unions, political parties). National and even international efforts continue to be important, apparently in the face of the inability of intermediate-sized units to operate effectively and the seemingly overwhelming complexity of interactions.

Irrespective of these forces, each human unit better serves itself and its larger entities with some sort of continuing search for change. Such a proposition would probably be unacceptable to some of the single-issue groups. Yet it is the key mechanism for them. The tuberculosis treatment and prevention group, for example, found its skills quite valuable and useful for the larger issue of lung diseases. Even units with conflicts and overlapping interests will each improve the quality and quantity of their efforts if *all* of them search for change. The opportunities for effective trade-offs increase as each unit becomes aware of its hierarchy of purposes, various ideal systems, items of regularity, and so on.

Improvements in all current systems and solutions for meeting new needs refers to the three conditions in which a system or solution exists—unsatisfactory, satisfactory, or future (Axiom 5). The unsatisfactory (noisy) ones get almost all the attention, and some attention is given to developing effective solutions for future needs. But the satisfactory (quiet) ones are seldom considered. Organizations unfortunately wait until they become unsatisfactory. ACCI therefore should focus attention on satisfactory conditions and future needs which the large percentage of projects will gradually start meeting.

The word *improvement* deserves a bit more explanation. It conveys the idea of incremental degrees of attainment, something humans have always sought (Figure 2-2). But its use here represents a key idea—searching and ACCI are able to produce "more" of the values, objectives and goals than would be attained without searching and ACCI. "More" relates to both practical and statistical significance in differences, but dwelling on providing conclusive evidence of these differences is not going to be fruitful. That is, a generalization that concludes that organizations with an arrangement to search for continuing changes will get an average of x% more benefits than others provides no method of predicting the specific increment for a specific organizational unit (Corollary 7a). What can be quite useful for obtaining the practical results a human unit wants is to do as much as possible about improving the several factors or variables the literature identifies as being present when significantly greater benefits are attained.

Such factors could be put together to serve as a rough indicator of an organization's *degree of readiness* for efforts in searching and ACCI. A poor climate for change or a low degree of readiness would mean that a continuing search effort would require a much different type of arrangement than would a high degree of readiness. The implications of this sentence are very critical: Each readiness factor as well as each method of searching and ACCI can be planned and designed. Each organization will have its own "amount" of readiness and arrangements for continuing search, none of which are ever at the "maximum" level. Thus each readiness factor and the form of ACCI can be improved through the perspective of a total P&D approach.

Measuring the degree of readiness is quite difficult. In addition, even determining which factors indicate readiness is not easy. For example, a 0.42 coefficient for a factor in one multiple path analysis equation was the highest significant one, hardly indicative of either satisfactory measurement or causal interpretation.

Yet some indicators can be identified to aid an organization or human unit in assessing itself. Perhaps the key people in the organizational unit could determine the amount of the factor present in the unit by using the 0-to-100 rating scale. (Appendix A lists several other techniques; see questionnaires, interviews, etc.) Zero represents the presence of absolutely none of the factor and one hundred absolutely all. If the measures for most factors are close to zero, then major efforts ought to be expanded in improving them. ACCI of the operational system may well need a slight delay. However, using PDA to develop the "measuring" system with the people involved will help change their climate of readiness, perceptions of needs, and directions in a healthy manner along the timeline.

The following readiness factors have been distilled from several sources; this list contains some unavoidable overlap and omissions:

Trust One person can believe what another says. Actions of one person or group are treated with credibility and integrity by others. Supportiveness. "Suspiciousness is absent in interpersonal relationships."[9] A good history of labor-management relations may indicate such trust.

Employment Conditions Job security is high, physical working conditions are people-oriented (noise, dust, heat/cold are greatly minimized), pay levels are comparable to or above area levels, safety is emphasized, career/promotion paths are known, and so forth.

Policy Commitments Explicit statements are made to guide actions of all organization members toward seeking the attainment of all societal values (Figure 2-1), generating interest in continuing change (education, time for group meetings, etc.), sharing gains of improvements, lowering the level of decision making, and so forth.

Resource Commitments Organization is willing to provide P&D professional services in the variety of roles and functions (Table 14-3), allocate top management time to the efforts (executives must not delegate corporate planning responsibility), coordinate and disseminate mechanisms; follow-up provided for implementation.

Open Communications People are not threatened, control over personal situation is maintained, data and information is shared, "power" relationships are considered, placing blame is not the objective of communications, decision making is shared, free discussion of P&D uncertainties and ambiguities takes place, confidences are maintained, and so on.

Conduct toward P&D and Change   Many people perceive change as necessary to organizational health, are willing to modify organizational structure if needed, focus on purposes and measures of effectiveness ("hungry" for change and improvement), seek to motivate others to search for change, feel that work produces one form of life's satisfactions, evaluations of efforts are received favorably, new goals and opportunities are sought to provide control over the change process, people seek to understand the nature and purposes of P&D in relation to other purposeful activities, learning of all types is encouraged, and so forth.

Data and Information   Measures of important factors of organizational results serve as a base of comparison (e.g., cost benefit ratio) for proposals and implemented changes, timelines are prepared to arrange availability of resources, measures describe *extent* of resource availability, *linkages* are established with sources of new ideas and research results, and so on.

Organizational Flexibility   Ability to respond to discontinuities, adaptiveness to technological advances, closeness of alignment to customer/client/user needs, degree of decentralization, complexity of processes and capital investments, compatibility of organizational levels and group norms toward directions and goals, cohesiveness in actions, willingness to experiment, surfacing and dealing with conflicts of all types (substantive questions—inventory levels, maintenance levels, markets, etc., as well as interpersonal styles, roles and functions, goal orientation, personality and interests, etc.).

No organizational unit "scores" high (say 70 to 75) on *each* of these readiness factors. Nor will more than just a few soon attain high scores on all of these factors or on any measures of "modern" organizations (open, participative, continually learning, humanized, etc.). A strong case can even be presented for attaining only minimal levels in another set of factors proposed to indicate good organizational performance and development:

Cooperation requires minimal *consensus* [so that] an organization can extract advantages from both consensus and dissension simultaneously. . . . Satisfaction rests upon minimal *contentment*. . . . Wealth arises from minimal *affluence* [which affords] a margin [that] absorbs consequences of fail-

ure [yet avoids] as serious a liability as . . . poverty. . . . Goals merit minimal *faith* [because] an organization should plan its future but not rely on its plans. . . . Improvement depends on minimal *consistency* [in seeking changes because] an organization can never be satisfied to continue behaving as it has, for perfection itself justifies dissatisfaction. . . . Wisdom demands minimal *rationality* [which too likely produces] oversimplifying models, . . . emphasizing means to the exclusion of ends, [and] developing rational answers to the wrong questions.[10]

The readiness factors point the way for estimating the probability of broadly searching and ACCI. They permit an organization to set priorities on what factors to enhance. At the same time, operational systems can be improved to the maximum amount possible under the conditions. The target set of readiness factors for which to strive should be getting better at the same time that current implementation of solutions is being accomplished to improve direct organizational performance and results.

How the ideas of ACCI might become operational is the major focus of this chapter. Several directions or thrusts are possible, but the specific *arrangements must be developed to fit a specific-situation human unit or organization.* It is impossible to specify arrangements that would be "best" for each of the combinations of the many contextual variables already discussed in this chapter. Then there are other locus-specific variables—"*type of organization* (economic/service/commonwealth), *societal type* (modern/modernizing), *task environment* (long-term stable/long-term unstable/short-term stable/short-term unstable), *change agent origin* (indigenous-internal/indigenous-external/nonindigenous-internal/nonindigenous-external), *mode of intervention* (unilateral/subordinate/delegative/collaborative), . . . *focus of change* (managers/staff/first-line supervisors/line/multiple levels), *focus of solution* (human/technological/structural/task/mixed), ..."[11]

The presence of so many variables demonstrates again, as does Figure 16-1, how the real world influences P&D. P&D focusses on influencing what goes on in the real world, but these "larger" organizational impacts bear special mention in relation to ACCI as a means of reinforcing the design-your-own-arrangement view. Without concerted efforts and commitments by key personnel in each "world," any arrangement is but a shell of bureaucracy.[12]

Another compelling reason for ACCI on a situation-specific basis is to improve the likelihood that the unique set of talented and creative P&D and other people in an organization will work together effectively. There is no rationale for any group to rehash old solutions and ideas or search arrangements from elsewhere when they should be diligently thinking up new ones.[13]

ACCI should encourage the establishment of a favorable P&D climate or culture. Even a high level of readiness is no assurance of continuing vigil against the entropic factors that cause deterioration in any organization or in the effectiveness of a solution. Several of these factors are especially insidious: (1) *Organizational myths.* Assumptions the organization or group has about itself are often far from the truth, long past gone, or horribly elitist (we serve the customer, we produce a quality product, we are cost-conscious, etc.). (2) *Disciplinary parochialism.* People continue to think in narrow or specialized patterns usually associated with their education (e.g., engineering, marketing) or area of initial successes. (3) *Organizational parochialism.* People view current successful endeavors as the center of affairs, putting aside new ideas or directions from inside the organization or from preferred external sources. Consider the electric companies that wouldn't buy Edison's light bulb patent, telegraph companies that did not adopt Bell's telephone, and duplicating companies that did not develop Carlson's xerography.[14]

Within the critical perspective of using the P&D approach in ACCI in the specific situation, four categories of arrangements are offered as illustrations rather than prescriptions of what specifically to set up. Parts of one or more can go together into an almost infinite variety of combinations. The four categories are specific betterment changes in each recommended solution, daily practice of favorable behaviors regarding search for continuing change and improvement, organizational policies promoting search for change, and institutionalized programs. These are listed roughly in the order of progression an organization might achieve in searching and ACCI.

A. ACCI BASED ON SPECIFIC BETTERMENT CHANGES IN EACH RECOMMENDED SOLUTION

Quite clear-cut ideas and specifications for future changes should be available when the initial solution is being installed. Sometimes these are contingency courses of action should certain conditions materialize. Mostly, the specifications should improve the solution. Use the manual, coded multiset carbon forms for nine months in a nursing medication system, but change then to the keyboard "typewriter" equipment for storing and transmitting the information. Set up an ad hoc national gypsy moth pest management board

now, but start it with the essential characteristics and roles it is expected to have when the desired staffing becomes available in a couple of years. Build the school to fit the current functions and purposes, but provide flexibility (movable walls, extra and easily accessible electrical outlets, portable equipment), even though changes are not expected for many years.

Sometimes the specification also sets up a mechanism to search for continuing change and improvement: a date for a planned betterment project to do P&D from "scratch", or the continual operation of the P&D committee after the new solution is installed. Establishing a date for future P&D recognizes that many developments (technological advances, legal changes, societal values, resource availability, etc.) might stimulate a significant shift in the concept underlying an existing, albeit satisfactory solution. Some examples include a six-year date for a betterment design of a university department's curriculum, a four-year date for a hospital medical records library system, a one-year date for redesign of a product component, a three-year date for a manufacturing inventory control system, a six-month date for redesign of a community's parking policy, and a four-year date for redesign of a person's career plans. A good "tickle file" is needed to bring the date to the attention of the appropriate people.

The continual operation of a P&D committee (or advisory group, or office, or section) after the solution is installed recognizes that the solution or system is large enough to warrant regular P&D efforts. This allows some cyclical focus on each of the smaller entities in the whole solution as well as early redesign of the overall target solution to keep it three or so years ahead. Some examples are the P&D committee associated with the national gypsy moth pest management board, the manufacturing facilities P&D committee in a company, a downtown area P&D committee to keep a target urban renewal plan four years ahead, a junior high school reading planning council, and an 11-county health system agency's continuing five-year planning committee. One architect, for example, proposed a four-year plan plus a method of P&D to keep the four-year plan up to date as his solution in a contest seeking a 20-year urban renewal master plan.

Both types of P&D mechanisms are likely to involve some evaluation to learn if the solution is "satisfactory" (step 1a, Chapter Twelve) and to prepare justifications of changes if needed. After all, change is not needed if advantages do not accrue. Thus the evaluation approach (Chapter Three) may be needed on occasion, and Phase 5 of the strategy is oriented toward setting the stage for this.

Consider how specific planned betterment ideas and/or a continuing P&D committee might have helped the General Foods' worker participation plan set up in the early 1970s in its new Topeka, Kansas, dog-food plant.[15]

Widely heralded as a model for the future, and General Foods claims that it still is, . . . the system, faced with indifference and outright hostility from some GF managers, has been eroding steadily. . . . A former employee . . . says, "There were pressures almost from the inception, and not because the system didn't work. The basic reason was power. We flew in the face of corporate policy. . . . *This system has to be changing or it will die.*" [A former GF manager] says "The system starts to be compartmentalized, and when you compartmentalize it, you degrade it." [Emphasis added.]

Important benefits of ACCI based on specific betterment changes in a particular solution are the early warning potentials it provides regarding deterioration of the solution, and the generation of "tension" as a stimulus to further change. People assigned such responsibility are likely to identify early where difficulties may occur and then *want* to correct the solution to meet its objectives. Turning over the installation to the operators and supervisors should occur only after sufficient assurance is available that the solution is in place. Many difficulties faced while developing and installing the solution can surface again in the early changeover period:

- Commitment of key decision makers and influentials may wane.
- Available resources may be modified.
- Training and education of people may be insufficient.
- Delivery times for needed equipment and devices may slip significantly.
- Costs may escalate beyond projections.
- Key organizations with power (e.g., unions, blocs of citizens, legislators, regulators) may decide they are "losing" too much even after installation.
- An unanticipated disturbance (e.g., oil embargo, tornado, strike of supplier) may occur.
- People operating the new system may experience adjustment difficulties.
- Elapsed time to full utilization of the solution becomes too great in face of a client/customer/country/user urgent need for the output(s) of the system.

The initial P&D group should really maintain such cognizance as part of good P&D. But having the betterment arrangement increases the likelihood that someone will cope with the difficulties after the initial P&D structure is disbanded. A word of caution, though, for the P&D professional, whether a consultant or a member of the internal staff: Avoid building yourself into the actual *operation* of the solution during installation, debugging, and turnover. The enthusiasm of a P&D professional may become so great that those who are supposed to operate the system demur to the professional's "suggested" decisions in resolving difficulties, thus never gain the experience needed to operate the system after the professional departs. The P&D professional may personally decide to become the operator-Manager permanently or for a while on a fixed-term contract basis, but this is a role change to operating and supervising that the P&D professional should make consciously.

A summary of ideas about *how* to get continuing changes in the solution itself includes:

- Assign unresolved questions in the target system and future dimension to research and development staff, to other P&D groups, or outside sources.
- Set up tickle dates for reviewing suggestions in the target system and future dimension for possible installation.
- Establish a continuing P&D committee for the locus area of the solution and redo the target system every *n* years to keep it two to four years ahead of the current solution (or assign this responsibility to a productivity circle or "worker's production problem committee"). The yearly update of the fifth-year target in corporate planning based on a five-year horizon is an illustration of building continuing changes in the solution itself.
- Schedule a complete betterment design and assign responsibility for initiating it (see Step 5I, Chapter Twelve).
- Schedule a time for setting up a new P&D system for the solution locus so it can determine if a betterment P&D project should be set up.
- Adopt a sunset law principle.
- Experiment with suggestions even if people feel that the solution is "great," or optimal specifications were developed.
- Set up a committee to meet once or twice a year to review the status of the solution (and whether regularities have changed, or new technology is available, etc.) and determine if a P&D effort should be started.
- Hold seminars regularly on topics related to the locus, where outsiders can review what's new to

keep people in the system apprised of possible change opportunities.

• Keep usual bargainers, negotiators, and grievance handlers alert to signals that may provide early warnings for a betterment design.

• Encourage and prepare people to practice better P&D attitudes in everyday activities (see below)

• Develop and put into effect organizational policies which encourage and reward continuing change (see below).

B. ACCI BASED ON THE DAILY PRACTICE OF FAVORABLE BEHAVIORS

The operational concept here is relatively simple: Practice and exhibit the behavior you want others to adopt. If you want people with whom you work to search for change, then you must practice searching for and adopting improvements. This expands Principle 9 in Table 16-1 to managers, supervisors, politicians, bureaucrats, teachers, etc. in their day-to-day activities. The concept is also applicable if you are neutral, do nothing about searching for change, resist improvements, or actively protect the status quo. These practices will tend to elicit comparable behavior from others. Protecting the status quo, incidentally, is not all bad, for example, when applied to maintaining democratic principles of government and protecting individual liberties under the Bill of Rights. The rest of this section obviously deals with practicing favorable change-oriented behaviors.

People often consider the words *attitude* and *behavior* to be synonyms, but be "wary of using attitudes to predict behavior and vice versa."[16] Because P&D is action-based, the word *behavior* will be used. It is operational and observable, regardless of the underlying attitudes and beliefs.

The P&D professional could treat this form of ACCI as a need or problem to which P&D should be applied. In other words, a P&D professional could help get any human unit to practice favorable behaviors by applying the P&D approach with them to develop appropriate methods. Expertise in several fields (organizational development, team building, communications, supervision, transactional analysis) are available to help in developing these kinds of solutions.

Even a P&D professional in a helping field (social work, counseling, career guidance, health care delivery) can foster this favorable conduct with clients so they are attuned to continuing search for change and improvement in their specific solution. Each client/

patient/case, for example, should understand not only the current course of action or therapy, but also the target to aim for in n months or years, the need to update the target every $0.5n$ or n or $2n$ period, and the interim improvements that can be implemented before the P&D of the next target.

The demeanor and behavior of managers/administrators/supervisors/principals/chairpersons are the major ingredients of the change climate or culture of the organization/community/institution. Action and responses are shaped by their behavior—the theories they put into practice (as contrasted with their espoused theories).[17] Good performances in organizations can be traced to the behavior and practice of these people. Some have called this a can-do spirit, an openness to suggestions, a persistence in practicing search behavior, a risk-taking perspective (at least for searching), an understanding that mistakes will be made. These people must take the initiative. Even a good initial spirit that manifests itself, say, in the development of the new dog food plant, must be maintained and nourished by favorable concepts or else the earlier benefits start to disappear. Similarly, practice of behaviors inimical to search for change and opportunities weakens, first, efforts for ACCI and second, the performance of the unit. One possible measure of commitment of P&D is the percentage of time the top person spends doing P&D. As the organizational complexity gets greater, the top person should spend more time on P&D, 25 to 35%, and less on supervising others.

Affective aspects are highly emphasized in ACCI to overcome the flaws that arise from only rationalism or systems modeling. "It is [difficult] for an organization to devote enough resources to searching its environment for opportunities [when rational attitudes] consume too many search resources [through] defensive responses to newly recognized problems."[18] Consider the response of an engineer to complaints about the poor performance and breakdowns of a jig for a drill press. After listening to the workers, the foreman, the maintenance person, and setup man and after looking over the drawings of the jig, he proclaimed that what all of them complained about couldn't be right "because the drawings show the difficulties could not be occurring"!

Organizational conduct and behavior are obviously dependent on cultural norms in the community, country, and society. The Japanese, for example, are major practitioners of PDA[19] because their culture emphasizes dealing with what the problem really is, if any exists at all, before any kind of discussion takes place about possible solutions. American culture emphasizes details of the present methods as prelude to finding solutions to the assumed problem. Other cultures emphasize waiting out a solution, or not even treating as a problem things we in the United States do consider problems: these problems are seen to be unimportant because this life is considered but a transitory stage of existence. Such philosophies do influence practice or behavior. Yet ACCI can be done in any culture if one does *not* assume that the initial new behaviors must be at the best or 100 level. To continue the example, just going from the 15 level to the 25 level in one year is to be applauded (Principle 7, Table 16-1). Then in the next year they can move to a "better" level, and so on.

Putting favorable behaviors into practice involves dwelling on the human unit as a whole rather than on the situation-specific solution. It requires little formality but much commitment. It seeks to build on the perceptiveness of those at any level in an organization. A concerned foreman can practice them as well as the company president, the grade level coordinator as well as the school district superintendent, and the head nurse as well as the top hospital administrator. Getting the top person involved with aiding the P&D professional to develop methods for improving favorable behaviors of others is a good way to get the top person to behave better! Even if the top person doesn't exhibit search-conducive behavior, others can in their own bailiwicks.

ACCI based on the daily practice of favorable behaviors may appear slow, even if successful, or not likely to result in changes and improvements. But consider the alternatives: Will the individual or the organizational unit establish good policies to encourage the search for change or set up a full-fledged program if they won't consider an effort to practice change-conducive behavior? And, if they did do either one without changing their own behavior, what would be the probability of success? Overall success in ACCI will necessarily be built on a large number of good performances on small efforts: exhibiting favorable behaviors, implementing built-in improvements on several projects, and so on.

The following factors directly related to behaviors are not exhaustive nor mutually exclusive. They portray a wide variety of considerations in practicing behaviors favorable to search for change:

- *Trust and Supportiveness*   See "trust" in readiness factors.
- *Open Communications*   See "open communications" in readiness factors. Share diverse types of information, including knowledge about the problems facing the unit. Set up a "hotline," monthly or

so meetings to discuss problems, high-reward suggestion systems, and so on.

- *Conduct toward P&D and Change*   See the same heading in readiness factors. Develop a sense of control over the process of P&D changes by following the timeline scenario, especially recognizing the realities of people and organizations (Chapter Five) as the initiating conditions.

- *Organizational Flexibility*   See "organizational flexibility" in readiness factors. Do individuals and groups look for the need to change, is there openness to experiment, is a potential for change and improvement maintained, is there high level commitment to human resource development as well as to effective product/service development?

- *Understanding*   Appreciate different personality types, interests, and capabilities of individuals and how each may need an individual "system" or effective psychological climate (especially if highly skilled, professional, scientific, etc.). Adapt to the group's psychostructure, sense of cohesiveness, balance of positions, and interdependence. Patience above all is critical to an understanding behavior.

- *Leadership*   Continued personal learning is an effective behavior and is frequently arranged for all personnel. Another is reducing the politics and gamesmanship that could sap efforts from the search for change, and the minimization of "power" plays and resulting inequities. Leadership for searching activities minimizes its own sense of loss of power by sharing and delegation to motivate others. Power may still be an effective behavior with external groups if a test is needed, if the solution has minimal or no room for compromise, or if rapid implementation is needed.

- *Promote Personal Growth of Personnel*   Provide continual *opportunity* for expanding the knowledge of all people, by participating in P&D projects, sharing goal development and evaluation, and treating all people equitably. People get "room to search," can form a good self-concept, and develop self-esteem through such growth possibilities.[20]

- *Use Groups or Teams*   Every solution involves several people who can influence the utilization of solutions as well as the search for change. Group projects foster this utilization and search, and provide means for giving employees some centrality to work processes in addition to their other "lives."

- *Be Alert to Emergent Needs*   Whenever one need is satisfied or a problem is solved, another need emerges. The most "perfect" solution in everyone's eyes today will give way to some dissatisfaction or new need tomorrow. These can be the catalysts to ACCI.

These behaviors are also far more likely to be effective in dealing with people's dispositions toward things, events, and ideas (the realities of Chapter Five) than using the exhortations and tired bromides usually offered to managers:

Get the workers to share the goals of the organization—not very likely because each person has many other "lives" with goals that may be considered more important.

Make work interesting and less routine by job enrichment and greater job control to the person—work is still not likely to be central to the worker nor is the imposition of an "enlarged" job likely to be accepted any better than currently imposed jobs based on division-of-labor ideas.[21]

Every manager should devote part of his or her time to planning—many managers feel that planning interferes with "my" work by introducing uncertainties and the unknown into "what I know best," and may expose their incompetencies in P&D efforts.[22]

Develop the loyalties of your people to the department/company/institution management—the several loyalties of professionals to the company, profession, and society[23] are also descriptive of the divided loyalties of other employees.

Motivate your people—the granddaddy of them all; this is usually translated into a simplistic act or two, such as personal compliments for something "good" or a specific monetary reward for desired performance, but many factors in addition to direct and indirect rewards are found to be involved, especially intrinsic ones—develop concept of self, pride in professional growth, feelings of control and efficacy, challenge of learning a difficult concept, self-esteem in craft, skill, and the like—which can sometimes be impeded by rewards.[24]

Which behaviors a manager practices emerge from personal style, cognitive processes, and personality type. A person is just not likely to bloom suddenly after learning about behavioral searching. If a conservative risk taker or sensation-thinking personality individual gains some confidence in ACCI through a project or two which have built-in solution improvements, the probability increases that the person will practice two or three of the behaviors. A large risk taker or intuitive-feeling personality may, on the other hand, do more with all behaviors sooner. ·

Some change in individual's ego states (Chapter Fourteen) usually occurs during the first project or two to help them practice favorable behaviors in searching

for change. One manager involved initially with a large-scale P&D project who then practiced behaviors for change put it this way in a letter to me:

When I first attended the P&D task force meeting, I was very close to the other managers in my poor attitude toward P&D. I know I continually played negative tapes in my head. Yet I found myself becoming interested in questions about purposes, hierarchies, and targets even while I kept associating everything that was said with my initial negative connotations. I think my attitude started to change as these interesting questions were raised, as I found I did not need to react in a way that defended my position, as I started to realize that the professional conducting the meetings was not going to lay a plan on us but we were going to do it ourselves, and as the other managers and I were starting to interact successfully. We had our arguments and disagreements, and some attacks were made on others, but I could feel everyone's attitude changing. All of us were being stroked positively and our jointly developed positions on the plan were being adequately reinforced. It was then that I started to realize that I was developing some positive tapes because I would use the approach with my own people. The positive experience, the winning with the successful interactions gave me the confidence that I could exert leadership and the power of my position to influence in a positive way the people toward good P&D and search for continuing improvement. What's more, we started to do it, even though none of them were involved with the original project.[25]

The effective behaviors of this manager led soon to the introduction of a P&D professional into the division. More on this case will be discussed in the following section.

C. ACCI BASED ON ORGANIZATIONAL POLICIES PROMOTING SEARCH FOR CHANGE

Behaviors favorable to continuing search for change constitute unwritten policies when practiced for a long period of time. Perhaps that would be sufficient as a policy base for an organization if everything were to remain the same over time. But people leave and enter, disturbances occur, external technological breakthroughs are announced, and, above all, normal operating and P&D changes are bound to occur if the search process is even minimally successful. Written policy guidelines or governing principles can capture the concepts implied by the favorable behaviors. The equivalent for an individual in personal planning is writing out "resolutions."

Formalized policies at the conceptual and strategic levels of an organization usually represent a commitment by management to operate and conduct affairs with certain guidelines. Resource commitments, budget allocations, time, rewards, and so forth are usually included. Even with the usual differences in interpretation and thus practice of the policies, they provide significant assurance of good working conditions.

Separating policies conducive specifically to searching and ACCI from those that are desirable for overall good organizational performance is an almost impossible task. Policies and efforts encouraging employees for example to take part in creating or restructuring company solutions very often incorporate concepts for encouraging them to be involved in operating and supervising decisions. Conversely, setting up operating systems that feature autonomous work groups that can hire and fire, set wage rates, settle grievances, allocate working times and shifts, select research topics, and so forth, very often incorporates policies for involving employees in P&D efforts.

It is likewise difficult to disassociate ACCI policies from the type of organization structure (assignment of responsibilities, functional versus geographical authority, degree of hierarchical formalism, etc.) or from the form of the budget (profit centers, line items versus decision/functional/program allocations, etc.). Some structures and budget formats tend to encourage the flexibility desired in searching for change, and others don't. Even though the relationships are so intertwined that sorting them out is not possible, policies that will work in ACCI in the midst of such complexity can be established by getting the people in the organization to plan and design them for the specific situation.

"Good" policies are unable in themselves to generate the search climate. In some organizations, policies are often the embodiment of the organizational mythology, stating platitudes that earlier were practiced but may have subsequently disappeared. Managers may *espouse* the policies, but their behaviors in day-to-day operation may belie them. Thus, major commitment to change in each P&D project and favorable behaviors are necessary ingredients in turning espoused concepts and policies into practical results.

Organizational policies promoting search for change will be reviewed in two categories: (1) possible areas or concerns and (2) policy positions about an area or concern that incorporates implementation perspectives.

1. Possible Areas or Concerns

The following list of possible policies is not exhaustive. It incorporates ideas from good operating policies, readiness factors, betterment or specific solutions, and favorable behaviors.

- *Employment Conditions*   See this heading in readiness factors.

- *Policy Commitments*   See this heading in readiness factors. Priorities for policy implementation and project selection may need to be made, with "potential for high payoff" as the main factor if all other criteria are equal.

- *Resource Commitments*   See this heading in readiness factors. Monetary allocations in the budget are the primary addition. Each organizational unit could budget money for P&D assistance and released time of employees. This helps to promote search by being based on future needs rather than on present or past expenditures. It provides better cost and scheduling estimates and enables effective trade-off questions to be raised early. It gets each person responsible for a budgetary/organizational unit to consider ACCI in budget projections.

- *Data and Information*   See this heading in readiness factors. An organization spends a great deal of money on data and information. How effectively these are used shows up in the time and effort put into arranging it for stimulating search. The I&K should continuously project what external organizations are likely to do and how they and the environment change, explore consequences of possible P&D actions, permit better trade-off determinations for the P&D alternative being developed, and monitor operational activities that are the subject of P&D efforts before and after the implementation.

- *Sharing Gains or Equitable Rewards*   Effective solutions usually generate measurable benefits that contribute to the longevity of the organization (e.g., lowered costs for the same or higher quantity of product, same costs for user-perceived higher-quality service, fast response time sought by clients). Some form of reward (e.g., bonus for maintaining costs below norms, profit sharing, incentive pay, gains sharing, productivity improvement sharing, stock option) for such good performance is considered for those working in the system. Policies in this area will also provide for employee security (e.g., retaining people whose jobs are eliminated as a result of a better manufacturing layout, avoiding peer pressure against an individual who develops an improvement). Both policy ideas create a change-conducive setting by providing monetary and possibly personal (ego satisfaction) benefits through implementing improvements. To paraphrase a humorous homily, "Money isn't everything, but it sure is far ahead of whatever is second." This does not disparage many survey results that show that workers value other factors on the job (e.g., interesting work, sociability, advancement prospects), but people do respond to sufficient differentials in take-home pay.

- *Grievances* Some events will cause some people to feel that an injustice or unfair action occurred. People within an operating unit or those who are suppliers/customers/clients may feel aggrieved, and all are more likely to take part in the search effort when they know mechanisms are available for dealing with complaints.

- *Life-stage Careers* People who change careers, even within one organization, four to six times in a lifetime may often bring a "fresh" outlook toward their new position. To learn the technical I&K of the new position, the person should apply the P&D approach to almost all problems. This removes blinders associated with the current solutions, yet identifies quickly what specialized I&K needs to be learned for the position. This is also a way of allowing practitioners (teachers, principals, curriculum developers, and superintendents in primary and secondary education) to cope with the vast amount of research available in many teaching content areas while solving P&D problems that focus on the individual student's learning: Give each practitioner the P&D approach skills to allow effective selection of what research I&K is needed and the practitioner will find it, thus developing greater specialization while solving real-world problems.[26] This is an updated P&D version of what some companies have found necessary in order to keep technical people (scientists, engineers, product specialists) at the forefront of I&K *in* the locus content areas and at the same time concerned with the total perspective of the organization. Involve them in conceptual P&D for the organization rather than with direct production or management, while advancing them "technically in the organization *and* outside professional groups where recognition can be obtained."[27]

- *Continuous Experimentation* This concern stems from the 1920 studies in the Hawthorne (Illinois) plant of Western Electric.[28] An experimental section was set up to determine the effect of different conditions (e.g., lighting) on productivity. The "Hawthorne effect" is a name associated with the unusual result of these experiments: productivity increased as the amount of light went up but it also increased when the amount of light decreased. The

explanation for this is that the people taking part in the experiment considered themselves special and were therefore highly motivated. Too often this is interpreted to mean that the installation of a solution "we managers found good" ought to be treated as an experiment, which, unfortunately, is often considered a way of duping the people. This will only work once, and, even if the experiment idea is real, people may be interested for only a short period of time in "experimenting" with other people's solutions. Maintaining a policy of real experimentation means continually searching and trying out ideas, with a willingness to remove a change if it fails to produce an improvement. Another perspective on experimentation involves setting up a budget for anyone who wants to try out an idea. Help the person prepare a "proposal" and estimate costs, and set up the project with that person. The people developing a proposal leading to an outside experiment should be involved if experimentation is needed.

- *Values Congruency* Searching for accommodation of the values of various constituencies in and related to an organization generates concomitant searching and ACCI, even through values congruency will not ever really be attained (except when survival is at stake). "Accommodation" seeks a modus operandi within which to operate and do P&D, even as values, objectives, and goals will continue to differ. Focusing on purposes and hierarchies is one effective meeting ground for structuring the accommodations. Another may be the "court" or "jury" arrangement that can include representatives of various interests.

- *People Involvement* The policy need here relates to operationalizing the forms and methods discussed in Chapter Fourteen for facilitating involvement and the deliberate search for ideas. One cannot just decree that involvement is to exist. Several organizational arrangements facilitate involvement and search for ideas: provide "on-company-time" for ad hoc groups to meet (the organization pays for the time), set regularly meeting P&D productivity improvement groups or teams, share knowledge (newsletter, bulletin boards, regular meetings, etc.), set up heterogenous groups (see step 1b, Chapter Twelve), top managers and administrators should formalize the mandate or charter for a group, and so on. Organizational behavior and policies regarding the role of P&D professionals are good harbingers of policies regarding people involvement. Assigning narrow (say, "measurer" and "modeler") roles to P&D professionals ("You just give me the facts, I'll take it from there'') instead of broad ones (Table 14-3) is an almost sure sign that people in the organization also are not likely to be significantly involved in P&D efforts.

Organizational Accommodation   This policy concern seeks to cope with power relationships and inequalities, reporting relationships in the usual hierarchical pyramid, high levels of specialization, interactions with operating units (finance, budgetary control, materials management, transportation, etc.), and similar real-world orientations. "Who wants to give up power," "who wants to change the people reporting to me," "who agrees my specialization is not deserving of a special niche in the organization," "who wants to minimize my control over organizational operations?" Such changes should not be made just for the sake of change but rather to aid in searching and ACCI. A policy, for example, that the vote of each member of a project team is equal, regardless of position, does not assure equality of power, but does start a group toward greater effectiveness. A policy that requires P&D projects to be identified in terms of purposes, values, objectives, and goals (instead of, say, by techniques of specialists) is a great help because it encourages the search of other specialities as sources of good plans and designs. A policy that sends every person to a seminar on advances in the person's field or a topic to broaden the individual is a major contributor to accommodating the real world to searching. A policy that provides channels for and protects (through devices such as an ombudsman, hotline for complaints, privacy code, hearing procedure) a person who protests or discovers difficulties with product safety, unethical activities, restrictive organizational policies regarding individual rights and due process, hazardous work areas, and so on contributes to search efforts by exposing possible P&D project areas at an early point.

2. Policy Positions That Incorporate Implementation Perspectives

This section illustrates policy statements most of which aggregate two or more of the policy areas or concerns. The total number of possible combinations of areas that can fit together into a policy statement is extremely large. Such a large number should stimulate each organization to *design its own set of policies*.

The following policy positions are therefore not "correct" or exhaustive, but are just illustrative. The specificity of each illustration will differ, with some illustrations seeming too specific to constitute a "pol-

icy." But this depends on the level from which the statement is considered—conceptual, strategic, tactical, or operational.

a Broad Range of Policies

More details will be included in presenting this set than in the following section.

1 Employee Security   The individual is the focus, for one person negatively affected finds no solace in a generalization that might read, "Seven of eight people will not be affected in any way by the implementation of a new solution." These policies seek to enhance the opportunity for each person to accept the challenge to develop personal mental capabilities and to determine what is ahead personally and for the organization.

Each employee is guaranteed work for a period of time (six months, twelve months at two-thirds pay) in the event the person's present job is eliminated by P&D or technological advances. Training for other jobs could be provided. Normal labor turnover almost always provides an opening. Also, a changeover to a new system could be postponed until a period of expansion when new jobs are being created by higher needs.

Some labor contracts contain specific clauses (sometimes called productivity bargains) related to severance and protection of employment. For example, one agreement says: (1) the organization must find productivity increases, and (2) it must take certain steps to ease the burdens of "released" employees, such as finding them alternative employment within the company, setting up joint consultation concerning number of released jobs, a commitment to select released employees, providing reasonable notice of termination of employment, and making severance allowances available. Another company and union have a severance pay plan to cope with increasing automation. Other companies have provisions on guaranteed annual salaries (for all employees) to stabilize employment. One such organization maintains an under-hour account for those who do not work 40 hours in a week, but are paid for 40 hours. The employee uses the account from which make-up hours are drawn when work over 40 hours is needed.

Base retention is guaranteed for 365 days to displaced employees in one company's statement of intent. Placement services are sometimes established to obtain jobs in other organizations for those laid off due to P&D improvements. Other methods include: Train employees, at organization expense, for new jobs; early retirement with adequate pension; transferability without personal expense to other sites; shorter workweek; incentives to move for those who fear a new location will not be to their liking; and maintenance of previous pay rates for employees moved to lower-paying jobs.

2 Sharing Gains of Improvements People are bound to ask "what's in it for me?" One plan provides a monetary reward for any changes, whether they result from P&D, normal operating changes (reduction of waste, increased equipment utilization), research results (improved product design, reduction of computer simulation runs), or new technology that becomes available.

Some usual ways of sharing the benefits of improvements are annual productivity wage increases, group bonuses to the people affected, good-sized lump-sum payments to the worker or workers making certain suggestions, stock ownership, deferred (for tax shelter reasons) and cash profit sharing[29] (or gains or savings sharing in nonprofit organizations on the basis of savings from budget), or increased base pay levels to encourage better-qualified people to apply and be hired for jobs in the organization.

3 Creating and Maintaining Interest in the Search for Change More than job security and gains sharing may be necessary: What can activate the internal interests of each individual for them to learn techniques and methods to search for change? Actions of others can only provide stimulations which we hope will catalyze and mobilize the inner impulses and drives toward searching. One view of motivation provides an intensely internalized perspective that deals with "bodily conditions, activity, emotion, stress, reinforcement, instinct, self-actualization, homeostasis (balanced equilbrium), hedonism (affective), sensitization—and anticipation—invigoration, mechanisms, and psycho-analysis."[30]

Another view describes many determinants: money, fringe benefits, promotion, supportiveness, group acceptance, effective behaviors of respected people, and ego involvement. A third view deals with intense communication, organizationwide recognition of individuals, participation in problem identification, employee goal setting, and frequent involvement in P&D scenarios.

Maintaining the interest of people is challenging. The hierarchy of needs (Chapter Two) intimates that people will seek "bigger" levels once smaller ones are effectively attained. As an individual is successful in the P&D improvement of, say, the particular work setting, greater control of it and larger systems are the next P&D focus. Policies to maintain interest therefore move into substantive issues of involvement in decision making about their own jobs, responsibility delegation, advancement, personal growth, and involvement in P&D of bigger systems. Not everyone will take part in such P&D, but the *opportunity* must be available for all (Chapter Fourteen). Maintaining interest also represents a policy position of the organization to eliminate the usual stress-induced, on-again, off-again improvement efforts (typical of these are cost reduction program, productivity improvement effort, energy conservation) and instead maintain strong pressures for searching all of the time.

Literally dozens of ideas fit this category:

- Publicity efforts, such as monthly "motivational" posters, descriptive material that emphasizes that eliminating jobs is not eliminating people, newsletters and article reprints that present "good" P&D results, and the telephone number IDEA (4331) people can call if questions arise or they have an idea.

- A departmental bonus program, or competition for the name of the search effort.

- External public relations to demonstrate how the organization is using a modern P&D approach for decreasing costs, increasing productivity, and developing total citizen usefulness. Speeches, advertisements, sales talks, newspaper articles, luncheons, and announcements on envelopes and statements are part of this idea.

- Special events, such as recognition dinners, progress reports, lectures and seminars, motion pictures, prizes for "project of the month," letting the family of an employee share in the pride of the results of the P&D activities, and distributing small novelty items (desk pen holder, tie clasps, pens and pencils, paper weights, message holders, etc.) with a message.

- Contracts between manager and each person regarding expected P&D results. A contract between an individual and a helping P&D professional is the equivalent for one-on-one projects.

- Give performance information to people on a regular and frequent basis. They will be in a much better position to keep their own search behavior up to date.

4 Education Our concern here centers around the P&D approach (theory *of* P&D) and its related aids and techniques (theories *in* P&D). A great deal of other education is certainly necessary to keep people up to date and enhance their competencies regarding advances in technology (theories *in* locus content area). This subject is too broad to cover here.

One company established P&D approach education for only one division as a start, before expanding it to other divisions. Those designing systems at a hospital just started to call their new applications "PDA" until others wanted to know about it, leading to educational sessions. Some effort is usually needed because few people get formal education in P&D ideas and methods as part of what should be considered a broad education.[31]

The amount of time for P&D education will vary for each level of an organization. In one company, top management received 10 three-hour sessions, the next levels of management 15 sessions, the staff levels 20 sessions, and the workers a simplified five sessions. About two-thirds of all the time is spent on specific applications. Even a half hour of discussion about the approach has sufficed just before a P&D project starts.

Outlines of material covered for specific organizations and groups of people obviously will vary, and should be developed to fit them. Many organizations develop training documents for their own situation. In most cases, a "learn-as-you-apply" concept is used. In some organizations where the product is somewhat complex (such as aerospace), the training programs are much longer for those who will be working with the product planning and design staffs.

Various teaching methods are included, such as system games, interactive computer programs, videotapes, simulation, video and audio recordings of a project team expanding functions, designing ideal systems, or discussing betterment projects.

Educating everyone in an organization becomes almost a physical impossibility as the organization gets large. There are at least two ways to handle this problem. First, for those not educated in P&D, explain the recommended system in terms of the overall approach and specific strategy steps. This at least gives them an opportunity to review the target and related information rather than thinking only about the present system. There is even the possibility that they may have a much better target or way of getting closer to the presented target. Second, a 60,000-employee company spread over five states includes a day and a half of P&D education as part of longer management development training to all people promoted from one level to another.

Several reasons spur the need for continuing education in P&D in addition to keeping abreast of new I&K *in* the locus content areas. In the first place, new conceptual material regarding the philosophies, ethics, and theories *of* the P&D approach will almost always be available (see Chapter Seventeen). Second, many new techniques and models *in* P&D will be developed by a wide variety of people. The formats for implementing such a policy are variable: in-house seminars,

paid educational leave, adult education courses available in a community, temporary full-time assignment to a P&D project staff, tuition aid for a degree program, and so on.

Each organization must design its own educational methods, for which the P&D approach can be used. Learning approach ideas (Chapter Three) can serve as the basis of education for I&K *in* locus content areas.

5 Group Arrangements This area concerns policies for implenention of the well-established concept of involving people (Chapter Fourteen). Policies can take advantage of findings showing that the associative instincts of humans overshadow individual self-interest and that utilizing this instinct improved *each person's ability* and outlook.[32] Associative desires can be incorporated in two forms: a continuing and regularly meeting workshop group, or the ad hoc project team.

The workshop group (or department committee or productivity circle or management council) concerns all the purposeful activities and problems. Workshop groups can be set up in all parts of the organization, usually along section or departmental lines of 10 to 20 people. The person normally in charge of the unit chairs the group (with a P&D professional's help if available) and one person is usually elected as group secretary. One person or the supervisor/foreman/forewoman/lead person serves on the workshop group at the next level, and so on to the management committee "workshop group." The effectiveness of each group is rejuvenated when new members replace others. Each workshop group usually meets once a month, more or less often as necessary. One-half hour per day was the initial schedule in one new American plant.

An ad hoc project team is composed of people from one or more locations if the organization is large, when a P&D project will extend over a long period of time (say over a year), is too involved, complicated, and big, or requires the talents of different experts. In organizations just starting P&D efforts, a project team working on an especially critical problem often precedes workshop groups. After the solution is implemented, the project team usually disbands.

Project teams that are long-lasting (say over one and a half or two years) or project-oriented organizations (matrix management is one illustration) do experience some problems with the human aspects:

Anxieties and feelings of frustration on the part of the members [occur when the project] is getting close to its eventual phaseout; . . . the members . . . don't feel they really know who their boss is; . . . displaced members . . . lose initiative [on] "make work" assignments . . . until productive jobs can be found for them . . . at as high a level of responsibility; . . . individuals who . . . are temporary members [on] a series of [team assignments] may feel a low sense of loyalty to the organization; . . . confusion and ambiguity are common; . . . personal development of individuals is random. . . . The work environment is one of intense competition . . . and conflict between members of . . . competing organizations; [and] members tend to become highly specialized, . . . narrow. . . . and limited in their potential for growth.[33]

Other reports, primarily at the anecdotal and case history level, note that project, task, or change teams may suffer from the manager's or administrator's sense of losing authority because unilateral decision making is minimized, and from the difficulties arising from a person serving concurrently on several teams.[34]

Coping with these potential difficulties involves setting up effective conditions for the other policies and behaviors. In essence, though, each project team can do this by incorporating these questions into the efforts for designing the P&D system (step 1b, Chapter Twelve).

b Specific Policy Arrangements

These illustrations overlap with institutionalized programs described in the next major section. The boundaries among ACCI levels will always be blurry. An organization that says it is setting up organizational policies and "lapses" into an institutionalized program *is to be encouraged.* That is precisely what ought to be done, and I hope many organizations make the same "mistake."

One company's policies were attempts to

reflect concern and mutual respect for personnel: the hiring process is a meaningful, two-way exchange. . . . Applicants and their spouses are invited in small groups to an after-dinner coffee. . . . Personnel people ask the newcomer to express . . . job preferences . . . for initial placement or for later transfer. . . .

There is no probationary period. . . . Although . . . supervisors may have to let someone go, the policy presumes that people are eager to work and to be dependable employees. . . .

The plants do not use time clocks, buzzers, or similar controls. . . . The company . . . assumes that individuals can accurately record their own times. . . .

All factory and office people . . . share the same benefit package. . . .

Office and factory supervisors hold departmental meetings at least once every two weeks to discuss issues that the employees themselves raise. . . .

The plant manager chairs a periodic roundtable with representatives from all office and factory departments who are

selected in whatever way the department decides. The participants prepare the agenda of concerns and the minutes. . . .

The personnel department and other staff people make a point of conducting business at the employee's workplace as well as at their own.

The manager invites some factory and office people to his weekly staff meetings. Similarly, there is regular factory representation at production planning meetings [and] methods, products, and process engineering committees.[35]

Another set of policies concerns the financial rewards stimulus for increasing productivity in any organization. Based on the principle of "improved productivity through sharing," the recommended policies of the "Improshare Plan" are described below:

Increased productivity of groups is shared by employees in the group. The input is the total man-hours worked by the group. The past average productivity level is used as the measurement base [of] average man-hours . . . to produce a unit of [output]. . . . The value of the output of the group is the total units produced multiplied by the past average man-hours [base]. . . . Productivity improvement is shared 50-50 between employees and management. Gains are calculated weekly, with a moving average to span several weeks. . . . Productivity is shared and paid weekly. Losses are absorbed into the moving average. Man-hour standards are frozen at the past average. Standards will not be changed when operations are changed by either management or the employees, except for capital equipment and technology changes. . . . Increased productivity will be shared with no attempt to pinpoint whether employees or management created the savings. An agreed ceiling is established on productivity sharing earnings. The excess over the ceiling will be carried forward to future weeks and eventually "bought back" from the [employees] by cash payments. . . . Total unit man-hour costs under the plan cannot exceed unit costs in the past. . . . Management rights are not changed. . . . Union contractual agreements are not altered.[36]

A third set of policies is proposed as a set of principles for design and improvement of large organizations. The objective of the principles is

to achieve smallness within large organizations [which can continuously strive to overcome the] natural bias and tendency [that] favor[s] order, at the expense of creative freedom. . . . The principles are: 1. The higher level must not absorb the functions of the lower one, on the assumption that, being higher, it will automatically be wiser and fulfill them more efficiently. . . . 2. The subsidiary unit must be defended against reproach and upheld by central authority. . . . Good government is always government by exception. . . . 3. A unit's success [on its operating and balance sheets] should lead to greater freedom and financial scope for the unit and failure should lead to restriction and disability. . . .

4. Motivation is the central problem of large organizations given the incomprehensibility that stems from large size and its bureaucratic structure, remote and impersonal controls and abstract rules and regulations. . . . 5. A middle axiom [is] required . . . between . . . the soft method of . . . exhortation [and] the tough method of . . . issuing specific instructions.[37]

To pick up the story of the manager discussed at the end of the "behavior" section, a little more can be added about policies:

One basic policy that did emerge stated that any P&D project would have to start with the design of the P&D system itself. We would literally spell out the needed specifications in terms of the P&D system matrix, although we didn't do a thorough job, looking primarily at the fundamental, measures, and interface dimensions. This really set up a P&D environment, with positive tapes "playing," conducive to searching and arranging for ACCI. What's more, norms of behavior and performance were well set, along with the needed stroking rewards and more acceptable statements of reprimand and penalities when required. We have only had two more P&D projects since the first one, but I personally have never experienced such *excellent solutions that were actually implemented so fast!* I am very confident we are on the road.

Here are some probing questions that may help a group to interrelate more effectively the peculiarities of the specific situation with the desired future policy conditions:

1 How can we generate positive interest in searching and ACCI? How will we help people see that it is beneficial always to *search* for improvement even though no direct change occurs?
2 What type and how much education is to be provided to all of the people regarding the basic P&D approach and improvement search idea? How will this differ for personnel at each level of the organization?
3 What awards or other recognitions for employee contributions might be designed into our policies?
4 How should the gains of change be shared among management, employees, clients, customers, and other stakeholders?
5 What provisions for employee security are needed if positions are eliminated through search and P&D projects?
6 How should the policy emphasis be directed? Will certain concepts be applied across the whole organization, or only on specific projects? Will emphasis be given to short-term returns, long-range goals, or towards those projects with the highest benefit/cost ratios?

7 What kind of publicity and promotion can be utilized to keep people continually informed about the policies?

D. ACCI BASED ON AN INSTITUTIONALIZED PROGRAM

Institutionalizing a betterment and search effort should draw on the benefits of the other three arrangements. The benefits hopefully produce the "harmony" or *wa* Japanese seek in their organizations to balance units by an identification with the whole.

A programmatic effort includes one or more P&D professionals, or a person who has a part-time assignment as the P&D professional. A program tends to be the vehicle for institutionalizing search processes in large organizations. A helping P&D professional, for example, would utilize project betterment and favorable behaviors, and would hardly get involved with organizational policies and programs. Besides, only large organizations are so subject to Corollary 5a (organizations tend toward unsatisfactory existence), or to Gresham's law (routine activities drive out planning). Overcoming this entropic direction requires energy and effort in the form of a program.

A feature of a program is its legitimization of all P&D and specifically of the search for change as important functions of the organization, comparable to personnel, accounting, marketing, operations, and so on. That is, search for P&D changes is just as critical a purposeful activity for the survival of the organization as these other activities. Its functions and activities should thus be organized and programmed just as the other survival functions are. This level of "respectability," however, must be matched by accomplishments of the *functions* of continuing change and improvement.

Another feature is axiomatic. The program for a specific organization should be designed by its people, especially managers, who will have to live with the structural, personnel, functional, and policy relationships. An organization should not jump into a programmatic effort just because the idea is good (such as participative management). Almost all organizations are far removed from the exemplary practices embodied in the descriptions of bettering each solution, favorable behaviors, and organizational policies.

A major concern of an institutionalized program is to keep the organization itself continually aware of and oriented toward the many changes that are taking place in the world around the organization, irrespective of its size. This means searching for P&D changes on a programmatic basis—posing future-type questions, identifying environmental trends, anticipating difficulties in organizational effectiveness and readiness factors (staffing, control, communications, facilities, purchasing, marketing, etc.), fostering and creating imaginative alternatives, maintaining contacts with many sources of I&K *in* locus content areas and *in* P&D, evaluating alternatives to aid the political choice process, seeking different views and theories *of* P&D, searching for changes in the institutional program itself, and so on.

This list is a tall order indeed. It represents the view that a program is always oriented towards becoming. It sets the stage for a stable organization based on continual changes that people expect rather than are shocked about. It represents a 100 ideal on a scale of "completeness of efforts in searching and ACCI."

How ready is an organization for such a program? A project or two may be needed initially to increase a factor's readiness before getting a whole program started.

1. Status of Readiness Factors for a Program

The history and behaviors of the organization will influence the amount of commitment to or readiness for implementing an institutionalized program. Putting together rough indicators of readiness for a program not only will lead to the most effective program for the organization, but may well avoid the difficulties found in organizations when they try to diffuse, for example, work restructuring or quality of working life principles throughout all divisions and sections. These difficulties (see Table 16-2) are virtual paraphrases of the explanations people offer for why individual project solutions are not adopted (see Chapters Four and Five). To the extent that developing a program is a P&D project that should follow the P&D scenario, these difficulties can be minimized by considering the level of readiness as part of step 1b, the design of the P&D system that will be put into place to then design the institutional program.

Measures of readiness factors can help identify the type of program that might be developed. *Type of program* will mean amount of completeness (e.g., programmatic search efforts, structured P&D systems for each project, education, etc.). This could be "measured" on a 0-to-100 scale. Each readiness factor could also be so measured. If all measures of all readiness factors were 0, it would be easy to conclude that no type of institutionalized program could exist (completeness = 0). If all readiness factors measured 100, a similar easy conclusion is that a totally complete program could exist (completeness = 100). Neither readiness factors nor program completeness will, of course, ever exist at either 0 or 100.

The idea of estimating the range of program completeness from the rough measures of readiness is portrayed in Figure 16-2. All of the curves represent hypothetical but mostly supportable relationships. The relationships portrayed are not and will likely never be highly reliable, thus are not useful for predicting the type of program to set up (Corollary 7a). Some illustrative interpretations about the types of programs identified along the ordinate in Figure 16-2 should help depict their range.

Position A: No efforts Changes occur by "accident," as, for example, when equipment required to replace a 25-year-old machine is much better. People in these organizations are often told when making an improvement suggestion, "Forget it, we're doing just fine. Besides, you are paid to work, not think."

Position B: Random An occasional idea is tried, but ideas are not encouraged or sought.

Table 16-2 Difficulties Found in Organizations Trying to Set up Quality of Working Life Programs throughout the Whole Organization*

- Regression in the pilot project
- Poor model for change because the initial project lacks either visibility or credibility or involves significantly different technology
- Confusion over what is to be diffused
- Higher management can botch up the way they formulate and communicate the diffusion policy
- Inappropriateness of labels employed
- Deficient implementation
- Lack of top management commitment and junior opposition
- Bureaucratic barriers of vested interests and existing organizational routines
- Threatened obsolescence of staff groups [and] first-line supervision
- Self-limiting dynamics of the "star-envy" phenomenon
- Shift in the reward structure with payoffs for pioneers providing a better benefit-risk picture than for subsequent users
- Early participants feeling special and superior
- Rivalry among those engaged in work restructuring
- Leaders skirmish with superiors and staff become aggressive in asserting their correctness and thus hurt their careers.

* Adapted from R. E. Walton, "Explaining Why Success Didn't Take," *Organizational Dynamics*, Vol. 3, No. 3, Winter 1975.

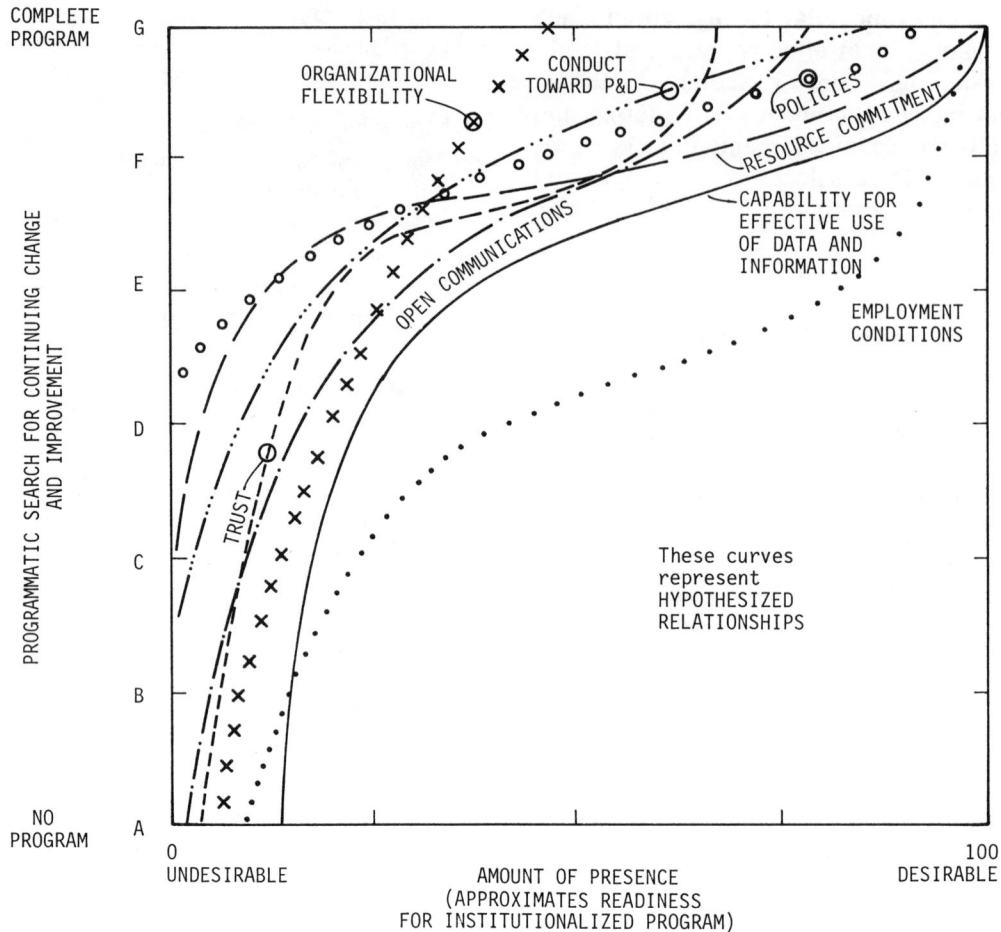

Figure 16-2 Relationship of readiness factors and programmatic efforts in search for P&D changes.

Position C: Crisis A special P&D or improvement effort is mounted to counteract a crisis (budget cut, price competition, sudden nonavailability of materials), but the organized effort is dropped when the crisis fades.

Position D: Positive Attitudes People search intuitively for possible P&D opportunities and this is encouraged. Or a "sharp" manager or top executive does seek and find continuing P&D opportunities, but usually finds it difficult to explain to others *how* it is done. The people get frustrated because they may not know how to proceed, and the manager gets frustrated because the others don't produce comparable results with their positive attitude.

Position E: Department of —— Commitment is translated to a department of —— staffed with professionals of the current rage in techniques or solutions: organizational development, operations research, work measurement, policy analysis, computer information systems, and so on. If you are a manager facing the real problem of, say, increasing costs per

unit, what is the likely response you get from the various specialists? The work measurement person will say: Measure more of the work, increase the number of jobs on incentives, give yourself greater control of the labor content. The operations research person will say: Build a mathematical model of cost relationships and get the optimum relationships. The industrial engineer will say: Flowchart the whole process and reduce the number of handlings, storage points, in-process inventory items, etc. The organization development person will say: Provide team skill training to employees, have them meet to work out the problems. The value analysis person will say: Go over each component to reduce the material costs. The quality of work life person will say: Enrich jobs, lower the level of decision making. The systems engineer will say: Do interpretive structural modeling and input-output analysis to determine the best information system for immediate diagnostic results for the manager. And so on.

Whose advice do you take? Or, if you believe two

or more should be put together, should you be the person who tries to bring together the various technique competitors? P&D professionals, after all, are supposed to help organizations achieve their objectives, not achieve P&D technique use. This position also occurs in large and complex political entities:

Congress keeps setting up its own official agencies to give it official advice. These are the Congressional Research Service, an arm of the venerable Library of Congress; the General Accounting Office, created in 1921 to investigate the workings of government programs and recommended improvements; the Office of Technology Assessment, established in 1972 to warn Congress about the unintended side effects of changing technology, and the Congressional Budget Office, set up in 1974 to keep score on Congress's spending plans.

All this agency-creation is part of the Capitol Hill syndrome of looking for the easy institutional fix, and adds to the already excessive growth of congressional staff.... But does a Congress need four separate coaches to sustain its independence? It seems doubtful.[38]

Position F: Improvement Program Usually separate from P&D (long-range planning, product design, information systems) but does coordinate techniques, focus on real-world problems; seeks to develop human resources, yet uses conventional approaches.

Position G: Complete Institutionalized PDA Program Seeks the same objectives as F but with the holistic perspective of the five intertwined factors.

Additional improvements in readiness factors enable an organization to change its position toward the 100 level. An organization at Position E, for example, may need improvements in organizational policies to start changing toward Position F, and one at Position B probably needs, say, seminars for improving communications and openness, and policies for employee security to change toward position C. A critical aid in any case is the total P&D approach, which can be used at any position to develop a solution for improving the factors that are most likely to "move" the organization more quickly toward 100, or at least toward the next position. Assuming that a change from, say, 50 to 100 can be made in a year is almost certainly going to lead to failure. If your organization is at position B now, then a move to C in a year is very good, and a move to D in the following year is excellent. Yes, it would be very desirable for all organizations to be at G *right now,* but that is highly unlikely ever to occur. Stability for tomorrow is defined as at least a constant increasing rate of change. This differs from today's definition of stability as a constant rate of change or yesterday's status quo.

2. Parts of an Institutionalized Program

These parts and the concepts they portray provide an explanation of Position G that can serve as an ideal target for specific designs. Early building blocks involved in ACCI concerned control functions (establish work norms, monitor performance, correct). Then came setting objectives, budgeting, operations planning (forecasting environment and demand), strategic planning (evaluation of forecasts and alternative selection), development planning (new project areas), and capability planning (long-term patterns and priorities).[39]

The following parts can be arranged in many different ways, especially to ensure that efforts in ACCI remain creative, responsive, open, participative, purpose-oriented, and exploratory:

A. Organizational Policies

Previously stated policies, favorable behaviors and project-specific betterment plans are the basis of this consideration. But the specific form of implementing, for example, the policy regarding assignment of responsibility for projects, can vary: Responsibility can be given to project teams that cut across organizational boundaries; P&D activities are controlled by the team; responsibility can be given to various existing organizational units depending on the stage and phase of the P&D activity (marketing can do *purposes*, engineering can do *system specifications*, manufacturing can do *production methods*, and so forth). Or responsibility can be given to any combination of units, if several P&D problems are being worked on.

A program could also be designed right from the start to incorporate the interim milestones of getting projects to incorporate betterment changes, develop favorable behaviors on the part of managers/administrators/supervisors, and establish policies in the various areas noted previously. In other words, organizational policies will reflect power and hierarchical relationships, already changing division/department coordination resulting from new products/services, extant levels of P&D, psychological types of the people involved, and so on. For example, the idea of a policy-making ladder in state government (Table 16-3) expresses hierarchical relationships that will influence such organizational policies.

B. Structure

The system matrix can characterize the complexity of institutionalized program structure. The idea of a P&D system for a particular project (Table 10-1) can be related to a program by calling the program and its structure a meta-P&D system. Reviewing these refer-

Table 16-3 Policy-Making Ladder
for State Government*

Governor

Legislative Leaders
Top Administrators
Supreme Court Justices

Top Party Leaders
Influential Legislators
High-Level Administrators
Elected Executive Officials

Other Legislators
Administrators
Other Judges

Interest Group Officials
Public Opinion Leaders
Lower-Level Party Leaders

Politically Active Citizens

Ordinary Voters

Nonvoters

* From C. E. Lindblom, *The
Policy-Making Process*. Englewood
Cliffs, N.J.: Prentice Hall, 1968, p.
103.

ences in the light of a meta-P&D system leads to critical questions about these structural factors of the whole organization.

Should there be a separate program department? If so, to whom should it report? If not, how should the search ideas be incorporated into the organization? Should the responsibility of supervising the program and long-range planning activities be given to an individual or a committee? For applicability throughout an organization, a program ACCI should report to someone with broad overall organizational responsibility and firm commitment to ACCI, such as the president, the executive vice president, or a committee from among those reporting to them. Some organizations have high-level and broadly defined personnel or controller vice-presidents who might take the responsibility.

Should searching and ACCI become part of some other department, such as management science, budgeting, corporate planning, information systems, productivity services, industrial engineering, or administrative systems? Yes, if the other department entails broad rather than narrow concepts. No, if they are technique-oriented rather than real-world/continual-change–directed. Be careful of the "De-

partment of Blank" myth. Too often an organization sets up such departments to which its executives can point with pride to show how progressive the organization is, but they are not really committed to ACCI and little gets done.

Should P&D operate on a project basis in the "matrix organization" format, with project teams appearing and disbanding as projects are started and finished? This is probably the most frequently used structure, and it is likely to be the easiest way of getting a program started if all the interpretations of ACCI are incorporated.[40]

Should a program be centralized or decentralized? Or should a central function and policy group be available to help decentralized P&D professionals located with real-world groups—sales people, engineers, teachers, hospital ancillary service people, financial experts, policy makers? Or should P&D professionals be one of the functional resources allocated along with other "specialists" in a matrix-type or project cluster structure? Most professionals believe they should work for the "top" person because they assume decisions only flow down and information up. This is not true even most of the time.

Should the P&D professionals be in-house, should they be shared among a group of similar organizations, such as hospitals, or should they be external consultants? Size of the organization tends to be large, medium, or small, respectively, for these three conditions. But size is far from *the* determinant.

What relationship should be set up with other search-for-change types of activities? Some of these are suggestion systems, cost containment, value analysis, management-by-objectives, corporate planning, profit or gains sharing, organizational development, "bonus saver of the month," and work simplification. No specific answer is given here, because the format an organization selects will depend on an almost infinite number of considerations.

Can a program be set up as a "collateral P&D organization" parallel to the "operating organization"? In effect, almost everyone operates and supervises in their existing organization, but "puts on a P&D hat" on a regular basis, perhaps with a different group.

How will disagreements between competing constituencies be resolved? Usual management processes can be used in most cases. Arbitrators, mediators, external panels, juries, and R&D are methods that could be used to resolve disputes among organizations (state-federal-private industry) as well as internal conflicts.

Other questions concerning structural matters *within* the program assume an answer to one or more of the above questions (e.g. determining the *de-*

partmental organization structure assumes that a department is the answer). Table 10-1 sheds some light on these critical intraprogram matters:

How should a program department operate? By having technique specialists operate in the "Department of Blank" mode (position F, Figure 16-2)? Or should the P&D professional be responsible for all solutions in a specific area of the organization coordinated by a central office, with advisors in technical fields? Figure 16-3 shows this type of structure.

What support services are available to the P&D efforts? Computer facilities and data banks, statisticians, graphic artists, and so forth may already be available.

Should P&D services be charged to various operating departments? This would apply to projects because overall long-range planning is probably a central overhead function. Some organizations do charge when each operating department is considered a profit center.

Should internal or external P&D professionals and staff personnel be involved? Are roles and functions (Table 14-3) that need emphasis now different from ones that will be needed later? Normal P&D professional preparation in models, techniques, and I&K *in locus* content areas is usually insufficient. Cooperative work with people of many backgrounds—technical, social, managerial, operational, private sector, public—means that special psychological characteristics are needed (see Chapter Fourteen).

How many people, primarily P&D professionals, are needed? This is so variable that I will not even refer to any numbers for fear that some one will interpret them as prescriptions. Usual factors to consider are the number of employees, intensity of capital investment (higher usually increases the number of P&D

professionals), degree of practice of favorable behaviors, existence of good policies, and so on. Fortunately the P&D scenario (Figure 16-1) is a good format for estimating person-hours and elapsed time per activity or phase along the timeline.

What is the source of P&D professionals, internal or external? Some professionals can only come from external sources—architects, engineers, health care professionals—whereas others may emerge from inside an organization and obtain specialized training through seminars and intensive courses—information systems designers, layout and facilities planners, interior designers. No person should be overlooked just because of a specific educational omission. That can always be added for someone with brains.

C. Audit and Review

A program inevitably has ups and downs, difficulties in application, and a share of adverse personality situations. To assume that it will proceed smoothly if it is planned properly sets the stage for deterioration. And if a program has no apparent present snags, a way to minimize them in the future is to look for program improvements now. The purpose of audit and review is to evaluate what has transpired and determine if the program's ends are being met.

Three highly interrelated levels of concern form the basis of audit and review. First is reviewing whether or not the measures of effectiveness for each implemented solution were attained, including originally built-in betterment changes and the search for each one's continuing improvement. This relates to two of the three P&D objectives—to maximize the effectiveness of solutions, and to maximize the likelihood of implementation. Second is the performance of the P&D efforts (department, office, project management,

Figure 16-3 A possible organization for a P&D department of ACCI.

group, etc.), including the program, in attaining the other P&D objective of maximizing the effectiveness of the P&D resources. Third is the preparation of basic evaluation information (see evaluation purposeful activity in Chapters Two and Three) about the first two levels of concern for presentation to top management and the organization as a whole.

1. Results Obtained from Each P&D Project and Search for Betterment

Individual project measures (increase in number of customers served, cost per unit produced or served, wait time, degree of acceptance, etc.) and some type of aggregation of the measures to portray "total" effects for a time period, usually a year, are the focus of this first level. Aggregation type factors are of many types. For example, productivity improvement efforts usually aggregate measures of material utilization, outputs of people's efforts and skills, resource (machines, tools, money) utilization, and customer/client satisfactions and/or demands for the products or services (see Phase 5 in Chapter Twelve). Each of these four measures can have several other factors for sublevel aggregations. Using data for these factors from the year's P&D projects helps to audit and review this level.

Another example is the aggregation of life-cycle cost measures. These could assess the effect of the past year's projects on products or systems as well as carry effectiveness ideas beyond the organization into use, disposal, recycling, and environmental factors. A P&D program effort is obviously not the only organizational activity that impacts on these figures, but they are still the essential ones that P&D projects are seeking to influence.

Other aspects of solution-finding and implementation endeavors to review are: How are the basic P&D philosophies being used? Are project design efforts, as an illustration, really developing ideal systems? How ideal are they, or how much do they get into advanced technology or ideas? Some gross and overall measures of these questions could include questionnaires, external assessments, interviews, and so on (see Appendix A). Project reports should be reviewed on a sampling basis to assess the performance of P&D teams: How many projects are started and proposals made in a given period of time? How many were accepted by the organization? Are changes being installed as soon as possible after they have been proposed and accepted? How did the cost estimate of a proposed solution compare with its later actual cost?

What is being done to give credit to individuals and groups for outstanding results? Such recognition helps to provide continual interest in P&D. Are the super-

visory staff members active in getting their people and themselves into P&D activities? Is any sort of achievement review being made of individuals, workshop groups, project teams, or other departments?

2. Performance Effectiveness of P&D Efforts

Quantitative and qualitative factors are involved. The quantitative factors are often closely related to what happens in the actual systems or solutions. But solution results are not always a direct measure of P&D performance since so many other organizational factors (e.g., good supervision, good purchasing, favorable policies) influence the solutions. At any rate, some possible quantitative measures of P&D performance include:

- Increased savings or benefits in real-world operations that resulted from P&D projects. Year-to-year actual and percentage increases in economic savings as a result of the projects (see Phase 5J in Chapter Twelve).
- Percentage economic savings per P&D staff person.
- Ratio of time and person hours taken on projects to the beginning estimates of time and person-hours.
- Ratio of P&D costs to economic savings.
- Ratio of actual to budgeted P&D expenditures.
- Absentee and voluntary turnover rates of P&D personnel.
- Ratio of P&D professionals' total time to time spent in meetings and communications with real-world personnel *during* projects.
- Percentages of milestone times and costs met within, say ±5% of estimates.
- Number of contacts about and amount of time spent on monitoring solution performance *after* implementation.
- Rating scale evaluation of each P&D professional in terms of individual performance on most of these factors.
- Effectiveness in managing time.
- Number of continuing education seminars and meetings attended per P&D professional on topics of organizational pertinence in all three areas of I&K.

A specific organization should not use survey generalizations from similar organizations as the only basis for auditing internal activities. One hospital, for example, had a radiology department with a productivity level 43% above the average of many hospitals. If next year's amount is 39%, a comparison with the generalization still looks fine, but a comparison with last year's amount in the *specific* hospital is far more important.

Quantitative factors will seldom be the only ones to consider. The quality of relationships is often the most important factor for the future. Some qualitative factors of P&D performance (even though some "measures" are found by questionnaires and interviews) include:

• Degree to which organization senses real purposes and goals are being met.
• Morale, motivation, and attitude of P&D professionals.
• Ease of working relationships between real-world units and P&D professionals.
• Image of P&D professionals in eyes of the organization.
• Sense of professionalism and performance orientation in doing P&D projects and presenting results.
• Ability to incorporate within projects and solutions only needed advanced and diverse areas of knowledge *in* P&D and *in* the locus content area.
• Minimization of political gamesmanship and connotations of "us" insiders and "you" outsiders.
• Ability to respond to emergency needs.
• Willingness of real-world units to seek P&D and program services.
• Ability to explain informally and in educational sessions the total P&D concept.
• Degree to which operational units feel a P&D project is a cooperative effort, not just a display of P&D professional expertise.
• Degree to which P&D programmatic efforts give operating units and personnel a better mode of "thinking" about problems, customers, and objectives.

Some of this audit and review (or performance auditing) might be conducted, say annually, by internal auditors, outside CPAs, consultants, or management teams from other areas.

3. Transmittal of Solution and P&D Performance Effectiveness Information to Top Management and the Whole Organization This is necessary to assess how well *organizational objectives and goals* are being met. A P&D group too often believes it is being effective by, for example, establishing more measurements and developing more models, whereas the real needs are being largely ignored. Properly summarizing the

measures from the first two levels and including pertinent anecdotal and qualitative references are the major forms whereby this information can be transmitted for top management's evaluation of P&D efforts. The P&D program or unit should seek to relate these factors to top management's directions, goals, and objectives. Thus, some *additional* factors ought to be assessed at this third level:

• Proportion of top priority *P&D* problems that were completed.
• Amount of acceptance by top management of the priorities for P&D projects proposed by the P&D unit.
• Degree to which expectations of P&D set up by top management are being met.
• Proportion of P&D projects in locus content areas that concern future conditions, satisfactory existing conditions, and unsatisfactory existing conditions. (The former two should be increasing as the latter one decreases.)
• Degree to which P&D changes and improvement are being reflected in the budget for each profit, cost, or departmental center, and whether planned, progressive P&D improvements are built into long-range budgeting.
• Success in obtaining budget commitments for speculative P&D projects in developing new solutions, encouraging technological innovations, and funding research and development projects recommended by P&D projects.
• Amount of assistance to the organization in increasing profitability or discretionary income, flexibility, sense of organizational identity, amelioration of organizational strain, growth and development of human resources, search for change as stability, survival, control over or forecasting environmental conditions and uncertainties, employee satisfaction, reliability of product or service, and creative and innovative behaviors.

One other idea is possibly part of this level. Sunset laws (in government) or concepts (in other organizations) proclaim that a system will be automatically abolished on a given date (three to seven years after inception of the system) unless a mandate is given to extend it. This would be done only after the whole effort were scrutinized as if it had no budget at all.

D. Research and Development in P&D

An organization that institutionalizes a program is likely to have an R and D program investigating new products, manufacturing, or operating processes, markets, and information and decision support systems concentrated *in* locus content areas (Chapter Fifteen). R and D concerning theories and knowledge *of* P&D tends to be done at universities and "think-tanks," just as "basic" research into, say, lasers, is done there while specific laser product and process R and D is done in organizations. Thus, R and D *in* P&D is the usual need in organizations.

In a broad sense, R and D in an institutionalized program gets specific information for and answers specific questions from workshop groups and project teams; distributes to various groups and teams pertinent information from the literature; evaluates techniques and approaches suggested by others (e.g., universities, research centers); develops new techniques as needed; and performs "laboratory" or field and survey research projects to supply needed information. Such R and D is the equivalent of the "intelligence" activities of a program ACCI.

The following specific types of R and D *in* P&D are just illustrative of what *some* organizations are doing. Each of the following topics may actually have started as a P&D project (design a system for project selection, plan an implementation procedure for all P&D projects, develop a method of measuring organizational effectiveness, etc.), but complexities, ambiguities, a wide range of possible organizational applications, and risk factors indicated that a "classical" research approach to investigate the possibilities of a generalization would quite likely be useful.

Project Selection (Step 1a Primarily)   How to gage prospective payoffs of possible P&D projects and implementation of solutions without limiting the prospects of a breakthrough that may occur during strategy steps? What P&D project selection model can cope with the variety of criteria needed—realism (of objectives, risks, people, technology level), capability to do a project (P&D skills, time availability, money), flexibility (adapt to start or terminate decisions, budget allocations), ability of many to use, cost to set up and run computer, and relationship to organizational needs.[41]

Implementation   What specific tools and techniques for the P&D professional and for the manager can incorporate implementation ideas immediately into a project? What prods or reminders can be used to get a P&D project effort to design its specific installation and implementation systems? Are there reward methods that would encourage operational people to take part in P&D and implementation efforts?

Organizational Impact   Many solutions change organizational relationships among positions, structure, and people. Can a method be developed for P&D professionals to adequately estimate the results of a solution on patterns of formal and informal information flow? Or estimate the future capacity to absorb growth within the current structure? What is the potential of the organization to adopt a new technology? How can the effectiveness of an organization be assessed so that internal changes and environmental conditions can be evaluated on the basis of consistent factors related to its survival, growth, and adaptability (profits or discretionary income are far from sufficient for the assessment)? Many *general* concepts are proposed to do these things, but they serve as checklists at best for a specific organization. One model, for example, investigating the utilization of technological and human resources, "treats personnel, technology, and organizational structure as simultaneous decision variables."[42] Another proposes that "technology, or the work done in organizations, is . . . the defining characteristic of organizations . . . that serves as a better basis for comparing them than the several schemes which now exist."[43]

Contents of Plans/Solutions/Designs   How can the solution framework/system matrix become organization-specific as a means of avoiding oversights on critical specifications? What methods can be used to document alternative futures? How can interactions among cells of the solution framework be identified?

P&D Interactions and Coupling   What is the appropriate mix and relationship between P&D and basic product/process/technology R and D? When should patch-up operating and supervising be terminated in favor of a P&D project? How can P&D establish effective communications on projects with related but not necessarily major thrust activities? How can advanced technology information be made available to P&D groups? Which of several functional components should be implemented as close to the FIST and as fast as possible while others have less of the target implemented now and then move on an accelerated basis in four to five years?

Forecasting Methods   Three basic questions about this critical P&D requirement need investigation: What formulation of data now available can show what naturally occurs (number of hours artificial lighting is needed in homes, number of 18-year-old persons in the country each year for the next 18 years)? Which model fits operating data on which P&D solutions are to be based (number of patients tested in the hospital emergency room each day, computer processing time of payroll checks)? Which type permits the most effective indicators of performance if conditional patterns of events did occur (impact on production schedules of reduced sales of oil-burning furnaces and of increased lower-margin electrics)? The benefits to each organization of doing R and D for itself is illustrated by the company with 40% of its product business in one market. Two national organizations predict yearly sales of the equipment the company's customers manufacture, but the company developed its own model which for four years in a row most closely predicted actual sales.

Technique Development and Evaluation How can the project team establish measures of effectiveness for the school district's purchasing department? What is the potential usefulness of linear programming for this project, or game theory, queuing models, etc.? What role can be played by any techniques that *assume* profit, cost, and other decision rules (which solidify the status quo) or cost more to utilize than present procedures?

Education in the Total P&D Approach for Executives and Managers To illustrate a far too typical situation, a good technical person became a vice-president of engineering. However, he contributed poorly to corporate planning, scheduling times and cost on departmental P&D projects, following solutions through to implementation, communicating effectively with the board of directors regarding plans, and getting people involved in P&D projects. What format would educate top-level people in the total P&D approach as a managerial concept? How can top executives and managers avoid a "picked-on" feeling if selected for an educational session?

E. Budget-Related Activities

Tying a program and P&D into the organizational budgeting process could be quite effective. The manager, coordinator, or facilitator of a program ought to spend most of the time with budgeting efforts of executives, managers and supervisors. This should be done on both the *guidance* information flow from top to the bottom, and the reverse *allocation* information flow to the next level of management, and so on.

Interrelating with major division and department heads on *budgetary* and cost matters enables the program manager to do the following:

- Learn when *new* systems are to be requested in the budget.
- Plan betterment programs.

- Reflect all savings in the budget or frame the budget request to show the savings in the face of other cost increases (such as merit raises, seniority, material increases, etc.)
- Inform the division or department head about P&D projects going on within that area of responsibility.
- Interest other department heads in participating in and providing encouragement for the departmental P&D projects.
- Get better follow-up in the installation and management of solutions.
- Provide another channel of information to the person which will support or cause adjustments to the budget requests
- Gain total support for P&D and ACCI.

One company established a capital expenditure budgeting procedure based on the three conditions of systems. A portion of the budget is set aside for original design projects, that is, those changes that constitute long-range development. Another portion is set aside for betterment design, and a third for correction design.

This tie is most essential when special techniques are set up, such as program-planning-budgeting system (PPBS) or zero-base budgeting (ZBB) (Appendix A). Both of these methods are developed around a *budget as the outcome*. Each starts with the *hope* that a program (ends to be sought—PPBS) or a basic decision package (a real need—ZBB) will become the basis from which budget dollar requirements are derived. Slippage from these objectives occurs as managers tend to concentrate on getting the *budget* part accomplished. Both *methods* (not necessarily their procedures, which bias the focus to *budgetary* details rather than purposes and "big-picture" decisions) are quite compatible with P&D and institutionalized programs. The P&D professional has an excellent opportunity to work with managers and the budget process when such techniques are used. As a matter of fact, using PDA may make the difference between success or failure of the techniques because it seeks the best possible solutions which can then be reflected in the budgets. In addition, each betterment schedule for a specific solution/plan/system/program sets up "start from zero" efforts, maybe three or more years apart. This is far more effective than the ZBB idea: "every thing each year starts from zero."

F. Name of the Program

As minor as it may appear, naming the program deserves some attention because it should have a "win-win" ring, should represent something positive the professionals are able to live with and the organization's personnel can understand and accept. "Continuing Planning and Design Change and Improvement Program" is hardly catchy. Even "Planning and Design Program" may lack pizazz. At least, the name and its possible acronyms should not be negative, embarrassing or laughable. Perhaps no new name is needed because searching and ACCI become a constituent part of the whole P&D effort. Some names that have been utilized are *improvement program, management engineering, management systems design, engineering office, planning and design office, value analysis, management services, productivity services, organizational development, strategic planning, cost containment and avoidance, better methods program, quality circles,* and *profit sharing* (or *gains sharing* or *cost reduction sharing* in a nonprofit organization).

Asking the following questions, as part of following the whole P&D approach, can help you in designing your own institutionalized program.

1 Does each P&D project have a complete betterment arrangement incorporated in its solution?

2 Are steps being taken to encourage effective individual and organizational behaviors?

3 Have effective organizational policies been established?

4 How should the program fit into the organization structure? To whom should it report? How can it be structured to fit organizational purposes that are to be achieved? What will be its ratio of overall P&D professionals to specialists?

5 How will the program be interrelated with existing incentive plans, corporate planning activities, suggestion systems, operations research, methods improvement, management by objectives, etc.?

6 What kind of publicity and promotion can be utilized to keep people continually informed about program *results* (and activities)?

7 What type of research and development capabilities should be incorporated into the program?

8 What type of audit and review mechanisms should be incorporated within the program? How often and what type of justification should be established for the program?

9 What should be the name of the program?

Illustrative Programs

The specific forms, policies, and structure of an institutionalized program differ from one organization to another. Some partial illustrations are included in Appendix B.

Other programs or arrangements in organizations were developed for purposes of improving operations, developing human resources, increasing productivity, reducing costs and waste, and so on. An institutionalized program in ACCI can be a worthwhile addition to an existing program if the program is successful, or the good parts in an otherwise poor effort can be incorporated into a more complete program.

Some of the alternative programs are reviewed briefly in Table 16-4. The mere fact that they exist (the equivalent of roughly position D or above in Figure 16-2) indicates some positive direction of thinking and level of readiness of the organization's policies. They almost always manifest the problems or shortcomings of current P&D (Chapters Four and Five), but have significant potential for growing into the type of institutionalized program described here. Other institutional arrangements, such as worker or union representation on boards of directors, productivity bargaining, workers councils, and collective bargaining, may exist independently or be a part of most other programs.

This section would seem incomplete if I omitted the major suggestion, repeated several times: Design your own arrangements for continuing search and improvement. Set up a P&D system to do the P&D of the effort. If this repeated message helps one more person to have the "ah-hah" experience and see the light, it is well worthwhile.

TIMELINE PERSPECTIVES ON THE FACTOR OF ACCI IN THE P&D APPROACH

A timeline view of arranging for continuing change and improvement would seem to be a redundancy. *Arranging* is a continual, time-based idea and *timeline* connotes dynamic and continuing perspectives. To a large extent, *how* the ideas might be useful through the phases and steps of a specific project is almost self-evident. The details of *how* to do this are related to the jointly performed perspectives of each step in the P&D scenario (Figure 16-1).

Put another way, though, the timeline perspective regarding ACCI during a particular project has to build on the real-world commitments expressed in favorable behaviors, conducive organizational policies, availability of various parts of a program and betterment details built into previous projects. A project team (or whatever form the P&D system takes) must have these ideas and resources current in the setting if ACCI is to have its greatest impact. If education in the P&D approach is needed during a project, then having such resources readily at hand influences what the group can

Table 16-4 Some Other Organizational Programs with Aspects of an Institutionalized ACCI Program

Name and Brief Description of Alternative Program	The Related Aspects and Possible Resource in ACCI
ANNUAL IMPLEMENTATION PLAN Health systems agencies are required to have a long-range health systems plan for ensuring quality and accessibility of health services in the area being served. An AIP is prepared annually to focus on practical and manageable goals and objectives for the year. Priorities are set for each item within broad functional areas after many people from the area served by the HSA have been involved.	Long-range "target." People involved. Yearly updates for detail (no set dates to update target). Priority setting.
COLLATERAL ORGANIZATION "A parallel, continuously coexisting organization [has] norms differing from those usually in force, [is] used to identify and solve apparently intractable problems, and is carefully linked to the 'regular' organization. No new people are required." D. E. Zand, "Collateral Organization: A New Change Strategy," *Journal of Applied Behavioral Science*, Vol. 10, No. 1, January–March, 1974, pp. 63+.	Similar to workshop groups with different representation. Operate and supervise is different from Planning and Design. (Note: could conceivably be the whole program.)
CORPORATE PLANNING Usually a five-year time horizon is used. Second year from now updated for quarters, one year from now for monthly budgets. Tends to be extrapolative and done by planning staff and managers. Can cover all elements and dimensions of the "corporation system," but usually focuses on financial ratios and monetary measures.	Continuous. Uses target ideas. Gets managers committed. Deals with total organization.
COST CONTAINMENT Deals with goals for reducing or maintaining costs of all line items in a budget or of all products/services. Infrequently seeks to get cost-cutting commitment that goes down six, seven, eight levels. Often set up on basis of fine-tuning measurements to provide control of costs. Many techniques are promoted for doing cost cutting: work measurement, charts, forms control, operations research modeling, computer analysis, statistical analysis, etc. See *Productivity improvement program*.	Focuses on results, albeit only monetary, which tends to be short-term–oriented.
MANAGEMENT BY OBJECTIVES A yearly cycle consisting of definition by management of organizational goals, delegation of prioritized goals down the hierarchy, manager and subordinate agreement on the subordinate's performance contract, implementation of all the contracts in a hoped for one-for-all and all-for-one helping relationship, and review of results to determine whether contracts should be changed. Some programs become overburdened with mechanics and paperwork, and focus only on short-term precise individual measures.	Mutual development of goals could develop team spirit.
MANAGEMENT *of* OBJECTIVES "The work of an organization is not the sum of many individual [operating and supervising] tasks, but is instead the achieving of an array of specified objectives, and these, whether they are ongoing or change objectives, usually require the coordinated contributions of several individuals in different departments. . . . The organization's objectives and functions can be coordinated contributions of several individuals in different departments. . . . The organization's objectives and functions can be coordinated on a grid . . . which then becomes the organization. [The former are] change [or] improvement objectives [and the latter] functional performance [or] performance maintenance objectives." D. D. Sherwin, "Management *of* Objectives," *harvard Business Review*, Vol. 54, No. 3, May–June 1976, pp. 149+.	Because two different purposeful activities are recognized, the arrangements for handling change and improvement are very close to an institutionalized program.
MANAGERIAL GRID People orientation and production orientation are each rated from 1 (very little) to 9 (very much) for each individual. A 9,9 score is the desirable climate, and movement toward this point on the grid is made through training to improve the appropriate skills. Often combined with *Organization development*.	Two values are recognized. Individual abilities to mesh the two are developed.
MATRIX MANAGEMENT Projects draw personnel on temporary basis from needed internal and external functions. A strong project manager or P&D professional handles all aspects of the project, after which all of the personnel return to their functional unit. A third dimension on activities or organizational service has been included in some cases.	Project teams and their responsibilities are stated to avoid two "bosses." Develops some open communication. (Note: could conceivably be the whole program.)
OPERATIONS RESEARCH/MANAGEMENT SCIENCE Although originally developed in the concept of multidisciplinary project teams, current OR/MS usually relies on seeking improvements through preprogrammed models and mathematical modeling of operations.	

Table 16-4 (*Continued*)

Name and Brief Description of Alternative Program	The Related Aspects and Possible Resource in ACCI
ORGANIZATION DEVELOPMENT Planned efforts managed by the executives to increase the effectiveness and health of the group and the organization through behavioral science. Attempts to move toward collaboration rather than competition among parts of an organization. Controls are interim managerial process on the way toward open communications and trust. A change agent is usually responsible for intervening with the problems of the organization.	Team building, training, multiple management, individual and group involvement.
PRODUCTIVITY IMPROVEMENT PROGRAMS Can range from equivalent of a program on ACCI to a series of measurements that are widely disseminated in the hope the numbers will encourage productivity increases. Many individual techniques are proposed: New pay plans, supportive participation, flexible work hours, job enrichment, etc. Usually involves a committee (cost effectiveness, productivity improvement, etc.). See *Cost containment*.	Measures are needed to justify changes and assess performance.
PROGRAM-PLANNING-BUDGETING SYSTEM See text.	
QUALITY OF WORKING LIFE Improving job satisfactions of workers by increasing the autonomy of each person's and group's work arrangement, maximizing their control of decisions, enriching scope of responsibilities and skills needed through job enrichment, continual learning, democratic processes, and providing healthy and safe work places. Results are projected as employees satisfied from work itself, social integration, positive impacts extending to family and community.	Most of the premises are desirable, although the approach would differ.
SOCIOTECHNICAL DESIGN OF ORGANIZATIONS To achieve institutional survival and adaptability, economic survival, institutional effectiveness in attaining goals, and quality of working life, 14 attributes of new designs are: "systemic structure and roles, organizations as open systems, design by joint optimization, organizational uniqueness, stated organizational values or philosophy, quality of working life as an essential objective, comprehensive roles, self-maintaining social units, flat structure, participation, minimal status differences, make large small, iterative evolutionary development, and minimal critical specifications." L. E. Davis, "Evolving Alternative Organization Designs: Their Sociotechnical Bases," *Human Relations*, Vol. 30, No. 3, 1977, pp. 261–273.	All the principles are worthwhile. The P&D approach would permit most of these to become incorporated in a redesign.
VALUE ANALYSIS ENGINEERING Although starting with functions and a limited version of a function hierarchy, a thorough analysis of present costs is made in preparation for assigning so much cost that ought to exist for the value of the component. Almost completely associated with products and components, efforts are underway to apply the same cost/value relationship in any type of system or service.	Cost/value ratio.
ZERO-BASE BUDGETING See text.	

do at that immediate point in time. If new I&K *in* a locus is needed for a project, then having an R and D resource at hand influences what a group does at a point in time. If questions about employment security arise during a discussion of a possible alternative solution, the group at that point in time is influenced by available policies regarding retention due to change, retraining, severance pay, and so on.

The timeline on a project is thus significantly affected by the levels to which previously reviewed factors in ACCI are or are not developed. Time may be necessary to develop an educational program, time may have to be allocated to develop employee security policies, time will just have to elapse before the specific I&K *in* the content area can be obtained. Con-

versely, *not* allocating time for those purposes has a direct bearing on the decisions made regarding the specific project in, for example, rejecting an alternative because the lack of employment security policies would cause massive personnel turmoil if it were adopted.

The "principal of congruence"[44] is what must be operable in a project. On the one hand, arrangements already set up for continuing change and improvement force the change needs of a project to conform at that point in time. On the other hand, project needs can set up pressures for getting better continuing change arrangements in place. The start of an approach must be embedded in the realities and characteristics of the organization itself at the particular point in time.

One method of accomplishing these objectives is to build in time and costs concerned with ACCI when developing the specific work program and allocations of people in steps 1a, 1b and 1c. Estimates are usually needed at that time, and all five factors in the holistic entities of P&D can contribute insights into what the project costs and times should involve. A pitfall of preparing project budgets and work programs is underestimating or overcommitting people's time. But just adding people is not necessarily satisfactory because the addition of each person does reduce the "efficiency" of the group. Interactions among ten people cause more inefficiencies than among five. The idea of optimality does enter because one may be clearly insufficient and 10 far too many, but very few techniques are available to calculate this. The timeline scenario of Figure 16-1 is thus an inestimable aid in determining these critical numbers.

As a project proceeds along the strategy path, individual aspects and parts of ACCI are likely to be used as needed. The opportunity for a project team to reach out and utilize an array of resources leads to the team doing so without necessarily scheduling all of it. Some aspects (education, audit and review) will have been preplanned into the project as the project timeline (step 1b, Chapter Twelve) is set up at the beginning. But the need for many other aspects (e.g., R and D, retraining) are likely to become known only as the project goes along.

The following comments recast many PDA concepts to help a P&D professional or team incorporate arrangements for continuing change and improvement as time goes on in a project.

Start a project with the psychostructure that exists. Criticizing a group because they are not truthful or do not have open communications or effective employment security policies is inappropriate. An organization cannot exist completely at Position G (Figure 16-2), so improvement in ACCI can always be expected.

Use the P&D principles organized on a change theory basis (Table 16-1). P&D principles' timeline basis can help you get through the normal cyclical euphoria and depression moods of a project. Some principles decline in importance over project time (see 3, 4 and 11 in Table 16-1) and others grow (see 8 and 13 as examples).

Get all constituencies involved early on a project (Column C, Table 14-2). Long-term continuing change and improvement arrangements may develop. For example, the growing number of joint labor-management committees in U.S. companies "are serious endeavors freely and cooperatively undertaken to enhance profits, jobs, and the workplace."[45]

Set up a checklist of key continuing change features available in the organization for review prior to each meeting.

Identify the factors of concern that have arisen in previous P&D projects. Figure 16-4 illustrates how a profile of a group, department, or organization might be portrayed with the aid of several measures. Everyone has the opportunity continually to seek movement of projects or groups from the current profile (connecting the values of each measure) toward the maximum 10 for each measure.

Treat any proposal from outside, usually "selling" a solution, as a learning purposeful activity. Even if the equipment, system, or whatever appears to be directly applicable, seems to have survived the tests of implementation elsewhere, and even if you have skilled people ready to implement it in your organization—nevertheless consider these siren songs to "accept and install" as out of bounds (Axiom 7). But *learning* about any apparently new idea provides constant stimulation for searching and ACCI.

Ask a key question each and every time a decision is made in a project: What impact will that choice have on the operation and improvement of the solution in *n* years?

The P&D process of continually searching for changes and improvements is the best game around—it will keep us playing.

SUMMARY

The interest of humans in improving their conditions is a long-term desire that needs short-term (from daily up to three- or five-year) arrangements to search for continuing change and improvement. Most PDA concepts already reviewed in early chapters support this continual search. The PDA principles, for example, can be placed in the timeline-oriented three steps of a change theory: getting started, developing specific solution recommendations, and implementing the solution within the context of continuing search for change.

Proposition 13 *An implemented P&D change can be considered complete only when the solution includes a closely interwoven set of future specifications, just as the human units where the changes occur should continually search for improvements in all current systems and for solutions to meet new needs.*

Each human unit will have different levels of readiness for efforts committed to searching for change. Several factors (trust and openness, communications,

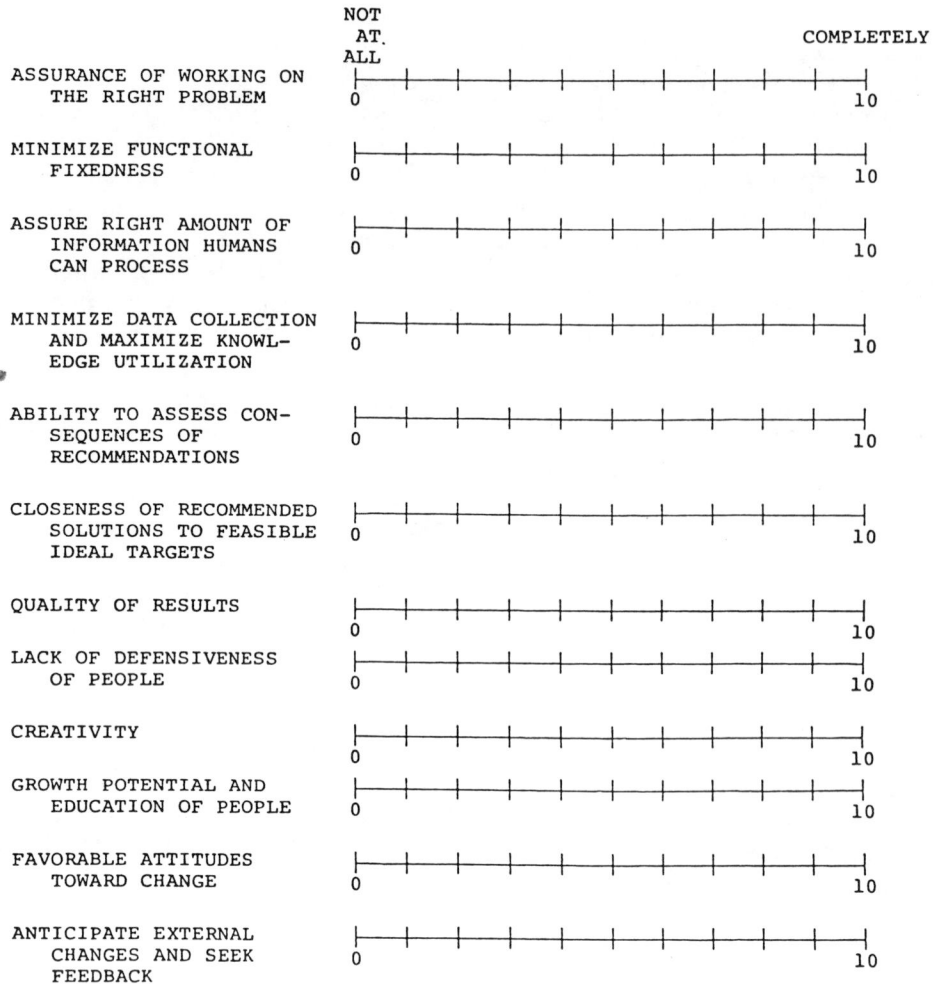

Figure 16-4 Profile work sheet to determine effectiveness of planning and improvement efforts in an organization.

policy level) can be assessed roughly to provide insights about readiness.

Arranging for continuing change and improvement can take place at four levels:

1 Including specific changes to be made in each solution after it is installed.

2 Developing day-by-day managerial practice of behaviors favorable to continual searching.

3 Formulating organizational policies (e.g., employment security, gains sharing, education) conducive to change.

4 Establishing an institutionalized program (structure, R and D, audit and review).

CHAPTER SEVENTEEN

Further Developments of a Total P&D Approach

As confident as I am that the prescriptive total P&D approach will significantly improve the performance of the P&D professions, I am equally convinced that the approach itself needs and will have many changes to increase its effectiveness. It is as incumbent on P&D professions to seek improvement in a good P&D approach as it is for an organization to continually search for them in its good solutions.

The theory *of* P&D presented in this book is a paradigm that should serve as an exemplar of the commonality of professional practice. Yet it is sufficiently open-ended to change as effective methods *in* P&D are developed to make it workable. Methods already exist, as will be shown in this chapter, to search for a paradigm shift.[1]

Our motivation in seeking such changes is to improve our P&D abilities to increase both parts of the paraphrased effective decision equation:[2] An effective P&D solution is equal to its quality times its acceptance. A brilliant solution (say 1 on a 0-to-1 scale) that is not accepted (0) is a 0 effective solution.

We already know many of the difficulties yet to be resolved in this paradigm. For example, the impact of technology on society is uncertain and often unknown. Whether or not a solution will be accepted is difficult to estimate, and for the type of trade-offs needed (e.g., almost instantaneous information transmission versus privacy of records, reliable power versus nuclear waste disposal) there are few if any P&D techniques to help. Better group processes for citizen involvement,

greater concern for politics, morality, religion, and esthetics,[3] improved forecasts and measures of impacts, and faster methods for generating innovative alternatives for effective technology-society interrelations are but illustrations of what P&D theorists must develop. And these do not even incorporate the very large number of unanswered questions raised in every chapter of the book.

These areas for P&D improvements intersect with quite a few academic disciplines. P&D is not just psychology, sociology, physics/chemistry, anthropology, mathematics, political science, nor economics. It *uses* knowledge from all fields, but it is none of them. P&D picks and chooses from their generalizations to further develop itself, but the P&D professions must now take the lead in identifying the questions and guiding some of the work regarding its improvements.

The comments thus far concern the needs for improvements in P&D, which themselves are part of the P&D approach. Yet they agree with what epistemologists and philosophers claim is needed for almost any kind of knowledge and concepts. ''What solid claims can *any* concepts and modes of thought have on our intellectual allegiance? . . . We can no longer afford to assume that our rational procedures, however impartial, find a guarantee in *unchanging principles*, . . . still less in some uniquely valid system of natural and moral philosophy. . . . The moment we stop assuming that the ideas of any milieu form static 'propositional systems,' and recognize that they constitute historically developing 'conceptual populations,' we are free to abandon also the philosophers' traditional assumption that rationality is a subspecies of logicality."[4]

This chapter provides a setting for and some questions about finding improvements of the PDA:

- Problems of P&D a theory *of* P&D should seek to ameliorate.
- Some of the progress of the theories *of* and *in* P&D in resolving these problems.
- The impact of the P&D problems and these theories *of* and *in* P&D on the education of P&D professionals.
- Areas *of* and *in* P&D where improvements are thus needed.
- Speculations about metaproblems where these theories *of* and *in* P&D may be fruitfully tried.

P&D PROBLEMS A THEORY *OF* P&D SHOULD SEEK TO AMELIORATE

Chapters Four and Five summarized a large number of problems relating to P&D. Elucidating a total approach to help resolve the problems has not eliminated all of them. The satisfactory solution for a P&D approach today may very well lapse into an unsatisfactory condition tomorrow, and new needs for P&D will certainly increase pressures to improve the total P&D approach. Consider the impact of only the new information and communications technology on society in general and the needs for new P&D methods and techniques becomes quite clear.

The education of P&D professionals is one major area where pressures to improve are severe. All students currently receive doubting game preparation almost exclusively (analysis, scientific aspects, research methods, modeling skills, theories and generalizations), which leaves the unstated assumption that purposes-objectives-implementation-politics aspects are someone else's job. So ingrained is this conventional reasoning and education that far too many P&D professionals accept assignments as given just because they can "see" the beauty of the model or analysis they would develop. They even fail to determine if the manager is committed to *doing something* about implementation and follow-up, not just the exercise of P&D. Education in conventional ideas continues to encourage people to practice all the poor aspects of P&D noted in Chapters Four and Five. As one possible indicator of the ineffectiveness of such education, studies on the creativity of engineers show it

drops significantly between their entry as freshmen and graduation as seniors. Other factors may also be at work (age, income) but one would at least expect no difference to occur in a *P&D* profession.

Conventionally-oriented professionals stress using their professional tools at the expense of solving real world problems. Building an innovative model of an existing situation becomes more highly regarded by the profession than the fact that it did not lead to any implementation because "they" didn't appreciate the model. Or the professional proclaims a focus on improving decisions, whereas managers want help so *they* can decide how to solve problems. Conversely, developing a "different" solution that the profession acclaims is innovative is more highly regarded than the ability of real-world people to use it effectively.

An informal survey of 125 P&D professionals in a variety of areas showed that the most frequent problems they and their colleagues faced were determining the right problem to work on; involving people; reducing the amount of analysis and data collection; getting the best and most from P&D resources; and achieving the most effective implemented solutions. The similar problems identified by so many different P&D professions can be explained partially by the conventional approaches most of them follow. A focus on research techniques, model building, and data analysis causes so much concentration on information *in* a locus content area and on the particular professional techniques that the person loses sight of approach ideas and even content knowledge from other P&D fields. So inward-looking does the conventional approach become that smaller specialties within a P&D profession are continually being formed, thus causing a lack of contact even among members of one P&D profession (engineering, architecture, social services). Protection of the status quo, failure to hire "different" professionals, focus on routines, fear of ridicule for unusual ideas, and reliance on "practical" or "tried-and-true" answers become endemic.

PROGRESS TOWARD RESOLVING P&D PROBLEMS

How is progress assessed in P&D? Three possible ways of reviewing the P&D concept are to examine it from a higher-level perspective or from "outside the concept"; to compare the approach with others proposed for the same end by means of suitable criteria or indicators; and to utilize the approach on real P&D projects and observe its effect and consequences. The first way is done rather thoroughly in Parts One and Two.

A starting point for a comparison is the statement of the three objectives of P&D (Chapter Four). These three literally explode into many other criteria as each major word is divided into its constituent factors. Consider only the word *effective*. In relation to *solutions*, it involves workability, creativeness, simplicity, timeliness, cost of operation, satisfactions of people operating the solution, risk/benefit ratios, operating or response time, sensitivity to individual and group needs and development, and many other factors that emerge from considering the spiral societal values of Figure 2-2. In relation to *utilizing P&D resources,* it can involve:

- Residual feelings of real-world people toward P&D professionals.
- Cost of developing the solution.
- Attitudes and morale of P&D personnel.
- Ability of real-life people to practice good P&D concepts after the project is completed.
- Elapsed time in developing the solution.
- Ratio of time taken to desired completion date (almost always insufficient time is available for P&D project).
- Adherence to betterment schedule for the artificials involved.
- Ability to set priorities for working on projects with the greatest potential impact.
- Degree of integration of all planning, design and improvement activities.
- Creativity in incorporating the latest information *in P&D* and *in* the broad "technology" of the locus.

Consider comparable potential lists for *implemented, solution, likelihood,* and so on. Thus, progress is a relative set of measures, where the amount of improvement is based on the degree of change from the present set of conditions, logic, assumptions, and practice. A comparison with some indicators or measures is used in Table 17-1 to portray the progress to date from the recommended P&D approach. A few other items difficult to fit into Table 17-1 are the following:

1 Many behavioral and organizational theorists offer evidence to support the ideas of involving people, search for change, continued learning, human betterment, and so on (Chapters Fourteen and Sixteen). Their suggestions for *how* to utilize these espoused theories are mostly exhortations and conventional approaches. The recommended P&D approach provides a prescriptive scenario to encourage the practice of espoused theories.

2 The individual P&D professional practicing on a one-to-one basis (architect, guidance counselor, social worker, interior designer) is a P&D system embodied in one person. If these professionals treat themselves as a separate P&D system to be designed each time to fit each individual client/owner/user, the relationship between the one-person real world and the one-person P&D world is very likely to be more effective.

3 A growing number of experiments and studies comparing all or parts of the recommended P&D approach with conventional approaches are showing the operational theories presented here to be significantly more effective. One survey of 48 manufacturing companies showed that the overall desirable features of the total P&D approach produced the economic benefits portrayed in Figure 17-1.[5] Three different strategies (conventional, PDA, and mixed) used by architecture students on interior space design problems did not result in differences in quality of solutions,[6] but the PDA group took less time and the information they used was solution- rather than problem-oriented. Health planners working on two real projects with three strategies (conventional with nominal groups, PDA in an interacting group mode, and unstructured) showed that PDA produced better results in terms of technical features, acceptance attributes, and implementability agreement, whereas the nominal group using conventional strategies introduced more situations, needs, or ideas not previously noted, and received more favorable reactions from the people involved.[7] As a result of this last experiment, much more use of the nominal group technique was introduced into PDA, such as for doing purpose expansions.

4 A good assumption base for P&D should, by definition, provide a framework within which non-P&D activities can be described. Chapters Two and Three provide this basis for the other purposeful activities. Books on the operating and supervising approach, evaluation approach, learning approach, and research approach, could each present its five factors, axioms, propositions, and so on. Other books and papers could address P&D professionals in specific locus content areas, such as education,[8] architecture,[9] health care delivery planning,[10] and manufacturing methods improvement.[11]

The third way of assessing progress represented by the recommended P&D approach is to report the effects and consequences of utilizing the approach on P&D projects. The case histories in Chapter One and

Table 17-1 Some Indicators of Progress in Theories *of* and *in* P&D

Criterion or Indicator	Conventional P&D Approaches	Recommended P&D Approach
Definition of problem	Mixture of undefined factors (goals, difficulties, types)	Substantive content or purposeful activities *and* values/objectives
Nature of P&D problem	Similar to any type of problem	One of seven purposeful activities. P&D is creating or restructuring situation-specific solution
Definition of an approach	Highly variable; many say research method, others say decision making, communication, creativity, group activity, information processing, problem solving, search, uncertainty and variety reduction, technology transfer	Five features in holism of P&D (pursuing a strategy, specifying and presenting solutions, involving people, using information and knowledge, and continuing change and improvement); all five intertwined with rational, affective, and chance behavior into a *total approach*
	Before-after snapshot perspective	Timeline scenario, selective and iterative
Orientation or direction of reasoning	Assign project to a professional "to dive into"	Develop a P&D structure for finding solution
	Doubting game	Believing game, and flexible
	Delve *into* what exists	Think purpose, what ought to be accomplished
	Use details about what exists as guide to finding solution	Purpose hierarchy(ies), regularities, and target are guides to finding solution
	More recorded information is better (exacerbates information overload)	Minimum collected data, use what people know, identify *needed* data
	Accept problem as given	Use hierarchies to find what ought to be worked on; no one knows in advance when a breakthrough may occur
	Reductionist: simple parts better	Holistic: all parts must be viewed from total view
Solution-finding	What are others doing?	Find solution to fit unique situation
	Patch up or satisficing	Know target as basis for recommendation
	One solution for everything and everyone	Regularity first, then pluralistic and multichanneled
	Limited number of alternatives considered	Many alternatives sought, creativity encouraged
Nature of solutions	Limited, internal scope	Best possible for conditions
	Discrete (problem is solved, now forget it)	Built-in changes identified and continuing search started
	Tradition-oriented or what has worked before; or apply advanced technology just because it's available	Innovative, exploratory, look for unusual ideas and future changes as well as workability; or let nature of circumstances dictate appropriate technology
	Incorporate details based on what intuition suggests	Use system context and solution framework
	Outcome usually measured by cost or quantified cost/benefits	Outcome assessed by costs, quality, satisfactions of users and of operators of solution
Role of People	Overcome their resistance	Deal with purposes, hierarchy, ideal systems, etc. to avoid defensiveness
	Confront people with collected information that shows how the problem is their fault (creates defensiveness)	Start with people's perception and expand; do not overload with information
	Groups get in the way	Groups needed and selected at beginning to lead to implementation; continue to give all *opportunity* to take part even if not attend early meetings
	Keep "them" happy and off our backs	People can grow and learn; can identify own needs and interests
	Tell people what change to make	People make a change when they help design it
	Passive attitude to improvement, wait until crisis arises	Continual internal and external search for change, seek signs of disturbances, new technologies

Table 17-1 (*Continued*)

Criterion or Indicator	Conventional P&D Approaches	Recommended P&D Approach
Role of P&D professional	Expert, measurer, modeler, or *the* designer	Facilitative in nature, with 36 possible roles, including measurer, etc. (see Chapter Fourteen)
	Rigid if someone else suggests "creative" idea	Flexible
	Closing quickly on a solution	Open as long as possible
	Solitary	Involve many
	Completed when plan/design presented	Implementation with built-in change is temporary end of project
Techniques used	Use latest sophisticated models and analysis	Know all techniques and use when strategy shows they are needed
	Quantitative factors and objectivity are most important	Qualitative factors and subjective concepts are often most important
	A focus on one or two techniques as *the* heart of P&D (e.g., computers, a group process, decision support systems, creativity, multiattribute decision models, gaming or simulation, conflict resolution)	Only the intermixed five features within the timeline scenario govern: all techniques may be usable as appropriate (Appendix A)
	Descriptive definitions of the word "system"	Prescriptive definition of "system" to handle all types of complexities and interrelationships
Communications perspectives	Final report plan/design is all that is needed	Continual interchange with real world at all stages and phases
	Power plays and political arrangements determine whether solution is accepted	All factors included along timeline, plus group is committed to and understands the solution, so support is significantly increased
	Take-it-or-leave-it solution view	Recommended solution is already a back-off position from FIST, so group knows other positions to accept that still leave open a future path to the FIST
	Minutes or meeting summaries concern actions or decisions	Minutes include alternatives and selected one, widely distributed to give others the opportunity to get involved
	Report is a standard format	Any type of format, including reports
Basic premises of the P&D approach	Almost always unstated; usually takes form of technological imperative, data collection to start, rationality, unbiased decision makers, hierarchical authority, and so on, most of which explain all of the above entries in this column	Explicit assumptions about purposeful activities and total approach, presentation of axioms and corollaries, propositions and corollary propositions, all of which explain and support the above entries in this column; effectively combines rational, affective, chance, incremental, mixed scanning, etc., approaches
	Solution/plan/design is answer	Implement as creative a solution as possible with built-in changes
	P&D resources should be allocated without accountability	P&D resources must be justified and methods sought to better utilize them
	Use solutions from elsewhere—don't "reinvent the wheel"	Find solution for the unique situation—make sure a wheel is needed before using it

Appendix B serve this purpose. In addition to showing how various parts and factors of the P&D approach benefit a project, they also portray the flexibility in using the prescriptive ideas. A few cases are rather dramatic in portraying breakthroughs that occurred as a result of an approach that always gives a project the *opportunity* for finding innovative solutions. Other projects show how "ordinary" results were obtained, where none had previously been obtained when a conventional approach was followed. The cases do show that, instead of saying "everybody knows you have to find out whose fault it is or the *real* causes of the problem," a focus of finding a solution for *real* purposes to be achieved is more effective. After all, identifying the

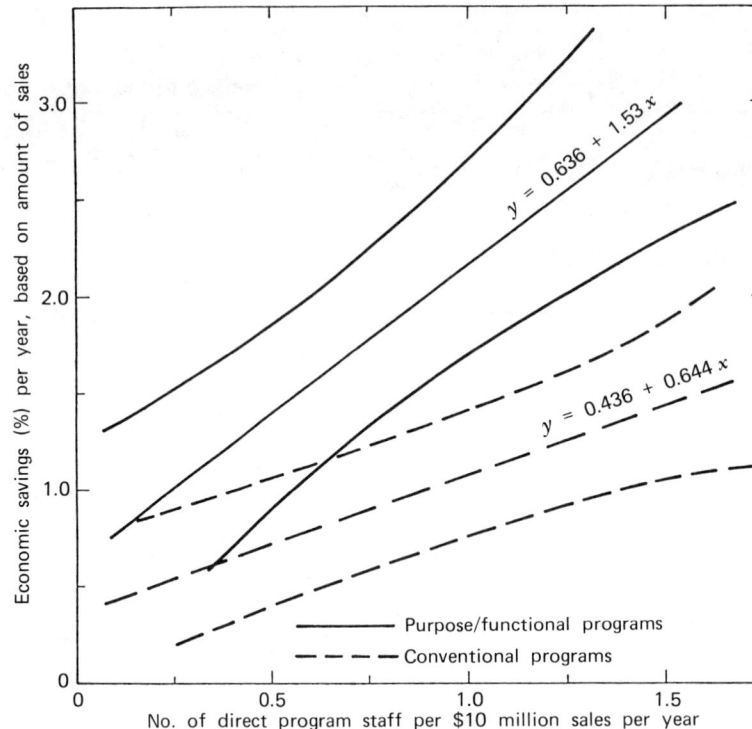

Figure 17-1 The effect of types of P&D orientation and direct program staff on economic results.

"right" culprit and the "right" causes is most often no assurance for a P&D effort that a solution is available or effective.

On rare occasions, usually for relatively small-scope projects, two relatively independent P&D teams are concurrently assigned to the same project. More often, a PDA team is set up after no results were obtained from a team using a conventional approach. Such comparisons show that PDA led to a better system, took less time to arrive at results, and included built-in change. For example, one group of engineers studied a 15-person die-casting production line to find a lower cost system. They used a conventional P&D strategy. At the same time, another engineering group, completely unknown to the first one, used PDA. The first group recommended a production line with six people whereas the second group recommended an automation system with no one. In addition, the second group recommended that some individuals could be retrained or moved to new assignments, and in one case one person could retire early with good severance pay. These recommendations were developed in less calendar time and with fewer person-hours than the recommendation of the first group.

A second illustration concerns a warehouse where an improvement program specialist using conventional P&D ideas recommended equipment costing $40,000

that would pay for itself in less than a year. A P&D professional on the vice-president's staff reviewed the project using PDA, and found that the warehouse should be sold, along with almost 20 others in the company. The warehouses were originally set up to protect the company against a 1920-type railroad strike. With different transportation modes now available, most of the warehouses weren't needed and could be sold. This is surely much better than a $40,000 capital expenditure per warehouse for a solution that ought not to exist at all. Company policies protected the employees through retraining, relocation, and severance pay.

A project group in another company used a conventional P&D approach for eight months and 2500 person-hours to redesign the company credit system, which was in unsatisfactory condition. The minimal modifications they recommended were not acted on because several details had been omitted. A few months later, a completely different group using PDA on the same system, and without reference to the previously collected information, took about two months and 900 person-hours to design a new system which, when installed, saved $2.5 million per year.

Many P&D professionals and real-world managers have reported significant feelings and attitudes *after* using PDA on projects. No thorough study has been done on this topic (this is a needed effort within the scope of suggestions in this chapter). The following are statements of people from many locus content areas:

- The approach makes me feel positive about future possibilities.
- I get a healthy feeling of self-sufficiency because I know I can always move toward the target.
- I get a much greater sense of pleasure from my design work with clients.
- We have a healthy and informal dissatisfaction with the status quo.
- Change is always possible because there are no permanent answers.
- I treat each person as a potential contributor to P&D by asking purpose and ideal system questions.
- I feel confident in the recommendations of a project team because the strategy gets us to generate many alternatives for each project.
- People are more convinced they exercise some control over their situations because the approach lets us treat them as interested, motivated individuals who are potential contributors. We know where we are going.
- Our solutions fit us. They involve appropriate technology for us.
- People present "radical" ideas now. They are not ridiculed for an idea "so far off the track." This is "practical idealism."

An intriguing comment came from one group: Older people using PDA can keep pace with younger ones. Because the approach deals with purposes (wisdom of age) and yields questions searching the forefront of any field (advanced technology of youth), both age groups acquire insight and knowledge from the others.

A subtle but critical sign of progress stems from the PDA view of time and change. Conventional P&D approaches tend to view time in discontinuous leaps between snapshots of analysis, and change as continuous incremental trends or evolutionary modifications. The PDA perceives time as a continuous framework of incremental human commitment to implementation, and change as discontinuous events and ever advancing targets. Rather than treating discontinuity[12] as a fearsome snapshot the conventional approaches and futurists develop, PDA treats it as but a target that allows today's actions to lead to the major change. Discontinuity in this sense is not fearsome but can *lead* to a desired high rate of change. PDA targets are future-oriented in terms of change whereas conventional P&D trends are past-oriented. PDA thus effectively

copes with time continuously for people purposes (perceptions, detailing, installing, participating, etc.) and change discontinuously for purposes of quality of results (ideal systems, targets, regularities, betterment, etc.).

THE IMPACT ON THE EDUCATION OF P&D PROFESSIONALS

Many books, papers and articles call for major educational reforms of one sort or another—revise the "innards" of the field, combine several P&D professions, integrate liberal arts as the basis of the profession, start P&D education in high schools, focus on three conceptual levels (-ics, -ing, and -tion, Chapter Fifteen), learn to live with a large number of imponderables. Also called for is a new kind of curriculum. This "curriculum in design . . . to take its place by the side of natural science in the whole engineering curriculum . . . includes at least the following topics: The evaluation of designs [involving] theory of evaluation, . . . computational methods [algorithms and heuristics, and] . . . the formal [imperative and declarative] logic of design, . . . the search for alternatives, . . . theory of structure and design organization, [and] representation of design problems."[13]

Environmental design education should include exposure of students to the difficulties of P&D, hardware and software technologies that support design, principles and theses of environmental systems, meshing factual knowledge and slices of reality, and concepts on how cultural, social, economic, and political factors influence design and can be influenced by design.[14] Such multifaceted exposure has as its goal an integrated approach to design: "the comprehensive design of environments eliminates the questionable distinctions between architecture and landscape architecture–industrial design–urban design–regional design, etc. These traditional divisions can no longer serve any useful purpose."[15]

I too have written about the poor preparation of P&D professions. I proposed, for example, that colleges of engineering should be organized along matrix lines. One axis would involve bodies of knowledge (e.g., control theory, not mechanical control or electrical control), and the other basic problem areas (transportation of people and things, not mechanical or civil engineering). I suggested that P&D ideas can best be taught in secondary education, starting at the fifth- or sixth-grade levels.[16] I have stated in speeches that a vice-president or vice-chancelor for the P&D professions would be a desirable organizational arrangement for universities not only to foster the interrelationship of P&D professions and synthetic modes of thought, but also to reduce *research* barriers among disciplines.

These "good" and "desirable" ideas suffer from a basic flaw well identified in this book: They are snapshots of a future, or seek to sell a solution, or fail to identify purpose, or, in effect, fail to consider the very P&D principles (Chapters Ten and Sixteen) they espouse. Especially critical is the purpose and purpose hierarchy of focusing on the *student*, the *person* being prepared, not just on the profession itself or its philosophical purity. The focus must be on designing the specific form in which specific students can learn the ideas or concepts.[17] When this is done, most of the other ideas pale into insignificance.

Education of P&D professionals can be significantly improved by considering several mandates that stem from PDA concepts:

Prepare a person for continuing life growth, starting with the specific P&D professional concepts. Worry far less about whether all engineers take the same science and technical curriculum in the first two years, and more about how the individual student can get a good foundation in theories *of* and *in* P&D (which ought to be common). Dozens of surveys have been conducted of graduates of curricula in urban and regional planning, engineering, architecture, business planning, educational planning, and so on about the skills and areas of knowledge they felt were important for their P&D professional lives. *Every* one shows overwhelmingly that the topics they needed most were never addressed in their P&D education! Topics mentioned by large majorities included interpersonal skills, communications ability, different P&D roles, integrative or total approaches to P&D, methods of organizing and synthesizing large amounts of information, ethical considerations, and operating and supervising skills.

Attention to these needs does not concurrently detract from content area I&K. The survey respondents used their locus content or technical knowledge only 10 to 20% of their time. But specific technical knowledge should constitute 70 to 80% of an educational program as long as it is imbedded in broad P&D background. Since this background may well spell the difference between so-so and outstanding professional performance for 80% or so of the students (the top 10% won't be "hurt" by any program, and the bottom 10% are unlikely to be helped), educators in P&D professional fields should focus their educational program on the students as a means of assuring the well-being and betterment of *their* own profession!

Design the specific educational program, organization structure, courses, and curriculum using PDA.

Specific arrangements, mix of topics, and other factors should be situation-specific. The P&D scenario (Figure 10-4), axioms, propositions, and so on should govern the process in each curriculum and institution. Obtaining an implemented solution with built-in change means starting with the human perceptions of those involved at any level (department, school, college, university, P&D professional society, group of practitioners, etc.). Reorganizing P&D professions at a university requires the people there to design it, not just the appointment of a vice-chancellor.

P&D education cannot be free of content or context. By definition, P&D is a purposeful activity addressing human needs and values. The specific locus or technology must include the field's history, sociology, psychological types, culture, epistemology, and so forth. This explains why none of the secondary purposeful activities in Table 3-9 (e.g., decision making, modeling) are very good educational programs by themselves. "Liberation from the claims of specialization is to be attained not by abandoning specialization, but through its sublimation and expansion in a given field."[18]

The question is therefore how and in what frame of reference specialized topics should be taught—as generalizations, as P&D, or both? Is the mean and variance of a research study sufficient, or should it also be related to impact on a P&D decision? Is the answer a student calculates in an exercise from an equation always "right," or should the students be questioned occasionally about when the "right" answer *wouldn't* be used in real-world situations? Do we have all the information, or is the information needed? Content can be effectively taught for P&D ends at the same time as it is presented for its research ends. At the present time, our society suffers when P&D ideas are omitted: "Society controls us by the knowledge it teaches us, since it does not teach us what we need to know to control and shape society."[19]

Theories of *and in P&D should be spread throughout all the years and all the locus content courses and activities.* The whole educational and specialization experience should be imbedded in a culture of the total P&D purposeful activity. Yet, to paraphrase a statement about engineering,

P&D education today, by striving to provide a strong analytical and content base, has ignored much of the professional development of the student. . . . One consequence of an analytically oriented faculty (and curriculum) has been a significant decrease in emphasis on preparing students to deal with complexities of P&D professional work. . . . Analysis is an essential ingredient of P&D professional education, but . . . [these] are means rather than ends. . . . Students [should be provided] with sufficient opportunities to make decisions and thus to develop the judgmental skills they will need.[20]

One illustration of how this might be done is to present an overview of P&D and many specific techniques in the first year, different purposeful activities with their associated approaches and how to select the appropriate one in the second year, axioms and propositions in the third year, and Part Three, on the five factors (especially the different P&D roles and functions in Chapter Fourteen) and a complete project in the fourth year. Most of the other courses in each year at the same time can incorporate the P&D context orientation noted above, thus giving students a continuing orientation about the content specialization (means of doing P&D) as well as the operational theories (ends of P&D). It is just too much to expect that two or three P&D courses at the end of a four-year program could overcome the analytical mindset produced by the usual curriculum.

The P&D theories should spur the search for better educational methods in all aspects of the P&D professions. More than creativity and expert designer capacities are involved in P&D. The facilitator role, for example, is one for which the P&D professional is almost always unprepared. The general populace and specifically high school students should receive insights into P&D, as suggested by a proposal[21] and an early experiment.[22] Most P&D fields seek to improve professional training by concentrating on, say, computerizing the techniques of the field. Unfortunately, in most cases, this makes more efficient that which ought not be done at all. On the other hand, a project on Dynamic Engineering Professional Training and Evaluation Review (DEPTER) provides students with "the opportunity to solve and practice developing solutions to real-world, time interactive problems engineers usually face. DEPTER is driven by a computer and will evaluate the subject's efforts at minimizing development costs, optimizing solution costs, containing risks, minimizing time to find and implement solutions, and finding effective integration and sequencing of information gathering."[23]

Another area of improvement needed in P&D is presenting the appropriate imagery of the timeline scenario. One student was reporting on the urban planning system of a city. He said that "planning was running to keep up with the real world." This misinterprets the timeline scenario idea. Say P&D uses a two-year time horizon for its targets. When the events or changes do occur, P&D is setting up the next two-year target which the student indicated was "running to keep up."! Because the real world is doing now what was planned two years ago, P&D is quite successful.

All of these needs lead to preparation of educational materials, most of which are not available—videotape of a real project group doing purpose expansion, audio cassettes on selection discussion, packets of exercises, and so forth.

Educators can influence professional roles and functions through teaching future practitioners. This is a classical role of a university, to encourage and experiment with new ideas. Students learning about different roles, for example, develop a questioning attitude about design tasks, which will then have a major impact on the profession. Educators stimulate this with the continual search of their own: "What is the changing nature of [P&D] practice? How can we learn more about the competencies appropriate to it, over the range of changing [P&D] situations and roles? How can we become better at detecting what students and faculty actually do learn from their interactions with one another? And how, in combination with substantive knowledge and techniques pertinent to [P&D], can we design better ways of communicating generic planning skills?"[24]

AREAS *OF* AND *IN* P&D WHERE RESEARCH AND DEVELOPMENT ARE NEEDED

This section was both easy and difficult to prepare. It was easy because developments are needed throughout the total P&D approach. Turn to any page of the book and read it until you have a question about the support (logic, experimental, analytical, empirical, etc.) for a particular point, the relationship of it to another point or idea, or the amount of weighting or priority it should receive in the entire P&D approach. On any page there will be several points needing development, because the P&D approach is presented on the premise that P&D is necessary and worth doing, even if all aspects are not clearly defined enough to do "perfectly." Chapter Sixteen even lists several topics for R and D into P&D which individual organizations may want to investigate.

It was difficult because selecting a frame of reference and set of priorities to illustrate the large number of possible needed improvements by definition omits many of them. So the broad-brush illustrations that follow should remind the professional of the need to keep abreast of reports about developments, and the student in a P&D profession of the need to keep an open and inquisitive mind about all aspects of the theories *of* and *in* P&D. Information and knowledge *in* locus content areas are also being improved as discussed in Chapter Fifteen, so all references about this extremely large amount of development are omitted.

A. Theory *of* P&D

Even though this theory is not likely to change significantly in the next 10 to 20 years, a great deal of "normal science"[25] (substantiation of the ideas and search for improvement) is needed. That is, the specific techniques and formulations in this book are subject to substantiation and improvement.

Theory construction was described in the Part Two introduction as usually involving six more or less sequentially developed parts.[26] One example of a conceptual theory concerns purposeful activities as describers of past, present, and future human perceptions of substantive matters. Most of the six theory parts are not available at the "usual" level of scientific thoroughness. But scientific thoroughness appears less available for any of the other concepts presented in Chapter Two in seeking a *usable* theory of human perceptions of substantive matters than for purposeful activities. Thus, although human purposeful activities emerged as a logically defensible and utilitarian array, continuing development is really needed to either substantiate the classification array or find a "better" set. Any set will have to fit the broader theories *of* the social and political circumstances in which P&D takes place (a socialist society is different from a market-based one, for example).

A second grouping concerns the assumptions, myths, or organizational beliefs that do and should accompany a P&D effort or program. The spiral of societal values, the translation of values into objectives and goals, the nature of P&D and its problems, axioms, and corollaries, and the premises of individual and group realities as starting points of an operational theory *of* P&D all need further investigation, substantiation and development.

A third grouping concerns the 13 propositions (and related corollary propositions) that make up the explicit statement of the theory *of* P&D. Each is stated in the format of a hypothesis that ought to be tested and verified with limits or threshold levels identified if needed. Getting such data is very difficult because it could interfere with activities in the real-world setting.

A fourth grouping concerns policies to motivate people at various levels of organizations and society to become involved with and implement P&D solutions. The whole range of policies needs investigation and

development, from national level tax laws and trade relationships to state, regional, and local land use and environmental laws and regulations, to the specific organization's operating procedures regarding incentives or profit sharing, facilitating participation, and employee security.

B. The Total P&D Scenario

The timeline (Figure 10-4) is a representation of the theory *of* P&D. It is placed here in a separate major category for further developments because it has a unique potential for portraying what goes on in actual P&D efforts. Figure 17-2 illustrates an overall format for displaying what happens during a project. The amount of time spent on each of the possible scenario functions listed in the left-hand column can be obtained by a review of minutes and logbooks, tape recordings of meetings or "thinking aloud" by P&D people, self-recordings, or direct observations. Notes about what is actually being done (what techniques, model, people, dimension or element of a system matrix, and so on) at each time can be placed on the form. Models depicting intensity of efforts along the timeline may even emerge. Then, measures of the dependent variables, and solution implementability and quality (e.g., creativeness, built-in change, costs, effectiveness) can be obtained (by means of expert judgment, actual cost, time to implement, reliability, etc.) to serve as a basis for testing all sorts of hypotheses concerning the many "independent" variables in a P&D scenario.

Several other timeline representations may also be tested with data in the form of Figure 17-2 from many projects. The rich variety of forms the timeline data may take for research as well as operational purposes is illustrated by the use of path analysis to trace influences on the dependent variables, major nodes or events through a network model to portray various P&D activities in relation to major events (nodes), and decision tree to sketch out alternatives at each choice point in time. Other types of research can also use the time data of Figure 17-2 for developments: Correlation, multiple regression, computerized search processes with rather minimal partitioning to identify likely influential variables, and multiattribute utility assessment could seek significant impacts on project selection, P&D system format, problem formulation, measures of effectiveness, and so on. Scenario-time information can thus provide gestalt perspectives as well as interaction and causal/reciprocal relationships of components and the total P&D scenario.

C. Theories *in* P&D

A major advantage of timeline scenario data is the substantial setting they provide for developments in theories *in* P&D. Because each technique, concept, process or method *in* P&D must be part of the larger theory *of* P&D, more effective development of this category than ever before can be expected. Those investigating project selection techniques, for example, are likely to consider factors in the whole setting not usually incorporated into past research. They are also likely to judge the state of "health" of the area and suggest further developments because of the context provided.

Here are a few prospective developments *in* P&D that might emerge from the scenario view:

Problem Formulation

Improve the role of semantic word meanings in constructing a purpose hierarchy. Develop guidelines for integrating semi-lattice and single channel hierarchical concepts. Provide some insight into the relationship between the P&D of implementation and the purpose hierarchy and selection of a level.

Measures of Effectiveness

Methods whereby the purpose/function hierarchy and selected level can be assessed without losing their gestalt continuity. Development of cost and benefit measures, even subjective, that reflect realism in, for example, the value of a human life (to supplant the grossly inadequate lost earnings because of early death) and the protection of health and safety in the workplace. Methods of interfacing various interpretations of individuals' measures of value and benefits that will aid in completing projects rather than becoming stumbling blocks.

Creativity

Methods within a project to get people to stop "imagining obstacles . . . with unabashed enthusiasm and with fluid ease so there is scarcely a niche or crack left into which to squeeze an imagined notion of how a highly desirable end can be achieved."[27] Development of methods to increase the probability that individuals, groups, and organizations will not satisfice (that is, accept the first workable answer), analyze possible solutions too early, consider only one person's ideas, or accept a person's statement that a constraint does exist.

In-depth Investigations of Sections of Figure 17-2

Using a graph with time as the abscissa and, say, "number of required criteria" as the ordinate, plot and compare how long various techniques take in getting a group to develop solution ideas that address all criteria or measures of effectiveness for a project.

Involving People

Determine the impact of different psychological types on each phase of a project. Develop and assess methods of interrelating different psychological type perspectives in decision phases and steps. Methods of identifying and selecting people for projects. Identifying appropriate points in the strategy for using various human dialectical exchange modes (argumentative, assumption testing, ideal-state comparisons, polar opposites, "debate," and so on). Methods to establish *effective* operating rules that groups generate and accept to meet their knowledge, psychological, control support, and task needs.

Organizational Arrangements

Chapter Sixteen listed several of these topics, especially those concerned with aggregations and generalizations from many organizations.

Implementation

Early in the project, develop measures of prospective implementation that various P&D system arrangements might produce. Identify individual and group attitudes, previous adoption/change behavior, conditions of readiness factors, and organizational "results" orientation that influence acceptance of the implementation concept as part of the beginning of a project. The relationships among educational background of P&D professional(s), organizational readiness, operating and supervising style of management, and rate and quality of successful implementation of P&D recommendations and betterments.

D. Each "Cell" of the P&D System Matrix

Table 10-1 describes the eight elements each in terms of the six dimensions. Even though each item or aspect in a cell is somewhat prescriptive, most items could be converted to hypotheses or propositions that could be explored, on the model of "the greater the ——— (user's need), the greater the likelihood of implementing the recommended solution (or of developing creative solutions, or of minimizing the cost of P&D)." Or comparisons of the items might establish the most critical or priority variables.

Another set of hypotheses, propositions, and derived corollaries can be developed in terms of the whole element or the whole dimension. The "values" dimension, for example, needs techniques and models

Functions to Be Accomplished
within Each Factor

Pursuing the P&D strategy

    Project selection
    P&D system structure
    Problem formulation
    Measures of effectiveness
    Creativity—idea generation
    Regularity—conditionals
    Target
    Recommended solution
    Approval
    Installation plan
    Preparation for operation
    Performance measures
    Turn—over to operators
    Interrupt—delay

Specifying and presenting
the solution

    Purpose
    Inputs
    Outputs
    Sequence
    Environment
    Human agents
    Physical catalysts
    Information aids

Involving people

    Decision maker 1
    Decision maker 2
    Influential 1 (elected)
    Influential 2 (business)
    Expert 1
    Expert 2
    Worker 1
    Worker 2
    P&D professional role 1
    P&D professional role 2
    Group process role 1
    Group process role 2
    Group process technique 1
    Group process technique 2
    Meeting condition 1
    Meeting condition 2

0   Time

Generate alternatives   Organize (hierarchy)   Select   Reorganize
                    Possible, organization select

Values dimension   All dimensions   Measures   Fundamental
                             Measures Creativity Regularity
    Values   Measures   Regularity
    Value   Measures Creativity Regularity
    Value

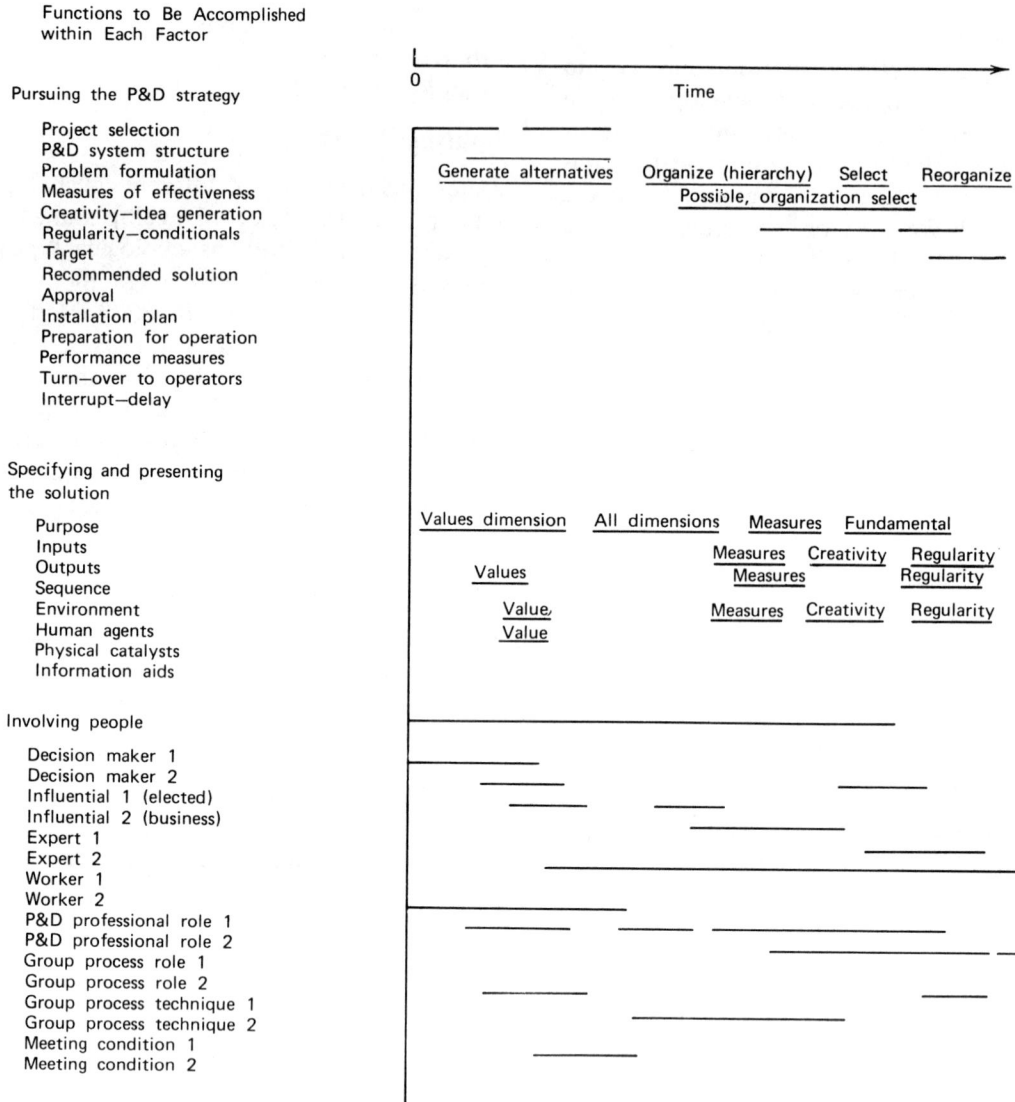

Figure 17-2 Timeline model for recording research data about a P&D project scenario. Functions to be accomplished within each factor vary from project to project.

to help establish values specifications for all elements in a solution. The values dimension is also important for P&D systems. What P&D system value aspects, for example, are assumed for an architectural professional who seeks esthetic appearances with a building design while manifesting little or no concern about what is to happen inside the building (whether house, factory, or office)?

All of the techniques listed in Appendix A are subject to further development. Not only should their purpose, cost, and effectiveness be improved, but the development of new techniques and evaluation of the utility of techniques from other fields should also occur.

E. Framework of Research and Development

The P&D system matrix can also stimulate a great deal of research by using, for example, the eight elements as columns in a framework. Each row could represent a research approach or method: experimental (field, two or more matched project groups, or laboratory), exploratory (cases, discursive), philosophical or conceptual, theoretical and analytical, action-based, and synthesis of literature. Such a framework gives rise to many specific research topics.

One of the advantages of a "complete" category of research possibilities is the avoidance of omitting important questions and issues. I was involved at the

Using information and
knowledge

    Theory of P&D—axiology
    Theory of P&D—philosophy
    Theory of P&D—epistemology
    Theory of P&D—history
    Theory of P&D pedagogy
    Information and knowledge in P&D 1
    Information and knowledge in P&D 2
    I&K in locus content area 1
    I&K in locus content area 2

    Utilizing what is available
    Developing new I&K
    Verifying the I&K
    Modifying the I&K

Arranging for continuing
change and improvement

    Readiness factors assessment
    Project betterment
    Favorable behavior
    Organizational policy 1
    Organizational policy 2

Institutionalized program

    Structure
    Education
    Workshop groups
    Project team
    P&D development and research
    Program audit

Other purposeful activities

    Operate and supervise
    Evaluate
    Research
    Learn

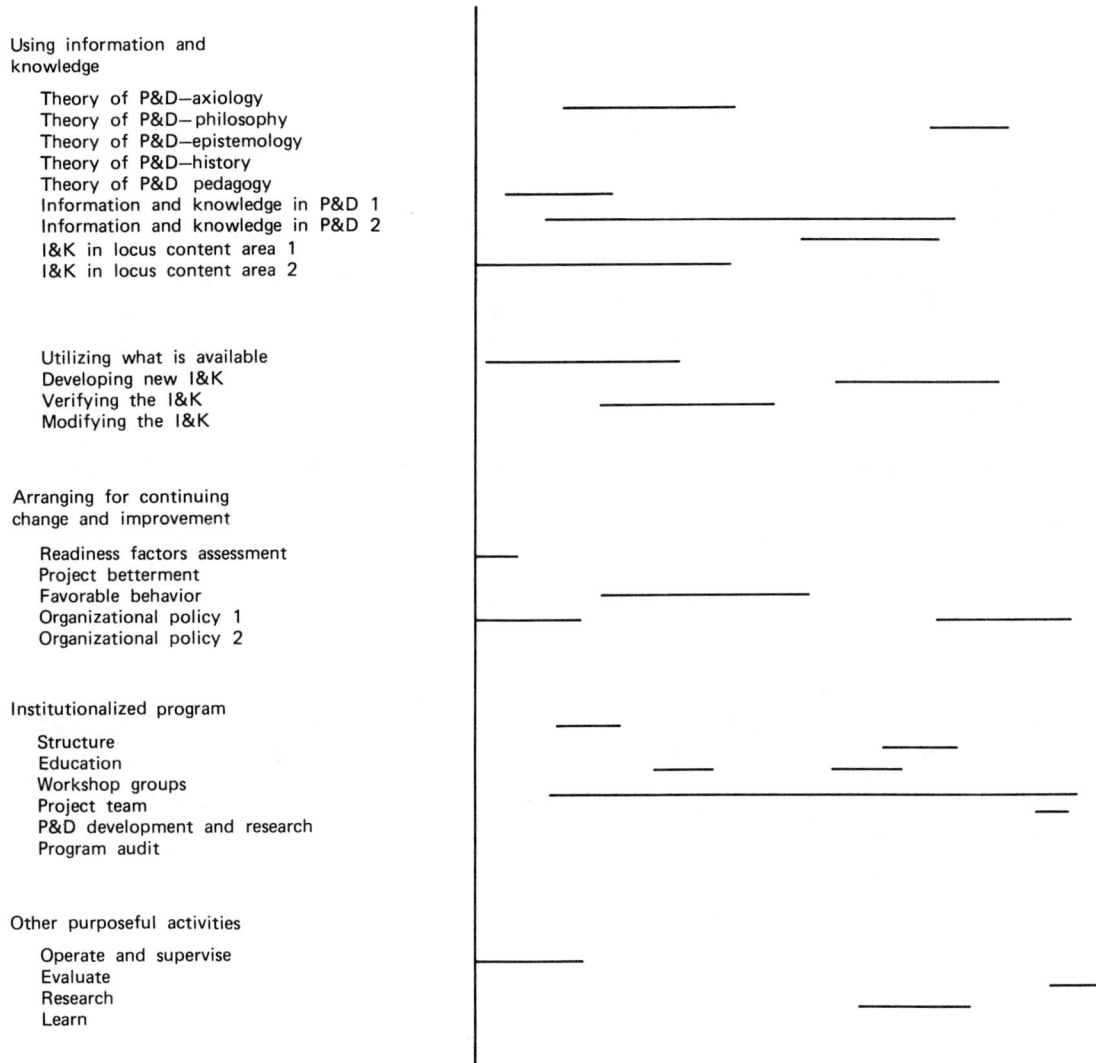

time of writing this chapter with a federally sponsored effort to find better ways of synthesizing research in educational processes so as to increase and improve field utilization of the research results. In setting forth the scope of the activity, several issues appeared to be overlooked and others were distorted. For example, the performance improvement of the clients was *ignored* in favor of the "beauty" of the synthesis format, and arguments about what type of research and synthesis ought to take place overshadowed the unraised question about what the client needs really were.

F. Lists of Research Topics

Many authors present lists that they prepare on the basis of their experiences and problems. Because these authors are erudite, committed to P&D im-

provements, and knowledgeable about the problems in P&D, such lists are valuable indicators of developments needed in theories both *of* and *in* P&D. Some of the lists refer to problems, but these can be translated to development needs. For example, Chapter Four presented some "dilemmas in a general theory of planning"[28] that are a start toward identifying where developments are needed. Almost every research paper and book on P&D methods and approaches will list what the author considers to be the next steps or the areas of research that are needed as a result of the reported work. I did this, for example, in conclusion to a paper reporting some early work in this field.[29] Two of the several journals concerned with P&D approaches, *Design Studies* and *Design Methods and Theories*, frequently enumerate possible topics.

The five factors used to characterize the total P&D

approach can each provide many other topics. They are introductions to related fields that themselves are constantly being changed and improved. The propositions, axiomatic bases, and basic assumptions and definitions presented in Chapters Two to Five all need development. Review of research in other fields is pertinent in these realms. For example, I follow to some extent the "problem-solving" literature in psychology, education, sociology, and cognitive processes. I need to be alert (for Chapters Two and Three) to any developments in typologies (e.g., for problem solving: transformation, arrangement, or induction of structure). I look for techniques to minimize the probability of working on the wrong problem (error of the third kind) and of working on the right problem but at the wrong time (error of the fourth kind).

Another list of topics may also be justified regarding the management of the P&D function in an organization. A major item would concern resource allocation, or relative amounts of money for the P&D function compared to that for other organizational functions, especially those that might be labeled "basic" science, "applied" science, research and development, product development, "improvement" programs, and so on. Many of these should be combined (Chapter Sixteen) to increase their effectiveness. Another question is: How can P&D techniques be flexible, provide early warning, and be normative? Natural resource scarcities and costs, for example, change P&D needs quickly. "Good" P&D projects in 1970 may be quite poor ones in 1980, as the price of fuel has changed so dramatically. There is strong evidence that "purposeful achievements" can be planned and money allocated effectively among the various organizational functions, so that at least applied, if not basic, research is somewhat controllable.[30]

Allocation and flexibility questions are crucial ones. They represent the point at which "words" about P&D get translated into "commitments" for P&D. A good theory *of* P&D may become a rallying point for all the P&D professions. Collective "clout" may be able to develop information and knowledge about better allocations for P&D efforts. Many executives stick only to operating and supervising current systems in the name of "survival" (according to 7000 top managers in one industrial classification) rather than pursue P&D concepts and efforts. Something is needed to put together such clout.

G. Relationships with Other Purposeful Activities

Many possible developments tie a P&D need directly to another of the purposeful activities. An example would be a requirement to develop methods for deter-

mining which purposeful activity is involved when trying to solve a problem, or one to determine indicators of when a P&D project needs a subproject dealing with another purposeful activity. Many additional topics arise when the interrelationships of the secondary purposeful activities are considered. An example of this would be to investigate the differences in effectiveness of creativity approaches within the different primary purposeful activities.

The words *research and development* associated with P&D mean humans will be involved in experiments and data collection. They cannot be treated in the classical experimental sense of "factors" to control beyond the simplest concepts (years of experience, degree, salary, etc.). "The required control is not only formidable but downright immoral."[31] Different methods for R and D have been noted previously.

SPECULATIONS ON SOLUTIONS TO METAPROBLEMS

The PDA premises and operational approach would seem to put the P&D professions on a better track to individual and collective prominence in coping with human, organizational, and societal needs for creating or restructuring situation-specific solutions. On the other hand, hoping that current P&D professional practitioners and educators will automatically adopt these ideas is far from accomplishment. The conventional approach to P&D is so ingrained in our society, starting at middle elementary school grades, that the problem of obtaining large-scale adoption of PDA ideas is immense. Lavoisier said, "I do not expect my ideas to be adopted all at once. The human mind gets creased into a way of seeing things. . . . It is the passage of time, therefore, which must confirm or destroy the opinions I have presented."[32] Darwin commented

Although I am fully convinced of the truth of the views given in this volume under the form of an abstract, I by no means expect to convince experienced scientists whose minds are stocked with a multitude of facts all viewed, during a long course of years, from a point of view directly opposite to mine. . . . Any one whose disposition leads him to attach more weight to unexplained difficulties than to the explanation of a certain number of facts will certainly reject my theory. I look with confidence to the future, to young and rising scientists who will be able to view both sides of the question with impartiality.[33]

In many ways, the changeover needed in P&D will involve intensive effort. There are far more P&D professionals today than there were scientists in the days of Lavoisier or Darwin. Yet this must surely be the time when a different approach to creating or restructuring situation-specific solutions is needed. We are certainly witnessing the failure of conventional P&D approaches to solve organizational and local problems, let alone national and international ones. Everyone seems to be decrying the poor rate of improvement in productivity, the decrease in innovations, the strangling attitudes of bureaucracy, the lack of personal will to do something, the failure of old solutions to solve current problems. "The current gloom may well be due to the gradual, perhaps still unconscious, realization that the problems we face are not amenable to the remedies conveniently at hand. Our political and our business leaders are really quite devoid of ideas but cannot afford to admit it. . . . Our country is once again confronted by problems that baffle the conventional wisdom, and bold, persistent experimentation is what we need today."[34]

The recommended P&D approach itself is not exactly an experiment, but a good experiment would be to try it on our nagging problems, to try it in preparing our P&D professionals, to try it in educating our children as a problem-solving approach *complementary* to the research approach. At the very least, trying it would force people to question their assumptions about problems and solution finding (Chapters Two and Three) so that a better set of assumptions and operational methods would be more likely to emerge. Think about some of the areas of organizational, national, and international problems that need creative solutions, where the total PDA could provide a much different perspective:

- Energy policies.
- International trade.
- Education—kindergarten through twelfth grade.
- Universities and post secondary education.
- Public and private policy for fostering innovation and productivity.
- Research on the future.
- Crime fighting, including white collar crime.
- Health care methods, access, and costs.
- Economic policies.
- Employment policies (unemployment, redundancy, training, etc.).

What about using PDA to redesign, for example, a whole school district to make it more effective for the cost involved? Industry is starting to do projects like this through its quality of work life programs. A company determines that classical production methods (division of labor) need to be turned around so that

autonomy and decision making can be a part of almost every job. Education could well use recent findings about individualizing student learning to turn around its "production" methods. Students, for example, would learn much more by using PDA to design their own study plans for required as well as elective topics. Such an approach would also get community citizens involved and allow much better utilization of restricted resources. Higher education can likewise benefit from the overall P&D approach. Why, for example, should a university maintain "global and rhetorical . . . singular mission statements"[35] when semilattice hierarchical purpose arrays are available to help cope along a timeline with human and organizational realities?

The recommended total P&D approach offers a reasonable, increased probability of creating or restructuring situation-specific solutions that are innovative and effective. It certainly offers a good chance for reinstituting the "can-do" spirit.

One final possibility should be mentioned here. What about establishing a National Planning and Design Foundation (NPDF) to complement the National Science Foundation (NSF) and the National Endowments for the Arts and for the Humanities (NEAH)? (In Great Britain, the proposal is to set up a Design Research Council to complement its Science Research Council). The United States also has complementary groups that reflect the thrust of other purposeful activities. The National Institute of Education relates to learning, and several relate to evaluation, such as the Office of Technology Assessment and the Government Accounting Office. Operating and supervising has many groups, such as the American Management Association and the Conference Board.

But activities whose purpose is to advance and develop all of the P&D professions are at best diffuse and at worst completely lacking. Some help for P&D is supplied by the honorific National Academy of Engineering which is supposed to complement the National Academy of Sciences. Current proposals to establish a sister group for the NSF in the form of a National Engineering Foundation, National Technology Foundation, or National Professions Foundation would be a mistake. A NPDF is far superior. It would bring engineering into a coordinated P&D relationship with other P&D professions that would balance all the coordinated sciences. The NPDF would focus on supporting and forwarding the development of theories, information, and knowledge *of* P&D and *in* P&D, while the NSF focus would remain disciplinary or *in locus* content areas. A good deal of interaction would take place with NSF and even NEAH. NPDF activities would raise questions that research through NSF ought to resolve. NSF-sponsored generalizations and findings (say in behavioral science) and NEAH-developed philosophies might influence the theories *of* and *in* P&D. The presence of a NPDF would help provide a good stimulus to types of research to perform since, "in almost every case a technological invention preceded much of the explosive growth in many subfields of physics"[36] and, "as the culture changes, so will the scientists, their findings, and their seminars."[37]

A NPDF would help perform the unifying service at a visible level for the whole country that a vice-president or vice-chancellor for the P&D professions would do at a single university. A large number of organizations are already available, primarily for lobbying and information exchange purposes, for many P&D professions. Yet their independence and lack of contacts with other P&D professions prevent a real attack on what this book identified as common problems. Working on the problems of P&D professions would be one major mission of a NPDF, seeking methods, for example, to improve the practice of specific P&D professionals or P&D firms. Another

purpose would be to serve as the catalyst for bringing all of the diverse planning and design professions together under the P&D umbrella, as the NSF does for all of the diverse sciences. A professional organization to complement a governmental NPDF could also emerge as, say, the American Association for the Advancement of Planning and Design (with functions similar to the American Association for the Advancement of Science). A P&D think tank or two for national policy issues could even emerge to concentrate on creating and restructuring solutions to meet all three P&D objectives (rather than analyzing and studying existing solutions or proposing futuristic snapshots for the year 2050, as most think tanks do today.)

Why not get the presidents of the P&D professional organizations together to design the P&D system that will be put in place to develop an implementable plan for a NPDF-type organization? And then the total P&D approach of asking the right questions could be used when the people involved in the P&D system first meet to . . .

APPENDIX A

Techniques and Models *in* P&D

The marvelous ability of humans to develop symbols, signs, and abstractions has led to a huge number of models, techniques, and tools. Most were proposed for the analysis and research methods of conventional P&D approaches. Yet most of them can be converted into valuable aids for all five factors of the total P&D approach (see Chapter Fifteen). All of the factors in the P&D scenario need the abstracting and estimating assistance models and techniques provide.

Appendix A provides a broad introduction to such techniques, models and tools by means of

- A listing of some of the available techniques by purposes or functions to be achieved in P&D
- A listing of techniques by the cells of the P&D system matrix (Table 10-1)
- Some selected references containing descriptions of many of the techniques

LISTING OF SOME AVAILABLE TECHNIQUES, MODELS, AND TOOLS BY PURPOSES/FUNCTIONS TO BE ACHIEVED

Analyze Alternative Options/Plans/Policies/ Programs/Contingencies/Functions

    Contingency analysis

    Contingency tables

    Function analysis diagram

    Gaming

    Goals-achievement analysis

Implementation, planning, and control technique (IMPACT)

Judgment analysis technique

Judgment policy analysis

Mathematical model

Mathematical programming technique

Multiattribute utility (MAU) models

Nominal group technique

Planning council

Planning, programming, and budgeting system (PPBS)

Queuing theory

Utility assessment

Value analysis

Voting technique

Zero-base budgeting (ZBB)

    Also see   Appraise/assess alternative options/ plans/policies/programs/contingencies/ functions

Analyze Investments

    Break-even analysis

    Mathematical model

    Operations research

    Optimization

    Proforma cash flow analysis

    Risk analysis

        Also see Appraise/assess investments

Analyze Job Methods and Motions

    Control charts

    Critical incident technique

    Job evaluation

    Maintenance chart

    Operations chart

    Process chart

    Productivity circles

    Relationship (Rel) chart

    Simultaneous motion (Simo) chart

    Task analysis

    Task timeline

    Time study

    Training

    Work measurement

Analyze Policy Setting and Decision-Making Variables

    See Analyze investments

        Analyze projects

        Analyze systems

        Appraise/assess investments

        Appraise/assess projects

        Appraise/assess systems

Analyze Product Quality

    See Identify (Product) opportunities

Analyze Projects

    ABC analysis (Pareto model)

    Critical path method

    Feasibility studies

    Gantt chart

    Map of activity and thought chains (MATCH)

    Management operations systems technique (MOST)

    Mathematical model

    Milestone chart

    New business project screening summary

    Network analysis

    Precedence diagram method

    Program evaluation and review technique (PERT)

    Purpose network analysis

    Resource allocation and multiproject scheduling (RAMPS)

    Risk analysis

        Also see Appraise/assess projects

Analyze Project Impacts on Society

    Cost-effectiveness analysis

    Cross-impact analysis

    Delphi

    Environmental impact statements

    Multiattribute utility (MAU) models

    Nominal group technique

    Planning balance sheet analysis

    Social cost-benefit analysis

    Utility assessment

    Voting technique

Analyze Systems

    Curry's model

    Decision worksheet

    Decision tree

    Function analysis diagram

    Gaming

    Gravity model

    Index numbers

    Linear models

    Mathematical model

    Mathematical programming technique

    Opportunity identification

    Optimizing model

    Path analysis

    Physical model

    Planning balance sheet analysis

    Planning council

    Planning model

    Planning, programming, and budgeting system (PPBS)

    Queuing theory

    Recursive programming model

    Relative space model

    Resource constrained scheduling heuristics

    Simulation model

    Value analysis

    Zero-base budgeting (ZBB)

        Also see Appraise/assess systems

Appraise/Assess Alternative Options/ Plans/Policies/Programs/Contingencies/Functions

    Contingency analysis

    Contingency tables

    Failure analysis

    Function analysis diagram

    Gaming

    Goals-achievement analysis

    Index analysis

    Indifference curves

Judgment policy analysis

Measurement model

Multiattribute utility (MAU) models

Needs analysis

Nominal group technique

Pair comparison

Planning council

Planning, programming, and budgeting system (PPBS)

Probability assessment

Program planning method

Psychological scaling

Subjective probability assessment

Utility assessment

Utility theory

Variance analysis

Value analysis

Voting technique

Appraise/Assess Investments

Cash flow model

Expected free cash flow model

Financial investment appraisal

Profit/volume (P/V) analysis

Return on investment

Risk analysis

Sensitivity analysis

Appraise/Assess Projects

Cash flow analysis

Critical path method

Demand analysis

Impact analysis

Input/output analysis

Map of activity and thought chains (MATCH)

Multiattribute utility (MAU) models

Network analysis

New product early warning systems

Observation model

Pair comparison

Procedence diagram method

Program evaluation and review technique

Purpose network analysis

RAMPS

Resource constrained scheduling heuristics

Risk analysis

Appraise/Assess Systems

A fortiori analysis

Cost-benefit analysis

Cross-impact analysis

Decision worksheet

Environmental impact statement

Gaming

Pair comparison

Planning balance sheet analysis

Planning council

Planning, programming, and budgeting system (PPBS)

Relative space model

Replacement model

Resource constrained scheduling heuristics

Sensitivity analysis

Simulation model

Social cost-benefit analysis

Utility theory

Value analysis

Zero-base budgeting (ZBB)

Approach Problems

Case histories

Conference

Counterplanning

Delphi

Digraphs

Function analysis diagram

Feasibility studies

Flow chart

Group process technique

Interviews

Meetings

Negotiation

Nominal group technique

Project teams

Purpose expansion

Questionnaire

Task force

Workshops

Categorize/Classify Alternatives

Abstract dimensioning

Classification

Control charts

Data dictionary

Fuzzy sets
Hierarchical clustering
Index analysis
Multiattribute utility (MAU) models
Pair comparison
Partitioning
Person-card sorting technique
Task timeline
Utility assessment

Collect and/or Organize Performance Information
Case histories
Cash flow analysis
Control charts
Critical incident technique
Delphi
Flow chart
Gantt chart
Histograms
Learning curves
Multiattribute utility (MAU) models
Management operations system technique (MOST)
Nominal group technique
Progress function
Time study
Training
Work measurement
    Also see Analyze job methods and motions
           Collect data and/or information
           Identify new product opportunities

Collect Data and/or Information
Activity sampling
Attitude surveys
Case histories
Central location testing
Charrette
Checklist
Citizen referendum
Climate analysis
Computer graphics
Counter planning
Critical incident technique
Data base system
Delphi
Ends-means chain
Environmental impact statements

Interviews
Job interviews
Learning curves
Managerial grid analysis
Media-based issue balloting
Meetings
Numbering/identification schemes
Nominal group technique
Observation model
Opportunity identification
Questionnaire
Standard data, charts, tables, and equations
Standard operating procedures
Telecommunications
Telephone polling
Time study
Training
Use testing
Wage scale
Work measurement
Workshops

Describe/Establish/Measure Relationships
Cause/effect assessment
Computer graphics
Correlation analysis
Data dictionary
Data transformation
Digraphs
Dynamic model
Factor analysis
Fault-tree analysis
Flow chart
Interaction analysis
Interpretive structural modeling
Mathematical model
Modeling
Network analysis
Oval diagrams
Pareto analysis
Physical model
Planning model
Profit/volume (P/V) analysis
Purpose network analysis
Statistical model
System matrix
Tree diagram

Detail Proposed Solution

  See Analyze job methods and motions

  Analyze systems

  Collect data and/or information

  Describe/establish/measure relationships

  Determining human ability and skill requirements for tasks

  Involve people

  Predict future conditions

  Provide graphic representations

Determine Human Ability and Skill Requirements for Tasks

  Aptitude test

  Critical incident technique

  Information content analysis

  Interviews

  Job evaluation

  Operation chart

  Performance/time measurement estimate

  Role analysis

  Task analysis

  Therblig chart

  Training

  Tree diagram

  Work measurement

Develop and Analyze Structure

  Computer graphics

  Critical path method

  Interpretive structural modeling

  Network analysis

  Precedence diagram method

  Program evaluation and review technique

  System matrix

Develop (Enhance) Creativity

  Bisociation

  Brainstorming

  Delphi

  Nominal group technique

  Morphological analysis

  Person-card sorting technique

  Synectics

    Also see Generate alternatives/ideas

Establish Priorities

  See Categorize/classify alternatives

  Organize alternatives

  Rank alternatives

  Rate conditions

  Weight criteria or factors

Establish Project Schedules and Basis for Measuring Progress and Performance

  Activity line balance evaluation (ABLE)

  Gantt chart

  Learning curves and progress functions

  Line of balance (LOB)

  Management operations systems technique (MOST)

  Milestone chart

  Network analysis

  PERT/cost

  Precedence diagram method

  Resource constrained scheduling heuristic

  Task timeline

Estimate Budget and Dollar Requirements

  Budget

  Cash flow analysis

  Expected free cash flow model

  Planning, programming, and budgeting system (PPBS)

  Zero-base budgeting

    Also see Analyzing investments

Evaluate Alternatives

  See Analyze alternative options/plans/policies/programs/contingencies/functions

  Analyze investments

  Analyze job methods and motions

  Analyze policy setting and decision making variables

  Analyze product quality

  Analyze project impacts on society

  Analyze projects

  Appraise/assess alternative options/plans/policies/programs/contingencies/functions

  Appraise/assess investments

  Appraise/assess projects

  Appraise/assess systems

Evaluate Interpersonal Relationships, Performance, and Effectiveness of an Organization

  Auditing

  Force field analysis

Index analysis
Organization mirror
Organizational sensing
Role analysis
Training

Generate a List of Possible Purpose/Function Statements

Brainstorming
Brain writing
Function analysis diagram
Nominal group technique
Purpose expansion
   Also see Generate alternatives/ideas

Generate Alternatives/Ideas

Analogies
Bisociation
Brain resting
Brainstorming
Brain writing
Case histories
Charrette
Citizen advisory committee
Conference
Counseling interviews
Delphi
Dialectical process
Fishbowl planning
Focused group interview
Forced connections
Interviews
Judgment analysis technique
Meetings
Morphological analysis
Nominal group technique
Productivity circles
Purpose expansion
Questionnaire
Random selected participation groups
Synectics
Team building
Telephone polling
Use testing workshops

Identify Management Styles

Attitude survey
Auditing technique

Interviews
Managerial grid analysis
Questionnaire

Identify (Product) Opportunities

Abstract dimensioning
Central location testing
Employee panels
Focus group testing
New-product early warning system
Opportunity identification
Product/service life cycle analysis
Substitution analysis
Use testing

Identify Problems, Overlaps, Conflicts

Bisociation
Brainstorming
Data dictionary
Delphi
Group process techniques
Interviews
Meetings
Morphological analysis
Nominal group technique
Person-card sorting technique
Purpose expansion
Questionnaire
   Also see Approach problems
             Identify management styles

Identify Project Opportunities

   See Analyze projects
           Identify (product) opportunities

Identify Regularities

Classification
Person-card sorting technique
Priority setting
System matrix
   Also see Weight criteria or factors

Inform and Involve Citizens

Citizen honoraria
Drop-in centers
Fishbowl planning
Group process technique
Judgment policy analysis

Media-based issue balloting
Meetings
Negotiation
Ombudsman
Open-door policy
Planning balance sheet analysis
Planning council
Public hearing

Involve People

Activity matrix
Brainstorming
Conference
Delphi
Interpretive structural modeling
Judgment analysis technique
Judgment policy analysis
Nominal group technique
Opinion polling
Planning council
Planning model
Productivity circles
Program planning method
Scenario writing
Telecommunications
Utility assessment
Value analysis
   Also see Inform and involve citizens

Measure Error

Control charts
Sensitivity analysis
Variance analysis

Measure Project Progress and Performance

   See Establish project schedules and basis for measuring progress and performance

Organize Alternatives

Classification
Couplet comparison technique
Data dictionary
Data transformation
Decision tables
Fuzzy sets
Hierarchical clustering
Hierarchical structures
Intent structures

Logical framework
Numbering/identification schemes
Objective tree
Person-card sorting technique
Program planning method
Purpose expansion
Psychological scaling
Scaling, subjective
Scheduling model
Specification listing
System pyramid
Team building

Plot and Analyze Data about the Performance of an Existing Installation

Budget analysis
Control charts
Index values
Learning curves and progress functions
Variance analysis

Predict Future Conditions

Adaptive forecasting
Budget
Contextual mapping
Control charts
Cross-impact analysis
Demographic forecasting
Econometric model
Forecasting
Index numbers
Learning curves
Markov chain
New-product early warning system
Operations research
Path analysis
Performance measures tally
PERT/cost
Probabilistic system dynamics
Probability assessment
Product/service life cycle analysis
Progress function
Queuing theory
Resource constrained scheduling heuristic
Regression analysis
Regression forecasting
Reliability theory

Risk analysis
Role playing
Sales force composite
Scenario writing
Scheduling model
Simulation model
Smoothing
Sociological projection technique
Subjective probability assessment
Substitution analysis
Technological assessment
Technological forecasting
Time series analysis
Trend analysis

Preserve an Image

Computer graphics
Data dictionary
Graphics
Modeling
Photographs
Physical model
Planning model

Portray an Order of Events

Critical path method
Decision tables
Delta charts
Flow chart
Gantt charts
Interpretive structural modeling
Machine-loading charts
Maintenance charts
Milestone chart
Network analysis
Operations chart
PERT/cost
Precedence diagram method
Process chart
Program evaluation and review technique
Resource constrained scheduling heuristic
Specification listing
Task timeline

Produce Consensus

Arbitration and mediation planning
Group process technique
Judgment analysis technique

Meetings
Negotiation
Nominal group technique
Ombudsman
Team building
Voting technique

Provide Graphic Representations

Computer graphics
Decision tree
Delta charts (cell 19)
Digraphs
Flow chart
Graphics
Graphy theory
Histogram
Influence diagram
Intent structure
Interpretive structural modeling
Network analysis
Objective tree
Oval diagrams
Partitioning technique
Performance measures tally
Physical model
Policy graphs
Progress function
Purpose network analysis
System pyramid
Templates
Tree diagram
   Also see Preserve an image
              Portray an order of events

Rank Alternatives

Contingency analysis
Cost effectiveness analysis
Goals-achievement analysis
Multiattribute utility (MAU) models
Measurement model
Nominal group technique
Pair comparison
Scaling, subjective
Social cost-benefit analysis
Utility assessment
Value analysis

Rate Conditions

Delphi

Job evaluation

Multiattribute utility (MAU) models

Questionnaire

Time study

Also see Weight criteria or factors

Stimulate Creativity of People

See Develop (enhance) creativity

Test Impact of Different Values of an Attribute/
Parameter/Variable

A Fortiori analysis

Scenario writing

Sensitivity analysis

Weight Criteria or Factors

Nominal group technique

Questionnaire

Subjective judgment

Utility theory

Voting

Also see Rate conditions

LISTING OF TECHNIQUES BY CELLS OF P&D SYSTEM (TABLE 10-1)

The techniques and models listed in each cell illustrate some that may be useful in accomplishing the functions of the cell. Others may well be applicable, but the following listing is an appropriate stimulator:

(1) Purpose, fundamental. Brain writing, couplet comparison technique, ends-mean chain, intent structures, interviews, map of activity and thought chains, multilevel approach, needs analysis, nominal group technique, objective trees, purpose expansion, relationship chart, relevance trees, sensitivity analysis, scenarios, semilattice tree, surveys, system pyramid.

(2) Purpose, values. Brainstorming, climate analysis, dialectical process, ends-means chain, intent structures, interviews, objectives tree, questionnaire, utility theory.

(3) Purpose, measures. Budgets, correlation analysis, financial investment appraisal, Gantt chart, index analysis, indifference curves, interpretive structural modeling, measurement model, monthly operating statement, needs analysis, nominal group technique, objectives or goals survey, objectives

pyramid, Planning, Programming, and Budgeting System, profit/volume analysis, return on investment, single-factor and multiattribute utility assessment, subjective probability assessment, subjective 0–100 scaling, variance analysis.

(4) Purpose, control. Annual report of P&D system activities and achievements, board of director review, budget control sheets, control charts, data transformation, external peer evaluation, influence diagram, management style questionnaire, participative review and control, Planning, Programming, and Budgeting System, trend analysis, value analysis, worst/best case analysis, zero-base budgeting.

(5) Purpose, interface. A fortiori analysis, arbitration and mediation planning, cause/effect assessment, correlation analysis, cross-impact matrix, digraphs, ends-means chain, graph theory, hierarchical structure, influence diagram, intent structures, interaction analysis, interpretive structural modeling, intersectoral analysis, negotiation, objectives tree, ombudsman, opportunity identification, policy graphs, purpose network analysis, relationship chart, sensitivity analysis.

(6) Purpose, future. Each of those in cells 1–5. Conditional demand analysis, extended scenarios, futures research, objectives tree, profits progress (learning) function, sociological projection techniques.

(7) Inputs, fundamental. Budgets, conditional demand analysis, contingency forecasting, demographic forecasts, monthly operating statements and balance sheets, nominal group technique, partitioning techniques, questionnaire, regression analysis, technological forecasting, telephone polling, time series analysis.

(8) Inputs, values. Brainstorming, dialectical process, group process technique, interviews, questionnaires, sociological projection technique, utility assessment, and utility theory.

(9) Inputs, measures. Budget, checklists, cost-benefit analysis, cost-effectiveness analysis, data transformation, information acquisition preference inventory, judgment analysis technique, judgment policy analysis, measurement model, planning and control technique, preference ordering, psychological scaling, sampling theory, sensitivity analysis, simulation, statistical model, subjective probability assessment, subjective scaling, voting techniques.

(10) Inputs, control. Attitude surveys, board of directors review, budget, checklists, citizen honoraria, control charts for human involvement measures and for information quality and quantity norms, control method, correlation analysis, data base system, employee panels, external peer evaluation, focus-group testing, a fortiori analysis, Gantt charts, group process technique, influence diagram, operational games, or-

ganization analysis, planning and control technique, program planning budgeting system, probability assessment, productivity circles, questionnaire, replicate information collection, role playing, sensitivity analysis, simulation, statistical model, task force, team building, telephone polling, use testing, value analysis, worst-case analysis, zero-base budgeting.

(11) Inputs, interface. Interface with outputs: charette, computer graphics, correlation analysis, drop-in centers, fishbowl planning, input-output analysis, media-based issue balloting, meetings, open-door policy, public hearing workshops. Others: arbitration and mediation planning, cross-impact matrix, influence diagram, interaction analysis, interaction matrix, intersectoral analysis, interpretive structural modeling, negotiation, ombudsman, profit/volume analysis, system pyramid, technology assessment.

(12) Inputs, future. Each of those in cells 7–11. Conditional demand analysis, contextual mapping, extended scenarios, forecasting, futures research, new-product early warning system, opportunity identification, progress ("learning") function for quality and quantity measures of effectiveness, regression forecasting, simulation, social indicators, technology assessments and forecasts, time series analysis.

(13) Outputs, fundamental. All available ones are possible as output representations, but a sample of them includes computer graphics, drawings, drop-in centers, fishbowl planning, hotline, input-output analysis, intent structures, interpretive structural models, media-based issue balloting, meetings, open door policy, oval diagrams, photographs, policy graphs, pro forma balance and operating statements, public hearing, public information program, scenario, system matrix, system or semilattice pyramid, workshops.

(14) Outputs, values. Brainstorming, dialectical process, intent structures, questionnaires, sociological projection technique, utility assessment.

(15) Outputs, measures. Benefit-cost analysis, break-even analysis, budget, correlation analysis, data transformation, a fortiori analysis, measurement model, PPBS, product or service life cycle analysis, profit/volume analysis, progress functions, psychological scalings, reliability theory, sensitivity analysis, simulation, subjective probability assessment, variance analysis.

(16) Outputs, control. Budget, cause-effect analysis, central location testing, checklists, control charts, control model, correlation analysis, counter planning, data transformation, decision matrix, employee panels, financial investment appraisal, influence diagram, return on investment, simulation,

tables reporting variance to norms, use testing, worst case analysis, zero-base budgeting.

(17) Outputs, interface. With inputs: computer graphics, correlation analysis, drop-in centers, fishbowl planning, input-output analysis, media-based issue balloting, meetings, open-door policy, public hearing, and workshops. With other elements: arbitration and mediation planning, cause-effect analysis, charrette, cross-impact analysis, diagraphs, environmental impact statements, fault tree analysis, impact analysis, influence diagram, interaction analysis, intersectoral analysis, negotiation, new business project screening summary, ombudsman, policy graphs, PPBS, profit/volume analysis, system or semilattice pyramid, and technology assessment.

(18) Outputs, future. Each of those in cells 13–17, plus additional techniques in cell 12.

(19) Sequence, fundamental. Because the P&D system sequence involves all aspects of time-based P&D, all of the techniques could be involved, especially the change principles (Table 16-2). The following just illustrate the differing types for each phase:

1 Delphi, forecasting techniques, function expansion, purpose hierarchy, intent structures, oval diagrams, semi-lattice, system pyramid, tree diagrams.
2 Analogies, bisociation, brain resting, brainstorming, brain writing, dialectical process, morphological box, search for diverse sources of options.
3 Cash flow analysis, causal diagram, cost effectiveness analysis, decision matrix, DELTA chart (decision, event, logic, time, activities), feasibility study, financial investment appraisal, flowchart, goals-achievement matrix, input-output matrix, layout-diagram, multilevel diagraph, operations research, optimization, pair comparison, Pareto analysis, return on investment, scenario, social cost benefit analysis, system matrix.
4 Same as 3 plus contingency analysis, cost-benefit analysis, decision tables, forecasting, multiple attribute utility assessment, parameter analysis, program planning method, simulation.
5 Same as 1, 2, 3, and 4 plus control charts, questionnaires (cells 21, 22, 23).

(20) Sequence, values. Brainstorming, dialectical process, group process technique, questionnaires, and utility theory.

(21) Sequence, measures. Activity balance line evaluation, break-even analysis, budget, correlation analysis, data transformation, decision tree, Gantt

chart, life cycle phasing, line of balance, management operations systems technique, measurement model, milestone chart, network analysis, operations chart, PERT or critical path method (manual or computerized), PERT/COST, precedence diagram method, process chart, RAMPS, statistical model, subjective probability assessment, timeline budget for phases, variance analysis.

(22) Sequence, control. Activity balance line evaluation, activity matrix, budget variance analysis, client/user/citizen/P&D peer review panels, contingency/worst case analysis, control charts, correlation analysis, data transformation, decision tables, DELTA chart, Gantt chart, influence diagram, line of balance, management operations systems technique, milestone chart, network analysis, operations chart, PERT/COST, PPBS, precedence diagram methods, process chart, RAMPS, scheduling model, simulation, statistical model, task force, zero-base budgeting.

(23) Sequence, interface. Arbitration and mediation, cause/effect assessment, change principles, contingency tables, correlation analysis, cross-impact analysis, decision tables, digraphs, force field analysis, improvement program, influence diagram, interaction matrix analysis, interface event control, intersectoral analysis, multiple criteria utility assessment, negotiation, ombudsman, policy graphs, scenarios, subjective probability assessment, surveys.

(24) Sequence, future. Each of those in cells 19–23. Some newer techniques are emerging: computerized Delphi, contingency forecasts, a fortiori analysis, parameter analysis, technological forecasting, worst-case analysis.

(25) Environment, fundamental. Causal diagrams, community attitude survey, Delphi, demographic analysis, dialectical process, dynamic model, gaming and simulation, goals program analysis, intersectoral analysis, interviews, matrix structure, organizational climate analysis, organizational sensing, oval diagrams, parameter analyses, productivity circles, project teams, preference ordering, scenarios, semilattice pyramid, telephone polling, tree diagrams, utility assessment, volunteer group status.

(26) Environment, values. Brainstorming, climate analysis, dialectical process, questionnaires, technology assessment, utility theory.

(27) Environment, measures. Budget, bureaucracy level analysis, cause/effect assessment, climate analysis, correlation analysis, counts and/or ratios of public attendance at P&D meetings, data transformation, demand analysis, econometric models, factor analysis, frequency of P&D system meetings, frequency of updating "pulse" of external environment

aspects, magnitude of external pressure, management grid analysis, measurement model, network analysis of P&D system, PPBS, regression analysis, rigidity versus openness analysis, role analysis, statistical model, subjective probability assessment, variance analysis.

(28) Environment, control. Budget, climate analysis trends, control charts, control model, correlation analysis, critical incidence review, data transformation, influence diagram, P&D peer review, PPBS, statistical model, utility assessment, zero-base budgeting.

(29) Environment, interface. Arbitration and mediation planning, cause/effect assessment, correlation analysis, demographic analysis, digraphs, environmental impact statement, factor analysis, fault-tree analysis, force field analysis, graph theory, human development continua, impact analysis, influence diagram, ISM, interaction analysis, intersectoral analysis, interviews, negotiation, ombudsman, organization mirror, organizational sensing, policy graphs, regression analysis, role analysis, surveys, technology and managerial control analysis, tree diagrams, trend analysis.

(30) Environment, future. Each of those in cells 25–29. Adaptive forecasting, contextual mapping, demographic forecasting, forecasting, Markov chains, probabilistic system dynamics, regression forecasting, sales force composite, smoothing, sociological projection technique, substitution analysis, technological forecasting, time series analysis.

(31) Human agents, fundamental. Attitude tests, contingency analysis, creativity techniques (analogy, morphological box, bisociation, brainstorming, brain writing, etc.), interviews, nominal group technique, ombudsman, oval diagrams, personality tests, personality type analysis, role analysis, semilattice pyramid, scenarios, subjective probability assessment, task analysis, task force, wage scale.

(32) Human agents, values. Brainstorming, dialectical process, group process technique, questionnaires, utility theory.

(33) Human agents, measures. Activity sampling, aptitude test, budget, correlation analysis, critical incident technique, data transformation, external examiner to assess performance, financial plans, Gantt chart, historical time/cost data in P&D, information content analysis, job evaluation, measurement model, performance measures tally, PPBS, progress functions and learning curves, quality of working life autonomy, salary versus job education curves, statistical estimation, statistical model, subjective probability assessment, user satisfaction surveys, variance analysis, wage scale, wage surveys, work measurement.

(34) Human agents, control. Aptitude test, budget, contingency analysis, control charts, control model, correlation analysis, counseling interviews, critical incident technique, critical path method, data transformation, Gantt charts, influence diagram, organizational analysis, peer review, PPBS, performance appraisal, RAMPS, regular retraining courses, semiannual sample tests or games, statistical model, task force, team building, training, zero-base budgeting.

(35) Human agents, interface. Arbitration and mediation planning, cause/effect assessment, correlation analysis, counseling interviews, cross-impact analysis, decision tables, digraphs, educational curriculum formats, group processes techniques, influence diagram, interaction analysis, interactive computer languages, intersectoral analysis, ISM, negotiation, ombudsman.

(36) Human agents, future. Each of those in cells 31–35.

(37) Physical catalysts, fundamental. Flow path diagrams, layout drawings, nomographs, photographs, physical and mathematical equations describing operating characteristics, physical model, specification listing, templates, three-dimensional models.

(38) Physical catalysts, values. Brainstorming, dialectical process, group process technique, questionnaires, utility theory.

(39) Physical catalysts, measures. Break-even analysis, budget, cash flow analysis, correlation analysis, cost benefit analysis, cost-effectiveness analysis, data transformation, downtime distribution, failure analysis, failure/reliability distribution, machine-loading charts, maintenance network, maintenance schedule graph, measurement model, PPBS, progress function, queuing models, social cost-benefit analysis, statistical model, subjective probability assessment, and variance analysis.

(40) Physical catalysts, control. Activity sampling, budget control sheets, control charts, control model, correlation analysis, critical path method, data transformation, influence diagram, interview surveys, maintenance charts, PPBS, RAMPS, replacement model, statistical mode, utilization indices and charts, value analysis, zero-base budgeting.

(41) Physical catalysts, interface. Arbitration and mediation planning, cause/effect assessment, climate analysis, contingency analysis, correlation analysis, cross-impact analysis, digraphs, graph theory, influence diagram, interaction analysis, interaction matrix diagram, intersectoral analysis, ISM, negotiation, ombudsman, semilattice pyramid, telecommunications.

(42) Physical catalysts, future. Each of those in cells 36–41. Modeling of conferences based on tech-

nologically advanced physical catalysts, technology assessment, technological forecasting.

(43) Information aids, fundamental. Abstract dimensioning, analysis of variance, career path analysis, case histories, charts, computer graphics, contingency analysis, continuing educational path, decision tables, decision trees, drawings, expected free cash flow model, graphics, graphs, group process techniques, hierarchical clustering, histograms, information content analysis, information flowcharts, lattice theory, mathematical and statistical tools (correlation analysis, factor analysis, histogram, Laplace transforms, risk distribution, variance, etc.), mathematical model, mathematical programming technique, modeling, performance/time measurement estimate, physical model, probability assessment, programming languages, recursive programming model, risk analysis, simulation languages, software in structures and packaging, standard operating procedures, system pyramid, time study, utility theory.

(44) Information aids, values. Brainstorming, dialectical process, group process technique, questionnaires, utility theory.

(45) Information aids, measures. Activity sampling, budget, cash flow analysis, computer simulation, contingency analysis, correlation analysis, cost-benefit analysis, cost-effectiveness analysis, data transformation, decision tables, downtime measurements, fault analysis, forecasting, a fortiori analysis, measurement model, morphological analysis, objective tree, PPBS, probability assessment, sensitivity analysis, social cost-benefit analysis, statistical model, subjective probability assessment, surveys, time between request and response, variance analysis.

(46) Information aids, control. Auditing technique, budget, budget control sheets, control charts, control model, correlation analysis, critical path analysis, data base system, data transformation, decision tables, decision trees, flowcharts, forecasting, Gantt charts, influence diagram, PPBS, priority setting or voting, replacement models, RAMPS, standard data charts and tables, statistical model, utilization indices, value analysis, zero-base budgeting.

(47) Information aids, interface. Cause-effect matrix, computer graphics, contingency analysis, correlation analysis, cross-impact matrix, digraphs, a fortiori analysis, influence diagram, interaction analysis, interaction matrix diagrams, intersectoral analysis, ISM, negotiation, ombudsman, parameter analysis, programming-computer interaction analysis, sensitivity analysis, survey questionnaires and interviews, telecommunications.

(48) Information aids, future. Each of those in cells 42–47. Computer programming research, com-

puterized Delphi, cost-benefit analysis, forecasting, gaming, and subjective probability.

SELECTED REFERENCES CONTAINING DESCRIPTIONS OF MANY TECHNIQUES

J. L. Adams, *Conceptual Blockbusting,* San Francisco: San Francisco Book Co., 1976.

R. J. Anderson, *The External Audit: Concepts and Techniques,* Toronto: Pitman, 1977.

R. D. Archibald, *Managing High-Technology Programs and Projects,* New York: Wiley, 1976.

J. S. Armstrong, *Long-range Forecasting from Crystal Ball to Computer,* New York: Wiley, 1978.

B. Auvine, B. Densmore, M. Extrom, S. Poole, and M. S. Hanklin, *A Manual for Group Facilitators,* Madison, Wis.: Center for Conflict Resolution, 1977.

M. M. Baldwin, Ed., *Portraits of Complexity: Applications of Systems Methodologies to Societal Problems,* Battelle Monograph No. 9, Columbus, Ohio: Battelle Memorial Institute, April 1973.

E. Buffa, *Modern Production Management,* 5th ed., New York: Wiley, 1977.

D. S. Clifton, Jr. and D. E. Fyffe, *Project Feasibility Analysis,* New York: Wiley, 1977.

R. G. Coyle, *Management System Dynamics,* London: Wiley, 1977.

N. Cross and R. Roy, *Design Methods Manual,* London: The Open University Press, 1975.

C. J. Dade, *An Introduction to Database Systems,* Reading, Mass.: Addison-Wesley, 1977.

K. A. DeGreene, *Sociotechnical Systems Factors in Analysis, Design and Management,* Englewood Cliffs, N.J.: Prentice-Hall, 1973.

A. Delbecq, A. Van de Van, and D. Gustafson, *Group Techniques for Program Planning—A Guide to Nominal Group and Delphi,* Chicago, Ill.: Scott-Foresman, 1975.

J. W. Dickey and T. M. Watts, *Analytic Techniques in Urban and Regional Planning,* New York: McGraw-Hill, 1978.

A. J. Duncan, *Quality Control and Industrial Statistics,* Homewood, Ill.: Irwin, 1974.

O. J. Dunn and V. A. Clark, *Applied Statistics: Analysis of Variance and Regression,* New York: Wiley, 1974.

T. R. Dyckman and L. J. Thomas, *Fundamental Statistics for Business and Economics,* Englewood Cliffs, N.J.: Prentice-Hall, 1977.

E. L. Grant, W. G. Ireson, and R. S. Leavenworth, *Principles of Engineering Economy,* 6th ed., New York: Wiley, 1976.

F. W. Horton, Jr., *Reference Guide to Advanced Management Methods,* New York: American Management Association, 1972.

G. P. Huber, *Managerial Decision Making,* Chicago, Ill.: Scott-Foresman, 1980.

J. C. Jones, *Design Methods,* 2nd ed., New York: Wiley, 1980.

R. L. Keeney and H. Raiffa, *Decisions with Multiple Objectives,* New York: Wiley, 1976.

D. A. Krueckeberg and A. L. Silvers *Urban Planning Analysis: Methods and Models,* New York: Wiley, 1974.

A. M. Law and W. D. Kelton, *Simulation Modeling and Analysis,* New York: McGraw-Hill, 1981.

M. LeBoeuf, *Imagineering,* New York: McGraw-Hill, 1980.

N. Lichfield, P. Kettle, and M. Whitbread, *Evaluation in the Planning Process,* Oxford, England: Pergamon, 1975.

G. L. Lippitt, *Visualizing Change,* Fairfax, Va.: NTL-Learning Resources Corporation, 1973.

W. J. Luzadder, *Basic Graphics,* 2nd ed., Englewood Cliffs, N.J.: Prentice-Hall, 1968.

N. Margulies and J. Wallace, *Organizational Change: Techniques & Applications,* Glenview, Ill.: Scott, Foresman, 1973.

F. G. Moore, and T. E. Hendrick, *Production/Operations Management,* 7th ed., Homewood, Ill.: Irwin, 1977.

G. Nadler, *Work Design: A Systems Concept,* Homewood, Ill.: Irwin, 1970.

N. H. Nie, C. H. Hull, J. G. Jenkins, K. Steinbrenner, and D. H. Bent, *Statistical Package for the Social Sciences,* New York: McGraw-Hill, 1978.

G. F. Pearce, *Engineering Graphics and Descriptive Geometry in 3-D,* New York: Macmillan, 1977.

E. S. Quade, *Analysis for Public Decisions,* New York: American Elsevier, 1975.

M. F. Rubenstein and K. R. Pfeiffer, *Concepts in Problem Solving,* Englewood Cliffs, N.J.: Prentice-Hall, 1980.

G. Salvendy, Ed., *Handbook of Industrial Engineering,* New York: Wiley, 1981.

P. G. Sassone and W. A. Schaffer, *Cost-Benefit Analysis: A Handbook,* New York: Academic Press, 1978.

W. G. Sullivan and W. W. Claycombe, *Fundamentals of Forecasting,* Reston, Va.: Reston, 1977.

M. Thompson, *Benefit-Cost Analysis for Program Evaluation,* Beverly Hills, Calif.: Sage Publications, 1980.

J. C. Thomson and K. M. Koritzinsky, *Guidelines for Facilitating Change in Secondary Schools,* Madison, Wis.: Wisconsin Research and Development Center for Cognitive Learning, 1976.

J. P. Van Gigch, *Applied General Systems Theory,* New York: Harper & Row, 1974.

H. M. Wagner, *Principles of Operations Research,* Englewood Cliffs, N.J.: Prentice-Hall, Inc. 1975.

J. N. Warfield, *Societal Systems: Planning, Policy and Complexity,* New York: Wiley, 1976.

S. C. Wheelwright and S. Makridakis, *Forecasting Methods for Management,* New York: Wiley, 1973.

R. E. Woolsey and H. F. Swanson, *Operations Research for Immediate Application: A Quick and Dirty Manual,* New York: Harper & Row, 1975.

G. Zaltman and R. Duncan, *Strategies for Planned Change,* New York: Wiley, 1977.

Case Histories Illustrating the Total P&D Approach (PDA)

The relatively complete PDA efforts reported in this appendix supplement the three brief cases reported in Chapter One. Many examples of PDA factors have been incorporated throughout the book. Because a real project is holistic, these case histories try to tell the "whole" story. I hope the reader will be able to detect how the five factors are intertwined throughout the project.

A particular technique may be emphasized occasionally. Some cases concentrate on one PDA factor or another (using information and knowledge, specifying and presenting solutions, etc.). Some of the cases occurred several years ago using the predecessors of the total PDA (Work Design, IDEALS Concept). But each case should contribute to an understanding of the total PDA even though some of the latest refinements were not formalized at the time.

All types of locus content areas and project or program "sizes" are also included. Not all content areas are depicted, nor are all the P&D professions represented. The breadth of types of cases should, however, illustrate that PDA can be used effectively in any size project in any locus content area. In addition, the cases should be interesting.

The titles of the cases are:

B1 Design of a National Gypsy Moth Pest Management System

B2 Unlocated Claim Files in an Insurance Company

B3 Student Planned Acquisition of Required Knowledge

B4 Improvement of Electric Fan Blade Packaging

B5 Nursing Practice Decisions in Emergencies

B6 Traffic Accident Information System

B7 "Saus-egg" Recipe Contest

B8 Practical Manufacturing Applications of the Purpose-Design Approach

B9 PDA in Architecture: The Design of a Small Space

B10 Planning a Six-day School Workshop

B11 Improving Productivity with Performance Measures and a Group Incentive Plan

B12 Bone Cement Stressing Rig for Hip Joint Replacements

B13 Preparing a Proposal for a Haifa Regional Housing Plan

B14 A Waitress Training System

Contact me if you would like the names of case histories not included here. For those not yet summarized in case history format (corporate planning for a manufacturing company, organization development in a hospital), I should be able to give you a name to contact.

CASE HISTORY B1

Design of a National Gypsy Moth Pest Management System

Situation

First imported to Massachusetts from France in 1869, the gypsy moth has since spread and become a major forest insect pest in 12 Northeastern states. Isolated infestations are found every year as far away as Florida, Wisconsin, and California. Each year from 1970 to 1976 gypsy moth larvae fed on from 0.75 to 1.75 million acres of forest, woodlot, and suburban vegetation. Continued heavy defoliation is predicted, especially as the insect spreads southward along the Appalachians.

Many problems confronted pest managers in their attempts to control the gypsy moth. Among the most important are the need to develop environmentally sound management techniques, the need to develop "integrated" management approaches that place maximum reliance on "natural" controls and take into account other kinds of pests and their interrelationships, and the need to coordinate management programs with programs of other functional and jurisdictional agencies. In addition, pest managers were operating in a difficult political and administrative environment.

The U.S. Department of Agriculture, under pressure from Congress, in 1973 began a five-year, three-phase program of expanded research and development to find solutions to the gypsy moth problem. Phases I and II were aimed at understanding the dynamics of the insect, quantifying and predicting the impact of the insect on the environment, and developing and improving direct and indirect control methods. The purpose of Phase III was to bring the results of the first two phases together and formulate practical systems for forest and pest management.

Phases I and II of the expanded research and development program produced a great deal of information about the behavior and impact of gypsy moths and developed a variety of techniques and tools for dealing with them. As Phase III got underway, however, it became increasingly apparent that despite the recent gains in knowledge from the research efforts, pest managers were still far from realizing *implemented solutions* to their problems.

In 1976, the U.S. Department of Agriculture (USDA) hired a consultant to gather together the in-

formation gained through the expanded research and development program and design a gypsy moth pest management system that could be implemented by federal and state agencies. The consulting company followed a conventional P&D approach, collecting data and information from government researchers and preparing a report that outlined alternative pest management systems and spelled out specific recommendations. Subsequent reports from the consultant presented cost-benefit and other in-depth analytical information about each of the alternatives.

Government officials discussed the recommendations of the reports at their meetings over the next several months. It was apparent during much of this time that the officials were having serious difficulties in taking action on any of the recommendations. First, the recommendations were all "snapshots" of desired systems five or more years in the future, and gave no idea of how pest managers should go about implementation then. Second, there was no consensus among the federal and state agencies that the recommended systems were the best for all agencies. Finally, the officials were aware that any changes in their operations would require a renegotiation of authority and responsibilities among the various federal, state, and private organizations involved. Just receiving and reviewing a consultant's recommendations had given them no reason or opportunity to do this. The net result of the consultant's recommendations was no action. The reports were quietly shelved.

Planning the Comprehensive Gypsy Moth Pest Management System (CGMPMS)

In July 1977 a meeting of 18 key federal and state gypsy moth program officials was held to plan a *planning system* that would be responsible for developing a Comprehensive Gypsy Moth Pest Management System (CGMPMS). The meeting was facilitated by personnel from the University of Wisconsin at Madison. By the end of the day, the group had identified a list of people from federal and state government agencies, private industry, and the university research community who would be involved in the planning project. Also identified were responsibilities, detailed planning activities, budget, expected products, and the overall project timeline (Figure B1-1). In subsequent stages of planning the timeline was twice amended and extended to better fit real-world conditions.

By October, final preparations and arrangements were complete, and work on the design of the CGMPMS began. The first meeting of 20 people began much as the July meeting had begun—with a great deal of catharsis from group members. It was apparent that they had experienced many frustrations over the past

David G. Hinds, 1979, Project Director, Gypsy Moth Pest Management Planning Task Force, Engineering Experiment Station, University of Wisconsin—Madison.

Timeline

September 1977	Begin planning and design of Comprehensive Gypsy Moth Pest Management System (CGMPMS)
October 1977 (two-day GMPTF meeting)	Generate purposes for the CGMPMS
	Prepare statement of need for CGMPMS
	Identify and define functional components of the CGMPMS
	Establish organizational framework (committees) of GMPTF
	Develop alternative Gypsy Moth Pest Management Systems
	Establish evaluative criteria for the selection of the target pest management system solution
	Identify CGMPMS major solution categories
	Identify most important conditions of the system
	Consolidate ideas from functional component committees
	Select target pest management system solution
Late October and November 1977	Meetings with states to exchange information
	Meetings with federal agencies to obtain feedback
	Discussion with or distribution of materials to Program Board about GMPTF activities
December 1977 (two-day GMPTF meeting)	Review details of target pest management system solution and incorporate feedback from state and federal agency meetings
Mid-December 1977	"National Meeting" on the gypsy moth (tentative)
February 1978 (two-day GMPTF meeting)	Identify less important conditions (exceptions) that must be considered in the CGMPMS
	Identify major categories of the recommended pest management system
	Define the broad outlines of the recommended CGMPMS
March 1978	Review outline CGMPMS with state and federal agencies
	Review outline with Program Board
April 1978 (two-day GMPTF meeting)	Define in detail the recommended CGMPMS
	Develop initial structure for Gypsy Moth Continuing Planning Committee (GMCPC)
June 1978	Develop the plan for implementation of the CGMPMS
	Identify phases of CGMPMS implementation
	Identify future research needs
July 1978	Discussion of CGMPMS and GMCPC with Combined Forest Pest Program Board
August 1978	Final detailing of the CGMPMS and GMCPC
September 1978	Submittal of CGMPMS and proposal for a GMCPC to Combined Forest Pest Program Board
	Assist federal and state governments in implementing the CGMPMS and the GMCPC

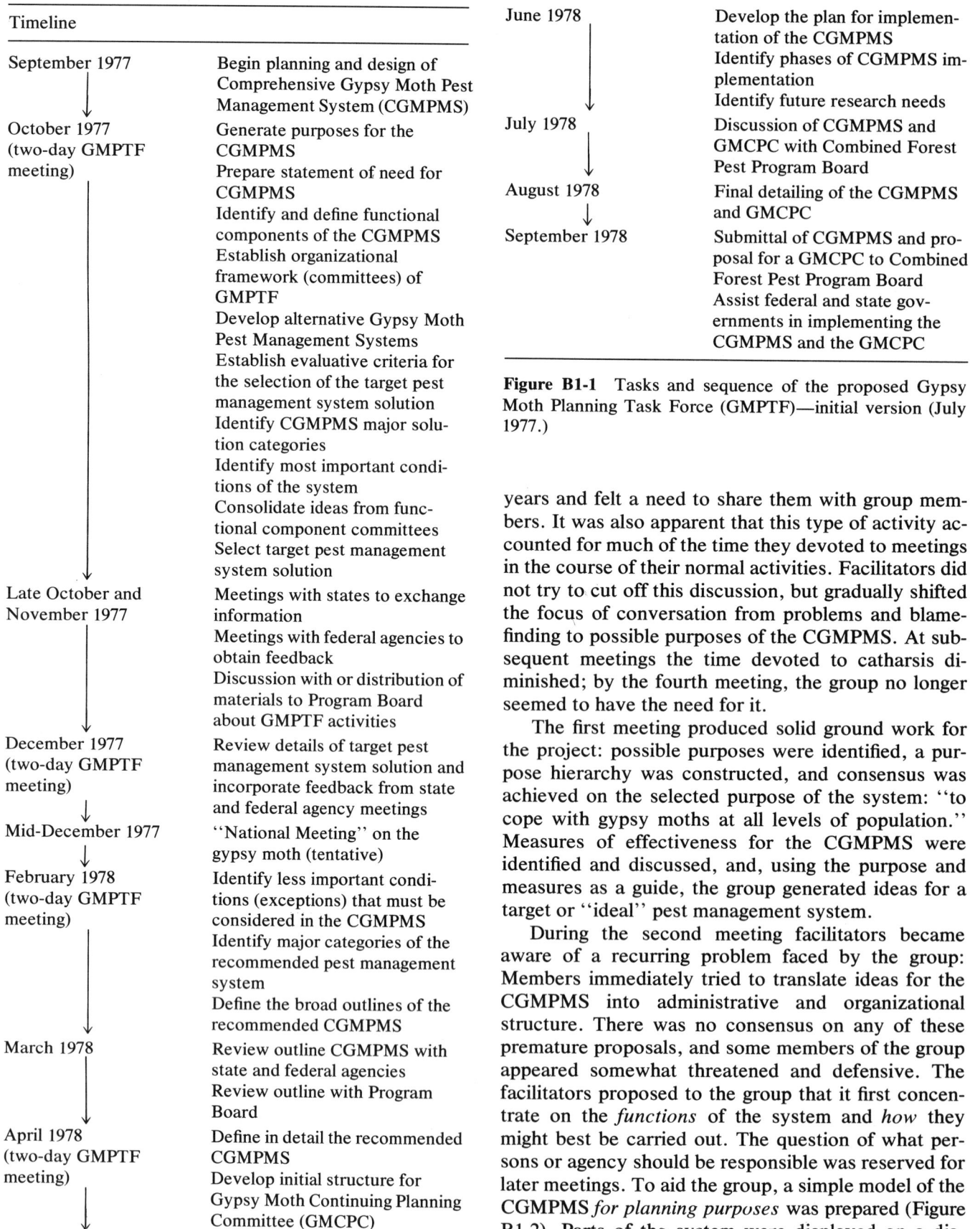

Figure B1-1 Tasks and sequence of the proposed Gypsy Moth Planning Task Force (GMPTF)—initial version (July 1977.)

years and felt a need to share them with group members. It was also apparent that this type of activity accounted for much of the time they devoted to meetings in the course of their normal activities. Facilitators did not try to cut off this discussion, but gradually shifted the focus of conversation from problems and blame-finding to possible purposes of the CGMPMS. At subsequent meetings the time devoted to catharsis diminished; by the fourth meeting, the group no longer seemed to have the need for it.

The first meeting produced solid ground work for the project: possible purposes were identified, a purpose hierarchy was constructed, and consensus was achieved on the selected purpose of the system: "to cope with gypsy moths at all levels of population." Measures of effectiveness for the CGMPMS were identified and discussed, and, using the purpose and measures as a guide, the group generated ideas for a target or "ideal" pest management system.

During the second meeting facilitators became aware of a recurring problem faced by the group: Members immediately tried to translate ideas for the CGMPMS into administrative and organizational structure. There was no consensus on any of these premature proposals, and some members of the group appeared somewhat threatened and defensive. The facilitators proposed to the group that it first concentrate on the *functions* of the system and *how* they might best be carried out. The question of what persons or agency should be responsible was reserved for later meetings. To aid the group, a simple model of the CGMPMS *for planning purposes* was prepared (Figure B1-2). Parts of the system were displayed on a dia-

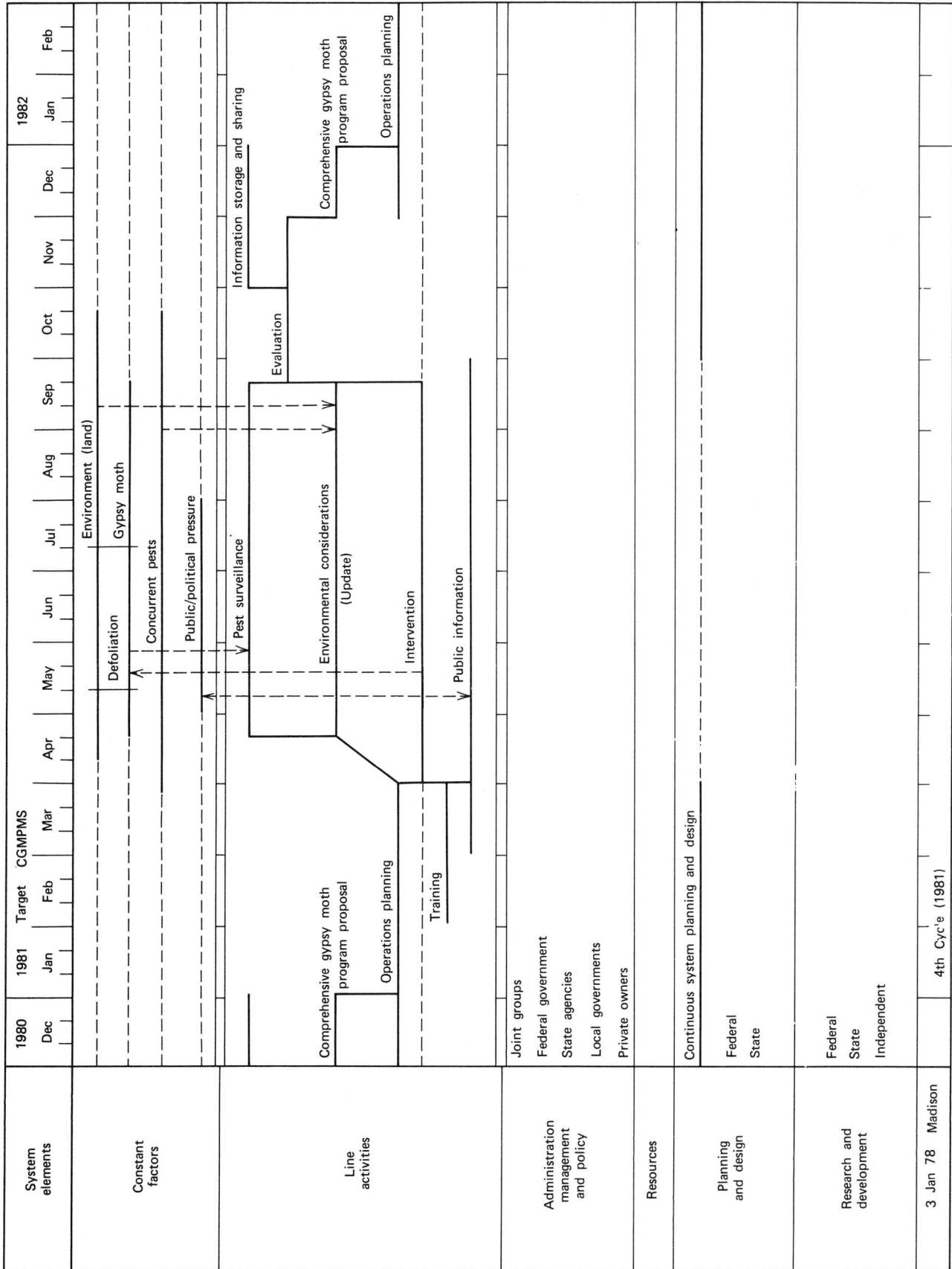

Figure B1-2 Target CGMPMS timeline.

gram, with the best known and agreed upon at the top and the least known at the bottom, as labeled on Figure B1-2. The group agreed that planning would proceed in this manner.

By January 1978 the planning group had developed the overall 1983 target system for the CGMPMS and decided to split up into committees to handle detailed work. Committees were formed to design each of the line activities identified earlier: operations planning, pest surveillance, environmental considerations, intervention, public communication, evaluation, information management, training, and policy formulation. Each of the committees treated its area of responsibility as a system and began by identifying purposes, measures, ideas for target systems and so on.

In June a special group was formed from the large group for the purpose of designing a system for gaining approval of the CGMPMS by the states, U.S. Forest Service, Animal and Plant Health Inspection Services, (APHIS), USDA Science and Education Administration (SEA), the Secretary of Agriculture's Office, and private groups. This group followed the same P&D approach used by the other group. The content and results, of course, were very different. A list of activities for obtaining approval was developed and arrayed on a timeline. Responsibilities for each of the activities were assigned to group members.

In implementing the approval system a serious problem developed when one of the group members became ill and failed to conduct preliminary briefing sessions for the three federal agencies' top managers. In the absence of information they would have received at the briefing sessions, each of the three agencies became suspicious of the motives of the other agencies and adopted "hard-line" stances against the proposed CGMPMS. It took the efforts of the chairman of the planning group and several other key people two months to ease apprehensions and restore trust. Implementation of systems must be monitored—even a system as small and temporary as an approval system—to avoid mistakes and misunderstandings.

By the end of August 1978, plans for the national level of the CGMPMS were complete and ready for implementation according to an agreed-upon schedule. The system was now being viewed as operating at three levels (Table B1-1). Level III (national), Level II (state and regional), and Level I (local, the "firing line"). The planning group decided to continue detailed planning for another year for Levels II and I, and to move ahead with implementation at the national level.

The target plan for the national level called for the creation of a National Gypsy Moth Management Board, with responsibility for overall system evaluation, policy formulation, program coordination, and fund raising (Figure B1-3). The National Board was to have a charter from the USDA and was to be funded and staffed through the same agency. A federal pest management coordinator was to be designated to coordinate all pest programs in USDA. The purpose of this proposal was to provide for the many problems associated with the interfaces between programs.

As the "planning world" was putting the final touches on its plans for the national level of the CGMPMS, the "real world" was moving ahead with

Table B1-1 Relationship of Activities to Structural Levels

Level I	Level II	Level III
Pest surveillance	Pest surveillance (broad scale)	
Concurrent pests	Concurrent pests (broad scale)	
Intervention	Intervention (broad scale)	
Local operations planning	Regional operations planning	
Local environmental considerations	Environmental considerations	
Logistics	Logistics	
Local public communication	Public communication	Public communication
Local planning and design	State and regional planning and design	National planning and design
	Training	
	Quarantine activities	
	Evaluation and information management	Evaluation and information management
	Research and Development	Research and development
	Resources	Resources
		Policy recommendations
		Systemwide coordination

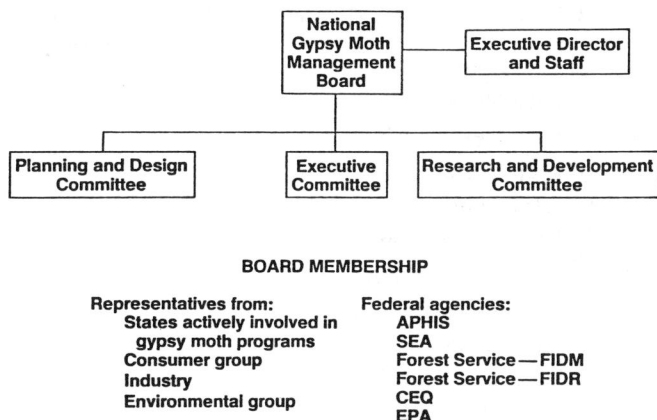

Figure B1-3 National gypsy moth management board.

decisions of its own. Feeling pressures from the Secretary of Agriculture's office to improve coordination among themselves (through the National Board), the three federal agencies (Forest Service, APHIS, SEA) met on their own and decided to form a "USDA Gypsy Moth Steering Committee," which would carry out some of the functions originally designated for the National Board.

The formation of the USDA committee was at first viewed as a setback by many members of the CGMPMS planning group, but their year's experience in planning and design quickly helped them to realize that planning is a continuing process and that "disturbances" should be dealt with positively. The group scheduled a series of meetings with the new USDA committee which were, in effect, a way of forming a broader planning group to replan Level III of the CGMPMS. A new plan was worked out, incorporating the USDA committee and redistributing functions and responsibilities. The procedure used to do this was first to achieve a consensus on the *functions* that needed to be carried out at the national level, and then *negotiate* the roles and responsibilities of each agency. Planning professionals leading the meetings had to be quick to realize at which point their role as planning facilitators became ineffective and the new role called for was that of negotiators.

Over the next eight months the National Gypsy Moth Management Board and the USDA Gypsy Moth Steering Committee began operations and planning for Levels II and I of the system (now under the auspices of the National Board). The three federal agencies, for the first time in their histories began to coordinate, at first cautiously, their gypsy moth work. As positive experiences of interagency activities accumulated, coordination became closer, and finally, in 1979, joint programs were undertaken.

By May 1979 the group facilitation work of the University of Wisconsin team was finished. Much remained to be done on Levels II and I of the system, but the CGMPMS framework was solidly established and the capability of the National Board and USDA agencies to continue planning and improvement was firmly in place.

As a final step in the initial planning effort, a report on the status of the CGMPMS was prepared. This, too, was treated as a system and designed using the P&D approach. A meeting with National Board members revealed that the report had to fulfill the purposes of three audiences: top level administrators, middle level pest managers, and people on the "firing line." Purpose hierarchies were developed for all three groups.[1]

What emerged from this P&D process[2] was a loose-leaf-bound report, specifically designed to be expanded and updated, section-by-section on a regular basis. Pages were color-coded for the different audiences, spaces titled and left blank for parts of the system yet to be developed, and a quick-reference table of contents was prepared. The report was produced according to a formal timeline of activities developed at the same time as the report plan.

At the time of this writing (early 1980) the National Board and the USDA agencies are continuing their development and improvement of the CGMPMS. As new systems are developed and existing systems modified, new sections of the report are printed and distributed.

Summary

This case offers several unique insights into the planning and design of a large-scale, complex system: First, the magnitude of the case was very large: Hundreds of people were either directly or indirectly involved; the area affected covered approximately one third of the United States; and many millions of dollars of research and development program funds were involved. Second, the pest management system had to relate to and integrate the activities of a wide range of people, from top-level policy makers in Washington to the most basic "front-line" field personnel scattered throughout the Northeast. Third, the people involved in planning had few incentives, obligations, or precedents to cooperate with each other beyond the professional formalities that existed.

In this case the use of PDA provided benefits that had been unobtainable before. Participants were afforded the environment and means for interacting and establishing a positive working relationship, developing a unique system to fit their special needs, and creating the right institutional arrangements to carry out and further their plans. Perhaps most important, the people involved found that P&D involves much more than collecting and analyzing data, developing recommendations, and publishing a report, which had made up most of their earlier experiences. Instead, they found that P&D called for their active participation in a well-organized process aimed at focusing on purposes, developing feasible targets and the means to achieve them, and following through with implementation and continuing planning and improvement.

CASE HISTORY B2

Unlocated Claim Files in an Insurance Company

Situation

Central Records is responsible for more than 600,000 claims, all filed numerically. In 1976 there was no control over these files; they were located in different facilities throughout Regina, Saskatchewan.

Unlocated claim files (an average of 200 at any given time) were the cause of considerable frustration. They led to a delay in claims processing, policy underwriting, inaccurate or late reporting of statistics, a poor public image, and generally poor morale within the department and other areas of Saskatchewan Government Insurance (SGI).

Searching for files—a time-consuming, monotonous, uninteresting task—required the services of one or two staff members each day. Staff in the different departments took exception to being bothered by junior clerks searching for files. The end result was that few files were actually found.

The P&D approach began with a carefully selected committee, including a senior clerk, a microfilm expert, a librarian-archivist, a new intermediate clerk serving as recording secretary, and myself as chairman.

At the first meeting, two hand-outs describing the approach were discussed and a seven-level purpose hierarchy was developed (Table B2-1).

The next meeting resulted in the "better" function expansion of Table B2-1. "Keeping claims files available" was selected as our aim—a broader and more positive objective than simply solving the problem of finding unlocated files.

At the next couple of meetings, several creativity techniques were used to generate ideas. As a result, we came up with 131 ideas—and had fun doing it. The ideas ranged from the simple and commonplace to those of a more complex nature employing the latest technology. At this point we assessed them as either "good" or "no good." There were 10 groups of

Table B2-1 Purpose Hierarchy for Unlocated Files

1	To locate files
2	To have files located
3	To have files available
4	To keep files available
5	To retrieve information
6	To have information
7	To supply information
8	To have information supplied
9	To fill requests
10	To have requests filled
11	To satisfy "system"
12	To improve service (to other departments)

"good" ideas, one possibly becoming an ideal solution. Various "experts" and representatives of "user" departments attended the next several meetings to help detail the alternatives.

Recommended Solution

An idea called "work station instructions" served as an informal "Feasible Ideal Solution Target." The system finally proposed included a charge-out system and color coding. The whole system involved a cost of $23,000 with a 2.2-year payback period. A three-person committee presented the recommendation to the executive officers of SGI. The response was positive.

Summary

There were several reasons for the PDA succeeding where other projects had failed:

1 The P&D process took place without disrupting necessary ongoing operations.

2 Morale was raised by involving people in solving their own problems.

3 Users, decision makers, and technical experts worked togeher without friction.

4 Participants were able to agree on an innovative procedure in Central Records.

Probably the most significant outcome of the project was determining the function of Central Records. I certainly feel much better about my department and job. What's more, we do in fact keep claims files available. (There are now, as of January 1980, virtually no unlocated files.)

Margaret McDougall, 1977, Central Records, Saskatchewan Government Insurance (SGI), Regina, Saskatchewan, Canada.

CASE HISTORY B3

Student Planned Acquisition of Required Knowledge (SPARK)

Situation

Individualization of instruction for each student is an objective educators at all levels extol. The rationale is axiomatic: each student is unique, has particular interests, learns in a unitary fashion, and develops at his or her own rate. Success at achieving "individualized learning" is rarely obtained.

Direct learning activities of each specific student seem to be rather overlooked in the literature. Students are treated in the aggregate or only superficially on an individual basis with data used in Computer Managed Instruction (CMI) or other records. Getting students involved in their own learning individualization needs a planning approach such as that formalized in SPARK.

Briefly, SPARK operates as follows:

1 Each unit of study (theme, topic, book, project, etc.) is presented to a class along with the minimum requirements the teacher expects from the unit.

2 Each student or group of students applies the

Distilled from G. Nadler, Margaret Norton, James V. Schultz, and James C. Thomson, Jr., *Educational Technology*, Vol. 18, No. 7, July 1978, pp. 15–18. (Also M. Norton, W. C. Bozeman, and G. Nadler, *SPARK*, Englewood Cliffs, N.J.: Educational Technology Publishers, 1980, Vol. 35 in the Instructional Design Library.)

CONTEMPORARY LIFE STUDY UNIT   NAME _Pat Hammer_

STEP ONE: Decide on the topic for your study this quarter as, for example,
           Ecology, Generation Gap, Drugs, Crime, Dissent or Conformity,
           New Morality, The Family, Life Styles, Future Shock, Ethnic Problems, etc.

STEP TWO: List as many possible purposes for studying this topic as you can
           possibly think of. You may do this as a group even though you
           plan to do your study by yourself. Sometimes the ideas that other
           people have will make it easier for you to think about what you are
           going to do. Work out on <u>scratch paper</u> to start with.

1. To read <u>Dig U. S. A.</u>

2. To recognize differing viewpoints.

3. To learn about Alcohol

4. To see how an Alcoholic lives.

5. To Understand how he feels being this way.

6. To see how his family feels about him

7. To Know if he respects himself

8. To know if he is losing any Friends

9. To know the type of friends he is making or already has

10. To learn how many different types of Alcoholics there are

11. To learn how the different alcoholics live

12. To know how many other problems they have after they become alcoholics besides their drinking

13. To learn how they became alcoholics

14. To Know what they're planning on doing about their problem if anything.

15. To find out what they like about drinking or what they did like about it

16. To know if they started drinking on their own or if someone encouraged them to in the beginning

17. To talk to people on the A.A. Plan and ask them different questions about alcoholism to get their opinions

18. to learn how an alcoholic affects his family

19.

20.

Figure B3-1 List of possible purposes.

CONTEMPORARY LIFE STUDY UNIT   NAME Pat Hammer

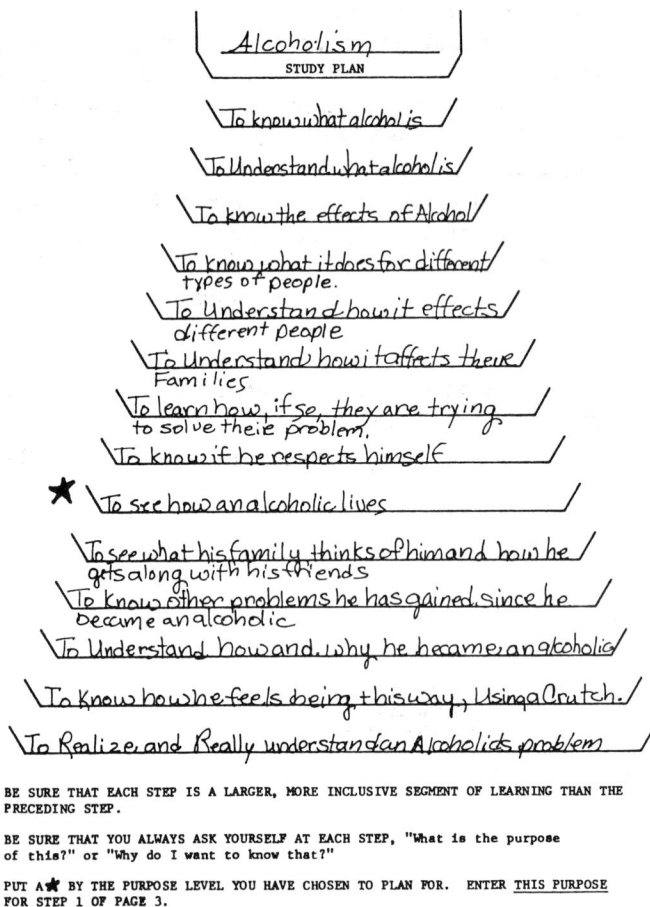

> _Alcoholism_
> STUDY PLAN
>
> To know what alcohol is
>
> To Understand what alcohol is
>
> To know the effects of Alcohol
>
> To know what it does for different types of people.
>
> To Understand how it effects different people
>
> To Understand how it affects their Families
>
> To learn how, if so, they are trying to solve their problem.
>
> To know if he respects himself
>
> ★ To see how an alcoholic lives
>
> To see what his family thinks of him and how he gets along with his friends
>
> To know other problems he has gained, since he became an alcoholic
>
> To Understand how and why he became an alcoholic
>
> To know how he feels being this way, Using a Crutch.
>
> To Realize and Really understand an Alcoholics problem

BE SURE THAT EACH STEP IS A LARGER, MORE INCLUSIVE SEGMENT OF LEARNING THAN THE
PRECEDING STEP.

BE SURE THAT YOU ALWAYS ASK YOURSELF AT EACH STEP, "What is the purpose
of this?" or "Why do I want to know that?"

PUT A ★ BY THE PURPOSE LEVEL YOU HAVE CHOSEN TO PLAN FOR. ENTER THIS PURPOSE
FOR STEP 1 OF PAGE 3.

Figure B3-2 Purpose hierarchy for Pat Hammer's study plan.

purpose-oriented planning strategy to the unit of study as a means of identifying his/her interests that will provide the needed motivation for learning.

3 The teacher reviews the resulting detailed study plan with the student or group to make sure that it fits within the framework provided by the topic and any requirements established by the teacher.

4 The student carries out his or her learning plans, including the reporting agreed upon in the plan, with teachers and others acting as resource persons, information sources, and advisors.

In one case, a seventh grade language arts teacher assigned the book _Dig U.S.A._[1] in a unit on Contemporary Life Study. "Step One" on Figure B3-1 summarizes what she wanted to accomplish, and items 1 and 2 were typed in to specify her requirements: to read the book and to recognize differing viewpoints.

Pat Hammer, one of the teacher's 288 students, used a set of worksheets the teacher had prepared to guide the students through the phases of SPARK. Figure B3-1 lists his possible purposes for studying his selected topic—alcoholism. Figure B3-2 shows Pat's hierarchy and selected purpose, which includes accomplishing the teacher's purpose.

Then the student is stimulated to use individual creative abilities to develop ideas on _how_ to achieve the purpose. The teacher acts as a resource by pointing out many alternative learning routes that may not have been considered. Student motivation is increased because the selected purpose is "owned" personally. As the teacher put it, "I did not have to react to grouchy students asking, 'Why do we have to read this?' They were too busy finding their own purposes and ideas."

After the student groups the many ideas into three to six relatively cohesive major possible plans of action, one is selected as most feasible, yet innovative, for "regularity" conditions. This feasible target plan of Pat's is shown in Figure B3-3 in a solution framework prepared by the teacher.

Responsibility for individual action in following the plan is fostered through the submission each week of "control dimension" reports (see Figure B3-3) by each student. Figure B3-4 illustrates one of Pat's reports.

Results of Using SPARK

The self-designed plans of students produced quite unusual results. For example, of 288 student plans one year, over 50% involved skits, oral reports with visual aids, debates, student-arranged and -chaired panel discussions with community representatives, complete audiovisual presentations, newspaper articles, and summaries of interviews students conducted in the community. Even the written report of each of the other students had a different focus and orientation.

There tended to be more family involvement when the SPARK process was used. For example, an older brother helped his sister with lettering on her charts, an aunt made clay figurines of Elizabeth I and Henry VIII to go with her niece's projects, parents took their daughter to the J. Paul Getty Museum so that she could get photographs for her report, and so on.

Students repeating this planning process on subsequent projects became quite proficient at planning and even more motivated to do so. Three boys who on the first project gave a one-hour presentation using charts, slides, and tapes were asked to present it again in another class. In a later project, their response to the question of how could they follow their first act

CONTEMPORARY THEMES STUDY UNIT — TOPIC Alcoholism

	RATE	CONTROL
1. Purpose: To see how an Alcoholic lives		Self control
2. Input - Me.		
3. Output: 1. A Report on Alcoholism - Oral	1 Report	
2. Me - with Knowledge		
4. Sequence (List steps to be followed in your plan to achieve purpose. List in order and in <u>detail</u>.	1st Week	Check-Friday - of 1st week For Completion)
1st week Read a book about alcohol-The effects of it Will get Book Monday -4/30/73 I will take one week to gather Material-Written Material from books, encyclopedias, Magazines, etc. Any type of Article Will finish during the Weekend.	1 book, 1 Encyclopedia 8 ila go look through 2 or 3 Magazines Any type of Article about it.	I changed from Reading a book to seeing Filmstrips
2nd Week Talk to different people about how alcohol effects them. Whether they are just a social drinker, a heavy drinking, or if they drink once in a while - Will be entitled - Personal Effects and Feelings towards alcohol	2nd Week Talk to 10 different people who drink heavy or light. including teenagers	Check Friday 2nd of x For Completion Wasn't Completed until 5th Week
3rd Week Take all of the Material I have collected and organize it into different Categories. proof read. Organize for oral Report.	3rd Week	Check Friday of 3rd For Completion Week
4th Week Copy all Material over. If happen to find Something to add to my work I will.	4th Week	Finish and Check For 4th Week
5th Week I will catch up on anything that I need to. I decided to do an oral Report, So I also got a book called Alcohol and Youth	5th Week Using a book alcohol and youth - And preparing for My oral Report on Wednesday	Check - and will be Finished Friday of 5th Week
5. Environment (What are the physical and psychological surroundings where you carry out plan?) In My Room, In the school Library, At School in class, at home.		
6. Physical Catalysts (What are tools, objects, materials used in plan. They do not change.) A Pen, Pencil, Paper, People, Book An Encyclopedia, A magazine, Film strips with tapes.		
7. Human Agents (Who will help you carry out your plan? teachers? aides? others? Teachers, My Mom, Other Students and Friends		
8. Information Catalysts (What must you find out in order to make plan work? a telephone number? speaker's name? an address? whether certain materials needed are available? etc.) I have to Find out about Alcoholism. I need to get material for my Report.		
	For RATE tell how many, how much, when items in column 1 will be worked on, learned, finished, etc.	For CONTROL tell how you are judging progress and success of what you are doing and what changes you make to make plan work as you want

Figure B3-3   Pat Hammer's solution matrix.

CONTEMPORARY LIFE STUDY UNIT
CONTROL DIMENSION REPORT

Circle: Week 1 2 3 4

NAME Pat Hammer

Date of report May 4

What did you say you would get done this week?

read 1 book, 1 encyclopedia, look through 2 or 3 magazines for information about alcoholics

What did you do this week?

In the encyclopedia at home, I read about the effects of alcohol and other information. I also looked in our Popular Science Book and found nothing much that helped me. I changed from reading the book to seeing filmstrips because I can not really understand the book.

What changes do you need to make to keep on target to finish work as planned?
none

Figure B3-4 Control dimension report.

was "the first presentation was nothing—wait until you see this one."

CASE HISTORY B4

Improvement of Electric Fan Blade Packaging

Plastic electric fan blades were injection-molded at Plant A and sent to Plant B for assembly. The blades were packaged to protect against damage during transportation and handling. There were no special problems concerning either quality or cost of the packaging, but this betterment study project was initiated to find a simpler and cheaper method for protecting the blades.

Determination of the System Function— Function Expansion

f1 To package electric fan blades.
f2 To protect the quality of electric fan blades.
f3 To protect the quality of electric fan blades from the environment during material handling and transportation.
f4 To protect the quality of electric fan blades from their physical distribution environment.
f5 To deliver electric fan blades to the assembly point.
f6 To deliver suitable amounts of electric fan blades to the assembly point.
f7 To supply the necessary amount of electric fan blades to the assembly point.

Fujio Umibe, 1975, Chief Specialist, Research and Development Center, Toshiba Corporation, Kawasaki, Japan.

f8 To assemble the necessary amount of electric fans.
f9 To manufacture electric fans that meet the requirement of the sales department.

Determination of the Function Level and Its Detailed Definition

Function level f4 was selected on the basis of management desires. A transportation subcontractor had a long-term contract that had to be honored. This project was to develop a solution suitable only for a period of time shorter than the contract term because a new factory would open then, where function f4 would not be necessary and f7 and f8 would be. The terms used in f4 were defined as follows:

- The quality of electric fan blades: the quality of electric fan blades passing inspection on the basis of the inspection specification.
- Physical distribution environment: the environment, consisting of shocks, vibrations, temperature, humidity, and their variations, the blades are in from Plant A until they reach the assembly point.

Identification of Regularities

Size of Blades There were six sizes (15, 20, 25, 30, 35, 40 cm) for the outer diameter, but the 30-cm size had the largest production volume and was used as the regularity for design.

Distribution Process Regularity was identified according to the situations in which the blades were being transported (Table B4-1).

Over 20 ideas were developed, and these were

Table B4-1 Identification of Regularities— Fan Blade Packaging

Classification	Regularity	Exception
In-plant materials handling	Forklift truck	Cart, conveyor, hand truck
Plant-to-plant transportation	Large truck	Small truck, railway, aircraft
Storage	In-plant warehouse	Leased warehouse, manufacturing shop
Handling	Manpower and conveyor, forklift truck	Drop or throw from truck

Table B4-2   Evaluation of Ideal Systems—Fan Blade Packaging

Evaluated Item	Direct-ness*	Number of Steps†	Simplic-ity	Cost	Techno-logical Ease	Automa-tion	Ease of Further Develop-ment
Pierced-blade container	2	1	1	1	1	2	1
Drawer-type container	2	2	3	2	2	3	2
Unit packaging and banding	1	3	2	3	3	1	3

* Directness: the degree of achieving the purpose directly.
† Number of steps: the fewer the steps the better.

grouped into five major alternatives, in two classifications:

1 Contemplative ideal systems (needing further research and development).

   a   Liquid container plan.
   b   Shock-absorbent material mixing plan.

2 Feasible ideal system ideas.

   a   Pierced-blade container plan.
   b   Drawer-type container plan.
   c   Unit packaging and banding plan.

The three feasible ideal systems were evaluated using the seven criteria shown in Table B4-2. The number 1 was used to indicate the most preferred and the number 3 was used to indicate the last preferred. The pierced blade-container plan was then selected.

Detail of the Plan

1 The flowchart of the process and the method of piercing the blades are shown in Figure B4-1.
2 The size of the container was determined so as to fit ordinary trucks efficiently.
3 The layout for the automatic pierced blade container system is shown in Figure B4-2.

The Recommended System and Implementation

The ideal system could not be installed as designed because there was a strong desire to minimize new investments. Furthermore, it was difficult to completely

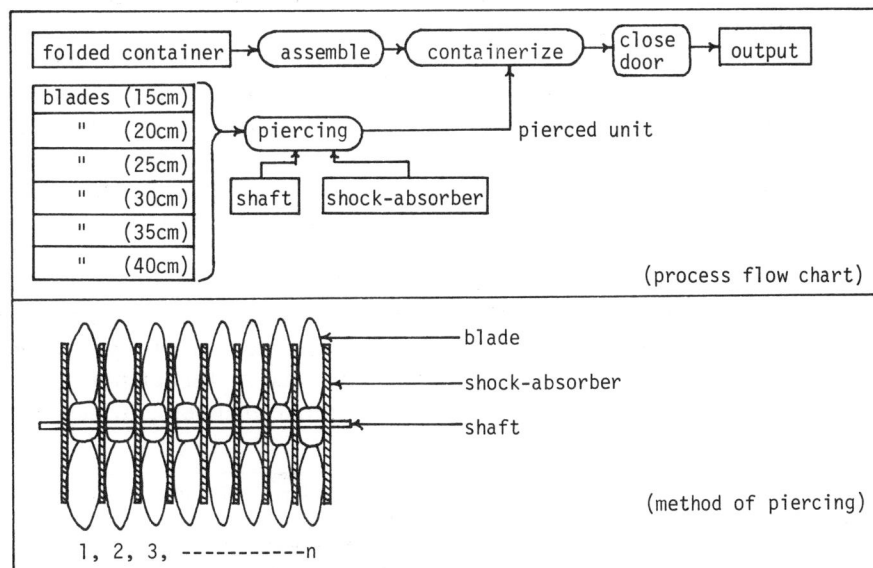

Figure B4-1   Some details of the plan—fan blade packaging.

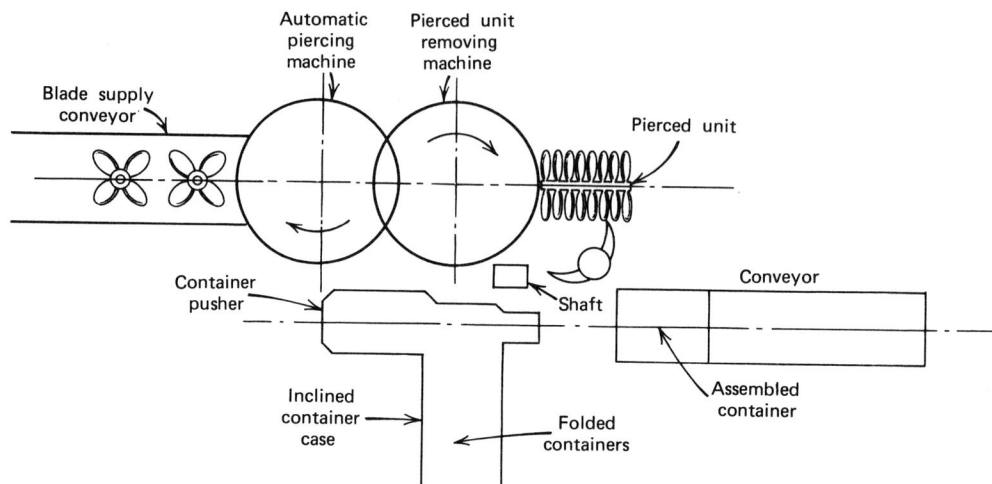

Figure B4-2 Layout of automatic pierced blade container system.

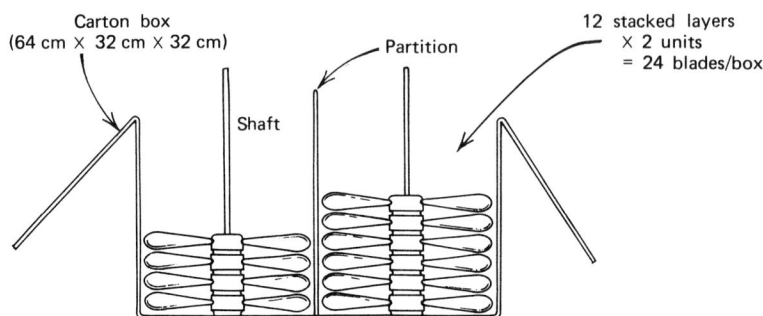

Figure B4-3 Actual system for fan blade packaging.

eliminate the operator fixing the pierced unit into the container. The implemented system shown in Figure B4-3 uses the available carton box and plastic spacers instead of shock absorbers in between the blades. The units were manually placed into the shipping box. Waste plastic obtained from subcontractors was used for the shafts and spacers.

The former method put individual blades into the carton box, partitioning each layer and each box containing fourteen blades. As a result of adopting the pierced container plan, costs were reduced by approximately 50%.

Several years later, the injection molding of the blades was implemented at the electric fan assembly plant, eliminating the need to ship the electric fan blades.

CASE HISTORY B5

Nursing Practice Decisions in Emergencies: A Course and How It Was Designed

At the University of Wisconsin-Madison School of Nursing, faculty and support services have been evaluating a newly implemented curriculum. This case will present a description of a planning process that was used to design a course to meet a subset of two needs identified through the evaluation efforts: increase student skills in setting priorities for the care they provide in clinical settings, and provide efficient learning opportunities for emergency and crisis care early in the students' programs. We believe the direction provided by this planning approach would benefit other course planners. In addition, the course design

Joy D. Calkin, R.N., Ph.D., and Mary W. Gulbrandsen, R.N., M.S.
(Adapted from *Journal of Nursing Education*, Vol. 17, No. 9, November 1978, pp. 30–37.)

may be of interest to those providing learning opportunities related to emergency and crisis care.

How the Course Was Designed

In the first phase of our preestablished four-month planning activity, the faculty recommended a required course (solution) to meet identified curriculum needs (purpose) within our curriculum constraints. The work group included three faculty members, each of whom represented one of the three divisions comprising the undergraduate curriculum faculty: one had worked with the curriculum implementation and evaluation; one had expertise in operating room nursing; and one had skills in group work facilitation and an interest in planning strategies. The IDEALS Concept was used as a basic planning framework for the course design.

The function of the subsystem course was to provide learning opportunities that would fill gaps in the curriculum. Then we raised questions about the kind of course we might design if we were not constrained by money, time, and so on. For example, ideally we would want students to deal with a patient in a clinical situation with a skilled teacher of crisis care available to the student. Questions were raised about what level of student with what requisite knowledge and skills (inputs) might best take the course. We considered the appropriate learning sequence for the students, and the human, equipment and informational resources we would like to have. We *gathered information* from participants about *proposed ideas* and noted *alternate solutions*. For example, it would be ideal to have small classes (proposed idea), but small-group work was required for only certain areas or situations.

The processes used by the group varied to facilitate search behavior and avoid early closure. When the interaction process led to expansion on ideas, checking information, and similar behavior, no change was made. When members began to search for new ideas the group switched to a modified form of the Nominal Group Technique or to "brainstorming." Problems were jotted down on a blackboard to depersonalize them as much as possible.

During a one-month period, the faculty member who was assigned the primary responsibility for course development moved back and forth within the steps of the planning strategy as she met with individuals with expertise in different areas such as emergency care and education, crisis intervention, instructional strategies, devloping audiovisual media, and dealing with a variety of emergencies. This provided us with a wide range of potential solutions, means of using a variety of human resources for planning, names of potential

resource people to teach the course, and a variety of literature sources.

A crucial human resource was nurses identified as particularly skilled in medical and traumatic emergency care. They discussed a process described as "preplanning," "prepackaging," "fantasizing," and "anticipating" for emergencies that *might* occur.

This information contributed a course approach that included the training of students to use a known planning strategy and to apply that strategy, with multiple iterations, to selected crisis and emergency situations.

The facilitator became skilled in working with the several kinds of experts, developing various conceptualizations of the course, and in providing and collating needed resource information. She assumed responsibility for administrative liaison to the resource controllers (e.g., budget) and to the faculty committee who would later review the course. The facilitator is a critical human resource to the planning process, requiring both the capacity for process facilitation and conceptual skills.

As multiple iterations of the planning steps were carried out, many of the committee's original notions were refined or replaced. The information on alternative approaches was evaluated in terms of how they might help students achieve the goals of the course. Time, money, and curricular limitations ruled out some approaches.

Finally, the *formulation of a system* to accomplish the functions for which the course was designed was completed and sent for review to the faculty screening committee. They identified components that would need careful evaluation: Will students be able to transfer the learning from critical incidents that describe emergencies to actual clinical practice? Would resource people continue to be available to provide a course requiring a variety of faculty expertise? How would the course be phased in? How would the course fit within the larger curriculum design?

The Result of Planning: The Course

The three-credit course, "Nursing Practice Decisions in Selected Emergencies," was implemented on a trial basis for one semester. A separate laboratory course of one credit may be taken with or following the main course to provide training in basic emergency care skills and cardiopulmonary resuscitation. Students intervene in simulated emergency care situations and can evaluate and explore their own psychomotor, cognitive and affective responses to such situations. These experiences are complementary to the three-credit course, but are not a mandatory part of the course objectives.

The first unit of the course focuses on the IDEALS planning process as used by the faculty members to develop this course, presented by means of a slide-tape format. Students are free to learn this material at their own pace.

In addition, the ability to preplan or fantasize the actions you might take when confronted by an emergency is presented as a *crucial* nursing skill to be learned. One process underlying this skill is that of planning and making decisions. To increase the student's appreciation of using planning for emergencies, role models are provided in the form of nurse clinicians who describe how they use planning strategies for emergencies.

Unit two concerns planning nursing interventions in usual or frequent crises. Through lectures, assigned readings, demonstration of crisis intervention, role playing, and evaluation of alternate interventions, the students are provided with opportunities to preplan interventions based on incidents described by clinicians. Students can determine their own responses to simulated crises as a basis for anticipating their responses and those of patients and others involved in real emergencies. They review what responses are effective or ineffective, what their strengths and limitations are, and a range of interventions that might be appropriate in the light of crisis theory.

The third unit, consisting of over 15, one-and-a-half-hour class periods, focuses on selected medical and traumatic emergencies (e.g., obstructed airway). This practices and expands the skills learned in the first two units. For each selected topic the students determine the disorganizing potential of the emergency to physical, psychological, and social systems, the differences in the nurse's responses as a function of the setting in which the emergency occurs, the physical and psychosocial manifestations of the patients and others in response to the emergency, the initial interventions appropriate to these manifestations and the actions to be taken subsequent to the immediate emergency intervention (for example, referral of patient to a suitable agency).

The conclusion of the course provides an opportunity for students to think about transferring their preplanning skill to future courses and practices in nursing: They consider some common health threats and anticipate potential crises; note examples of emergencies that require advanced therapeutic skills; and promote the continued use of the preplanning strategy.

Students' progress is evaluated primarily through their demonstrated ability to select appropriate inter-vention for simulated situations (e.g., written critical incidents, role playing, videotaped incidents).

This is how we dealt with the several curriculum gaps that were found through curriculum evaluation. The planning approach used provided both structure and richness for course design. The efficiency and effectiveness of faculty members were enhanced through the use of the IDEALS planning approach.

CASE HISTORY B6

Traffic Accident Information System

Background

The desirability of improved accident data has been recognized in Saskatchewan for approximately 10 years. The major problem with the old system was the inability to determine the real cause of the accident. We wanted to develop countermeasures to try to decrease accidents but were unable to determine where to place our emphasis. Locations were usually not precise.

The old accident reporting form contained a policeman's narrative describing the accident. To determine what really happened someone would have to read these narratives and then try to determine the precise location and cause. It was easy to get information from the form about the driver (such as age, sex), to determine which driver was most accident-prone, but the form was of no value in determining how the accident could have been prevented.

System Design Approach

In the spring of 1977, Saskatchewan Highways and Transportation was given the funds and mandate to develop and implement a traffic accident information system to meet the needs of the province. A User/Steering Committee was established to manage the project. This committee had representatives from Saskatchewan Highways and Transportation, the Highway Traffic Board, the Transportation Agency, Saskatchewan Government Insurance, the Police, Municipal Affairs, and the City Engineering Department.

The User/Steering Committee began meeting twice monthly in the fall of 1977 to develop a complete system. Throughout their deliberations the IDEAL SYSTEMS approach was used. The overall system goal was "to reduce significantly social and economic losses due to traffic accidents, by correcting traffic

A. I. Massier, 1978, Management Services Branch, Saskatchewan Highways and Transportation, Regina, Canada.

accident problems.'' The selected design level function was "a means to identify problems to determine inadequacies of driver, vehicle, and environment.'' Measures of effectiveness were defined as value of information obtained, ease of operation, cost, timeliness of the information, and accuracy of data.

Each accident data user agency identified *what* information they required to manage their responsibility; *why* or what is the purpose for this information; and *how* the information they needed can be obtained. The regularities were determined to be that two vehicles are involved in the majority of accidents, and that the police visit the accident scene. Three alternate solutions emerged from the Committee's deliberations. The target solution is a completely "on-line" system where each police force puts in its own data and each user retrieves his own information from a remote terminal. This was the only solution that would allow us to achieve the target in the future.

After the desired outputs were determined, work began on an input form that would become the accident report form for field use. The objective was to make the new form comprehensive, simple to complete and the data to be amenable to rapid coding processing.

System Trial

A one-page accident report form was developed with an overlay template for coding significant information about the accident. Training seminars were held during July 1978 in six areas of the province and the form was field-tested. A number of improvements and corrections to the form were made as a result.

The report form was designed with the enforcement personnel in mind. The layout of the form is broken into logical sections for location, driver and vehicle, and description. Narratives and diagrams are eliminated. A check-off system is used to describe the accident and related information. The one-page form reduces paperwork and takes less time to complete than the present form. The data processing system is close to what the target solution called for, and can be expanded as needed.

Another component of the traffic accident information system is a bimonthly newsletter. The purpose of the newsletter is to keep all agencies concerned with traffic safety informed of the efforts, progress, and results of the provincially funded Traffic Accident Information System.

A number of accident prevention measures have been undertaken on the basis of information generated since the sytem was implemented: two uncontrolled rural intersections have now been controlled by stop signs; two highway intersections with major roads

have been placed on the program for interchanges because of the number and types of accidents occurring there; some slippery sections of highway have been identified for surface treatment; and a number of urban locations have been identified as unsafe.

CASE HISTORY B7

The Wisconsin "Saus-egg" Recipe Contest

Situation

The Wisconsin Department of Agriculture, Trade and Consumer Protection, and the Sausage and Egg industries sponsored a contest on 30 April 1980 to develop new recipes for sausages and eggs. The recipe categories were cold salads and sandwiches; the recipes were to use a minimum of one egg and one ounce of Wisconsin sausage per serving for four to six servings. The judging criteria were originality, nutritional value, taste, and appearance.

Mrs. H. learned about this contest only a week before the entry deadline. She decided to use PDA for entering the contest in the category of cold salads. I served as the facilitator.

Figure B7-1 shows the purpose hierarchy for the recipe finding system. She selected a bigger purpose (number 5) instead of just developing the sausage and egg recipe. Then she developed the values and measures of effectiveness as shown in Table B7-1.

Next she used several creativity techniques to generate ideas for ideal recipes to achieve the selected purpose. Twenty major ideas resulted. She organized these 20 major ideas with the Person-Card Technique (Appendix A) into three major alternatives.

She selected the "Egg Roll Salad" (Table B7-2) as her ideal recipe target. She submitted this recipe and she was selected as one of the finalists. She had only three days to prepare for the final contest on May 10 at Southridge, Milwaukee, Wisconsin. She detailed her recipe to achieve the purpose and meet the values and measures within those three days.

This recipe won first place in the salad competition and was awarded the grand prize in the whole contest.

Summary

PDA provided some important benefits:

1   In spite of the very short time available, Mrs. H.

S. Hibino, 1980, Professor, Chukyo University, Nagoya, Japan, and Honorary Fellow in 1979–80, Department of Industrial Engineering, University of Wisconsin-Madison.

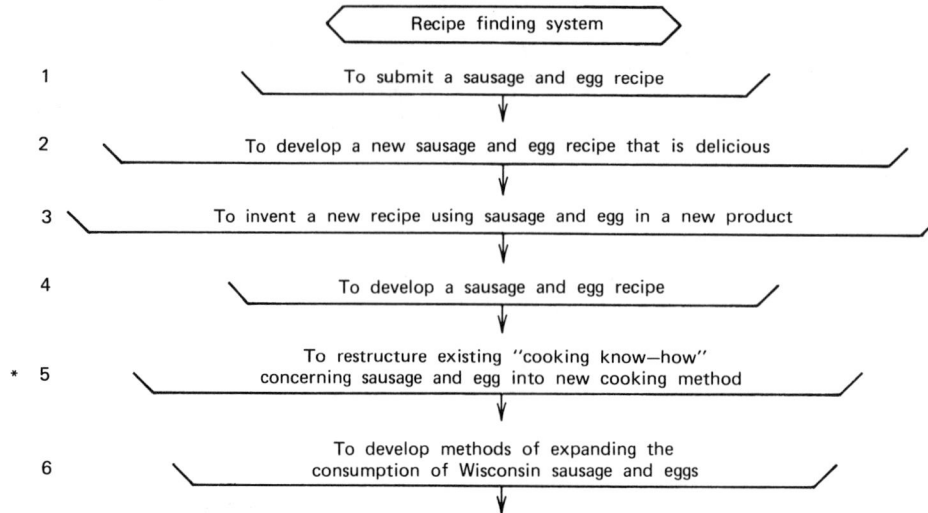

Figure B7-1   Purpose hierarchy for recipe-finding system.

Table B7-1   Values and Measures of Effectiveness for Salad Recipes

1   Eat delicious and appetizing fresh vegtables
2   Eggs and sausage should enhance the fresh vegetables
3   Get nutrition from vegetables
4   Satisfy the desire to eat fresh foods
5   Keep nutritional balance
6   Help maintain a healthy diet
7   Originality—number of innovative features
8   Taste: 90% of people will find the dish delicious
9   Nutritional value: number of calories
10 Appearance: beautiful, looks delicious, arrangement, shape, cutting, color arrangement, freshness
11 Easy to prepare: easy to get ingredients, short time to prepare, technically easy to cook

Table B7-2   Recipe for Egg Roll Salad

8 slices thinly sliced Wisconsin sausage, cut into strips	1 medium carrot, cut into strips
½ head lettuce, torn into bite-sized pieces	8 Wisconsin eggs
	½ tsp. salt
2 medium tomatoes, cut into strips	3 different kinds of thick-style dressing
2 cups sliced mushrooms	
1 green pepper, cut into strips	

Beat eggs slightly, add salt, and mix well. Heat greased 8-inch skillet over medium heat. Pour 3 tablespoons egg mixture into skillet and immediately rotate pan. Cook until golden, turn and cook on other side. Make 8 thin sheets and cool. Cut into ¼ fan shape. Roll salad ingredients with thin egg sheets. Arrange them on the platter with dressing. Serves 4.

could develop *several* creative recipes and prepare for the final recipe.

2   The use of the purpose hierarchy enabled her to free herself from past limitations and to restructure her existing cooking know-how into a new cooking method.

3   The PDA process enabled her to concentrate her resources (her ability, time, and materials) on one purpose.

CASE HISTORY B8

Practical Manufacturing Applications of Purpose Design

The industrial engineering department of Container Corporation of America consists of 10 industrial engineers, who are strategically located throughout the country to serve the 88 domestic plants and 57 international plants as internal consultants. To maximize the effectiveness of this small staff, all the industrial engineers have had training in using the purpose-design approach (PDA). We have found it yields the maximum results with the minimum amount of engineering time, since massive and sometimes useless studying of existing operations is usually not required. It also gets us to the heart of the system quickly, thereby avoiding time-consuming blind alleys.

The purpose or function of *any* system is the emphasis in its design, investigation, or improvement. For example, at a bag plant we wanted to cover an entire press cylinder with a plate to give overall printing.

C. E. Geisel, 1978, Corporate Manager of Industrial Engineering, Container Corporation of America, Chicago, Illinois.

The press cylinder consisted of one half that was solid and one half that contained a reel slot for securing the tail of normal canvas and rubber printing plates. We made several attempts at filling the slot with various materials so the printing plate could be glued over it, but they all failed. However, when we determined that the required function was to provide a smooth solid circular surface under the plate, the answer became apparent: Use two solid halves to make the cylinder and glue the plate on (see Figure B8-1).

The wording of our function statement serves as a guide to our design. We do not use restrictive words. We expand whatever restrictions someone suggests. For example, form a can end rather than stamp it, store information rather than file it, and communicate dimensions and form rather than make a drawing.

We helped get a maintenance group to start thinking about preventive maintenance when the group realized its function was not to repair equipment, but to keep it running. This led to the development of an extensive equipment reliability program for all divisions.

We defuse a lot of arguments about time standards when we point out that the function of standards is not to measure productivity, but to point out areas for improvement. A thermometer cannot warm up a room; you need a furnace. Changes in standards will not increase productivity; you need new systems.

In that famous pasture of sacred cows, the accounting department, many have been slaughtered in the process of determining the function. A study of CCA's accounts receivable department revealed excessive handling of checks and record keeping. Once we had convinced everybody that the function of the department was to "apply payments to proper ac counts," the people in the department stopped trying to justify all the alphabetizing, check handling, and excess recording in the present system.

When CCA wanted to reduce its crew's exposure to noise in some of its paper mills and corrugated and can plants, a massive study was proposed to quiet the machinery or put soundproof "dog houses" around them. This would have cost several millions of dollars. When we asked what was the function of quieting the machinery, the answer was to "provide a quiet workplace." When asked why a quiet workplace, the answer was "to assure workers that their exposure to noise is under OSHA limits." Starting with this function, we started redesigning the job methods and machine control locations to enable the worker to perform essential functions outside noisy areas, which were identified by noise contour charts.

The design and operation of systems to accomplish certain purposes and functions can lead you down some bizarre paths. While designing a composite (paper) can to hold tobacco presently being packed in a tin can, the first level function of the can was "to hold the tobacco under vacuum." A composite can could not hold the vacuum. When we expanded the function, we asked what was the function of holding the tobacco under vacuum. After some investigation, we found that the function of the vacuum was to provide a hiss when the customer opens the can to denote freshness. The vacuum wasn't necessary for freshness.

At CCA all the industrial engineers have had extensive training in using the purpose-design approach. We have also taught the concepts at all levels throughout the organization. A recent example of avoiding doing efficiently that which ought not be done at all occurred when the industrial engineering department was asked to analyze the die cutting operation for a corrugated box designed to hold and dispense large plastic storage bags. Because of the complexity of the die cutting required in the box design (see Figure B8-2), the waste was running at 25% and the downtime around 30%.

Instead of doing studies on the die cutting operation, we made a function expansion where we continued asking the question, "What is the function?" until we arrived at the function: "Provide the customer

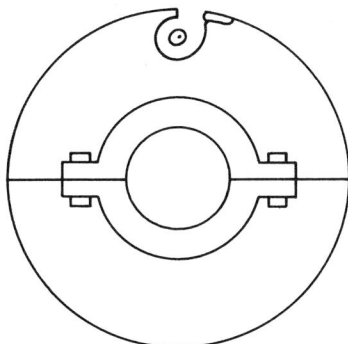

Figure B8-1 Press cylinder.

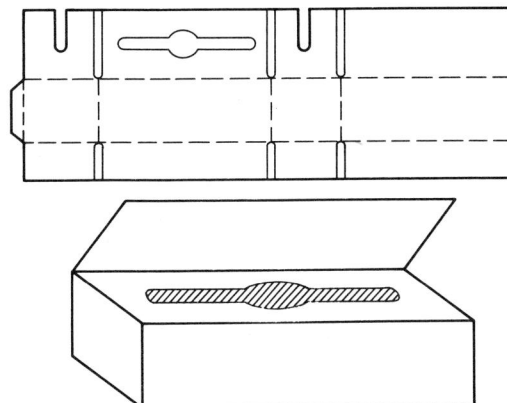

Figure B8-2 Original box design.

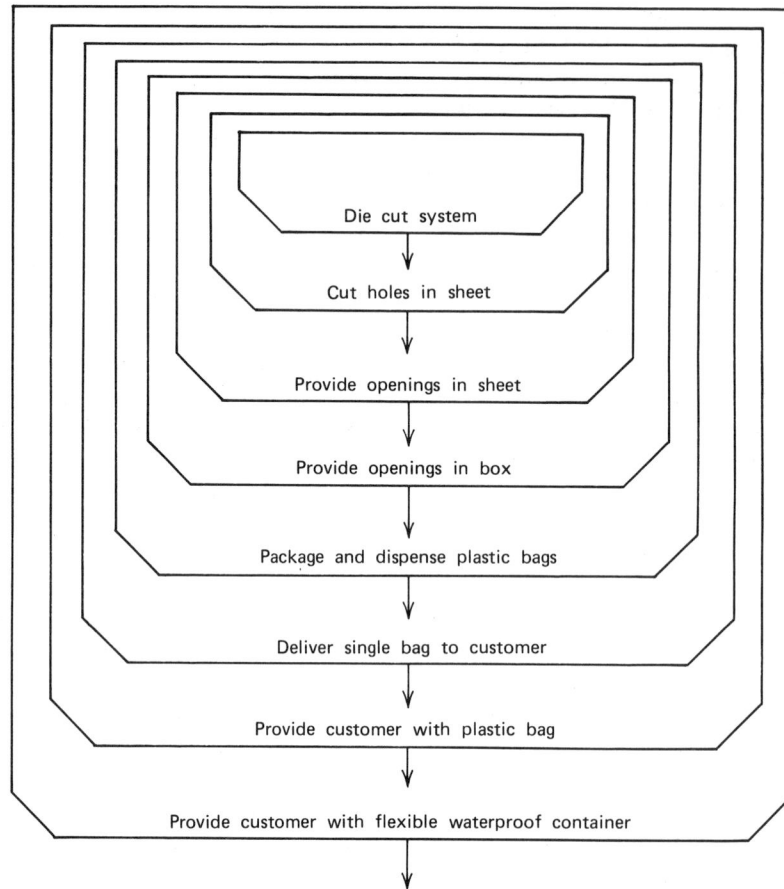

Figure B8-3 Function expansion for box die-cut system.

Table B8-1 System Design Matrix for Package and Dispense Bags

	Constraints	Regularity
Input	Must use corrugated	
Output	Must not damage bag	Storage bags
	Must be easy to open	
	Must dispense only one bag at a time	
	Bag must be easy to grab	
	Package must be attractive	
Sequence	Packaged before reaching store	
Environment	Store	Hardware store and supermarket
Equipment	None	
Human factor	Package must be under 25 pounds and easy to handle	

with a flexible waterproof container'' (see Figure B8-3). Then backing up we decided to design a system for the function level "package and dispense plastic bags."

After developing several ideal systems, we constructed a system matrix in which we identified the necessary constraints and the regularity (i.e., what would normally be expected of the system) for six of the system elements. (See Table B8-1)

The resulting design consisted of a box that did not require any die cutting and still met the customer's specifications. Therefore, the troublesome die cutting operation was eliminated entirely (see Figure B8-4).

In a bag plant, we recorded paper delivered to the bag machine on little delivery tags that were sent to accounting to reduce inventory. The tags were getting lost and were difficult to read. We were asked to design new forms. Instead, we did a function expansion (see Figure B8-5) and decided to design a system to "communicate paper usage to inventory control." We listed the measures and regularity of the system and began to consider all possible ideal systems, contemplative and technologically workable. When we began to think in terms of communication instead of

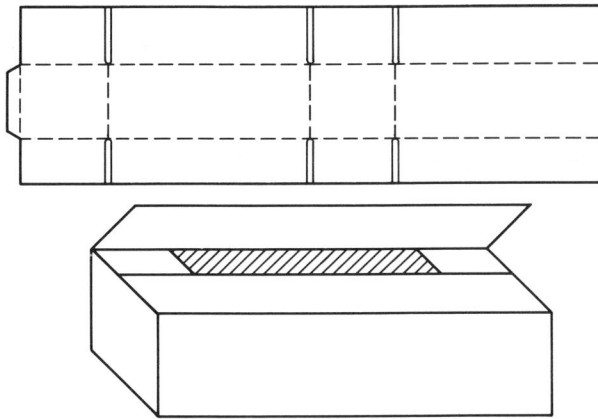

Figure B8-4 Improved box design for package and dispense bags.

forms, the system designed was to place microphones at the machines where the operators could record verbally on tape the paper used. This tape would then be transcribed directly to the inventory cards. The need for the forms was eliminated entirely.

When asked to study the order processing from first sales inquiry to final shipment along with inventory, supply, and other supporting systems for 16 plants, we did not begin a massive analytical study. Instead, we used PDA. The approach was outlined to management, who readily accepted it and selected a test plant. The function expansion was made (Figure B8-6), and the function "provide production people necessary information, materials, and tooling to pro-

duce cartons required" was selected for design. Since it was a large system, it was broken down into functional components (Table B8-2). During the development, we did keep our focus on the functions to be performed and were not permitted to use present titles such as scheduler, planner, and estimator since such references may prejudice the design of the system.

Necessary information transmission was determined before a form was considered. Present forms were used only when they exactly met information requirements. Supervisors, planners, salespeople, and everyone else connected with the function were interviewed to determine exactly what information, materials, and supplies they must have to process and produce an order.

The resulting system required fewer people in the order processing function, reduced the number of forms from as high as 95 in some plants to 37, eliminated confusion, minimized "running down" information,

Table B8-2 Functional Components for "Provide Production People Necessary Information"

1 Interact with customer and plant to establish specifications to produce order
2 Estimate cost to produce according to specifications
3 Determine events required to produce order
4 Procure materials and tooling to produce order
5 Determine time and sequence of events to produce order

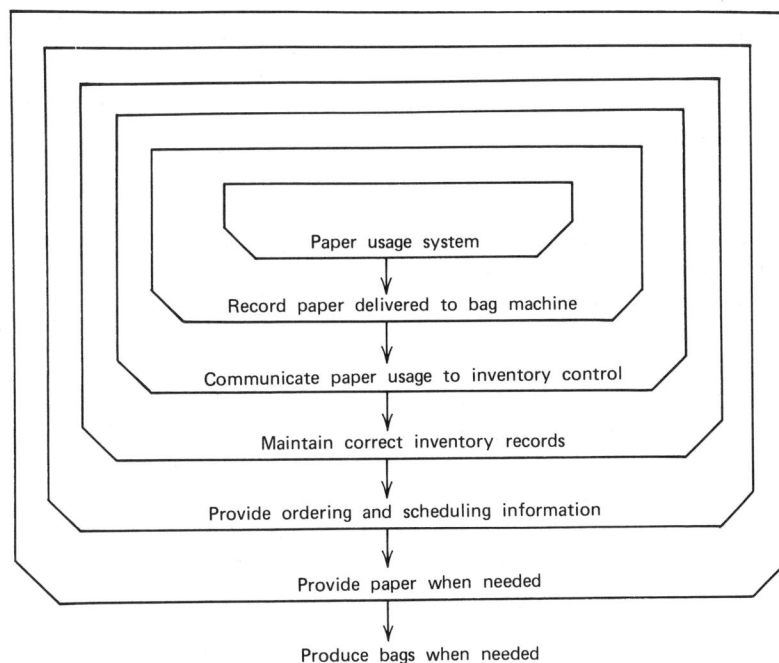

Figure B8-5 Function expansion for paper usage system.

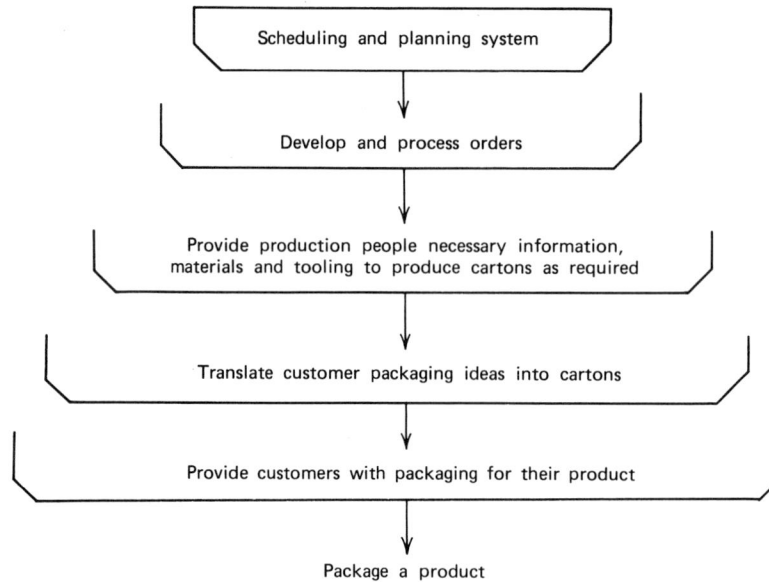

Figure B8-6 Function expansion of scheduling and planning system.

reduced the floor supervisor's workload by 10 to 30%, and reduced inventory levels and errors.

PDA is used on all types of problems and assignments, from the design and improvement of small systems (e.g., workplace layout) to the development and implementation of very large and complex systems (e.g., operation and management of a large corporation) in production and service areas. We have found better solutions to problems and better designs for new systems by beginning each effort with the purpose/function questions.

CASE HISTORY B9

PDA in Architecture: The Design of a Small Space

Situation

When I learned about PDA, my initial reaction was to reject the idea of its claim to universal applicability in any P&D situation, especially in architectural design. Experienced persons who have tried to transplant methods into architectural design from other fields, especially from operations research and management science, are aware that most transplants have failed miserably.[1]

On learning more, it occurred to me that the approach *could* be applied to architectural problems. It is a people-oriented process and has a great deal in com-

mon with what good architects do naturally and intuitively.

I decided to redesign my Technion office to accommodate the new approach. Many more details than might be used are included here because I used this project to help learn how to apply PDA. The effort ended in a workable solution which I implemented. The resulting space has been successfully used for many PDA team sessions.

Project Description

A list of purposes for my office was developed, as shown in Table B9-1. The smallest purpose was care-

Table B9-1 Purposes for Office—Random List of Purpose Statements

To enable work with a small group

To create space near the blackboard

To shelter private workspace from outside disturbances

To store semiprocessed administrative paperwork

To have access to such material

To prevent such material from cluttering my desk

To enable production of graphic material

To have horizontal work surface

To keep work space uncluttered

To have work space naturally lit from the left

To enable me to rest horizontally or to sleep

To enable the projection of slides and transparencies*

To have vertical surfaces for display of graphic material

To store and to display plans and models

---

* The smallest purpose.

Daniel Gat, 1977, Technion-Israel Institute of Technology, Faculty of Architecture and Town Planning, Haifa.

fully expanded into a purpose hierarchy (Table B9-2). Functional components were identified in the subsystems in a system pyramid format shown in Table B9-3. On inspecting my system pyramid I decided, on the basis of prior experience, that the most demanding function is group work, especially the nominal group process. Therefore my strategy began with designing the physical setting for conducting nominal group work sessions. The complete "system for enabling me to work" is not being redesigned, just its architecture. This restricts the discussion to architectural criteria or measures of effectiveness. There appear to be three distinct though interacting ways in which architecture will influence an individual.[2] These are illustrated and made specific in my own design project, as shown in Table B9-4.

Keeping in mind the focus purpose, I proceeded to brainstorm a list of possible ways to achieve the purpose (see Table B9-5). Because internal communication is of critical concern, the dominating design consideration is interpersonal physical orientation. This

Table B9-2 Purpose Hierarchy for My Office

To enable projection of slides and transparencies

To transfer visual information to an intimate audience

To share information with a group

To enable communication within a group

To enable a group to communicate and carry out other functions

To create conditions for a group to function

To enable me to conduct a group working session

To enable me to work (in several modes)*

To produce work products

To obtain products that serve purposes

* Purpose level selected.

Table B9-3 Functional Components

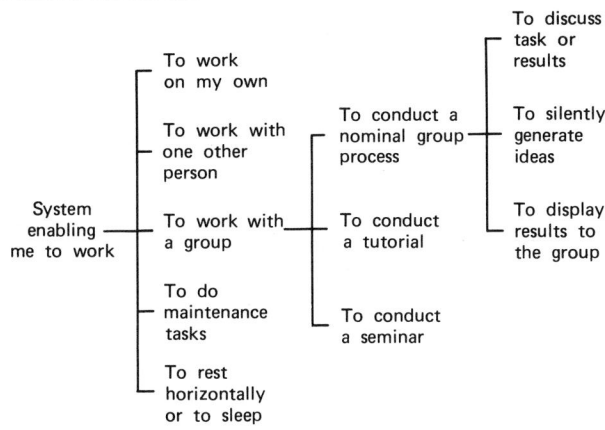

Table B9-4 Values Criteria and Measures of Effectiveness

TERRITORIAL ZONING AND COMMUNICATION CONTROL A nominal group process takes place in one zone requiring these communication controls:

1 The zone should be isolated; audio and some visual privacy is necessary for group work. Work may be interrupted occasionally, but not constantly.
2 Each person should have two-way visual and audio communication with other group members.
3 Each group member should have visual (and sometimes physical) access to graphic display surfaces.

COMFORT AND FUNCTIONAL PHYSICAL CONDITIONS

1 The zone should be climatically suitable for sedentary work
2 The zone should keep out noise and support group conversations.
3 There should be sufficient lighting for seeing faces, noticing facial expressions, writing and reading. Blackboard glare should be minimized.
4 All participants should have comfortable seating.
5 Individuals should be provided with adequate writing equipment (e.g., easel pads, marking pens) for the display of group work.
6 There should be several options for the display of group work with preference given to simultaneous and continuous display (e.g., easel pad sheets, slides, drawings).

MESSAGE ENCODING Some requirements simply reflect my own tastes. Others are instrumental to the system's purpose.

1 Should make it clear that the major function of the space is to support group work.
2 Should be inviting to a wide range of audiences.
3 Should be casual rather than formal.
4 Should provide an outside view.
5 Should be attractive.
6 Should display some of my work products.

requires that seating arrangements constitute the major portion of the solution: round table, conference table, army T-style, sit on floor—mattress or carpet, lounge style, or floor pit.

These solution ideas were evaluated through an application of the design criteria. On the first iteration "sitting on carpeted floor" and "floor pit" were eliminated. Table B9-6 displays the evaluation of the remaining four based on relevant criteria.

Table B9-6 clearly shows the preferability of "lounge" and "round table." The "conference table" and "army T" are dropped and the FIST (feasible

Table B9-5   List of Possible Solution Ideas

1   Round table
2   Conference table
3   Army-style T-table arrangement
4   Floorspace is one big mattress to sit on
5   Sit on wall-to-wall carpet
6   Sit around a central space, lounge style
7   Sit inside a floor pit
8   Sit on a couch
9   Sit on a swivel chair
10 Sit on chairs with built-in writing board
11 Distribute unattached writing tablets
12 Use blackboard for graphic display
13 Use flip chart and easel
14 Place flip chart on blackboard shelf
15 Use overhead projector
16 Use slide projector
17 Cover the walls with softboards for continuous display
18 Hang display sheets from the blackboard shelf
19 Use all modes of display one at a time
20 Use all modes of display simultaneously
21 Use natural cross ventilation to cool place during summer
22 Use forced ventilation
23 Install air conditioning unit
24 Use standard electric wall panel for heating during winter
25 Install an electrically heated carpet
26 Add thermal insulation to reduce thermal control energy intake
27 Use wicker basket to store large paper sheets rolled up
28 Store plans and sheets inside standard drawer cabinet
29 Use top of such cabinet for placing paperwork trays
30 Install dart board and coffee equipment for use during workbreak

ideal system target) was developed with the remaining two seating arrangements.

The system for regularities was specified by prescribing each of its elements and dimensions in a modified system matrix (with architecture as a ninth element, and only conceptual, quantitative, interface, and control dimensions). An architect who constructs a "brief" or "program statement" is engaged in describing the other eight elements of the system. That is why the system matrix is an effective framework for architectural programming. I found it helpful even to treat each of the nominal group modes as a small system, as shown in Table B9-7.

Having stated all of the pertinent system prescription data, I began the architectural design phase for the FIST regularities. For conversation, a round inward-facing lounge layout was suggested. For silent idea generation, the participants would be seated *facing away from each other* to facilitate maximum concentration. This layout requires individual writing surfaces. Since silent idea generation follows the conversation mode, the use of swivel chairs is suggested. This solution is too expensive for my situation and will have to be saved for some future opportunity. Other possibilities for idea generation with the participants facing each other include an inward facing lounge or a round table.

Figures B9-1 and 2 show spatial arrangements suited for displaying information to a small audience using various visual aids. Figure B9-3 shows the FIST spatial arrangement for the entire nominal group process, combining and relating the modes. The passage from one mode to any other, within this spatial layout, is immediate. There is a minimal need to shuffle furniture, equipment, or people.

Workable Solution

I like the location of my existing room and the view from it, and besides, all other rooms are assigned. For these reasons, the workable solution must use the existing room.

The major system that now has to be incorporated is "my personal work system." Table B9-8 describes it in terms of system elements. Several spatial arrangements were sketched out for the existing room that leave sufficient space for the regularity activity. Figure B9-4 is a floor plan of the workable solution. Leaving out some of the details, it clearly shows the spatial arrangements for nominal group activities (perfect also for seminar and tutorial), my personal work, "one-on-one" conversations, resting horizontally, and storage.

In addition, several preset conditions are met: An air conditoning unit provides desired summer coolness while allowing closure of doors and window for maximum isolation, sound insulation, and speech privacy; filing cabinet and my own attaché case are at fingertips while open files are reachable but not obtrusive; storage space for large sheets of paper is provided by drawer cabinet behind the door, while the top holds sets of open files; and graphic display is versatile and simultaneous (blackboard; flip chart; finished sheets on continuous display; overhead projector).

Figure B9-5 shows the spatial layout of my room prior to this exercise. Comparing it with the workable solution, the difference in quality between the two layouts may be assessed.

Table B9-6 Evaluation of Four Major Alternatives

		Round Table	Conference Table	Army T-style	Lounge Style
A	Communication				
A.2	Personal proximity and orientation to each other and to group leader	Excellent	Fair Difficult to see person at your side; leader is advantaged	Fair Same as with conference table	Excellent
A.3	Orientation and access to graphic display surface	Good Visual access for all; physical access obstructed by table	Good Same as in round table	Fair Leader's table blocks visual and especially physical access	Excellent All can see well; all may walk to display surface
B	Physical conditions				
B.2	Speech privacy	Excellent Proximity allows low conversational intensity	Fair Length of table may cause people to raise their voices	Fair As in conference table	Excellent As in round table
B.3	Comfort	Excellent	Fair Orientation toward leader may cause muscular strain	Fair As in conference table	Excellent
B.5	Writing conditions	Excellent	Excellent	Excellent	Varies: Bad if no writing surface is provided Good to excellent, depending on type of writing surface
C	Message encoding				
C.3	Casualness, informality	Good On the casual side of formal	Fair Formal	Bad Very formal, emphasizing leader's location	Excellent

Table B9-7 Mode-Specific System Descriptions for Nominal Group Technique

	Conversational Mode	Silent Generation Mode	Graphic Display Mode
Purpose	To allow task identification, evaluation of results, and modification or retrackng of the process	To individually generate purposes, criteria, solution, ideas and other P&D items in the presence of other group members	To collect and display items generated by each member
Input	The idea in a group member's mind	The idea in a group member's mind	The idea on the individual's card
Output	The idea received by the minds of the rest of the group	The idea on a card	The idea on flip chart paper
Process	Leader states task, then each person may clarify by speaking in turn	Person writes down the ideas without talking to other group members	Leader turns to each participant in round robin fashion, asks for one item, and then writes it on the flip chart paper
Environment	Oriented for conversation and discussion, and privacy	Complete silence; individual writing conditions	Capable of continuous or temporary display of graphics
Equipment	Seats oriented inward	Individual writing surface table or personal tablets, etc.	Blackboard, flip chart, overhead projector, etc.

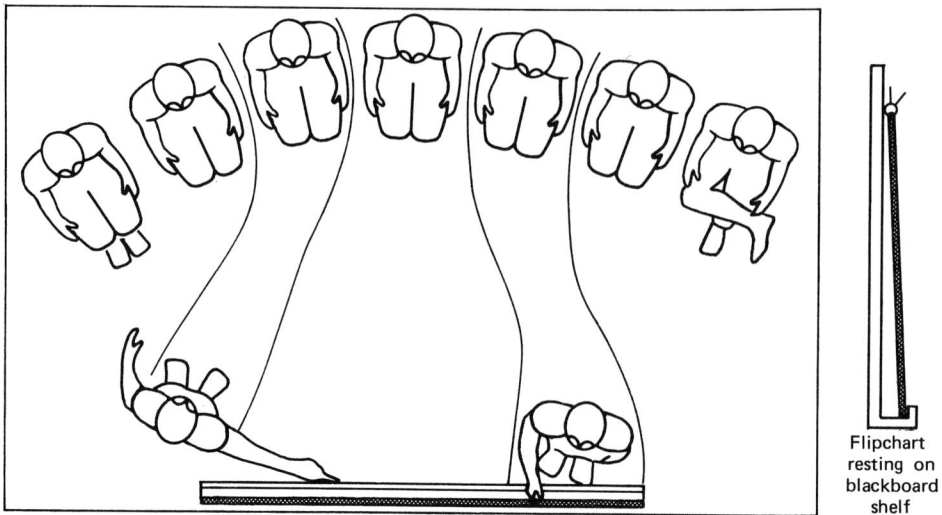

Figure B9-1 An "ideal" configuration for displaying information.

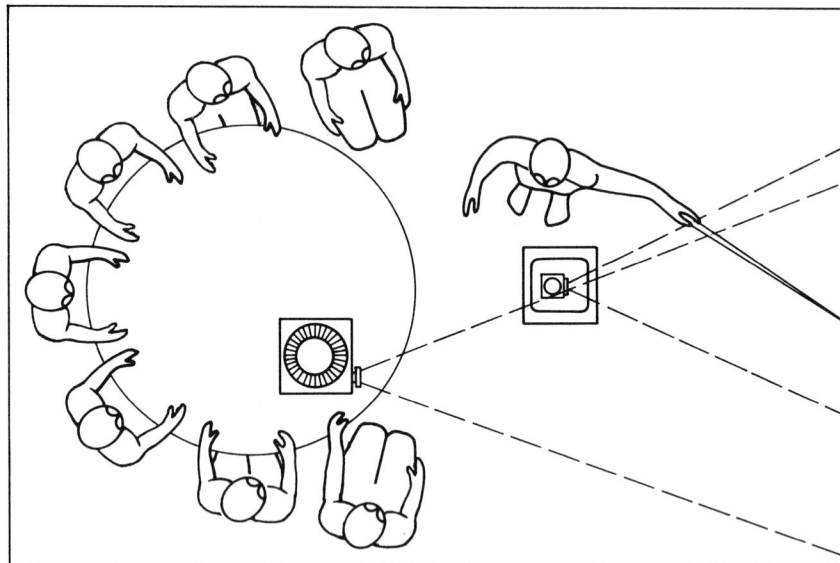

Figure B9-2 An "ideal" configuration for using visual aids.

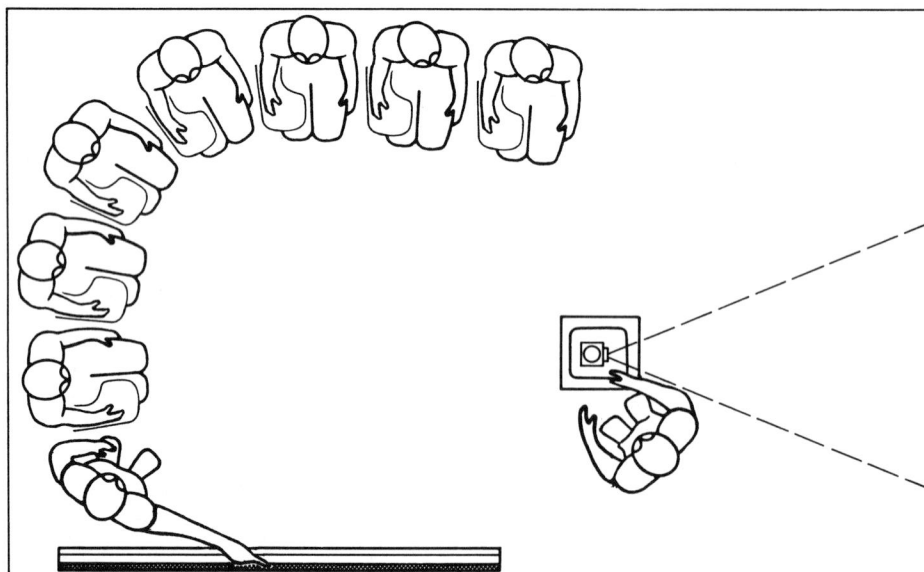

Figure B9-3 The FIST (feasible ideal system target) for regularity conditions.

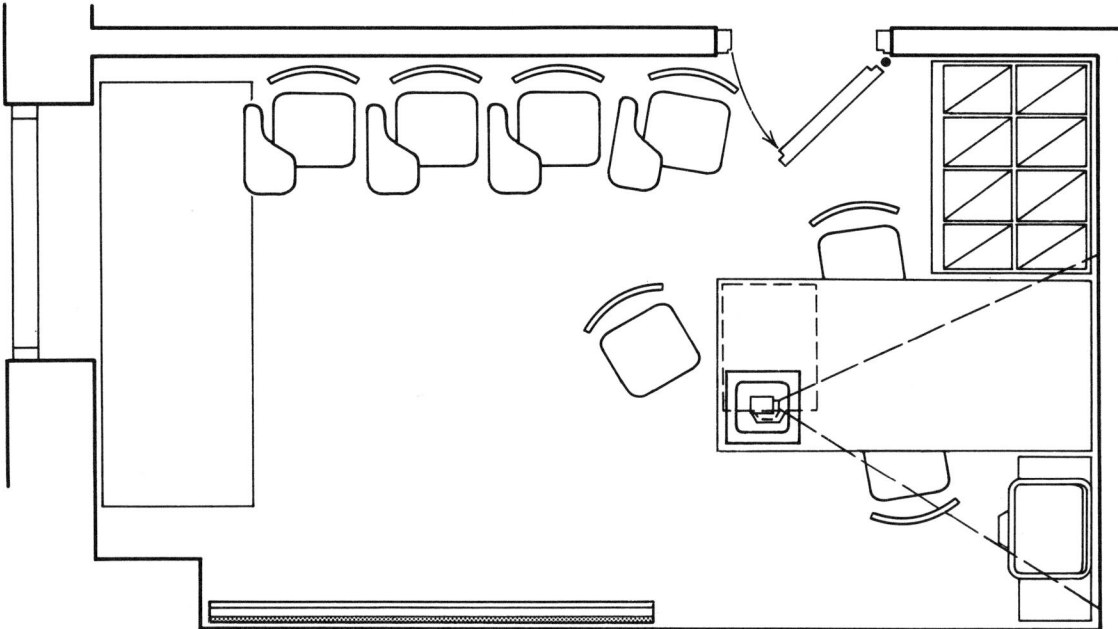

Figure B9-4 The workable solution as installed.

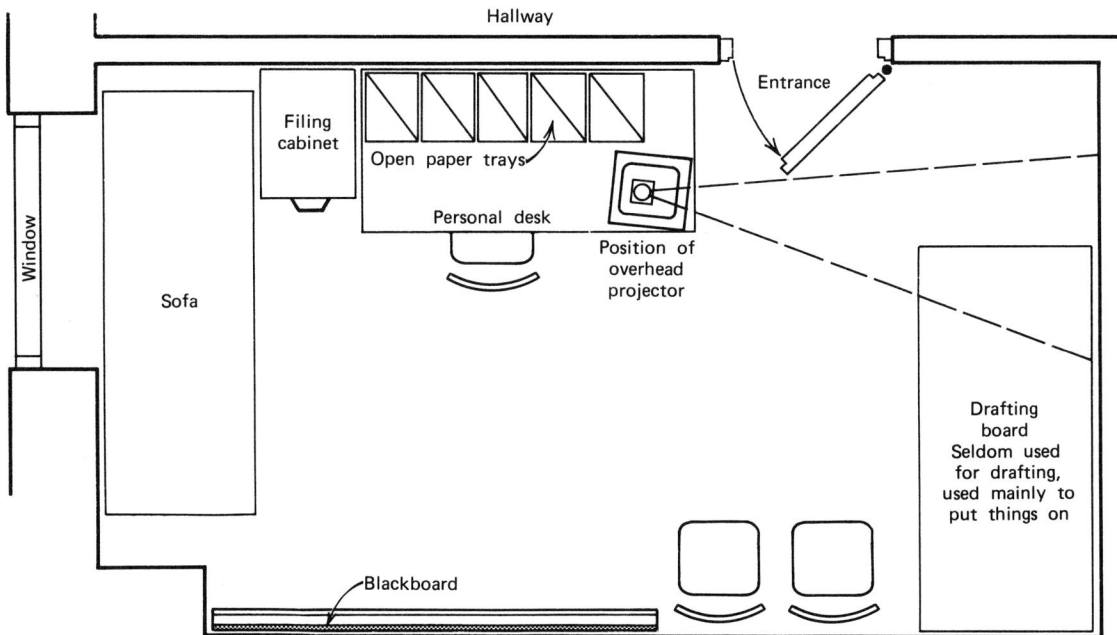

Figure B9-5 The original layout of the office.

Table B9-8 System Description for my Personal Work

Purpose	To enable me to work alone
Outputs	Instructional material
	Papers, essays, articles
	Letters and memos
	Waste material (mostly paper)
Inputs	Paper and writing materials
	Information from books, articles, etc.
	My time and effort
	Coffee
Process	Thinking
	Sketching
	Writing
	Reviewing and comparing
	Reading
	Reaching for material from open and closed files and from attaché case.
Desired	Large horizontal surface for writing, sketching and for spreading materials instruments and "things"
	Natural lighting and view from left hand side
	Area should be relatively sheltered visually when door is in open position
	Open files accessible, but must not clutter work surface
	Locked files and attaché case immediately accessible
	Acoustic, climatic, and privacy conditions as in nominal group
Human agents	Me
Information aids	Desk diary
	Memo cards and board for tacking them up
	Books, journals, copied material
Physical catalysts	See sketches to follow

CASE HISTORY B10

Planning a Six-Day School Workshop

Determine the Possible Purposes for the Workshop

The planning group brainstormed a list of *possible* purposes for the workshop.

Determine the Most Specific Purpose from the List of Possible Purposes

This discussion helped the group move toward concensus on what should be done at the workshop by

Staff members from the Individually Guided Education/Secondary (IGE/S) Project (Wisconsin Research and Development Center for Cognitive Learning) and teachers from Winnequah Middle School, 1976, Monona, Wisconsin.

clarifying and resolving different ideas on the focus and direction of the workshop.

Construct Hierarchy of Purposes for the Winnequah Workshop

Constructing the hierarchy in itself achieved three ends: it helped the group to organize their purpose ideas for the workshop in relation to the bigger level purposes of the school, the community, society, and the student; it gave the group a way of getting together on a focus toward which all members could direct their thinking; and it gave the group agreed-on criteria (in terms of bigger purposes) for making decisions about what to include and what not to include in the workshop. The resultant hierarchy is shown in Figure B10-1.

Select the Focus Purpose for the Workshop

The planning group considered first the biggest purpose (to improve life on earth) and then worked its way toward smaller and more specific purposes until a purpose level was reached that seemed feasible for the workshop (marked with an asterisk in Figure B10-1).

Determine Possible Ways to Achieve the Focus Purpose

As part of brainstorming to get ideas to achieve the selected purpose, the group reviewed the list of possible purposes for the Winnequah Workshop to incorporate ideas suggested there. Thirty-three possible ways to achieve the focus purpose were developed.

Categorize the Possible Ways to Achieve the Focus Purpose

The group decided that the ideas could be divided into four major types of activities for the workshop schedule and one category that had to do with generally operating the workshop. The categories in order of emphasis priority are staff development activities, presentation of new ideas and concepts, planning procedures and techniques, and post-workshop planning. Criteria for selecting a plan that incorporated many "how" ideas were identified as follows:

1   Include parents and students if possible.
2   Vary types of activities to maintain interest.
3   Avoid using jargon.
4   Obtain closure at the end of each session.
5   Demonstrate a variety of group planning and learning procedures.
6   Evaluate workshop progress on an ongoing basis.
7   Modify workshop as necessary to achieve selected purpose.

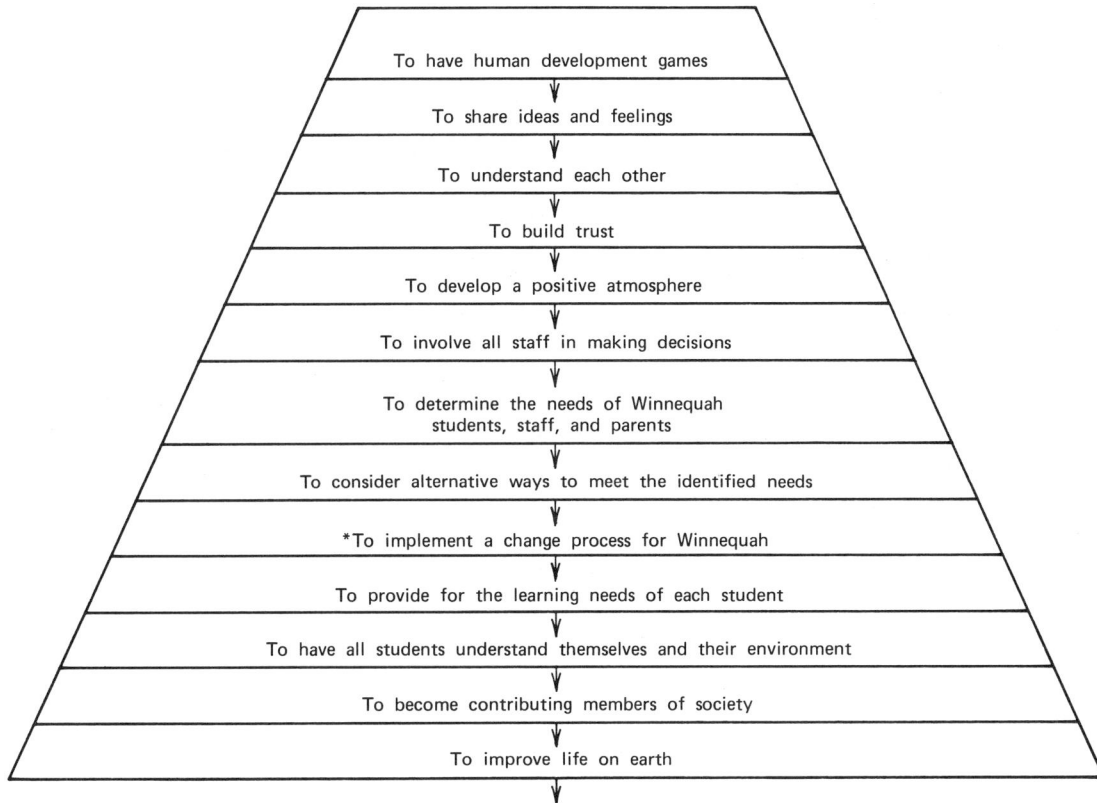

Figure B10-1 Winnequah workshop purpose hierarchy.

Detail Each of the Major Activity Categories and Develop a Rough Target Schedule

The group split into four subgroups (one R&D Center person and one Winnequah person), each of which worked up a plan based on ideas from the list of possible "hows." Each detailed plan consisted of specific recommendations about how a particular category should be handled at the workshop, including type and number of sessions, specifically what should be done at the sessions, how the workshop participants should be organized, and so on.

The planning group then met as a whole, each subgroup presented its ideas, and the group as a whole discussed the various alternatives and organized the ideas into a rough target schedule for the workshop, shown in Figure B10-2. Modifications, deletions, and additions were then made, shown also in Figure B10-2, to arrive at the final target workshop schedule.

Target Workshop Plan

The overall target workshop plan was concurrently developed.

1 Four types of sessions will take place: staff development, conceptual development, planning, and business.
2 Workshop activities will follow the target schedule.
3 The staff and planners will meet at the end of each day to evaluate progress and make any necessary schedule changes.
4 A staff evaluator will evaluate and document workshop activities.

Finalize the Details of the Workshop Schedule

The specific details for each session were devloped, including the materials needed and the exact timing involved. In addition, a staff member was assigned to lead each session, procedures were specified for ongoing evaluation of workshop progress and for modification of the plan if necessary, and general workshop operating tasks (e.g., coffee) were assigned.

Implement the Workshop Plan

The workshop actually began as planned on Wednesday, August 13, at approximately 8:00 A.M. This is the step that makes all the others worthwhile.

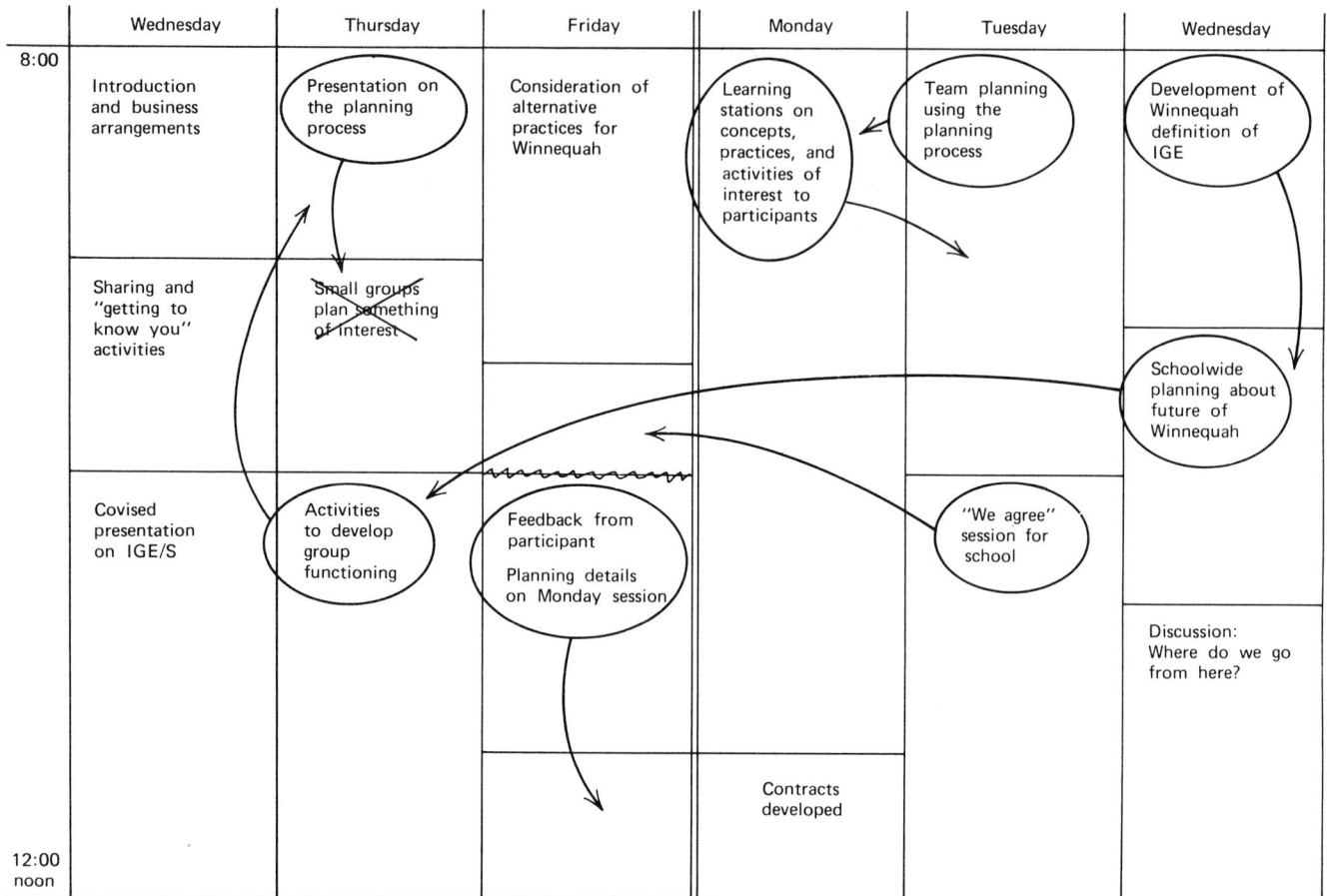

Figure B10-2 Rough workshop schedule.

CASE HISTORY B11

Improving Productivity with Performance Measures and a Group Incentive Plan: a Case Study

Situation

When wage incentive plans are proposed, the industrial engineer usually thinks of highly developed individual incentive systems that require elaborate time standards and record-keeping procedures for each job and person covered by the incentive plan. But these individual plans may be too expensive and time-consuming for many companies, especially small businesses, to develop and maintain. A group incentive plan can be a successful and profitable alternative for improving labor, clerical, and mangerial productivity.

This case concerns a factory manufacturing heavy wire-rope and electromechanical cable. The 30-year-old individual incentive plan in the rope mill was

thought to be inadequate because of many recent technological changes and frequently occurring problems in calculating incentive pay. Consequently, management initially wanted a documentation of the present job methods in the rope mill, individual time standards for each job, and a better way to determine the wages of each employee. The revised system had to be operational within six weeks, when the factory management would purchase the plant from the parent company. This paper examines the methodology used by a consulting team to develop, *instead* of document present job methods, an inexpensive incentive system within the short time allowed.

Design Approach

To put the Work Design (IDEALS Concept) Approach into practice, the consulting team spent several days interviewing individuals from all levels of management and the direct-labor work force to gather as many suggestions as possible concerning the incentive system's objectives, desired functions, and functional performance requirements. A work design committee of labor and management representatives was then es-

J. Byron Nelson (University of Missouri-Rolla), *Proceedings of the American Institute of Industrial Engineers*, 1977 Spring Annual Conference.

tablished to review all of these suggestions, with the consulting team acting as a catalyst to the committee's deliberations. The accomplishments and characteristics of an ideal incentive system were finally decided upon and used later as a target for the consulting group. Care was taken to separate imaginary and insignificant constraints from the real and significant limitations that the industrial environment would impose on the incentive system design. Using the target ideal system as a guide, the consultants then developed a recommended system that was compatible with the minimum set of real restrictions.

A number of goals for the incentive system were adopted. In addition to the usual objectives of having a fair and equitable plan, adequate employee wages, increased productivity, and good product quality, the following major goals guided the project. The plan should cover all direct-labor jobs in the departments, should be simple and inexpensive to administer, must be easy to understand so employees and supervisor can easily calculate daily incentive earnings and encourage necessary corrective action during any two-week pay period, should encourage separate and joint cooperation of labor and management in seeking better work methods and procedures, and should encourage employees to assist each other during such situations as machine downtime, temporary bottlenecks, and so forth.

To get a plan that meets such goals operational within a few weeks supported the idea of a single group incentive plan instead of individual job standards covering approximately 25 direct-labor employees on each of three work shifts. Several features were designed into the group incentive plan to promote a joint concern for increased productivity. A suggestion system was established in which everyone could participate. The work-design committee became permanent to study all suggestions and make recommendations.

The production vice-president was responsible for final decision making and implementation of worthy ideas. To provide both employees and management an adequate reward in their respective efforts to improve productivity, the employees would receive 75% of the group bonus and the company 25%.

A productivity score board was designed and placed in several locations in the production area. Each day's performance, as well as the cumulative performance, was posted daily so that employees and supervisors could readily see how they were progressing through the two-week pay period. The performance of several previous pay periods was also posted for comparison purposes. After reviewing nine possible performance measures, pounds per man-hour was selected as the basis for the group incentive (it had a small coefficient of variation, and was easily calculable from company records).

Results and Conclusions

During the initial six months with the new group incentive system, the average direct-labor productivity increased 9% over that of the old individual incentive plan. More significant than this increase, however, is the present cooperation among fellow workers and between employees and supervision, as well as the *substantial cost reductions in administering the incentive program*. Considerable reduction in supervisory, employee, and staff paperwork requirements has resulted. Employee earnings can now be calculated without voluminous data, complex formulas, and procedures. Workers cannot earn incentive bonuses at the expense of other workers, because the success of each employee is directly related to the success of the entire factory. Consequently, employees' goals and those of management are more closely aligned. For the future, this joint partnership and sharing of performance responsibility should provide the opportunity for greater productivity, lower overall costs, and sound labor-management relations.

Instead of analyzing the shortcomings of the existing incentive plan and attempting to modify it (Conventional Improvement Approach), the inexpensive group-incentive plan was developed using the Work Design or IDEALS Concept Approach. Without the Work Design philosophy, many of the features of the installed incentive plan probably would not have been developed and implemented. Attempts at modifying the previous incentive system would have required too much management and engineering time and effort, and would have resulted in an inferior system as well.

CASE HISTORY B12

Bone Cement Stressing Rig

Orthopaedic surgeons have been using an acrylic cement for supporting metallic replacement of defective hip joints in the human body for the last 18 years (Figure B12-1). Thousands of these replacements have been made throughout the world and they have been declared a huge success,[1, 2] particularly in the case of the aged in the restoration of normal walking ability. However, some surgeons have become alarmed to find

J. B. Mantle, 1976, Professor of Engineering, University of Regina, Saskatchewan, Canada. This work was performed while the author was Visiting Professor of Mechanical Engineering, University of Queensland, Brisbane, Australia.

that marked deterioration of the bone-cement interface, a so-called "late infection," has shown up in an increasing number of patients who have carried implants without problems for several years. It is suspected that continued application of body forces at the interface is leading to a breakdown of the cement.

The author was encouraged by Dr. R. Cooke, orthopaedic surgeon of the University of Queensland surgery department, and Dr. E. J. Evans, Visiting Lecturer in Mechanical Engineering, University of Queensland, to try to simulate this breakdown under laboratory conditions. The cooperation of the University's chemistry department (Dr. J. O'Donnell), in tackling the problem was obtained. A program was developed in which samples of the bone cement were prepared and test coupons (2 × ¼ × ⅛ inch) were machined for testing in the chemistry department. Unloaded coupons were stored in various chemical solutions equivalent to body fluids, and at various temperatures (body temperature and somewhat above). The stored coupons were then tested to destruction in an Instron machine (model 1026) after having been stored for varying periods of time. Chemical analyses of the material and the stored fluid were conducted to determine whether any chemical or structural changes were occurring in the bone cement.

One facet of the program was to simulate body

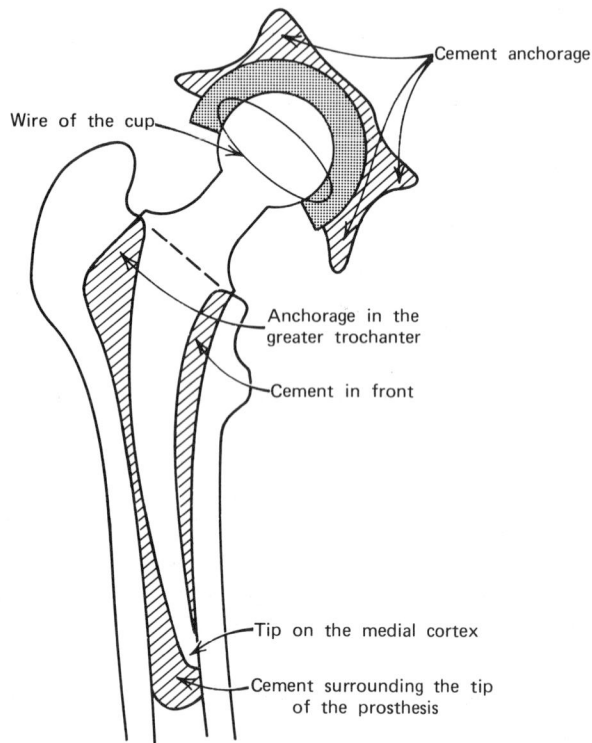

Figure B12-1 Total hip prosthesis.

Table B12-1 Function Expansion

Design a system to . . .

1 Apply compressive stress continually to plastic under simulated body conditions
2 Apply stress continually to plastic under simulated body conditions
3 Simulate body force acting on plastic*
4 Simulate plastic used with implants
5 Find out why some plastic implants fail in use
6 Assist orthopaedic surgeons in their practice
7 Reduce human misery
8 Make this a better world to live in

* Selected system to be designed—Level 3.

Table B12-2 Ideal Systems List Number 1*

FUNCTION LEVEL: "TO SIMULATE BODY FORCES ACTING ON PLASTIC"

C	F	Number	
	✓	1	Dead weights acting on compression test piece
	✓	2	Dead weights acting on test piece in bending
	✓	3	Forces applied to test piece in bending by means of Euler columns
	✓	4	Forces applied to test piece in bending by means of negator springs
	✓	5	Forces applied to test piece in bending by means of ring dynamometer
	✓	6	Repeated loads applied to test piece in bending by means of magnetic field
	✓	7	Repeated loads applied to test piece in bending by means of shaker machine
	✓	8	Repeated loads applied to test piece in bending by means of rotation with dead weights
	✓	9	Loads applied to test piece by means of hydraulic pistons
	✓	10	Loads applied simultaneously to numerous test pieces
✓		11	Embed plastic in body and observe periodically
	✓	12	Loads applied to test piece by means of vacuum
	✓	13	Loads applied to test piece by means of screw
	✓	14	Loads applied to test piece by means of spacer or wedge
	✓	15	Loads applied to test piece by means of centrifugal force
✓		16	Embed plastic in body and apply forces externally

* C = contemplative, F = feasible.

forces acting on coupons of the bone cement while the coupons were under the simulated body environments. In all probability, except for accident, the cement in the body would be subjected to its most severe loading state during normal walking, climbing stairs, and so forth. This loading would be compressive and cyclical in nature. In solving the problem of determining loading limits, we decided to use the IDEALS approach.

Define the Function or Purpose

As a first approximation it was agreed to develop a simplistic system for applying compressive stress to the bone cement coupons while in the simulated body environments. Table B12-1 shows the function expansion.

Develop Ideal Solution

Brainstorming with the author's colleagues resulted in the list of IDEAL solutions shown in Table B12-2 with

"feasible" and "contemplative" solutions indicated. The Feasible Ideal System Target (FIST) selected was "to apply repeated loads by rotation of dead weights" and "loads applied simultaneously to numerous test pieces".

Develop the Practical Solution

It was considered that a stress level of approximately 5000 pounds per square inch should be exerted on the plastic with an accuracy of ±5%. It was not practical, at this stage, to design a repeated load scheme for the material in its environment. A first effort was made to devise a gadget to apply and maintain three-point bending loading on the coupon. There was a strong tendency for the material to creep under load so that application by simple screw loading was ruled out. The methods of load application that seemed most feasible were through the use of "Euler column" or "screw-loaded ring dynamometer." Design specifications

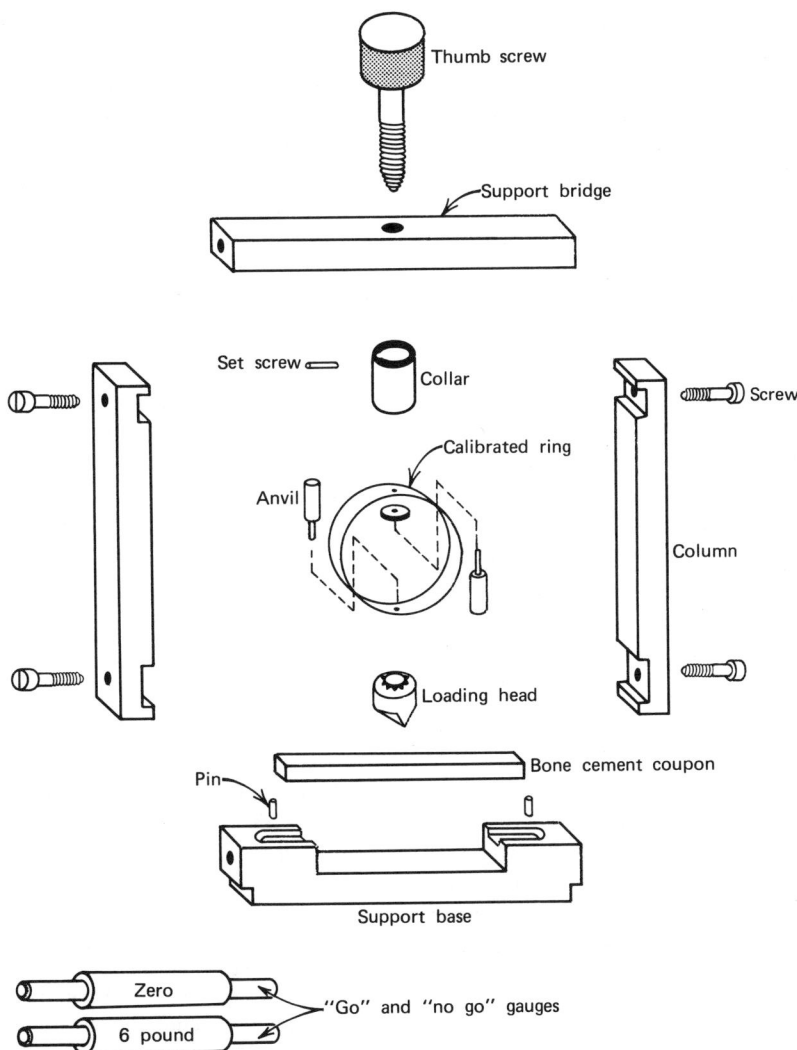

Figure B12-2 Exploded view of stressing rig for bone cement.

Table B12-3 Ideal Systems List Number 2*

FUNCTION LEVEL: "TO MEASURE AND MAINTAIN RING DEFORMATION"

C	F	Number	
	√	1	Electrical resistance strain gauges on ring surface
	√	2	Mechanical strain gauge across diameter of ring
	√	3	Anvils with "go" and "no go" plug gauges
	√	4	Observation with calibrated microscope across diameter
	√	5	Photoelastic disc dynamometer in series with ring
	√	6	Dial gauge in contact with ring diameter

* C = contemplative, F = feasible.

were made for both of these possibilities. The force to be applied was 6 pounds. For the ring dynamometer a simple method was needed to measure and maintain ring deformation. This was brainstormed, resulting in the list shown in Table B12-3. The idea of using two anvils attached to the ring and the use of cylindrical "go" and "no go" gauges to indicate zero and design loads emerged as the most practical.

Do It That Way

A ring of stainless steel (approximately 1 inch in diameter × ¼ inch wide × 0.018 inch wall thickness) was machined and then calibrated to measure suitability. With 6 pounds applied diametrically, the change in diameter was approximately 0.035 inch. The prototype design was then drawn up and submitted to the shop. An exploded pictorial view of the rig is shown in Figure B12-2. Upon fabrication the prototype was submitted to various test runs. It became apparent that an unforeseen advantage of the design was the ease of resetting the ring if it should be accidently overloaded. This could be done simply by squeezing the ring across the horizontal diameter and checking the unloaded distance between anvil faces with the zero "go" and "no go" gauge. The difference between the diameters of "go" and "no go" was approximately 0.003 inch, which meant that the accuracy of force application was within the tolerance allowed. Several of these stressing rigs were then made and put into service. Future improvement will be aimed at the FIST, simultaneous application to several coupons and repeated loadings.

CASE HISTORY B13

Preparing a Proposal for a Haifa Regional Housing Plan

Situation

In 1977 the Center for Urban and Regional Studies at the Technion was approached by the Israel Housing Ministry and asked to submit a detailed proposal for a regional housing plan. Land suitable for housing within the boundaries of the city of Haifa was becoming scarce, and there remained only scattered, very expensive Mount Carmel sites. Therefore, it was suggested that the search for new sites should extend beyond the city limits and into the surrounding countryside.

Structure of the Proposal

The sequence of steps proposed closely resembled the PDA strategy of purpose clarification followed by solution generation that proceeds from the ideal to the workable. The flow chart (Figure B13-1) graphically shows the major steps along the center band, while the supporting activities appear on the flanks.

After determining the general structure, the proposal described each of the activities as a small system, relying on the PDA system matrix elements. Thus each task was described in terms of its purpose, sequence of small steps, work and data inputs, specific outputs, as well as the professional skills and specialties needed for its successful completion.

Purpose Clarification

This phase was begun even as the proposal was being prepared. It involved a "taking apart" of the contents of the letter of intent. Out of that, a random list of purposes was drawn. A small purpose was chosen from that list and expanded into a purpose hierarchy (Table B13-1). A level within that hierarchy was selected to guide the plan.

Ideal Solutions

Based on the PDA notion that "many minds are better than one," the circle of solution concept generators was enlarged. The process engaged in was similar to a nominal group session, though modified and expanded. A list of people was drawn up to include persons who are intimate with the region, known to have

Daniel Gat and Daniel Havkin, 1977, Faculty of Architecture and Town Planning, Technicon, Israel Institute of Technology; Haifa. The study team included Daniel Havkin (Project Director), Daniel Gat (Deputy Director), Shaul Amir, Baruch Kipnis, Anat Gonen, Doron Balasha, Yoram Ben Yaaco, Esther Gilboa, and Sanda Kaufman.

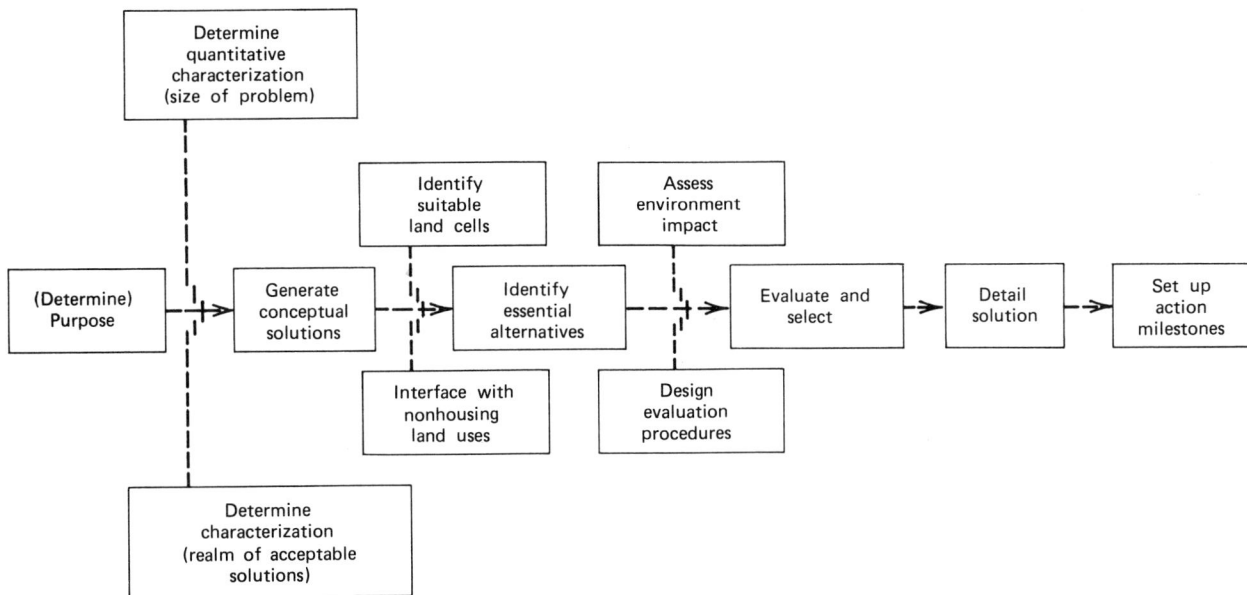

Figure B13-1 The proposed mainstream and support activities in planning for the Haifa regional housing plan.

ideas for the region, and considered to be creative planners.

All were invited to participate in a "one day sketch" workshop. It began in the morning with a short briefing, outlining the task and stressing the desire for concept—not detail. It lasted till the evening as many of the participants demonstrated their solution ideas and explained them to the others.

Table B13-1 Purpose Hierarchy for Haifa Regional Housing Plan

---

1 To identify sites suitable for housing in the Haifa region
2 To rank sites according to their suitability for publicly sponsored housing
3 To include these sites in a housing development plan
4 To obtain control over these sites
5 To enable development of the sites
6 To enable construction of publicly sponsored housing (on these sites)
7 To supply housing to "qualified populations" in Haifa region*
8 To supply housing to "qualified populations" in the country
9 To respond to housing needs of Israeli society
10 To respond to "life support" needs of Israeli society
11 To support the life quality of the Israeli citizen

---

* Purpose level selected to be achieved for the planning project.

From Ideal to Workable Solution

More than 20 ideal solutions were conceived during the special workshop. These were all standardized so as to enable comparison. Broad criteria were used to narrow down the choice into a smaller set, each member of which was then quantified. Out of this reduced set a preferred solution was isolated and made ready for detailed processing and refinement. For this step a fine aerial grid of cells representing 3 acres each was made to contain needed data. Only data dictated by measures of performance was collected for cells that were clearly associated with the preferred solution. This parsimonious use of data reflects the PDA approach and is not characteristic of land use planning studies. The textbook approach specifies a very long and tedious overall survey.

The fine data was processed and manipulated using a specially developed computerized system for the purpose of finalizing the preferred solution by sharply defining the best sites for housing, commerce, industry, and recreational open space.

Final Note

The client participated closely in the plan-making process. A senior member representative continuously associated with the team and helped interpret the letter of intent and formulate the purpose hierarchy. A steering committee reviewed each stage, weighted the criteria, and helped narrow the array of alternatives. Thus the final detailed plan came as no surprise to the client team, and it was accepted with little opposition.

CASE HISTORY B14

A Waitress Training System

Situation

Seven years ago, 20 kids from Chicago opened The Ovens of Brittany, a restaurant dedicated to the creation of a harmonious work place and a unique dining experience for guests. Satisfaction of the former means that there are no locked storerooms or time clocks, and extremely informal operating and supervising procedures exist. In theory, self-actualization, not external controls, characterizes the "new age."

Key to the special Ovens dining experience are a high employee-to-guest ratio, the finest culinary ingredients, classical music, fresh flowers, linen napkins, and a unique waiting staff. The emphasis is on gracious service without sanctimoniousness. Easygoing informality characterizes the Ovens ambience, as well as its management.

As senior waitress, I was asked by Bob Gore, nominal Ovens head, to train six new waitresses. We have had the same staff for almost seven years, but are losing three waitresses. It is assumed that with three extras we won't have to train others for some time to come.

I did set up a timeline of events and milestones for the project, simply to remind me of time constraints and to notify clients in advance. Bob, Dave, and Richard were to be involved in the first two weeks of October, Lynn in addition in the third week, all plus the trainees in the fourth week, and then Bob, Lynn, and Richard in the last week.

I developed a list of over 25 possible purposes. I also discussed purposes with my clients, Bob and Dave. They wanted me to take the major responsibility. Also, they felt I had a special relationship to the Ovens staff and trainees (Ovens earth mother) and that anything I came up with would be acceptable to them. They were also skeptical of formalized interaction techniques among friends. I didn't feel I had the time to persuade them, but I did use the methods indirectly. To get purpose statements from them I asked what it was they wanted me to do and why. Values and mission were intertwined. When I suggested separation they stated emphatically that given the philosophical

context of the Ovens operation, they should remain linked. They are linked in P&D theory too: purpose always has a value dimension.

After I used the couplet method, purpose number 1 emerged as the most specific purpose. I must say I found the method tiresome because it was intuitively obvious to me that this was the case.

My purpose hierarchy is shown in Figure B14-1. I also asked Bob and Dave to make a purpose hierarchy. Theirs was heavy on value statements and jumped, I felt, too quickly into very large purposes. However, when I pointed out to Bob and Dave that most of their purpose hierarchy simply could not be entirely achieved by a waitress training system, they were willing to limit their scope. I did, however, find their purpose hierarchy an invaluable guide to the value system underlying the restaurant's operations.

Table B14-1 shows how the purpose level was selected. Purpose levels 1 to 3 are too small, purpose levels 6 to 11 are too big; that leaves 4 and 5. I chose 4 because both 5's seemed like an M of E (measure of effectiveness)/value statement hybrid. Bob and David agreed to this, with the caveat that level 4 remain securely in the context of the value statements in their hierarchy, as well as the larger context of my own. When I explained that not losing sight of larger purposes was the "raison d'etre" of the purpose hierarchy it was clear that PDA had scored a minor victory.

An M of E performance standard checklist was developed in thinking about subcomponents of purpose statements. One of the major purposes of a training system is to ensure that each trainee knows how to

Table B14-1   Selecting the Focus Purpose

Purpose Level	Criteria 1	2	3	4
1	+	+	−	−
2	+	+	−	−
3	+	+	+	−
4	+	+	+	+
5	+	+	+	+
6–11	−	−		

Criteria for selection

1 Purpose should be achievable in six weeks, by November 12, 1979.

2 Purpose should require no more than 10 hours to achieve.

3 Purpose should assure waitresses capable of performing all items on M of E performance standard checklist.

4 Purpose should be cost-effective but not at the expense of three operational values: respect for the trainees, "esprit de corps," group social goals.

W. Diller, 1979, as the first project in a course on Sociotechnical Design Concepts, University of Wisconsin-Madison. (This case not only portrays another application area, but is also a good illustration of the whole P&D approach. The project area was real, at the place of employment of the student in the course. More details are included in this case history than in the others to illustrate many of the operational ideas presented in Chapters Eleven through Sixteen.)

1. To have a waitress training system

2. To familiarize trainee with the responsibilities of each time slot

3. To demonstrate set up, clean up, and interaction procedures

*4. To ensure that each trainee's skills are at an acceptable level before waitressing

5a. To provide other staff with relief in performing waitress duties   5b. To ensure high standards of guest/waitress interaction

7. To maintain the restaurant's ambience

8. To ensure each guest a "special evening"

9. To protect the Oven's reputation

10. To protect the Oven's financial investment

11. To ensure the Oven's continued existence

12. To promote the social goals of the group

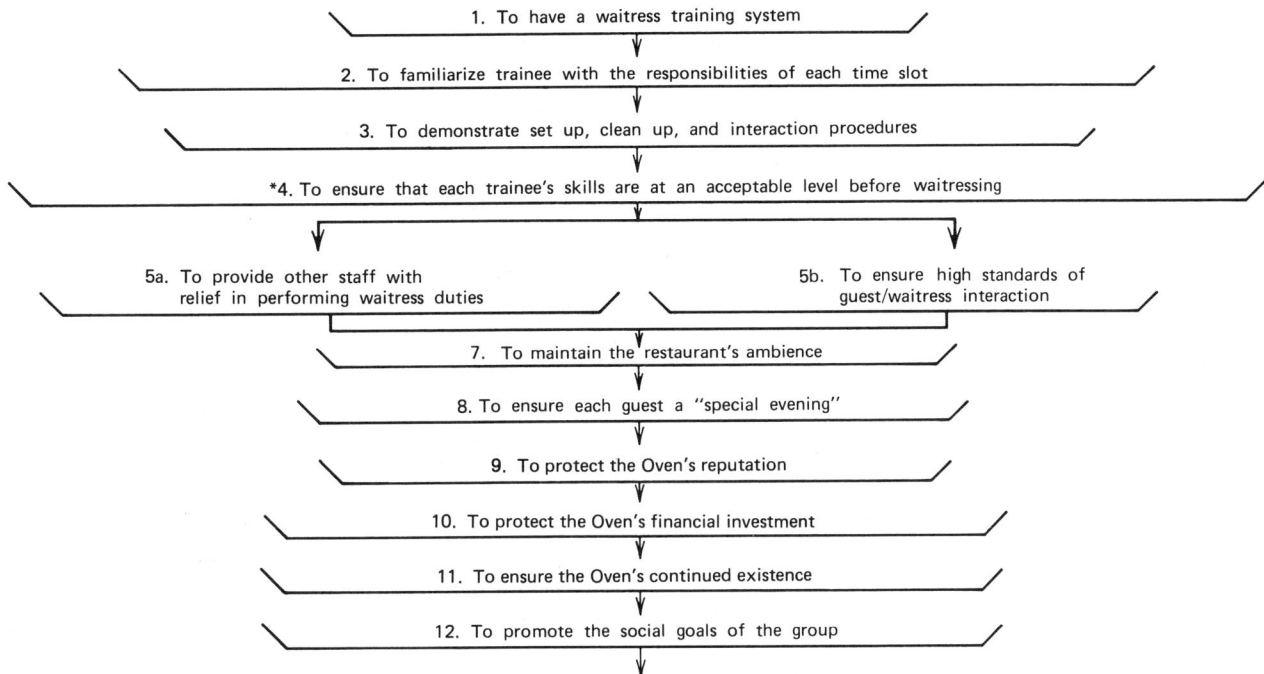

Figure B14-1 Purpose hierarchy: Ovens waitress training system.

perform each checklist item. It is of course possible, however, to perceive the checklist as an M of E of outputs rather than purpose. The checklist had four parts, each with many subparts: Proper setup procedure, clean-up procedure, good service/customer satisfaction, and interemployee harmony.

Nearly 30 ideas were generated by many techniques: brainstorming; analogy; stimulator words; breaking the problem into components; adaptations of utopian solutions; and interactions with Lynn and Clare, head waitresses.

The regularity conditions (Table B14-2) were developed by considering the purposes and the unique opportunities of the system elements: inputs (regularity conditions 2, 3); human agents (1, 5); the environment (4, 6); outputs (7). M of E were formally stated at this point, to reflect most of the ideas characterizing the restaurant. Table B14-3 summarizes these.

Five major alternatives were developed from all of the ideas. Each has a training, testing/evaluation, and continuing change and improvement (CC&I) component. Table B14-4 shows both the major alternatives and the major components. Solution criteria can then be applied to each component engendering a FIST based on the strongest in each category. Major components (12) and (2) will be important details of any training and testing/evaluation component, as (27) and (28) will be of any CC&I component. (1) was elimi-

nated on its face as being too competitive; but it might make for a fun restaurant party.

In evaluating the alternatives I decided to subject each of the three components first to the M of E (Table B14-3) via a decision worksheet. However, it was clear that M of Es 5 and 8 were go–no go; so I first checked each alternative against these. All emerged unscathed.

Table B14-2 Regularity Conditions

1 Seven staff are available for long-term training

2 All of the trainees have come up through the ranks at subsidiary operations; the minimum term of employment has been three years; consequently, they have already had exposure to the overall philosophy

3 Any waitressing experience in subsidiary operations is not the same as the radically different pacing and ambience of the Ovens

4 The restaurant is open from 11 A.M. until midnight; thus, there are time constraints on the use of the Ovens area

5 Most of the Ovens staff are willing to give training time without pay

6 Within reason, there are no financial constraints on training materials, because good waitresses are such a key element in a good restaurant

7 It is assumed that a great deal of learning will occur after the initial training in the process of waitressing

Table B14-3 Measures of Effectiveness of Good Waitress Training System

1 Increase guest enjoyment (measured by tips, remarks to maitre d', volume of business)
2 Decrease in accidents and snafus, avoidance of bureaucracy
3 Increase staff harmony and esprit de corps (because everyone is doing their job correctly others don't feel put upon and harried)
4 Increase trainee self-confidence
5 Trainees able to perform all items on performance standard checklist
6 Participants pleased with program
7 Changes in system in response to evaluation
8 Take no more than 10 hours to complete
9 Logistical complications kept to a minimum

Procedural Notes

M of Es 1 to 3 were developed as measure of purpose; 4 and 5 in relation to outputs; 6 in relation to inputs and human agents; and 7 as an M of E for continuing change and improvement.

Each alternative was measured against the others in relationship to the other M of E. The scale was 1 to 5, with 1 meaning best. I weighted the MEs equally, however it was clear later than number 9 was less important to me than the others. Table B14-5 shows the three decision worksheets.

Alternative 2 emerged the winner in decision worksheet A. It had, however, a major flaw. Careful and creative thought would have to go into FIST detailing so as to minimize the logistical complications. I also felt that alternative 5 was a better way to meet M of E 1, which, given regularity condition 4, is particularly important. Consequently, one element of the FIST training component would include trainees observing experienced waitresses on the job.

In worksheet B, I decided to use M of E 5 because I was interested in which alternative evaluated proficiency most accurately. In the training worksheet this was a go–no go because all solutions *had* to result in learning all checklist items. Alternative 2 was again number 1; again it had logistical problems. Alternative 3 scored much higher on logistics and informality, but the nature of this solution was so fundamentally different from 2 that these elements could not really be pirated.

Alternative 4 is the winner in worksheet C. How-

Table B14-4 Major Alternatives/Major Components*

Training	Testing/Evaluation	CC&I
Notebook (2)	Olympic games (1)	Assign waitress to trainee on job (13)
Night school (4)	Waitress observe and evaluate dress rehearsal (11)	Maitre d' evaluation one month later between him and trainee (14)
En masse (8)	Performance standard checklist (12)	Brunch for group evaluation
Assign different waitresses on job training (9)	**a** Checked off by trainee herself	Immediate written evaluation (16)
Film/discussion (10)	**b** Checked off by instructor	Trainees evaluate program later (23)
Dress rehearsal (11)	Exam given by head waitress (29)	Staff evaluation system deficiencies (28)
Staff who interface system plan and participate in training (21). (21) details include best traits of each waitress (17), best waitresses teach specialty (18), cooks explain ingredients (19), stewards discuss wine (20), explain waitress input to bookkeeping (2)		Written trainee evaluation deficiencies (27)
		Staff/trainee evaluation over wine (26)

* Numbers in parentheses refer to the original list of ideas in the report. The list is not reproduced here, so some of the ideas on the original list are missing.

Major alternatives from the solution list are

1 Big sisters (3)
2 Ground school (5,6)
3 Self-instruction/staff evaluation (7)
4 Night school (4)
5 Traditional

Table B14-5 Selecting components for the Five Major Alternatives

DECISION WORKSHEET A—TRAINING COMPONENT

M of E Number	1	2	3	4	5
1	2	3	3	3	1
2	1	2	3	3	3
3	4	1	4	2	3
4	3	1	2	2	3
6,7	5	1	4	2	3
Total	15	8	16	12	13

DECISION WORKSHEET B—TESTING/EVALUATION COMPONENT

M of E Number	1	2	3	4	5
1	4	1	4	4	4
2	2	3	1	4	5
3	2	1	3	3	3
5	3	1	3	3	1
6,7	3	1	3	3	1
9	3	5	1	2	4
Total	17	12	15	19	18

DECISION WORKSHEET C—CONTINUING CHANGE AND IMPROVEMENT

M of E Number	1	2	3	4	5
2	3	3	5	2	3
3	2	1	2	1	3
9	2	4	2	1	1
Total	7	8	9	4	7

ever, there may be a problem with the decision process there because some M of Es were not relevant. This component may, however, need an M of E somewhat in conflict with M of E 2, namely, a solution that has some kind of formalized way of ensuring that evaluations are acted upon, both in the creation of a new training system, and in correcting the current batch of trainee's "on the job" deficiencies. Thus the CC&I component will probably be a combination of 4, 2, and 2, plus a coordination element.

To develop the FIST, Alternative 6, I took the winners from each worksheet, pirating other elements where possible. I then subjected each element to the regularity conditions not expressly incorporated in the M of E. I really wanted an ideal solution. The FIST is given in Table B14-6.

The FIST was given to Bob and Dave on November 1. They were quite carried away, until they realized that closing the downstairs for one day would cost the restaurant at least $1500. This exceeded the "within reasonable limits" of regularity condition 6. We agreed that the downstairs was not essential for session 1, but was for sessions 2 and 3 (dress rehearsal). Lynn suggested that we hold session 1 in the employees' lounge and session 2 after work on Sunday night, as the guests are seldom there after 9:30.

We also toyed with the idea of simply having the assigned big sister run through the checklist with her trainee after work on the evenings when the trainee was observing. But it didn't take long to conclude that doing it together would be more fun, bring people closer together, and probably result in better training. Lynn was particularly pleased by the dress rehearsal idea, because in talking to the prospective trainees she felt they were rather intimidated by the more formal

Table B14-6 The FIST—Alternative 6

1 Prior to an all-day marathon for all trainees, they will receive a loose-leaf notebook containing a map of Ovens layout and location of equipment, a statement of the Phoenix philosophy, a statement of waitresses' responsibilities, and the marathon's agenda

2 One day will be set aside for training purposes: a three-hour morning session, where various staff members will explain and demonstrate different aspects of waitressing (philosophy of service, grace in movement, emergencies, floor behavior, wine, food, etc.); a three-hour afternoon session with individual demonstration of each item on the performance standard checklist; then individual testing of trainee

3 Evening dress rehearsal: staff play guests, mock food, evaluation of trainee by "guests" and other staff (the videotaping was scrapped because it would be too time-consuming and create unnecessary nervousness on the part of trainees)

4 Bread, wine, and cheese for all participants

5 Each trainee will observe on one "real" work evening, without participating, so as to get a feel for pacing and ambience

6 Each trainee will be assigned to an experienced waitress who will keep an eye on her performance for a month and whom she can ask questions

7 After trainee's first on-the-job evenings, interested staff can get together over house wine and offer complaints and compliments

8 After one week on the job the trainee will submit a written evaluation of the training session indicating what it did not prepare her for; one month later the staff will evaluate training results in writing; these reports will be kept in Bob's office for future reference

Ovens waitressing procedures. The dress rehearsal was to be scheduled in the morning hours, before 10:00, when the Bakers' Rooms (a related fast-food restaurant) opened.

Bob asked Lynn and me to be responsible for implementing the new FIST. He also asked me to develop a long-term system, including selection criteria for future trainees, and a method for training when there is only one trainee, not six. He also gave me a file drawer where written elements of the program, including evaluations, could be kept for future reference. We set the week of December 16–22 as our target date for the training program, as we wanted to avoid holiday time conflicts, but train before January, when Lynn, Claire, and Patrick would be leaving.

Lynn and I let trainees and staff know what we were doing through informal networks—talking individually to trainees and staff, and posting a copy of the proposed plan in the employee lounge. We asked people to write comments on the posted paper. We asked Claire to be dress rehearsal coordinator, I took session 1 and Lynn session 2.

Based on the responses, we developed a recommended solution. It differs from the FIST in two respects. Trainee observation of waiting staff in action precedes the training sessions. And, because everyone liked the notebook idea and wanted one, Lynn and I decided to xerox a packet of materials and give it to trainees and waiting staff to place in their own loose-leafs.

In addition, while detailing the solution, the following irregularity conditions needed to be considered:

1 The training environment may be occupied by guests after 10:00 P.M. on session 2 training night.
2 Some staff may feel put-upon, giving time without pay.
3 Trainees and staff may have time conflicts.
4 Individual emergencies may prevent trainees from attending sessions.
5 Emergency may prevent "teacher" from attending.

Table B14-7   Implementation Schedule

November 5–7	Selection of coordinators Funds allotted into packet Proposal posted in lounge
November 9–10	Notify contributors to info packet Notify participants session 1 meeting Notify staff meeting session 2
November 12	Performance checklist review meeting Assign "big sisters"
November 15	Session 1 agenda meeting
November 18	Revised performance checklist to Zoe's office
November 20	Dress rehearsal agenda meeting Session 1 agenda developed Session 2 agenda developed Performance checklist reedited, typed
November 24–25	Complete training agenda sent to Zoe to type Participants notified about tentative session dates
November 25–30	Staff trainee time conflicts considered; new date set if necessary
December 1	Session dates posted Information packet contributors give material to Zoe
December 4	Information packet material typed, copied, collated
December 9–15	Trainee observation nights
December 10	Info packet distributed to trainees
December 16	Session 1
December 18	Session 2
December 20	Dress rehearsal
December 28	Written trainee evaluations to office
January	CC&I activities

Condition 1 Participants will meet in the employee lounge before going downstairs; Maitre d' will seat all 8:00 tables in Fountain Room, so Fireplace Room will be available for trainees.

Condition 2 The waitresses make a fortune in tips; we won't complain. As for the other staff, a copy of the training proposal will be posted in the lounge; anyone interested in participating can let Lynn or me know via the informal "rumor mill", that way no one is put on the spot.

Condition 3 Dealing with schedule conflicts is incorporated into the implementation schedule (Table B14-7); however, it is expected that trainees and waitstaff will make time.

Condition 4 If a trainee misses a session, her "big sister" and the rest of us will just have to make an

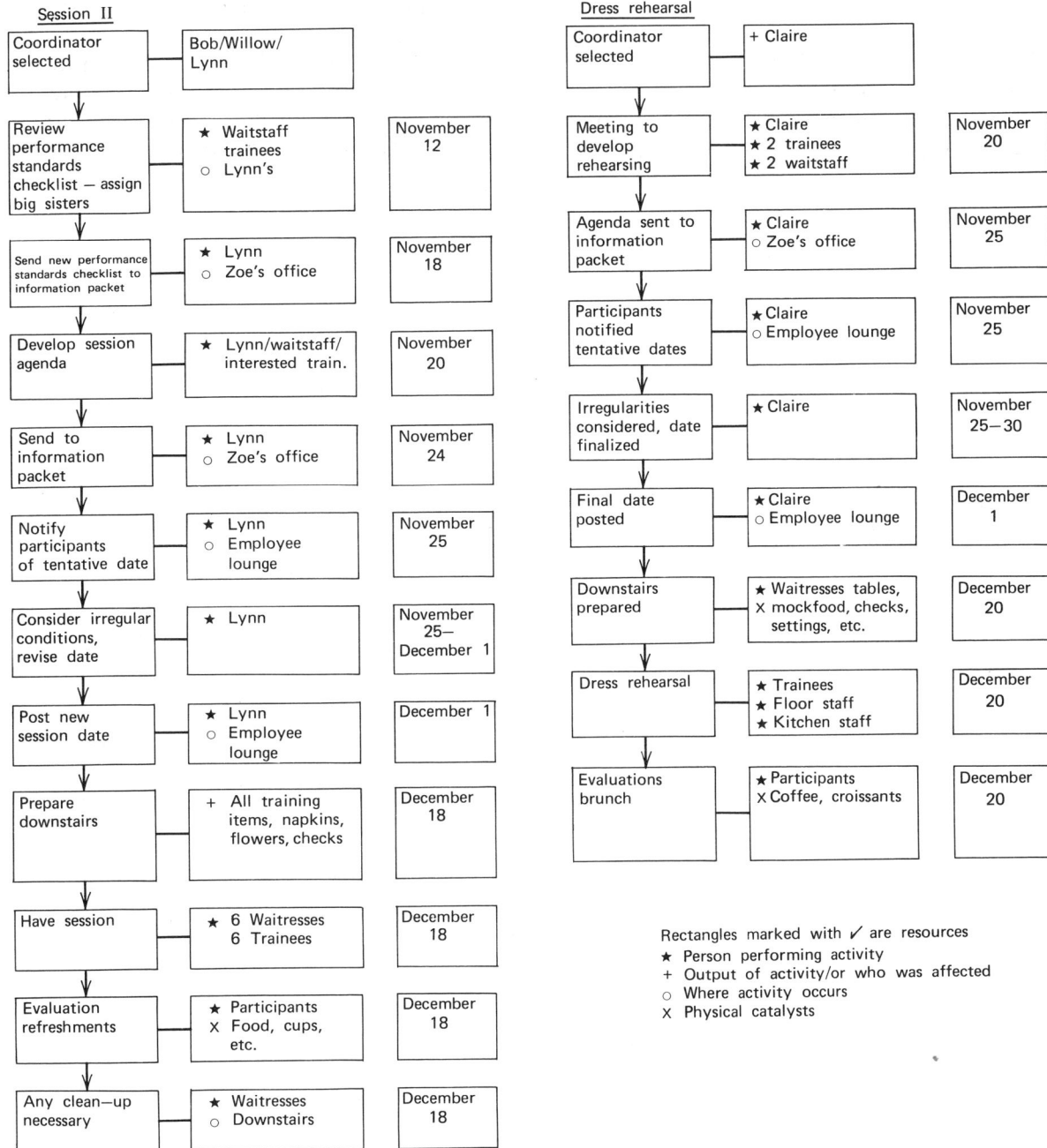

Figure B14-2 Two of five major segments of recommended solution shown in timeline fashion.

extra effort to help her, perhaps after hours on working evenings. The trainee may need to have more "observation" nights, before starting work. Rob may tape session 1, which would enable at least an aural repeat for trainee.

Condition 5 Speakers for session one will be asked to share information with a backup in case of an emergency; if we are short a training waitress in session 2 we can double up; dress rehearsal participants are pretty expendable.

In order to get a handle on the implementation schedule, I reviewed the solution matrix and divided the plan into its major segments: the information packet, session 1, session 2, dress rehearsal, and continuing change and improvement. The latter refers to evaluating the program and establishing change chan-nels. I then made modified flowcharts indicating activity sequence, resources, and projected dates; session 2 and dress rehearsal of the five major segments are shown in Figure B14-2.

Postscript The training system was installed and implemented almost exactly as designed and scheduled. As of January 1981, there was still no turnover among waitresses. Thus, no training programs were needed after the December 1979 program was implemented. When a new training program will be needed, information will be available from the evaluation forms that were completed in December 1979. A new person—Claire—has been now designated as head waitress, and she is monitoring all customer and waitress complaints and quality of presentation as a means of arranging for continuing change and improvement.

NOTES

CHAPTER TWO

1 W. Gomberg, "Enterepreneural Psychology of Facing Conflict in Organization," in G. Fisk, ed., *The Frontiers of Management Psychology,* New York: Harper & Row, 1964, pp. 50–67.

2 G. A. Davis, *Psychology of Problem Solving: Theory and Practice,* New York: Basic Books, 1973.

3 E. de Bono, *Lateral Thinking: Creativity Step by Step,* New York: Harper & Row, 1970.

4 A. W. Kimball, "Errors of the Third Kind in Statistical Consulting," *Journal of the American Statistical Association,* Vol. 57, 1957, p. 133.

5 R. K. Merton, *Social Theory and Social Structure,* New York: Free Press, 1957.

6 L. Price, *The Scientific Estate,* Cambridge, Mass.: Harvard University Press, 1965, as reported in H. Lambright, *Governing Science and Technology,* New York: Oxford University Press, 1976.

7 C. H. Kepner and B. B. Tregoe, *The Rational Manager,* New York: McGraw-Hill, 1965.

8 P. Drucker, *Management: Tasks, Responsibilities, Practices,* New York: Harper & Row, 1974.

9 R. A. Johnson, F. E. Kast, and J. E. Rosenzweig, *The Theory and Management of Systems,* 2nd ed., New York: McGraw-Hill, 1967.

10 E. Cassirer, *An Essay on Man,* New Haven, Conn.: Yale University Press, 1975; G. Holton, *The Scientific Imagination,* Cambridge, England: Cambridge University Press, 1978; and G. S. Stent, *Paradoxes of Progress,* San Francisco: W. H. Freeman, 1978.

11 A. H. Maslow, *Motivation and Personality,* rev. ed., New York: Harper & Row, 1970.

12 V. F. Weisskopf, "The Frontiers and Limits of Science," *American Scientist,* Vol. 65, No. 4, July–August 1977, p. 405.

13 Maslow, op. cit.

14 R. W. White, "Motivation Reconsidered: The Concept of Competence," *Psychological Review,* Vol. 66, 1959, pp. 297–333; J. Cherfas and R. Lewin, *Not Work Alone,* Beverly Hills, Calif: Sage, 1980.

15 Maslow, op. cit.

16 R. Nisbet, *History of the Idea of Progress,* New York: Basic Books, 1979.

17 J. J. Servan-Schrieber, *The American Challenge,* New York: Atheneum, 1968.

CHAPTER THREE

1 J. S. Buchler, *The Concept of Method,* New York: Columbia University Press, 1961.

2 G. Nadler, "Relating Systems Concepts and Public Planning," *Policy Sciences,* Vol. 12, No. 3, October 1980, pp. 283–299.

3 C. W. Churchman, "Morality in Planning," *Design Methods and Theories,"* Vol. 10, No. 3, July–September 1976, pp. 165–194. Copyright, Design Methods Group.

4 G. Zaltman and R. Duncan, *Strategies for Planned Change,* New York: Wiley, 1977, Chapter 13.

5 E. Burke, as quoted in N. Cousins, "History ⊔ld Happenstance," *Saturday Review,* 20 August 1977, p. 6.

6 D. W. Ewing, "Discovering Your Problem–Solving Style," *Psychology Today,* Vol. 12, No. 7, December 1977, pp. 69–73+.

7 C. G. Jung, *Man and His Symbols,* New York: Doubleday, 1964, p. 38.

8 J. Hadamard, *An Essay on the Psychology of Invention in the Mathematical Field.* Princeton, N.J.: Princeton, 1945.

9 A. Rapoport, "Modern Systems Theory," *General Systems,* Vol. 14, 1970, p. 17.

10 For examples, see R. Lilienfeld, *The Rise of Systems Theory: An Ideological Analysis,* New York: Wiley, 1978; I. R. Hoos, "Engineers as Analysts of Social Systems: A Critical Enquiry," *Journal of Systems Engineering* Vol. 4, No. 2, 1976 p. 81; D.

Berlinski, *On Systems Analysis,* Cambridge, Mass.: MIT Press, 1976; and G. Majone and E. S. Quade, eds., *Pitfalls of Analysis,* New York: Wiley, 1980.

11 I. I. Mitroff, "Towards a Theory and Measure of Total Problem Solving Performance," *Proceedings,* MIT Conference on Implementation, 1975.

12 W. Barrett, *The Illusion of Technique,* New York: Anchor/Doubleday, 1978.

13 C. W. Churchman, *The Design of Inquiring Systems,* New York: Basic Books, 1971.

14 S. Toulmin, "From Form to Function," *Daedalus,* Journal of the American Academy of Arts and Sciences, Vol. 106, No. 3, Summer 1977, pp. 143–162. Reprinted by permission.

15 R. W. Sperry, "Lateral Specialization of Cerebral Functions in Surgically Separated Hemispheres," in F. J. McGuigan and R. A. Schoonover, eds., *The Psychology of Thinking,* New York: Academic Press, 1973, pp. 209–229.

16 J. Levy, "Psychological Implications of Bilateral Symmetry," in S. J. Dimond and J. G. Beaumont, Eds, *Hemispheric Function in the Human Brain,* New York: Wiley, 1974.

17 J. E. Bogan, "Some Educational Aspects of Hemispheric Specialization," *UCLA Educator,* Vol. 17, 1975, pp. 24–32.

18 P. Elbow, *Writing Without Teachers,* New York: Oxford University Press, 1973, Appendix Essay.

19 Buchler, op. cit.

20 T. S. Kuhn, *The Structure of Scientific Revolutions,* Chicago: University of Chicago Press, 1962.

21 N. Cochran, "Society as Emergent and More Than Rational," *Policy Sciences,* Vol. 12, No. 2, August 1980, pp. 113–129.

CHAPTER FOUR

1 H. A. Simon, *The Sciences of the Artificial,* Cambridge, Mass.: MIT Press, 1969.

2 A. Koestler, "Beyond Atomism and Holism—The Concept of the Holon," in A. Koestler and J. R. Smythies, eds., *Beyond Reductionism,* London: Hutchinson, 1969, pp. 192–232. Also see the appendix on the hierarchy of complexity and stable sub-assemblies in H. A. Simon, op. cit.

3 H. G. J. Aitken, *Syntony and Spark,* New York: Wiley, 1976, p. 311.

4 W. Hurst, "Consensus and Conflict in Twentieth-Century Public Policy," *Daedalus,* Journal of the American Academy of Arts and Sciences, Vol. 105, No. 4, Fall 1976, pp. 89–101. Reprinted by permission.

5 T. Kotarbinski, *Praxiology: An Introduction to the Sciences of Efficient Action,* New York: Pergamon, 1965.

6 W. Bevan, "Science in the Penultimate Age," *American Scientist,* Vol. 65, No. 5, September–October, 1977, p. 538.

7 S. Mandelbaum, "A Complete General Theory of Planning Is Impossible," *Policy Sciences II,* Amsterdam: Elsevier, 1979, pp. 59–71.

8 E. Layton, "Conditions of Technological Development," in I. Speigel-Rosing and D. de Solla Price, eds. *Science, Technology and Society,* Beverly Hills, Calif.: Sage, 1977; P. Kelly and M. Kranzberg, *Technological Innovation,* San Francisco: San Francisco Press, 1978, p. ix.

9 H. W. J. Rittel and M. W. Webber, "Dilemmas in a General Theory of Planning," *Design Methods Group–Design Research Society Journal,* Vol. 8, No. 1, January–March 1974, p. 31–39.

10 Ibid.

11 D. N. Michael, *On Learning to Plan—and Planning to Learn,* San Francisco: Jossey-Bass, 1973, p. 18.

12 M. Inbar, *Routine Decision Making: The Future of Bureaucracy,* Beverly Hills, Calif.: Sage, 1979.

13 E. Bardach, *The Implementation Game,* Cambridge, Mass.: MIT Press, 1977.

14 H. Cross, "Problems in the Quest for Productivity," in *Proceedings, Conference on Productivity and the Professional/Technical Work Force,* Crotonville, N. Y.: General Electric Company, 1976.

15 P. Davidoff, "Advocacy and Pluralism in Planning," in A. Faludi, ed., *A Reader in Planning Theory,* New York: Pergamon, 1973.

16 G. Nadler, "An Investigation of Design Methodology," *Management Science,* Vol. 13, No. 10, 1967, pp. B642–B655.

17 J. Diebold, "Why Things Don't Work Anymore," *Newsweek,* 18 July 1977, p. 9.

18 B. D. Karl, "Philanthropy, Policy Planning, and the Bureaucratization of the Democratic Ideal," *Daedalus,* Journal of the American Academy of Arts and Sciences, Vol. 105, No. 4, Fall 1976, pp. 124–149. Reprinted by permission.

19 L. G. Sprague and C. R. Sprague, "Management *Science?*" *Interfaces,* Vol. 7, No. 1, November 1976, p. 57.

20 G. Nadler, "Is More Measurement Better?" *Industrial Engineering,* Vol. 10, No. 3, March 1978, pp. 20–25.

21 D. MacRae, Jr., *The Social Function of Social Science,* New Haven, Conn.: Yale University Press, 1976, pp. 25–28. Copyright © Yale University.

22 R. S. Morison, "A Further Note on Visions," *Daedalus,* Vol. 109, No. 1, Winter 1980, pp. 55–64.

CHAPTER FIVE

1 S. M. Zifferblatt and C. G. Hendricks, "Applied Behavioral Analysis of Societal Problems," *American Psychologist,* Vol. 29, No. 10, October 1974, pp. 750–761; and A. Tversky and D. Kahneman, "The Framing of Decisions and the Psychology of Choice," *Science,* Vol. 211, 30 January 1981, pp. 453–458.

2 I. R. Hoos, "Engineers as Analysts of Social Systems: A Critical Enquiry," *Journal of Systems Engineering,* Vol. 4, No. 2, 1976, p. 87. Also see G. Majone and E. S. Quade, eds. *Pitfalls of Analysis,* New York: Wiley, 1980.

3 N. R. F. Maier, *Problem Solving and Creativity in Individuals and Groups,* Belmont, Calif.: Brooks/Cole, 1970.

4 H. Gilliam, "The Fallacy of Single-Purpose Planning," *Daedalus,* Journal of the American Academy of Arts and Sciences, Vol. 96, No. 4, Fall 1967, pp. 1142–1157. Reprinted by permission.

5 J. A. Mecklenburger and J. A. Wilson, "Learning C.O.D.: Can the Schools Buy Success?" *Saturday Review,* 18 September 1971, pp. 62–65+. All rights reserved. Reprinted with permission.

6 A. Schlesinger, Jr., "The Futility of Futurism," *Wall Street Journal,* 12 December 1977, Editorial page.

7 H. A. Simon, *The Sciences of the Artificial,* Cambridge, Mass.: MIT Press, 1969.

8 A. C. Shapiro, "Incentive Systems and the Implementation of Management Science: A Spare Parts Application," *Interfaces,* Vol. 7, No. 1, Part 1, November 1976, p. 14.

9 A. Faludi, ed., *A Reader in Planning Theory,* New York: Pergamon, 1973.

10 H. Mintzberg, D. Raisinghani, and A. Theoret, "The Structure

of 'Unstructured' Decision Processes," *Administrative Science Quarterly,* Vol 21, No. 2, June 1976, pp. 246–275.

11 P. C. Nutt, "An Experimental Comparison of the Effectiveness of Three Planning Procedures," *Management Science,* Vol. 23, No. 5, February 1977, pp. 378–394.

12 D. M. Murtha, "A Comparison of Problem-Solving Approaches Used by Environmental Designers," Ph.D. Dissertation, Department of Industrial Engineering, University of Wisconsin-Madison, 1973.

13 G. Nadler, "Increasing the Effectiveness of Productivity Services Through a Systems Perspective," *Proceedings, 1977 Congress of European Federation of Productivity Services,* Vienna, 22 April 1977.

14 G. Nadler, "I. E. Problem Solving," *Industrial Engineering,* Vol. 8, No. 4, April 1976, pp. 36–39.

15 G. Nadler, "An Investigation of Design Methodology," *Management Science,* Vol. 13, No. 10, June 1967, pp. B642–B655.

16 G. Nadler, "Is More Measurement Better?" *Industrial Engineering,* Vol. 10, No. 3, March 1978, p. 20–25.

17 W. Edwards, L. D. Philips, L. W. Hayes, and B. C. Goodman, "Probabilistic Information Processing Systems: Design and Evaluation," *IEEE Transactions on Man, Science and Cybernetics,* Vol. 4, No. 248, 1968; and J. G. Miller, *Living Systems,* New York: McGraw-Hill, 1978, pp. 151–156.

18 I. I. Mitroff and T. R. Featheringham, "On Systemic Problem-solving and the Error of the Third Kind," *Behavioral Science,* Vol. 19, No. 6, November 1976, p. 383.

19 P. Watzlowick, J. H. Westland, and R. Fisch, *Change: Principles of Problem Formulation and Problem Resolution,* New York: Norton, 1974.

20 R. A. Swalm, "Utility Theory Insights into Risk Taking," *Harvard Business Review,* Vol. 44, No. 6, November–December 1966, p. 123.

21 I. L. Janis and L. Mann, *Decision Making,* New York: Free Press, 1977.

22 M. H. McCaulley, "Psychological Types in Engineering: Implications for Teaching," *Engineering Education,* Vol. 66, No. 7, April 1976, pp. 729–736; and C. G. Jung, *Psychological Types,* Vol. 6 of collected works, Princeton, N.J.: Princeton University Press, 1971.

23 C. W. Churchman, *The Systems Approach and Its Enemies,* New York: Basic Books, 1979, pp. 206–207.

24 Janis and Mann, op. cit.

25 D. G. Myers and H. Lamm, "The Polarizing Effect of Group Discussion," *American Scientist,* Vol. 63, No. 3, May–June 1975, pp. 297–300.

26 D. Cartwright, and A. Zander, eds. *Group Dynamics,* Evanston, Ill.: Bow/Peterson, 1960.

27 J. G. Wilson, *The Investigators,* New York: Basic Books, 1978.

28 E. C. Banfield, "Ends and Means in Planning," *International Social Science Journal,* Vol. 11, No. 3, 1959, p. 199. Reproduced by permission of UNESCO.

29 M. Inbar, *Routine Decision Making: The Future of Bureaucracy,* Beverly Hills, Calif.: Sage, 1979.

30 R. M. Kanter, *Men and Women of the Corporation,* New York: Basic Books, 1977.

PART TWO

1 With permission. From *Webster's New World Dictionary,* College Edition. Copyright © 1968 by the World Publishing Company.

2 J. Hage, *Techniques of Theory Construction in Sociology,* New York: Wiley, 1972.

3 E. C. Banfield, "Ends and Means in Planning," *International Social Science Journal,* Vol. 11, No. 3, 1959, p. 199.

4 W. W. Gasparski, "Praxiological-Systemic Approach to Design Studies," *Design Studies,* Vol. 1, No. 2, October 1979, pp. 101–106.

5 S. Toulmin, *Human Understanding,* Vol. 1, Princeton, N. J.: Princeton University Press, 1972, p. 21.

6 Ibid.

CHAPTER SIX

1 T. Mann, *The Magic Mountain,* translated by H. T. Lowe-Porter, New York: Knopf, 1962.

2 E. Taschdjian, "Time Horizon: The Moving Boundary," *Behavioral Science,* Vol. 22, No. 1, January 1977, p. 41.

3 R. L. Henshel, *On The Future of Social Prediction,* Indianapolis, Ind: Bobbs-Merrill, 1976, p. 8.

4 F. E. Emery and E. L. Trist, *Towards a Social Ecology,* New York: Plenum Press, 1973.

5 Specific point-in-time predictions of physical relationships are relatively certain and thus not particularly subject to the flaws that follow. The tensile strength of a steel beam in a building 50 years from now, for example, can be predicted fairly well.

6 H. Bergson, *An Introduction to Metaphysics,* London: MacMillan, 1913, translated by T. E. Hulme, p. 58.

7 C. J. Hitch, "Unfreezing the Future," *Science,* Vol. 195, 4 March 1977, p. 825. Copyright 1977 by the American Association for the Advancement of Science.

8 P. Marris, *Loss and Change,* New York: Pantheon, 1974.

9 M. Greenfield, "What Happens Now?" *Newsweek,* 19 November 1975, p. 176.

10 A. Rosenfeld, "The New LSD: Life-span Development," *Saturday Review,* 1 October 1977, pp. 32–33. All rights reserved. Reprinted with permission.

11 J. D. Levinson, et al., *The Seasons of a Man's Life,* New York: Petrocelli/Charter, 1975.

12 A. Wildavsky, "Doing Better and Feeling Worse: The Political Pathology of Health Policy," *Daedalus,* Journal of the American Academy of Arts and Sciences, Vol. 106, No. 1, Winter 1977, p. 105. Reprinted by permission.

13 N. T. Feathers, *Values in Education and Society,* New York: Free Press, 1975.

14 A. C. Filley, *Interpersonal Conflict Resolution,* Chicago, Ill.: Scott, Foresman, 1975.

15 B. L. Hedberg, P. C. Nystrom, and W. H. Starbuck, "Camping on See Saws: Prescriptions for a Self-Designing Organization," *Administrative Science Quarterly,* Vol. 21, No. 1, March 1976, p. 42.

CHAPTER SEVEN

1 R. L. Ackoff, "Beyond Problem Solving," *General Systems,* Vol. 19, 1974, pp. 237–239.

2 J. G. Miller, "The Nature of Living Systems," *Behavioral Science,* Vol. 20, No. 6, November 1975.

3 B. K. Karl, "Philanthropy, Policy Planning, and the Bureaucratization of the Democratic Ideal," *Daedalus,* Journal of the

American Academy of Arts and Sciences, Vol. 105, No. 4, Fall 1976, pp. 129–149. Reprinted by permission.

4 A. Korzybski, *Science and Sanity*, 4th ed., Lakeville, Conn.: Institute of General Semantics, 1958.

5 H. A. Simon, *The Sciences of the Artificial*, Cambridge, Mass.: MIT Press, 1969.

6 Korzybski, op. cit.

7 Ibid.

8 Miller, op. cit.

9 S. Beer, "On Heaping Our Science Together," in C. W. Churchman, ed., *Systems and Management Annual*, New York: Petrocelli/Charter, 1975.

10 Simon, op. cit.

11 J. G. Miller, *Living Systems*, New York: McGraw-Hill, 1978.

12 Ackoff, op. cit.

13 R. L. Ackoff and F. E. Emery, "On Ideal-Seeking Systems," *General Systems*, Vol. 17, 1972, p. 17–24.

14 S. Makridakis, "The Second Law of Systems," *International Journal of General Systems*, Vol. 4, No. 1, 1977.

15 P. Watzlawick, J. H. Weakland, and R. Fisch, *Change: Principles of Problem Formulation and Problem Resolution*, New York: Norton, 1974.

CHAPTER EIGHT

1 A. Korzybski, *Science and Sanity: An Introduction to Non-Aristotelian Systems and General Semantics*, Lakeville, Conn.: Institute of General Semantics, 1958.

2 S. I. Hayakawa, *Language in Thought and Action*, London: Allen & Unwin, 1952.

3 P. Watzlawick, J. H. Weakland, and R. Fisch, *Change: Principles of Problem Formation and Problem Resolution*, New York: Norton, 1974.

4 Quotation in this paragraph and paragraph following are from Hayakawa, op. cit.

5 Ibid.

6 J. R. Platt, "Strong Inference," *Science*, Vol. 146, No. 3642, October 16, 1964, pp. 346–53.

7 C. W. Churchman, *The Systems Approach and Its Enemies*, New York: Basic Books, 1979.

8 R. B. Braithwaite, *Scientific Explanation*, New York: Harpers, 1960.

9 Ibid.

10 J. N. Shuman, "Mathematical Model Building and Public Policy: The Games Some Bureaucrats Play," *Technological Forecasting and Social Change*, Vol 9, No. 3, 1976, pp. 309–334. Copyright, Elsevier North Holland, Inc.

11 S. W. Sutherland, *Systems: Analysis, Administration, and Architecture*, New York: Van Nostrand, 1975.

12 L. A. Zadeh and E. Polak, eds., *System Theory*, New York: McGraw-Hill, 1969.

13 Hayakawa, op. cit.

14 F. Heisenberg, *Physics and Philosophy*, New York: Harpers, 1958.

15 M. H. Bradley, "Zero—What Does It Mean?", *Science*, Vol. 208, 4 April 1980, p. 9.

16 B. L. Hedberg, P. C. Nystrom, and W. H. Starbuck, "Camping on Seesaws: Prescriptions for a Self-Designing Organization," *Administrative Science Quarterly*, Vol. 21, No. 1, March 1976, p. 41.

17 W. S. Baer, L. L. Johnson, and E. W. Merrow, "Government-Sponsored Demonstrations of New Technologies" *Science*, Vol. 196, 27 May 1977, pp. 950–957.

18 J. W. Lorsch, "Making Behavioral Science More Useful," *Harvard Business Review*, Vol. 57, No. 2, March–April 1979, pp. 171–180.

19 S. Toulmin, "From Form to Function: Philosophy and History of Science in the 1950s and Now," *Daedalus*, Vol. 106, No. 3, Summer 1977, p. 143.

20 L. Lipson, "Technical Issues and the Adversary Process," *Science*, Vol. 194, 26 November 1976, p. 890.

CHAPTER NINE

1 N. Cousins, "Cop-out Realism," *Saturday Review*, 2 September 1978, p. 48.

2 A wide variety of hypotheses that could be explored for interface dimensions is presented in J. G. Miller, *Living Systems*, New York: McGraw-Hill, 1978, pp. 90–114.

CHAPTER TEN

1 H. Leventhal, "Changing Attitudes and Habits to Reduce Risk Factors in Chronic Diseases," *American Journal of Cardiology*, Vol. 31, No. 5, May 1973, pp. 571–580.

2 Michael, D. N., *On Learning to Plan—and Planning to Learn*, San Francisco: Jossey-Bass, 1973.

3 G. T. L. Land, *Grow or Die: The Unifying Principle of Transformation*, New York: Random House, 1973.

4 F. E. Emery and E. L. Trist, *Towards a Social Ecology*, New York: Plenum, 1973.

5 H. I. Ansoff, "The State of Practice in Planning System," *Sloan Management Review*, Vol. 18, No. 2, Winter 1977, pp. 1–24.

6 R. E. Walton, "Explaining Why Success Didn't Take," *Organizational Dynamics* (AMACOM, a division of American Management Associations), Vol. 3, No. 3, Winter 1975, pp. 2–22.

7 L. G. Sprague and C. R. Sprague, "Management *Science*?" *Interfaces*, Vol. 7, No. 1, November 1976, pp. 57–62.

8 B. Taylor, "Strategies for Planning," *Long Range Planning*, Vol. 8, No. 4, August 1975, pp. 27–40.

PART THREE

1 M. Greenfield, "The People's Revenge," *Newsweek*, 19 June 1978, p. 92.

CHAPTER ELEVEN

1 P. C. Nutt, "An Experimental Comparison of the Effectiveness of Three Planning Methods," *Management Science*, Vol. 23, No. 5, January 1977, pp. 499–511.

2 N. Seshadri and G. Nadler, "A Further Study of the Experiment on Environmental Designers," Project Report, Department of Industrial Engineering, University of Wisconsin-Madison, May 1974.

3 O. Friedman, "The Economic Effect of Cost Control Programs in the Mid-West Industry", Masters thesis, University of Wisconsin-Madison, 1973.

4 P. Elbow, "The Doubting Game and the Believing Game," in P. Elbow, *Writing Without Teachers*, New York: Oxford, University Press, 1973.

5 Ibid.

6 Ibid.

7 C. W. Churchman, *The Systems Approach and Its Enemies,* New York: Basic Books, 1979.

8 S. A. Gregory, "Towards Design Science: Review of Twenty Years," Birmingham, England: University of Aston, Department of Chemical Engineering, 1977.

9 Ibid.

10 R. L. Keeney and H. Raiffa, *Decisions with Multiple Objectives: Preferences and Value Tradeoffs*, New York: Wiley, 1977. For other definitions, see G. P. Huber, *Managerial Decision Making*, Glenview, Ill.: Scott, Foresman, 1980, Chapter 1.

CHAPTER TWELVE

1 S. Alter, "Implementation Risk Analysis," in R. Doktor, R. L. Schultz, and D. P. Slevin, eds., *Implementation of Management Science*, Studies in the Management Sciences, New York: Elsevier North Holland, 1980.

2 This list of purposes could be put into a hierarchy of its own, but is not presented as such. The reasons for seeking a hierarchy of purposes for a problem are different for each situation, thus each purpose in this list could be at different levels for different projects.

3 R. J. Volkema, "An Empirical Investigation of Problem Formulation and Problem-Purpose Expansion," Ph.D. dissertation, University of Wisconsin-Madison, 1980.

4 R. L. Ackoff, "Beyond Problem Solving," *General Systems,* Vol. 19, 1976, pp. 237–329; and A. Tversky and D. Kahneman, "The Framing of Decisions and the Psychology of Choice," *Science*, Vol. 211, 30 January 1981, pp. 453–458.

5 J. S. Buchler, *The Concepts of Method,* New York: Columbia University Press, 1961, p. 108.

6 R. L. Keeney and H. Raiffa, *Decisions with Multiple Objectives: Preferences and Value Tradeoffs,* New York: Wiley, 1976.

7 J. Kraegel, V. Mousseau, C. E. Goldsmith and R. Arora, *Patient Care Systems,* Philadelphia: Lippincott, 1974.

8 A. Koestler, *The Act of Creation,* New York: Macmillan, 1964.

9 H. Mintzberg, D. Raisinghani, and A. Theoret, "The Structure of 'Unstructured' Decision Processes," *Administrative Science Quarterly,* Vol. 21, No. 2, June 1976, pp. 245–275.

10 G. R. White and M. B. W. Graham, "How to Spot a Technological Winner," *Harvard Business Review,* Vol. 56, No. 2, March–April 1978, pp. 146–152.

11 L. Jakobson, "The Sketch Plan Concept and Its Application to Central Tunisia," Discussion Paper, Regional Planning and Area Development Project, International Studies and Programs, University of Wisconsin-Madison, October 1980.

12 Mintzberg, Raisinghani, and Theoret, op. cit.

13 Second National Conference on Higher Education/State Relations, Columbus, Ohio, 25–27, October 1977. As reported in *NEA Advocate,* December 1977.

14 E. Bardach, *The Implementation Game,* Cambridge, Mass.: MIT, 1977. Also see Chapter 9 in G. Majone and E. S. Quade, eds., *Pitfalls of Analysis,* New York: Wiley, 1980.

15 Bardach, op. cit.

16 Ibid.

17 J. L. Pressman and A. Wildavsky, *Implementation,* Berkeley: University of California Press, 1973.

18 Bardach, op. cit.

19 Ibid.

20 Mintzberg, Raisinghani, and Theoret, op. cit.

CHAPTER THIRTEEN

1 W. R. King and D. I. Cleland, *Strategic Planning and Policy,* New York: Van Nostrand, 1978.

2 J. W. Sutherland, *Systems: Analysis, Administration, and Architecture,* New York: Van Nostrand, 1975.

3 H. Mintzberg, "Patterns in Strategy Formation," Faculty of Management, McGill University, Montreal, Canada, March 1976.

4 E. Bardach, *The Implementation Game,* Cambridge, Mass.: MIT Press, 1977.

5 *A Framework for Business Planning,* Report No. 162, Menlo Park, Calif.: Stanford Research Institute, 1963.

6 G. Zaltman and R. Duncan, *Strategies for Planned Change,* New York: Wiley, 1977.

7 P. G. Herbst, *Socio-Technical Design: Strategies in Multidisciplinary Research,* London: Tavistock Publications, 1974.

8 "Proposed Resolution," *Tranet,* Winter 1976, p. 1.

9 M. Milne, as reported in W. J. Mitchell, *Computer-Aided Architectural Design,* New York: Petrocelli/Charter, 1977.

10 G. J. Wacker and G. Nadler, "Myths About Implementing Quality of Working Life Programs," *California Management Review,* Vol. 22, No. 3, Spring 1980, pp. 15–23.

11 J. N. Warfield, *Societal Systems,* New York: Wiley, 1976.

12 G. Holton, "On the Role of Themata in Scientific Thought," *Science,* Vol. 188, 25 April 1975, pp. 328–334.

13 King and Cleland, op. cit.

14 A. W. Wymore, *Systems Engineering Methodology for Interdisciplinary Teams,* New York: Wiley, 1976.

15 Warfield, op. cit.

16 A. Locker and N. A. Coulter, Jr. "A New Look at the Description and Prescription of Systems," *Behavioral Science,* Vol. 22, No. 3, May 1977.

17 H. W. J. Rittel and M. M. Webber, "Dilemmas in a General Theory of Planning," *Policy Sciences,* Vol. 4, No. 2, June 1973, p. 155.

18 R. A. Rettig, Review of *Fish Protein Concentrate,* in *Science,* Vol. 203, 26 January, 1979, p. 349.

19 Mintzberg, op. cit.

20 W. Hurst, "Consensus and Conflict in Twentieth-Century Public Policy," *Daedalus,* Journal of the American Academy of Arts and Sciences, Vol. 105, No. 5, Fall 1976, pp. 89–101. Reprinted by permission.

21 N. B. Hannay and R. E. McGinn, "The Anatomy of Modern Technology," *Daedalus,* Vol. 109, No. 1, Winter 1980, pp. 25–54.

CHAPTER FOURTEEN

1 A. Rosenfeld, "Learning to Give Up," *Saturday Review,* 3 September 1977, pp. 36–37.

2 P. Elbow, "The Doubting Game and the Believing Game—An Analysis of the Intellectual Enterprise," in P. Elbow, *Writing Without Teachers,* New York: Oxford University Press, 1973.

3 D. A. Kolb, I. M. Rubin, and J. M. McIntyre, *Organizational Psychology: An Experimental Approach*, Englewood Cliffs, N.J.: Prentice-Hall, 1971.

4 D. G. Myers and H. Lamm, "The Polarizing Effect of Group Discussion," *American Scientist,* Vol. 63, No. 3, May–June 1975, pp. 297–303.

5   Ibid.

6   B. E. Collins and H. Guetzkow, *A Social Psychology of Group Processes for Decision-Making,* New York: Wiley, 1964.

7   R. Schrank, *Ten Thousand Working Days,* Cambridge, Mass: MIT Press, 1978.

8   C. P. Snow, address at Washington University, St. Louis, Mo., February 1963. Also see H. A. Otto, "New Light on the Human Potential," *Saturday Review,* 20 December 1969, pp. 14–17.

9   N. H. McMillan, *Planning for Survival,* Chicago: American Hospital Association 1978, p. 79.

10 Ibid.

11 Other information about characteristics of groups can be found in G. L. Lippitt, *Visualizing Change,* Fairfax, VA.: NTL-Learning Resources, 1973.

12 R. M. Kanter, *Men and Women of the Corporation,* New York: Basic Books, 1977, p. 68.

13 For another perspective, see H. J. Leavitt, L. R. Pondy and D. M. Bojo, eds. *Readings in Managerial Psychology,* Chicago: University of Chicago Press, 1980.

14 L. E. Greiner, "Patterns of Organizational Change," in G. Dalton and P. Lawrence, *Organizational Change and Development,* Homewood, Ill.: Irwin, 1970.

15 C. Argyris, *Intervention Theory and Method: A Behavioral Science View,* Reading, Mass.: Addison-Wesley, 1970.

16 E. Howe and J. Kaufman, "The Ethics of Contemporary American Planners," *Journal of the American Planning Association,* Vol. 45, No. 3, July 1979, pp. 243–255.

17 D. G. Hinds, "An Evaluation of Planning and Design Theory and Practice Using Criteria Derived from Transactional Analysis," Independent Study Paper, Department of Industrial Engineering, University of Wisconsin—Madison, August 10, 1977.

18 C. M. Steiner, *Scripts People Live,* New York: Bantam, 1974, p. 41.

19 Eric Berne, *What Do You Say After You Say Hello?* New York: Bantam, 1972, p. 11.

20 Steiner, op. cit.

21 R. D. Abell, *Own Your Own Life,* New York: McKay, 1977, p. 54.

22 Abell, op. cit.

23 Berne, op. cit.

24 Charles Albano, *Transactional Analysis on the Job,* in T. Rendero, Ed., *Communicating with Subordinates,* New York: AMACOM, a division of American Management Associations, 1974, p. 9.

25 Berne, op. cit.

26 Abell, op. cit.

27 Ibid.

28 Ibid.

29 Hinds, op. cit.

CHAPTER FIFTEEN

1   P. F. Drucker, "India and Appropriate Technology," *Wall Street Journal,* 1 March 1979, Editorial page.

2   A. J. Large, "Congress Wrestles With Technology," *Wall Street Journal,* 21 April 1978, Editorial page.

3   M. J. Adler, *Philosopher at Large: An Intellectual Autobiography,* New York: Macmillan, 1977.

4   B. Archer, "Whatever Became of Design Methodology? The Three Rs," *Design Studies,* Vol. 1, No. 1, July 1979, pp. 17–20.

5   M. Tribus, "The National Significance of Public Understanding of Technology," in E. M. Hawk, ed., *Technology and Society Courses at the College Level,* University Park: Pennsylvania State University, 1976.

6   K. Strike and G. Posner, "Types of Synthesis and their Criteria," in S. Ward and L. Reed, Eds., *Knowledge Structure and Use,* Washington D.C.: National Institute of Education, 1981.

7   T. Levitt, "Management and the 'Post-Industrial' Society," *The Public Interest,* Number 44, Summer 1976, pp. 69–103. Reprinted with permission of the author. Copyright © 1976 by National Affairs, Inc.

8   N. Caplan, A. Morrison, and R. J. Stambaugh, "The Use of Social Science Knowledge in Policy Decision at the National Level," Ann Arbor, Mich.: Center for Research on Utilization of Scientific Knowledge, Institute for Social Research, University of Michigan, 1975.

9   M. Greenfield, "Why We Don't Know Anything," *Newsweek,* 18 December 1978, p. 112.

10 R. L. Sinsheimer, "The Presumptions of Science," *Daedalus,* Journal of the American Academy of Arts and Sciences, Vol. 107, No. 2, Spring 1978, pp. 23–36. Reprinted by permission.

11 W. D. Carey, "Concerning the Technology Base," *Science,* Vol. 203, No. 4379, 2 February 1979. Copyright 1979 by the American Association for the Advancement of Science.

12 B. Dervin, "Information As a User Construct," in S. Ward and L. Reed, Eds., *Knowledge Structure and Use,* Washington, D.C.: National Institute of Education, 1981.

13 "Technology Transfer and Utilization," Washington, D.C.: National Academy of Engineering, 1974. For an industrial perspective, see T. J. Allen, *Managing the Flow of Technology,* Cambridge, Mass.: MIT Press, 1977.

14 S. Hibino and G. Nadler, "Transfer of Technology Approached Logically and Systematically (TOTALS)," *Journal of Technology Transfer,* Vol. 5, No. 1, Fall 1980.

15 B. Archer, K. Baynes, and R. Langdon, *Design in General Education, Part One,* London: Royal College of Art, Department of Design Research, 1976.

16 Ibid.

17 P. Schrecker, *Work and History,* Princeton N.J.: Princeton University Press, 1948.

18 E. M. Hawk, "Technology and Society Audio-Visual Resources Digest," University Park: Pennsylvania State University, STS Program, 1977.

19 L. Jennings, "Counting Our Troubles," *The Futurist,* Vol. II, No. 2, June 1977, pp. 184–185.

20 G. Nadler and W. C. Bozeman, "The Role of Purposeful Planning and Knowledge Synthesis," in S. Ward and L. Reed, Eds., *Knowledge Structure and Use,* Washington, D.C.: National Institute of Education, 1981.

21 J. Ziman, *Reliable Knowledge,* New York: Cambridge University Press, 1979.

22 C. W. Churchman, *The Systems Approach and Its Enemies,* New York: Basic, 1979.

23 G. Bateson, *Steps to an Ecology of Mind,* New York: Chandler, 1972.

24 A. Kuhn, "Dualism Reconstructed," *General Systems,* Vol. 22, 1977, p. 91.

25 R. L. Henshel, *On The Future of Social Prediction,* Indianapolis, Ind.: Bobbs-Merrill, 1976.

26　J. L. Simon, "Resources, Population, Environment: An Over-supply of False Bad News," *Science,* Vol. 208, 27 June 1980, pp. 1431–1437; and "Letters: Bad News—Is It True?" *Science,* Vol. 210, 19 December 1980, pp. 1296–1308.

27　I. I. Mitroff and R. H. Kilmann, *Methodological Approaches to Social Science,* San Francisco: Jossey-Bass, 1978.

28　R. Hesse, "Gallia Est Omnis Divisa in Partēs Trēs . . . ," *Interfaces,* Vol. 7, No. 4, August 1977, pp. 47–49.

29　I. R. Hoos, "Engineers as analysts of Social systems: A Critical Enquiry," *Journal of Systems Engineering,* Vol. 4, No. 2, 1976, pp. 81–88.

30　R. A. Frosch, "A New Look at Systems Engineering," *IEEE Spectrum,* September 1969, pp. 24–28.

31　S. C. Wheelwright and D. G. Clarke, "Corporate Forecasting: Promise and Reality," *Harvard Business Review,* Vol. 54, No. 6, November–December 1976, p. 40.

32　J. Novak, *A Theory of Education,* Ithaca, N.Y.: Cornell University Press, 1977.

33　J. W. Sutherland, *Systems: Analysis, Administration and Architectures,* New York: Van Nostrand, 1975.

34　M. Gandelsonas, "Linguistic and Semiotic Models in Architecture," in W. R. Spillers, ed., *Basic Questions of Design Theory,* New York: American Elsevier, 1974.

35　K. Strike and G. Posner, "Epistemological Problems in Organizing Social Science Knowledge for Application," in S. Ward and L. Reed, Eds., *Knowledge Structure and Use.* Washington D.C.: National Institute of Education 1981.

36　G. Nadler, "Is More Measurement Better?," *Industrial Engineering,* Vol. 10, No. 3, March 1978, pp. 20–25.

37　S. P. Sethi, "Getting a Handle on the Social Audit," *Business and Society Review/Innovation,* No. 4, Winter 1972–1973, pp. 31–38. Copyright, Warren Gorham & Lamont, Boston.

38　I. Kristol, "People Who are S-S-ST," *Wall Street Journal,* 24 July 1978, Editorial page.

39　G. B. Kolata, "Polling the Professors: Survey Draws Protest," *Science,* Vol. 199, 17 February 1978, pp. 751–755.

40　D. M. Murtha, "A Comparison of Problem Solving Approaches Used by Environmental Designers," Ph.D. dissertation, Industrial Engineering, University of Wisconsin-Madison, 1973.

41　D. R. Coleman, "Plant Layout: Computers Versus Humans," *Management Science,* Vol. 24, No. 1, September 1977, pp. 107–112.

42　R. E. Pugh, *Evaluation of Policy Simulation Models,* Washington, D.C.: Information Resources Press, 1977.

43　Pack, et al., "The Use of Urban Models in Urban Policy Making: Report on Research to Refine the Relevant Questions and to Provide an Appropriate Research Design," Philadelphia: The Fels Center of Government, University of Pennsylvania, 1974, pp. 4–11, in Pugh, op. cit.

44　L. M. Branscomb, "Information: The Ultimate Frontier," *Science,* Vol. 203, 12 January 1979, pp. 143–147.

45　J. M. Ziman, "The Proliferation of Scientific Literature: A Natural Process," *Science,* Vol. 208, 25 April 1980, pp. 369–371.

46　C. M. Eastman, "Information and Data Bases in Design: A Survey of Uses and Issues in Building Design," DRC-15-4-79, Design Research Center, Carnegie-Mellon University, Pittsburgh, September 1979.

47　S. L. Alter, "How Effective Managers Use Information Systems," *Harvard Business Review,* Vol. 54, No. 6, November–December 1976, p. 97.

48　I. I. Mitroff, J. Nelson, and R. O. Mason, "On Management Myth-Information Systems," *Management Science,* Vol. 21, No. 4, December 1974, pp. 371–382.

49　Novak, op. cit.

50　S. A. Gregory and M. W. Commander, "New Materials Adoption Study: Some Contributions to Design Knowledge," *Design Studies,* Vol. 1, No. 2, October 1979, pp. 107–112.

51　Ibid.

52　R. Ricklefs, "Publish or Perish? Professors Discover Perishing Is Simpler," *Wall Street Journal,* 25 May 1979, p. 14.

53　Gregory and Commander, op. cit.

54　For examples, see D. Okrent, "Comments on Societal Risk," *Science,* Vol. 208, 25 April 1980, pp. 372–375, and D. T. Spreng and A. M. Weinberg, "Time and Decentralization," *Daedalus,* Vol. 109, No. 1, Winter 1980, pp. 137–143.

55　H. L. Dreyfus, *What Computers Can't Do,* New York: Harper & Row, 1972; and M. Henrion, "Automatic Space-Planning: A Postmortem?" Pittsburgh Carnegie-Mellon University, Institute of Physical Planning, Research Report 72, January 1978.

56　J. W. Sutherland, op. cit.

57　S. A. Gregory, "Toward Design Science: Review of Twenty Years," Birmingham, England: University of Aston, July 1977.

58　K. J. Arrow, *The Limits of Organization,* New York: Norton, 1975, pp. 39–41.

59　Ibid.

60　C. Weiss, Jr., "Mobilizing Technology for Developing Countries," *Science,* Vol. 203, 16 March 1979, pp. 1083–1084.

61　M. J. Cetron and A. Clayton, "Investigating Potential Value Changes," Chapter V.4. in H. A. Linstone and W. H. C. Simmonds, eds., *Futures Research: New Directions,* Reading, Mass.: Addison-Wesley, 1977.

62　R. L. Nolan, "Managing the Crises in Data Processing," *Harvard Business Review,* Vol. 57, No. 2, March–April 1979, pp. 115–126, and A. Tversky and D. Kahneman, "The Framing of Decisions and the Psychology of Choice," *Science,* Vol. 211, 30 January 1981, pp. 453–458.

63　W. H. Stockmayer, "Data Evaluation: A Critical Activity," *Science,* Vol. 201, 18 August 1978, Editorial page.

64　A. L. Blumenthal, *The Process of Cognition,* Englewood Cliffs, N.J.: Prentice-Hall, 1977.

65　S. Kierkegaard, *The Concept of Irony* as quoted in S. Toulmin, *Human Understanding,* Vol. I, Princeton, N.J.: Princeton University Press, 1972, p. 51.

CHAPTER SIXTEEN

1　B. L. T. Hedberg, P. C. Nystrom, and W. H. Starbuck, "Camping on Seesaws: Prescriptions for a Self-Designing Organization," *Administrative Science Quarterly,* Vol. 21, No. 1, March 1976, pp. 41–65.

2　E. E. Lawler, III, "The Motivating Work Climate: An Endangered Species?", General Electric Conference on Productivity and the Professional/Technical Work Force, Crotonville, N.Y., 18–21 July 1976.

3　"Stonewalling Plant Democracy," *Business Week,* 28 March 1977, p. 78.

4　W. R. Spillers, ed., *Basic Questions of Design Theory,* New York: American Elsevier, 1974, foreword.

5　S. Alter, "Implementation Risk Analysis," in R. Doktor, R. L. Schultz, and D. P. Slevin, eds. *Implementation of Management Science,* New York: Elsevier North Holland, 1980.

6 G. Zaltman and R. Duncan, *Strategies for Planned Change,* New York: Wiley, 1977, pp. 13–15.

7 M. Fein, Book review of S. A. Tucker, *The Complete Machine-Hour Rate System for Cost-Estimating and Pricing.* (Englewood Cliffs, N.J.: Prentice-Hall, 1975), in *Industrial Engineering,* Vol. 8, No. 12, December 1976, p. 52. Copyright, American Institute of Industrial Engineers, Norcross, Ga.

8 The literature is growing regarding implementation, but it does not distinguish among many factors identified in this book— purposeful activities, total approaches, factors in an approach, timeline scenario, purposes-design strategy versus research strategy, and so forth. The variables listed here were garnered from several sources such as Zaltman and Duncan, op. cit.; Doktor, Schultz, and Slevin, op. cit.; E. Bardach, *The Implementation Game,* Cambridge, Mass.: MIT Press, 1977; and many articles in such journals as *Human Relations, Organizational Dynamics, Harvard Business Review, Administrative Science Quarterly, Interfaces,* and *Applied Behavioral Science.*

9 L. W. Porter, E. E. Lawler, III, and J. R. Hackman, *Behavior in Organizations,* New York: McGraw-Hill, 1975, p. 497.

10 Hedberg, Nystrom, and Starbuck, op. cit.

11 W. N. Dunn and F. W. Swierczek, "Planned Organizational Change: Toward Grounded Theory," *Journal of Applied Behavioral Science,* Vol. 13, No. 2, April–June 1977, pp. 135–155. Reproduced with special permission, NTL Institute.

12 "Stonewalling Plant Democracy," op. cit.

13 R. P. Lutz, "High-Technology Companies Don't Act the Way Professors Say They Do," *New Engineer,* Vol. 6, No. 11, December 1977.

14 W. R. King and D. I. Cleland, *Strategic Planning and Policy,* New York: Van Nostrand, 1978.

15 "Stonewalling Plant Democracy," op. cit.

16 Zaltman and Duncan, op. cit.

17 C. Argyris and D. A. Schon, *Theory in Practice,* San Francisco: Jossey-Bass, 1974.

18 Hedberg, Nystrom, and Starbuck, op. cit.

19 Several Japanese books and many papers have been written on this P&D approach, a national society has been founded to promote its ideas and techniques in aiding the overall thought process, seminars are offered frequently, and so on.

20 M. Rosenberg, *Conceiving the Self,* New York: Basic Books, 1979.

21 G. J. Wacker and G. Nadler, "Myths About Implementing Quality of Working Life Programs," *California Management Review,* Vol. 22, No. 3, Spring 1980, pp. 15–23. Reprinted by permission of The Regents, University of California.

22 H. I. Ansoff, "The State of Practice in Planning Systems," *Sloan Management Review,* Vol. 18, No. 2, Winter 1977, pp. 1–24.

23 D. W. Ewing, "Multiple Loyalties," *Wall Street Journal,* 1 May 1978, Editorial page.

24 M. R. Lepper and D. Greene, eds., *The Hidden Costs of Reward: New Perspectives on the Psychology of Human Motivation.* New York: Wiley, 1978.

25 Personal communication, to author, 1978.

26 G. Nadler and W. C. Bozeman, "The Roles of Purposeful Planning and Knowledge Synthesis", in S. Ward and L. Reed, eds., *Knowledge Structure and Use,* Washington, D.C.: National Institute of Education, 1981.

27 H. E. O'Kelley, "How to Motivate and Manage Engineers," *New York Times,* 26 November, 1978, Editorial Section.

Copyright © 1978 by the New York Times Company. Reprinted with permission.

28 F. J. Roethlisberger and W. J. Dickson, *Management and the Worker,* Cambridge, Mass.: Harvard University Press, 1939.

29 The Rucker and Scanlon profit-sharing plans, which also emphasize participation in decision making and solving operating problems are well known; see, for example, F. G. Lesieur and E. S. Puckett, "The Scanlon Plan Has Proved Itself," *Harvard Business Review,* Vol. 47, No. 5, September–October 1969, pp. 109–18.

30 C. N. Cofer and M. H. Appley, *Motivation: Theory and Research,* New York: Wiley, 1964.

31 L. B. Archer, "Design as a Discipline: Whatever Became of Design Methodology? The Three Rs," *Design Studies,* Vol. 1, No. 1, July 1979, pp. 17–20.

32 Roethlisberger and Dickson, op. cit.

33 C. Reeser, "Some Potential Human Problems of the Project Form of Organization," *Academy of Management Journal,* Vol. 12, No. 4, December 1969, pp. 459–467.

34 W. W. George, "Task Teams for Rapid Growth," *Harvard Business Review,* Vol. 52, No. 2, March–April 1977, pp. 71–80.

35 D. N. Scobel, "Doing Away with the Factory Blues," *Harvard Business Review,* Vol. 53, No. 6, November–December 1975, pp. 136–137.

36 M. Fein. "Motivation—Financial," in G. Salvendy, ed., *Handbook of Industrial Engineering,* New York: Wiley, 1981.

37 E. F. Schumacher, *Small is Beautiful: Economics as if People Mattered,* New York: Harper & Row, 1973.

38 A. J. Large, "Congress Wrestles With Technology," *Wall Street Journal,* 21 April 1978, Editorial page.

39 H. I. Ansoff, "The State of Practice in Planning Systems," *Sloan Management Review,* Vol. 18, No. 2, Winter 1977, pp. 1–24. A comparable indicator of maturing status in national development in third world countries is described in M. G. Blase, *Institution Building: A Source Book,* Washington, D.C.: Agency for International Development, U.S. State Dept., 1973.

40 S. M. Davis and P. R. Lawrence, "Problems of Matrix Organizations," *Harvard Business Review,* Vol. 56, No. 3, May–June 1978, pp. 131–142.

41 P. Kelly and M. Kranzberg, *Technological Innovation: A Critical Review of Current Knowledge,* San Francisco: San Francisco Press, 1978, p. 107.

42 J. S. Dyer, R. A. Millen, and J. J. Morse, "A Framework for the Study of Work Settings," *Management Science,* Vol. 24, No. 13, September 1978, pp. 1393.

43 Charles Perrow, "A Framework for the Comparative Analysis of Organizations," *American Sociological Review,* Vol. 32, No. 3, April 1967, pp. 194–195.

44 D. G. Bowers, J. L. Franklin, and P. A. Pecorella, "Matching Problems, Precursors, and Interventions in OD: A Systemic Approach," *Journal of Applied Behavioral Science,* Vol. 11, No. 4, October–December 1975, pp. 391–408.

45 W. L. Batt, Jr., and W. Weinberg, "Labor-Management Cooperation Today," *Harvard Business Review,* Vol. 56, No. 1, January–February 1978, pp. 96–104.

CHAPTER SEVENTEEN

1 T. S. Kuhn, *The Structure of Scientific Revolutions,* Chicago: University of Chicago Press, 1962.

2 N. R. F. Maier, *Problem Solving and Creativity in Individuals and Groups,* Belmont, Calif.: Brooks/Cole, 1970.

3 C. W. Churchman, *The Systems Approach and Its Enemies,* New York: Basic Books, 1979.

4 S. Toulmin, *Human Understanding,* Vol. 1, Princeton, N.J.: Princeton University Press, 1972.

5 O. Friedman, "The Economic Effect of Cost Control Programs in Midwest Industry," Masters thesis, University of Wisconsin-Madison, 1973.

6 D. M. Murtha, "A Comparison of Problem-Solving Approaches Used by Environmental Designers," Doctoral dissertation, University of Wisconsin-Madison, 1973.

7 P. C. Nutt, "An Experimental Comparison of the Effectiveness of Three Planning Methods," *Management Science,* Vol. 23, No. 5, January 1977, pp. 499–511.

8 M. Norton, W. C. Bozeman, and G. Nadler, *Student Planned Acquisition of Required Knowledge,* Englewood Cliffs, N.J.: Educational Technology Publishers, 1980.

9 D. Gat, "Architecture, System Design and Human Purposeful Activities," Haifa, Israel: Technion, Faculty of Architecture and Town Planning, 1976.

10 G. Nadler, *Strategic Planning,* Chicago: American College of Hospital Administrators, 1978.

11 C. E. Geisel, "The Role of Methods Design," in G. Salvendy, ed., *Handbook of Industrial Engineering,* New York: Wiley, 1981.

12 P. F. Drucker, *The Age of Discontinuity,* New York: Harper & Row, 1969.

13 H. A. Simon, *The Sciences of the Artificial,* Cambridge, Mass.: MIT Press, 1969.

14 H. W. J. Rittel, "Some Principles for the Design of an Educational System for Design," *DMG Newsletter,* Vol. 5, No. 1, January 1971, pp. 3–11.

15 S. Chermayeff, "Design as Catalyst," *Socio-Economic Planning Sciences,* Vol. 1, 1967, pp. 63–69.

16 Norton, Bozeman, and Nadler, op. cit.

17 Ibid.

18 T. Kotarbinski, *Praxiology: An Introduction to the Sciences of Efficient Action,* New York: Pergamon, 1965.

19 A. Gorz, "On the Class Character of Science and Scientists," Chapter 4, in H. Rose and S. Rose, eds., *The Political Economy of Science,* New York: Holmes and Meier, 1977, p. 64.

20 W. R. Lynn, "Engineering and Society Programs in Engineering Education," *Science,* Vol. 195, January 1977, pp. 150–155.

21 B. Archer, *A Framework for Design Scholarship,* London: Royal College of Art, Department of Design Research, 1979.

22 Norton, Bozeman, and Nadler, op. cit.

23 Proposal prepared by DEPTER committee, College of Engineering, University of Wisconsin—Madison, G. Nadler, Chairman, May 1980.

24 D. A. Schon, N. S. Cremer, P. Osterman, and C. Perry, "Planners in Transition," *AIP Journal,* Vol. 42, No. 2, April 1976, pp. 193–202.

25 Kuhn, op. cit.

26 J. Hage, *Techniques of Theory Construction in Sociology,* New York: Wiley, 1972.

27 E. Land, Chairman's letter to Polaroid Corporation, Stockholders, 1977. Copyright, Polaroid Corp.

28 H. W. J. Rittel and M. W. Webber, "Dilemmas in a General Theory of Planning," *DMG-DRS Journal,* Vol. 8, No. 1, January–March 1974, pp. 31–39.

29 G. Nadler, "An Investigation of Design Methodology," *Management Science,* Vol. 13, No. 10, June 1967, pp. B642–B655.

30 H. P. Binswanzer, V. W. Ruttan et al., *Induced Innovation: Technology, Institutions and Development,* Baltimore: Johns Hopkins University Press, 1978.

31 Churchman, op. cit.

32 A. L. Lavoisier, as reported in D. L. Hull, P. D. Tessner, and A. M. Diamond, "Planck's Principle," *Science,* vol. 202, 17 November 1978, pp. 717–723.

33 C. Darwin, as reported in Hull et al., op. cit.

34 A. Schlesinger, Jr., "The Decline-and-Fall Mood," *Wall Street Journal,* 5 June 1979, Editorial page.

35 R. Chait, "College Mission Statements," *Science,* Vol. 205. 7 September 1979, p. 957.

36 H. Brooks, "Physics and Polity," *Science,* Vol. 160, 26 April 1968, pp. 396–400.

37 J. A. Lee, "Behavioral Theory Vs. Reality," *Harvard Business Review,* Vol. 49, No. 2, March–April 1971, pp. 20–28.

CASE HISTORY B1

1 A technical note. Although several purpose statements were identical in each hierarchy, the levels at which they appeared were dramatically different. "Sell ideas developed by the National Management Board" was the biggest level in the hierarchy for administrators, the second smallest in the hierarchy for mid-level people, and fourth smallest in the hierarchy for "firing line" people. Other statements likewise appeared in different arrangements.

2 A summary of this miniproject is available by request from the Department of Industrial Engineering, University of Wisconsin—Madison, 1513 University Ave., Madison, Wisconsin 53706.

CASE HISTORY B3

1 A. Daigon and R. T. LaConte, eds., *Dig U.S.A.,* New York: Bantam, 1970.

CASE HISTORY B9

1 C. Alexander, interviewed by Max Jacobson, *Design Methods Newsletter,* March 1971, Vol. 5, No. 3, pp. 3–7.

2 A. Rapoport, "Architecture, Communication and Meaning," lecture given at the Design Colloquium, Technion's Faculty of Architecture, Haifa, July 1976.

CASE HISTORY B12

1 J. Charnley, "Acrylic Cement in Orthopaedic Surgery," London: E. and S. Livingstone, 1970.

2 "The Hip Doctor," *Time Magazine,* 25 November 1974, p. 69.

Index